CANADIAN EDITION

PRINCIPLES OF FOOD, BEVERAGE, AND LABOUR COST CONTROLS

Paul R. Dittmer

J. Desmond Keefe III

Gary Hoyer

Tim Foster

WILEY

JOHN WILEY & SONS CANADA, LTD.

Library and Archives Canada Cataloguing in Publication

Principles of food, beverage, and labour cost controls / Paul R. Dittmer ... [et al.]. -- Canadian ed.

ISBN 978-0-470-15818-0

1. Food service--Cost control--Textbooks. I. Dittmer, Paul

TX911.3.C65P75 2009   647.95068'1   C2009-901909-4

Production Credits
Acquisitions Editor: Darren Lalonde
Vice President & Publisher: Veronica Visentin
Vice President, Publishing Services: Karen Bryan
Creative Director, Publishing Services: Ian Koo
Marketing Manager: Anne-Marie Seymour
Editorial Manager: Karen Staudinger
Developmental Editor: Gail Brown
Editorial Assistant/Permissions Coordinator: Rachel Coffey
Typesetting: Interrobang Graphic Design
Cover Design: Interrobang Graphic Design
Cover Images: Andersen Ross, Getty Images and iStockphoto.com
Printing and binding: Edwards Brothers Incorporated
Printed and bound in the United States.
1 2 3 4 5 EB 14 13 12 11 10

John Wiley & Sons Canada, Ltd.
6045 Freemont Blvd.
Mississauga, Ontario L5R 4J3
Visit our website at: www.wiley.ca

PREFACE

TO THE STUDENT

Successful restaurant personnel, including chefs, restaurant managers, food and beverage controllers, dining room managers, and stewards, have many skills. Among them is the ability to keep costs at predetermined levels. To furnish a profit, they understand that successful operations require costs to be carefully established and monitored. After all, many profitable foodservice operations have less than a 10 percent profit margin on sales after taking all costs into consideration. Food, beverage, and labour costs generally use up 60 to 70 percent of the total revenue of a restaurant. If the remaining 40 to 30 percent does not cover all additional costs and generate some profit, the operation will probably not succeed. No matter what type of business is considered, if expenses like these and certain other operational costs are not carefully established and monitored, they can gradually increase until profit is eliminated and losses are sustained. While this text focuses on everything necessary to control expenses, we do not want you to lose sight of the fact that generating sales is also essential for profitability. *Without sales, costs are uncontrollable—even for the world's best managers.*

To produce sales requires an intelligent, well-organized, and multifaceted effort on a continuing basis. Sales have to be generated at a level that will pay all costs, including goods, labour, rent or mortgage, and many others. It should also pay those who invested money in the business and are taking a risk on its success. Throughout the life of a business, there are times when it is more important to cut expenses and other times when increasing sales becomes imperative. Maintaining the proper balance of sales and expenses is always essential.

Principles of Food, Beverage, and Labour Cost Controls, Canadian Edition is written to provide you with knowledge of the principles necessary to keep restaurant costs under control and to manage a profitable operation. Putting these principles into practice will not guarantee a profit, because there are other essential elements to a successful restaurant, but they are absolutely necessary if a profit is to be maintained. Chain operations such as Tim Hortons, Swiss Chalet, Earls, and Kelsey's have long ago learned the necessity of keeping costs under control. They also work to ensure that enough sales will be generated to allow for profitability, supplying quality products to their customers and establishing procedures that guarantee food, beverage, and labour costs will be kept within pre-determined goals. Independent restaurants must do the same if profits are to be realized. Learn these principles and you will know how to achieve success in your chosen profession.

TO THE INSTRUCTOR

This text has been developed for use in courses introducing food, beverage, and labour cost controls to students preparing for careers in the food and beverage industry—careers as managers and chefs in all types of foodservice facilities, hotels, restaurants, resorts, clubs, institutions, sports facilities, caterers, and other enterprises where this knowledge is necessary. This text consists of 21 chapters, divided into four parts, as follows:

Part I offers an introduction to food, beverage, and labour cost controls, defining a number of key terms and concepts and providing a foundation for the balance of the work as well as some sense of its scope. It identifies working definitions for the terms *cost* and *sales*, discusses the control process in some detail, and introduces the basics of cost/volume/profit analysis.

Part II addresses the application of the four-step control process to the primary phases of foodservice operations: purchasing, receiving, storing, issuing, and production. Specific techniques and procedures for each phase are explained and discussed in detail. Three chapters are devoted to determining costs and using them as monitoring devices in foodservice operations. One chapter deals specifically with menu analysis. Another discusses food sales control, offering a broad definition of the term and providing detailed discussion of several approaches to sales control.

Part III discusses the application of the four-step control process to the various beverage operations: purchasing, receiving, storing, issuing, and production. Here, too, specific techniques and procedures for each phase are explained and discussed in detail. One chapter is devoted to the principal methods used to monitor beverage operations. The final chapter in Part III specifically addresses beverage sales control, offering a broad definition of the term and providing detailed discussion of several approaches to controlling beverage sales.

Part IV is a four-chapter exposition of labour cost control. The first of the four explores the factors affecting labour cost and labour cost percentage. Admittedly, some of these are beyond the control of management, but it is important for managers to know about them. The second chapter discusses the need for performance standards. This leads naturally to a chapter on training, a topic many believe to be central to labour cost control. The concluding chapter in Part IV deals with monitoring performance and taking corrective action.

The authors recognize that most food and beverage operations are computerized to a great extent. Thus, each of the chapters in parts I, II, and III incorporate a discussion of computer use in food and beverage operations. Additionally, spreadsheet exercises using Excel are provided at the end of each chapter.

In developing the text, flexibility has always been a key concern. For example, each of the four parts can generally stand alone. Except for Part I, eliminating any other part will not make it difficult to use the remaining parts.

Thus, in courses without beverage components, instructors may prefer to skip Part III. And instructors in courses that do not include labour cost control can choose to skip Part IV.

The book has a greater number of chapters than many instructors use in a one-term course. In our view, this is a virtue, because it provides instructors with opportunities to select chapters dealing with specific topics identified in their course syllabus. We believe this is the best way to meet the varying needs of instructors in the broad range of courses and programs in this field.

Because many chapters include more questions and problems than most will be inclined to assign, instructors will find it easy to make selective use of the end-of-chapter exercises for written assignment or for in-class discussion. For those instructors who will use this text as a supplement to train management personnel, Chapter 20 is particularly useful. It outlines specific training methods, and provides various thoughts on training methods best used in different circumstances.

A Note about the Metric and Imperial Systems of Measurement

The topic of converting from one system of measurement to another can become confusing, as the imperial (British and Canadian) system differs from the U.S. system, and both differ considerably from the metric system. The metric system is the International System of Units, a system of measurement using decimal graduations. Canada adopted the metric system gradually starting in 1972, but later slowed the process. What can be confusing is that the use of both imperial and U.S. measurement units still persists in Canada, despite the adoption of the metric system. This is probably due to historic context, the continuing use of the traditional imperial system of measurement units in Canada, and our close proximity and close affiliation economically to the United States.

Butter is an example of an item that has multiple implied unit references. Because consumers still think of butter in pounds, it is normally sold in 454-gram blocks, which equals one pound. It may become more confusing in certain contexts because of rounding. Actually, the avoirdupois pound is 453.59237 grams or 0.45359237 kilogram.

The measurement of fluids is even more of a challenge. In Canada, an imperial fluid ounce is 28.4130625 millilitres (ml) or 0.0284130625 litre (L). A U.S. fluid ounce is 29.5735295625 ml or 0.0295735295625 L. Beer is another good example of complication: beer often comes in cans of 12 U.S. fluid ounces (or 355 ml), but beer in bottles is usually 12 imperial fluid ounces (or 341 ml). When a pint of draught beer is sold in Canada it is 20 imperial fluid ounces, or 568.26125 ml, and in the United States a pint is 16 U.S. fluid ounces or 473.176473 ml.

The foodservice industry in Canada still presents some measurements using mixed systems. In this text, conversions are based on accepted international standards and calculations are rounded for both mathematical and industry presentation, so that a 225-gram or 0.225-kilogram salmon steak might be thought of as being equivalent to 8 ounces or one half pound (although in reality 8 ounces equals 226.796185 grams, using 453.59237 grams per pound divided in half); and a 6-ounce glass of wine (Canadian imperial) would be equivalent to 170 ml even though it should contain almost one half of a millilitre more. (Even the best bartender won't get that out of the bottle.)

Our challenge for the Canadian edition of *Principles of Food, Beverage, and Labour Cost Controls* was to present measurements as they are currently used in the industry. We hope our readers learn all of the different systems of measurement, their usage, and applications in internal controls.

FEATURES

Chapters are organized in the following manner:

1. Chapter objectives are listed at the beginning of each chapter and are repeated throughout the chapter where they apply.
2. Chapter 1 illustrates a hypothetical restaurant, and each chapter thereafter continues a discussion of that restaurant, relating the control procedures discussed in that chapter to the hypothetical restaurant, *Bistro Quatre*. This discussion is identified by an icon.
3. A discussion of established computer programs that perform control procedures in each chapter is included. Links to the sources for these computer programs are available on the textbook's website.
4. Things to consider that relate to the topics discussed, as well as chapter essentials and key terms, are shown at the end of each chapter discussion.
5. Substantial numbers of questions and problems are listed at the end of each chapter.
6. At the end of every chapter is one or more exercises to be completed in Excel, including those for a hypothetical restaurant. Details for those exercises are provided on the textbook's companion website.

An additional feature is the glossary of key terms at the end of the text.

SUPPLEMENTARY MATERIALS

An instructor companion website and a student companion website containing supplementary resources for this textbook are available at *www.wiley.com/canada/dittmer*. Resources include PowerPoint slides, web links, Excel exercises and their solutions, as well as the Instructor's Manual, which contains the test bank and answers to the end-of-chapter questions and problems.

WebCT and BlackBoard on-line courses are available on demand for this textbook. For more information, contact your Wiley sales representative.

WileyPLUS

WileyPLUS, a powerful yet easy-to-use technology solution, provides instructors and students with a suite of interactive resources, including a complete on-line version of the text and tools that allow instructors to assign and grade homework and quizzes.

ACKNOWLEDGEMENTS

We would like to thank those who reviewed chapter material for the Canadian edition of *Principles of Food, Beverage, and Labour Cost Controls*. Their insights and feedback were invaluable and contructive.

Vince Bourque, Niagara College

Simon Day, University of Guelph

David Fairbanks, Algonquin College

Ian Grady, George Brown College

David Keindel, Algonquin College

Alan Kerr, Niagara College

Joseph Mariani, Algonquin College

Warren Pendree, Red River College

Klaus Theyer, Humber College

Ken Upton, SAIT Polytechnic

Scott Warrick, Algonquin College

We would also like to thank the contributors who worked on the textbook's supplementary material: Ian Grady (Instructor's Manual), David Keindel (PowerPoint slides), Vince Bourque (Excel exercises), and John Frantz (quizzes).

Finally, we want to express very special appreciation to our respective families, for their endless support and encouragement during our work on this book. This book is dedicated to them and to the spirit of hospitality.

Gary Hoyer, Tim Foster
Toronto, Ontario
December, 2009

BRIEF CONTENTS

CONTENTS

PART I

INTRODUCTION TO FOOD, BEVERAGE, AND LABOUR CONTROLS

This text outlines the elements and procedures for food, beverage, and labour cost control. Initially, it is necessary to define the terminology used in the text and to discuss two other very important preliminary topics: the concept of control and determining the break-even point. These are outlined in the first three chapters.

Chapter 1 is devoted to the basic concepts of costs and sales and their many variations and uses. Chapter 2 examines the concept of control—what exactly do we mean by it and what are the many ways we institute it. Chapter 3 deals with break-even analysis and the various ways an establishment can calculate the sales it must achieve to prevent loss and achieve profit. Chapter 3 also discusses the relationships among cost, volume, and profit, and the financial consequences of inadequate cost controls.

As you begin your journey into this subject, keep in mind that cost control is absolutely necessary for a profitable operation. Learn the principles outlined in this text well, because all foodservice personnel at the supervisory level and higher have an obligation to control those costs under their jurisdiction.

CHAPTER 1

Cost and Sales Concepts

• **LEARNING OBJECTIVES** •

After reading this chapter, you should be able to:

1.1 Define *costs* and provide an example of the following types of costs: fixed, variable, directly variable, semivariable, controllable, noncontrollable, unit, total, prime, historical, and planned.

1.2 Define *sales* and provide several examples illustrating monetary and nonmonetary sales concepts.

1.3 Describe the significance of cost-to-sales relationships and identify several cost-to-sales ratios and the formulas used to compute cost percent and sales price.

1.4 Describe factors that cause industrywide variations in cost percents.

1.5 Explain the value of comparing current cost-to-sales ratios with those for previous periods.

INTRODUCTION

Il Giardino

Until she decided to purchase a restaurant two years ago, Joan Clairoux had been a successful advertising executive. Her annual income was substantial, and she augmented it by investing in some profitable real estate ventures with her brother. However, her position in advertising required that she travel several days a week, and over time the travel became wearisome to her. This made her decide to give up the advertising business in favour of operating her own business. On the advice of her brother, she decided to go into the restaurant business, even though she lacked previous experience in the field. After all her years of travel, she thought she knew more about restaurants from the customer's point of view than most restaurateurs. So she began to look around for an appropriate property. Fortunately, she soon found a place just 12 kilometres from her home, located on a main road on the outskirts of a city of 75,000 people. The building and equipment were only six years old and apparently in fine condition, and the retiring owner was anxious to sell at a very fair price. The owner's books revealed a successful operation, with a restaurant profit of approximately $165,000 per year. Joan decided to buy. The restaurant, Il Giardino, had 150 seats. It was open seven days a week, from 5:00 to 10:00 p.m., serving a varied menu but emphasizing northern Italian food and operating with a middle range price point. Joan believed she would be able to run it successfully with a small and dedicated staff.

In the first year, Joan's profits were less than those of the previous owner. After two years, profits were continuing to decline. The restaurant was simply not showing an adequate profit, even though Joan had increased the volume of business over that of the previous owner. The place was reasonably busy, her customers often complimented her on the food, and her staff appeared to be loyal and helpful in every way. The truth was that Joan was operating a popular, but not very profitable, food and beverage business. At the end of the second full year of operation, the statement of income prepared by her accountant revealed a restaurant profit of $48,455 (see Figure 1.1).

It quickly became apparent to Joan, her family, and her accountant that unless something could be done to make the restaurant more profitable, the operation would not be worth the effort required.

• FIGURE 1.1 •

Il Giardino Income Statement, Year Ended December 31, 20XX

Sales		
Food	$1,686,740	
Beverage	$297,660	
Total Sales		$1,984,400
Cost of Sales		
Food	$708,431	
Beverage	$95,251	
Total Cost of Sales		$803,682
Gross Profit		$1,180,718
Controllable Expenses		
Salaries and Wages	$535,788	
Employee Benefits	$133,947	
Other Controllable Expenses	$242,660	
Total Controllable Expenses		$912,395
Income before Occupancy Costs, Interest, Depreciation, and Income Taxes		$268,323
Occupancy Costs	$132,608	
Interest	$27,060	
Depreciation	$60,200	
Total Occupancy Costs, Interest, and Depreciation		$219,868
Restaurant Profit		$48,455

Bistro Quatre

Just a few kilometres down the road from Il Giardino, Bistro Quatre is owned and operated by Bill Kowalchuk. After three years in the Canadian Forces, Bill had worked for an insurance company for a few years before enrolling in a nearby college to study hospitality management. His interest in the food and beverage sector of the hospitality industry began during his high school days, when he worked part time at the local unit of a national fast-food chain. Although his interest had grown steadily over the years, it took considerable courage for him to give up a fairly promising insurance career to go back to school. He earned a degree in hospitality management and then went to work as the assistant manager in a local restaurant. Over the next several years, he worked in three food and beverage operations in the area, including Il Giardino, before deciding that he was ready to own and operate his own restaurant.

With the help of his family and a local bank, Bill was able to purchase Bistro Quatre, a fairly popular establishment with the same type of menu as Il Giardino, as well as comparable prices and hours of operation. The only differences to the casual observer were size and location: Bistro Quatre had only 75 seats and was in a somewhat less favourable location on the other side of town. The menu for Bistro Quatre is illustrated in Figure 1.2.

• FIGURE 1.2 •

Bistro Quatre Menu

APPETIZERS

DUCK EMPANADAS
Tender roast duck encased in an empanada purse,
served with roasted poblano sauce
$7.65

GRILLED VEGETABLE TARTLETS
Semolina and potato tartlet shells filled with grilled sliced zucchini,
fennel, and fire-roasted tomato, garnished with shaved parmesan
$6.50

SAVOURY SMOKED SALMON CROUSTADE
Smoked salmon and Gruyère cheese baked in a savoury crust
served with Cucumber Dill Cream sauce
$8.20

OYSTERS ROCKEFELLER
Six Malpeque Bay oysters baked on the half shell
with spinach, onions, and hollandaise sauce
$9.35

EGGPLANT ROULADE
Thinly sliced fresh eggplant stuffed with ricotta, mozzarella, and
goat cheese and served with a tomato basil sauce
$5.50

SHITAKE MUSHROOM BUREKS
Sautéed wild mushroom and goat cheese layered in phyllo dough
$5.50

SOUPS

ANASAZI BEAN AND ROASTED CORN WITH CHILIES
beautiful purple beans with corn, chilies,
celery, onions, and just enough spice
$4.95

(continued)

• FIGURE 1.2 • (continued)

MANHATTAN STYLE FISH CHOWDER
Traditional tomato-based soup
with haddock, shrimp, and scallops
$8.25

SALADS

MESCLUN GREENS TOPPED WITH HAZELNUTS AND CHEVRE
Warm herbed chevre cheese and Dijon vinaigrette
$4.95

CRACKED WHEAT SALAD
Tossed with cucumber, tomato, and a citrus and green onion vinaigrette
$4.75

CAESAR SALAD
Topped with roasted garlic croutons and classically dressed
$5.45

MAINS
All main dishes are served with fresh seasonal vegetables and your choice of pasta, frites, or
rice pilaf and choice of house salad or traditional Caesar salad.

BLACK ANGUS NEW YORK STRIP STEAK
8-ounce prime steak charbroiled and topped with crimini mushrooms
$23.65

TOURNEDOS BISTRO
Two 3-ounce fillets of beef pan-seared and topped
with fresh asparagus and a Madeira sauce
$24.75

ROASTED MUSCOVY DUCK BREAST
Maple-infused jus lie, cashew and scallion rice, and spaghetti squash
$21.40

ROASTED LEG OF ONTARIO LAMB
Succulent lamb served with a sage and lavender sauce and angel hair pasta
$21.50

BARBEQUED BABY BACK RIBS
Slow smoked pork ribs with our own barbeque sauce
$20.50

TAMARIND AND GINGER SHRIMP
Gulf shrimp, bean sprouts, snow peas, enoki mushrooms, and scallions
in an Asian glass noodle stir-fry with a light ginger-sesame dressing
$18.00

GNOCCHI
Handmade semolina and ricotta gnocchi with roasted tomatoes and fresh basil
$16.50

(continued)

• **FIGURE 1.2** • (continued)

DARJEELING-SMOKED WILD B.C. SALMON
Lightly smoked and roasted in the oven, accompanied by Italian white beans,
fusilli, and saffron broth served with baby spinach.
$19.20

PAELLA
With chicken, mussels, peas, Bomba rice and cuttlefish ink aioli
$16.50

CHARRED BIG EYE TUNA
Fresh tuna with Nicoise salad
$20.85

MISO-GLAZED BLACK COD
Roasted and served with tatsoi and sweet pepper salad
$24.75

GRILLED BREAST OF CHICKEN
With shallots and artichoke in an Ontario Pinot Noir sauce
$16.45

TAGLIATELLE
Tossed with braised Swiss Chard, sweet peas, sorrel, and crème fraîche
$19.00

FRESH SCALLOPS
Pan-seared, with Aloo Gobi and roasted carrot fondue
$19.95

CAPELLINI
Lobster, shrimp, and scallops tossed in a light basil cream with fresh romano,
served over angel hair pasta
$21.40

CATCH OF THE DAY
Fresh sustainable daily fish
$16.50

DESSERTS

GINGER-LIME CHEESE TARTLETTES
Served with crystallized ginger
$3.85

CHOCOLATE TORTE WITH CHERRY ICE
Chocolate, walnuts, and vanilla baked in a soufflé cup served
with a cherry, ricotta, and maple syrup ice.
$4.40

FRESH FRUIT TART
Prepared with the finest and freshest fruit of the season
$2.75

Under the previous owner, the restaurant had shown a profit of $65,000 per year. But Bill felt sure he could increase the profit by applying the principles he had learned in the college's hospitality management program. The employees he inherited with the restaurant were both loyal and co-operative, and he found them receptive to the changes that he made gradually over the first year of operation. None of the changes were dramatically apparent to the customers; in fact, at the end of the first year, most had not noticed any changes at all. In general, they were as pleased with the establishment as they had been when Bill first took it over, and they continued to return. In addition, newcomers tried the restaurant, liked it, and became regular customers. At the end of the first full year of operation, Bill's accountant presented him with a statement of income showing a restaurant profit of $128,702 (see Figure 1.3).

• FIGURE 1.3 •

Bistro Quatre Income Statement, Year Ended December 31, 20XX

Sales		
Food	$891,687	
Beverage	$157,356	
Total Sales		$1,049,043
Cost of Sales		
Food	$312,090	
Beverage	$39,339	
Total Cost of Sales		$351,429
Gross Profit		$697,614
Controllable Expenses		
Salaries and wages	$209,809	
Employee benefits	$47,207	
Other controllable expenses	$162,602	
Total Controllable Expenses		$419,618
Income before Occupancy Costs, Interest, Depreciation, and Income Taxes		$277,996
Occupancy Costs	$89,169	
Interest	$13,875	
Depreciation	$46,250	
Total Occupancy Costs, Interest, and Depreciation		$149,294
Restaurant Profit		$128,702

The statement confirmed Bill's expectations. It proved to him that his management of the operation was effective in the ways he had anticipated. At the end of his first year, he looked to the future with confidence.

A comparison of the statements of income for these two restaurants reveals some very important facts. As one might expect, Il Giardino, with twice as many seats as Bistro Quatre, as well as a comparable menu and comparable prices, shows approximately twice the dollar volume of sales. However, despite the apparently favourable sales comparison, the restaurant profit for Il Giardino is considerably less than for Bistro Quatre. Because the difference between sales and restaurant profit on each statement of income is represented by costs of various kinds, we can infer that part of the difficulty with Il Giardino is somehow related to cost. The costs of operation seem to be in more favourable proportion to sales at Bistro Quatre. Initially, we must look to the nature of these costs and their relations to sales to find the differences between the two establishments. It is possible that the costs of operation are not well regulated, or controlled, by Il Giardino. It is also possible that sales are not well controlled, and that if Joan Clairoux is going to increase her profit to a desirable level, she must begin by exercising greater control over the several kinds of operating costs, as well as over sales.

The statement of income from Bistro Quatre suggests that Bill Kowalchuk has kept both costs and sales under control, and, as we shall see, this is critically important to the success of his business. Comparative investigation of the two restaurants would reveal that Bill had instituted various control procedures in Bistro Quatre that are noticeably absent in Joan's business. These control procedures are overseen by a computer program that plays a significant part in the operation of Bistro Quatre. These procedures have helped Bill to manage his business more effectively. It will be important, therefore, to look closely at the nature and effect of these control procedures in succeeding chapters. However, before proceeding, it will be useful to establish clear definitions of the terms *cost, sales,* and *control*, as a thorough understanding of these concepts is essential to success. Cost and sales will be defined and discussed in this chapter; control will be covered in Chapter 2.

COST CONCEPTS

Definition of Cost

LEARNING OBJECTIVE 1.1
Define *costs* and provide an example of the following types of costs: fixed, variable, directly variable, semi-variable, controllable, noncontrollable, unit, total, prime, historical, and planned.

In our industry, **cost** is defined as the expense to a foodservice establishment for goods or services when the goods are consumed or the services are rendered. Foods and beverages are considered "consumed" when they have been used, wastefully or otherwise, and are no longer available for the purposes for which they were acquired. Thus, the cost for a piece of meat is incurred when the piece is no longer available for the purpose for which it was purchased, regardless of whether it has been cooked, served, thrown away, spoiled, or even stolen. The cost of labour is incurred when people are on paid duty, whether or not they are working and whether they are paid at the end of a shift or at some later date. The cost of this labour can also be incurred regardless of an associated sale being made.

The cost of any item may be expressed in a variety of ways: weight, volume, or total dollar value. The cost of meat, for example, can be expressed as a value per piece, per kilogram, or per individual portion. The cost of liquor can be expressed as a value per bottle, per drink, or per millilitre. Labour costs can be expressed as value per hour (an hourly wage, for example) or value per week (a weekly salary).

Costs themselves can be viewed in several different ways, and it will be useful to identify some of them before proceeding.

Fixed and Variable Costs

The terms *fixed* and *variable* are used to distinguish between those costs that have no direct relationship to business sales volume and those that do.

Fixed Costs

Fixed costs are normally unaffected by changes in sales volume. They are said to have little direct relationship to business volume because they do not change significantly when the number of sales increases or decreases. When a lease stipulates a set dollar amount every month, then rent is a fixed cost unaffected by sales volume. Property taxes, insurance premiums, and depreciation on equipment are also examples of fixed costs. Property taxes are set by governmental authorities and are based on a government's need for a determined amount of total revenue. The property taxes for an individual establishment are based on the appraised value of the assessed property as real estate. Property taxes do not change when the sales volume in an establishment changes.

All fixed costs change over time, sometimes increasing and sometimes decreasing. However, changes in fixed costs are not normally related to short-term changes in business volume. They are sometimes tied indirectly to long-term volume changes. For example, an increase in the cost of insurance premiums may be attributable to an insurance company's perception of increased risk associated with higher volume. Even though the increase in insurance cost is somehow related to an increase in volume, the cost of insurance is still considered a fixed cost. Advertising expense is another example: Larger establishments tend to spend more on advertising because their larger sales volume makes larger amounts of money available for the purpose, but advertising expense is still considered a fixed cost if establishments allocate a set dollar amount to it without considering how it relates to sales.

The term *fixed* should never be taken to mean forever static or unchanging, but merely to indicate that any changes that may occur in such costs are related only indirectly or distantly to changes in volume. Sometimes, in fact, changes in fixed costs are wholly unrelated to changes in volume, as with property taxes. Other examples of costs that are often considered fixed include repairs and maintenance, most utility costs, and the costs of professional services, such as legal and accounting.

Variable Costs

Variable costs are clearly related to business volume. As business volume increases, variable costs will increase; as volume decreases, variable costs should decrease as well. The obvious examples of variable costs are food, beverages, and hourly labour. For example, every time you sell a steak you must buy one to have it available. If you control that relationship, when you sell more, you must buy more: if you sell 10 steaks, you will need to buy 10. This variable cost of steaks means that the relationship of costs to sales is constant. If each steak costs $10.00 and you sell each for $25.00, no matter how many or how few steaks you sell, that relationship should be maintained. Drinks are similar. We can use the example that one bottle of beer sold should indicate one purchased and consumed. These food and beverage costs are considered directly variable costs. **Directly variable costs** are directly linked to the volume of business, so that every increase or decrease in volume brings a corresponding increase or decrease in cost. Total directly variable costs increase or decrease—or at least *should* increase or decrease—in direct proportion to sales volume. There are, however, significant differences between the behaviour of food and beverage costs and the behaviour of labour costs.

Payroll costs (including salaries and wages and employee benefits, and often referred to as **labour costs**) present an interesting contrast. Foodservice employees may be divided into two categories: those whose numbers will remain constant despite normal fluctuations in business volume, and those whose numbers and consequent total costs should logically (and often will) vary with normal changes in business volume. The first category often includes such personnel as the manager, chef, cashier, and bookkeeper. They are fixed-cost personnel, probably on a weekly *salary*. That means that no matter what the sales volume is, they must be paid the amount of their salary weekly. Their numbers and costs may change over time, but not because of short-term changes in business volume.

The second category includes the cooks, servers, hosts, and cleaners—staff who work for wages, usually on a weekly schedule. Their schedule or daily hours vary with expected changes to customer numbers, so as business volume changes, their numbers and total costs should increase or decrease accordingly. Both fixed-cost and variable-cost employees are often included in one category on the statement of income: *salaries and wages*. Because payroll cost has both the fixed element and the variable element, it is known as a **semivariable cost**, meaning that the variable portion of it should change with short-term changes in business volume and the fixed component should not.

It must be noted that each establishment must decide which employees should be fixed-cost personnel and which should be variable-cost. In some specialized cases, it is possible for payroll to consist entirely of either fixed-cost or variable-cost personnel. For example, there are some restaurants in which the entire staff works for hourly wages. In these cases, numbers of hours worked and consequent costs are almost wholly related to business volume. Conversely, in some smaller restaurants with consistent sales numbers, employees may all be on regular salaries, in which case labour cost is considered fixed.

Controllable and Noncontrollable Costs

Costs may also be labelled *controllable* and *noncontrollable*. **Controllable costs** can be changed in the short term. Variable costs are normally controllable. The cost of food or beverages, for example, can be changed in several ways, such as by changing portion sizes, ingredients in a recipe, or the quality of the products purchased. Thus food costs are normally variable and controllable.

The cost of labour can be increased or decreased in the short term by changing scheduling of hours, increasing or decreasing the hours of work, or, in some instances, by increasing or decreasing wages, hiring additional employees, or by laying some off.

In addition, certain fixed costs are controllable, including advertising and promotion, utilities, repairs and maintenance, administrative and general expenses, office supplies, postage, and telephone expenses, among others. It is possible for owners or managers to make decisions that will change any of these in the short term.

In contrast, **noncontrollable costs** cannot normally be changed in the short term. These are usually fixed costs, and a list of the more common ones would include rent, interest on a mortgage, property taxes, licence fees, and depreciation. Managers do not normally have the ability to change any of these costs in the near term.

Unit and Total Costs

It is also important to distinguish between **unit costs** and **total costs**. The units may be food or beverage portions, as in the cost of one steak or one beer, or units of work, as in the hourly rate for an employee. It is also useful to consider costs in terms of totals, as in the total cost of all food served in one period, such as a week or a month, or the total cost of labour for one period. The costs on a statement of income are all total costs of a specified type, rather than unit costs.

These concepts are best illustrated by example. In Bistro Quatre, where steaks are cut from strip loins, a strip loin was purchased for $98.25. If one entire strip were consumed in one day, the total cost would be $98.25. However, the cost per unit (the steak) depends on the number of steaks cut from the strip. If 15 steaks are cut, then $98.25 ÷ 15 gives a unit cost average of $6.55. Because it is not normally possible for a butcher to cut all steaks to exactly the same weight, no two of the 15 steaks are likely to have identical costs. That's why in the food and beverage business, we often deal with average unit costs, rather than actual unit costs. It is important to know unit costs for purposes of establishing menu prices and determining unit profitability. Total costs, including those that appear in statements of income, are normally used for broader purposes, including determining the relationship between total costs and total sales—as discussed later in this chapter—and determining overall profitability of operations.

It is important to note that, as business volume changes, total and unit costs are affected in different ways. Assume that a restaurant has a fixed cost for rent of $2,000 per month. If 2,000 customers were served during a period of one month, the fixed cost of rent would be $2,000 ÷ 2,000 or $1.00 per customer. If, in the succeeding month, the number of customers increased to 4,000, the total fixed cost for rent would not change, but the fixed cost for rent per unit (customer) would be reduced from $1.00 to $0.50.

A similar analysis may be done with variable costs. The variable cost for the steak described earlier is $6.55 per unit. If 240 customers in a given month order steak, the total variable cost would be 240 × $6.55 or $1,572. If, in the following month, 300 customers order steak, the variable cost per unit (the steak) should remain at $6.55, whereas the total variable cost for 300 steaks would increase to $1,965.

The preceding paragraphs illustrate cost behaviour only as business volume increases, but it is important to recognize that costs *should* behave similarly as business volume decreases. The relationships hold true. Figure 1.4 illustrates the behaviour of fixed and variable costs per unit and in total.

These concepts of control are essential to profitability and success. Anticipated sales must be sufficient to at least satisfy fixed costs. Variable costs once established in their relationship to sales must be controlled and that relationship maintained. Understanding these relationships is essential to cost/volume/profit analysis and the calculation of break-even points, which are discussed in Chapter 3.

• FIGURE 1.4 •

Cost Behaviour as Business Volume Changes

	Unit Costs	*Total Cost*
Fixed cost	Changes	Does not change
Variable cost	Does not change	Changes

It must be noted that this relationship does not always hold true. As volume increases, some variable costs have a tendency to decrease. This is particularly true with variable labour costs, because workers become more productive with greater time utilization. Food can be purchased cheaper in larger quantities and can thus reduce variable costs.

Prime Costs

Prime cost is a term our industry uses to refer to the costs of goods sold and labour incurred: food, beverages, and payroll. Unfortunately, although everyone agrees that total food costs and total beverage costs should be included in prime cost, there is no general agreement on the payroll cost component. Some would include all payroll costs, whereas others would include only the cost of kitchen staff. In this text, prime cost is defined as the sum of food costs, beverage costs, and labour costs (salaries and wages, plus employee benefits). Referring to Figure 1.3, these costs for Bistro Quatre are $351,429 (food and beverage costs), $209,809 (salaries and wages), and $47,207 (employee benefits). These, taken together ($608,445), represent by far the largest portion of total costs for virtually all foodservice operations. In addition, management can typically alter these costs more easily than most fixed costs. Consequently, prime cost is of the greatest interest to most owners and managers. *The level and control of prime cost plays a large part in determining whether an establishment will meet its financial goals.* In this text, we therefore concentrate on those controllable costs that are most important in determining profit: food cost, beverage cost, and labour cost.

Historical and Planned Costs

Two additional cost concepts are important for those seeking to comprehend cost control: **historical costs** and **planned costs**. The definition of cost at the beginning of this chapter carries with it an implication that all costs are historical; that is, that they can be found in business records, books of account, financial statements, invoices, employees' time cards, and other similar records. Historical costs are used for various important purposes, such as establishing unit costs, determining menu prices, and comparing present with past labour costs. However, the value of historical costs is not limited to these few purposes. Historical records of costs are of particular value for planning—for determining in the present what is likely to happen in the future. Planning is among the most important functions of management, and, in order to plan effectively, managers use historical costs to develop planned costs—projections of what costs will be or should be for a future period. Thus, historical costs are necessary for effective planning. This kind of planning is often called *budgeting*, a topic to be discussed in Chapter 2.

SALES CONCEPTS

Now that food and beverage operations have been briefly introduced, it will be useful to establish a working definition of the term *sales* and to examine some of the principal sales concepts required for an understanding of control in foodservice.

    The term *sales* is used in several ways among professionals in the foodservice industry. For the term to be meaningful, one must be specific about the context in which it is used. The following paragraphs therefore define the term and explore some of the many ways it is used in the industry.

LEARNING OBJECTIVE 1.2
Define *sales* and provide several examples illustrating monetary and nonmonetary sales concepts.

Sales Defined

In general, the term **sales** is defined as revenue resulting from the exchange of products and services for value. In our industry, food and beverage sales are exchanges of the products and services of a restaurant, bar, or related enterprise for value. We normally express sales in monetary terms, although there are other possibilities. Actually, there are two basic groups of terms normally used in food and beverage operations to express sales concepts: monetary and nonmonetary.

The Importance of Sales

Sometimes, what is most obvious is taken for granted. Any business, foodservice or otherwise, that operates for profit must generate revenue. In our industry, we incur costs by purchasing and preparing goods for sale and paying occupancy, utilities, and other costs. Without sales dollars these costs would not be paid and our business would quickly fail. It is *essential to plan and execute a business properly* so that there is good opportunity for sales to be made at a scale necessary to pay all expenses and, hopefully, leave additional money for profit. In today's competitive and low-margin foodservice environment, having a good concept, in a good location, with excellent service, products, and value for customers is critical. Marketing to achieve necessary sales levels and improving on them is needed to create, maintain, and increase customer counts. Management can train staff to sell high profit margin items and increase sales to each customer. Any sales earned and any increase in sales will help to pay costs. In chapters 12 and 17, we will discuss food and beverage sales controls further.

Monetary Terms

Total Sales

Total sales is a term that refers to the total volume of sales expressed in dollar terms. This may be for any given time period, such as a week, a month, or a year. For example, total dollar sales for Bistro Quatre was expressed as $1,049,043 for the year ending December 31, 20XX.

Total Dollar Sales by Category. Examples of **total dollar sales by category** are total food sales or total beverage sales, referring to the total dollar volume of sales for all items in one category. By extension, we may see such terms as *total steak sales* or *total beer sales*, referring to the total dollar volume of sales for all items in those particular categories.

Total Sales per Server. **Total sales per server** is the total dollar volume of sales for which a given server has been responsible for in a given time period, such as a meal period, a day, or a week. Management sometimes uses these figures to make judgements about the comparative performance of two or more employees. It may be helpful, for example, to identify those servers responsible for the greatest and least dollar sales in a given period.

Total Sales per Seat. Total sales per seat is the total dollar sales for a given time period divided by the number of seats in the restaurant. The normal time period used is one year. This figure is most frequently used by chain operations as a means for comparing sales results of one outlet with those of another. In addition, the Canadian Restaurant and Foodservices Association determines this average nationally so that individual operators may compare their results with those of other similar restaurants.

Sales Price. Sales price refers to the amount charged to each customer purchasing one unit of a particular item. The unit may be a single item (e.g., an appetizer or a main dish) or an entire meal, depending on the manner in which a restaurant prices its products. Figure 1.2 showed the sales prices for each of the dinner menu items at Bistro Quatre. The sum of all sales prices charged for all items sold in a given time period will be total dollar sales for that time period. Figure 1.5 shows the sales on one particular Saturday. Total dollar sales for all items including soups, appetizers, main dishes, and desserts is shown as $3,902.30.

• FIGURE 1.5 •

Bistro Quatre Daily Sales and Covers, Saturday, February 6, 20XX

Menu Item	Number Sold	Sales Price, $	Total Sales, $
Anasazi Bean and Roasted Corn with Chilies	16	$4.95	$79.20
Manhattan Style Fish Chowder	24	8.25	198.00
Duck Empanadas	13	7.65	99.45
Grilled Vegetable Tartlets	9	6.50	58.50
Savoury Smoked Salmon Croustade	16	8.20	131.20
Oysters Rockefeller	17	9.35	158.95
Eggplant Roulade	9	5.50	49.50
Shitake Mushroom Bureks	14	5.50	77.00
Black Angus New York Strip Steak	13	23.65	307.45
Tournedos Bistro	10	24.75	247.50
Roasted Muscovy Duck Breast	5	21.40	107.00
Roasted Leg of Ontario Lamb	8	21.50	172.00
Barbequed Baby Back Ribs	6	20.50	123.00
Tamarind and Ginger Shrimp	9	18.00	162.00
Gnocchi	6	16.50	99.00
Darjeeling-Smoked Wild B.C. Salmon	13	19.20	249.60
Paella	9	16.50	148.50

(*continued*)

• **FIGURE 1.5** • (continued)			
Menu Item	Number Sold	Sales Price, $	Total Sales, $
Charred Big Eye Tuna	7	20.85	145.95
Miso-Glazed Black Cod	8	24.75	198.00
Grilled Breast of Chicken	11	16.45	180.95
Tagliatelle	9	19.00	171.00
Fresh Scallops	6	19.95	119.70
Capellini	9	21.40	192.60
Catch of the Day	11	16.50	181.50
Ginger-Lime Cheese Tartlettes	15	3.85	57.75
Chocolate Torte with Cherry Ice	25	4.40	110.00
Fresh Fruit Tart	28	2.75	77.00
Total Covers	140		
Total Sales			$3,902.30

Average Sale. An **average sale** in business is determined by adding individual sales to determine a total and then dividing that total by the number of individual sales. There are two such averages commonly calculated in food and beverage operations: average cheque and average sale per server.

Average Cheque. **Average cheque** is the result of dividing total dollar sales by the number of sales or customers. In the foodservice industry, customers (diners) are also known as covers. The term *cover* is defined in greater detail later in the chapter.

This average is determined as follows:

Average cheque = Total dollar sales ÷ Total number of covers

Figure 1.5 shows total sales of $3,902.30 and 140 covers. Thus,

Average sale = $3,902.30 ÷ 140
= $27.87

Note that appetizers and desserts are not included when determining the number of covers. The assumption is that each customer ordered a main dish and that appetizers and desserts were additional orders placed by the same customers. This figure is for food only and does not include beverages. Many restaurants keep food and beverage figures separate when calculating average sale per customer. Please note that in today's market there are restaurants that sell only smaller plates and don't differentiate between appetizers and main dishes. In these cases, any customer who purchases items is a cover.

The average dollar sale is used by foodservice operators to identify sales trends, and to compare the effectiveness of various menus, menu listings, sales promotions, or to compare one server's performance with another's.

This figure is of considerable interest to managers, who are likely to be watching business trends. If the average sale decreases over time, management will probably investigate the reasons for the changes in customer spending habits. Possibilities include a deterioration in service standards, customer dissatisfaction with food quality, inadequate sales promotion, changes in portion sizes, or even deteriorating economic conditions.

Average Sale per Server. **Average sale per server** is total dollar sales for an individual server divided by the number of customers served by that individual. This, too, is a figure used for comparative purposes, and it is usually considered a better indicator of the sales ability of a particular individual because, unlike total sales per server, it eliminates differences caused by variations in the number of persons served. If Bistro Quatre had four servers on duty, and Vijay, one of the servers, had 30 customers and total dollar sales of $565 on Saturday night, February 13th, average sale per server for Vijay would be calculated as follows:

Average sale for Vijay = Total sales for Vijay ÷ Number of customers for Vijay
= $565 ÷ 30
= $18.83

The average sale per server for Vijay would be compared with other servers. If his average sale per customer was considerably lower than other servers, management might look into the reason why, and possibly decide to retrain Vijay in sales techniques.

All of these monetary sales concepts are common in the industry and are likely to be encountered quickly by those seeking careers in food and beverage management. Yet several nonmonetary sales concepts and terms should also be understood.

Nonmonetary Terms

Total Number Sold

Total number sold refers to the total number of steaks, shrimp cocktails, or any other menu items sold in a given time period. This figure is useful in several ways. For example, foodservice managers use total number sold to identify unpopular menu items in order to eliminate such items from the menu. In addition, historical records of total numbers of specific items sold are useful for forecasting sales. Such forecasts are critical in making decisions about purchasing and production. The total number of a specific item sold is a figure used to make judgements about quantities in inventory and about sales records, as discussed in later chapters. For example, Figure 1.5 shows that only five orders of roasted duck breast, six orders of baby back ribs, and six orders of gnocchi were sold on the day these calculations were made. The purchasing steward would track these items carefully so as not to order too much. Additionally, the manager might consider eliminating these three items from the menu if the number sold consistently underperforms the other menu items.

Covers

Cover is a term used in the industry to describe one diner, regardless of the quantity of food he or she consumes. An individual consuming a continental breakfast in a hotel coffee shop is counted as one cover. So is another individual in the same coffee shop who orders a full breakfast consisting of juice, eggs, bacon, toast, and coffee. These two diners are counted as two covers.

Total Covers. Total covers refers to the total number of customers served in a given period—an hour, a meal period, a day, a week, or some other period. Foodservice managers are usually particularly interested in these figures, which are compared with figures for similar periods in the past so that judgements can be made about business trends and action can be taken if necessary to improve numbers. As shown in Figure 1.5, there were 140 covers for that Saturday night.

Average Covers. An **average number of covers** is determined by dividing the total number of covers for a given time period by some other number. That number may be the number of hours in a meal period, the number of days the establishment is open per week, or the number of servers on duty during the time period, among many other possibilities. The following calculations are some of the more common ones used:

> Covers per hour = Total covers ÷ Number of hours of operation
> Covers per day = Total covers ÷ Number of days of operation
> Covers per server = Total covers ÷ Number of servers

The averages so derived can be of considerable help to a manager, attempting to schedule and control labour costs make judgements about the efficiency of service in the dining room, the effectiveness of a promotional campaign, or the competence of a particular server.

Seat Turnover

Seat turnover, most often called simply *turnover* or *turns*, refers to the number of seats occupied during a given period (or the number of customers served during that period) divided by the number of seats available. For example, Figure 1.5 shows 140 customers served during that one Saturday meal. The restaurant has 75 seats, so seat turnover would be calculated as follows:

$$\text{Seat turnover} = \text{Number of customers served} \div \text{Number of seats}$$
$$= 140 \div 75$$
$$= 1.87 \text{ turns}$$

In other words, each seat in Bistro Quatre was occupied an average of 1.87 times during that Saturday dinner meal.

Seat turnover may be calculated for any period, but is most often calculated for a given meal period.

Sales Mix

Sales mix is a term used to describe the relative quantity sold of any menu item as compared with other items in the same category. The terms *popularity index* and *menu mix* are related and widely used in the industry, as we will see in chapters 7 and 11, respectively. The relative quantities are normally percentages of total unit sales and always total 100 percent. Figure 1.6 shows the number of main dishes sold for each of the main dish items, and the sales mix at Bistro Quatre for Saturday, February 6. Note that the percentages vary from 3.57 percent to 9.29 percent. These percentages will be significant when we discuss menu engineering in Chapter 11.

• FIGURE 1.6 •

Bistro Quatre Sales Mix, Saturday February 6, 20XX

Menu Item	Number Sold	Sales Mix, %
Black Angus New York Strip Steak	13	9.29
Tournedos Bistro	10	7.14
Roasted Muscovy Duck Breast	5	3.57
Roasted Leg of Ontario Lamb	8	5.71
Barbequed Baby Back Ribs	6	4.29
Tamarind and Ginger Shrimp	9	6.43
Gnocchi	6	4.29
Darjeeling-Smoked Wild B.C. Salmon	13	9.29
Paella	9	6.43
Charred Big Eye Tuna	7	5.00
Miso-Glazed Black Cod	8	5.71
Grilled Breast of Chicken	11	7.86
Tagliatelle	9	6.43
Fresh Scallops	6	4.29
Capellini	9	6.43
Catch of the Day	11	7.86
Total Covers	140	100.00

THE COST-TO-SALES RATIO: COST PERCENT

LEARNING OBJECTIVE 1.3
Describe the significance
of cost-to-sales relationships
and identify several cost-to-
sales ratios and the formulas
used to compute cost percent
and sales price.

Raw dollar figures for directly variable and semivariable costs are seldom, if ever, of any particular significance for control purposes. Because these costs vary to some extent with business volume, they become significant only when expressed in relation to sales volume. These ratios are usually described as a percentage. Foodservice managers calculate costs in dollars and compare those costs with sales in dollars. This enables them to discuss the relationship between costs and sales, sometimes described as the **cost per dollar of sale**, the ratio of costs to sales, or simply as the cost-to-sales ratio. The industry uses the following basic formula for calculating cost-to-sales ratio.

$$\text{Cost} \div \text{Sales} = \text{Cost per dollar of sale}$$

The formula normally results in a decimal answer, and any decimal can be converted to a percentage if one multiplies it by 100 and adds a percent sign (%). This is the same as simply moving the decimal point two places to the right and adding a percent sign. This is the formula used to calculate **cost percents**; it is commonly written as

$$\text{Cost} \div \text{Sales} \times 100 = \text{Cost \%}$$

This formula can then be extended to show the following relationships:

$$\text{Food cost} \div \text{Food sales} \times 100 = \text{Food cost \%}$$
$$\text{Beverage cost} \div \text{Beverage sales} \times 100 = \text{Beverage cost \%}$$
$$\text{Labour cost} \div \text{Total sales} \times 100 = \text{Labour cost \%}$$

Consider Figures 1.1 and 1.3, the statements of income for the two establishments described earlier—Il Giardino and Bistro Quatre. In the case of Bistro Quatre, we saw that food costing $312,090 ultimately resulted in sales of $891,687. To determine the percentage of sales represented by cost, we divide cost by sales, as in the preceding formula, and multiply the resulting decimal answer by 100 in order to convert it to a percentage. The costing triangle illustrated in Figure 1.7a is very useful when solving cost percent formulas. It should be noted that the costing triangle can be used to solve for cost percent as well as for cost and sales. The idea is that any number over another number indicates division; therefore, in Figure 1.7a, cost divided by sales multiplied by 100 is equal to cost percent. Similarly, when solving for sales, the cost would be over the cost percent figure, as shown in Figure 1.7b, thus cost divided by cost percent (after converting to a decimal) is equal to sales. Finally, when using the costing triangle to solve for cost, the cost percent and sales numbers are side by side, as shown in Figure 1.7c. In this case, we multiply to find the unknown cost, remembering always to convert percents to decimals before using them in a formula:

$$\$312{,}090 \div \$891{,}687 = .35 \text{ and } .35 \times 100 = 35.0\%$$

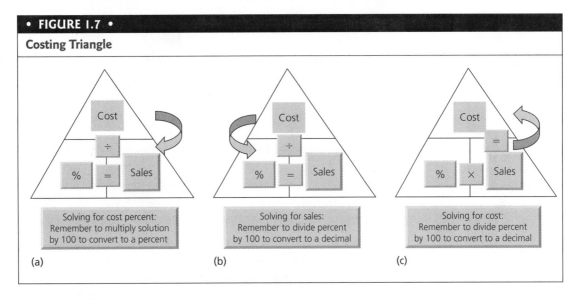

• FIGURE 1.7 •

Costing Triangle

(a) Solving for cost percent: Remember to multiply solution by 100 to convert to a percent

(b) Solving for sales: Remember to divide percent by 100 to convert to a decimal

(c) Solving for cost: Remember to divide percent by 100 to convert to a decimal

Thus, we learn that the food cost percent, or the food cost-to-sales ratio, in Bistro Quatre over the past year has been 35 percent. This tells us that 35 percent of the income from food sales over the year has gone to cover the cost of the food. Because the cost of food represents $0.35 out of each $1.00 in sales, we can also say that food cost per dollar sale is $0.35. Following the same formula, we may now take the figures for food costs and food sales from the statement of income for Il Giardino and calculate both the food cost percent and the cost per dollar of sale for purposes of comparison:

$$\$708{,}431 \div \$1{,}686{,}740 = .42 \text{ and } .42 \times 100 = 42.0\%$$

So, in the case of Il Giardino, the food cost per dollar of sale is $0.42, and the food cost percent is 42 percent.

Cost percents are useful to managers in at least two ways: (1) they provide a means of comparing costs relative to sales for two or more periods of time; and (2) they provide a means of comparing two or more operations. When comparing cost percents for two or more operations, it is important to note that the comparisons are valid only if the operations are similar. Thus, one can compare two fast-food restaurants offering similar products, but one cannot compare a high-priced French restaurant with a local inexpensive neighbourhood diner and expect the comparison to be meaningful.

Useful information from the comparison of the two case study restaurants is shown in Figure 1.8.

• **FIGURE 1.8** •		
Comparison of Costs and Sales, Bistro Quatre and Il Giardino		
	Bistro Quatre	*Il Giardino*
Food Sales	$891,687	$1,686,740
Cost of Food Sold	$312,090	$708,431
Cost per dollar of sale	$0.35	$0.42
Food cost %	35%	42%

It is only at this point that the figures can begin to take on some real meaning and that one can begin to compare them intelligently. It is significant that a principal difference between the two restaurants lies in the fact that the food cost per dollar of sale is $0.07 higher in one. Expressed another way, one can say that the cost-to-sales ratio for food is 7 percent higher at Il Giardino. It is not until raw dollar figures have been converted to this form that there is any useful way of comparing them.

Because food cost is variable, it increases and decreases with sales volume. It would not be possible to make useful comparisons between operating periods for one restaurant or between similar restaurants (as in a chain, for example) unless one were to work with cost percents, or with costs per dollar of sale. Because cost-control figures in the hospitality industry are most commonly expressed in terms of cost percents, we will deal with those figures in this text. In addition, because real dollar figures in real restaurant operations seldom result in round numbers, our percents will be expressed in tenths of 1 percent—35.9 percent or 36.2 percent, for example. This, too, is common in the hospitality industry and permits a greater degree of accuracy. After all, in the case of Bistro Quatre, one-tenth of 1 percent of sales is $891.69, which is a considerable number of real dollars.

• **FIGURE 1.9** •		
Comparison of Cost Percents, Bistro Quatre and Il Giardino		
	Bistro Quatre	*Il Giardino*
Food cost as a % of food sales	35.00%	42.00%
Beverage cost as a % of beverage sales	25.00%	32.00%
Combined food and beverage cost as a % of total sales	33.50%	40.50%
Payroll as a % of total sales	24.50%	33.75%
Overhead as a % of total sales	29.73%	23.31%
Prime cost as a % of total sales	58.00%	74.25%
Profit before taxes as a % of total sales	12.27%	2.44%

Using the preceding formula, it is now possible to develop a chart (Figure 1.9) comparing cost percents in the two restaurants.

It is both interesting and significant that the cost percents for prime cost as well as the components of prime cost—food, beverages, and labour—are all higher at Il Giardino than they are at Bistro Quatre. The remaining costs are lower at Il Giardino when expressed as a percent of sales. In food service, these remaining costs are often referred to as **overhead** costs. In this text, the term *overhead cost* is used to mean all costs other than prime cost. Overhead normally consists of all the fixed costs associated with operating the business. One of the reasons that the overhead costs of Il Giardino are lower than those of Bistro Quatre did, when expressed as a percentage of sales, is the higher sales volume of Il Giardino. It is normal for high-volume restaurants to have a lower overhead cost percent than restaurants with lower volume of sales. It may seem obvious that if Il Giardino controlled its variable costs to the same extent as Bistro Quatre did, it would produce a far greater dollar profit. Because it does not, Bistro Quatre still makes a higher dollar profit and a much higher profit percentage.

Let's look at other ways to use the cost-to-sales ratio: as explained in Figure 1.7, sometimes the formula

$$\text{Cost} \div \text{Sales} \times 100 = \text{Cost \%}$$

is rearranged algebraically to facilitate other calculations. For instance, suppose a banquet manager has been directed by her boss to ensure that all banquet functions operate at a given food cost percent, and she wants to quote a sales price for a particular menu item, the cost of which is known. The calculation of sales price is simplified if the formula is rearranged in the following form:

$$\text{Cost} \div \text{Cost \% (expressed as a decimal)} = \text{Sales (or sales price)}$$

Remember: When working with percents, one must convert to a decimal before using it in a formula.

If the given cost percent were 30.0 percent and the food cost for the item were $3.60, the appropriate sales price would be $12.00, as illustrated here:

$$\text{Cost \% must be changed to a decimal, so } 30.0\% \div 100 = 0.3$$
$$\$3.60 \div 0.3 = \$12.00$$

Suppose this banquet manager is dealing with a group willing to spend $15.00 per person for a banquet, and the same 30.0 percent cost percent is to apply. Calculation of the maximum permissible cost per person to achieve the 30 percent food cost is facilitated by rearranging the formula once again:

> Sales × Cost % (expressed as a decimal) = Cost
> Cost % must be changed to a decimal, so 30.0% ÷ 100 = 0.3
> $15.00 × 0.3 = $4.50

So the maximum cost per person can be calculated as $4.50.

In summary, the cost percent formula can be written and used in any one of three possible forms:

> Cost ÷ Sales = Cost %
> Cost ÷ Cost % (expressed as a decimal) = Sales
> Sales × Cost % (expressed as a decimal) = Cost

The foregoing discussion has assumed that food and beverage costs are relatively stable over time and that one can readily predict future costs accurately. Unfortunately, that is not normally the case. However, it is often necessary to quote prices for functions to be held some months in the future. To do so with some reasonable degree of accuracy, one should consider both seasonal fluctuations in costs and inflation rates. Prices change seasonally. As an example, the prices of most salad greens are higher in Canada during the winter months when produce is shipped from the U.S. or Mexico, and this fact should be taken into account when quoting prices in July for a function to be held in January. Moreover, in times of inflation, various food costs increase at various rates. These can frequently be anticipated by management from published information and should be taken into account when quoting future sales prices. An example is the case of an establishment quoting a banquet price for a date six months in the future when the current rate of inflation is 5 percent on an annual basis. If the current food cost for one item is calculated to be $4.00, the manager may be reasonably sure that the cost will be somewhat higher in six months. Although it is not possible to predict a future cost with perfect accuracy, it is possible to approximate it. A simple way is to assume that one-half of the annual inflation rate will apply to the first six months of the upcoming year, and thus use 2.5 percent (one-half of 5 percent) as the approximate future cost—$4.10, in this case. Assuming a pre-established food cost percent of 30 percent, sale price will be increased from $13.33 to $13.67, as illustrated here.

> 30.0% ÷ 100 = 0.3
> $4.00 ÷ 0.3 = $13.33 versus $4.10 ÷ 0.3 = $13.67

Mathematicians will recognize that this calculation is not wholly accurate. However, it does offer a simple system for taking inflation into account.

INDUSTRYWIDE VARIATIONS IN COST PERCENTS

LEARNING OBJECTIVE 1.4
Describe factors that cause industrywide variations in cost percents.

Cost percents vary considerably from one foodservice operation to another. There are many possible reasons for these variations, several of which are discussed in the following paragraphs. Some of the factors contributing to these variations are type of service, location, price structure, and menu.

In very broad terms, there are two basic types of foodservice operations:

1. those that operate at a low margin of profit per item served and depend on relatively high customer counts and
2. those that operate at a relatively high margin of profit per item and therefore do not require such high customer counts.

It is apparent that if two operations—one of each type—were to have any menu items in common, the menu price would tend to be lower in the operation of the first type.

The following examples of the cost structures of establishments in these two categories are intended to serve only as illustrations of relative costs. The examples should not be taken to imply either that these are standards for the industry or that any particular restaurant should have or should strive to achieve the illustrated cost structure. The cost structure for each individual restaurant must be determined for that restaurant alone, the obvious point being that, as percentages of sales, costs must always total less than 100 percent if the operation is to be profitable.

Restaurants that depend principally on convenience foods—the so-called fast-food or quick-service restaurants (or QSRs)—are generally included in the first (low-margin) category, because of relatively lower menu price operations. The food cost percents in these types of restaurants tend to be high, often because the restaurants use processed or convenience foods that are more expensive than raw ingredients and processed with their own labour. They are, in effect, outsourcing the labour on these products so the food cost actually contains that portion of labour cost. However, to run their operations, they hire lower-skilled personnel, pay lower wages, and keep the number of employees at a minimum. This makes it possible for these restaurants to offset high *food cost* percent with low labour cost and low labour cost percent. A typical cost analysis for such a restaurant is shown in Figure 1.10.

• FIGURE 1.10 •	
Cost Analysis for Typical Low-Margin Restaurant	
Cost of food and beverages	40%
Labour cost	20
Other controllable and noncontrollable costs	30
Profit before income taxes	10
Total	100%

Restaurants in the second (high-margin) category tend to depend less on convenience foods, catering to customers who prefer more sophisticated foods with more personal service. The food cost percent in such establishments tends to be lower as they buy raw products, not processed ones. A good example is bread. If a casual low-margin restaurant buys bread for resale and it costs $3.00 a loaf, the food cost is $3.00 per loaf and there is no labour cost involved. In essence, the product is outsourced (we will discuss outsourcing in Chapter 2). If a high-margin restaurant makes its own bread from scratch, it might pay $1.00 for the yeast, flour, salt, water, and other ingredients, so the food cost is $1.00 per loaf. But the labour cost to make the bread, which might be $2.00 per loaf, means the total cost for the bread is also $3.00. As you can see, for both types of restaurants, the bread cost is $3.00 but their food cost percents and labour cost percents will be completely different. What is interesting is that the prime cost for each restaurant will be the same, $3.00 per loaf. Both operations could be profitable even though they have vastly different food and labour cost ratios. In Chapter 3 we will see how dollar volume and contribution margin may help to determine profitability.

Buying and preparing raw products tends to keep the cost of labour higher in high-margin restaurants than in QSRs as they are incurring the labour of processing raw products (manufacturing) as well as all other operational labour costs. This type of food preparation and service requires a greater number of personnel who are more skilled and often better paid. An analysis of costs for a typical restaurant of this type would resemble that in Figure 1.11.

• FIGURE 1.11 •	
Cost Analysis for Typical High-Margin Restaurant	
Cost of food and beverages	25%
Labour cost	35
Other controllable and noncontrollable costs	30
Profit before income taxes	10
Total	100%

It is important to note that operations in the first category require greater numbers of customers to achieve a given dollar volume of sales. In the second example, partly because of higher menu prices, fewer customers are required to reach a given dollar volume. In general, it is possible to achieve a profit with fewer customers if menu prices are high, because margins are better. We will discuss contribution margin further in Chapter 3.

In the two examples cited, profit as a percentage of sales is shown to be 10.0 percent. It must be remembered that these figures are not to be taken as industry standards or even as necessarily desirable standards. Some experts believe that 5.0 percent profit is desirable; others think that a lower percentage of profit will help ensure customer satisfaction and will induce customers to return regularly. If true, this would likely lengthen the business life of a restaurant. Many operators now report profit margins of 3 to 10 percent after all expenses.

The appropriate percentage of profit for a given restaurant must be based on other factors, such as desired return on investment, the real and perceived risks of being in the foodservice business as compared with other forms of investment, the return one might expect to earn in some other business, and a whole range of considerations involving the competition in a specific market. In the last analysis, evaluations and judgements about costs, sales, and profits must be made on an individual, case-by-case basis. Although many similarities exist, each restaurant tends to be unique.

MONITORING COSTS AND SALES

It is obvious that total sales must exceed total costs if a foodservice enterprise is to be profitable. If costs exceed sales for an extended period of time, the enterprise may eventually face bankruptcy. At the very least, the owner will have to put additional funds into the business to keep it going. It is the job of the manager—and the cost controller, if there is one—to be constantly aware of the costs of operating the business and to keep these costs below the level of sales. Fortunately, many smaller operations and most larger operations have the benefit of computers and industry-specific computer programs that automatically calculate the data described in this chapter (see Chapter 2 for an example of such a program). Daily reports printed out by the computer allow management to monitor various cost and sales information, as well as the important ratios (percents). These ratios are compared with the same ratios from previous periods, and judgements are made about whether the ratios are satisfactory. If not, remedial steps must be taken to bring these ratios into line with those of previous more profitable periods.

It is important that the cost and sales data used to calculate these ratios be from like periods. Customarily, comparisons are made for specific days of the week—Monday of last week compared with Monday of this week, for example. Sometimes comparisons are made of like weeks in two different months—the first week in June compared with the first week in July, for example. Sometimes trends can be identified by those who track these ratios from week to week. However, there are still many establishments in which cost and sales data are seldom examined and ratios are rarely calculated. Some of these operators are successful anyway, but they are rare, and they may be missing additional profits because of this. At best, not keeping on top of such information is risky and can lead to problems that are difficult to diagnose and correct.

Establishments that gather cost and sales information only monthly, quarterly, or annually may not be able to take effective and immediate remedial

LEARNING OBJECTIVE 1.5
Explain the value of comparing current cost-to-sales ratios with those for previous periods.

action, because the information is not sufficiently timely to shed light on current problems. Costs, once incurred, cannot be recouped.

THINGS TO CONSIDER

There is a high failure rate in restaurants, and in retail businesses generally. A restaurant's costs are varied and numerous. What seems like a relatively easy task—spending less to cover costs than sales dollars earned—often turns out to be more difficult than anticipated. In today's world of high overhead, profits are small, even in successful operations. Foodservice businesses generate average profits of 3 to 10 percent. Because profit margins are shrinking, understanding how to achieve sales and control costs is fundamental. Most successful hospitality and foodservice operators in Canada realize where, how, and why money comes into and goes out of the business. They manage to maximize sales and control expenses.

It must be understood that a good business plan and a proper set-up are essential. Before a business can become a reality, a good concept and intimate knowledge of the market and the correct position to take in it are crucial. This is true for all retail businesses, but especially so for restaurants, hotels, and caterers. Many businesses fail even before they begin because the proprietor neglects these fundamental initial steps.

Knowing who your customers are, what they want, how much they will pay for products and services, how often they will frequent, how many of them you can count on as clients, who the competition is, and what strengths and weaknesses competitors have are all key elements to creating a successful enterprise. In addition, choosing a proper location, ensuring that the ambience and service matches or exceeds guests' quality standards and expectations, picking the right price point, selling the right products and menu items, and making certain that every detail is appropriate to the level of standards to excite and entice your targeted market will help to ensure prosperity. Performing market surveys and feasibility studies and developing a good business plan are integral to proper business start-up. Timing may be critical as well. Many types of foodservice operations can succeed if the concept is appealing and the target customers exist in sufficient numbers to allow for profitability. Service quality is a key factor in determining success, but value is also crucial at every level of quality or position in the marketplace. In fact, with competition everywhere, all aspects of operations are significant.

After all of these factors are researched and evaluated, a good business plan is produced, and a good start-up is implemented, the business has an excellent foundation before it even opens! Once the business is operational, management must ensure success by working to maximize sales and control all the myriad costs associated with operating in our industry. That is the focus of this text, and when you have finished studying it you will know how to control costs and sales.

CHAPTER ESSENTIALS

In this chapter, we defined *cost* as the term is used in the foodservice industry and showed that all industry-related costs can be viewed from several perspectives, including fixed versus variable (with some variable costs being directly variable and others being semivariable), controllable versus noncontrollable, total versus unit, and historical versus planned. We defined the term *prime cost* and showed how the components of the prime cost relate to one another as well as to total sales. We defined *sales*, showed their importance to cost control and profitability, and illustrated special terms commonly used in the industry to discuss and compare various ways of identifying and expressing sales. Monetary expressions of sales include total sales; total sales by category, by server, and by seat; sales prices; and average sale per customer and per server. We defined the term *cover* and identified such nonmonetary expressions of sales as total number sold, total covers, average covers, seat turnover, and sales mix. We defined the cost-to-sales ratio and provided the formulas used in the industry for various common calculations. We also showed how cost-to-sales ratios may vary from one establishment to another throughout the industry. Finally, we discussed the importance of monitoring cost and sales data and of calculating significant ratios regularly. An understanding of these concepts will provide the necessary foundation for those seeking to understand and apply the control process in food service.

KEY TERMS IN THIS CHAPTER

QUESTIONS AND PROBLEMS

1. Given the following information, calculate cost percents. Round your answers to the nearest tenth of a percent.
   a. Cost, $200.00; Sales, $500.00
   b. Cost, $150.00; Sales, $500.00
   c. Cost, $178.50; Sales, $700.00
   d. Cost, $216.80; Sales, $800.00
   e. Cost, $127.80; Sales, $450.00
   f. Cost, $610.00; Sales, $2,000.00

2. Calculate cost, given the following figures for cost percent and sales:
   a. Cost percent, 28.0%; Sales, $500.00
   b. Cost percent, 34.5%; Sales, $2,400.00
   c. Cost percent, 24.8%; Sales, $225.00
   d. Cost percent, 31.6%; Sales, $1,065.00
   e. Cost percent, 29.7%; Sales, $790.00
   f. Cost percent, 21.2%; Sales, $4,100.00

3. Calculate sales, given the following figures for cost percent and cost:
   a. Cost percent, 30.0%; Cost, $90.00
   b. Cost percent, 25.0%; Cost, $500.00
   c. Cost percent, 33.3%; Cost, $1,000.00
   d. Cost percent, 27.3%; Cost, $1,300.40
   e. Cost percent, 24.5%; Cost, $88.20
   f. Cost percent, 34.8%; Cost, $1,113.60

4. List three examples of foodservice costs that are fixed. Are they controllable? Explain your answers.

5. List three examples of foodservice costs that are variable. Are they controllable? Explain your answers.

6. Write a short paragraph illustrating why a comparison of raw dollar costs in two restaurants would not be meaningful, but a comparison of the cost percents for food, beverages, labour, and overhead might be.

7. The present cost to Lil's Restaurant for one à la carte steak is $3.20. This is 40 percent of the menu sales price.
   a. What is the present sales price?
   b. At an annual inflation rate of 5 percent, what is this steak likely to cost one year from today?
   c. Using the cost calculated in (b) above, what should the menu sales price be for this item in one year if the cost percent at that time is to be 38 percent?
   d. If you were a banquet manager planning a function six months from now and planning to use this item, what unit cost would you plan for?
   e. The banquet manager in (d) above has already calculated that the other items, not including the steak, in this banquet menu will have increased in cost in six months from $2.00 to $2.11. What should the sales price

per person be for this banquet if the desired cost percent is 40 percent (include the steak in your calculation.)

8. At the Loner Inn, total fixed costs for October were $28,422.80. In that month, 14,228 covers were served.

   a. What was the fixed cost per cover for October?

   b. Assume that fixed costs will increase by 2 percent in November. Determine fixed cost per cover if the number of covers decreases by 10 percent in November.

9. Joe's Downtown Restaurant purchases domestic red wine at $9.20 per bottle. Each bottle contains 3 litres. The wine is served per glass in 150 millilitre portions, and management allows for 30 millilitres of spillage per 3-litre bottle.

   a. What is the average unit cost per drink?

   b. What is the total cost of 60 glasses of wine?

   c. The banquet manager is planning a function for 120 persons for next Friday evening. Each guest will be given one glass of wine. How many bottles should be ordered for the party?

   d. What will be the unit cost of the wine? The total cost?

10. Sales records for a luncheon in the Newmarket Restaurant for a recent week were:

    Item A, 196

    Item B, 72

    Item C, 142

    Item D, 24

    Item E, 112

    Item F, 224

    Item G, 162

    Given this information, calculate the sales mix.

11. Calculate the average cheque from the following data:

    a. Sales, $1,000.00; Number of customers, 125

    b. Sales, $1,300.00; Number of customers, 158

    c. Sales, $8,720.53; Number of customers, 976

12. The following table indicates the number of covers served and the gross sales per server for one three-hour period in Sally's Restaurant. Determine (a) the average number of covers served per hour per server, and (b) the average sale per server for the three-hour period.

SERVER	COVERS SERVED	GROSS SALES PER SERVER
A	71	$237.40
B	66	$263.95
C	58	$188.25

13. Use the information about Sally's Restaurant identified in Question 12 to complete the following:

    a. Calculate the average cheque.

    b. Calculate the turnover for the three-hour period if there are 65 seats in the restaurant.

14. Given the information about Sally's Restaurant identified in questions 12 and 13, assume the restaurant had 85,629 customers per year and gross sales were $352,783.40.

    a. Calculate the average cheque.

    b. Calculate sales per seat for the year.

15. The financial records of the Colonial Restaurant reveal the following figures for the year ending December 31, 20XX:

Depreciation, $25,000

Food sales, $375,000

Cost of beverages sold, $30,000

Other controllable expenses, $60,000

Salaries and wages, $130,000

Beverage sales, $125,000

Employee benefits, $20,000

Cost of food sold, $127,500

Occupancy costs, $55,000

    a. Following the form illustrated in Figure 1.1, prepare a statement of income for the business.

    b. Determine the following percentages:

      Food cost percent

      Labour cost percent (payroll plus payroll taxes and employee benefits)

      Beverage cost percent

      Combined food and beverage cost percent

      Percentage of profit before income taxes

    c. Assuming the restaurant has 75 seats, determine food sales per seat for the year.

16. Define the key terms in this chapter.

EXCEL EXERCISES

The companion website for this text provides computer exercises for students using Microsoft Excel. Bring up the exercises for each chapter on your Excel spreadsheet and complete the problems. Students using another spreadsheet program can complete these exercises, but must construct their own templates, using the illustrations in the text as examples.

    Barnaby's Hideaway is a 140-seat restaurant located on the outskirts of a city of 250,000 population. Its menu is shown as Figure 1.12.

Exercise 1.1

Complete the income statement for Barnaby's Hideaway by inserting the following figures in the appropriate places. Print your completed income statement. This will give you printed information for completing exercises 1.2, 1.3, and 1.4.

Sales

Food, $1,120,964

Beverage, $465,200

Cost of Sales

Food, $392,337

Beverage, $102,344

Salaries and Wages, $396,541

Employee Benefits, $99,135

Other Controllable Expenses, $275,330

Occupancy Costs, $75,230

Interest, $25,600

Depreciation, $79,099

Exercise 1.2

On your Excel spreadsheet, calculate food cost percent and labour cost percent for Barnaby's Hideaway.

Exercise 1.3

On your Excel spreadsheet, calculate overhead as a percentage of total sales for Barnaby's Hideaway.

Exercise 1.4

On your Excel spreadsheet, calculate prime cost as a percentage of total costs for Barnaby's Hideaway. When completed, add the cost percents for prime cost, overhead costs, and profit to arrive at 100 percent.

Exercise 1.5

Sales for one Friday night are shown on the textbook's companion website. On your Excel spreadsheet:

a. Calculate the average cheque (assume one customer for each main dish sold).

b. Calculate the sales mix.

c. Eight servers are on duty that night. Calculate the average sales per server.

d. Calculate the seat turnover for the meal period.

Exercise 1.6

Follow the instructions on the textbook's companion website to complete this exercise.

• FIGURE 1.12 •

Menu for Barnaby's Hideaway

SOUPS

Black Bean Soup
$5.95
New England Style Clam Chowder
$6.95

APPETIZERS

SHRIMP COCKTAIL
Five jumbo shrimp served with a zesty cocktail sauce
$8.95

OYSTERS ROCKEFELLER
Six oysters on the half shell baked with spinach, onion, bread crumbs, bacon, and spices
$12.95

PROSCIUTTO AND FIG BRUSCHETTA
Bruschetta covered with Italian prosciutto and figs
$9.95

JEWELS OF THE SEA IN PUFF PASTRY
Select shellfish served with a delicious sauce in puff pastry
$10.95

SALADS

WILD MUSHROOM AND QUINOA SALAD
With fresh thyme, goat cheese, and shallot vinaigrette
$8.95

CARMELIZED APPLE SALAD
With walnuts and spicey orance vinaigrette
$7.95

CAESAR SALAD
Topped with roasted garlic bread croutons and our own dressing
$7.95

MAINS

All entrées served with pasta, baked potato, or wild rice;
vegetables du jour; and choice of salad

NEW YORK STRIP STEAK
12-ounce prime steak charbroiled and topped with crimini mushrooms
$23.65

PRIME RIB OF BEEF
10-ounce prime beef with corn-poblano pudding
$22.50

BABY BACK PORK RIBS
Barbecued ribs with our own barbecue sauce
$20.50

(continued)

• FIGURE 1.12 • *(continued)*

ROAST LEG OF LAMB
Roast lamb with honey, balsamic vinegar, and fresh mint paste
$21.50

LOIN OF PORK À MAISON
Tender pork served with our sauce du jour
$17.45

MEATLESS MANICOTTI*
Pasta stuffed with a delicious low-fat cheese filling
$10.45

CHICKEN BREASTS AU SOY*
Breasts marinated in soy sauce and honey
$12.45

TEA-SMOKED SALMON*
Italian white beans, fusilli, and saffron broth served with salmon
on a bed of lemon baby spinach
$17.45

BAKED STUFFED SHRIMP
Five large shrimp stuffed with a crab dressing
$19.50

CHICKEN ALBUFERA
Chicken breast sautéed with shallots, brandy cream sauce, and artichoke hearts
$14.45

FRUITES DE MER
Lobster, shrimp, and scallops tossed in a light basil cream with fresh romano,
served over thin pasta
$19.45

CATCH OF THE DAY
Fresh fillet of fish sautéed and served with lemon
$14.50

DESSERTS
Deep-Dish Apple Pie
$3.50
Banana Beignets with Orange-Caramel Sauce
$4.00
Caramelized Apple-Blackberry Cobbler
$3.50

*heart-healthy items

CHAPTER 2

The Control Process

• LEARNING OBJECTIVES •

After reading this chapter, you should be able to:

2.1 Define *control* and provide examples of its significance in food and beverage management.

2.2 List the four steps in the control process in food and beverage operations, and pinpoint responsibility for control.

2.3 Cite eight control techniques used in food and beverage operations.

2.4 Describe the steps involved in preparing an operating budget, and prepare a budget given fixed and variable costs for a restaurant.

2.5 Explain why the cost–benefit ratio is significant when making control decisions.

2.6 Identify what to consider when deciding whether to make a product in-house or to outsource.

INTRODUCTION

A considerable part of the previous chapter on costs and sales was devoted to explaining the meaning of those terms as they relate to the food and beverage industry. This chapter will define control, discuss the relationship of control to costs and sales, and outline how a manager plans, organizes, and institutes control in an enterprise. Later chapters will go into the specific procedures used to control various phases of food and beverage operations; this chapter addresses control and the control process in general terms.

CONTROL

LEARNING OBJECTIVE 2.1
Define *control* and provide examples of its significance in food and beverage management.

In general, **control** means exercising governing power over events and situations such that an outcome can be achieved or prevented. In our personal lives, we can normally exercise governing power over our actions, to achieve or prevent various outcomes. For example, we leave our homes for work or school each day early enough so that we arrive at a specific time. We drink alcoholic beverages to achieve a desired glow, but we must limit the amount we drink if we do not want to get drunk or sick. Many people establish a budget so they manage how much they spend on a specific item, like groceries, ensuring there will be enough money left from their paycheque to cover other expenses, like rent, utilities, clothing, and entertainment.

If we do not arrive at school on time, there is the possibility of a penalty for being late for class. If we spend too much on groceries, perhaps we can't afford to go to a club on the weekend. In each of these situations, if we do not establish and follow certain control measures we may face undesirable consequences.

Managers of businesses make rules and establish procedures of various kinds for their employees. In the foodservice industry, knowing what affects costs and how to control them is essential to instituting controls and achieving success. There are varied and numerous types of costs in our industry. Some operators produce 10-page income statements that include over 100 types of costs. They are diverse in nature, and knowing what to expect and what can be done to control or reduce these costs is key to profitability.

Exercising control generally means that there is some human involvement. Humans either take some form of action or prevent others from taking an action in order to achieve an outcome. It is important to point out that in the food and beverage industry, control often means controlling people rather than things. Consider the following: Food does not disappear by itself, without help. Excess quantities of liquor do not get into drinks unless put there by bartenders. Employees' wage calculations are not based on the wrong numbers of hours unless someone gives the wrong information to the paymaster. Food is not consumed by rodents unless human beings make that food accessible. Customers seldom leave without paying unless staff members make that possible. In every one of these instances, the problem is the result of human action or lack of it. If a business is to operate profitably and reach its financial goals, people's actions must be managed, or, in some cases, limited. It is necessary, of course, to provide employees with the tools and resources they need to meet these controls, including the necessary time, money, equipment, and training.

"People" may include more than simply the personnel of the food and beverage operation; they may include customers of the establishment and, in some cases, intruders who seek to steal the resources of the establishment—obviously, without the knowledge and consent of management. Thus, installing locks on both the front and back doors is one of the most basic control measures one can use to prevent intruders from entering and stealing food, beverages, equipment, and cash when the operation is closed. Locating the cashier near the front door helps prevent customers from leaving without paying for their food and beverage charges.

There are several kinds of control devices. Instituting various sanitation procedures may effectively control infestation by insects and rodents. Requiring employees to use a time clock serves many purposes, one of which is to prepare accurate payroll records so that labour costs will be correct. Another good control is the bartender's use of a measuring device to ensure that each drink will contain the correct amount of a particular alcoholic ingredient.

In the food and beverage business, control is a process used by managers to direct, regulate, and restrain the actions of people so that an enterprise's established goals may be achieved. Probably the most common goal for all private enterprises is financial success—a particular profit or return on investment. Other goals may include operating the best restaurant in the city, having a low labour turnover (dedicated employees who stay with the restaurant for many years), or promoting better customer health by providing healthy and nutritious cuisine.

To achieve these goals, management must set up subgoals or objectives compatible with its primary goals. These tend to be more specific and usually more immediate in nature. For example, to achieve the goal of operating the best restaurant in the city, it might be necessary to have subgoals of hiring an excellent chef and purchasing the finest ingredients. To have a low labour turnover, it generally is necessary to have subgoals of establishing a desirable working environment, providing good pay, and offering suitable fringe benefits.

On the assumption that appropriate goals have been established, the discussion in this chapter is restricted to the control procedures employed by foodservice managers to achieve one basic goal of business: operating profitably, because losing money usually results in business failure. Therefore, the focus is on establishing control over costs and sales in food and beverage operations. Attention is centred on the particular methods and procedures used by foodservice managers to direct, regulate, and restrain the actions of people, both directly and indirectly; to keep costs within acceptable bounds; to account for revenues; and to earn a profit.

Cost Control

Cost control is defined as the process used by managers to regulate costs and guard against excessive costs. Cost control is an ongoing process and involves every step in the chain of purchasing, receiving, storing, issuing, and preparing food and beverages for sale; training and scheduling the personnel involved; and ensuring revenues are accounted for and properly used. The particular methods used to control costs vary from one establishment to another, depending in part on the nature and scope of operations, but the concepts behind these principles are universal and the methods are consistent. The obvious objective is to eliminate excessive costs for food, beverages, and labour—to exert some governing power over costs in all areas, ensuring that the enterprise will operate at a profit.

Two of the principal causes of excessive costs are inefficiency and waste. For example, storing food in refrigerators that are not cold enough or bottled beer in a warm, sunny room will cause spoilage and excessive cost. So will the preparation of an inedible pasta dish or an unpalatable drink. When the pasta is thrown into the composting bin or the drink is poured down the drain, costs are increased, but sales are not. Because profit is essentially the difference between sales and costs, it is apparent that any increase in cost that does not lead to a corresponding increase in sales can have only one effect: a reduction in profits. Clearly, management must take steps to guard against such excessive costs.

THE CONTROL PROCESS

LEARNING OBJECTIVE 2.2
List the four steps in the control process in food and beverage operations, and pinpoint responsibility for control.

As indicated in the previous paragraphs, control in the food and beverage business is defined as a process by which managers attempt to direct, regulate, and restrain the actions of people in order to achieve desired goals. The **control process** consists of four steps:

1. Establish standards and standard procedures for the operation.
2. Train all individuals to follow established standards and standard procedures.
3. Monitor performance and compare actual performances with established standards.
4. Take appropriate action to correct deviations from standards.

Sometimes investigation reveals that an established standard is actually unrealistic or inappropriate. If that is the case, management should consider changing the standard. Often the standard cannot be met because of a lack of time, money, or material available to complete the job to standard. This situation must be corrected by management if standards are to be met.

To illustrate the relevance of the control process to food and beverage management, consider the following example: Imagine a restaurant owner who has taken great care to establish goals for her business. One of those goals is to serve the finest food in the area. To reach this goal, the owner has established standards and standard procedures that help define her vision of "the finest food." For one menu item—prime New York strip loin steak is indicated—the standard is made clear by the use of the term *prime*, which specifies certain characteristics in beef. The standards and standard procedures for the chef and the steward reflect the owner's wish that only prime New York strip loin is to be purchased for this menu item. Employees receiving deliveries of meat from purveyors (suppliers) have been trained to follow standard procedures, which include checking the quality of the beef delivered by examining it and verifying that the Canada Prime grade stamp is present. The restaurant manager must monitor operations regularly, checking personally to see that the beef purchased meets the standards set. This may be done in several ways, one of which is by examining the raw beef. The manager knows that if operations are not monitored and orders are placed for a lower grade of beef, regular customers will notice the difference. Some will complain; most will not—they will simply find a restaurant that has the prime beef they desire. Therefore, whenever the manager finds that the quality of beef purchased deviates from the standards, appropriate remedial action must be taken to correct the deviation.

There is a clear need for control in every phase of food and beverage operations. Control is one key to successful food and beverage management and must be established if success is to be achieved. Experience throughout the industry has long proven that establishing control means instituting the four-step process identified in the preceding list.

Sales Control

Although cost control is critically important to the profitable operation of any business, cost control alone will not ensure profitability. Additional steps must be taken to ensure that all sales result in appropriate income to the business (**sales control**). For example, profits will be adversely affected if a steak listed in the menu for $18.95 is sold to a customer for $15.95, or if the drink priced to sell for $4.50 is sold for $2.50, or if food and drink are given away for free. Therefore, it is important to require that each employee records each sale accurately. In addition, it is useful to compare sales records with production records to ensure that all quantities produced are accounted for. Although it is unfortunate that some employees are not completely honest, it is a fact of life that must be taken into account in food and beverage operations. Therefore, guest cheques are usually numbered to ensure accountability. Sometimes duplicate copies of the cheques, clearly identified as duplicates so they are not confused with the originals, are used to reconcile kitchen production with recorded sales. When the cheques and duplicates are numbered sequentially, missing numbers can be noted and investigated at once.

Establishments that use industry-specific computer programs find that control is much easier to institute than without such programs. For example, this chapter illustrates one such program that makes it difficult for menu items to be priced incorrectly; makes it easy to reconcile kitchen production with recorded sales; and allows management to determine that all sales have been accounted for, either in cash or by credit. Other techniques will be discussed in Chapters 12, which include a more thorough treatment of this complex topic.

Responsibility for Control

Responsibility for every aspect of any food and beverage enterprise rests with management. Control, therefore, is clearly a responsibility of management. In some food and beverage enterprises—probably the majority—managers take personal charge of directing and supervising the control procedures in every phase of operations. In others, managers delegate some or all of the work to subordinates. The nature, size, and scope of operations help determine the extent to which managers can exercise direct control rather than delegate that control to someone else. In general, the larger and more complex the operation, the more likely it is that control procedures will be supervised by subordinates. Job titles for these subordinates include chef, kitchen or floor supervisor, sous-chef, assistant manager, food controller, beverage controller, and others.

Throughout this text, several job titles are used for those having responsibility for supervising food, beverage, or labour control procedures. In most food and beverage enterprises, one is likely to find control procedures supervised directly by managers, so that title is used most often. In larger operations, one may find food controllers and beverage controllers. Today, there are comparatively few of these, but the job titles are still useful in discussions of control principles and will appear in various chapters. The use of one job title rather than another in this text is not intended to suggest that any particular task should be assigned to any particular job title. In that sense, the specific job titles used are of little importance. The significant point is that management is ultimately responsible for seeing that appropriate control procedures are established, either by attending to the work personally or by assigning it to others.

Instituting Control

The food and beverage business can be characterized as one that involves raw materials purchased, received, stored, and issued for the purpose of manufacturing products for sale. In respect to these functions, there are many similarities between the food and beverage business and other manufacturing businesses. For example, consider the steps involved in the production of wood furniture.

The furniture manufacturer must determine the kinds of wood that are best suited to the types of furniture to be manufactured and must purchase appropriate quantities of lumber at favourable prices. When the wood is delivered, the shipment must be checked to ensure that the material delivered is exactly as ordered. Then it must be moved into appropriate storage facilities, partly to prevent theft and partly to ensure that the characteristics of the wood will not be adversely affected by climate. The wood must then be issued in appropriate amounts for the production of various kinds of tables and chairs. During the manufacturing process, some effort must be made to maintain balanced quantities of parts so that, for example, one tabletop is made for each four legs. After the tables have been manufactured and sold to customers, care must be taken to ensure that each sale is properly recorded, that the correct price is charged for each table sold, and that the total dollar value of each sale is collected.

The motel coffee shop, the school cafeteria, the hotel dining room, and the resort cocktail lounge all share the same need for purchasing, receiving, storing, and issuing raw materials for the production of finished products for sale. In food and beverage operations, we deal with fruits, vegetables, meat, poultry, and many other foods—fresh, frozen, and canned—as well as alcoholic beverages in many establishments; but these really serve the same purposes in our business that wood serves in the furniture manufacturing business. Thus, in a very real sense, the food and beverage industry is a manufacturing business. All restaurants take raw material and "manufacture" them into a final product. Some restaurants use raw materials to a greater extent than others. A fine-dining establishment, for example, will use relatively few convenience foods. By contrast, fast-food restaurants and institutional operations will generally purchase foods that require less preparation to serve.

In both restaurants and manufacturing operations, the quality of raw materials must be carefully selected, always with the desired final products in mind, and appropriate quantities of each must be ordered to meet expected production needs. Orders for materials are placed with a vendor at the most favourable price. As materials are received, they are checked to see that the business is getting what it pays for. Then the materials are stored properly until needed. When the person in charge of production requests materials from storage, they are made available for the production of finished items for sale. When sold, the revenue generated must be accounted for and used properly to pay expenses.

There are also some differences between foodservice operations and other types of manufacturers. The furniture manufacturer may sell its products wholesale, while a foodservice operation may also be a retailer and a service provider. This requires different expertise, additional planning, organizing, and controls. It is far easier to control labour costs in the furniture industry through the use of set production schedules that allow for proper scheduling and purchasing as there are fewer fluctuations in demand. Often in our industry, we will be at full capacity from noon to 1:30 p.m., and from 6:30 to 9:30 p.m., so controlling costs of production in this environment is more difficult both at these peak times as well as the off-peak times of 1:30 to 6:30 p.m., when all of a sudden much less staff and product are required. Another aspect is the perishable nature of the products used. For example, fresh berries have a much shorter shelf life than wood. More attention, therefore, has to be given to purchasing proper amounts so that spoilage and waste do not increase costs. An additional factor is the lessening of quality and its potential harm to customer satisfaction. Before the berries go completely bad and unsalvageable, they lose quality and, if sold in an inferior state, may cause a good customer not to return, potentially incurring a substantial loss of revenue over time had that customer continued to eat and enjoy fresh berries there.

For all types of operations, it is necessary to institute control in order to prevent problems at every stage in the business process. Control may be accomplished in a variety of ways, and anyone who attempts to manage a food and beverage operation should be aware of the range of techniques available.

The particular techniques selected for use in a given situation depend on the nature of the process requiring control and on the expense and degree of difficulty inherent in instituting such control. Deciding on the appropriate control technique to adopt in a given situation is not always simple. Some of the more common techniques are discussed in the following paragraphs.

Control Techniques

LEARNING OBJECTIVE 2.3
Cite eight control techniques used in food and beverage operations.

Managers must plan and organize in order to succeed in instituting appropriate controls. The control techniques available to managers include the following:

1. Establishing standards
2. Establishing procedures
3. Training personnel
4. Setting examples and directing personnel
5. Observing and correcting employee actions
6. Requiring records and reports
7. Disciplining employees
8. Preparing and following budgets

Establishing Standards

Standards are defined as rules or measures established for making comparisons and judgements. In business these standards are set by management and are used for judging the extent to which results meet expectations. They are consistent with and appropriate to the business, its concept, and its position in the market. To achieve these standards is to succeed in delivering the promise that the business or brand makes. Many types of standards are useful in establishing control over food and beverage operations. It is important to develop a working understanding of these types of standards before proceeding.

Quality standards are used to define the degree of excellence of raw materials, finished products, and, by extension, work. In one sense, establishing quality standards is a grading process. Most food items are graded according to degree of excellence (many of them by government: the Canadian Food Inspection Agency and similar agencies in other nations), and management should establish a quality standard for each food item that is to be purchased. Beef, for example, is generally available in different grades of quality for restaurant and institutional use, and it is important to determine which grade will be used for the preparation of a particular menu item.

Beverage items also require quality standards. For example, some spirits improve with age, and a 12-year-old Scotch whisky is generally considered to be of a higher quality than one that is only 8 years old. Management in beverage operations must determine which beverage items are of appropriate quality to ensure their customers' satisfaction.

Quality standards must also be determined for the workforce. In some hotels and fine restaurants, higher degrees of skill and education are required for the production and service of elaborate menu items. Lower levels of skill would probably be acceptable in the average roadhouse diner.

Quantity standards, defined as measures of weight, count, or volume, are used to make comparisons and judgements. Management must establish several quantity standards. Standard portion sizes for food and beverage products and standards for work output are simple examples. The portion size for every food item served must be clearly established. Each shrimp cocktail should contain a predetermined number of shrimp of specified size, a certain measure of sauce, and clearly identified quantities of garnishes. A portion of soup should be identified according to its volume, the size of bowl or cup to be used, or the size of the ladle used to portion it, and the quantity of any garnish to be added. Similarly, main course items must be identified according to the number of grams or pieces. Surrounding items, such as vegetables, should be portioned with a spoon of a particular size, as with peas, or identified by count, as with asparagus spears.
In bar operations, management must establish a standard quantity for each measure of liquor used. In many instances, bars operate with standard drink recipes indicating the specific quantities of ingredients to be used in preparing particular drinks.

Quantity standards are often important in the control of labour costs as well. When planning staff schedules, it is useful to know, for example, the number of tables or seats a server can cover during a given period or the number of sandwiches a pantry worker can make per hour. In addition to quality and quantity standards, it is ultimately necessary to determine and set cost standards, more commonly referred to as standard costs.

The term **standard cost** is defined as the cost of goods or services identified, approved, and accepted by management. They are models set at predetermined cost levels. Standard costs are used for various purposes. They may be compared with actual costs in order to make judgements about the actual costs, and they may be used as a basis for establishing sales prices. Paradoxically, a standard cost is simultaneously both realistic and an ideal. For example, if one bottle of wine containing 750 millilitres costs $16.00 to purchase and contains four portions, then each millilitre has a value of $0.021, and the standard cost of one glass is $4.00, based on the actual purchase price of the bottle. However, this is an ideal: It does not take into account the possibility of spillage or over-pouring, either of which may occur and affect actual cost.

Standard costs are useful in measuring the effectiveness of operations in food and beverage establishments. As discussed later, comparing standard costs with actual costs can help determine how effectively food and beverage materials and labour resources are being used in day-to-day operations. Standard costs are particularly useful in cost control because they provide a means for management to compare what is actually happening in an enterprise with what should be happening, given the standards established.

There are various methods for calculating standard costs, each of which is discussed in detail in later chapters. In the case of food and beverages, various kinds of calculations are necessary. In the case of labour, determination of standard cost is more complex.

Establishing Procedures

In addition to establishing standards for quality, quantity, and cost, food and beverage managers must establish standard procedures. **Procedures** are the methods employed to prepare products or perform jobs. **Standard procedures** are those that have been established as the correct methods, routines, and techniques for day-to-day operations. As discussed in later chapters, maintaining effective control over food, beverage, and labour costs requires establishing standard procedures for every phase of operations.

Production procedures must be standardized for several reasons. One of the most important of these is customer satisfaction. Quality must be consistent. Any given item should be produced by the same method and with the same ingredients every time it is served. It should also be served in the same quantity each time, so that regular customers will be given a consistent portion each time they order the item, and to maintain cost standards. All of the standard production procedures can be achieved through the use of standardized recipes that include standard ingredients, quantities, costs, and procedures for making each menu item to ensure consistent preparation techniques and final product. Standardized recipes are discussed in detail in Chapter 6.

Ordering and purchasing procedures must be standardized to ensure that ingredients used to make food and beverage products are purchased at appropriate times in needed quantities, at the most favourable prices, and are of appropriate quality for their intended use. Receiving procedures must be standardized so that all goods received conform in quality, quantity, and cost to those ordered. Standard storing procedures must be put into effect to guard against both spoilage and theft, which reduces their value, and leads to excessive costs.

Issuing, which in foodservice is defined as distributing purchased goods from the storeroom to the kitchen, must be standardized so that food and beverage items will be used in the order in which they are received, thus preventing spoilage and the resulting excessive costs. To further guard against spoilage and theft, the quantities of food and beverages issued must be linked carefully to pre-determined production needs. Records of issues can also be used to calculate cost per item produced; they can then be compared with standard costs to determine the efficiency of production and the effectiveness of operations. Procedures must also be in place to ensure that the revenue generated from sales gets into the business' account and is used appropriately. These procedures on controlling revenue are discussed in Chapter 12.

Training Personnel

Although establishing standards and standard procedures is necessary for control, staff must then meet those standards. It is of vital importance initially to recruit, screen, and hire good staff. Hiring competent personnel who do not need constant direction and supervision will make any operation more efficient and successful. Once that is accomplished, the employees will have to be trained to become aware of and be able to meet established standards. **Training** is the process by which managers teach employees how work is to be done, given the standards and standard procedures established. For example, if management has established a standard 100 gram portion size for hamburgers, then all employees responsible for producing portions of hamburgers must be made aware of this. Moreover, each employee must be trained to produce portions of the standard size at his or her workstation, using the correct equipment and supplies provided for doing so. Having the correct supplies and equipment is part of achieving standards; without them, standards are often unattainable. If all employees are not aware of the relevant standards and standard procedures established for their work and are not trained to follow these standards, the standards are useless.

Any foodservice manager who trains employees would doubtlessly agree that training is difficult, time-consuming, and, in the short run, costly. Perhaps that is why a substantial number of poor managers ignore training and simply put new employees to work without devoting any time to demonstrating and explaining how to do their job. Sometimes a new employee is merely introduced to a co-worker, who is then expected to train the new person. Occasionally this works reasonably well; often it does not, frequently because the co-worker is either unwilling or unable to train the new employee. After all, the typical foodservice employee is not hired for his or her ability to train others, and probably has not been trained for that purpose.

If employees are not suitably trained to follow established standards and standard procedures, the control aspects of the manager's job become difficult, at best; sometimes control becomes impossible and the operation fails. This topic is discussed further in relevant sections of the text and in the chapters on labour control.

Setting Examples and Directing Personnel

Sometimes the process of establishing standards and standard procedures is not quite as formal as the foregoing discussion may suggest. In many instances, standards are established informally. Employees in an operation follow the examples set by the manager: the manager's behaviour, manner, responses to questions, or even a failure to speak or take action in some situations. In general, the behaviour of individuals in a group tends to be influenced by the actions, statements, and attitudes of their leaders.

It is the duty of the manager to direct staff to perform according to the established standards. They must also consistently meet these standards. The attitudes and work habits of a manager are evident as he or she performs various tasks in the course of a workday. The behaviour of the manager will influence the manner in which employees perform their work. If the manager who has occasion to help employees plate food for the dining room serves incorrect portion sizes, employees will be more likely to do the same when the manager is not there. Similarly, if a manager is inclined to wrap parcels of food to take home for personal use, employees will be more likely to do so. And if the manager observes them doing so and fails to end the practice, the amount of food leaving the premises will usually increase.

Managers must be consistent in setting examples, as well as in directing, regulating, and restraining employees and their actions. In far too many cases, managers appear not to have long-range and short-range goals in mind as they go about managing. Consequently, their examples, actions, directions, and responses to employees' questions do not present a clear and consistent view. Such inconsistency confuses employees and works against the control processes and procedures in effect.

Observing and Correcting Employee Actions

If a manager were to see a bartender mixing drinks without measuring the ingredients and did not take the time to remind the individual to measure quantities carefully, then the bartender may reasonably assume that his or her work met the manager's standards. The manager would have missed an excellent opportunity to improve the bartender's work habits and to maintain control. Similarly, if a manager were to observe a receiving clerk failing to verify that quantities of meat delivered conformed to the quantity on the invoice and did not correct the individual, the employee might never know that his or her performance was unacceptable.

One of a manager's important tasks is to observe the actions of all employees continually as they go about their daily jobs, judging those actions in light of the standards and standard procedures established for their work. If any employee fails to follow standards, it is a manager's responsibility to correct their performance.

Requiring Records and Reports

Obviously, no manager can be in all places at all times to observe employees' actions. The owner/manager of a small operation can observe employee actions to a far greater extent than can the manager of a larger operation—one consisting, for example, of several bars and dining rooms, seating hundreds of guests and employing hundreds of personnel. The larger the establishment, the more likely it is that managers' observations must be indirect rather than direct. Their "observations" must be abstracted and inferred from a variety of records and reports.

An example of such a report is the statement of income illustrated in Chapter 1. The statement of income summarizes cost and sales information for a particular period. The figures in the statement of income can be used to calculate cost-to-sales ratios of various kinds. These are normally compared with ratios for previous periods, and judgements are made about operations on the basis of these comparisons. If the comparisons are considered satisfactory to management, this implies, in general, that employee performance has been acceptable during the period covered by the statement. If the comparisons are unsatisfactory, the implication is that some or all of the standards and standard procedures have not been followed. This type of report may raise a red flag, alerting the manager to problems, but may not pinpoint specific problems. Other more specific and timely reports and records are usually required. Some of these may be developed daily, others weekly or monthly, as discussed in later chapters. At this point, it is important to recognize that managers need timely information to determine whether primary goals and subgoals are being met. If timely records and reports are not available, opportunities for taking corrective action may be lost. The variety and extent of the records and reports developed and used for control purposes are discussed in greater detail in later chapters.

Disciplining Employees

Discipline is defined as action taken to admonish, penalize, or reprimand an employee for work performance or personal behaviour that is incompatible with established standards. It is a term with negative connotations, suggesting the threats and punishments used on children by some parents. Discipline, therefore, is a difficult topic to address.

Foodservice managers must know all labour laws and union guidelines pertinent to disciplining staff. They generally prefer to avoid the need for discipline by improving the hiring practices in their organizations. By selecting the right people for various jobs—those with the education, experience, skill, and personal characteristics that match the job requirements—the number of individuals requiring some level of discipline can be reduced to a bare minimum. However, every manager must face the fact that, at times, an individual staff member must be disciplined.

Discipline is used as a control technique in many food and beverage operations and may take many forms, as discussed in the following paragraphs. It is a valuable technique if used properly and judiciously.

Discipline is not the same as observing and correcting employee actions; it is the next step beyond that. Before resorting to discipline, managers are assumed to have made reasonable, though unsuccessful, efforts to correct the actions of an employee. Discipline is called for only if corrective action, such as retraining, has failed to correct the problem, often after two or three warnings.

At this point, managers commonly resort to some words or actions that employees normally regard as punishing, in the broadest sense of that term. One must assume that the standards for work performance and personal behaviour are known and understood by all employees because of proper training and instruction by management or because they should be aware of the norms for acceptable behaviour in the workplace.

On one hand, it must be understood that the objective of discipline is to change or modify employees' job performance or personal behaviour—to improve performance so that the work is done in conformance with the standards and procedures that management has identified as those most likely to achieve the organization's goals and objectives. On the other hand, it should be apparent that disciplinary action generally has negative connotations in the minds of employees, most of whom would normally prefer to avoid any such unpleasantness. If certain behaviour patterns (those that follow the standards and procedures established by management) lead to positive and pleasant rewards, like thanks for a job well done, and others (those that ignore management's standards and procedures) bring the negative and unpleasant consequences associated with disciplinary action, then most employees will generally work toward the former and avoid the latter. The very fact that employees know that continual failure to follow established standards can lead to unpleasantness tends to have the desired effect of making job performance and personal behaviour conform to those standards, promoting a pleasant experience. If this is not the case, discipline may be the only option, yet it may not necessarily have the desired effect. In some cases, the relationship will not work and should be terminated.

Preparing and Following Budgets

Preparing and following budgets may be the most common technique for controlling business operations; it may also be one of the most useful. A **budget** is defined as a financial plan and may be described as a realistic expression of management's goals and objectives expressed in financial terms. Many businesses establish budgets for specific aspects of operations. Thus, there are sales budgets, cash flow budgets, capital equipment budgets, and advertising budgets, among others.

Food and beverage operations also use budgets—many of the same types of budgets that are used in other businesses. Many restaurants prepare capital equipment budgets, for example, because of the ongoing need to replace equipment that wears out and to purchase new types of equipment that become available in the market. Capital equipment is typically very costly, and a financial plan must be established before making such purchases. Advertising budgets are established so that appropriate levels of funds can be made available to generate a particular level of sales.

The most important type of budget a food and beverage manager can prepare is an **operating budget**. Stated in dollar terms, this is a forecast of sales activity and an estimate of costs that will be incurred in the process of generating sales. By extension, the budget indicates the profit that should result after the costs of producing those sales have been met. An operating budget is clearly a financial plan for the period it covers. In this text, the discussion of budgets is restricted to operating budgets, because the operating budget is most closely aligned with food, beverage, and labour cost control.

For established restaurants, preparation of an operating budget normally begins with historical information—the financial records of the business. In addition, one needs to estimate any anticipated changes in costs and sales due to the business environment. Thus, if federal or provincial/territorial laws will affect wage rates paid to employees in the period covered by the budget being prepared, this information must be factored into the planning. Similarly, if the establishment's municipal property tax rates have increased or decreased, that information should be reflected in the budget. More difficult to deal with, but equally important, are the effects of poor weather conditions on future crops, anticipated shortages of beef due to ranchers' reductions in herds, and other such general conditions, including trends in the local and national economy that may affect future costs and sales.

For new operations, forecasts for sales are based on customer markets and what portion of them can be captured for sales. Forecasts of costs are based on standards developed by management using their experience and expertise or by checking industry averages. When no market analysis is available, or when the manager is not widely experienced in the food and beverage business, or both, it may be that no effort is made to prepare a budget. This is a missed opportunity for control.

Preparing an Operating Budget

As previously stated, an operating budget is normally prepared using historical information from previous budgets and other financial records. This information, together with anticipated changes in sales and costs, provides the basic data needed to prepare an operating budget for an upcoming period. Operating budgets can be prepared for any period of time—a day, a week, a month, a quarter, six months, or a full year. Typically, an operating budget for one full year is prepared first and then broken down into smaller units for shorter time periods, usually a month or a four-week period. Budgets for these shorter periods may not reflect equal sales and costs in every instance. This is the case in seasonal restaurants. For example, if the budget for a restaurant forecasts $1.6 million in sales for the year, each quarter would not necessarily forecast sales of $400,000. The first and fourth quarters might be busy periods for the restaurant, whereas the second and third quarters might be slow. The manager might forecast $500,000 in sales for the first and fourth quarters and only $300,000 in sales for each of the second and third quarters. In addition, the manager might forecast substantial profits for the busy quarters and very little for the slow quarters. Therefore, breaking down the budget into quarters or months would be very helpful for planning and control.

LEARNING OBJECTIVE 2.4
Describe the steps involved in preparing an operating budget, and prepare a budget given fixed and variable costs for a restaurant.

To illustrate the preparation of a budget, consider as an example Bistro Quatre described in the introduction to Chapter 1. The statement of income and relevant percentages derived from it are reproduced in Figure 2.1. The illustration of budget preparation is for a static budget. A **static budget** is prepared for only one level of business activity for the period (i.e., $1.6 million in sales for the year).

In the previous chapter, distinctions were drawn between controllable and noncontrollable costs and between fixed and variable costs. To prepare an operating budget, it is necessary to determine which costs are fixed and which are variable. That can be more complex than it sounds, and the determinations made by management in one restaurant may be incorrect or inappropriate for another. Figure 2.2 lists the assumptions about fixed and variable costs that were used in the preparation of the operating budget illustrated in Figure 2.3.

• FIGURE 2.1 •

Bistro Quatre, Income Statement, Year Ended December 31, 20XX

			Percent of Sales
Sales			
Food	$891,687		85.0%
Beverage	157,356		15.0%
Total sales		1,049,043	100.0%
Cost of Sales			
Food	$312,090		35.0%
Beverage	39,339		25.0%
Total cost of sales		$351,429	33.5%
Gross Profit		$697,614	66.5%
Controllable Expenses			
Salaries and wages	$209,809		20.0%
Employee benefits	47,207		4.5%
Other controllable expenses	162,602		15.5%
Total Controllable Expenses		$419,618	40.0%
Income before Occupancy Costs, Interest, Depreciation, and Income Taxes		$277,996	26.5%
Occupancy Costs	$ 89,169		8.5%
Interest	13,875		1.3%
Depreciation	46,250		4.4%
Total Occupancy Costs, Interest, and Depreciation		$149,294	14.2%
Restaurant Profit		$128,702	12.3%

• FIGURE 2.2 •

Fixed and Variable Costs in Bistro Quatre

Fixed Costs

Occupancy costs	$ 89,169
Other controllable expenses	$162,609
Fixed salaries	$125,885 (60% of salaries and wages)*
Employee benefits	$ 31,471 (25% of fixed salaries and wages)
Interest	$ 13,875
Depreciation	$ 46,250

Variable Costs

Cost of food	35% of food sales
Cost of beverages	25% of beverage sales
Wages	9.4% of food sales**
Employee benefits	18.8% of variable salaries and wages

*Salaries and wages are semivariable costs, so they must be divided into their fixed and variable components. In the example, we have assumed that 60% of total salaries and wages are fixed while the remaining 40% are variable.

**Variable salaries and wages are assumed to be associated with food sales. Therefore, other salaries and wages will not increase or decrease with changes in business volume. Variable salaries and wages—40% of $209,809 or $83,924—are 9.4% of food sales.

• FIGURE 2.3 •

Bistro Quatre, Projected Operating Budget, Year Ended December 31, 20XX

			Change	Upcoming Year
Sales				
Food	$891,687		$ 44,584	$ 936,271
Beverage	$157,356		$ 7,868	$ 165,224
Total sales		$1,049,043	$ 52,452	$1,101,495
Cost of Sales				
Food	$312,090		$ 15,605	$ 327,695
Beverage	$ 39,339		$ 1,967	$ 41,306
Total cost of sales		$ 351,429	$ 17,572	$ 369,001
Gross Profit		$ 697,614	$ 34,880	$ 732,494
Controllable Expenses				
Fixed salaries	$125,885		$ 5,035	$ 130,920

(continued)

			Change	Upcoming Year
• **FIGURE 2.3** • *(continued)*				
Variable wages	$ 83,924		$ 4,085	$ 88,009
Employee benefits	$ 47,207		$ 2,052	$ 49,259
Other controllable expenses	$162,602		$ 6,500	$ 169,102
Total Controllable Expenses		$ 419,618	$ 17,672	$437,290
Income before Occupancy Costs, Interest, Depreciation, and Income Taxes		$ 277,996		$ 295,204
Occupancy Costs	$ 89,169		$ 2,000	$ 91,169
Interest	$ 13,875			$ 13,875
Depreciation	$ 46,250			$ 46,250
Total		$ 149,294		$ 151,294
Restaurant Profit		$ 128,702		$ 143,910

Using those assumptions, we begin the process of preparing an operating budget for Bistro Quatre for the coming fiscal year. The initial step in this process is to examine sales figures from the recent past to note evident trends, if any. In some establishments, the examination of sales records may reveal regular increases in sales from year to year; in others, decreases may be seen; in still others, changes from year to year may show no discernible pattern. In any case, it is the responsibility of the owner or manager to analyze past sales for this purpose. Information from such an analysis can be of great value in projecting sales levels for the period to be covered by the budget.

The next step in the budgeting process is to examine the external environment and assess any conditions or factors that could affect sales volume in the coming year. These include general economic conditions in the nation and in the immediate geographic area; population changes; changes that may affect transportation to the establishment, including new highways and bus routes; and any number of other external variables, including new or increased competition from other restaurants.

Another important step is to review any planned changes in the operation that will affect sales volume. For example, any plans to increase or decrease menu prices will clearly affect sales volume, and the impact of such changes must be clearly assessed. The impact of such varied possibilities as anticipated changes in the number of seats in the restaurant, in services or markets, in the number of items listed in the menu, in the particular menu items offered, or in levels of advertising must also be considered.

After conducting the aforementioned assessments, the next procedure is to determine the nature and extent of changes in cost levels, some of which will be dictated by anticipated changes in sales volume, while others will occur independent of volume changes. Some variable costs are certain to be affected by changes in volume, but may also be affected by other factors. A union labour contract may include a new hourly wage for all employees. There are many other possibilities for cost increases—a clause in a lease dictating a rent increase effective on a particular date, higher utility rates, anticipated increases in the costs of particular foods, and any number of others. Any anticipated changes in cost and sales levels must be considered and factored into the new operating budget.

Assume that the management of Bistro Quatre has carefully examined past cost and sales figures and has assessed the impact of various anticipated changes in both internal and external conditions on costs and sales.

The following changes are anticipated:

1. Both food and beverage sales are expected to increase by 5 percent.
2. Fixed salaries will increase by 4 percent.
3. Wages will increase by 4 percent.
4. Variable salaries and wages will continue to be the same percentage of sales.
5. The cost of employee benefits will increase, but will continue to be the same percentage of salaries and wages.
6. Other controllable costs will increase by $6,500.
7. Occupancy costs will increase by $2,000.
8. Food and beverage cost percents will remain the same.
9. Interest and depreciation will remain the same.

Based on these anticipated changes, the budget for Bistro Quatre for the coming fiscal year will be as illustrated in Figure 2.3.

Assuming that the projections in the operating budget for sales, costs, and profits are acceptable to management, the budget will be adopted as the plan of action for the covered period. If the projections are unacceptable, management will re-examine both the assumptions on which the budget was based and the budget figures. A re-examination of this nature may suggest the desirability of additional changes affecting sales or costs that may lead to more accurate results. Before the adoption of the budget, the effects of such potential changes can be tested by means of the techniques of cost/volume/profit analysis, the principal subject of the following chapter.

Once an operating budget is accepted and adopted for an upcoming period, it becomes a standard against which operating performance is measured as the fiscal year progresses. To use it effectively for this purpose, the operating budget may be broken down into smaller units for shorter time periods, as discussed earlier. This may result in monthly or quarterly budgets, with sales and cost projections with which actual figures can be compared. The budget projections become the standards or targets for the covered periods. If cost and sales figures for a given period do not meet expectations as identified in the budget, there will be an effort to identify the causes. Once the causes have been identified, it is possible and desirable to take remedial actions to ensure better performance in the next operating period. If, for example, sales do not meet budget projections and costs are too high for the level of sales recorded, some remedial action will clearly be required. If payroll or any other controllable cost is greater than the amount budgeted, then management should attempt to determine the causes of the excessive costs and take appropriate measures to keep future costs at more suitable levels.

One must recognize that budget projections are merely targets and are often misstated or difficult to meet. Sales levels are often higher or lower than projections, because the people who prepare budgets—owners, managers, and accountants—are seldom able to predict the future accurately. Sometimes this is caused by their failure to take all of the information at hand into account when preparing the operating budget. A new office building down the street, for example, may generate additional luncheon business that was not accurately anticipated, or planned advertising may bring in more customers than the manager had expected. Conversely, unexpected road construction outside a restaurant may cause a significant decrease in sales volume for some period of time, or the unexpected closing of a nearby manufacturing facility may bring about a loss of business.

To counteract the inherent shortcomings of fixed operating budgets, a manager can prepare a budget designed to project sales and costs for several levels of business activity. This is called a **flexible budget**. Flexible budgets are normally prepared for levels of business volume above and below the expected level. The idea is that if the level of sales is higher or lower than expected, management already has a new operating budget available with appropriate projections of costs for the particular sales level with which to compare actual sales. The process of preparing a flexible budget is essentially the same as preparing a static budget. Different cost assumptions are made for each level of business volume. In order to keep the budget discussion in this chapter at a basic level, we will not prepare a flexible budget for Bistro Quatre. We will assume that the projections shown in Figure 2.3 will be accurate.

CONTROL SYSTEMS

Control system is the term used to describe that collection of interrelated and interdependent control techniques and procedures that are in use. Historically, and in certain instances still, foodservice control systems employed paper-and-pencil methods that were difficult and time-consuming. Often nowadays, operations rely on electronic cash registers, programmed to keep records of numbers of portions sold and to print out simple reports to management at the end of a day. Many restaurants depend on computers, with software designed to accumulate and summarize information that was simply not available in the past. Still others have invested in amazingly complex computer systems to assist in maintaining control over operations in ways that previously were not possible.

One of the primary reasons that Bistro Quatre has been able to control its costs so well is that it has a computer system with software designed specifically for restaurant operations. A schematic diagram of the restaurant's layout is shown in Figure 2.4. A file server located in the general managers office functions as the hub of the computer network. Terminals with touch-screen monitors and printers, as well as credit-card imprinters, have been installed at two servers' stations. One workstation is on the manager's desk. Remote printers have been installed at the bar and in the kitchen.

The control features for purchasing, receiving, issuing, producing, and selling described in the following chapters have been programmed into the software. In addition, the system provides managers with full access to sales and cost information at any time.

Operations proceed along the following lines: Servers arriving for work change into uniforms on a lower level (not shown on the diagram) and then proceed to the manager's office to sign in. They record their arrival for work much as they would with a traditional time clock, except they log in at the terminal in the manager's office.

Guests enter the dining room, leaving coats in the coatroom. They are seated by the supervisor, who leaves menus at the table. A server greets the guests and takes their orders for drinks; the orders are written on a pad rather than on a guest cheque. Having taken the orders, the server proceeds to a terminal and opens an account stored in the computer's memory. This account is equivalent to a guest cheque. The process requires the server to enter a personal identification code, the table number, and the number of guests. With the account opened, the server manipulates a touch-screen point-of-sale (POS) system to enter the customers' orders for drinks. This information, along with the time of the order, is now in computer memory, which has been programmed with correct prices for all drinks. The system is programmed to send the recorded drink orders to the bartender at the bar, where they are printed on a remote printer. The hard copy, provided by the remote printer, is an order for the bartender to prepare the drinks. This hard copy includes the server number, table number, and order time. The bartender removes the order from the printer, makes the drinks, and places the printed order on the tray with the drinks, thus eliminating questions about which drinks are for which server and what time the orders were entered.

At the appropriate time, the server follows similar procedures for placing food orders. The computer is programmed to send food orders only to the remote printers in the kitchen. All ordered items are stored in memory, but the only items appearing on the remote printer at any preparation station are those

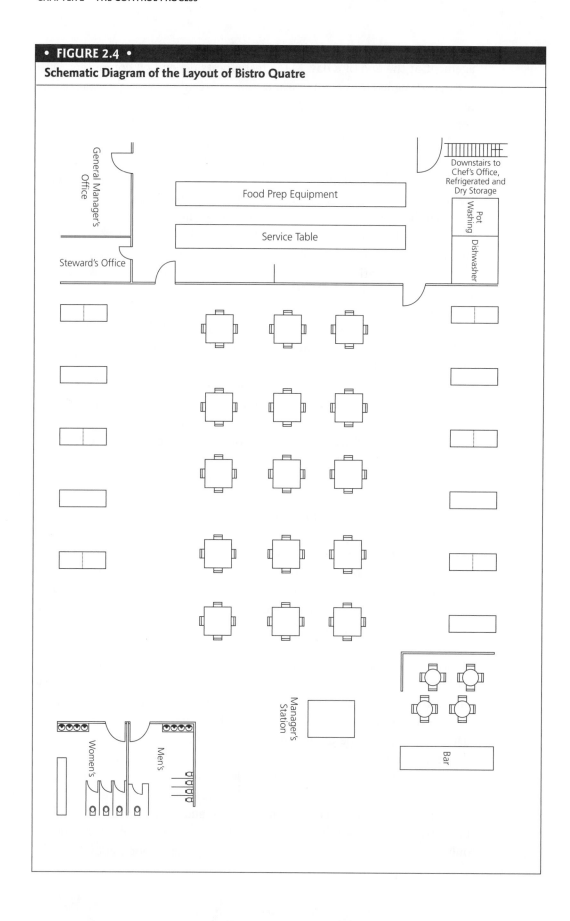

• **FIGURE 2.4** •

Schematic Diagram of the Layout of Bistro Quatre

appropriate to that station. Thus, food orders are not sent to the bar, and orders for coffee, handled by the servers, do not appear on any remote printers.

After a diner has finished the meal, the server obtains the guest cheque by requesting it via the terminal and prints it at the side stand. With this system, the guest cheque is merely a copy of the data file stored in the computer, accessed by table and server number. This hard copy is taken from the printer and given to the diner. In Bistro Quatre, each server acts as a cashier for his or her own cheque, and settlement is recorded for each cheque as the server receives cash or a credit card. At the end of a shift, the server reports to the manager's office to turn in the cash, cheques, and credit card vouchers for his or her sales. Bill Kowalchuk, the owner, sits at his terminal to obtain summary data showing charge and cash sales for that particular server. He collects cash and charge vouchers accordingly. Before changing out of uniform and leaving the premises, each server logs out, using the manager's terminal.

At any time of day, Bill can monitor operations. Data includes gross sales volume, numbers of customers served, numbers of cheques outstanding, numbers of portions of particular items sold, sales mix, and many other kinds of information that may be of special interest at given times throughout the day.

At the conclusion of business, Bill prints a detailed breakdown of the day's business. The software has been programmed to provide total dollar sales categorized into cash sales and charge sales, with the charge sales divided by type of credit card; total dollar sales separated into food sales and beverage sales, with the food sales broken down into dollar sales by menu category or by individual menu items; average dollar sale per customer, per server, per seat, per table, or per hour, or any combination of these; seat turnover; number of customers per server, per hour, per meal, and per day; number of orders of each food and beverage item sold (a reflection of the sales mix); total dollar sales per hour; sales in any category for the period to date; total payroll cost for the day, for any part of the day, or for the period to date; and a vast amount of food and beverage cost data, including standard costs.

Today most food and beverage operators are using some type of computer control system as an aid to managing restaurants. For some, the computer system is simply a modern electronic cash register with features that earlier cash registers were not able to provide. In growing numbers of operations, however, the computer systems are increasingly complex and designed to provide both quick access to needed information and sophisticated managerial control over most or all operations in the restaurant.

COST–BENEFIT RATIO

An important concept in the control process is the **cost–benefit ratio**: the relationship between the costs incurred in instituting and maintaining a single control or control system, compared with the benefits or savings derived by

LEARNING OBJECTIVE 2.5
Explain why the cost–benefit ratio is significant when making control decisions.

doing so. It should be obvious that no control measure can be instituted without some cost. Sometimes that cost is relatively insignificant. Yet sometimes it is so great that careful consideration must be given to the extent of the expected benefit before the cost can be justified. Occasionally the cost may prove to be completely prohibitive. A relatively insignificant cost is required to institute one basic control measure: locking the front and back doors at night to prevent burglary. In contrast, relocating a restaurant cashier's desk to a position judged to be more suitable for preventing customers from leaving without paying the bills may be somewhat more costly. Installing a sophisticated new computer system and hiring a new employee trained to operate it would require even greater, ongoing costs. Establishing a new control department, hiring a food and beverage controller and appropriate support staff, and supplying the staff with equipment and supplies would obviously require large—and possibly prohibitive—amounts of money.

In judging whether the cost of any control procedure is justified, one must take into consideration how long a period of time will be required for the savings to pay for the cost of the new procedure—the payback period. For example, purchasing and installing locks for food storage facilities to prevent employee theft costs a relatively small amount of money and could result in immediate savings. The payback period might be only one month or less and would be easily justified. Relocating the cashier's station to a more suitable position may result in only minimal savings, and might have a payback period of a year or longer. Purchasing a new computer system might have a payback period of more than one year, but be judged necessary anyway. Establishing a new control department and hiring a food and beverage controller and appropriate support staff may have annual costs that would exceed the financial savings and thus would never justify the costs incurred.

One must keep clearly in mind the primary purposes of cost and sales control measures: to guard against excessive costs and to ensure that all sales result in appropriate income. In other words, some identifiable financial benefit must be obtainable from the introduction of any control device or control procedure or from the hiring of any staff member responsible for instituting controls. Benefits must always exceed costs. Before instituting any new procedures for control, management should first determine that the anticipated savings will be greater than the cost of the new procedures. If controls cost more than the benefits they deliver, their value is doubtful. In normal circumstances, it is not sensible to institute any controls that cost more than they save. Stated in other terms, one might say that one should not normally spend a dollar to save a dollar. In numeric terms, one might say that the ratio of cost to benefit should always be 1:2 or greater. Some operators require at least 1:3 or 1:4 ratios.

It is important to note that the benefit from instituting a control may not be easily measured in dollars. For example, a control measure established to determine that all food received is of the designated quality would be designed to ensure that the quality of food served in the dining room meets the standards set by management and to reduce the amount of purchased food returned to the purveyor. This should pay off in increased customer satisfaction and additional customers. However, the benefits are very difficult to measure in dollars. If customers provide more positive reviews of the food quality to management, we know that the control is working. Similarly, if the number of customers increases, we can perhaps assume that it is because of the more consistent food quality. However, even though we are satisfied that the cost of instituting the control is worth the expenditure in additional labour cost or other cost, we would have a very difficult time measuring the benefit in dollars, as it would be difficult to specifically identify the reason for additional sales.

Additionally, before instituting any control procedure and incurring the consequent dollar costs, one should also look at the negative nonquantifiable effects. Control systems and procedures generally affect many aspects of an operation, sometimes in negative ways not anticipated by management. For example, a system designed to verify that all food transported by servers from kitchen to dining room is appropriately recorded on guest cheques may slow down service, reduce seat turnover, and even result in cold food being served to guests. Similarly, the installation of a time clock to obtain accurate data for payroll purposes may cause resentment among long-time, loyal, and valued employees, some of whom might seek other employment rather than start to punch a time clock. Thus, management should carefully estimate the nonmonetary outcomes of any control system or procedure before putting it into effect.

Determining Whether to Make In-House or to Outsource

Many operators face the decision of whether to make a menu item on the premises from scratch or buy a prepared convenience product from a supplier. This is known as the **make in-house versus outsource determination**. An example of such an item is french fries. Many restaurants buy them frozen, ready to fry. Others make them fresh from scratch. As you will see, there are many determining factors in deciding whether to make in-house or outsource.

The first consideration is what standard of quality can be obtained in a convenience product, as these products are produced by others and the operator will not have control over their standards. Next, the reliability and service of the supplier are important. If a product and supplier are found to meet those requirements then price becomes an essential issue. The cost of the convenience product is easily calculated. To determine the cost of the house-prepared item, food and labour costs will have to be considered as well as any additional utility or energy costs that may be incurred. Even equipment maintenance, depreciation, and additional insurance costs may be a factor. Generally, other issues are also considered: whether there is skilled staff needed and on hand to produce the item efficiently and if they can do it without incurring additional labour cost by finding extra time in their day to produce the item. Perhaps as a nonmonetary benefit, making items in-house may improve: customer satisfaction, employee morale, or help to recruit good staff eager to learn new skills. The final decision may involve many factors, comparing quality, cost, and other

LEARNING OBJECTIVE 2.6
Identify what to consider when deciding whether to make a product in-house or to outsource.

operational aspects. It is important that the final decision fits with the standards of the operation, making sense on many levels.

THINGS TO CONSIDER

Good managers prepare operating budgets, stating, in financial terms, what sales they are expecting and listing the costs that should be incurred in generating those sales. Often these figures are based on historical income statements that are modified to indicate expected trends in sales and adjustments to costs. For new operations, market share multiplied by average cheques may forecast sales, and costs may be based on industry standards, experience, or by investigation.

Either way, a yearly, month-by-month picture is created that will be used as a standard guide and reference that can be compared with actual sales and costs as the months pass. The operating budget is an extremely useful tool for managerial control, especially when flexible, offering different scenarios. The practical applications may involve searching for divergences between budgeted and actual sales, perhaps demonstrating a need to promote more sales to meet targets. Divergences in costs may pinpoint areas where control procedures need to be reinforced. Each month, the differences between the operating budget and actual sales and costs should be analyzed and used to improve the operation. If it is determined that anticipated sales or costs are unachievable, changes to standards or to the business model must be made to ensure success. In these instances, a revised operating budget should be created and used accordingly.

Using operating budgets to analyze and improve operations is perhaps the most effective way to ensure success, and may help to make an organization an industry leader.

CHAPTER ESSENTIALS

In this chapter, we established working definitions of the terms *control, cost control,* and *sales control.* We fixed responsibility for control and demonstrated that control is needed in all phases of operating a successful enterprise. We identified eight common control techniques, illustrated their use in food service, and explained their value to managers seeking to establish control. Emphasis was given to budgeting—the preparation and use of the operating budget—as a control technique. We identified the four-step process of control and described its use in food and beverage operations. We defined cost–benefit ratio, explaining its significance in determining the extent to which proposed control measures are worth being implemented, and finally, we discussed the make versus outsource determination, outlining what to consider when deciding to make a product in-house or to buy it already prepared.

KEY TERMS IN THIS CHAPTER

Budget, p. 52
Control, p. 40
Control process, p. 42
Control system, p. 58
Cost control, p. 42
Cost–benefit ratio, p. 61
Flexible budget, p. 58
Make in-house versus
 outsource determination, p. 63
Operating budget, p. 52

Procedures, p. 48
Quality standards, p. 46
Quantity standards, p. 47
Sales control, p. 43
Standard cost, p. 47
Standard procedures, p. 48
Standards, p. 46
Static budget, p. 54
Training, p. 49

QUESTIONS AND PROBLEMS

1. Compare the quality standards that may be used in a school cafeteria with those that may be used in a fine-dining restaurant for one standard portion of ravioli.
2. Would the quality standards for workers in a fine-dining restaurant be the same as those for workers in a school cafeteria? Why or why not?
3. Is discipline the only control technique that has negative implications? Why or why not?
4. The manager of Phil's Bar & Grill has purchased and directed bartenders to use a device that automatically measures the quantity of any alcoholic beverage poured. The bartenders were formerly permitted to mix drinks without measuring. What positive and negative effects do you think this will have on bar operations?
5. From your own working experience, cite an instance in which a manager's inconsistency in setting examples or giving directions has led to confusion in day-to-day operations.
6. How can budgets be used as control devices in food and beverage operations?
7. What is the purpose of cost control? What is the purpose of sales control?
8. Imagine that you are the manager of a fine-dining restaurant. You are faced with the problem of a server who refuses to follow the service standards and techniques established by the owner. It is apparent to you that the

server's techniques result in faster service, but they are clearly better suited to a roadhouse. Two of the owner's goals are profitability and elegant service. Discuss the possible actions that you might take to bring the employee's performance into line with established standards and to work toward achieving the owner's goals.

9. One of the items on the menu in the Central Restaurant is chopped steak. Each cook has his or her own idea about what a chopped steak is, and each prepares it differently. Using the four steps in the control process as the basis for your response, explain how a new manager might eliminate this problem.

10. The new manager of Jill's Place has decided that all employees should be searched before they leave the premises each day because she believes this will reduce the problem of employee theft. Discuss the possible costs and potential benefits the manager should consider before instituting this policy.

11. Define standard procedures, and give two examples from your own experience.

12. The following information has been prepared by the manager of the Market Restaurant. It represents his best estimates of sales and various costs for the coming year. Using this information, prepare an operating budget for the Market Restaurant for the coming year, following the illustration provided in this chapter.

Food sales: $820,000
Beverage sales: $290,000
Cost of food: 36 percent of food sales
Cost of beverages: 24 percent of beverage sales
Variable salaries and wages: 20 percent of food sales
Total of fixed salaries and wages: $102,000
Employee benefits: 25 percent of total salaries and wages
Other controllable expenses: $95,000
Depreciation: $65,500
Interest: $55,000
Occupancy costs: $56,000

13. In the current year, the manager of the Downtowner Restaurant has been following the operating budget reproduced here:

Sales		
Food		$630,000
Beverage		140,000
Total sales		$770,000
Cost of Sales		
Food	$252,000	
Beverage	35,000	

Total costs		$287,000
Gross Profit		$483,000
Controllable Expenses		
Salaries and wages	$173,250	
Employee benefits	45,045	
Other controllable expenses	82,000	
Total Controllable Expenses		$300,295
Income before Occupancy Costs, Interest, Depreciation, and Income Taxes		$182,705
Occupancy Costs	64,000	
Interest	$10,000	
Depreciation	28,500	
Total Occupancy Costs, Interest, and Depreciation		$38,500
Restaurant Profit		$80,205

For the coming year, the following changes are expected:

a. Food sales will increase by 10 percent.

b. Beverage sales will increase by 6 percent.

c. Food cost percent and beverage cost percent will remain the same.

d. Fixed salaries and wages—$69,300 for this year—will increase by $8,000. Variable salaries and wages will be 16 percent of expected food sales.

e. Employee benefits will remain the same percentage of salaries and wages.

f. Controllable expenses will increase by $12,000.

g. Occupancy costs will increase by $5,000.

h. Interest and depreciation will remain the same.

Given these anticipated changes, prepare an operating budget for the Downtowner Restaurant for the coming year.

14. Referring to Question 13, assume that the operating budget you prepared for the upcoming year has been adopted. After the first six months of the year, financial records reveal the following:

a. Food sales have increased by 12 percent rather than by the 10 percent anticipated.

b. Beverage sales have increased by 5 percent rather than by 6 percent.

c. Food cost percent is 1 percent lower than budgeted, but beverage cost percent is 2 percent higher.

d. Variable salaries and wages are 14 percent of food sales, rather than the 16 percent anticipated.

Assuming that the trends evident in the first six months continue for the rest of the year and that both sales and costs are equally divided between the two halves of the year, prepare a revision of the budget for the second six-month period.

15. Define each of the key terms in this chapter.

EXCEL EXERCISES

Exercise 2.1

Bring up the income statement for Barnaby's Hideaway on your Excel spread-sheet. It is listed on the companion website for this text as Exercise 2.1.

The following changes are anticipated in the coming year:

1. Both food and beverage sales are expected to increase by 5 percent.
2. Food and beverage cost percents will remain the same.
3. Salaries and wages will increase by 4 percent.
4. The cost of employee benefits will increase, but will continue to be the same percentage of salaries and wages.
5. Other controllable costs will increase by $6,500.
6. Occupancy costs will increase by $2,000.
7. Interest and depreciation will remain the same.

Prepare an operating budget for Barnaby's Hideaway for the coming year, using Figure 2.3 in the text as a model for your budget.

Exercise 2.2

Follow the instructions on the textbook's companion website to complete this exercise.

CHAPTER 3

Cost/Volume/Profit Relationships

• LEARNING OBJECTIVES •

After reading this chapter, you should be able to:

3.1 State the cost/volume/profit equation and explain the relationships that exist among its components.

3.2 Define the terms *variable rate* and *contribution rate*.

3.3 Apply the formulas used to determine sales in dollars, sales in units, variable costs, fixed costs, profit, contribution rate, contribution margin, variable rate, and break-even point.

INTRODUCTION

In the introduction to Chapter 1, statements of income were provided for two comparable restaurants: Il Giardino and Bistro Quatre. It was apparent that profit earned in Bistro Quatre was substantially larger than that earned in Il Giardino for the period covered by the statements. In Chapter 1, we noted that the relationships of costs to sales in Bistro Quatre were more favourable than in Il Giardino. In fact, the food cost percent, the beverage cost percent, and the labour cost percent in Bistro Quatre were all about 7 percent lower than those for Il Giardino.

However, one cannot assume that "good" cost-to-sales relationships automatically result in profit for a restaurant. It was stated in Chapter 1 that many restaurants operate with higher than normal cost percents and are able to obtain a satisfactory profit. Indeed, it is possible that a higher food cost percent—obtainable by lowering menu prices or by increasing food costs, thus giving each customer more for his or her money—may result in sufficient additional customers to increase profitability despite the higher food cost percent. It is also possible that lower cost percents—achieved by raising menu prices or lowering costs—may result in fewer customers and lower profits. Another possibility is that lower menu prices will lessen profit because there is an insufficient increase in the number of customers to offset the higher cost percent. The effect on profit from lowering costs or changing menu prices must be judged by management. Management must examine the cost/volume/profit relationship for that particular foodservice operation in light of many factors, including its market, the type of clientele targeted, its competition, customers' willingness to pay higher prices, the effect of lowering costs on quality of food, beverage, and service, and other factors.

This chapter examines the nature of the cost/volume/profit relationships. An understanding of these relationships is the key to fully comprehending cost control in food and beverage operations when costs are established. The following examples illustrate the nature of the cost/profit/volume relationship.

At Bistro Quatre, the given level of sales ($1,049,043) and total costs ($920,341), produced satisfactory profit ($128,702). It is also possible, however, to earn acceptable profit at some sales level other than $1,049,043, even if prime cost, as a percentage of sales, increases. Figure 3.2 illustrates this concept.

• FIGURE 3.1 •		
Bistro Quatre, Current Sales and Prime Costs		
Sales	$1,049,043.00	100.00%
Cost of sales	$ 351,429.00	33.50%
Cost of labour	$ 257,016.00	24.50%
Cost of overhead	$ 311,896.00	29.70%
Profit	$ 128,702.00	12.30%

• **FIGURE 3.2** •

Bistro Quatre, Necessary Sales Level to Earn an Acceptable Profit When Prime Costs Increase as a Percentage of Sales

Sales	$1,500,000.00	100.00%
Cost of sales	$ 600,000.00	40.00%
Cost of labour	$ 450,000.00	30.00%
Cost of overhead	$ 311,896.00	20.79%
Profit	$ 138,104.00	9.21%

Although the costs and cost-to-sales ratios for the components of prime cost have increased (cost of sales from 33.5 percent to 40 percent, and cost of labour from 24.5 percent to 30 percent), a satisfactory profit was still realized, because lowered menu prices resulted in many new customers, and the number of dollars required for overhead was the same in both cases. Consequently, as sales volume increases, the number of dollars required for overhead represented a smaller percentage of sales. Profit as a percentage of sales is considerably lower, but the dollar amount of profit is higher.

By contrast, suppose that lowering menu prices resulted in relatively few new customers—only a sufficient number to maintain total sales at the given level of $1,049,043. In that case, profit would be reduced to zero, as shown in Figure 3.3.

• **FIGURE 3.3** •

Bistro Quatre, Illustration of Zero Profit with Reduced Prices and Sales at Original Level

Sales	$1,049,043.00	100.00%
Cost of sales	$ 419,617.00	40.00%
Cost of labour	$ 317,530.00	30.27%
Cost of overhead	$ 311,896.00	29.73%
Profit		0.00%

In the preceding exhibit, total sales remained at the original figure, but prime costs expressed as a percentage of sales increased because of lowered menu prices and increased labour cost to service the increased number of customers.

Now assume a decrease in sales in the restaurant, as illustrated in Figure 3.4. In this instance, cost percents for the components of prime cost are the same as they were in Figure 3.1. However, the operation shows a loss rather than a profit, because of fewer customers. The fixed element for overhead, still $311,896, now accounts for 47.98 percent of sales dollars, rather than the 29.7 percent it represented at the sales level illustrated in Figure 3.1. A key lesson in the preceding examples, then, is that although percentages are very useful in

• FIGURE 3.4 •		
Bistro Quatre, Illustration of Loss Resulting from Decreased Sales (Prime Costs as a Percentage of Sales Remains as Originally Planned)		
Sales	$ 650,000.00	100.00%
Cost of sales	$ 217,750.00	33.50%
Cost of labour	$ 159,250.00	24.50%
Cost of overhead	$ 311,896.00	47.98%
Profit	(38,896)	25.98%

comparing operations and judging a single operation, one should not rely on them to provide all of the information necessary to judge profitability.

The key to understanding cost/volume/profit relationships lies in understanding that there are fixed costs in any operation, regardless of sales volume, and that it is necessary to generate sufficient total volume to cover both variable and fixed costs. This is not to say, however, that ratios of variable costs to sales are to be ignored. In fact, if the ratio of variable costs to sales is very high, it may not be possible to generate sufficient volume to cover fixed costs. After all, the seats in a dining room can be turned over only a limited number of times in any given meal period. Conversely, if the ratio of variable costs to sales is too low, it may not be possible to generate adequate sales volume, simply because potential customers perceive that prices are too high for the value they receive. If this is the case, they are likely to dine elsewhere.

THE COST/VOLUME/PROFIT EQUATION

LEARNING OBJECTIVE 3.1
State the cost/volume/profit equation and explain the relationships that exist among its components.

From the foregoing discussion, it should be apparent that there are relationships between sales, cost of sales, cost of labour, cost of overhead, and profit. In fact, these relationships can be expressed as follows:

> Sales = Cost of sales + Cost of labour + Cost of overhead + Profit

Thus, in Bistro Quatre, using the numbers from Figure 3.1:

> $1,049,043 = 351,429 + 257,016 + 311,896 + 128,702

Because cost of sales is variable, cost of labour includes both fixed and variable elements, and cost of overhead is fixed, one could restate this equation as follows:

> Sales = Variable costs + Fixed costs + Profit

In fact, this is the basic **cost/volume/profit equation**.

Using the first letters of the terms to stand for those terms, this basic equation can be written as a formula:

$$S = VC + FC + P$$

Throughout this chapter, then,

S = Sales
VC = Variable costs
FC = Fixed costs
P = profit

In proceeding with the chapter, the reader will do well to keep three points in mind:

1. Within the normal range of business operations, the relationship between variable costs and sales remains relatively constant. That relationship is a ratio that is normally expressed either as a percentage or as a decimal. However, expressed in dollar amounts, both increase or decrease in tandem.
2. In contrast, fixed costs tend to remain constant in dollar terms, regardless of changes in dollar sales volume. Consequently, whether expressed as a percentage or as a decimal, the relationship between fixed costs and sales changes as sales volume increases and decreases.
3. Once appropriate levels are determined for costs, they must be controlled if the operation is to be profitable.

Before considering cost/volume/profit relationships in detail, it is necessary to understand some important concepts, abbreviations, and terms. These are illustrated using figures from the statement of income for Bistro Quatre, reproduced in Figure 3.5.

• FIGURE 3.5 •

Bistro Quatre, Income Statement, Year Ended December 31, 20XX

Sales		
Food	$891,687	
Beverage	$157,356	
Total Sales		$1,049,043
Cost of Sales		
Food	$312,090	
Beverage	$39,339	
Total Cost of Sales		$351,429
Gross Profit		$697,614
Controllable Expenses		
Salaries and wages	$209,809	
Employee benefits	$47,207	

(continued)

• FIGURE 3.5 • (continued)

Controllable Expenses		
Other controllable expenses	$162,602	
Total Controllable Expenses		$419,618
Income before Occupancy Costs, Interest,		$277,996
Depreciation, and Income Taxes		
Occupancy Costs	$89,169	
Interest	$13,875	
Depreciation	$46,250	
Total Occupancy Costs, Interest, and		
Depreciation		$149,294
Restaurant Profit		$128,702

The first step is to determine total variable costs for Bistro Quatre. Total variable costs consist of food cost, beverage cost, and the variable portion of labour cost. As discussed in Chapter 2, the cost of labour includes both a fixed element and a variable element. Figure 3.6, taken from Chapter 2, is the basis for the following discussion.

• FIGURE 3.6 •

Fixed and Variable Costs in Bistro Quatre

Fixed Costs

Occupancy costs	$89,169	
Other controllable costs	$162,602	
Fixed salaries	$125,885	(60% of salaries and wages)*
Employee benefits	$31,471	(25% of fixed salaries and wages)
Interest	$13,875	
Depreciation	$46,250	

Variable Costs

Cost of food	35% of food sales
Cost of beverages	25% of beverage sales
Salaries and wages	9.4% of food sales**
Employee benefits	18.8% of variable salaries and wages

*Salaries and wages are semivariable costs, so they must be divided into their fixed and variable components. In the example, we have assumed that 60% of total salaries and wages are fixed while the remaining 40% are variable.

**Variable salaries and wages are assumed to be associated with food sales. Therefore, other salaries and wages will not increase or decrease with changes in business volume. Variable salaries and wages—40% of $209,809, or $83,923—are 9.4% of food sales.

By referring to Figure 3.5, one can determine that food cost is $312,090 and beverage cost is $39,339. The variable portion of labour cost will be 40 percent of total payroll expense (salaries and wages, plus employee benefits). Total payroll expense is $257,016, and 40 percent of that total is $102,806. One can then determine total variable costs by adding the following three figures:

Food cost	$312,090
Beverage cost	39,339
Variable labour cost	102,806
Total variable costs	$454,235

The next step is to determine total fixed costs for the restaurant. Total fixed costs includes all costs other than the variable costs. From Figure 3.1, these are the fixed portion of the labour cost (60 percent of $257,016, or $154,210), other controllable expenses ($162,602), occupancy costs ($89,169), interest ($13,875), and depreciation ($46,250). One can then determine total fixed costs simply by adding these five figures:

Fixed labour cost	$154,210
Other controllable expenses (fixed)	162,602
Occupancy costs	89,169
Interest	13,875
Depreciation	46,250
Total fixed costs	$466,106

Given the preceding figures, the basic cost/volume/profit equation for Bistro Quatre at the level of sales indicated is:

Sales ($1,049,043) = Variable costs ($454,235) + Fixed costs ($466,106) + Profit ($128,702)

or

S ($1,049,043) = VC ($454,235) + FC ($466,106) + P ($128,702)

VARIABLE RATE AND CONTRIBUTION RATE

Two additional terms must be introduced and defined before proceeding: *variable rate* and *contribution rate*.

LEARNING OBJECTIVE 3.2
Define the terms *variable rate* and *contribution rate*.

Variable Rate

Variable rate is the ratio of variable costs to dollar sales. It is determined by dividing variable costs by dollar sales and is expressed in decimal form. It is similar algebraically to a cost percent equation:

$$\text{Variable rate} = \text{Variable costs} \div \text{Sales}$$

Variable rate is normally abbreviated as VR, so the equation can be written as

$$VR = VC \div S$$

In the preceding example, variable costs (VC) are \$454,235, and sales (S) are \$1,049,043. Therefore,

$$\text{Variable rate} = \text{Variable costs (454,235)} \div \text{Sales (1,049,043)}$$
$$VR = .433$$

This is the same as stating that 43.3 percent of dollar sales is needed to cover the variable costs, or that \$0.433 of each dollar of sales is required for that purpose. As sales increase, the total dollars spent to cover these costs will increase, but the percentage will not change.

Contribution Rate

If 43.3 percent of dollar sales is needed to cover variable costs, then the remainder (56.7 percent) is available for other purposes, namely:

1. Meeting fixed costs
2. Providing profit

As sales increase, an increasing number of dollars will be available to be used to meet fixed costs and provide increased profit. Thus, \$0.567 of each dollar of sales or 56.7 percent is available to contribute to covering fixed costs and providing profit. This rate or ratio is known as the **contribution rate**, abbreviated as CR.

The contribution rate is determined by subtracting the variable rate from 1.

$$CR = 1 - VR$$

Indeed, one can easily see that after paying all fixed costs for a period, dollars from additional sales (after deducting variable costs) will generate contribution dollars that can go directly to increasing profit.

For Bistro Quatre, the CR is .567, determined by subtracting the VR of .433 from 1.

$$CR = 1 - .433$$
$$= .567$$

BREAK-EVEN POINT

Determining the break-even point is an excellent way for managers to view and analyze the dynamic relationships between sales, costs, and profit.

No business enterprise can be termed profitable until all of the fixed costs have been met. If dollar sales volume is insufficient to cover both variable and fixed costs, then the enterprise will operate at a loss. If dollar sales are sufficient to cover both variable and fixed costs exactly, but insufficient to provide any profit (i.e., profit is zero), then the business is said to be operating at the break-even point. The **break-even point**, usually abbreviated as BE, is defined as the point at which the sum of all costs equals sales, so that profit equals zero. So,

> BE = Break-even point

Profitability can also be viewed as existing on a scale, as shown in Figure 3.7. The midpoint on the scale, indicated by the zero, is the break-even point, at which operational expenses are equal to sales revenue.

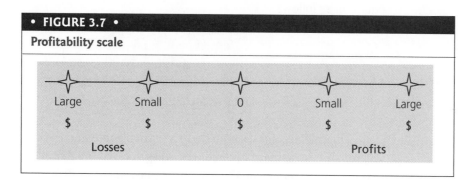

• FIGURE 3.7 •

Profitability scale

| Large | Small | 0 | Small | Large |
| $ | $ | $ | $ | $ |

Losses   Profits

COST/VOLUME/PROFIT CALCULATIONS FOR BISTRO QUATRE

We now have the following information about Bistro Quatre:

Sales = $1,049,043
Variable costs = $454,235
Fixed costs = $466,106
Profit = $128,702
Variable rate = .433
Contribution rate = .567

An additional formula must be introduced at this point:

> Sales = Fixed costs + Profit ÷ Contribution rate,

LEARNING OBJECTIVE 3.3
Apply the formulas used to determine sales in dollars, sales in units, variable costs, fixed costs, profit, contribution rate, contribution margin, variable rate, and break-even point

which is abbreviated as

$$S = FC + P \div CR$$

This formula can be used to determine the level of dollar sales required to earn any profit that one might choose to put into the equation.

To prove that the formula works, one can substitute the preceding figures in the formula, as follows:

$$\$1,049,043 = \$466,106 + \$128,702 \div .567$$
$$= 594,808 \div .567$$
$$= \$1,049,043$$

The alert student will note that the above division actually results in a figure that is $1.00 higher. This is because of rounding.

To determine the break-even point for Bistro Quatre, the point at which profit would be equal to zero dollars, one would simply let P = 0 and solve the equation as follows:

$$S = FC + P \div CR$$
$$= \$466,106 + \$0.00 \div .567$$
$$= \$466,106 \div .567$$
$$= \$822,056$$

The calculations assume that the variable rate and the contribution rate will remain the same at the reduced sales volume. At that level of sales, variable costs (VC) remain at 43.3 percent of sales, or $355,950. Thus, VC of $355,950 plus FC of $466,106 equals S, or $822,056, leaving no profit.

$$S\ (\$822,056) = VC\ (\$355,950) + FC\ (\$466,106) + P\ (0)$$
$$\$822,056 = \$822,056$$

No profit-oriented business ever wants to operate at break-even, and Bistro Quatre was no exception. The sales level achieved in Bistro Quatre was $1,049,043, which was $226,987 beyond BE. As mentioned, although there are no additional fixed costs to cover after the break-even point is reached, each additional dollar of sales does have variable costs associated with it. In Bistro Quatre, these costs were identified as $0.433 for each dollar of sale, which is the same as saying that VR = .433. Variable costs can be determined by multiplying S (sales) by VR (variable rate).

$$VC = S \times VR$$
$$= \$226,987 \times .433$$
$$= \$98,285$$

If one multiplies dollar sales of $226,987 by VR .433, one determines that variable costs associated with those sales beyond BE is $98,285. If this $98,285 in variable costs is subtracted from sales of $226,987, the result ($128,702) is equal to the profit (P) for the period. It consists of $0.567 of each dollar sale beyond BE.

$$P (\$128,702) = S (\$226,987) \times CR (.567)$$
$$\$128,702 = \$128,702$$

It must be stressed that this is true only for sales beyond BE: Before BE, there is no profit. Furthermore this assumes that the VR is always controlled, consistently maintained at .433 despite fluctuations in sales. It is normally more difficult, with diminished sales, to precisely maintain that ratio in a real operation than it is in theory.

To reduce the amount a business needs to break even, variable costs must be reduced. There are several ways to do this, including reducing labour costs, lowering the quality of products, reducing quantities and portion sizes, and raising prices. Be advised, however, that each of these methods, although effective in a strict sense of reducing costs, may do more harm than good, driving customers away and reducing sales.

Contribution Margin

Each dollar of sales, then, may be divided into two portions:

1. one portion that must be used to cover variable costs associated with the item sold and
2. the second portion that remains to cover fixed costs and to provide profit.

The dollar amount remaining after variable costs have been subtracted from the sales dollar is defined as the **contribution margin**, abbreviated as CM. Thus,

CM = Contribution margin
= Selling price − Variable costs of that item

Thus, if a menu item sells for $12.00 and it costs $5.00, the contribution margin is $7.00:

$$\$7.00 = \$12.00 - \$5.00$$

This holds true for each menu item and for the total of all menu items. Again considering the statement of income for Bistro Quatre, food sales were $891,687 and food costs were $312,090. The contribution margin of food sales at Bistro Quatre can be derived from these numbers:

Food sales	=	$891,687
− Food costs	=	312,090
Contribution margin	=	$579,597

The final figure is also referred to as the gross margin and the gross profit on food sales.

When sales reach a level sufficient to cover all variable costs and all fixed costs, with an additional amount left over, that additional amount is profit. The importance of the contribution margin in food and beverage management cannot be overemphasized. Clearly, any item sold for which variable costs exceed sales price results immediately in a negative contribution margin, which is an immediate financial loss to the business. A prime sirloin steak with a variable cost of $4.00 must be sold for an amount greater than $4.00, or there will be a loss. Furthermore, in establishing a sales price for the steak, provision must be made for each sale to result in an adequate contribution margin—one that, when combined with all other contribution margins from all other sales, will be sufficient not only to cover fixed costs of the operation, but also to provide for an additional amount beyond break-even that will be the desired profit.

Number of Customers Required to Break Even

Managers often want to know the number of sales required to break even or make a desired profit. Calculating that figure will allow managers to determine how many customers are required, and will provide an alternative means of determining whether financial goals are being met.

As previously discussed, the total of the contribution margins for all sales is used to cover fixed costs and provide a profit. If one knows the average contribution margin per customer sale and the dollar figure for fixed costs, it is then possible to calculate the number of sales, or customers, needed to cover fixed costs and the desired profit.

For example, if the financial records of a small restaurant indicated sales of $48,000 and variable costs of $18,000 in a period when 3,000 customers were served, then:

$48,000 sales ÷ 3,000 customers = $16.00 average sales

Similarly,

$18,000 variable costs ÷ 3,000 customers = $6.00 average variable costs

Using that information, it is possible to determine average contribution margin, defined previously as average sales minus average variable cost. Thus:

Average S	$16.00
Average VC	− 6.00
Average CM	$10.00

Before using this figure to complete calculations to determine the required number of customers, an important limitation on its use must be noted. An establishment with a stable sales mix can obtain more reliable data from the following calculations than can one with large fluctuations in the sales mix. Fluctuations in the sales mix typically cause the average sale and the average variable cost to change. These changes typically produce inaccurate results. Mathematically, the number of customers required to reach the break-even point may be calculated by the following formula:

> **Break-even Point in Customers = Fixed costs ÷ Average Contribution margin**
> **BEP in Customers = FC ÷ Average CM**

If management wishes to determine the number of customers required to achieve a given profit, one simply adds profit to fixed costs and divides by average contribution margin. Thus:

> **Number of Customers = FC + Profit ÷ Average CM**

In the small restaurant in our illustration, the average sale is $16.00, the average variable cost is $6.00, and the average contribution margin is $10.00. Assume that fixed costs for the period were $30,000. Thus for a BE calculation:

> **Number of Customers = $30,000 ÷ $10**
> **= 3,000 customers**

Applying this formula to Bistro Quatre, we can find the number of customers necessary to break even or make a desired profit if we know the average sale and the average contribution margin.

In Chapter 1, the average sale was calculated to be $27.87. Even though that did not include liquor, for purposes of this discussion, we will assume that the average sale of $27.87 is correct for food and that there will be little fluctuation in that figure throughout the year.

Referring to the statement of income in Figure 3.5, one can calculate that liquor sales represent 15 percent of total sales ($157,356 ÷ $1,049,043), and food sales represent 85 percent of total sales. Thus, the average sale can be calculated by dividing $27.87 by .85:

> **$27.87 ÷ .85 = $32.79 Average Sale**

We previously calculated the average contribution rate of .567. Thus, to find the average contribution margin, we multiply the average contribution rate times the average sales price.

Average sales price	$32.79
Average CR	× .567
Average CM	$18.59

Fixed costs for Bistro Quatre were previously calculated to be $466,106. We apply the formula for the number of customers necessary to break even:

$$\text{Number of Customers} = \text{FC} \div \text{Average CM}$$
$$= \$466,106 \div \$18.59$$
$$= 25,073$$

For an interesting exercise, to determine the number of sales achieved for the profit shown in Figure 3.5, the profit of $128,702 is added to fixed costs:

$$\text{Number of Customers} = \text{FC} + \text{P} \div \text{Average CM}$$
$$= \$466,106 + \$128,702 \div \$18.59$$
$$= \$594,808 \div \$18.59$$
$$= 31,996$$

To prove that the formula works, we multiply the number of sales (31,996) times the average sale ($32.79) to arrive at $1,049,149, the approximate gross sales figure shown in Figure 1.3. The small difference of $106.00 results from rounding.

Thus, Bistro Quatre received 6,923 (31,996 − 25,073) more customers than were necessary to break even. Assuming that the restaurant is open 365 days during the year, the restaurant averaged 88 sales or covers each day (31,996 ÷ 365). Of course, some days had fewer customers and some days had more.

A detailed discussion of evaluating the contribution margin for individual menu items is found in Chapter 11.

COST CONTROL AND THE COST/VOLUME/PROFIT EQUATION

Earlier in this chapter, we emphasized that cost must be controlled by the means discussed in Chapter 2 if an operation is to achieve planned profits. It is useful to consider what happens to planned profits when costs are not controlled. To illustrate, we refer to the operating budget for Bistro Quatre for the coming year, developed in Chapter 2 and reproduced in Figure 3.8.

To determine the variable rate (VR) for the coming year, one must add the budgeted variable costs for food and beverages ($369,000) and the variable portions of salaries and wages and employee benefits.

In Chapter 2 in the discussion of the budget for Bistro Quatre for the coming year, it was stated that sales were expected to increase by 5 percent and that

• **FIGURE 3.8** •

Bistro Quatre, Projected Operating Budget, Year Ended December 31, 20XX

			Change	*Upcoming Year*
Sales				
Food	$891,687		$ 44,584	$ 936,271
Beverage	$157,356		$ 7,868	$ 165,224
Total sales		$1,049,043	$ 52,452	$1,101,495
Cost of Sales				
Food	$312,090		$ 15,605	$ 327,695
Beverage	$ 39,339		$ 1,967	$ 41,306
Total cost of sales		$ 351,429	$ 17,572	$ 369,001
Gross Profit		$ 697,614	$ 34,880	$ 732,494
Controllable Expenses				
Fixed salaries and wages	$125,885		$ 5,035	$ 130,920
Variable salaries and wages	$ 83,924		$ 4,085	$ 88,009
Employee benefits	$ 47,207		$ 2,052	$ 49,259
Other controllable expenses	$162,602		$ 6,500	$ 169,102
Total Controllable Expenses		$ 419,618	$ 17,672	$437,290
Income before Occupancy Costs, Interest, Depreciation, and Income Taxes		$ 277,996		$ 295,204
Occupancy Costs	$ 89,169		$ 2,000	$ 91,169
Interest	$ 13,875			$ 13,875
Depreciation	$ 46,250			$ 46,250
Total		$ 149,294		$ 151,294
Restaurant Profit		$ 128,702		$ 143,910

variable costs would remain at the same percentages as before. Therefore, the ratio of variable costs to sales (the variable rate, or VR), calculated as .433 from figures in the income statement earlier in this chapter, is budgeted to remain the same for the coming year. Because this is true, the contribution rate (CR), defined as 1 – VR, will also be the same: .567. Budgeted fixed costs for the coming year are as follows:

Fixed salaries and wages	$130,092
Fixed employee benefits	32,523
Other controllable expenses (fixed)	169,102
Occupancy costs	91,169
Interest	13,875
Depreciation	46,250
Total fixed costs	$483,011

Assume that this new year has begun. The new budget has been adopted and is in effect. However, the manager has not been controlling variable costs adequately. As a result, excessive variable costs are developing, largely through inefficiency and waste. Such problems as spoilage of raw materials and poor scheduling of staff are common causes of these excessive costs.

Now assume that these excessive variable costs have had the effect of increasing the variable rate from .433, a figure calculated earlier from figures in the income statement, to .515. This is the same as saying that the amount needed to cover variable costs has increased from a planned .433 to .515.

We now use the formula developed earlier in the chapter to determine the sales level required to earn the $143,910 profit indicated in the budget (Figure 3.8) if the variable rate is .515. Using the formula

$$S = FC + P \div CR$$
$$CR = .485 \, (1 - .515)$$

we substitute numbers in the formula to find that

$$S = 483,011 + \$143,910 \div .485$$
$$= \$626,921 \div .485$$
$$= \$1,292,621$$

This indicates that an additional $191,126 ($1,292,621 − $1,101,495) in sales will be required to earn the target restaurant profit.

The reason these additional sales are required is simply that excessive variable costs have had the effect of increasing the variable rate unnecessarily. The planned profit could have been earned at the sales level of $1,101,495 if management had done a better job of controlling variable costs at the levels budgeted. This could have been done, conceivably, without any change in quality or quantity standards and without raising prices.

This situation illustrates that an understanding of cost/volume/profit relationships is central to full comprehension of the need for cost control in food and beverage operations. On the one hand, one must understand that lowering contribution margins will necessitate increasing volume in order to achieve a given target profit. Sometimes the higher volume may not be attainable in a given operation because of limited seating capacity, unrealistic turnover rates, or even the limited size of the market. On the other hand, higher contribution margins, because of reduced variable costs, may increase profit in some instances. However, if this is accomplished by raising sales prices beyond the capacity or willingness of customers to pay, sales may suffer and budgets may not be met. Some establishments with low menu prices and low contribution margins are very successful because they are able to maintain high volume. Some, with similar prices, contribution margins, and sales volume, may be unsuccessful because of their higher fixed costs. There are other food and beverage operations with high contribution margins and low sales volume; some are successful, but others are not. The differences from one to another in their levels of profit and relative success can normally be traced to differences in their fixed costs, market, or positioning. The ideal restaurant would have high contribution margins, high sales volume, and low fixed costs.

Once satisfactory levels have been determined for costs, sales, and sales volume, it is clearly necessary for management to control costs if the enterprise is to achieve the profit level planned in its budget.

THINGS TO CONSIDER

The cost/volume/profit (CVP) relationships are fundamental, their elements dynamic. For instance, any changes to menu item costs affect variable and contribution rates. Most successful foodservice operations change menus seasonally or annually, but try to maintain food cost percents even as new items are added. The food cost-to-sales ratio is kept the same. Be aware that this does not guarantee all variable costs will stay the same. If new menu items require more labour to produce and serve, the variable rate will increase, changing the contribution rate and break-even point. It is necessary to recognize the effects new menu items will have on profitability. That doesn't mean that new recipes requiring more labour to produce and serve can't be added to a menu. There are many ways to adjust for increased costs, including lowering the food cost percent to compensate for increased staff costs.

Another problem many managers face in maintaining healthy CVP ratios is sales mix. When food costs are calculated, they include the effect of all of the individual menu item costs as a weighted average of sales. Because most menus combine a mix of different food and labour cost percents for the various items they contain, changing the weighting of items in a calculation of total items sold will affect overall variable cost percents. Often, when menus are changed the sales mix also changes. Sometimes customers change their buying habits with the same result. These changes will affect variable and contribution rates, as well as the break-even point. To overcome this problem, low-cost items can be made more popular and sales can be directed by staff toward those items with the best prime costs.

It is important to monitor any changes to variable costs. They change for a number of reasons and a good operator will adjust as necessary to maintain ratios and CVP relationships to protect profits. We will discuss the controls necessary to accomplish this throughout the text.

CHAPTER ESSENTIALS

In this chapter, we have shown that knowledge of cost/volume/profit relationships is important for those seeking to understand the need for control. We have given the basic formulas used in cost/volume/profit analysis and illustrated their use. We have defined several key terms, including *break-even point, variable rate, contribution rate*, and *contribution margin*. Finally, we have illustrated the effect of excessive or uncontrolled costs on profits.

KEY TERMS IN THIS CHAPTER

Break-even point, p. 77   Cost/volume/profit equation, p. 72
Contribution margin, p. 79   Variable rate, p. 75
Contribution rate, p. 76

QUESTIONS AND PROBLEMS

1. Given the following information, determine total dollar sales:
   a. Cost of sales, $46,500; cost of labour, $33,247; cost of overhead, $75,883; profit, $3,129.
   b. Cost of sales, $51,259; cost of labour, $77,351; cost of overhead, $42,248; loss, $41,167.
2. Given the following information, find contribution margin:
   a. Average sales price per unit, $13.22; average variable cost per unit, $5.78
   b. Average sales price per unit, $14.50; average variable rate, .36
   c. Average sales price per unit, $16.20; average contribution rate, .55
   d. Average variable cost per unit, $6.20; average variable rate, .3
   e. Average variable cost per unit, $3.60; average contribution rate, .6
   (From this point on, the term *average* is eliminated from the problems. This will affect neither the problems nor the solutions.)
3. Given the following information, find variable rate:
   a. Sales price per unit, $19.25; variable cost per unit, $6.70
   b. Total sales, $164,328; total variable cost, $72,304.32
   c. Sales price per unit, $18.80; contribution margin, $10.72
   d. Sales price per unit, $16.37; total fixed costs, $142,408; total unit sales, 19,364; total profit, $22,952.80

4. Given the following information, find contribution rate:

   a. Sales price per unit, $18.50; contribution margin, $10.08

   b. Sales price per unit, $17.50; variable cost per unit, $6.95

   c. Total sales, $64,726; total variable costs, $40,130.12

   d. Sales price per unit, $16.50; profit, $33,381.80; number of customers, 18,440; total fixed costs, $136,137

5. Given the following information, find break-even point in dollar sales:

   a. Fixed costs, $48,337.80; contribution rate, .6

   b. Variable rate, .45; fixed costs, $155,410.31

   c. Variable cost per unit, $5.85; sales price per unit, $17.40; fixed costs, $164,065.60

6. Given the following information, find break-even point in number of customers:

   a. Fixed costs, $113,231.64; contribution margin, $2.28

   b. Sales price per unit, $17.22; fixed costs, $215,035.68; variable cost per unit, $6.98

   c. Contribution rate, .6; sales price per unit, $18.20; fixed costs, $219,423.16

7. Given the following information, find dollar sales:

   a. Fixed costs, $60,000; profit, $18,000; sales price per unit, $8.00; variable cost per unit, $5.00

   b. Variable rate, .45; profit, $21,578.10; fixed costs, $58,382

   c. Sales price per unit, $16.60; profit, $21,220; contribution margin, $9.29; fixed costs, $126,000

8. Given the following information, find number of customers:

   a. Fixed costs, $58,922; profit, $9,838; contribution margin per unit, $3.82

   b. Profit, $33,603; sales price per unit, $17.00; fixed costs, $97,197; contribution rate, .6

   c. Variable cost per unit, $5.30; profit equal to 18 percent of $211,000; sales price per unit, $16.30; fixed costs, $86,609

   d. Sales price per unit, $16.20; fixed costs, $129,425.36; variable rate, .4; profit, $44,000

9. Given the following information, find fixed costs:

   a. Total sales, $104,672; profit, $18,000; variable rate, .42

   b. Profit, $12,000; number of customers, 32,392; variable cost per unit, $4.63; sales price per unit, $10.34

   c. Sales price per unit, $14.60; profit, $34,000; number of customers, 26,712; variable rate, .35

   d. Contribution rate, .65; sales price per unit, $18.40; number of customers, 26,549; profit, $33,000

10. Given the following information, find profit:

   a. Fixed costs, $82,449.40; total sales, $167,543.20; variable costs, $55,629.60

   b. Variable rate, .4; number of customers, 26,412; fixed costs, $193,764.40; sales price per unit, $17.60

c. Total sales, $190,830.66; variable cost per unit, $5.64; fixed costs, $75,919.70; sales price per unit, $16.22

11. The owner of the Barn Lodge Restaurant estimates that fixed costs for the coming year will be $360,000. Based on his investment in the business, he wants a profit of $120,000 for the year. Experience has shown that the average cheque is $12.00.

a. If total variable cost is $720,000, what level of dollar sales will be required to earn the target restaurant profit?

b. Given total variable costs are and total sales figures calculated in Question 11a, what variable rate is the owner projecting?

c. Given the variable rate calculated in Question 11b, determine the contribution rate.

d. Given the contribution rate calculated in Question 11c, determine the average contribution margin based on a $12.00 average sale.

e. At what level of dollar sales will the restaurant break even?

12. The following information is from the records of Wing's Restaurant:

Sales	$800,000
Variable costs	$342,400
Fixed costs	$345,600

Assume that sales volume equals 40,000 covers:

a. Calculate profit.

b. Calculate average dollar sale.

c. Calculate dollar sales required to earn a profit of $125,000, assuming variable rate does not change.

13. Define each of the key terms in this chapter.

EXCEL EXERCISES

Exercise 3.1

The budgeted income statement for Barnaby's Hideaway is produced on an Excel spreadsheet on the companion website for this text. Assume that the following constitute the fixed and variable costs for the upcoming year:

Fixed Costs for the Upcoming Year

1. 40 percent of labour (representing salaries)
2. Employee benefits—40 percent of employee benefits (that correspond to salaries).
3. Other controllable expenses
4. Occupancy costs
5. Interest expense
6. Depreciation

Variable Costs for the Upcoming Year

1. Cost of food
2. Cost of beverages
3. 60 percent of salaries and wages
4. Employee benefits—60 percent of employee benefits

Using the Excel spreadsheet:

1. Calculate total fixed costs for the upcoming year.
2. Calculate total variable costs for the upcoming year.
3. Calculate the variable rate for the upcoming year.
4. Calculate the break-even point for Barnaby's Hideaway for the upcoming year.
5. Assuming that the average contribution margin per unit is $14.50, calculate the number of customers necessary to break even.

Exercise 3.2

Using the Excel spreadsheet:
1. Assume that variable costs are not controlled and that budgeted costs of sales for food and beverage increase to $600,000 and total sales are as budgeted ($1,665,472.20). Calculate profit for Barnaby's Hideaway. All other costs remain the same.
2. Calculate the new variable rate and new contribution rate, assuming the same variable salaries and employee benefits.
3. Calculate the break-even point for Barnaby's Hideaway using the new contribution rate.
4. Using the new contribution rate, calculate the sales level necessary for Barnaby's Hideaway to earn the budgeted profit of $166,794.43.
5. Assume that the new contribution margin falls to $12.60. Calculate the number of customers necessary to break even.

Exercise 3.3

Follow the instructions on the textbook's companion website to complete this exercise.

PART II

FOOD CONTROL

Now that we have built a foundation by discussing the three topics central to this text—*cost*, *sales*, and *control*—we can start addressing some specific elements of food control. This part of the text addresses various means of controlling food costs, from purchasing through to production and sales, by setting standards and implementing systems and processes in order to achieve profitability. First we will discuss the typical chain of daily events that make up the foodservice business, from initial purchase of raw materials right through to the sale of the products that were prepared from those materials. We will consider techniques for measuring food costs and investigate ways of analyzing those costs in relation to food sales. From there we can engineer solutions to improve performance. Let's begin by discussing food purchasing and receiving controls.

Food Purchasing and Receiving Control

• LEARNING OBJECTIVES •

After reading this chapter, you should be able to:

4.1 Describe how quality and quantity standards for food purchases are established.

4.2 List six reasons that standard purchase specifications are important, and provide examples of specifications for both a perishable and a nonperishable food item.

4.3 Describe the process used to determine the quantity of perishable and nonperishable food to be purchased.

4.4 Determine order quantities using the periodic and perpetual order methods.

4.5 Describe the procedures for purchasing perishable and nonperishable foods at the most favourable prices.

4.6 Describe the various purchasing methods.

4.7 Describe the duties of a receiving clerk, and outline the essential equipment and supplies needed for proper receiving.

4.8 Describe the steps in a standard receiving procedure.

4.9 List the information contained in the receiving clerk's daily report, and explain the report's function.

4.10 Explain the difference between directs and stores, and provide examples of each.

INTRODUCTION

All foodservice businesses, regardless of size or type, have certain processes in common. Whether the foodservice business is a fast-food restaurant or a fine-dining establishment, it must purchase supplies from purveyors (suppliers) by phone, e-mail, Internet, fax, letter, or through a salesperson who calls at the establishment. Both types of establishments must control how supplies are received, so that someone must verify that the quantity, quality, and price are the same as ordered. The food must be moved directly to production or be put away properly in storage. When needed, the food must be taken from storage and prepared for customers who order it. Finally, the food must be served to the customers whose collected payments must be recorded and secured, so that the money is used appropriately for the business.

All foodservice establishments, once they have established their menu and business standards, have the following sequence of operations:

1. Purchasing
2. Receiving
3. Storing
4. Issuing
5. Producing
6. Selling and serving
7. Securing and recording sales

In each of these steps, it is possible for excess and unwarranted costs to develop. For example, a purchasing steward can order more of an item than is needed, resulting in excess supplies that go bad before they can be used. Food can be improperly stored so that it spoils prior to production. The cooks can prepare food improperly so that it cannot be served and must be thrown out. In each of these instances, excessive costs are incurred and profit suffers.

This chapter deals with measures that can be taken to prevent unnecessary costs from developing during purchasing and receiving. Succeeding chapters discuss measures to prevent excessive cost in storing, issuing, production, and sales. As seen in Figure 4.1, there are several stages in the flow of food through a foodservice operation, and at each stage it is imperative to prevent waste and/or spoilage.

THE CONTROL PROCESS: PURCHASING AND RECEIVING

In Chapter 2, *control* was defined as a process used by managers to direct, regulate, and restrain the actions of people so that the established goals of an enterprise may be achieved. The control process was identified as a four-step

• FIGURE 4.1 •

The Flow of Food through a Food Service Operation

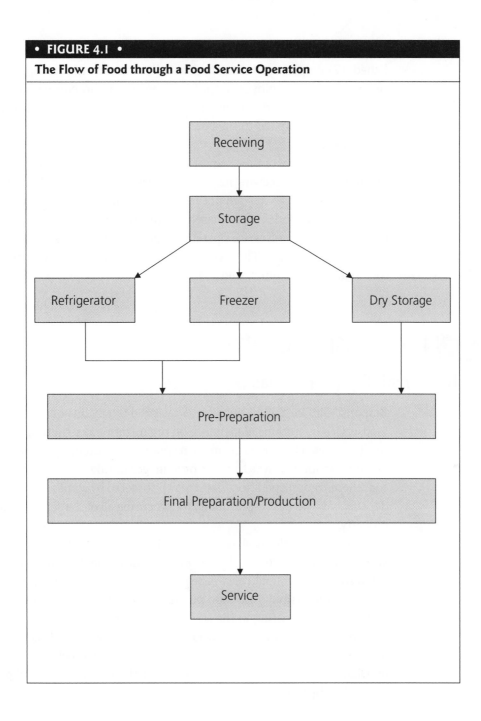

approach, requiring that (1) standards and standard procedures be established, (2) employees be trained to follow those standards and standard procedures, (3) employee output be monitored and compared with established standards, and (4) remedial action be taken as needed. This general process can be applied to the control of any activity in foodservice or in any other business.

The objective of this chapter is to apply the control process to the tasks of purchasing and receiving food. Our discussion emphasizes the standards and standard procedures needed in these areas so that the appropriate quantities and qualities of foods are purchased and received, preventing excess costs from developing. For foodservice operations, purchasing food is the initial step, so we will start with that. The second part of this chapter deals with receiving the food that has been purchased.

PURCHASING CONTROL

Responsibility for Purchasing

Responsibility for purchasing can be assigned to any one of several persons in foodservice operations, depending on organizational structure and management policies. The chef is normally responsible for ordering, although it is not uncommon for a steward, owner, or manager to take on the responsibility. In some hotel/motel operations, food may be ordered by someone in a purchasing department who has responsibility for procuring all of the supplies used on the property.

To facilitate discussion at this point, responsibility for food purchasing is arbitrarily assigned to a chef. This does not mean that the authors believe that this responsibility should always be given to a chef; determining who should be assigned responsibility for food purchasing must be based on the situations and conditions existing in the specific foodservice operation. The important point here is that, for control purposes, the authority to purchase foods and the responsibility for doing so should be assigned to one competent individual. That individual can then be held accountable for the system of control procedures established by the business.

Types of Food Purchased: Perishables and Nonperishables

The types of foods to be purchased for any foodservice enterprise can be divided into two categories: perishables and nonperishables. Because there are significant differences between the approaches to purchasing foods in these categories, it is important to differentiate between them.

Perishable foods are those items, typically fresh foods, that have a comparatively short useful life after they have been received. Various kinds of fruit, vegetables, and fresh fish and seafood, for example, begin to lose their quality very quickly. Some fresh meats and cheeses will retain their quality for somewhat longer periods, but the quality of these foods will begin to deteriorate much sooner than will the quality of many nonperishables—bottles of olive oil, for example. Perishables, then, should be purchased for immediate use in order to take advantage of the quality desired at the time of purchase. If a chef is always careful to purchase the best quality available for intended use, it would be wasteful and costly not to maintain and use that carefully selected quality.

Nonperishable foods have longer shelf lives. Frequently referred to as groceries or staples, they may be stored in the packages or containers in which they are received, often on shelves and at room temperature, for weeks or even months. They do not deteriorate quickly as long as they are unopened and kept at recommended temperatures and humidity levels. Nonperishables are typically purchased and stored in cans, bottles, bags, and boxes. The storage area in which they are kept, usually called a storeroom, resembles the shelves of a supermarket. Frozen foods are generally considered to be nonperishables, because they last a considerable period of time when they're kept frozen.

Because these foods do not deteriorate quickly, it is possible to keep a reasonable supply of them on hand, for use as needed. For example, a restaurant that uses an average of four No. 10 cans of whole, peeled tomatoes daily (more than four cases per week) can keep a supply of eight cases on hand without running any risk of spoilage. Foods that typically fall into this category of nonperishables include salt, sugar, legumes, spices, and oils.

It is important to note that each foodservice operation must determine which foods are considered perishable and which foods are considered nonperishable. There is little disagreement over the perishability of fresh ripened tomatoes or lettuce, or the nonperishability of most canned goods. However, many would disagree over whether to consider meats, eggs, or frozen products perishable or nonperishable.

Geographic location frequently determines whether particular foods are considered perishable or nonperishable. Businesses on the east or west coast will frequently consider seafood a perishable because they have delivery daily. By contrast, restaurants located in the centre of the country are more likely to purchase a larger portion of seafood frozen, and therefore less frequently. This would lead them to categorize seafood as a nonperishable. In addition, the type and style of restaurant will also dictate which foods fall into each category. A fine-dining establishment such as Bistro Quatre will purchase fresh seafood and consider it perishable, whereas a fast-food restaurant would be more likely to purchase seafood frozen and consider it nonperishable.

Meats can also be considered perishable or nonperishable. Many establishments order and receive fresh aged meats daily and purchase only a sufficient supply to last a few days. This would be considered perishable. Others purchase meats in larger quantities, age it on the premises, or buy it frozen. This would be considered nonperishable.

In general, the farther away that foodservice establishments are located from seafood and meat-producing areas, the more likely that fish and meat will be considered nonperishable. Rapid transportation allows many establishments to obtain fresh perishables very quickly, even in remote areas. However, the high transportation cost of obtaining fresh perishable foods in these areas may cause many establishments to purchase frozen products at a lesser price.

The category that each establishment puts various foods into is not critical. The importance of categorizing each food into perishable and nonperishable has to do with the amount of each food that should be purchased, how often it should be purchased, and how its cost is treated when calculating a daily, weekly, or monthly food cost. These issues are discussed next.

DEVELOPING STANDARDS AND STANDARD PROCEDURES FOR PURCHASING

LEARNING OBJECTIVE 4.1
Describe how quality and quantity standards for food purchases are established.

The primary purpose of establishing control over purchasing is to ensure a continuing supply of sufficient quantities of the necessary foods, each of the quality appropriate to its intended use, purchased at the most favourable price. Therefore, we will discuss purchasing from this point of view first by establishing the essential standards and standard procedures for effective purchasing. Standards must be developed for the following:

1. Quality of food purchased
2. Quantity of food purchased
3. Prices at which food is purchased

Establishing Quality Standards

Before any intelligent purchasing can be done, someone in management must determine which foods, both perishables and nonperishables, will be required for day-to-day operations. The quality of these foods should correspond with the quality of the operation, its clientele's needs and desires, and the market's accepted price point. This list of needed foods stems from the menu and the ingredients of its standard recipes. Selecting the quality of ingredients, however, does at times get complicated. For example, most restaurants use tomatoes and tomato products for a variety of purposes—as salad ingredients, as sauce ingredients, and so on. At the same time, tomatoes and tomato products are available for purchase, fresh and processed, in various grades. Before purchasing, important decisions must be made about degree of freshness, sizes, packaging, grades, and brands, among other things.

Developing a complete list of foods and their characteristics for a foodservice operation is complex and time-consuming. It must be done, though, to establish effective control over purchasing. If a restaurant is to produce products of consistent quality, it must use raw materials of consistent quality.

Therefore, it is important that the chef, in cooperation with other members of the management team, draw up the list of all food items to be purchased, with details of the specific and distinctive characteristics that best describe the desired quality of each. These carefully written descriptions are known as **standard purchase specifications** and are often based on grading standards established by the federal government or, in some instances, when federal grading standards are considered too broad, on grading standards common in the appropriate marketplace. When necessary, specifications are written solely for an individual operation that are far more precise and thus more useful for indicating to purveyors the exact quality desired. Once these standard purchase specifications have been developed, they can be printed and distributed to potential purveyors to ensure that each fully understands the restaurant's exact requirements. Figure 4.2 gives five examples of standard purchase specifications written for Bistro Quatre.

• FIGURE 4.2 •

Standard Purchase Specifications

Black Angus Strip Loin, short cut
IMPS number 180
Boneless 25 cm trim
Canada AAA
Range #2, minimum 5.5 kg, maximum 6.5 kg
1.0 to 2.0 cm fat, except for seam fat
Chilled upon delivery
Free from objectionable odours, no evidence of freezing

Salmon
Whole, dressed, fresh day of delivery
Minimum 3.5 kg, maximum 5.5 kg
Fish firm and elastic, meat pink and slightly translucent
Gills free from slime and reddish-pink in colour
Scales adhere tightly to the skin
No stale odours of ammonia

Crimini (Italian Brown) Mushrooms
Canada No. 1
Medium, 3.2 to 4.5 cm in diameter
Light tan to brown in colour
Thin-skinned, tender, delicate flesh
No visible spotting or bruising on skins
Packed in 4.5 kg containers

Canned Cherries
Dark sweet, pitted, canned
Canada Fancy, packed in medium syrup
800 ml: 30 to 35 cans

(*continued*)

> **• FIGURE 4.2 •** *(continued)*
>
> Federal inspector's certificate of grade required
>
> Packed 24 to a case
>
> **Shrimp (headless, frozen)**
>
> Shell-on
>
> 16/20 count
>
> Packed in 4 kg blocks
>
> Delivered at −12°C or below
>
> Packed 6 blocks to a case

Standard purchase specifications, if carefully prepared, are useful in at least six ways:

LEARNING OBJECTIVE 4.2
List six reasons that standard purchase specifications are important, and provide examples of specifications for both a perishable and a non-perishable food item.

1. They force chefs, owners, or managers to determine exact requirements in advance for any product.
2. They are often useful in menu preparation. For example, it is possible to use one cut of meat to prepare several different menu items.
3. They eliminate misunderstandings between buyers and purveyors.
4. They make true competitive bidding possible because specifications for one product are circulated to several purveyors.
5. They eliminate the need for detailed verbal descriptions of a product each time it is ordered.
6. They facilitate checking food as it is received.

Although specifications are written at one particular time, they need not be considered fixed for all time. If conditions change, they can be rewritten and recirculated. Chefs who use computers may have an easier time rewriting specifications.

This critically important step—determining quality standards and developing standard purchase specifications—helps ensure that all foods purchased will be of the desired quality for their intended use.

Establishing Quantity Standards

LEARNING OBJECTIVE 4.3
Describe the process used to determine the quantity of perishable and nonperishable food purchased.

Although purchase specifications can be established initially and merely updated on occasion, quantity standards for purchasing are subject to continual review and revision, often on a daily basis. All foods deteriorate, some more quickly than others, and it is the chef's job to establish a system to ensure that quantities purchased will be needed immediately or in the relatively near future. In cooperation with the steward or the food controller, the chef does this by instituting procedures for determining the appropriate quantity for each item to be purchased. These procedures are based principally on usage and the useful lifespan of the commodity.

For purchasing purposes, foods are divided into the two categories previously discussed: perishables and nonperishables. The procedures for determining their purchase quantities differ and are discussed separately.

Perishables

The very nature of perishable products suggests the importance of always using up those quantities already on hand before purchasing additional quantities. Therefore, the purchasing routine must provide for determining quantities already on hand. Decisions must also be made as to total quantities needed. Once these amounts have been arrived at, the difference between them is the correct amount to order.

There is a term commonly used in industry for the quantity needed: **par**, or **par stock**. Par stock is defined as the amount on hand necessary to satisfy anticipated customer demand for a specific period of time. A basic requirement of the purchasing routine is taking a daily inventory of perishables. In some cases, this daily inventory may be an actual physical inventory. In others, it may be only an estimate based on physical observation. For example, the chef or steward would probably count the actual number of ribs of beef, but only estimate the quantity of chopped beef. A very important and useful tool for the steward to employ in taking this daily inventory is a standard form called the **Market Quotation List**, partially illustrated in Figure 4.3. A similar form, generally available from stationers who cater to the hotel and restaurant industry, is a list of the most common perishables, arranged by types, with several blank lines provided for the special requirements of each restaurant. Foodservice operators who have incorporated computers into the purchasing routine can readily prepare their own, as shown. Doing so makes it possible to limit the number of items on the form to those used by the establishment and to easily add and subtract items as the need arises. The form shown in Figure 4.3 has more items than are needed for the menu of Bistro Quatre. These additional items are listed because they might be needed for special menu items. When the forms are computer-generated, a steward can also have separate sheets for different food groups: one for meat, another for dairy, and so on.

To take the daily inventory of perishables, the steward or chef goes through refrigerators and freezers (if items in the freezer are considered perishable by the establishment) with the form in hand. Next to the appropriate items in each category, the steward fills in the column on the left marked "On Hand." After completing this survey, the steward has a relatively accurate inventory of perishable products. The question of whether items in the freezer are considered perishable, and thus inventoried daily, is a matter for each operation to determine. For example, many seafood establishments freeze portions of fish and shellfish when received in order to prevent those items from deteriorating in quality. Portions of these items are removed from the freezer each day for immediate use. Stewards might treat these items as perishables, because they are ordered frequently and in limited quantities.

The next step in the routine requires that a determination be made as to anticipated total needs—in effect, par stocks—for each item, based on future

• FIGURE 4.3 •

Market Quotation List, Partial List

On Hand	Article	Par	To Order		Quotations	
	Beef					
	Corned beef					
	Beef, chopped					
	Butts					
	Chuck					
4	Fillets	6	2			
3	Strip steaks	5	2			
	Ribs					
	Lamb					
	Chops					
	Loin					
4.5 kg	Legs	9 kg	4.5 kg			
	Racks					
	Saddle					
	Poultry					
20	Chicken breast	32	12			
	Chicken roast					
	Chicken broilers					
	Capons					
10	Duck breast	10	0			
	Guinea hens					
	Guinea squab					
	Turkey					
	Shell Fish					
	Clams, chowder					
	Clams, cherrystone					
	Crabs, hard					
	Crab meat					
	Lobster meat					
10	Lobsters, whole	20	10			
2 doz.	Oysters, boxed	2 doz.	0			
2 kg	Scallops	6 kg	4 kg			
4 kg	Shrimp	11 kg	7 kg			

menus, and often on experience as well. Depending on the establishment, the total anticipated needs can be determined by any—or a combination—of several key personnel: chef, manager, or steward. If the computer form illustrated in Figure 4.3 is used, the par stock figure for total anticipated needs is written in the "Par" column.

Then, for each required item, the steward subtracts the amount on hand from the par figure to determine the proper order quantity. This difference is the amount that should be ordered to bring supply up to the total quantity required. This amount is written in the "To Order" column at the right. If the amount needed is small, as shown for "Duck breast" in Figure 4.3, the chef or steward may not order that item at all, deciding that the amount on hand is sufficient to last until the next order is delivered.

Referring to the Market Quotation List illustrated in Figure 4.3, for example, lamb chops are on the menu, and a total of 9 kilograms will be required to meet the anticipated demand. This number is recorded in the "Par" column. Because the daily inventory indicates 4.5 kilograms, written in the "On Hand" column, the quantity to be purchased is 4.5 kilograms, recorded in the "To Order" column, and is found by subtracting the quantity on hand (4.5 kilograms) from the established par stock (9 kilograms).

Nonperishables

Although nonperishable foods do not deteriorate quickly, having too many on inventory is unnecessary and ties up funds that may be put to better use paying operating expenses. Therefore, one goal of purchasing nonperishables should be to avoid having excessive quantities on hand. Additional benefits from maintaining reduced quantities include reduced overconsumption, diminished possibilities for theft, reduced storage space requirements, and possibly reduced personnel required to maintain the storage area.

Another important factor is establishing a permanent location for each nonperishable item. Labelling the storeroom shelves so that each product has only one location ensures proper inventory figures and may prevent overordering. Another benefit of identifying fixed single locations for products is that it is easier to find things, especially for new personnel. For the convenience of stewards or chefs, a form can be obtained from some stationers that list nonperishables, just as the Market Quotation List itemizes perishables. This form is not widely used, however, because lists of groceries are not as universally applicable as lists of perishables. Most purchasers prefer to make up their own lists of storeroom contents to properly itemize amounts to be ordered.

There are two suitable methods for determining proper purchasing amounts for nonperishables:

1. Periodic order method
2. Perpetual inventory method

LEARNING OBJECTIVE 4.4
Determine order quantities
using the periodic and
perpetual order methods.

Periodic Order Method. Perhaps the most common method for maintaining inventories of stores at appropriate levels is the so-called **periodic order method**, which, in contrast to methods for ordering perishables, permits comparatively infrequent ordering. Because nonperishables have longer shelf lives than perishables, it is possible and desirable to order them less frequently. By doing so, the steward or chef has more time available for ordering perishables, which typically requires considerable attention. When the periodic order method is followed, regular dates for ordering with fixed intervals between them are established. Then, on a regular basis—once a week, every two weeks, or even once each month, depending on storage space available and management policies as to the amount of money to be tied up in inventory— the steward or chef reviews the entire stock of nonperishable items and determines how much of each to order to ensure a supply sufficient to last until the next regularly scheduled order date. Calculating the amount of each item to order is comparatively simple:

> Amount required for the upcoming period
> − Amount presently on hand
> + Amount wanted on hand at the end of the period to last until the next delivery
> = Amount to order

An example can illustrate how the system works. At Bistro Quatre, where orders for nonperishables are placed every two weeks, one of the items ordered is crushed tomatoes, purchased in cans, packed 6 cans to a case. The item is used at the rate of 7 cans per week, and delivery normally takes five days from the date an order is placed. If the chef or steward in this establishment found 9 cans on the shelf, anticipated a use of 14 cans during the upcoming period of approximately two weeks, and wanted 10 cans on hand at the end of that period, the calculation would be the following:

> 14 cans required
> − 9 cans on hand
> + 10 cans to be left at the end of the period (desired ending inventory)
> = 15 cans to be ordered on this date

However, because orders are normally placed for this item in cases rather than in cans, the chef or steward would probably round the order up to the next highest purchase unit (three cases), placing an order for three cases, consisting of 18 cans. Although rounding an order upward in this way appears, at first glance, to be overpurchasing, in fact the steward must order a full case because wholesalers normally do not sell less than full cases at the wholesale price. The slight overpurchase will not affect the quality of the product, because of its longer shelf life and the fact that the additional inventory doesn't represent much money.

One may ask how the steward or chef would know the quantity of an item required for an upcoming period. Storerooms have hundreds of items, and it is impossible for a person to know, without records, the total quantity required for each item in the inventory. In some smaller operations, the purchaser simply guesses, knowing that each subsequent order date will provide an opportunity to improve the accuracy of the figures. In larger restaurants, experienced staff get to know and remember the approximate quantities used in a period and keep this information in mind when ordering. In some establishments that rely on a single supplier for most of their needs, purchasers may seek help from the supplier, who keeps records of previous orders. With that information, one can look on the storage shelf and make an approximate determination of the amount used by subtracting the quantity remaining from the quantity last ordered.

Although such informal methods are probably better than ignoring usage entirely, one must keep in mind that they all fail to take into account the amount on hand at the beginning of any period. Nevertheless, these informal methods are often used in the food and beverage industry.

A more systematic method of determining usage requires additional steps. For establishments without computers, a desirable first step is to make shelf labels more useful by adding information on them. For example, if a label is somewhat larger than standard size, it is feasible in many establishments to record the quantities added to and taken from shelves right on the label. When used in this form, such labels are known as **bin cards**, an example of which is shown in Figure 4.4.

• **FIGURE 4.4** •								
Bin Card								
Item		Crushed tomatoes		**Desired Ending Inventory**				10
Date	In	Date	Out	Date	Out	Date	Out	Balance
1-Oct	Order 18							9
		2-Oct	1	3-Oct	1	4-Oct	1	6
6-Oct	18	5-Oct	1	6-Oct	1	7-Oct	1	21
		8-Oct	1					

As each delivery is received and placed on the shelf, both the date and number of units are entered on the bin card. As quantities are issued for use, those dates and amounts are recorded as well. More spaces are provided for items issued than for items received, for the obvious reason that purchases are comparatively infrequent but issues may occur daily. A balance column is provided so that a steward or chef can determine and enter amounts on hand at any desired time, such as when a salesperson calls or when the periodic ordering date arrives.

At such times, it is quite simple to determine approximate usage by looking on the card for the balance on hand on the date the last order was placed, adding to that figure the number of units placed on shelves when the last order was received, and subtracting the balance currently on hand. The result will be the approximate usage in the most recent period, regardless of the length of that period. That amount can be used to determine purchase quantities.

The assumption is made that this quantity was used productively, although this may not always be the case and should be considered in determining the amount to order for the next period. When such a system is followed, it is normally wise to compare the balance on the bin card with the number of units of the item actually on the shelves in order to be sure that all items issued have been suitably recorded. If there is a discrepancy, the balance shown on the bin card will not be entirely reliable as a measure of actual usage during the period, and the missing items, presumably issued, must be added to the derived usage figure to achieve a more accurate figure.

If the amount used in the preceding period is the amount ordered for the coming period, there is a strong possibility that no units of the item will be left on the shelf at the end of the coming period. Because this may make it impossible to produce some menu items or may make it necessary to obtain some emergency supply to last until the next delivery date, foodservice operators who follow the periodic method must establish the quantity that should be on hand at the end of any period. That quantity should be an amount sufficient to last until the next delivery is received. Once established, this quantity, known as the **desired ending inventory (DEI)**, is recorded on the bin card. Both delivery time and daily usage for the period must be used to determine the DEI. Furthermore, it is advisable to include some additional quantity to serve as a safety factor, just in case the normal delivery is delayed or business volume is higher than expected in the coming period. For the example given, the calculations for DEI would be as follows:

> Daily usage × Number of days in delivery period = Normal usage
> Normal usage + Safety factor (50%) = DEI

Thus:

> 14 cans per week ÷ 7 days = 2 cans per day
> 2 cans per day × 5 days in delivery period = 10 cans normal usage
> 10 cans normal usage + 50% safety factor = 15 cans DEI

It should be obvious that a bin card system requires considerably more manual record keeping than most operators would like. Many do not have the time, the labour, or the trained personnel required to keep the bin cards up-to-date.

Therefore, one will often see shelf labels in food storerooms, but may never see bin cards used for keeping records of foods received and issued. It may, however, be worthwhile to track high-priced items like dried wild mushrooms with bin cards.

In computerized foodservice operations, shelf labels are still useful for many of the purposes identified earlier, but are not needed as bin cards. The information formerly recorded manually on bin cards is now an integral part of inventory records in the computer. As deliveries of any given item are received and placed on shelves, quantities are entered in the computerized inventory records. When units are removed from the shelf for use, those quantities are also entered. If the records are accurately maintained, a balance figure for each inventory item is readily available at all times, and accurate orders can be placed at the appropriate time.

Regardless of the system, other useful information about inventory items should be maintained as well. The container size and the latest purchase price, as well as the current supplier, for example, can be available as an integral part of the record; the ready availability of this information can help the steward or chef prepare purchase orders quickly and easily.

It is important for anyone planning to go into the foodservice industry to realize that those using the periodic order method must constantly review two quantities used in the formula: normal usage and DEI. After all, many changes occur in usage from period to period, and the steward or chef who fails to take changes into account is mismanaging. For example, as the seasons and menus change, some foods will be used in greater quantities. If demand for some menu items increases, usage for related inventory items will increase as well; the reverse is also true. Thus, before ordering, it is normally advisable to compare usage in similar periods in preceding years.

Perpetual Inventory Method. The perpetual inventory method has two primary purposes:

1. to ensure that quantities purchased are sufficient to meet anticipated need without being excessive and
2. to provide effective control over those items being stored for future use.

The **perpetual inventory method** requires the maintenance of perpetual inventory records, similar to that illustrated in Figure 4.5. Successful use of this method requires complete and accurate records. Some operations attempt to maintain perpetual inventories manually; more prefer computerized approaches. The primary difference is that those without computers must keep the records on paper cards and perform the calculations manually; computer users maintain the records on hard drives or discs, with the computers doing all of the calculations.

• FIGURE 4.5 •						
Perpetual Inventory Card						
Item		Crushed tomatoes	Cost		$19.98 per 6-Can Case	
Size		#10 can	Par Stock		15	
Supplier		ABC Co.	Reorder Point		10	
		18 120th St.	Reorder Quantity		12	
		Calgary				
Date			Order #	In	Out	Balance
1-Oct			#222-24		1	9
2-Oct					1	8
3-Oct					1	7
4-Oct					1	6
5-Oct					1	5
6-Oct				12	1	16

Perpetual inventory cards, although similar to the bin card illustrated in Figure 4.4, include some additional information and are used differently. One very important difference is that the perpetual inventory card is not normally affixed to the shelf on which the covered item is kept. It is kept in a location other than the storeroom and is maintained by someone who does not work in the storeroom. The quantity of food purchased is recorded, and, as units of product are issued for use, those quantities issued are similarly recorded. If the quantities recorded accurately reflect the movement of items into and out of storage, it is possible at any given time merely to consult the perpetual inventory card to determine how much of an item is in stock at the moment. This system makes it possible to compare balances on the perpetual inventory cards with actual items on shelves to determine if all items are accounted for.

The additional information, including the name and address of the supplier and the most recent purchase price for the item, facilitates ordering. Three additional items included on the card—reorder point, par stock, and reorder quantity—are also of considerable use in facilitating purchases.

The **reorder point** is, quite simply, the number of units to which the supply on hand should decrease before additional orders are placed. Thus, if the reorder point for a given item is 10 cans, then no order for that item should be placed until the supply shown in the balance column has reached that number. To establish a reorder point for any item, it is necessary to know both normal usage and the time needed to obtain delivery. Furthermore, it is advisable to include in the calculations a certain additional amount to allow for delivery delays and for possible increased usage during that period. In effect, the reorder point in the perpetual inventory method is the equivalent of the DEI in the periodic method.

Reorder point is calculated in the following manner. If normal usage is 14 cans per week and it takes five days from date of order to get delivery, then the basic number of cans needed is 10. However, because delivery may be delayed, because usage may increase for unforeseen reasons, or because both of those possibilities may occur at once, it is advisable to increase that amount somewhat. The amount of the increase is a matter for management to decide. For our purposes, we will add 50 percent to our calculation so that the reorder point would be set at 15 cans. Under the periodic method, the DEI would similarly be calculated as 15 cans.

The perpetual inventory card also provides for a par stock figure for each item in stock. (Par stock was defined earlier in the chapter as the quantity of any item required to meet anticipated needs in some specific, upcoming period.) With nonperishables, that quantity can be determined only after carefully weighing the following considerations:

- Storage space
- Limits on total value of inventory prescribed by management
- Desired frequency of ordering
- Usage
- Purveyors' minimum order requirements

Storage space is limited for all but a few very fortunate owners and managers, so it is obviously necessary to calculate the maximum amount of storage space available for all nonperishables and then to allocate the use of that space carefully and wisely. For example, for those items normally purchased in comparatively large packages, such as bulk flour and sugar, it may be necessary to restrict space to a one-week supply.

Management may restrict the amount of cash invested in inventory. If cash flow is a problem (i.e., if cash for meeting payroll and for paying outstanding bills is in comparatively short supply), then management is likely to restrict the size and value of inventory and to require more frequent ordering of smaller quantities. In some cases, it may be possible to accomplish this by restricting only the purchase of the more expensive items in the inventory without effecting any change in purchases of less costly products.

Obviously, management must determine how often foods should be ordered. In addition, although the foods involved are typically referred to as nonperishables, some are, in fact, more perishable than others, and this should be taken into account. Determination of par stock should always take into account the relative quantities of an item used, which may change over time. If anticipated consumption of an item is expected to be high in a given period, then the par stock should be higher than at, say, another time or season when consumption is rather low. Also, most purveyors prefer to supply items in standard wholesale purchase units, such as cases and 40 kilogram bags; these quantities as purchased may affect par stock. Finally, the minimum order requirements of purveyors must also be taken into account. With the high costs of transportation and labour, many suppliers maintain a minimum purchase amount for delivery. Only orders over $150 and in some cases over $500 will be shipped. Others may require a delivery surcharge if a minimum order is not met.

Once all of these factors have been considered and a par stock figure has been established for each inventory item, it is entered on the appropriate perpetual inventory card. The final consideration is the establishment of a reorder quantity. **Reorder quantity** is the amount that will be ordered each time the quantity of a particular item diminishes to the reorder point. The quantity ordered should be sufficient to bring the total inventory up to the par stock level. Remember the adjustment to the reorder point? Let's add the quantity needed to cover the usage between the order date and the delivery date:

	Par stock	20
−	Reorder point	15
=	Subtotal	5
+	Normal usage until delivery	10
=	Reorder quantity	15

However, food is normally purchased in case lots of 6, 12, 24, or some other quantity per case, depending on the item and size of container, and this must be taken into account. If the establishment needs 15 units of an item packed 6 to the case, the order placed must be in some multiple of 6. In this case, the reorder quantity will be three cases, or 18 cans, rather than the 15 determined to be needed. Upon delivery, the stock is brought to 23 units, or approximately to par.

Hybrid Methods. Many establishments do not use either the periodic order method or the perpetual inventory method as described here. Some fear the comparative absence of control in the periodic method. Others appreciate the value of having perpetual inventory records removed from the control of those who receive and issue food. For these and other reasons, some have developed what amount to hybrid systems that selectively employ the more desirable features of both systems.

One such system is essentially a perpetual method, but with reorder points and par stocks set sufficiently high so that orders need not be placed at precisely the moment that reorder points are reached. Such establishments may use a reorder point as a signal that a particular item should be ordered on the next regularly scheduled day for placing orders and may merely add the item to a list. If the reorder point were set high enough, there would be little danger of consuming the remaining quantity through normal usage before the next delivery.

The final determination of a routine—one of those illustrated earlier or some variation—must be based on the needs of the individual operation and the policies established by management. The important point is that the purchasing procedure must take into account the need for determining, on an ongoing basis, the quantity of each product that will be adequate for meeting anticipated demand. It must guard against overpurchasing (the purchasing of unneeded quantities). In the case of perishables, overpurchasing increases the possibilities for loss through overconsumption, spoilage, or theft. It increases the possibilities for overproduction and consequent waste. It also may lead to diminished quality of menu items. Because food deteriorates over time, by overpurchasing, staff may be using older inferior foods that are not spoiled but are not up to quality standards. If a guest consumes an item that is inferior and consequently does not return, thousands of dollars of potential sales may be lost. This result of overpurchasing could be the most costly. It may have been less damaging to the business to have thrown away the product and its value. In the case of nonperishables, overpurchasing clearly increases the possibilities for theft, it may increase the need for personnel, and it certainly can tie up unwarranted amounts of money in inventory. Because control systems guard against these conditions, it is important to set up procedures for determining appropriate quantities for ordering.

Assume that management elects to maintain supplies of nonperishables by the perpetual inventory method and that all relevant records are in a computer, including reorder point, reorder quantity, previous purchases and issues, and any other information that would be useful in making purchase decisions. With all such data available, management can quickly determine the current status of the entire inventory, including a list of those items at or below reorder point. In effect, the perpetual inventory card for each item would be a file in a computer database, rather than a card in a file drawer.

Using one of the programs currently available, it is comparatively simple to create a computer inventory for nonperishable foods. Depending on the specifics of the software used, one can record such information as the items in the inventory, various vendors, purchase units, current prices, quantities purchased, and quantities issued. The purchases and issues for each item can be used to determine a quantity on hand, which can be compared with the reorder point, and a report can be generated listing those items for which the quantity on hand has reached the reorder point. In the case of an individual restaurant, this report can be used by the steward or chef to place orders. In a chain organization, similar reports from all units can be transmitted electronically to a home office, where they can be used to generate one complete list of purchases to be made centrally for the entire organization, conceivably at considerable savings.

Although there are many advantages to maintaining food inventories by computer, this approach is not without its problems. For example, perpetual inventory files in a computer must be kept current in the same basic manner as perpetual inventory cards in a file drawer. Someone must be responsible for recording and updating all purchases and issues. Unless this information is recorded with complete accuracy, the records will be useless for making purchasing decisions. Moreover, recording data in a computer terminal requires as much time and concentration as recording this data on index cards. If management directs that computers be used as aids in record keeping and decision-making, it must be prepared to accept an expense for the time that one or more employees will spend at the computer terminal keeping the records current. Computer use is most common in larger restaurants and in chain organizations, because it is still somewhat more difficult for small operators to identify sufficient tangible benefits to justify the cost. Some small operators and chefs know their par stock and inventory levels so well, being so aware of daily operations, that they run these systems without the aid of bin cards or computers. This method also has challenges.

Computer Applications

One of the best applications of a computer system in our industry is purchasing. A good program will allow the manager to track the rise and fall of food costs automatically, and it should also generate customized reports on such items as purchases and price variances. Many programs today have the additional convenience of being compatible with a personal digital assistant (PDA) or smart phone, allowing the manager to conduct a physical inventory electronically, thus eliminating paper inventory worksheets. These devices can upload spreadsheets to the restaurant's computer, and inventory values can be calculated.

In addition, many programs can then generate orders based on par levels and reorder points and determine which vendor to purchase from based on lowest price. Many reports can be generated, including those tracking purchases by inventory category, account category, or location. These reports can be extremely helpful in analyzing trends in excessive costs. Systems can be custom programmed to the manager's specifications to flag price increases and decreases and exaggerated fluctuations in purchasing amounts. They can also monitor if inventory values become too high or if certain items have been in storage too long and should be used up.

One such program is Comtrex, a point-of-sale (POS) system. Ordering can be performed by an order wizard. Information from past sales periods is kept in memory and the wizard forecasts needed supplies based on anticipated sales. Another system comes from Restaurant Plus. It combines inventory and sales data to generate purchase orders based on inventory reorder points and economic order quantities, and will even e-mail the orders to established purveyors. Many operations using up-to-date computer software systems are linked to their purveyor, with access to databases enabling ordering and generating inventory calculations and historical reports.

These computer systems are just two of the many available. The authors cite these as examples of computer programs that include the principles outlined in the text. We do not necessarily endorse them or any of the others cited throughout this text. Students are encouraged to visit the web links provided on this textbook's companion website to further investigate these programs' features and services.

Inventory in large warehouse operations can be tracked by bar code or by radio frequency identification (RFI), which stores all of a product's information on tags that can be accessed by receiver readers that track and issue items. These supply chain systems make controlling the flow of products and inventory easy and accurate.

Establishing Price Standards

Having established purchase specifications indicating the appropriate quality to buy, and procedures to determine the quantity to buy, one can turn to the question of price. Because it is desirable to buy products of the appropriate quality in adequate quantities at the lowest possible price, it is important to ensure that food purchases are made based on competitive prices obtained from several possible suppliers.

LEARNING OBJECTIVE 4.5
Describe the procedures for purchasing perishable and non-perishable foods at the most favourable prices.

The availability of supply sources varies considerably from one location to another. Major metropolitan areas, for example, tend to offer the greatest number of possibilities, both in terms of the different categories of suppliers and the number of suppliers in each category. In contrast, remote rural areas tend to offer few possibilities; sometimes establishments in remote areas must be content with what they can get. Increasingly, some items can be purchased on the Internet and shipped anywhere. This makes some things easier to find and widely accessible. Cost may become a factor, but finding diverse products is certainly easier. Below is a list of the different types of suppliers that foodservice operators might use:

- Wholesalers
- Local producers
- Manufacturers
- Packers
- Local farmers
- Retailers
- Cooperative associations

In most instances, the foodservice operator will deal with several of these sources to obtain the necessary foods. For example, a restaurant may turn to a local producer for dairy and bakery products, a wholesaler for fresh meats, and a different wholesaler for fruits and vegetables.

In recent years, there has been a trend for wholesalers to diversify their product lines in an attempt to better meet the needs of their restaurant customers. In some instances, one supplier may be able to provide virtually all of a restaurant's food-related needs. In general, a chef or steward will deal with as many suppliers as may be necessary to ensure the supply of foods of appropriate quality at the lowest prices. To ensure that purchases are made at the most favourable prices, the operation must obtain prices from several competing suppliers for each product that is needed. The procedures differ for perishables and nonperishables.

Means of Obtaining Price Quotations

Today purchasers have several means of finding purveyors, obtaining price quotations, and ordering supplies:

- Internet
- Telephone
- Fax and fax modem
- Quotation sheets obtained by mail
- Information supplied by salespersons who call on customers
- Direct computer links with purveyors via the Internet or dedicated telephone line

The Internet is a worldwide source of purveyors, wholesalers, producers, and products. From a website you can source products and specifications, get price quotes, make purchases, and arrange for delivery.

Direct computer links with purveyors enable the purchaser to access price lists on a computer. Fax messages provide the advantage of obtaining written information very quickly. Fax modems enable one to obtain fax messages without a separate machine. Telephone quotations, obtaining quotes from salespersons who call at the establishment, and obtaining price lists by mail are the traditional means of gaining information. However, as computers, fax machines, and modems become more common in restaurants, fewer establishments are relying on traditional means.

Virtually all purveyors have fax machines to provide price quotations to customers and to receive orders. In addition, many purveyors now have websites that enable purchasers to obtain prices for their entire range of products and place orders. Purchasing via the Internet is becoming increasingly common and will likely continue to gain in popularity.

Perishables

Because prices for perishables generally change daily, it is necessary for the steward or chef to contact several different suppliers by one or more of the aforementioned means to determine current prices each time an order is to be placed. If copies of specifications have previously been sent to suppliers, the purchaser has reasonable assurance that each is quoting on products of comparable quality. The Market Quotation List, shown in Figure 4.3, provides columns for price quotations on each product, with space for the supplier's name. Ideally, the steward will obtain prices from several suppliers for each item and will select the lowest price. In reality, other considerations should also be taken into account. These include delivery time, minimum orders, managers' preferences for particular dealers, the reliability of dealers in providing foods that meet specifications, and the number of individual items that can be ordered from any one dealer. Once price quotations have been obtained, the steward or chef selects the most favourable and places the order with the chosen dealer, who is often the lowest bidder. As the order is placed, the steward circles the particular price quotation next to the item to be supplied. Thus, when all perishables have been ordered, the operation has a complete record of products ordered as well as records of prices, quantities, and suppliers. As discussed in the receiving controls section later in this chapter, this list will be valuable for receiving purposes when the food is delivered.

Nonperishables

Procedures used to obtain competitive prices for nonperishables may be somewhat different from those used for perishables. Sometimes stewards and chefs obtain nonperishables from the same supplier that provides perishable products. This is particularly true in smaller establishments that do not purchase large quantities of any one item. Stewards generally prefer to deal with fewer suppliers for nonperishables. In fact, many obtain extensive price lists from wholesale supply houses (e.g., by mail, by fax, or by turning to the suppliers' web pages), each of which may be able to supply most of the nonperishable products that restaurants are likely to order. With these lists in hand, stewards can compare prices and make selections at greater leisure than is possible with the purchase of perishables.

Although a purchaser normally selects the lowest price consistent with the quality desired, there are exceptions here as well. For example, if dealer A is offering all but one item at a lower price than dealer B, and dealer B's price for that one item is only $0.02 per can lower, an operation would be likely to place an order for 12 cans with dealer A despite the higher price, the difference being only a matter of $0.24. The expenditure would be more than justified by the simplification of the order and the savings in bookkeeping costs. In addition, it is possible that dealer B may not accept an order as small as 24 cans of a single item, because the profit may be more than offset by the cost of making the delivery.

PURCHASING METHODS

Centralized Purchasing

Centralized purchasing systems are widely used by chain operations and occasionally established by small groups of independent operators with similar needs. Under a centralized purchasing system, the requirements of individual units are relayed to a central office, which determines total requirements of all units and then purchases that total, either for delivery to the individual units by the dealer or for delivery to a central warehouse, with subsequent distribution by the central office. The advantages and disadvantages to these centralized systems are discussed below.

LEARNING OBJECTIVE 4.6
Describe the various purchasing methods.

Advantages of Centralized Purchasing

1. Foods and beverages can be purchased at lower prices due to volume.
2. Desired quality or variety may be obtained more readily because the purchasing agent has a greater choice of markets.

3. Larger inventories can be maintained, ensuring reliable supply to individual units.
4. The possibilities for dishonest purchasing in individual units are reduced.

Disadvantages of Centralized Purchasing

1. Each unit may have to accept the standard item in stock with little freedom to purchase for its own particular needs.
2. Individual units may not be able to take advantage of local specials at reduced prices.

There are different types of operations using centralized purchasing. Most franchises would not allow individual units to change menus and requisition different goods. Some multi-unit operations may allow more flexibility with menus and ingredients, while some resort complexes that include diverse food-service operations may centrally purchase whatever any operation wants. Regardless of the entity, decisions about whether to adopt a centralized purchasing system are normally made by top management, not by food controllers. However, there are times when food controllers are asked to give their advice and opinions. To do so, they must understand the advantages and disadvantages of centralized purchasing.

Purchase Orders

Purchase orders are formal agreements that a product is going to be bought at a specific price. Purchase orders are submitted by a purchaser to the purveyor. This is a promise to purchase goods; it is not an invoice.

A written purchase order provides many benefits, including the following:

1. Written verification of the quoted price
2. Written verification of the quantity ordered
3. Written verification of all goods ordered
4. Written and special instructions to the receiving clerk, as needed
5. Written verification of conformance to product specification
6. Written authorization to prepare vendor invoice for payment

One-Purveyor Buying or One-Stop Shopping

One-purveyor buying is used by many regional and national chains, as a large purveyor can supply all of the specified foodservice items the individual units may need. While convenient and possibly time-saving, being tied to only one supplier has obvious shortcomings, including possibly higher product costs.

Open Bid

An **open bid** is essentially sending out specifications to several purveyors for competitive bidding. The buyer can discuss one purveyor's quote with another in an effort to obtain the best price and will ultimately decide on the best bid.

Cost Plus

Cost plus is an arrangement where the buyer and purveyor agree to a fixed dollar or percentage markup for an item. This type of arrangement may save time and money for the purchaser, and if a good relationship can be established, it may be mutually beneficial.

Contract Purchasing

Contract purchasing guarantees a set price for an item for a given term. It is often used to smooth fluctuating seasonal prices for perishable items. If contracts are negotiated properly and unaffected negatively by market factors, they may work well in reducing costs.

Food Brokers

Food brokers work as liaisons and negotiate sales of products between producers and manufacturers of food products and buyers. The producer/manufacturer may save the expense of maintaining its own sales force. Since brokers may represent a large number of producers, buyers can easily access many items. They also expedite distribution and keep everyone up to date on market conditions.

Standing Orders

Although it is desirable for the needed quantity of a given item to be determined with great care each time an order is placed, purchasers commonly make arrangements with certain purveyors for the delivery of goods without specific orders. These arrangements are known as **standing orders** and typically take one of two forms.

One arrangement calls for the delivery of a specific quantity of a given item each day (e.g., 12 loaves of bread). The order remains constant unless specifically changed by the chef. The second arrangement calls for the replenishing of stock each day up to a certain predetermined number. For instance, the operation may arrange with a dairy supplier to leave a sufficient quantity of bulk milk each morning, to bring the total supply up to a predetermined figure, such as 70 litres. Although these arrangements are convenient, they do present possibilities for waste and excessive development costs.

RECEIVING CONTROLS

LEARNING OBJECTIVE 4.7
Describe the duties of a receiving clerk, and outline the essential equipment and supplies needed for proper receiving.

If great care is taken to establish effective controls for purchasing, equal attention must be given to receiving controls. After all, ordering specific quantities and qualities at optimum prices constitutes no guarantee that the products ordered will actually be delivered. Purveyors may deliver incorrect quantities of foods, foods of higher or lower qualities, foods with prices other than those quoted, or all three. Therefore, the primary objective of receiving controls is to verify that quantities, qualities, and prices of timely food deliveries conform to orders placed.

In our discussion, we use the job title *receiving clerk* to identify the individual to whom management assigns full responsibility for receiving food deliveries and carrying out the control procedures set up by the chef, steward, and food controller. In larger operations, particularly those with complete food control systems, one person may be so designated. In smaller operations that deem the payroll expense of a receiving clerk unwarranted, food deliveries may be received by any of several individuals, including the chef, sous-chef, owner, or manager. Although we use the job title *receiving clerk* extensively in this chapter, we are aware that others do receive deliveries. The job title is not important; what is important is the development of a set of standard procedures for receiving food deliveries to verify that these deliveries conform to purchases in every way.

Establishing Standards for Receiving

The primary purpose of receiving control is to verify that the quantity, quality, and price of each item delivered conforms to the order placed, and is on time. To ensure that this is the case, it is necessary to establish standards to govern the receiving process, as follows:

1. The quantity delivered should be the same as the quantity listed on the Market Quotation List, and this should be identical to the quantity listed on the invoice, or bill, that accompanies the delivery.
2. The quality of the item delivered should conform to the establishment's standard purchase specification for that item.
3. The prices on the invoice should be the same as those circled on the Market Quotation List.
4. The goods are received at the time specified.

The Invoice

Every time food is delivered to an establishment, it should be accompanied by a document that lists the items being delivered. For food, the document is normally an **invoice**, which is the same as a bill. A typical invoice is illustrated in Figure 4.6.

• FIGURE 4.6 •

Invoice

Invoice
Market Price Meat Co.
300 Market St.
Calgary, Alberta

To   Bistro Quatre   Date 11-Jun

Quantity		Unit		Description		Unit Price		Amount
13.6		kg		Strip loin		22.99		$312.66
4.54		kg		Veal loin		27.17		$123.35
								$436.01

An invoice is usually presented to the receiving clerk in duplicate by the person making the delivery, who will expect the receiving clerk to sign and return the second copy. This serves as an acknowledgement to the purveyor that the establishment has received the products listed on the invoice and consents to pay for them as agreed. The original is a bill that must be routed to the bookkeeper or other individual responsible for paying bills. This routing procedure is dealt with later in this chapter. The acceptance of invoices that do not list prices should be discouraged: Prices should be checked as the food products are received. Otherwise, it is possible that a purveyor may bill at the wrong prices, either by accident or by design.

ESTABLISHING STANDARD PROCEDURES FOR RECEIVING

LEARNING OBJECTIVE 4.8
Describe the steps in a
standard receiving procedure.

Although exact procedures and techniques for receiving vary from one establishment to another, it is useful to examine one standard procedure that many managers have found appropriate for use in their establishments. This procedure has five steps:

1. Verify that the quantity, quality, and price for each item delivered conform exactly to the order placed.
2. Acknowledge that quantity, quality, and price have been verified by stamping the invoice with an invoice stamp provided for that purpose.
3. List all invoices for foods delivered on a given day on the Receiving Clerk's Daily Report for that day and complete the report as required, or enter appropriate information directly into computer software.
4. Forward completed paperwork to proper personnel.
5. Move food to appropriate storage or production areas.

Verifying Quantity, Quality, and Price

To carry out the verification procedure suggested here, the receiving clerk must have certain supplies and equipment available, including the following:

- A permanent copy of the standard purchase specifications
- Appropriate equipment for determining weight, including such items as a hanging scale (for whole fish and large meat items) and a platform scale (for boxed items)
- Certain paper forms, tags, rubber stamps, and related office supplies

Quantity verification entails weighing, counting, or otherwise enumerating the quantity of a particular food delivered by the vendor, and then checking to see that the same quantity appears on both the invoice and the order (the Market Quotation List). In some larger establishments, a purchase order may be used for staples in place of the Market Quotation List.

Quality verification requires knowledgeable inspection to ensure that the quality of the food delivered matches the quality established in the standard purchase specifications. For example, the individual receiving strip loins of beef should be able to determine that the beef conforms to the restaurant's standard purchase specifications. Given the specification for beef strip loin short cut illustrated in Figure 4.2, inspection should reveal Black Angus Canadian AAA, IMPS #180, boneless, weighing in the range of 5.5 to 6.5 kilograms, with fat limited to 1.0 to 2.0 centimetres except for seam fat, free from objectionable odours or evidence of freezing. In addition, the loins should be delivered in a refrigerated truck. Each item delivered should conform to the standard purchase specification written for it.

Price verification requires comparing the unit price appearing on an invoice with the price quote circled on a Market Quotation List or a purchase order.

In the event that the quantity, quality, or price of foods delivered does not conform to the orders placed, appropriate steps should be taken. Sometimes this will involve returning inferior foods with the delivery driver. Sometimes it will involve changing the quantities listed on the invoice and having the delivery driver initial the change. For purposes of this discussion, it is important to mention that each discrepancy should be noted and attended to at the time of delivery. However, drivers frequently do not have time to wait for verification to be completed. Therefore, it is important to maintain good working relationships with vendors so that any discrepancy found after the driver has left can be readily resolved by a telephone call or some other informal means. From time to time, some foodservice operators have found it necessary to put aside unacceptable food for return to the vendor at the earliest opportunity.

As mentioned, deliveries must be made when agreed to so that supplies arrive when they are needed, and at appropriate times for receiving. Purveyors sometimes deliver food during times of the day when receiving personnel are busy attending to other duties. Most foodservice operations are busiest during the traditional meal periods of breakfast, lunch, and dinner. As a result, those periods are not the optimal times to receive goods, because those responsible for receiving are frequently directly involved with production in one way or another. To alleviate this dilemma, the establishment should make it clear to the purveyor and ultimately the delivery driver that deliveries will not be accepted at certain times of day and that deliveries should be made during specific times (generally before 11:00 a.m. or after 2:00 p.m.). This reduces the possibility of improper receiving procedures.

Receiving personnel are required to have a great deal of expertise. They must be able to recognize whether particular items meet established standard purchase specifications. They should be able to examine meats, for example, to determine grade, degree of freshness, and extent of trimming, among other considerations. With produce, they should be able to determine variety, degree of ripeness, and grade, at the very least. In other words, receiving personnel really need extensive knowledge if they are to do a proper job of checking quality. Most employees can be taught to weigh and count, but only a few can make necessary quality judgements.

This may explain, in part, why so many restaurateurs do not require receiving clerks to check for quality as foods are delivered. They know that their receiving clerks do not have the requisite knowledge. Instead, they rely on another employee to check the quality after the receiving process has been completed. Some depend on the chef, sous-chef, or a knowledgeable steward to do this. It is essential that quality be confirmed. If the proper judgements about food quality are not made by the staff, the customers will make the final determination. It may not be a good one.

Stamping the Invoice

It is generally good practice to provide the receiving clerk with an **invoice stamp**—a rubber stamp to be used on all invoices. This invoice stamp—a suggested form is illustrated in Figure 4.7—is used for several reasons. It allows for the following:

- Verification of the date on which the food was received
- The signature of the clerk receiving the food, who vouches for the accuracy of quantities, qualities, and prices
- The steward's or chef's signature, indicating that he or she knows the food has been delivered
- The food controller's verification of the arithmetical accuracy of the bill
- Signatory approval of the bill for payment by an authorized individual before a cheque is drawn

• FIGURE 4.7 •

Invoice Stamp

Invoice Stamp	Date	11-Jun
Received	*J. Wilson*	
Steward		
Prices and Extensions Verified		
OK for Payment		

Listing Invoices on Receiving Clerk's Daily Report

LEARNING OBJECTIVE 4.9
List the information contained in the receiving clerk's daily report, and explain the report's function.

For establishments that do not use a computer to keep track of inventories, the **Receiving Clerk's Daily Report** is an important accounting document. For all establishments, food is divided into at least two different categories, because some foods are purchased for immediate use and others are purchased to be kept in inventory until needed. The former become part of cost immediately, whereas the latter are not included in cost until they are issued from the inventory into production. In foodservice control, all foods that are charged to cost immediately are called *directs*, and all foods that are charged to cost when issued from inventory are called *stores*. An understanding of the differences between the two, as well as their working definitions, will be increasingly important in later chapters.

LEARNING OBJECTIVE 4.10
Explain the difference between directs and stores, and provide examples of each.

Directs are those foods that, because of their extremely perishable nature, are purchased on a more or less daily basis for immediate use. The quality of these foods tends to diminish quickly, and if they are not used very soon after the time of purchase, they become unusable. Foods that typically fall into this category are fresh fruits and vegetables, fresh baked goods, and most dairy products. Ideally, the quantities of such foods purchased on any given day should be sufficient for that day alone. Therefore, because they are purchased for immediate use, they are considered to be issued as soon as they are received and are included in food cost figures on the day of delivery. The working definition is that *directs* are those items that will be issued and charged to food cost as they are received.

Stores, by contrast, are those foods that, although ultimately perishable, will not diminish significantly in quality if they are not used immediately. They can be held in storage and carried in inventory for a day or so or, in some instances, for considerable periods of time. Meats, for example, if stored under proper conditions, can be maintained for reasonable periods of time. So, too, can grocery items that are purchased in cans, bottles, and boxes. All of these items are purchased on the basis of anticipated needs, not necessarily immediate, and are kept in inventory until they are needed. When the need arises, they are released from inventory and issued to the kitchen. Because cost occurs when food is issued or used, these items will be included in the food cost figures when they are issued for use. The working definition is that *stores* are those items that will be charged to food cost as issued.

There are no industrywide rules to indicate that any food item is always categorized with directs or with stores. The decision depends on how the item is stored and issued. In some establishments, for example, fresh fish is included with directs, because it is purchased for use on the day of delivery. Other places may buy whole fish, which are cleaned and otherwise prepared for use the following day or perhaps frozen for later use, and they thus include fresh fish with stores. Management must decide how to classify foods in that particular establishment on the basis of its use. It should be noted that many foodservice operations, particularly smaller ones, do not bother to classify food into directs and stores. They simply verify that the food received is that which has been ordered, and then they send the invoice to accounting for payment. This procedure certainly simplifies the receiving procedure, but it does not allow an accurate food cost calculation to be made until a physical inventory is taken, typically once a month. In the meantime, excessive food cost can take place without the knowledge of management.

If management can control food costs on a day-to-day basis by direct supervision, they may be successful. This may be achievable in a smaller operation, but does require vigilant monitoring. For larger operations, this system will not work. The separation of food into directs and stores is necessary, and a Receiving Clerk's Daily Report form should be filled out whenever food is received. Alternatively, this same information can be entered into the computer. The Receiving Clerk's Daily Report, illustrated in Figure 4.8, is a summary of invoices for all foods received on a given day.

• FIGURE 4.8 •

Receiving Clerk's Daily Report

Receiving Clerk's Daily Report

No.   1

Date 11-Jun

Quantity	Unit	Description	Unit Price	Amount	Total Amount	Food Direct	Food Stores	Sundries
		Market Price Meats						
13.6	kg	Strip loin	$22.99	$312.66				
4.54	kg	Veal loin	$27.17	$123.35	$436.01		$436.01	
		Ottman Meats						
6.8	kg	Pork tenderloins	$13.97	$ 95.00	$ 95.00		$ 95.00	
		Jones Produce & Fruit						
1	Crate	Lettuce	$16.50	$ 16.50				
1	Bag	Onions	$12.75	$ 12.75				
1	Box	Grapefruit	$18.30	$ 18.30				
1	Crate	Peaches	$22.60	$ 22.60	$ 70.15	$70.15		
Totals				$601.16	$601.16	$70.15	$531.01	

Purchase Journal Distribution

The Receiving Clerk's Daily Report is prepared by a receiving clerk, who merely records data from each invoice in appropriate columns on the report and then enters the total for each invoice into one of the three columns under the general heading **Purchase Journal Distribution**—"Food Direct," "Food

Stores," or "Sundries." These are the three rightmost columns in Figure 4.8. In the exhibit, the invoice shown in Figure 4.6 has been entered as the first invoice of the day, with the individual items and the totals recorded. The total dollar value of food listed on that invoice, $436.01, has been recorded in the "Food Stores" column, because these items have been purchased for future use and will be held in inventory until needed, at which time they will be charged to food cost. In contrast, the third invoice on the report, from Jones Produce and Fruit, totaling $70.15, is found in the "Food Direct" column, because the listed items have been purchased for immediate use and will thus be charged to food cost on the day they are received.

In computerized control systems, the information may be keyed into records directly as the goods are received. In some operations, this information is entered by the purchasing steward when the records of received goods are provided. It is still necessary to keep separate records of those foods treated as directs and those treated as stores, in order to facilitate the calculation of daily food costs.

Forwarding Completed Paperwork

By the time all deliveries for the day are in, preferably as early in the day as possible, the receiving clerk will have stamped and signed all invoices and entered them on the Receiving Clerk's Daily Report, often referred to simply as the receiving sheet. This sheet, with the invoices attached, should then be sent to the steward or chef, who signs the invoices and routes them to the food controller, who checks the arithmetical accuracy of each invoice. When the checking has been completed, the controller sends the receiving sheet and the invoices on to the accounting department, where the figures will be entered in the purchase journal.

However, while the food controller still has the receiving sheet, a very important total figure is recorded: the total cost of directs. Because directs are charged to the food cost as received, the food controller will need this figure in order to calculate the daily cost of food sold. When we reach the chapter concerned with calculating daily food cost (Chapter 9), it will be important to keep in mind that the daily cost of directs comes from the receiving sheet or from computer records.

Moving All Delivered Food

Once deliveries have been received in the manner described, it is important that foods be moved to appropriate storage areas as quickly as possible, first putting away those that will most quickly deteriorate at room temperature. The spoilage and theft that may occur between receiving and storing foods can be a major cause of excessive cost. Therefore, the food controller should check from time to time to be sure that foods are being moved to storage areas expeditiously.

The purpose of establishing control procedures for receiving is to ensure that the establishment receives food as needed in the quantities ordered, in the qualities specified, and at the prices quoted. These steps are basic and should be common to all foodservice operations, regardless of size. More complex systems of control, typically operated with a greater number of personnel and more equipment and procedures for checking, obviously offer greater measures of protection, but do so at a greater cost. However, even a small owner-operated restaurant should take these basic steps to guard against excessive costs that may develop as a result of improper receiving.

Completing the Control Process

In Chapter 2, we outlined the complete control process, which has four steps:

1. Establish standards and standard procedures for operation.
2. Train all individuals to follow established standards and standard procedures.
3. Monitor performance and compare actual performance with established standards.
4. Take appropriate action to correct deviations from standards.

In order for the control process to be completed, it is obviously necessary to complete steps 2, 3, and 4. Management has the responsibility to complete the process or delegate these tasks to other individuals in the organization. If all of the steps in the control process are not completed, it is probable that control will not truly exist in food and beverage operations and that excess costs will develop despite establishing standards and standard procedures.

The essential means of completing steps 2, 3, and 4 are found in the labour section of this text. We will not repeat these in this section or the section on beverage control, except where specific measures for training, monitoring, or taking corrective action for a particular standard or standard procedure warrants discussion. Keep in mind that enacting these controls requires equipment and resources to be available. Having working scales, adequate refrigeration, good software and hardware for computer systems, invoice stamps, and making time available to staff to allow for proper purchasing and receiving are all necessary for control.

THINGS TO CONSIDER

Some aspects of foodservices operations are more difficult to control than others. Food purchasing is critical, as the ingredients received become the end product that guests consume and use to base their decision on whether or not to return. Chefs work hard to ensure that perishable products are at the peak of freshness and flavour to optimize the diner's experience. To do this, they put a lot of effort into sourcing the best ingredients and buying just the right amounts so that fresh products are used and replenished daily—not an easy task. It just makes sense that any purveyors they buy from do the same thing.

When a wholesaler purchases perishable products, it must also source the best ingredients at the most favourable prices and buy appropriate amounts so that turnover occurs on a timely basis. Occasionally, both the chef and the wholesaler may have to refuse a product not up to quality standards. For the wholesaler, this means that a product will be out of stock. For the chef, this means it will be unavailable to the guest.

Despite not ever wanting to be out of a menu item, perhaps there are times when it is advisable. It would be preferable to tell a client that a menu item is unavailable that day rather than serve an inferior version of the dish. By not having the product on a rare occasion, perhaps the wholesaler is actually doing an exceptional job, not compromising by buying inferior quality when it is the only thing available. This might be a good supplier to buy from.

CHAPTER ESSENTIALS

In this chapter, we described the application of the four-step control process as it relates to food purchasing and receiving. We emphasized the need for fixing responsibility for purchasing and establishing appropriate quality and quantity standards, and described methods for determining optimum purchase prices. Specific procedures for the purchase of perishable and nonperishable foods were outlined, including the two most common methods for purchasing nonperishable foods: the periodic order method and the perpetual inventory method. The most common sources of supply used by foodservice operators were listed, means of communicating with purveyors were discussed, and various considerations that affect selection of particular suppliers were described.

We also described centralized purchasing and discussed its advantages and disadvantages. We defined purchase orders, one-purveyor buying, open bids, cost plus contracts, and standing orders, and discussed their use.

We described the application of the control process to the receiving function in a foodservice enterprise, explaining why foods received should conform to orders placed in respect to quantity, quality, and price, and the need for on-time delivery. We listed and explained common standards and standard procedures for receiving and then described various forms and pieces of equipment required for proper receiving, including the invoice, invoice stamp, and Receiving Clerk's

Daily Report. We distinguished between directs and stores and established useful working definitions for each. We pointed out the importance of effective receiving control in preventing excessive costs. We discussed the importance of training receiving personnel and pointed out their need for considerable knowledge of foods if they are to be effective.

KEY TERMS IN THIS CHAPTER

Bin card, p. 105

Centralized purchasing, p. 115

Contract purchasing, p. 117

Cost plus, p. 117

Desired ending inventory (DEI), p. 106

Directs, p. 122

Food brokers, p. 117

Invoice, p. 119

Invoice stamp, p. 122

Market Quotation List, p. 101

Nonperishable foods, p. 97

One-purveyor buying, p. 116

Open bid, p. 117

Par, p. 101

Par stock, p. 101

Periodic order method, p. 104

Perishable foods, p. 96

Perpetual inventory card, p. 108

Perpetual inventory method, p. 107

Purchase Journal Distribution, p. 124

Purchase order, p. 116

Receiving Clerk's Daily Report, p. 122

Reorder point, p. 108

Reorder quantity, p. 110

Standard purchase specifications, p. 99

Standing orders, p. 117

Stores, p. 123

QUESTIONS AND PROBLEMS

1. List 10 items considered perishable and 10 considered nonperishable in the foodservice industry.
2. Write a standard purchase specification for each of the following:
   a. Leg of lamb
   b. Fresh tomatoes
   c. No. 10 cans of green beans
3. Write a one-paragraph explanation of why the standard purchase specifications for eggs used for producing a breakfast menu would differ from the specifications for eggs used for producing baked goods.
4. Nestor's Restaurant uses the periodic order method, placing orders every two weeks. Determine the quantity of canned peaches to order today, given the following:
   a. Normal usage is one case of 24 cans per week.
   b. Quantity on hand is 10 cans.
   c. Desired ending inventory is 16 cans.

5. Abdul's Restaurant uses the periodic order method, ordering once a month. Determine the proper quantity of tomato juice to order today, given the following:

   a. Normal usage is one case of 12 cans per week.

   b. Quantity on hand is 6 cans.

   c. Desired ending inventory is 18 cans.

   d. The coming month is expected to be very busy, requiring 50 percent more tomato juice than normal.

6. The Downtown Restaurant uses the perpetual inventory method. One of the items to be ordered is canned pears. Determine the reorder point and reorder quantity, given the following:

   a. Normal usage is 21 cans per week.

   b. It takes four days to get delivery of the item.

   c. Par stock is set at 42 cans.

   d. Cans come packed 12 to a case.

7. The Last Chance Restaurant uses the perpetual inventory method. One of the items in the inventory is virgin olive oil in one litre bottles. Determine the reorder point and reorder quantity, given the following:

   a. Normal usage is 2 bottles per day.

   b. It takes five days to get delivery of the item.

   c. Par stock is 29 bottles.

   d. Bottles come packed 6 to a case.

8. Assume you have been hired as the purchasing steward of a new restaurant located in an area that is completely unfamiliar to you. You have never lived here before, and you have no friends or family in the area. How would you obtain information on sources of supply for perishable and nonperishable foods?

9. How can managers use computers to establish control over food purchasing?

10. Explain several significant effects of improper receiving controls.

11. Why is each of the following necessary for effective receiving control?

    a. Platform scale

    b. Hanging scale

12. Assume you are a receiving clerk in a fine-dining restaurant. Twenty kilograms of strip steak have been delivered. The quality meets the restaurant's specification, but the quantity and price are different from those listed on the Market Quotation List. You have not yet signed the invoice, and the driver is still present. How would you deal with the apparent problems?

13. Why is it necessary for the receiving clerk to have a complete set of the establishment's standard purchase specifications?

14. What possible cost effects might there be if food deliveries all arrived at the same time?

15. Distinguish between directs and stores.
16. Is it possible for proper receiving to take place in the absence of standard purchase specifications? Explain your answer.
17. The manager of Rupert's Restaurant does not believe in using the Receiving Clerk's Daily Report form. Instead, she has her receiving clerk check each item delivered against the invoice. What are the possible advantages and disadvantages of this alternative procedure?
18. The Uptowner Restaurant treats all meats as directs. What are the immediate effects of this procedure on food cost? What are the possible ultimate effects?
19. The receiving clerk in the Holiday Restaurant is also the dishwasher and has had no previous education or training in foods or in the food and beverage business. Discuss the possible effects on restaurant operations of having this individual responsible for receiving.
20. In many restaurant operations, the steward who purchases food also functions as the receiving clerk. What are some of the possible positive and negative effects of this procedure?
21. Define the key terms in this chapter.

EXCEL EXERCISES

Exercise 4.1
Barnaby's Hideaway uses its own computer-generated Market Quotation Sheet. Par stock and the amount on hand for beef, poultry, and shellfish are shown on the companion website for this text for Exercise 4.1. Bring up the Market Quotation List on your Excel spreadsheet and complete the amounts for the "To Order" column.

Exercise 4.2
Barnaby's Hideaway uses the perpetual inventory method for its nonperishable foods. Given the following information, determine the reorder point and the reorder quantity for each of the following items. Add 50 percent to the amount you calculate as the amount needed until delivery as a safety factor when determining the reorder point.

Canned Tomato Juice
Normal usage, 2 cans per day
Time to get delivery, 5 days
Par stock, 24
Number of cans to a case, 6

Canned Peaches
Normal usage, 3 cans per day
Time to get delivery, 4 days
Par stock, 36
Number of cans to a case, 12

Canned Black Olives
Normal usage, 1 can per day
Time to get delivery, 5 days
Par stock, 12
Number of cans to a case, 12

Exercise 4.3

Assume that Barnaby's Hideaway will change its ordering system from a perpetual system to a periodic system, ordering nonperishables every two weeks. Given the following amounts of each found on the shelf, determine the amounts to order for each of the items in Exercise 4.2. Add 50 percent to the amounts calculated as a safety factor.

Canned Tomato Juice, 10 cans
Canned Peaches, 9 cans
Canned Black Olives, 6 cans

Exercise 4.4

Complete the Receiving Clerk's Daily Report as shown in Exercise 4.4 on the companion website for this text.

Exercise 4.5

Complete a Purchase Order using the data provided in Exercise 4.5 on the companion website for this text.

CHAPTER 5

Food Storing and Issuing Control

• LEARNING OBJECTIVES •

After reading this chapter, you should be able to:

5.1 List and explain three causes of unplanned costs that can develop while food is in storage.

5.2 List and explain five principal concerns that can be addressed by implementing standards for storing food.

5.3 Explain the importance of establishing standards for storage temperatures for foods, storage containers for foods, shelving, and cleanliness of storage facilities.

5.4 Identify optimum storage temperatures for the five classifications of perishable foods.

5.5 Explain the importance of assigned locations for the storage of each particular food.

5.6 Explain the principle of stock rotation as applied to food service.

5.7 Distinguish between issuing procedures for directs and those for stores.

5.8 Describe the process used to price and extend a food requisition.

5.9 Explain the difference between interunit and intraunit transfers, and give two examples of each.

5.10 Explain the significance of transfers in determining accurate food costs.

INTRODUCTION

The previous chapter was devoted to explaining the need for establishing control over purchasing and receiving and to describing the application of the control process to ensure that the proper foods are purchased at optimum prices and that items purchased are received precisely as specified. When a foodservice operator selects particular qualities and quantities of food and places orders at particular prices, he or she is, in effect, creating and accepting the costs for food that will be served in the establishment. Eventually, these costs will be reflected in the income statement. Having accepted a particular level of cost, it is clearly in the operator's best financial interest to take all necessary steps to prevent the development of additional, unplanned costs before the foods are sold to customers. These unacceptable costs normally develop from spoilage, waste, or pilferage (the industry's term for theft). "Shrink" is another term for excess costs. As we discussed in the previous chapter, potential sales losses from products that have lost quality can be devastating to a business. Improper storing and overpurchasing can result in inferior food items that, although not wasted, do not satisfy quality standards and may result in unhappy clientele and lost sales. There are many types of storerooms used in foodservice to protect the integrity of a wide range of products and to maintain their value. Storerooms are used for dry goods and groceries, refrigerated and frozen foods, linen, paper goods, and sundries. In this chapter, we describe how the control process can be applied to storing and issuing to reduce or eliminate the development of unplanned and unwarranted costs.

STORING CONTROL: ESTABLISHING STANDARDS AND STANDARD PROCEDURES FOR STORING

In general, the standards established for storing food should address five principal concerns:

1. Condition of facilities and equipment
2. Arrangement of foods
3. Location of storage facilities
4. Security of storage areas
5. Dating and pricing of stored foods

Condition of Facilities and Equipment

The factors involved in maintaining proper internal conditions include temperature, storage containers, shelving, and cleanliness. Problems with any or all of these conditions may lead to spoilage and waste. It should be noted that all provinces and many municipalities have sanitation and health codes that must be followed by all foodservice facilities. These codes specify storage temperatures, storage containers, and storage procedures, among many other requirements (hot water temperatures, sanitation requirements, and so on). Inspectors regularly visit establishments and grade them on their adherence to the codes. It is thus imperative that foodservice employees have a detailed knowledge of sanitation and health codes for their particular areas.

Temperature

One of the key factors in storing foods is the temperature of the storage facilities. This is particularly important for perishables. Food life can be maximized when food is stored at the correct temperature and at the proper level of humidity. The food controller should keep a log on each refrigeration unit, to record temperatures daily. The following temperatures are generally accepted as optimum for storing the foods indicated:

LEARNING OBJECTIVE 5.4
Identify optimum storage temperatures for the five classifications of perishable foods.

> Fresh meats: 1 to 2° C
> Fresh produce: 1 to 2° C
> Fresh dairy products: 1 to 2° C
> Fresh fish: -1 to $+1$° C
> Frozen foods: -18 to -23° C

If temperatures are permitted to rise above these levels, shelf life is shortened and the risk of food spoilage is increased for perishables.

Proper temperature can also be a key factor in preventing spoilage of nonperishables. Storage facilities for staple food products should usually be room temperature, approximately 18°C to 21°C. Sometimes, particularly in older establishments, staples are kept in facilities that are either too warm because of their proximity to hot stoves or steam pipes running through the ceiling, or too cold because they are located in unheated parts of a building. Although the degree of risk is not as great with staples, it should be remembered that all foods are ultimately perishable and that the shelf life of food is increased by storage at proper temperatures.

Storage Containers

In addition to maintaining foods at proper temperatures, care must be given to storing them in appropriate containers. Many staples are purchased in airtight containers, but others are purchased in unsealed containers—paper bags, boxes, and sacks—which are susceptible to attack by insects and vermin. Whenever practicable, products purchased in unsealed packages should be transferred to tight, insect-proof containers. In the case of perishables, both raw and cooked, care should be given to storing them in whatever manner will best maintain their original quality. Many raw foods, such as apples and potatoes, may be stored as purchased for reasonable periods; others, such as fresh fish, should be well wrapped and then packed on ice and placed in a pan that will drain as the ice melts. In general, cooked foods and opened canned foods should be stored in stainless steel containers, either wrapped or appropriately covered.

Shelving

For perishable foods, shelving should be slatted to permit maximum circulation of air in refrigerated facilities. For nonperishables, stainless steel wire shelving is usually preferred. At no time should any food product be stored on the floor. Appropriate shelving raised 15 centimetres or more above floor level (check local health department regulations) should be provided for larger and heavier containers.

Cleanliness of Storage Facilities

Absolute cleanliness should be enforced in all food-storage facilities at all times. In refrigerated facilities, this will prevent the accumulation of small amounts of spoiling food, which can give off odours and may affect other foods. In storeroom facilities, it will discourage infestation by insects and vermin. Storerooms should be swept and cleaned daily, and no clutter should be allowed to accumulate. A professional exterminator should be brought in regularly to prevent rodents and vermin from reaching population levels large enough to cause damage and disease.

Arrangement of Foods

The factors involved in maintaining an appropriate internal arrangement of foods include keeping the most-used items readily available, fixing definite locations for each item, and rotating stock.

Keeping the Most-Used Items Readily Available

It is usually helpful to arrange storage facilities so that they are central to receiving and production and that the most frequently used items are kept closest to the door. Although it has no effect on spoilage or theft, this arrangement does tend to reduce the time required to move needed foods from storage to production and thus tends to reduce labour costs.

Fixing Definite Locations

LEARNING OBJECTIVE 5.5
Explain the importance of assigned locations for the storage of each particular food.

Each particular item should always be found in the same location, and attention should be given to ensuring that new deliveries of the item are stored in the same location. All too often, one product is stored in several locations at once (e.g., six cans on a shelf and two partially used cases in two other areas). This increases the chances for overpurchasing, spoilage, and theft. In addition, it makes the monthly process of taking a physical inventory, which is discussed in Chapter 8, more difficult. Incidentally, separate facilities for storage of different classes of foods should be maintained whenever practicable and possible. Eggs, for example, should not be stored with fish, cheese, or other foods that give off odours, because their shells are quite porous and they will absorb flavours from other foods. Fish are best stored in separate facilities.

Rotating Stock

The food controller must establish procedures to ensure that older quantities of any item are used before any new deliveries. The procedure used to do this is known as the **first-in, first-out method of stock rotation**, commonly called FIFO in the industry. The steward, chef, and staff must be held responsible for storing new deliveries of an item behind the quantities already on hand, ensuring that older items will be used first. This reduces the possibilities for spoilage. If this procedure is not followed and those who store foods are permitted to put new food in front of old food on shelves, the chances are increased that the older items will spoil before they are used, and if not yet spoiled, will result in inferior products getting to the customer. Stock rotation is particularly important with perishables, but it should also be practised with nonperishables.

LEARNING OBJECTIVE 5.6
Explain the principle of stock rotation as applied to food service.

Location of Storage Facilities

Whenever possible, the storage facilities for both perishable and nonperishable foods should be located between receiving areas and preparation areas, preferably close to both. Such locations facilitate the moving of foods from the receiving areas to storage and from storage to the preparation areas. A properly located storage facility will have four effects:

1. Speeding the storing and issuing of food
2. Maximizing security
3. Reducing labour requirements
4. Helping to minimizing infestation of rodents

Sometimes storage facilities are located in areas that are also used for other purposes. For example, some restaurants locate their preparation kitchen in the storage area, because it is more convenient to do preparation work near the supplies. Although it might be desirable to locate preparation areas within the areas used as the food source for efficiency purposes, theft and waste are likely to increase. Additionally, temperature and sanitary conditions in storage areas may be inadequate for food preparation. Storage areas should be used only for storage.

Dry storage areas should be sealed and, whenever possible, located in areas not susceptible to rodents and other unwanted creatures. For example, sometimes dry storage areas are located adjacent to construction sites or other spaces that are breeding grounds for mice, rats, and so on. Under these circumstances, it may be nearly impossible to completely seal the storage area sufficiently to prevent these rodents from entering. Exterminators treat the area, but the rodents return a few days later. It is wise to select an exterminator who guarantees results and will return at the first sign of a problem.

Security of Storage Areas

Food must be kept secure. One way to help accomplish this is to move products from the receiving area to storage as quickly as possible. Once in storage, appropriate security must be maintained at all times. A storeroom for staple food products should never be left open and unattended. Employees should not be permitted to remove items at will. Typically, a storeroom is kept open and supervised at specified times for specified periods well known to the staff and is otherwise closed to enable the storeroom clerk to attend to other duties. When the storeroom is closed, it should be locked, and the single key should be in the storeroom clerk's possession. In such cases, one additional emergency backup key is usually kept by the manager or in the office safe.

Security is also an important consideration in storing perishables, particularly in the case of high-cost items such as meat and fish. The importance of security obviously increases with the value of the items stored. It is sometimes advisable to establish separate control procedures for steaks, liquor, and other high-cost items.

In the case of chemical and cleaning supplies, storage is also important. Access must be controlled and given only to appropriate personnel. Security is essential to prevent loss, accidents, and misuse.

Dating and Pricing of Stored Foods

It is desirable to date items as they are put away on shelves, so that the storeroom clerk can be certain of the age of all items and make provisions for their use before they can spoil. Of particular concern are items that are used infrequently. The storeroom clerk should visually check the stock frequently to ascertain which items are beginning to get old and then inform the chef, so that items can be put to use before they spoil.

In addition, all items should be priced as goods are put away, with the cost of each package clearly marked on the package. Following this procedure will greatly simplify issuing, because the storeroom clerk will be able to price requisitions with little difficulty. If items are not priced as they are put away, the storeroom clerk will waste considerable time looking up prices when goods are sent to the kitchen. Computer users need not price goods if the program and inventory cards already have this information. As illustrated later in this chapter, the latest prices are recorded on inventory records, enabling the steward to easily calculate the cost of goods issued.

ISSUING CONTROL: ESTABLISHING STANDARDS AND STANDARD PROCEDURES FOR ISSUING

In Chapter 4, definitions were given for directs and stores. *Directs* were defined as those foods charged to cost as received, and *stores* as those carried in inventory and charged to cost as issued. That distinction is particularly important in a discussion of issuing.

There are two elements in the issuing process: (1) the physical movement of foods from storage facilities to food preparation areas and (2) the record keeping of the cost of the food issued.

Physical Movement of Foods from Storage Facilities

As described in the discussion of standards and standard procedures for storing, foods should be stored in fixed locations and under secure conditions to ensure that they will be available readily and in the proper quantities when needed. When a cook needs a particular item, it must be removed from a storage facility and transported to the preparation area. Practices for doing this vary from one establishment to another. In some operations, all facilities are locked, and cooks must list all of their needs on requisitions, which are turned over to a steward, who sees to the issuing of the various items and their delivery to preparation areas. In other operations, storage facilities are unlocked and any cook who needs an item simply goes to get it. In many establishments, some of the storage facilities are locked (the storeroom and the walk-in refrigerators for meat, for example), whereas others are left unlocked (refrigerators containing produce or leftovers, for example).

There is no universal practice, but it should be obvious that establishments that take greater precautions tend to have greater control over unauthorized issuing. At the same time, it must be noted that these establishments tend to make issuing more time-consuming, and thus costly, by requiring written requisitions that must be filled by additional specialized personnel. In general, small establishments tend to follow more informal practices, and large organizations are more likely to rely on specific procedures requiring paper records and specialized staff. Standards and standard procedures for the physical movement of foods must be determined specifically for a given establishment, often on the basis of a cost–benefit ratio. Whether an operation is large or small, controls must be maintained. In a small restaurant, having a chef or manager constantly on duty to monitor the storage, preparation, and production of food is critical. This can be accomplished by vigilant supervision and facilitated by a well-trained and loyal staff. Although no formal procedures for storing and issuing are in place, they are still enacted successfully in an informal manner. Let's discuss record keeping for issues in a large operation and remember that these controls are critical for every operation.

Record Keeping for Issued Foods

Directs

Directs are charged to food cost as they are received, on the assumption that these perishable items have been purchased for immediate use. Theoretically, these foods will be sent directly to the kitchen and be used entirely in food preparation on the day they are received. In practice, this is not normally the case. Some of the directs received on a given day are likely to be left over and used the following day; in fact, most establishments purposely purchase more than one day's supply of many directs. Although this greatly simplifies the record keeping associated with determining the cost of directs, it does immediately introduce some inaccuracy in costs recorded.

As discussed later, establishments that determine daily food costs use the total dollar figure in the "Food Direct" column on the Receiving Clerk's Daily Report as one component of the daily cost of food. This is based on the presumption that all directs received on a given day have been consumed and should thus be included in food cost for that day. Because this is not strictly true, these daily costs tend to be artificially high on days when all directs received have not been consumed and artificially low on days when directs included in costs for previous days are actually being consumed. When several days are averaged together, as in a week-to-date food cost, these discrepancies will eventually be smoothed out by costing over a longer period of time. This will not help to resolve any issues associated with excessive costs during the first days of the week, but by a combination of daily and to-date monitoring, more accurate averaged costs can be gauged without resorting to daily physical inventory.

For record-keeping purposes, then, directs are treated as issued the moment they are received, and no further record of those particular items is kept. The alternative is to follow an issuing procedure similar to that described for stores in the next paragraph, which requires significant additional time and labour. Finally, it should be obvious that waste, pilferage, or spoilage of directs will result in unwarranted additions to food cost figures.

Stores

The food category known as stores was previously described as consisting of staples. When purchased, these foods are considered part of inventory until issued for use and are not included in cost figures until they are issued. Therefore, it follows that records of issues must be kept in order to determine the cost of stores. For control purposes, a system must be established to ensure that no stores are issued unless authorized kitchen personnel submit requisition lists of the items and quantities needed.

The Requisition. A **requisition**, illustrated in Figure 5.1, is a form filled in by a member of the kitchen staff, usually the chef or sous chef. It lists the items and quantities of stores that the kitchen needs for the current day's production. Each requisition should be reviewed by the chef, who should check to see that all required items are listed and that the quantity listed for each is accurate. If the list of items and quantities is correct, the chef signs and thus approves the requisition. It is then given to the storeroom clerk, who fills the order.

LEARNING OBJECTIVE 5.8
Describe the process used to price and extend a food requisition.

• FIGURE 5.1 •

Requisition

Supply Main Kitchen   Date   8-Sep

Quantity		Description	Unit Cost		Total Cost	
3		#10 cans artichoke hearts				
22		kg sugar				
9		kg boneless duck breasts				
14		kg strip steak				

Charge to   *Food*   Dept.
             J.J. Lemon
                 Chef

For computer users, the requisition process may be slightly different. If the chef has a computer in his or her office, the chef may input the information directly into the computer and then send the requisition electronically to the storeroom. The quantity of each item requisitioned will automatically be deducted from inventory, and it will then simply be a matter of gathering the foods indicated on the requisition.

Whenever practical, it is advisable to require that requisitions be submitted in advance to enable the storeroom clerk to prepare the order. In some places, it has been found practical to insist on requisitions being submitted the day before food is needed. This has the desirable effect of forcing kitchen personnel to anticipate needs and plan for the following day's production. In some operations, the requisition is also used to inform the steward of unusual items that will be needed for upcoming functions. It is therefore helpful to submit requisitions as far in advance as possible to give the steward adequate time to properly purchase and obtain the items.

It is also desirable, whenever possible, to set definite times for the storeroom clerk to issue food. The storeroom clerk, after all, has other duties to perform, including keeping the storerooms and refrigerators clean, maintaining stocks of staples on shelves, rotating stock, and doing considerable paperwork. Some operations have achieved good results by restricting the times for issuing food to two hours in the morning and two hours in the afternoon. Naturally, such decisions must be left to management in any particular operation and exceptions may be made. The customer's needs take priority, however, so if one particular item runs out because it sold in much greater quantity than anticipated, then an additional "emergency" requisition may be filled by the storeroom clerk outside of the defined issuing schedule.

Pricing the Requisition. After stores have been issued from the appropriate storeroom, refrigerator, or freezer, it may be the storeroom clerk's responsibility to record on each requisition the cost of listed items and to determine the total value of the foods issued. If the requisition has been printed by the computer, prices should already be recorded. As will be discussed in Chapter 9, this information is necessary for determining daily food costs.

The items listed on requisitions fall into two categories: staples and meats, and mains. The unit cost for staples is derived from one of the following, depending on the system in use:

1. The most recent purchase price for each item is listed on a perpetual inventory card or in the computer.
2. The unit cost of each item is marked on each container as it is stored, making it readily available to the storeroom clerk.
3. A book, card, or computer file is maintained for all staple items, one page, card, or file per item. As prices change, the most recent purchase price is entered.
4. The storeroom clerk keeps a mental record of the orders placed and usually remembers the purchase prices because of constant use.

Computer users who use purchasing programs will employ the third method. The computer program keeps track of the prices paid for all purchases and is thus able to provide accurate information for all issues. For example, the Comtrex computer software discussed in Chapter 4 depletes stock in inventory when issued. It is done on a first-in, first-out basis and provides the food cost for all issues, as well as a value of all remaining stock. This obviously saves considerable time and effort over other methods.

The second method is generally preferred by those still using a manual system. However, it unquestionably involves considerable labour and consequently is costly to maintain. Therefore, though preferred, this is not the method in general use. More often than not, prices come from the storeroom clerk's head. Although the accuracy of this system leaves much to be desired, it is the method requiring the least time and labour.

The costs for meats and main dish items are determined differently. As discussed in the previous chapter, meats can be considered as either directs or stores. Many operations purchase meats daily in the same way they purchase other directs, such as lettuce, fresh vegetables, and fruits. These meats are typically precut in individual portions similar to purchasing at a retail grocery store. Essentially, the butchering process is done by the wholesaler. The establishment may trim the meat and remove excess fat, but preparation of the meat for cooking involves little else. These operations can treat meat as either directs or stores. If large amounts are purchased at one time, the establishment might treat meat purchases as stores, in which case the cost of meats is charged to food cost when issued. If meats are purchased for daily use in smaller quantities, they are treated as directs and charged to the cost of food when received.

Once the unit cost of each item on the requisition—both staples and meats/mains—has been recorded, it becomes possible to determine the total value of the food issued. For each listed item, the unit value is multiplied by the number of units issued. This is called **extending the requisition**. Computer-generated requisitions are automatically extended. When the values of the various items on the requisition have been extended, each requisition is totalled, as illustrated in Figure 5.2. At the end of each day, all requisitions are sent to the food controller.

Thus, each morning the food controller will have figures available for the principal components of a daily food cost for the preceding day:

1. Cost of directs from the receiving sheet
2. Cost of stores from the requisitions

• FIGURE 5.2 •					
Requisition					
Supply Main Kitchen			Date 8-Sep		
Quantity		Description	Unit Cost		Total Cost
3		#10 cans artichoke hearts	$5.79		$17.37
22		kg sugar	0.86		18.92
9		kg boneless duck breasts	8.38		75.42
14		kg strip steak	22.99		321.86
					433.57

Charge to _____*Food*_____ Dept.

_____*J.J. Lemon*_____

Chef

The importance of having accurate and timely data developed in this way will become apparent in Chapter 9, which discusses a method for determining daily food cost and its significance.

As previously illustrated, the first step in the control process—establishing standards and standard procedures—is the proper beginning in storing and issuing control, which must be followed by three additional steps: training staff, monitoring performance, and taking corrective action as required.

FOOD AND BEVERAGE TRANSFERS

LEARNING OBJECTIVE 5.9
Explain the difference between interunit and intraunit transfers, and give two examples of each.

LEARNING OBJECTIVE 5.10
Explain the significance of transfers in determining accurate food costs.

So far in our discussions we have assumed that a restaurant purchases, receives, stores, and issues food for use in one kitchen in which all production is accomplished. By doing so, we have quite purposely ignored the existence of several possible complications, which will be useful to consider at this point. For example, even in small restaurants, food production in the kitchen may require the use of certain beverage items, such as wines and liquors, not purchased specifically for kitchen use. Conversely, many establishments purchase some food items knowing that they will be used at the bar for drink production. Whole oranges and lemons, as well as cream, are good examples. On one hand it is important that the kitchen be charged for the wine it takes from the bar to use for cooking. If the bar was charged for the wine, the cost will have to be moved to the kitchen's costs. On the other hand, the bar should assume the cost for the lemons it uses to garnish drinks, because the kitchen paid for the case of lemons. In addition, in some large hotel and motel operations, more than one kitchen is in operation, and it may be necessary or desirable to transfer food from one kitchen to another. Transfers may also occur in chain operations. For example, a single unit may produce such items as baked goods for other units in the chain, or one unit in the organization that is running short of needed items may be encouraged to secure them from another unit. In these cases, a failure to record the nature and value of transfers will result in food costs that are inaccurate.

Because the goals of food control include determining food cost as accurately as possible and matching food cost with food sales, it is often necessary to maintain records of the cost of the food transferred. The costs incurred must be distributed accurately to the appropriate department. When the amounts involved are relatively insignificant and have little appreciable effect on cost and on the cost-to-sales ratio, they may be, and usually are, disregarded. But when the amounts become somewhat larger and have more significant effects, records of some type must be developed.

Intraunit Transfers

Intraunit transfers are food and beverage transfers between departments of a food and beverage operation. They include transfers of food and liquor between the kitchen and bar, and between two kitchens in larger operations that have multiple food outlets.

Between Bar and Kitchen

Food and beverage transfers between bar and kitchen occur frequently in operations of all sizes. Many kitchens use beverage items such as wine, brandy, and even ale to produce sauces, charcuterie, sweets, and certain baked items Occasionally, these beverages are purchased by the food department for use in the kitchen, kept in a storeroom until needed, and then issued on requisitions directly to the kitchen. In such cases, additional records are not required; the quantities and values listed on the requisition from storage are sufficient to permit accurate calculations of cost. In most instances, however, when these beverages are needed in the kitchen, appropriate amounts are obtained directly from the bar. After all, if sufficient supplies are already being maintained at the bar, it makes little sense to keep additional quantities for specific use in food production.

The same may be said of certain food items in the directs category used by bartenders in drink production. If supplies of oranges, lemons, limes, cream, and eggs are already available in a kitchen, it makes little sense to purchase specific supplies of these items for exclusive use at the bar. It is far simpler merely to secure the needed items from the kitchen. When it becomes necessary or desirable to achieve a high degree of accuracy in determining costs to match with sales, records of these transfers between the food and beverage departments must be maintained. The form used to maintain these records is the Food/Beverage Transfer Memo, illustrated in Figure 5.3.

• **FIGURE 5.3** •

Food/Beverage Transfer Memo

From   Bar

To   Main Kitchen   Date   8-Sep

Quantity		Description	Unit Price		Amount
1		750 ml Sneed's sherry	$11.99		$11.99
1		750 ml red wine	$12.30		$12.30
			Total		$24.29

Sent by   *Joe—Bartender*

Received by   *Paul—Chef*

As transfers are made, items and amounts are recorded. These records are sent to the food controller, who can use them to adjust food cost figures to achieve greater accuracy, and then routed to the food controller and an accounting office, where the appropriate adjusting entries can be made in the financial records.

Between Kitchen and Kitchen

In some of the larger hotels that operate more than one kitchen and dining room, it is common practice to determine food costs for each outlet separately and to match the costs for each operating unit with the sales generated by that unit. When some food items are transferred from one kitchen to another, higher degrees of accuracy in determining food costs may be achieved by keeping records of items and amounts transferred.

Recording the value of the items returned on transfer memos or on similar forms makes possible a more accurate determination of individual food costs and, consequently, of cost-to-sales ratios for operating periods. This is true even in cases in which items are not transferred but are merely returned to a central kitchen or commissary for reissue to the same or to other units on succeeding days.

Interunit Transfers

Interunit transfers are transfers of food and beverages between units in a chain. The two examples that follow illustrate interunit transfers and the effect of such transfers on food costs.

In some instances, small chains produce some items (e.g., baked goods) in only one unit and then distribute those items to other units in the chain. If the ingredients for the baked goods come from that particular unit's regular supplies, then some record must be made of the cost of the ingredients used. Failure to record such costs can result in overstating the food cost of the producing unit by the value of the ingredients used, and in understating the food costs of the receiving units by the value of the foods they receive. In addition, if the matching principle is to be followed and if food sales are reported separately for each unit, then food cost figures that do not include the cost of all those foods sold, including the baked goods from another unit, cannot be said to be truly matched with sales. Under such conditions, if one of management's goals is to match costs and sales with a reasonably high degree of accuracy, it is necessary to use a transfer memo or a similar form to record the value of ingredients used to produce finished products transferred to other units.

With such records available, it is possible to decrease the cost of the producing unit by the amount transferred. Appropriately increasing the food cost figures of the receiving units may pose more of a problem. If each unit receives an equal share of the goods produced, then one could simply divide the cost of the goods produced and credited to the producing unit by the number of units to which items have been transferred, and then increase the food cost of each by one equal share. However, if the total produced for distribution to the various units is not divided among them equally, then some more equitable means for apportioning cost must be found. A possible solution is to record the values of transferred items at standard costs. The question of calculating standard costs of production for this and other purposes is considered in the next chapter.

Another problem involving the value of foods transferred from one unit to another may be seen in those chain organizations that permit or encourage unit managers to obtain foods from other units when their own supplies run low and additional purchases are precluded by lack of time. Occasions may arise when a unit nearly exhausts the supply of an important item and does not discover this shortage until it is clearly too late to purchase an additional amount. In some organizations, when units are comparatively close to one another and offer identical menus, items are borrowed and returned within a day or so as a matter of course, and no complications arise as long as all borrowed items are returned. However, not all cases are quite so simple, as, for example, when a perishable item borrowed by one unit does not appear on the menu again for some considerable period of time. Rather than maintain records over long periods to ensure the return of borrowed items, it is often simpler to record such transfers of foods on transfer memos and to use the information so recorded to increase the cost of the unit that has been borrowed and correspondingly decrease the cost of the supplying unit.

Inventory Control Software

Many companies sell computer inventory programs to assist restaurateurs in ordering, receiving, keeping track of inventory, and issuing food. These programs reduce and sometimes eliminate paperwork, as all information is entered directly into the computer terminal. They keep track of orders to purveyors, prices of ordered food, and inventory balances. Some of them even alert the steward when an order should be placed, based on established par figures. Additionally, they can alert management to food items that are priced greater than standard. They enable management to more easily spot waste and theft. When food is wasted or missing, additional food cost is incurred. Obviously, unwarranted increases in food costs directly affect the restaurant's bottom line. Each dollar of excess food cost reduces profit by a dollar. One software program in use in many foodservice operations is ChefTec. ChefTec has some very helpful features that will enable the foodservice manager to maintain accurate records for inventory control. The foodservice manager creates an "invoice" for the menu being produced, which is costed out based on the prices that have been entered into the software by the steward. This "invoice," as it is referred to by ChefTec, is essentially a requisition. An important duty of the steward will be to update prices from invoices into the software in order to have the most recent prices paid when costing out one's invoices. Figure 5.4 is an example of an invoice created using ChefTec.

• FIGURE 5.4 •

Invoice Created Using ChefTec

ChefTec Software

Invoice

Date: 10/3/20XX

Time: 11:31 AM

Bistro Quatre

Vendor	Thar She Blows Fish Co.	**Invoice Number**　b123
Contact Address	123 Crustacean Way	**Date**　10/3/20XX
	Unit C	**Item Count**　7
	Halifax, NS B3J 1A2	**Total Amount**　$275.50
Phone	(902) 123-4567	
Fax	(902) 123-4568	
Cust ID	123456789	

Prod Code	Inventory-Item	Quantity	Units	Cost	Cost/Unit	% Change
	salmon fillets	1	kg	$4.00	$8.00/kg	
	lobster, 1 – 1 1/2 lb	1	ea	$50.00	$50.00/kg	
	scallops 16–30 ct, sea	2	kg	$40.50	$20.25/kg	
	shrimp 16–20 ct	5	kg	$105.00	$21.00/kg	
	clams, cherrystone	3	dozen	$18.00	$6.00/dozen	
	mussels	2	dozen	$6.00	$3.00/dozen	
	halibut fillets	4	kg	$48.00	$12.00/kg	

Conclusion

In this industry, there are a reasonably large number of transfers of the various types discussed here, but there are also a large number involving comparatively small amounts of food of relatively insignificant value. Consequently, because the amounts involved are usually negligible in most places, records are often not used. If and when the amounts become significant, provision must be made for maintaining adequate records to ensure that food cost figures include all incurred costs for products used regardless of where they are from, and that costs are credited for transfers to other departments or units, to accurately compare costs to sales.

THINGS TO CONSIDER

When issuing product from a storeroom, it is important to establish a system for checking the requisition. Checks should be for product identification, quantity, and cost. Many operations will establish a type of checkout procedure that designates a staff member to double check that all of the products specified are in fact there, that amounts are correct, and that prices are accurate. This can save time and labour in avoiding additional requisitions and disputes over items that were charged for but not delivered. Double checking that the requisition is accurate will benefit the kitchen, and ensure that the issuer has done a proper job, while protecting him or her from honest mistakes.

CHAPTER ESSENTIALS

In this chapter, we described the application of the control process to the storing and issuing functions in a restaurant. We explained that unwanted costs can develop from spoilage, waste, and pilferage, and that products of diminished quality can lead to losses in sales. We listed the five principal concerns that standards for storing must address: conditions of facilities and equipment, arrangement of foods, location of facilities, security of storage areas, and dating and pricing of stored foods. Included were discussions of temperature, storage containers, shelving, cleanliness, food locations, and rotation of stock. We distinguished between issuing procedures for directs and stores and indicated the importance of the requisition in issuing stores. We defined food and beverage transfers and illustrated several types, pointing out the possible effects on food costs that such transfers may have. We described the means for maintaining records of transfers to introduce greater accuracy into food and beverage cost determination. Finally we discussed the role computers play in controlling costs and alerting management to excess costs.

KEY TERMS IN THIS CHAPTER

Extending the requisition, p. 143
First-in, first-out (FIFO)
   method of stock rotation, p. 137
Interunit transfers, p. 146

Intraunit transfers, p. 144
Requisition, p. 141

QUESTIONS AND PROBLEMS

1. What are some of the possible problems implicit in allowing the chef, receiving clerk, or dining room manager to have keys to the storeroom?
2. Even with restricted access to storeroom keys, it is sometimes desirable to change locks. Under what specific conditions would you, as a food controller, advise a manager to change locks?

3. Explain how excessive food costs may be reduced by properly rotating stock.
4. List and explain the disadvantages of locating a storage area at some distance from the receiving and preparation areas. Are there any advantages?
5. If a new storeroom clerk discovers an item on the shelves that is still in good condition but is six months old, what, if anything, should be done about it? Why?
6. Referring to the price list provided in Figure 5.5, calculate the total value of each of the requisitions in figures 5.6 through 5.9.

• FIGURE 5.5 •

Price List

Item	Purchase Unit	Unit Price
Applesauce	#10 can	$2.85
Beets, sliced	#10 can	$2.90
Carrots, diced	#10 can	$2.90
Clams, minced	#10 can	$9.70
Cocktail sauce	litre	$2.00
Coffee	kilogram	$12.00
Corn, whole kernel	#10 can	$5.20
Cranberry sauce	#10 can	$7.45
Flour, all-purpose	kilogram	$0.90
Fruit cocktail	#10 can	$6.20
Garlic powder	500 gram can	$7.20
Ketchup	340 ml	$1.05
Linguini #18	kilogram	$1.90
Mushrooms, whole	#10 can	$9.20
Mustard	227 ml	$3.10
Olive oil	litre	$4.00
Peaches, halves	#10 can	$5.20
Pepper, black	kilogram	$16.00
Pepper, white	kilogram	$25.00
Pineapple, crushed	#10 can	$4.70
Rice	kilogram	$2.00
Salt	kilogram	$0.50
Sauerkraut	#10 can	$5.15

(continued)

• FIGURE 5.5 • (continued)

Item	Purchase Unit	Unit Price
Sugar, granulated	kilogram	$0.95
Tomato, puree	#10 can	$3.60
Tomato, whole peeled	#10 can	$3.20
Vinegar	litre	$3.23

• FIGURE 5.6 •

Requisition

Supply   Main Kitchen   Date   6-Jul

Quantity		Description			Unit Cost		Total Cost
24-227 ml		Mustard					
24-340 ml		Ketchup					
10 kg		Salt					
1 kg		Black pepper					
20 L		Olive oil					
20 L		Vinegar					
5 kg		Sugar					
					Total:		

Charge to   _____*Food*_____

Dept.:   _____*H. Sneed*_____
                    Maitre D'

• FIGURE 5.7 •

Requisition

Supply   Main Kitchen   Date   6-Jul

Quantity		Description			Unit Cost		Total Cost
12-#10		Tomatoes, whole					
12-#10		Tomatoe puree					
5 kg		Coffee					
1 kg		White pepper					
20 kg		Salt					
20 kg		Flour, all-purpose					
2-#10		Sauerkraut					
3-#10		Carrots, diced					
1-#10		Fruit cocktail					
					Total:		

Charge to _____*Food*_____

Dept.:   _____*P. Noir*_____
                   Sous-Chef

• FIGURE 5.8 •

Requisition

Supply Main Kitchen   Date 6-Jul

Quantity		Description			Unit Cost		Total Cost
3-#10		Corn, whole kernel					
6-#10		Beets, sliced					
3-#10		Peaches, halves					
2-#10		Applesauce					
12 kg		Rice					
3-#10		Cranberry sauce					
4 L		Cocktail sauce					
2-#10		Mushrooms, whole					
					Total:		

Charge to *Food*

Dept.: *G. Chambvertain*
                Chef

• FIGURE 5.9 •							
Requisition							
Supply Main Kitchen					Date 6-Jul		
Quantity		*Description*			*Unit Cost*		*Total Cost*
2-#10		Clams, minced					
2 kg		Linguini #18					
1-500 g can		Garlic powder					
6-#10		Pineapples, crushed					
				Total:			

Charge to _____*Food*_____

Dept.: _____*P. Chardonnay*_____
                    Relief Chef

7. The Somerset Restaurant Company owns and operates three small units in one community. Gross food sales and food costs as recorded on the books of each unit are as follows:

	Unit A	Unit B	Unit C
Sales	$155,400	$98,300	$228,000
Food cost	80,808	30,473	77,520

The preceding figures do not include the values of food transferred from Unit A to the other two units. These are all baked goods used in the chain, which are produced in one bakeshop located in Unit A. During the period, transfers from Unit A to the other two units totalled $20,000, of which $8,000 was sent to Unit B and the rest to Unit C.

a. Calculate food cost percents before transfers are taken into account.

b. Adjust food cost figures by the amounts of the transfers to determine more accurate food costs.

c. Calculate food cost percents based on the costs determined in (b).

8. Food cost percent is often one of the elements used to judge a chef's ability to control food costs. Explain how failure to take the value of transferred foods into account before calculating food cost percents can affect the performance ratings of chefs who send food items to other units, and of chefs who receive food from other units.

9. Lunch Inn is a small chain that operates four units in one city. Each unit purchases for its own needs and produces for its own sales on premises. Each produces its own rolls, cakes, and pies. However, when one unit underproduces, the manager is encouraged to secure needed quantities from another unit in the chain before purchasing from the outside. One item, apple pie, costs $1.35 to produce in-house and is available for $2.75 from nearby bakeries. What would be an appropriate transfer price for apple pies sent from one unit to another? What effect would this transfer price have on the volume of transfers between units?

10. Why should food not be stored on the floor at any time? What may happen to food stored this way?

11. Define each of the key terms in this chapter.

EXCEL EXERCISES

Exercise 5.1
The chef at Barnaby's Hideaway has prepared a requisition as shown on the companion website for this text as Exercise 5.1. Using the price list reproduced on the website and shown as Price List Exercises 5.1 and 5.2, complete and total the requisition.

Exercise 5.2
The bar at Barnaby's Hideaway has prepared a transfer memo for supplies from the kitchen. Complete and total it, getting your prices from the price list on the website.

CHAPTER 6

Food Production Control I: Portions

• **LEARNING OBJECTIVES** •

After reading this chapter, you should be able to:

6.1 Explain the importance of standard portion sizes, standard recipes, and standard portion costs to foodservice operations.

6.2 Identify four methods for determining standard portion costs, and calculate standard portion costs using these four methods.

6.3 Use yield factors derived from recipe detail and cost card, butcher tests, and cooking loss tests to determine correct purchase quantities.

6.4 Use cost factors derived from butcher tests to calculate portion costs.

6.5 Use cost factors derived from cooking loss tests to calculate portion costs.

6.6 List the advantages and disadvantages of using standardized yield figures versus in-house yield tests.

INTRODUCTION

In Chapter 4, we explained that all foodservice establishments have a sequence of operations consisting of purchasing, receiving, storing, issuing, producing, selling, serving, and securing and recording sales. Each of these operations can be considered a system in itself, and the foodservice establishment can be considered to be composed of interrelated systems, each with specific goals. The purchasing system, for example, is designed to ensure the availability of an adequate supply of the ingredients required to meet customer demand, each of a carefully selected quality and acquired at an optimum price. The receiving system has a primary goal of making sure all food is received in a timely manner and conforms to the quality, quantity, and price ordered by the purchasing system. The best means for ensuring that these systems will achieve their aims—that events will conform to plans—was shown to be instituting control processes. This is true not only for the purchasing and receiving systems, but also for the systems designed for storing and issuing foods. As we will see, it is equally true for the production system.

Following the pattern established in earlier chapters, we now describe the application of control to the production phase of foodservice operations.

FOOD PRODUCTION CONTROL: ESTABLISHING STANDARDS AND STANDARD PROCEDURES

LEARNING OBJECTIVE 6.1
Explain the importance of standard portion sizes, standard recipes, and standard portion costs to foodservice operations.

The standards and standard procedures for production control are designed to ensure that all menu item portions conform to standards and that, as much as possible, all portions of the same menu item are identical. Portions of a given menu item should be identical to one another in five respects:

1. Types of ingredients
2. Proportions of ingredients
3. Production method
4. Quantity
5. Appearance or presentation

To reach this goal, it is necessary to develop the following standards and standard procedures for each menu item:

1. Standard portion size
2. Standard recipes
3. Standard portion cost

Standard Portion Size

One of the most important standards that any foodservice operation must establish is the **standard portion size,** defined as the quantity of any menu item that is to be served each time that item is ordered. In effect, the standard portion size for any item is the fixed quantity of a given menu item that management intends to give each customer in return for the fixed selling price identified on the menu. It is possible and desirable for management to establish these fixed quantities in very clear terms. Every item on a menu can be quantified in one of three ways: by weight, by volume, or by count.

Weight

Weight, normally expressed in grams (or ounces, if the U.S. or Imperial system is used), is frequently used to measure portion sizes for many menu items. (Please note that we are rounding our measurements for most examples in this chapter. For instance, 225 grams, not 227, is equal to 8 ounces and 125 grams, not 113, is equal to 4 ounces.) Meat and fish are two of the most common items whose portions are determined by weight. Steak, for example, is served in portion sizes of varying weights, typically ranging from 175 to 450 grams (6 to 16 ounces), with the particular size for a specific restaurant being set by management. For example, Bistro Quatre serves a 350-gram (12-ounce) portion for its strip steak, and two 90-gram (3-ounce portions) of filet mignon for its Tournedos Bistro. Vegetables are often portioned by weight as well.

Volume

Volume is also used as the measure for portions of many menu items. Liquids (e.g., soups, juices, coffee, and milk) are commonly portioned by volume expressed as millilitres (fluid ounces in the Imperial system). A cup of soup may contain 150 millilitres (5 fluid ounces), and a bowl of soup may contain 225millilitres (8 fluid ounces); a portion of orange juice may be 120 millilitres (4 fluid ounces); a glass of milk may contain 300 millilitres (10 fluid ounces).

Count

Count is also used by foodservice operators to identify portion size. Such items as bacon, link sausage, eggs, chops, shrimp, and asparagus are portioned by count. Some foods are purchased by count, and this plays a major role in establishing portion size. Shrimp, for example, are purchased at Bistro Quatre in the common purchase size of 16/20 count, meaning you get 16 to 20 pieces of shrimp in a pound (or 450 grams), and then they are portioned by number per shrimp cocktail—five in one order. Potatoes and grapefruit are purchased by count per purchase unit, which clearly serves as a determinant of portion size. Potatoes for baking, for example, can be purchased in 50-pound (about 23 kilogram) boxes with a particular number per box specified. The higher the count per box (e.g., 120 rather than 90), the smaller the size of the portion served to the customer. Bistro Quatre serves 90-count baked potatoes. Count is important even with some dessert items, such as pie, with the portion size expressed in terms of the number of slices of equal size to be cut from one pie.

 An interesting variation occurs with those items portioned by means of implements such as scoops or slotted spoons. A portion size is stipulated to be one or more such measures, but the measuring device selected holds a particular quantity of the item to be portioned. Many devices are available to help foodservice operators standardize portion sizes. Among the more common are the aforementioned scoops and slotted spoons, as well as ladles, portion scales, and measuring cups. Even the number scale or dial on a slicing machine, designed to regulate the thickness of slices, can aid in standardizing portion size: A manager may stipulate a particular number of slices of an item on a sandwich and then direct that the item be sliced with the dial at a particular setting.

Standard portion sizes help reduce customer discontent, which should be viewed as a major cause of lost customers and sales. If standard portion sizes are established and served, no customer can compare his or her portion unfavourably with that of another customer and feel dissatisfied or cheated. In addition, repeat customers will be more inclined to believe that they receive fair measure for their money on each visit.

Standard portion sizes also help eliminate animosity between kitchen staff and dining room personnel, which can lead to delays in service and make personnel antagonistic to patrons. When portion sizes are left to the whims of the kitchen staff, arguments can and do develop over whether a certain cook is giving larger portions to one particular server to give his or her customers, thus ensuring larger tips, which can be shared with the cook.

Standard portion sizes also help eliminate excessive costs. The cost for any item is closely linked to the quantity served to the customer. It stands to reason that a 225-gram (8-ounce) portion of an item costs about twice as much as a 120-gram (4-ounce) portion of the same item. If 120 grams cost $5.70, 225 grams will cost roughly $11.40. Except in rare instances, selling prices for menu items do not vary with portion sizes. Prices are typically printed on a menu and usually are not changed until the menu is reprinted.

Even when not printed, prices cannot be changed from customer to customer (except in instances in which customers receive discounts for various reasons; however, even in these instances the prices printed on the menu are the same for all menus). If the menu price of an item is $18.95, and one customer receives a 120-gram portion costing $5.70 and a second customer receives a 225-gram portion of the same item costing $11.40, it is apparent that costs are not under control. To anyone experienced in foodservice, it is also obvious that there will be many dissatisfied customers and employees.

Serving portions of varying sizes can have unpleasant consequences: Customers complain, never return, or both. Servers argue with one another and with the customers, and some may quit. From a food controller's point of view, perhaps the most important undesirable consequence is that costs are not under control and excessive costs develop. In addition, under such conditions, contribution margins vary on sales of the same item. Using the preceding example, contribution margin is $13.25 on the sale to the first customer, and $7.55 on the sale to the second. As discussed in a later chapter, permitting varying portion sizes, varying costs, and varying contribution margins makes it impossible to be profitable.

Once standard portion sizes have been established for menu items, it is important that each person producing portions of a given item knows the correct portion size. Methods for accomplishing this vary, but having standardized recipes posted that indicate standard portion size and how to obtain them are usually the most appropriate and effective.

Standard Recipes

The recipe is the basic tool for controlling portion consistency. A recipe is a list of the ingredients and the quantities of those ingredients needed to produce a particular item, along with a procedure or method to be used. A **standard recipe** is the recipe that has been designated the correct one to use in a given establishment for a specific item.

Standard recipes help to ensure that the quality and quantity of any item will be consistent each time the item is produced. Figure 6.1 provides the standard recipe for Capellini, an item on the menu of Bistro Quatre. If the same ingredients are used in the correct proportions and the same procedure is followed, the results should be nearly identical each time the standard recipe is used, even if different people are doing the work. In addition, returning customers will be more likely to receive items of identical size and quality.

Standard recipes are also very important to food control. Without standard recipes, costs cannot be controlled effectively. If a menu item is produced by different methods, with different ingredients, and in different proportions each time it is made, costs will be different each time any given quantity is produced. For example, the standard recipe for Capellini calls for 50 grams of scallops, 80 grams of shrimp, and 50 grams of lobster meat for each portion served. If the item is prepared according to recipe, its quality and cost will be maintained according to management's desire. However, if more or less of each major ingredient is used, the cost can be considerably higher or lower and the quality will vary. Additionally, if substitutions are made in the ingredients (e.g., cod in place of lobster), the cost and taste will be different than management desires.

• FIGURE 6.1 •

Standard Recipe

Capellini   **Yield: One 350-gram portion**

50 g scallops (20–30 ct.)

80 g shrimp (21–25 ct.) peeled and deveined

50 g lobster meat

5 g chopped garlic

15 mL olive oil

30 mL white wine

100 mL heavy cream

15 mL chiffonade of fresh basil

15 g freshly grated Romano cheese

130 g fresh capellini pasta

salt and pepper to taste

1. Sauté scallops and shrimp in olive oil and garlic until they begin to lose translucency; add lobster meat and continue to sauté one more minute; remove.

2. Deglaze with white wine and reduce by one-half.

3. Add heavy cream. Simmer until a light sauce consistency is achieved.

4. Meanwhile, immerse fresh pasta in salted boiling water for 2 minutes and drain.

5. Add basil, seafood, and cooked pasta to sauce and toss until thoroughly incorporated and hot. Season appropriately.

6. Serve on 13-inch plate. Garnish with Romano cheese and a basil leaf.

Some people have the mistaken impression that standard recipes are those developed for use in schools, hospitals, and similar public institutions and that they use ingredients of poor quality and yield menu items of even lower quality. Such impressions are absolutely false. The term *standard* merely means that a recipe will produce an item of acceptable quality for a particular operation, regardless of the level of cost or sophistication. Any recipe can be adopted as a standard recipe. Sometimes such recipes are taken from cookbooks or magazines. Sometimes they are developed by the chef in a given restaurant, then tested and modified until they result in the production of an acceptable product. At that point, the recipe becomes the standard—the recipe that will be used each time the product is to be made.

In many operations, these standard recipes are written or printed on cards to be used by kitchen workers. They are made readily available to any workers responsible for producing menu items. If handwritten, the writing must be clear and legible so that the standard recipes can be easily followed. Sometimes they are printed on special cards that are then laminated in plastic for durability. Computer-printed recipes are stored in a program and can be easily changed and reprinted. In some establishments, these recipe cards include either drawings or photographs of the finished products, to illustrate for the production staff exactly how the final product should look when served to the customer. Because they help provide uniform appearance for all portions of a given menu item, illustrated recipe cards are particularly important in restaurants that have photographs in their menus. Even the front staff benefits from these drawings or photos, enabling them to compare an item's appearance before it is served to a guest, and having it redone if necessary.

Along with establishing standard recipes, standard portion sizes, and standard preparation and portioning procedures, standard portion costs must be developed.

Standard Portion Cost

A standard portion cost can be calculated for every item on every menu, provided that the ingredients, proportions, production methods, and portion sizes have been standardized as previously discussed. In general, calculating standard portion cost merely requires that one determine the cost of each ingredient used, then add the costs of the individual ingredients to arrive at a total. The total recipe cost is divided by the number of portions produced to obtain a single portion cost. There are several other techniques for determining portion cost.

Before considering the different ways of determining portion costs, it is important to understand that the portion costs determined by these techniques will only be calculated portion or planned portion costs. These indicate what portion costs *should* be. Actual portion costs may be quite different. There are many possible reasons for this variance. For example, if the employee making shrimp tempura gives customers seven shrimp rather than five (the number established by management as the standard), the real portion cost will be greater than the calculated or planned cost. If the employee gives customers three, the real portion cost will be less than planned. Real portion costs for these shrimp may be either higher or lower than planned.

Real portion costs will also be different from planned costs if employees fail to use portion scales, use improper portioning devices, fail to follow standard recipes, purchase ingredients other than those stipulated by standard recipes, or procure them at different costs than specified in the recipe and in purchasing standards.

Calculated, or planned, portion costs are best known by the term *standard portion costs*. **Standard portion cost** is defined as the dollar amount that a standard portion should cost, given the standards and standard procedures for its production. The standard portion cost for a given menu item can be viewed as a budget for the production of one portion of that item.

There are several reasons for determining standard portion costs. The most obvious is that a clear idea of the cost of a menu item should precede establishing a menu sales price for that item. For control purposes, there are additional reasons for determining standard portion costs, including the need to make judgements in the future about how closely real or actual costs match standard costs, as well as the extent to which operating efficiency can be improved. These topics are discussed in later chapters.

CALCULATING STANDARD PORTION COSTS

LEARNING OBJECTIVE 6.2
Identify four methods for determining standard portion costs, and calculate standard portion costs using these four methods.

There are several methods for calculating standard portion costs:

1. Formula
2. Recipe detail and cost card
3. Butcher test
4. Cooking loss test

Owners, managers, chefs, and others with responsible positions in food-service operations should be familiar with and able to use all of these methods.

Formula

LEARNING OBJECTIVE 6.3
Use yield factors derived from recipe detail and cost card, butcher tests, and cooking loss tests to determine correct purchase quantities.

For many (perhaps even for a majority) of the menu items prepared in foodservice establishments, determining standard portion cost can be very simple. For a large number of items, one may determine portion cost by means of this formula:

$$\text{Standard portion cost} = \frac{\text{Purchase price per unit}}{\text{Number of portions per unit}}$$

For example, consider an establishment serving eggs on the breakfast menu, with two eggs as the standard portion. One can determine the standard cost of the portion of the eggs by dividing the cost of a 15-dozen case of eggs—at, say, $30.00—by the number of two-egg portions it contains (90) to find the standard portion cost of $0.333.

$$\frac{\$30.00 \text{ purchase price per case}}{90 \text{ standard portions per case}} = \$0.333 \text{ cost per portion}$$

This simple formula can also be used to find the standard cost of each of the additional items served in a typical breakfast, including the juice, bacon, toast, butter, and coffee. The sum of the standard costs of the individual items will thus be the standard cost of the whole breakfast, possibly offered in a particular restaurant as Breakfast Special #3, at a $5.95 menu price.

In many restaurants today, large numbers of menu items are purchased already portioned by vendors. Determining the cost of one portion of any of these items is very simple: One divides the purchase price by the number of portions.

Frankfurters purchased in multiples of 12 for $2.40 cost $0.20 each. Frozen heat-and-serve entrées are often purchased in individual units, in which case the purchase price is the portion cost. Many frozen preportioned foods come packed in cartons marked to show the exact number of portions in the carton. In most fast-food restaurants, portion costs for the majority of menu items can be determined by means of this simple formula.

Determining the portion cost of a large number of menu items may be done easily, by applying a very basic formula. Not all foods, however, may be so simply portioned after purchase, and other techniques must be developed to determine the standard portion costs of more complex items, such as those prepared from standard recipes.

Recipe Detail and Cost Card

For menu items produced from standard recipes, it is possible to determine the standard cost of one portion by using a form known as a **recipe detail and cost card**. A sample of that form is provided in Figure 6.2.

• FIGURE 6.2 •

Recipe Detail and Cost Card

				S.P.	$21.40
				Cost	$ 7.23
Item	Capellini	Menu	Dinner	F.C.%	33.79%
Yield	1 Portion	Portion Size	500 g	Date	6/22 20XX

Ingredients	Quantity	Unit	Cost	Ext.
Scallops	50 g	kg	$20.25	$1.013
Shrimp	100 g	kg	$21.00	$2.100
Lobster meat	50 g	kg	$50.00	$2.500
Chopped garlic	5 g	kg	$5.50	$0.028
Olive oil	15 mL	L	$10.80	$0.162
White wine	30 mL	1.5 L	$11.20	$0.224
Heavy cream	100 mL	L	$4.00	$0.400
Basil	15 mL	bunch (225 mL)	$4.00	$0.267
Romano cheese	15 g	kg	$11.60	$0.174
Capellini pasta	130 g	box (500 g)	$1.40	$0.364
Salt and pepper				
Total				$7.232

A standard recipe yields a predetermined number of standard portions. Thus, it is possible to determine the standard cost of one portion by dividing the number of portions produced into the total cost of preparing the recipe. The standard recipe for Capellini shown in Figure 6.1 is for one portion rather than several portions because it is prepared individually as the orders are placed in the kitchen. To find the cost of a recipe, one lists each ingredient and quantity from the standard recipe on the recipe detail and cost card and then multiplies the quantity of each ingredient by the unit cost for that ingredient. In the example given, the third ingredient is 50 grams of lobster meat. If 1 kilogram costs $50.00, then 50 grams costs $2.50 ($50.00 × .050). That figure is entered in the column on the right headed "Ext." the abbreviation for *Extension*. We have carried out the calculations to three decimal places for greater accuracy.

Determining the cost of an ingredient can sometimes be complex. If, for example, a recipe calls for three diced onions, it will be necessary to determine the average number of onions in a sack and then determine the price of one onion by dividing the total number into the price of the sack of onions. Multiplying the price of one onion by three gives the price for the onions in the standard recipe. It may be more accurate, though, to determine the weight of the three onions and cost them by multiplying the weight by the price per unit. In general, it is advisable to list the recipe ingredient quantity in the same unit it is purchased. So if the onions are purchased for $1.99 per kilogram, then list the recipe ingredient quantity in kilograms or grams. This will simplify changes to recipe ingredient costs if the price paid for the ingredient before processing—known as the **'as purchased'** (AP) price—changes. If we determine that the onions weigh 200 grams each, then three weigh 600 grams, and they cost $1.99 per kilo. The extended cost of the ingredient in the recipe is $1.194.

Ingredient	Quantity	Unit	Cost	Extension
Onions	3 pc or 600 grams	kilogram	$1.99	$1.194

Adding Yield and Edible Portion to the Recipe Detail and Cost Card

Yield (Y) must also be considered. It is defined as the ratio of the useful amount left after cleaning or trimming to the whole. Let's say a recipe calls for 600 grams of chopped onion instead of three 200-gram onions; the cost must be calculated for the onion as purchased, skin on, and then divided by the yield to determine the **edible portion** (EP) cost. In other words consideration must be made for the loss of skin and core in the raw onion as purchased to ensure that the yield remaining meets the 600 grams specified by the recipe. To make this calculation, let's use this formula:

$$\frac{\text{Edible Portion}}{\text{As Purchased}} = \text{Yield}$$

$$\text{or } \frac{EP}{AP} = Y$$

If we clean 10 kilograms of similarly sized onions and find that the skins and cores represent 1 kilogram waste or loss, and that the remaining 9 kilograms or 90 percent represents cleaned, ready-to-use (EP) onion, then

EP of 9 kg ÷ AP of 10 kg = 0.90 or 90 percent yield

In place of weighing AP and EP amounts to determine yield, there are many reference books available that list the yield of common foods after cleaning and trimming. We will discuss their use later in the chapter.

As purchased price, edible portion cost, and yield can also be used to calculate the cost or amounts of ingredients needed.

In costing our recipe ingredients we will use the yield percent divided into the AP price per unit to determine the EP cost. If the onions we require cost $1.99 per kilogram AP, we can divide that by the yield to determine the price per kilogram of the EP.

Our formula is:

AP price per kg ÷ Y = EP cost per kg

In our example, AP price of $1.99 per kilogram ÷ 0.90 (90 percent as a decimal) = EP cost of $2.211 per kilogram.

Using a yield to determine an ingredient cost must be done with many foods that are purchased in a natural state then cleaned before using in a recipe. Some examples are mushrooms, garlic, leeks, and turnips, but there are many more. This yield method is used for ingredients where the product's waste portion has no value. This is an important distinction as we shall see when we examine a butcher yield test.

We can also use this formula in another way to determine how much we will need to buy AP when we know the EP amount needed and the yield. We divide the yield into the ingredient amount expressed in EP units to determine the AP we would need to start with before processing.

For example, if we require an EP of 600 grams of chopped onions, how many grams of unpeeled onions will we need AP?

The formula now is:

EP ÷ Y = AP required or

600 g ÷ 0.90 = 667 g

We will need to buy 667 grams of unpeeled onions in order to yield 600 grams after cleaning them.

Let's try another example. If you require 10 kilograms of cleaned potatoes for a recipe, how many would you have to buy, skin on, to yield that amount? Divide by the yield. From our formula EP ÷ AP = Yield we can now solve for AP by reformulating to EP ÷ Yield = AP. If a potato has a 90.9 percent yield after peeling, divide 10 kilograms by 0.909 to determine that you will need to purchase 11 kilograms.

We can use our formula now to solve for another variable. Let's say we wanted to know how many cleaned potatoes we would get from an as-purchased amount.

This time we will use the following formula:

$$AP \times Y = EP$$

So, if we bought a 10-kilogram bag of potatoes, skin on, and had a yield of 90.9 percent after peeling, then $10 \times .909 = 9.09$. We would have 9.09 kilograms of cleaned potatoes to work with. We will talk more about yield later in this chapter.

Other Considerations When Costing Recipes

Another instance of additional complexity in determining the cost of an ingredient would be using house-made chicken stock as an ingredient. It would be necessary to refer to a separate recipe detail and cost card to determine the cost of one measure of stock prepared according to that standard recipe.

For ingredients used in small quantities, such as 5 millilitres of basil, it may not be worthwhile to calculate the actual value. For such ingredients, the figure entered is some token amount, like $0.15, which is generally more than enough to cover the cost. Alternatively, several books provide resources to managers and give yields for all items in both as-purchased and edible portion forms. For example, a manager could look up fresh basil in one of these books and find the following information:

70.9 Grams per Bunch	39.7 Grams of Stemless Leaf per Bunch	56% Weight EP per Bunch	59 Leaves per Bunch	96 Millilitres of Chopped Leaf per Bunch

Thus, if the price of one bunch of fresh basil is $2.00, and given the fact that there are 96 millilitres per bunch, the cost of a 5-millilitre portion would be $0.104 ($2.00 ÷ 96 = $0. 02083 per ml × 5 ml). Further, if we know that there are 59 garnish leaves per bunch, we can determine the cost of one garnish sprig as follows: $2.00 ÷ 59 = $0.0339, or $0.034.

Let us consider the manager who is completing calculations for dry herbs and spices. The first step is to determine what unit the item is purchased at. For example, if we are using curry powder in a recipe, it is common to purchase it in 1 kilogram units. At this point, it will be necessary to find some weight-to-volume conversions. One that is helpful is the number of millilitres per gram. To find the number of millilitres per gram, one would simply fill a container, say a 15-millilitre spoon, with curry powder and then weigh the results, making sure the weight of the spoon is considered. The 15 millilitres now converted into grams can be costed by extension.

Once the cost of each ingredient has been established, the total cost of preparing the recipe is determined by adding the costs of the individual ingredients. This total, divided by the number of portions produced (again called the yield), gives the cost of one standard portion. As long as ingredients of standard quality are purchased as specified and at relatively stable prices, this should be the cost of producing one standard portion in actual operations, provided there is no waste. Thus, in Figure 6.2, the standard cost of Capellini is calculated at $7.232 per portion. At a sales price of $21.40, the food cost percent is 33.79 percent. However, one must remember that salad is included in the price of the meal. Assuming that the salad cost is $0.400, this brings the portion cost to $7.632, and results in a food cost percent of 35.66 percent.

The cost percent can be changed dramatically if the standard recipe is not followed. For example, assume that a cook prepares the recipe using 100 grams of scallops and 100 grams of lobster meat, rather than the quantities listed in the standard recipe. Scallops would cost $2.025 instead of $1.013, and lobster would cost $5.00 instead of $2.50. The additional cost would be $3.513, for a total of $10.745 for the recipe. The food cost, including salad at $0.400, would be $11.145, and the cost percent would be 52.08 percent, which are both unacceptably high costs.

Standard costs of standard portions must be recalculated as purveyors' prices of the ingredients change. The frequency of the recalculations will depend largely on conditions in the market, as well as the availability of personnel to do the calculating. If market conditions and prices remain fairly constant, it should not be necessary to recalculate standard portion costs more frequently than every three or four months.

Determining the standard recipe and portion cost may require further calculations for some items (steaks portioned in-house from wholesale cuts of beef, or portions of roast lamb, for example); neither the basic formula nor the recipe detail and cost card is useful for determining standard portion cost. For these items and others like them, portion costs cannot be determined until after some processing has taken place. The processing may include trimming, butchering, cooking, or some combination of these steps. During this processing, fat, bone, and other inedible or unnecessary parts are removed. In some cases, this is accomplished by cutting these parts away. In other cases (e.g., roasts), fat is removed by rendering and dehydrating during the cooking process.

Any such processing results in products' weight loss: the quantity available for portioning weighs less than the quantity originally purchased. The true quantity available for portioning is not known until after the processing has been completed, and the item to be portioned cannot be weighed to determine the quantity available for portioning until after processing.

Two special techniques are used to determine standard portion costs for items requiring the kinds of processing described: the butcher test and the cooking loss test. In general, the **butcher test** is used to determine standard portion costs for those items portioned before cooking, and the **cooking loss test** is used for those items portioned after cooking. In some instances, both tests may be required to determine standard portion costs.

Butcher Test

LEARNING OBJECTIVE 6.4
Use cost factors derived from butcher tests to calculate portion costs.

When meat, fish, and poultry are purchased as wholesale cuts, the purchaser pays the same price for every kilogram of the item purchased, even though, after butchering, the resulting parts may have entirely different values. If, for example, a particular cut of beef is approximately half fat and half usable meat, the two parts clearly have different uses and different values, even though they were purchased at the same price per kilogram because both were part of one wholesale cut. Among other purposes, the butcher test is designed to establish a rational value for the primary part to be used. A butcher test is usually performed under the supervision of a chef or food controller, who would ask a butcher to assist in testing a particular item. The butcher uses his or her special skills to break the item down into its respective parts, keeping the parts separate so that they can be weighed. As the butcher prepares to begin, the other individual records some basic information about the item being tested at the top of the butcher test card (Figure 6.3).

Figure 6.3 indicates the results of a butcher test performed on a whole beef tenderloin, Canada AAA, weighing 4 kilograms, purchased at $19.80 per kilogram from the XYZ Meat Company on March 21. The purchase price for the piece was $79.20.

As the butcher works, he or she keeps the parts separated so that their individual weights may be determined after the work is completed. The parts are indentified and recorded in the column at the left under "Breakdown," and the weights of the parts go into the next column to the right. Ideally, the total

• FIGURE 6.3 •

Butcher Test Card

Item	Beef Tenderloin			Grade	Canada AAA			Date		3/21/20XX	
Pieces	One			Weighing	4 kg			Average Weight			
Total Cost	$79.20			At	$19.80 per kg			Supplier		XYZ Meat Co.	

Breakdown	No.	Weight kg	Ratio to Total Weight	Value per kg	Total Value	Cost of Each Usable kg	Portion Size	Portion Cost	Cost Factor per kg	Cost Factor per Portion
Fat		0.6	15%	$0.00						
Loss in cutting		0.1	2.5%	$0.00						
Tip meat		0.8	20.0%	$13.20	$10.56					
Usable meat		2.5	62.5%		$68.64	$27.456	0.175 kg	$4.805	1.387	0.243
Total		4.0	100%		$79.20					

weight of the individual parts equals the total original weight. However, some small measure of weight is usually lost during the butchering as particles of moisture, blood, or fat, and it is common to find an entry in the "Breakdown" and "Weight" columns for loss in cutting.

Calculating Butcher Cost

In Figure 6.3, the entries made in the "Breakdown" column are for fat, loss in cutting, tip meat, and usable meat for tournedos. The weights for each have been written in the "Weight" column: 0.6 kilograms for fat, 0.8 kg for tip meat, and 2.5 kg for usable meat. The weight for loss in cutting, 0.1 kg, is determined by adding the weights for the three known parts and then subtracting that total from the purchased weight.

Fat	0.6 kg
Tip meat	0.8 kg
+ Usable meat	2.5 kg
= Total of butchered parts	3.9 kg
Purchased weight	4.0 kg
= Loss in cutting	0.1 kg

The next column, labelled "Ratio to Total Weight," indicates the percentage of each part in relation to the whole. The ratio of each weight to the whole is calculated by following the formula:

$$\frac{\text{Weight of part}}{\text{Weight of whole}} = \text{Ratio to total weight}$$

$$\frac{0.6 \text{ kg}}{4.0 \text{ kg}} = 0.15 \text{ or } 15.0 \text{ percent fat}$$

$$\frac{0.1}{4.0 \text{ kg}} = 0.025 \text{ or } 2.5 \text{ percent loss in cutting}$$

$$\frac{0.8}{4.0 \text{ kg}} = 0.2 \text{ or } 20.0 \text{ percent tip meat}$$

$$\frac{2.5}{4.0 \text{ kg}} = 0.625 \text{ or } 62.5 \text{ percent usable meat}$$

These ratios can be of particular interest to those attempting to compare similar cuts of meat supplied by two or more purveyors. Performing butcher tests on similar pieces and then comparing ratios of usable parts may help determine which supplier offers better yield. In addition, these ratios may be used to compare meats of different qualities to determine which is more economical to serve. This ratio is known as a *yield percentage,* or a *yield factor.* The "Value per Kilogram" is possibly the simplest to complete. The values per kilogram for all parts except the principal part are the current prices that each of the portions of trim would cost if purchased separately in the open market. In most instances, restaurants and other foodservice operations obtain these figures from one of their regular suppliers. The use of these dealer prices for the various parts is based on the fact that one would pay this price to buy each of the parts separately. Theoretically, the value recorded for each part thus represents a reasonable market value. These values are given knowing that there will be a use for these products that will generate sales. No value per kilogram for the principal part is entered. That value is derived last after the total values for all other parts have been calculated and recorded in the next column, marked "Total Value."

The total value for the parts identified as trimming is obtained by multiplying the value per kilogram by the weight. The total value of the primary part is determined by

1. Adding the total values of the trim parts, and
2. Subtracting that figure from "Total Cost," indicated at the top of the form.

In Figure 6.3, there is no value for the fat. The trim part with value is tip meat, which would cost $13.20 per kilogram, if purchased separately. Bistro Quatre will save these pieces and freeze them until there is enough accumulated to use as a special item on the menu. Thus, subtracting the value of the tip meat ($10.56) from the value of the entire piece ($79.20) leaves $68.64 as the value of the usable meat of the tenderloin, for the Tournedos Bistro dish.

With both the weight and total value of the usable meat known, the cost of each usable gram or kilogram—the next column to the right—can be determined by some simple division:

$$\frac{\text{Total value of usable meat}}{\text{Weight of usable meat}} = \text{Cost per usable kg or g}$$

$$\frac{\$68.64}{2.5\text{ kg}} = \$27.456 \text{ per kilogram}$$

The standard portion size, stated in kilograms, is entered in the next column, "Portion Size." This is obviously a quantity standard established by management. The portion cost is calculated by multiplying the portion size in kilogram by the cost of each usable kilogram.

$$\text{Portion size} \times \text{Cost per usable kg} = \text{Portion cost}$$
$$.175\text{ kg} \times \$27.456 = \$4.805$$

The remaining two columns are used for recording the **cost factor per kilogram** and **cost factor per portion**, both of which require explanation.

Cost Factors

Purveyors' prices of meat, fish, and poultry change weekly, and sometimes daily. As prices change, the foodservice operator's usable kilogram costs and portion costs change as well. Therefore, it is good to have some simple means for calculating both usable unit costs and portion costs whenever supplier prices change, so that it is unnecessary to complete a new physical butcher test each time. The cost factors serve this purpose and are calculated in the following manner:

Cost Factor per Kilogram:

$$\frac{\text{Cost per usable kg}}{\text{As purchased price per kg}} = \text{Cost factor per kg}$$

$$\frac{\$27.456}{\$19.80} = 1.387$$

Cost Factor per Portion:

$$\frac{\text{Portion cost}}{\text{As purchase price per kg}} = \text{Cost factor per portion}$$

$$\frac{\$4.805}{\$19.80} = 0.243$$

These factors are extremely useful. Suppose the purchase price per kilogram for beef tenderloin was expected to increase from the present $19.80 to $20.80. This price increase would increase portion cost, but those in foodservice management must know more than this obvious truth: they must know the standard portion cost at the new, higher dealer price. One could proceed to complete a new set of butcher test calculations, but although that could be done, it would take time and cost money. A simpler, faster method uses the cost factors and the formulas provided, as follows:

$$\text{Cost factor per kg} \times \text{new dealer price per kg}$$

Cost of a usable kilogram at new dealer price:

$$1.387 \times \$20.80 = \$28.8496 = \$28.85$$
$$\text{Cost factor per kg} \times \text{new dealer price per kg}$$

Cost of a portion of same size at new dealer price:

$$0.243 \times \$20.80 = \$5.0544 = \$5.05$$
$$\text{Cost factor per portion} \times \text{new dealer price per kg}$$

By this means, one can determine quite specifically that the $1.00 increase in the dealer price per kilogram will lead to an increase of $1.39 in the cost of a usable kilogram and $0.24 in the portion cost.

These formulas provide chefs, managers, and owners with the means for determining new food costs as purchase prices change. They also enable management to determine when changes in menu sales prices may be required to maintain relatively stable cost-to-sales ratios.

To ensure the accuracy of figures derived by this method, it is necessary to perform butcher tests regularly on reasonable numbers of pieces. The test on one piece alone is not reliable, because the piece may not be typical, even if it was purchased according to specifications. It is better to have test results on several different pieces in order to arrive at averages. Another important consideration is the comparative size of the cuts to be butchered. Using head-on, gutted coho salmon as an example, you would have a substantially different yield of usable meat from a 3-kilogram fish than from a 6-kilogram fish. This is generally true with meats and poultry as well. Often the larger things grow, the higher the yield. It is important when using cost factors to ensure they were derived from similar sized samples.

Establishments that do butcher tests find several other important uses for the results:

1. Menu prices can be more intelligently planned, because exact costs are known.
2. Butcher tests conducted periodically allow the manager to appraise the extent to which any one supplier is adhering to specifications.
3. Butcher tests on pieces purchased according to specifications from two or more suppliers may give results that are useful in determining which to buy from.

Those with experience in foodservice will recognize that comparatively few establishments do regular butcher testing today. That was not the case in years past, however. A primary reason for the change has been the availability of preportioned entrées from vendors: steaks, chops, and other items portioned before cooking. Additionally, several books available provide standardized information that can be used to approximate yield information. However, the butcher test is still extremely valuable to the manager who wants to compare the cost of a preportioned item purchased from a vendor with the cost of an identical item portioned in the restaurant. Typically, one would expect to find a lower standard portion cost for the item portioned in the restaurant, but this figure takes into account only food cost for the item, not labour cost. On the other hand, the portion cost for the preportioned item purchased from a vendor includes the vendor's labour cost. Therefore, to make a valid comparison, management would have to determine labour cost per portion for items portioned in the restaurant.

Although the butcher test makes it possible for foodservice operators to determine portion costs for entrée items portioned before cooking (steaks, chops, and fillets), it is of no value for determining portion costs for items that cannot be portioned until after cooking. Products that require cooking loss tests to determine true costs are certain prepared foods, often sold in markets and shops. These stores have been a growing part of our industry recently and are employing many cooks and chefs to produce meals to sell alongside aisles of grocery items. For those chefs working in this growing sector it will be essential to know how to properly cost butchered and roasted meats, poultry, and fish. After butchering, portion costs for these items—typically roasts of beef, pork, lamb, and other meats—still cannot be determined until after the cooking process is complete. A different procedure, known as the cooking loss test, is required.

Cooking Loss Test

LEARNING OBJECTIVE 6.5
Use cost factors derived from cooking loss tests to calculate portion costs.

The primary purpose for the cooking loss test is the same as that for the butcher test: determining true standard portion cost. The cooking loss test is used for those items that cannot be portioned until after cooking is complete. With these items, one must take into account the weight loss that occurs during cooking. Therefore, one cannot determine the quantity remaining to be portioned until cooking is completed and portionable weight can be determined. Cooking loss varies with cooking time, temperature, and moisture loss, and it must be taken into account in determining standard portion costs.

Before considering a detailed explanation of the cooking loss test, it is useful to note that the butcher test form and the cooking loss form have many similarities (see Figure 6.4). A glance at the form shows that the column headings are the same as those on the butcher test form. The major difference between the forms lies in the "Breakdown" column: On the butcher test form (Figure 6.3), terms are written in this column as the butcher test progresses; on the cooking loss test form, they are preprinted ("Original Weight," "Trimmed Weight," and so on). It is important, then, to learn the meanings of these terms in order to understand the cooking loss test.

The cooking loss test is perhaps best explained by illustration. Figure 6.4 shows a completed set of test results for one pork loin served as a special at Bistro Quatre. As purchased, the pork weighed 7.5 kilograms. At an AP price per kilogram of $13.99, the purchase price for the loin was $104.93. All this information is recorded on the first line of the test form, "Original Weight." The loin required some butchering before it could be cooked. The butcher cut away unnecessary parts, primarily fat, to prepare the loin for roasting. After butchering, the loin was found to weigh 6.5 kilograms. This weight is recorded on the line marked "Trimmed Weight."

Next, trimmed weight of 6.5 kilograms is subtracted from original weight of 7.5 kilograms, and the difference of 1.0 kilograms is recorded on the line marked "Loss in Trimming." Original weight, then, represents the piece as purchased; trimmed weight represents the piece after in-house butchering, if any; and "loss in trimming" represents the difference between the two.

• **FIGURE 6.4** •

Cooking Loss Test

Cooked   Hours   One   Minutes   Ten   At   175° C

Breakdown	No.	Weight kg	Ratio to Total Weight	Value per kg	Total Value	Cost of Each Usable kg	Portion Size	Portion Cost	Cost Factor per kg	Portion
Original Weight			7.5	100%	$13.99	$104.93				
Trimmed Weight			6.5	86.67%						
Loss in Trimming			1.0	13.33%						
Cooked Weight			5.5	73.33%						
Loss in Cooking			1.0	8.00%						
Bones and Trim			0.5	6.67%						
Salable Weight			5.0	66.67%	$104.93	$20.986	150 g	$3.148	1.500	0.225
Remarks	Item	Pork Loin	Portion Size 150 g		Portion Cost Factor .225					

At this point, the trimmed pork loin is put into an oven to roast. After cooking for 1 hour and 10 minutes at 175 degrees Celsius (350 degrees Fahrenheit), it is removed from the oven and weighed. The weight, 5.5 kilograms, is recorded on the line marked "Cooked Weight." Next, cooked weight of 5.5 kilograms is subtracted from trimmed weight of 6.5 kilograms to determine the entry for the following line, "Loss in Cooking"—1.0 kilogram.

Because the cooked piece includes cooked bone and cooked fat, not all 5.5 kilograms can be portioned. Usable meat must be removed from the bone and weighed to determine the quantity available for portioning. After that is accomplished, the weight of the portionable meat is recorded on the line marked "Saleable Weight"—5.0 kilograms, in this instance. This is subtracted from the cooked weight of 5.5 kilograms to determine the amount of waste, noted on the line marked "Bones & Trim"—0.5 kilograms.

Having completed the entries in the "Weight" column, one can proceed to fill in the "Ratio to Total Weight" column. The percentage recorded on each line is the ratio of the weight of that part to the original weight of the piece as purchased. These ratios are calculated in exactly the manner described in the discussion of the butcher test.

This is a most important step. These ratios may be used productively by chefs and managers to make various comparisons. For example, cooked weight ratios calculated for several pieces of meat may be compared to determine which of several available grades would yield the maximum quantity of saleable meat. Similarly, cooked weight ratios may be used to compare the results of cooking several pieces at different temperatures, or for different lengths of time, to determine the optimum cooking times and temperatures. Once optimum cooking time and temperature for a given type of roast have been determined, these may be established as the standards.

The "Value per Kilogram" column is used only once in cooking loss tests. The only value recorded is that on the first line, "Original Weight." This is actually the purveyor price per kilogram for the original piece as purchased. With each step in processing, the decreased weight assumes a greater value per kilogram, so that the costs of all nonportionable kilograms are transferred to the saleable weight, as nothing else is of value. This clearly underscores the need for the cooking loss test. It is impossible to determine portion costs until cooking loss has been calculated.

Once the weight and value of the saleable meat are recorded and the portion size is entered from the restaurant's list of standard portion sizes, the remaining calculations are performed in the same manner as in the butcher test.

The foregoing discussion was based on a piece of meat not requiring extensive butchering before cooking. However, in many instances, meats require considerable butchering (e.g., in cases where the parts trimmed away have usefulness and value to the establishment). In these instances, the original and trimmed weights on the cooking loss test will appear as very different figures, because a butcher test has first been performed to determine weights and assign values to the trimmed parts. The weight and value of the primary usable part becomes the weight and value entered on the cooking loss test as trimmed weight. The original weight and value remain that of the piece of meat as purchased. Figure 6.5 illustrates this concept.

The original weight for the lamb loin was 10.0 kilograms and the original cost was $64.10. After in-house butchering, the value of the usable meat for the loin was determined to be $49.18. Both of these figures are entered in the cooking loss test. The $14.92 listed as loss in trimming is actually the value of the kidneys and flanks shown in the butcher test. Those two items, along with the fat trimmed during in-house butchering, constitute 50 percent of the total weight before cooking. The final cost per kilogram and per portion are then calculated in the same manner as previously explained. The cost of each kilogram of usable meat turns out to be $16.393, and a 0.150-kilogram portion costs $2.459. By adding the cost of other items served with the meal, it is possible to establish a selling price that will bring the desired profit margin and food cost percent.

Computer users can find programs for all of these methods for finding the standard cost of any item on the menu. Programmers have provided templates within many of these programs for users to input information—food ingredients and prices, for example—that are the basis for portion costs. When specific recipes are input, these programs use the ingredient and price information to determine and output recipe and portion costs automatically, at obviously great savings of time and labour over the manual methods of the past. Although it is comparatively easy to make provision for cooking loss tests and even butcher tests in such programs, they are not as common as one might expect.

• **FIGURE 6.5** •

Butcher Test Card

Item	Lamb Saddle		Grade	Canada AAA	Date	3/21/20XX
Pieces	One		Weighing	10 kg	Average Weight	
Total Cost	$64.10		At	$6.41 per kg	Supplier	Ewe too Meat Co.

Breakdown	No.	Weight kg	Ratio to Total Weight	Value per kg	Total Value	Cost of Each Usable kg	Portion Size	Portion Cost	Cost Factor per kg	Portion
Fat		1.0	10%	$0.00						
Kidneys		0.4	4%	$11.00	$2.35					
Flanks		2.8	28%	$8.80	$12.57					
Loss in Cutting		0.8	8%	$0.00						
Usable Meat		5.0	50%		$49.18					
Total		10.00	100%		$64.10					

				Cooking Loss Test						
Cooked Hours One Minutes Ten At					385° F (195° C)					
Breakdown	No.	Weight kg	Ratio to Total Weight	Value per kg	Total Value	Cost of Each Usable kg	Portion Size	Portion Cost	Cost Factor per kg	Portion
Original Weight		10	100%	$6.41	$64.10					
Trimmed Weight		5	50.00%		$49.18					
Loss in Trimming		5	50.00%		$14.92					
Cooked Weight		4	40.00%		$49.18					
Loss in Cooking		0.5	5.00%							
Bones and Trim		0.5	5.00%							
Salable Weight		3	30.00%		$49.18	$16.393	150 g	$2.459	2.557	0.384
Remarks	Item	Lamb Loin	Portion Size 150 g		Portion Cost Factor 0.384					

0.15 × 16.393
=

ADVANTAGES AND DISADVANTAGES OF STANDARDIZED YIELD

As previously discussed, several books provide standardized yields for most foods. The following are the general advantages and disadvantages of using standardized yields versus performing yield tests in-house.

Advantages to using standardized yields from industry resources:

LEARNING OBJECTIVE 6.6
List the advantages and disadvantages of using standardized yield figures versus in-house yield tests.

1. They reduce labour costs involved in the time-consuming process of performing yield tests, and will give results that are approximately accurate.
2. These resources generally use yield percentages and weight-to-volume equivalents, which help managers make decisions about how much raw food to buy or requisition.
3. The weight-to-volume equivalents are very helpful when converting a recipe from foods purchased by weight (AP) but often used by volume.

Disadvantages to using standardized yields from industry resources:

1. Standardized yields cannot allow establishments to compare purveyors' prices and quality, making it more difficult to determine who to purchase from.
2. Standardized yields are not as accurate as in-house calculations. Standardized yields are based on averages that may or may not apply to a specific food or purveyor.
3. Standardized yields do not take into consideration standard purchase specifications for specific establishments.

The final determination as to which method to use will be up to the individual establishment. It is possible to use a combination of both methods, using the standardized yields for lower-priced items, and performing yield tests on higher-priced items such as meats and fish.

MORE USES FOR YIELD PERCENTAGES

We discussed using yield to properly price the EP cost per unit of ingredients in a recipe detail and cost card. Let's now examine it in relation to the butcher and cooking loss tests. Remember, the **yield percentage** (or **yield factor**) is defined as the percentage of a whole purchase unit of meat, poultry, fish, or any other ingredient that is available for portioning after any required in-house processing, trimming, peeling, or cleaning has been completed. This percentage is calculated by dividing the portionable weight by the original weight of the purchase unit before processing. These calculations are included in the butcher test and cooking loss test calculations. On the butcher test, the yield percentage is found in the "Ratio to Total Weight" column on the line reserved for the usable meat. For example, in Figure 6.3, the "Ratio to Total Weight" for the usable meat is 62.5 percent. On the cooking loss test, the yield percentage is found in the "Ratio to Total Weight" column on the line labelled "Saleable Weight." On the cooking loss test illustrated in Figure 6.4, the "Ratio to Total Weight" for the "Saleable Weight" is 66.67 percent.

Once again, yield percentage can be used in a number of quantity calculations. The general formula for these is:

$$\text{Quantity} = \text{Number of portions} \times \text{Portion size (as a decimal)} \div \text{Yield percentage}$$

As with any formula, it is possible to solve for any one of the terms, provided the other three are known. Thus, given quantity, portion size, and yield factor, one could determine the number of standard portions that should be produced from the given quantity. Or, given quantity, number of portions, and yield factor, one could determine the portion size that should be served to feed a given number of people with a given quantity of meat. The following are three variations on the basic formula:

$$\text{Number of portions} = \text{Quantity} \times \frac{\text{Yield percentage}}{\text{Portion size}}$$

$$\text{Portion size} = \text{Quantity} \times \frac{\text{Yield percentage}}{\text{Number of portions}}$$

$$\text{Yield percentage} = \text{Number of portions} \times \frac{\text{Portion size}}{\text{Quantity}}$$

Although there are many practical uses for the basic formula and its variations, one illustration will suffice. It is possible to use the basic formula to determine the quantity of a given item that must be purchased to serve portions of a given size to a particular number of people.

Suppose a chef wanted to buy the proper quantity of pork loin to provide 150-gram portions of pork loin for 64 people, and he had previously calculated the yield percentage given in the cooking loss test in Figure 6.4 at 66.67 percent. Using the formula provided earlier,

$$\text{Quantity} = \text{Number of portions} \times \frac{\text{Portion size (as a decimal)}}{\text{Yield percentage}}$$

the chef would calculate as follows:

$$\text{Quantity} = 32 \text{ portions} \times \frac{0.150}{.667 \text{ Yield percentage}}$$

$$= 7.196 \text{ kg or round up to } 7.2 \text{ kg}$$

To confirm the accuracy of the calculation, refer to the pork loin used for an example in the cooking loss test, the calculations for which appear in Figure 6.4. Given similar pork loins, one can see that the loin would produce 33 portions, because each portion weighs 0.150 grams, and there are 5.0 kilograms of salable weight (5.0 ÷ 0.150). One can also see that if 64 portions were desired, two pork loins would be needed.

It is important to note that the preceding formula assumes that future purchases of pork loin will provide the same yield as the tested loin. This means that the meat would contain the same relative amounts of bone, fat, and lean meat and that it would be cooked at the same temperature for the same period of time so that shrinkage would be relatively the same as in the tested pork. Calculations using yield percentages are reliable only if one is able to trust the repeated accuracy of these assumptions.

RECIPE SOFTWARE

The importance of using standard recipes cannot be overemphasized; therefore, at this point, readers will want to familiarize themselves with the various recipe software programs available to the foodservice manager. Recipe software programs allow users to create recipes in a standard format and edit or modify recipes to suit the occasion. In addition, they can cost recipes. Many also provide nutritional analysis information. Most software also allows the user to insert a photograph of the finished product. Many also have a library of recipes, all of which can have the ingredients listed in a requisition format. There are websites for many of the recipe software programs. These sites frequently provide technical support and discussion boards on how to best optimize each of the program's benefits. For example, the Meal Cost System allows the user to cost out a menu item in about 30 seconds. Its ingredients and current costs are programmed into the system. Finding the cost of any menu item is simply a matter of calling it up. This system also allows the controller to test different ingredients for a recipe or a meal and determine its cost, all in a matter of minutes.

THINGS TO CONSIDER

Some chefs and restaurants do not value the trim and secondary cuts that are by-products of butchering. In our butcher test example (Figure 6.3), we put a dollar value to the trimmed tip meat as well as the primary usable meat. When we butchered the beef tenderloin, we used a market price for the tip meat of $13.20 per kilogram that we got from our purveyor. That left us $27.46 per kilogram as the value of our usable meat.

Unfortunately, not all chefs make this consideration. If they discard the by-products, it transfers the whole purchase price to the usable meat. In our example, the $79.20 total cost would become the cost of the usable tournedo meat. Under this method, the meat would have a value of $79.20 / 2.5 kilograms or $31.68 per kilogram. We would have to charge a higher menu price for our Tournedos Bistro because of this increase to cost. On the other hand, the tip meat with no assigned value attached to it can be sold at a lower cost. If the tips are used for a dish such as tenderloin sauté with merlot and mushrooms, the only costs of the dish would be the sauce and garnish, as the meat is "free." This would enable us to sell the dish for a lower price.

This method may seem erroneous, but if the demand for Tournedos Bistro is much greater than for tenderloin sauté with merlot and mushrooms, it may lead to a wise pricing decision. As long as the customers are satisfied, by reducing the price and increasing sales of the tenderloin sauté, an equilibrium can be reached between the tip and the usable meat, ensuring that the entire beef tenderloin is purchased and consumed.

Another important consideration is metric conversions. Many recipes used in Canada are written in U.S. measurements because of Canada's physical proximity to the U.S. and because the fact that the United States is a much bigger market than Canada. Similarly, most ovens are calibrated in Fahrenheit because manufacturers sell 10 times as many units in the United States than they do in Canada. That's probably why Canadians are still not generally comfortable cooking and baking using metric measurements. They are just not used to it. If you are converting from U.S. measurements to Canadian Imperial, keep in mind that a U.S. cup is 8 fluid ounces and ours in Canada is 10; a U.S. pint is 16 fluid ounces, ours is 20; a U.S. quart is 32 fluid ounces and ours is 40; and a U.S. gallon is 128 fluid ounces, while ours is 160. Also keep in mind that volume-to-weight comparisons differ depending on the ingredient. A cup of flour will weigh 125 grams approximately, but a cup of sugar will weigh about 225 grams. Care must be taken in such conversions.

CHAPTER ESSENTIALS

In this chapter, we explained the application of the control process to the production phase of foodservice operations. We listed and discussed the standards and standard procedures required for control, including standardization of ingredients, proportions, production methods, and portion sizes. We described the importance of the standard recipe in maintaining standards and suggested possible consequences of failing to maintain production standards. Having established basic production standards, we listed and explained in detail four methods for determining standard portion costs: formula, recipe detail and cost card, butcher test, and cooking loss test. We described the procedures for calculating cost factor per kilogram, AP or as purchased, EP or edible portion, portion cost factor, yield, and yield factor. We listed the advantages and disadvantages of using standardized yield tests. Finally, we explained and illustrated the use of yield tests for calculating portion costs as purveyor prices change and for solving specific quantity problems faced by those who purchase and produce food.

KEY TERMS IN THIS CHAPTER

As purchased, p.166	Standard portion cost, p.163
Butcher test, p.170	Standard portion size, p.159
Cooking loss test, p.170	Standard recipe, p.161
Cost factor per kilogram, p.172	Yield, p.166
Cost factor per portion, p.172	Yield factor, p.179
Edible portion, p.166	Yield percentage, p.179
Recipe detail and cost card, p.165	

QUESTIONS AND PROBLEMS

1. In each of the following cases, determine the selling price for 1 portion of a recipe yielding 30 portions, when the standard recipe cost and desired cost-to-sales ratio are as indicated in the following table:

Recipe cost	Cost percent for one portion
a. $55.25	30.0%
b. $22.58	18.0%
c. $124.50	45.0%
d. $105.00	21.0%
e. $12.60	40.0%

2. Using the form illustrated in Figure 6.3, complete butcher test calculations on a beef tenderloin, Canada AAA, from the following information:

Weight as purchased:	4.0 kg
Dealer price:	$9.25 kg
Portion size for filet mignon:	227 g

   Breakdown
Fat: 2 kg; value per kg:	$0.00
Loss in trimming:	0.16 kg
Tidbits: 0.340 kg; value per kg:	$5.49
Filet mignon:	1.5 kg

3. Using cost factors derived from the butcher test in Question 2, determine:
   a. Cost of the 227-gram portion if the supplier increases the price for beef tenderloin to $10.00 per kilogram

b. Cost of each usable kilogram at the $10.00 price

c. Cost of a 170-gram portion at the $10.00 price

4. Using the forms for the butcher test and the cooking loss test illustrated in figures 6.3 and 6.4, complete butcher test and cooking loss test calculations for a rib of beef, Canada AAA, weighing 17.665 kilograms and purchased from a dealer at $8.80 per kilogram.

Breakdown

Fat: 2.95 kg; value per kg:	$0.00
Bones: 1.928 kg; value per kg:	$1.00
Short ribs: 1.474 kg; value per kg:	$8.80 kg
Chopped beef: 1.2 kg; value per kg:	$4.39
Loss in cutting:	113 g
Oven-ready rib:	10 kg
Cooked weight:	9.19 kg
Loss in cooking:	0.243 kg
Bones and trim:	0.567 kg
Portion size for roast beef:	227 g

5. Records of cooking loss tests done on legs of lamb in the Hearthstone Restaurant provide the following factors for roast lamb:

Yield factor: .425

Kilogram cost factor: 2.1387

a. Determine the number of kilograms of uncooked oven-ready leg of lamb that must be purchased to produce 48 125-gram portions of roast lamb.

b. Determine the number of kilograms of uncooked, oven-ready leg of lamb that must be purchased to produce 55 150-gram portions of roast lamb.

c. Determine the costs of the portions in Questions 5a and 5b if the dealer price per kilogram for leg of lamb is $7.00.

6. The following information, taken from records in the Circle Restaurant, provides the results of butcher tests on 10 legs of veal, Canada Grade A1, purchased over the last several weeks from George's Meats, Inc. Veal legs are purchased to produce 150-gram portions of veal cutlets. The restaurant paid $814.28 for the 10 legs, which weighed a total of 112.3 kilograms as purchased.

Breakdown:

Fat: 18.824 kg; value per kg:	$1.00
Bones: 25.628 kg; value per kg:	$1.00
Shanks: 8.959 kg; value per kg:	$7.50
Trimmings: 21.432 kg; value per kg:	$4.99
Loss in cutting:	1.134 kg
Veal cutlets:	36.288 kg

a. Given the preceding information, complete butcher test calculations to determine the standard cost of the 150 grams, as well as yield factor, portion cost factor, and kilogram cost factor.

b. Find the cost of the standard 150-gram portion at each of the following dealer prices:

1. $7.00 per kg
2. $7.50 per kg
3. $7.99 per kg

c. Find the cost of each of the following:

1. A 175 g portion, if dealer price is $7.00 per kg
2. A 125 g portion, if dealer price is $7.50 per kg
3. A 125 g portion, if dealer price is $7.65 per kg

d. The owner of the Circle Restaurant wants portion cost for veal cutlet to be $2.65, regardless of variations in purchase price. Determine the correct portion size if

1. Dealer price is $7.65 per kg
2. Dealer price is $0.00 per kg

e. Develop a chart showing the costs of 125-gram, 150-gram, and 175-gram portions at purchase prices per kilogram of $7.00, $7.10, and so on in $0.10 increments up to $8.00 per kilogram.

f. How many kilograms of veal leg (as purchased) will be needed to prepare and serve 150-gram portions to 235 people?

g. Given the weight of the average leg of veal, as determined in the butcher test, how many legs should the steward order to prepare and serve 175-gram portions to 235 people?

h. Records show that the Circle Restaurant used 48 legs of veal last month. How many standard 150-gram portions should have been produced from these 48 legs?

i. The restaurant has a banquet for 500 people scheduled for tonight, and the manager has promised to serve veal cutlet as the main dish. The steward neglected to order veal legs for this specific party, but there are 24 legs of veal in the house and veal cutlet is not on the regular dining room menu for tonight. Using these 24 legs of veal for the party, what size portion should be prepared so that all 500 people can be served?

7. The steward of Phil's Restaurant uses specifications to purchase oven-ready legs of lamb, Canada AAA. They are used to produce 200-gram portions of roast lamb. Over a period of several weeks, records were kept of the original weights, cooked weights, and saleable weights of 15 legs selected at random from the total number purchased. These records are summarized as follows:

Original weight (15 pieces): 61.235 kg
(Purchased @ $4.63 per kg—$283.52)

Cooked weight: 54.43 kg

Saleable weight: 34.02 kg

a. Using the preceding data, complete cooking loss test calculations for the 15 legs of lamb to determine yield factor, standard cost of the 200-gram portion, portion cost factor, and kilogram cost factor.

b. Find the cost of the standard 200-gram portion at each of the following dealer prices:

1. $4.99 per kg

2. $5.50 per kg

3. $4.00 per kg

c. Find the cost of each of the following:

1. A 175-gram portion, if dealer price is $4.99 per kilogram

2. A 150-gram portion, if dealer price is $5.50 per kilogram

d. Assume that purchase price increases to $4.99 per kilogram and the manager of Phil's wants a portion cost to be $1.65. What size portion should be served?

e. How many average-size legs of lamb should be purchased to serve 175-gram portions to 270 people?

f. Last month, this restaurant used 82 legs of lamb. How many standard 200-gram portions should have been produced from these 82 legs?

g. If the standard portion size had been 175 grams, how many portions could have been produced from the 82 legs of lamb used last month?

h. The restaurant has only 30 legs of lamb on hand today, and these must be used for a banquet function tonight for 350 people. What size portion should be served?

8. List and discuss three possible customer reactions to nonstandard portion sizes.

9. How can failure to follow standard recipes affect portion costs and quality of menu items?

10. Stella's Restaurant does not have standard cooking times and temperatures for roast prime ribs of beef, one of the principal items on the menu. Two full standing ribs were roasted yesterday. One was well done, and the other was rare. Standard portion size is 300-grams. Do 300-gram portions cut from the rare roast have the same portion costs as those cut from the well-done roast? Why?

11. Using any standard cookbook, select one recipe that could be used as a standard recipe in a foodservice establishment. Following the form illustrated in Figure 6.2, use current wholesale prices to determine the standard cost of one standard portion of the item. Determine an appropriate menu sales price for the item if the desired food cost percent is 35.0 percent.

12. Define each of the key terms in this chapter.

EXCEL EXERCISES

Exercise 6.1
Complete the recipe detail and cost card for beef stew. Costs for the various ingredients are shown on the companion website for this text. Calculate the cost per portion and food cost percent. The selling price for beef stew is $7.50 per portion.

Exercise 6.2
Complete the butcher's test card for beef tenderloin. If the price of the whole piece goes to $15.43 per kilogram, what would be the new price per kilogram and per portion for the usable meat?

Exercise 6.3
Complete the butcher's test card and cooking loss test card for the lamb loin. Calculate figures for the right-hand side of the cooking loss test; there is no need to calculate these figures for the right-hand side of the butcher's test card.

Exercise 6.4
Follow the instructions on the textbook's companion website to complete this exercise.

Food Production Control II: Quantities

• **LEARNING OBJECTIVES** •

After reading this chapter, you should be able to:

7.1 Define the standard for controlling production volume and explain its importance.

7.2 List and describe three standard procedures that enable managers to gain control over production volume.

7.3 Define *sales history* and describe two methods for gathering the data from which a sales history is developed.

7.4 List three basic approaches to arranging data in a sales history.

7.5 Define popularity index and use a popularity index to forecast portion sales.

7.6 Describe the production sheet and calculate needed production for menu items.

7.7 Describe a void sheet and explain its use.

7.8 Complete a portion inventory and reconciliation.

7.9 Describe a procedure used for controlling high-cost, preportioned main course items.

INTRODUCTION

In the preceding chapter, the focus of attention was the portion: establishing control over the ingredients in a portion, the proportions of the various ingredients to one another, and the size of each portion. The reason for establishing control over these three elements was to be able to gain control over a fourth: portion cost.

In this chapter, we will assume that control has been established over individual portions and will shift our focus to the number of portions produced for each item on a menu for a given day or meal. After all, if the cost of a portion of some item is controlled at, say, $4.50 per serving, and the establishment produces 100 portions but sells only 40, there will be 60 portions unsold. These may or may not be saleable on another day. Even if they are saleable, these portions are likely to be of lower quality than when they were first produced. It is also possible that they cannot be sold in their original form, but must be converted into some other item that will be sold at a lower sales price. Sometimes, if none of these possibilities are feasible, it may be necessary to throw the food away. In any case, there is excessive cost—either the cost of the food or the cost of additional labour that would not have been required if the establishment had produced 40 portions rather than 100. Such excessive costs can be reduced or eliminated by applying the four-step control process to the problem of quantity production.

FOOD PRODUCTION CONTROL: ESTABLISHING STANDARDS AND STANDARD PROCEDURES

LEARNING OBJECTIVE 7.1
Define the standard for controlling production volume and explain its importance.

LEARNING OBJECTIVE 7.2
List and describe three standard procedures that enable managers to gain control over production volume.

The standard for controlling production volume is to determine and produce, for any menu item, the number of portions that is likely to be sold on any given day. It is essential that foodservice establishments know this number with some reasonable degree of accuracy, so that intelligent plans can be made for purchasing and production. If, for example, it can be determined that 40 portions of an item are likely to be sold, this can readily be translated into the proper purchasing of the ingredients for producing that number of portions. Failure to set up procedures for establishing the number of portions to be produced can lead to excessive purchasing and labour, with their obvious implications for cost.

To achieve any aim, it is necessary to establish appropriate procedures. To control production volume, three standard procedures are required:

1. Maintaining and analyzing sales history
2. Forecasting portion sales
3. Determining production quantities

Maintaining Sales History

A **sales history** is a written record of the number of portions of each menu item sold. It is a summary of portion sales. In some establishments, sales histories are maintained for every item on the menu, from appetizers to desserts. In others, the only records kept are for main course items. In many instances, the extent and complexity of the sales history is related to the length and scope of the menu itself. In all instances, information obtained from a sales history can be used to improve operations. Its maintenance cannot be justified unless it leads to improved production controls.

LEARNING OBJECTIVE 7.3
Define sales history and describe two methods for gathering the data from which a sales history is developed.

Because a sales history records customers' selections, the basic information is gathered by those who record these selections: the sales staff, servers, or wait staff. To see how the basic information is incorporated into the sales history, it is necessary to understand the two methods used for recording customers' selections: manual and electronic.

Manual Method

Establishments that record customer selections manually are those that use the traditional guest cheques—paper forms that become itemized bills given to customers at the conclusion of their meals. Essentially, there are two kinds of guest cheques: single cheques and cheques that come in pads of 25, 50, or another amount. Servers commonly record customer selections on these cheques manually, using pen or pencil, and the cheque is ultimately given to the customer as a bill to be paid. Payment is made to a cashier or to the server, and the establishment retains the cheque. Assuming that all selections have been recorded completely and legibly on the cheque, it is clearly a source document for the development of a sales history. The key is to set up a routine for abstracting the data from the cheque.

Abstracting information from guest cheques may be accomplished in any of several ways. The simplest method involves maintaining a running count of portion sales as they occur. The work is often assigned to a cashier, who records information from the cheques as customers present them. The information may be recorded on a copy of the menu, on a special score sheet, or on one of several types of mechanical counting devices widely available to the industry. Figure 7.1 illustrates a score sheet, one that might be used if Bistro Quatre were keeping a manual count of portion sales for Monday, February 1.

At the conclusion of a meal or at some other appropriate time, such as the end of the day, the information is given to the individual responsible for maintaining the sales history (e.g., manager, chef, food controller, steward, dining room manager), so that it can be added to the accumulated records previously developed.

• **FIGURE 7.1** •

Portion Sales Breakdown

Bistro Quatre

Day	Monday	Date	1-Feb				Meal	Dinner		

Item	Number of Portions							Total
Strip Steak	11111 11111							10
Tournedos Bistro	11111 1111							9
Duck Breast	111							3
Leg of Lamb	11111 111							8
Baby Back Ribs	1111							4
Tamarind and Ginger Shrimp	11111 11							7
Gnocchi	11111							5
Darjeeling-Smoked Salmon	11111 11111 11							12
Paella	11111 11111 1							11
Big Eye Tuna	1111							4
Miso Glazed Black Cod	11111 1111							9
Chicken Breast	11111 111							8
Tagliatelle	11111 11							7
Scallops	11111							5
Capellini	11111 1							6
Catch of the Day	11111 111							8
Total								116

In some operations, where the cashier may be too busy to take on this extra work, the food controller or another member of the management staff may take the guest cheques after the meal or at the close of business and prepare an abstract of the portion sales, usually on a score sheet. In a variation on this approach, the cashier gives the cheques to someone from accounting, who records the necessary information and forwards it to the individual responsible for maintaining the sales history.

Electronic Method

Clearly, electronic terminals are becoming the most common method of recording food sales. Some interface with complex computer systems, whereas others are little more than electronic versions of the old mechanical cash registers. Some of these machines have the capacity to maintain cumulative totals of the numbers of portions of menu items sold.

Given the many electronic sales terminals available, developing sales history data has become simpler and faster than it was in the past. With standalone sales terminals, it is comparatively easy at the end of a day or a meal period to print out a report of portion sales, which can be added to a manually maintained history. With sales terminals integrated into a local area network (LAN), portion sales data may merely be stored for future reference in a file maintained on the server. It would be simple to create a database program for rendering the data in a form useful for forecasting.

Essentially, there are three methods for inputting portion sales data. The first is accomplished by depressing a key on an electronic terminal marked with the name of the menu item selected. The second is a variation of the first method using a touch-screen computer screen. A server touches the menu item displayed on the monitor. The third method employs a 10-key numeric keypad. A server presses a two- or three-digit price lookup code for each menu item selected. Regardless of the method used, at the end of a day or a meal period, management can obtain a printout from the terminal listing all menu items available and the number of portions of each that was sold.

One good example of computer software that provides this information easily is SilverWare POS. Daily sales statistics and server end-of-shift reports can be printed at any time. The software keeps track of historical sales information and provides over 100 built-in reports to management.

Data mining is a software-based information gathering and modelling technique that helps to process consumer information and find patterns and preferences from sales history databases. It can also be used to improve the guest's experience and the operator's effectiveness. Some savvy operators will maintain an individual data file on customers, noting their preferences, birthdays, anniversaries, etc. When the customer returns, the information is brought up on the computer and the guest is asked if she would like the same table and cocktail she had during her last visit. It provides a distinct customer service advantage.

The portion sales data is added to the cumulative records to date. If an establishment uses the manual methods described earlier, the data will be added to master records kept on file cards or in an analysis book. If electronic methods are used, the data may be transcribed manually on cards or in a book or added to a computer database or spreadsheet designed for this purpose. Regardless of whether the portion sales records are stored manually or electronically, they are likely to be arranged in one of three ways:

1. By *operating period*, such as one week or month, so that all sales records for an entire operating period can be viewed together on one page, card, or screen. See Figure 7.2 for the sales history of Bistro Quatre for the first 10 days of February.
2. By *day of the week*, so that all sales records for a given day (e.g., Tuesday) for a period of several weeks can be compared.
3. By *menu item*, so that the degree of popularity of a given item can be seen over time.

LEARNING OBJECTIVE 7.4
List three basic approaches to arranging data in a sales history.

• **FIGURE 7.2** •

Sales History

**Portions Sold
For the Period February 1–10**

Weather	Snow	Fair	Cold	Fair	Fair	Snow	Cold	Cold	Snow	Fair	Fair
Day	M	T	W	Th	F	S	S	M	T	W	Th
Date	1	2	3	4	5	6	7	8	9	10	11
Strip Steak	10	11	10	11	13	12	12	10	12	10	11
Tournedos Bistro	9	11	12	10	10	11	12	10	12	11	
Duck Breast	3	4	5	6	5	4	4	4	3	4	
Leg of Lamb	8	7	10	8	8	9	7	7	8	9	
Baby Back Ribs	4	6	6	7	6	5	5	5	7	7	
Tamarind and Ginger Shrimp	7	9	8	10	8	10	7	6	8	9	
Gnocchi	5	4	3	6	4	5	4	6	5	4	
Day	M	T	W	Th	F	S	S	M	T	W	Th
Date	1	2	3	4	5	6	7	8	9	10	11
Darjeeling-Smoked Salmon	12	11	13	10	13	12	11	11	9	12	11
Paella	11	9	8	11	7	10	9	12	8	9	
Big Eye Tuna	4	5	7	6	5	6	4	5	7	8	
Miso Glazed Black Cod	9	7	9	7	9	8	9	10	6	7	
Chicken Breast	8	11	7	11	11	10	9	7	9	8	
Tagliatelle	7	6	7	9	7	8	9	6	6	6	
Scallops	5	6	8	4	6	7	7	4	7	6	
Capellini	6	7	8	9	9	8	10	7	8	9	
Catch of the Day	8	9	11	9	11	10	9	9	9	10	

Many establishments have found it desirable to combine two of these systems to provide an overall picture of sales for the entire week at one glance. In addition, this approach provides some indication of the relative popularity of menu items as compared with other items on the same menu. Figure 7.3 illustrates a sales history arranged this way for Bistro Quatre.

• FIGURE 7.3 •

Sales History, by Weekday Portions Sold Arranged by Day of Week; Dates: February 1–10

Portions Sold — Arranged by Day of Week — Dates: February 1–10

Weather	Snow	Cold		Fair	Snow		Cold	Fair	Fair	Fair	Fair		Fair			Snow	Snow		Cold	Cold	
Day	Monday			Tuesday			Wednesday			Thursday			Friday			Saturday			Sunday		
Date	1	8	15	2	9	16	3	10	17	4	11	18	5	12	19	6	13	20	7	14	21
Item																					
Strip Steak	10	9		11	10		10	11		11			13			12			9		
Tournedos Bistro	9	10		11	12		12	11		10			10			11			12		
Duck Breast	3	4		4	3		5	4		6			5			4			5		
Leg of Lamb	8	7		7	8		10	9		8			8			9			7		
Baby Back Ribs	4	5		6	7		6	7		7			6			5			5		
Tamarind and Ginger Shrimp	7	6		9	8		8	9		10			8			10			7		
Gnocchi	5	6		4	5		3	4		6			4			5			4		
Darjeeling-Smoked Salmon	12	11		11	9		13	12		10			13			12			11		
Paella	11	12		9	8		8	9		11			7			10			9		
Big Eye Tuna	4	5		5	7		7	8		6			5			6			4		
Miso Glazed Black Cod	9	10		7	6		9	7		7			9			8			9		
Chicken Breast	8	7		11	9		7	8		11			11			10			9		
Tagliatelle	7	6		6	6		7	6		9			7			8			9		
Scallops	5	4		6	7		8	6		4			6			7			7		
Capellini	6	7		7	8		8	9		9			9			8			10		
Catch of the Day	8	9		9	9		11	10		9			11			10			9		
Total	116	118		123	122		132	130		134			132			135			125		

LEARNING OBJECTIVE 7.5
Define popularity index and
use a popularity index to
forecast portion sales.

Popularity Index

In addition to keeping records of numbers of portions sold, many foodservice operators use the data to determine a popularity index. **Popularity index (PI)** is defined as the ratio of portion sales for a given menu item to total portion sales for all menu items (or to items in the same category; comparing one appetizer with all appetizers sold or one main dish to all main dishes sold, for example), as illustrated in Figure 7.4. It represents the main dish sales at Bistro Quatre for the month of February.

The popularity index is calculated by dividing portion sales for a given item by the total portion sales for all menu items in the category and then multiplying by 100 in order to convert to a percentage. The index may be calculated for any time period, even for a single meal. When calculated for a single meal, the index is usually referred to as the sales mix, as was shown in Chapter 1. For example, the popularity index for Strip Steak at Bistro Quatre for the month of February is calculated as follows:

$$\text{Popularity index} = \frac{\text{Portion sales for item}}{\text{Total portion sales for all menu items}} \times 100$$

$$\frac{188}{1,937} = 0.09706 \text{ and } 0.09706 \times 100 = 9.706\%$$

These ratios are of far greater use in determining an item's popularity than the raw figures that simply indicate number of portions sold. For example, the sales history may show portion sales of Roasted Muscovy Duck Breast from a low of three portions (see Figure 7.2) to a high of six portions. This data would not be as useful as information indicating that Roasted Muscovy Duck Breast represented 3.252 percent of total sales for the month of February (see Figure 7.4). In many operations, particularly those with relatively stable menus, the popularity index is a key element in forecasting sales. The popularity index can also be useful in determining whether to continue offering a certain item on the menu. If an item consistently represents only 3.252 percent of total sales whenever it appears, serious consideration should be given to removing it from the menu and substituting a more popular item.

• FIGURE 7.4 •

Bistro Quatre Popularity Index, Month of February

Menu Item	Number Sold	Popularity Index %
Strip Steak	188	9.706
Tournedos Bistro	158	8.157
Duck Breast	63	3.252
Leg of Lamb	125	6.453
Baby Back Ribs	55	2.839

(continued)

Menu Item	Number Sold	Popularity Index %
• FIGURE 7.4 • *(continued)*		
Tamarind and Ginger Shrimp	164	8.467
Gnocchi	84	4.337
Darjeeling-Smoked Salmon	144	7.434
Paella	102	5.266
Big Eye Tuna	86	4.440
Miso Glazed Black Cod	107	5.524
Chicken Breast	166	8.570
Tagliatelle	122	6.298
Scallops	81	4.182
Capellini	123	6.350
Catch of the Day	169	8.725
Total Covers	1,937	100.000

Other Information in Sales Histories

Good managers can use their experience and knowledge to help predict fluctuations in future sales, and their input will be valuable to forecasting. In addition, sales histories often include provisions for recording additional relevant information—internal and external conditions that affect sales volume. One of the most common of these conditions is the weather. Most foodservice operators find that weather conditions have a noticeable impact on sales volume. In many establishments, bad weather has a clearly negative impact on sales volume, so including some information about the weather each day can often help explain why sales were high or low on that day. Interestingly, hotels and motels in major metropolitan centres often find the impact of weather on sales to be the opposite of that experienced by neighbouring free-standing restaurant operators: bad weather seems to increase food and beverage sales in these properties, probably because it discourages guests from going out to nearby restaurants. Figure 7.3 shows the weather for the first 10 days in the month.

Special events can decidedly influence sales and are often included in sales histories. The occurrence of a national holiday on a particular day or the presence of a particular convention group in a hotel can affect sales considerably. So can such varied conditions as faulty kitchen equipment, street construction in front of the restaurant, or a major sale at a nearby store. In hotel restaurants, the *house count*—or the number of people registered in the hotel on a particular day—is often included so that an organization can determine the percentage of registered guests who are using the hotel's restaurants. With this information, judgements can be made regarding numbers of portions to prepare for a given rate of occupancy. In general, one should include in the sales history any information about conditions and events that have affected sales and that should be considered in future forecasts.

Forecasting Portion Sales

Sales forecasting is a process in which managers use data and intuition to predict what is likely to occur in the future. It amounts to intelligent, educated guesswork about future events. If one can predict the future with reasonable accuracy, appropriate plans can be made to prepare an enterprise for dealing with the predicted events. In the food industry, which deals with highly perishable products, predicting accurately and planning properly can be major factors in operating profitably.

Forecasting is a principal element of cost control. If sales volume can be predicted accurately, then plans can be made for purchasing and preparing appropriate quantities of food. Purchasing unneeded quantities can be avoided, thus reducing the possibilities for waste, spoilage, and pilferage. In addition, plans can be made for producing particular numbers of portions for sale on particular dates, thus reducing the possibilities for excessive costs of food and labour. Moreover, establishing control over purchasing can lead automatically to control over production: It is impossible to prepare a greater number of portions than necessary if the raw materials for overproduction do not exist.

A usual first step in forecasting is to predict total anticipated volume: total numbers of customers anticipated for particular days or particular meals. To arrive at a figure, one refers to the sales history to find the total number of sales recorded on each of a number of comparable dates in the recent past. When great differences are apparent, reasonable efforts must be made to determine the reasons for the differences. The causes are often revealed by information in the history relating to weather and other external conditions that existed at the time of the sales. The effect of each of these conditions must be assessed—some increase sales, others decrease them. In Figure 7.5, the initial sales forecast for Thursday, February 11, at Bistro Quatre indicates management initially expects 134 customers.

When the effects of surrounding conditions have been evaluated, the next step is to judge the extent to which these conditions will affect sales on the particular date or dates for which one is preparing the forecast. This may involve checking a local calendar for coming events, following weather forecasts, and looking into various other relevant sources of information. Figure 7.5 shows an adjusted forecast of 120 persons, rather than the 134 originally forecasted, because of predicted snow that will fall and decrease the number of customers expected. After these steps have been taken, it is possible to estimate the total business volume that may be anticipated for the period.

The next step is to forecast the sales of each item on the menu. This is simpler to do if the menu is identical to those that have appeared on Thursdays in the past. However, it can also be done for changing menus if the sales history is set up to reflect the relative popularity of individual items as compared with a changing variety of other items appearing on the same menu. This type of forecasting is more difficult, but by no means impossible. When restaurants use many daily specials, forecasting can still be fairly accurate. Again, maintaining a sales history of previous specials will

FOOD PRODUCTION CONTROL: ESTABLISHING STANDARDS AND STANDARD PROCEDURES ■ 199

• FIGURE 7.5 •

Production Sheet

Day _Thursday_   Date _February 11, 20XX_

Menu Item	Total Forecast		PI		Portion Forecast	Adjusted Forecast		PI		Adjusted Portion Forecast
					Volume Forecast					
Strip Steak	134	X	0.09706	=	13	120	X	0.09706	=	12
Tournedos Bistro	134	X	0.08157	=	11	120	X	0.08157	=	10
Duck Breast	134	X	0.03252	=	4	120	X	0.03252	=	4
Leg of Lamb	134	X	0.06453	=	9	120	X	0.06453	=	8
Baby Back Ribs	134	X	0.02839	=	4	120	X	0.02839	=	3
Tamarind and Ginger Shrimp	134	X	0.08467	=	11	120	X	0.08467	=	10
Gnocchi	134	X	0.04337	=	6	120	X	0.04337	=	5
Darjeeling-Smoked Salmon	134	X	0.07434	=	10	120	X	0.07434	=	9
Paella	134	X	0.05266	=	7	120	X	0.05266	=	6
Big Eye Tuna	134	X	0.0444	=	6	120	X	0.0444	=	5
Miso Glazed Black Cod	134	X	0.05524	=	7	120	X	0.05524	=	7
Chicken Breast	134	X	0.0857	=	11	120	X	0.0857	=	10
Tagliatelle	134	X	0.06298	=	8	120	X	0.06298	=	8
Scallops	134	X	0.04182	=	6	120	X	0.04182	=	5
Capellini	134	X	0.0635	=	9	120	X	0.0635	=	8
Catch of the Day	134	X	0.08725	=	12	120	X	0.08725	=	10
Total					134.0					120.0

be extremely beneficial in developing production forecasts. When the main ingredient of the new special matches the historical one, sales forecasts should be similar. For example, if on a Wednesday evening last month a Calves' Liver Special sold 10 portions, forecasted sales of a similar Calves' Liver Special this Wednesday night, with a similar number of covers expected, should also be for 10 portions.

If the sales history shows both portion sales and popularity index, the popularity index is the easier to use for predicting. For example, if Strip Steak has represented 9.706 percent of total sales (see Figure 7.4) in the past, it would be fairly safe to predict that Strip Steak would represent the same percentage of the anticipated 120 sales, or 12 portions. Thus, to forecast portion sales of a given item, one multiplies total forecasted portion sales by the decimal equivalent of the popularity index (PI) for the given item:

$$\text{Popularity index} \div 100 = \text{decimal equivalent of PI}$$

thus:

$$9.706 \div 100 = 0.09706$$

$$\text{Total forecasted portion sales for all menu items} \times \text{decimal equivalent}$$
$$\text{of PI} = \text{Forecasted sales of individual menu item}$$

Thus:

$$120 \times .09706 = 11.647 \text{ or } 12 \text{ portions}$$

After this has been done for every item that will appear on the menu, the result is a forecast of anticipated sales for a particular day or period. However, this forecast must be considered flexible, subject to change as conditions change. A change in the weather forecast, for example, might indicate a need to change the number of sales forecast if there is sufficient time to do so. Also, specific information about particular situations also enters into the forecast. Thus, the adjusted forecast shows one additional portion of Scallops beyond the initial forecast based on some specific knowledge of customers coming into the restaurant that Thursday and their preference for that menu item.

After one member of the management team has developed the forecast, another member of the team should review it. Forecasting is educated guess-work, and two heads are usually better than one. The completed forecast represents management's best judgement of the sales volume anticipated and should be shared with appropriate personnel. The chef can use this information to schedule appropriate amounts of staff both for preparation and for service. The dining room manager will also develop a schedule for the wait staff based on these numbers. The aim is to have sufficient personnel on duty for each meal while avoiding excess staff and controlling labour costs. Purchasing can also be done accurately. With information about anticipated portion sales for each menu item, the chef is better equipped to order properly, or to advise the steward on the appropriate quantities of food to have on hand. If sales of 12 portions of strip steak are forecasted for Thursday, the restaurant need not purchase a greater quantity of the perishable ingredients than necessary. The consequent control of purchasing can be one of the most important factors in limiting excessive costs. When needed quantities are known, only those quantities should be purchased.

It should be noted that the popularity index is not the only method for forecasting sales in the hospitality industry. The random walk, in which the forecast is based on the previous day's sales (i.e., yesterday's actual sales is equal to today's forecasted sales) is clearly the simplest method, but it is also the least accurate and can only be used efficiently in operations where business volume varies little from day to day, such as an office cafeteria. Another method that is often employed by foodservice managers is the moving average, in which the manager looks at the business volume for the previous two or three days and then finds the average business volume for the corresponding two or three days, and that becomes today's forecast. For example, if the previous two days' sales volume were recorded as 453 and 465, then we would find the forecast as follows:

$$453 + 465 \div 2 = 459 \text{ total anticipated sales}$$

This may not work well where sales vary greatly each specific day of the week. For example, many restaurants are consistently 100 to 300 percent busier on Saturday than on Monday.

Forecasting Without a Sales History

In a new operation or an expansion, it takes a bit more educated guesswork to forecast sales. New businesses will obviously have great volatility, but forecasting is still necessary and with proper management will improve quickly. Most new restaurants do not want to run out of menu items and may forecast higher numbers to avoid that problem. Some operations make allowances for excessive food cost the first few days or weeks, then trim those tolerances over time. Although it is difficult to make forecasts with no sales history, having an experienced manager who knows the marketplace, who can "guesstimate" numbers of covers, and who can reasonably assess what the popularity index of the menu items may be, will be of great benefit. Once the first few days of operation are behind it, a restaurant's sales history accrues rapidly. After only one day, there is a bank of data to draw from, and by the end of the week the value of the historical sales data increases greatly. When production numbers and sales are reconciled and analyzed, there is a steep learning curve and production estimates can gain efficiency quickly.

Forecasting Software

There is now software offering forecasting for hotels, casinos, and food and beverage outlets. One company producing such software is Carnus Systems, which develops and implements automated demand forecasting and scheduling software for the hospitality industry. These packages combine sales history and other data with artificial intelligence to predict numbers of sales, covers, and guests. Those forecasts can then be converted into work schedules. The system works over the Internet and is a highly sophisticated way to forecast demand and control costs by controlling scheduling and production.

DETERMINING PRODUCTION QUANTITIES

The Production Sheet

LEARNING OBJECTIVE 7.6
Describe the production sheet and calculate needed production for menu items.

A **production sheet** is a form to list the names and quantities of all menu items that are to be prepared for a given date or service. Production sheets such as that illustrated in Figure 7.5 translate management's portion sales forecasts into production targets. Production sheets list menu items and quantities in terms that the chef and staff can use for production. In some cases (e.g., with sirloin steaks), quantity is stated in portions. In others (e.g., beef stew and chicken noodle soup), quantity may be stated in terms of total production rather than number of portions. The production sheet is best viewed as a tool used by management to control production and eliminate waste.

Production sheets vary in form and complexity from one kitchen to another. A very simple form appears in Figure 7.5. It would be filled out by a manager and forwarded to the chef as many days in advance as possible. Upon receiving it, the chef would have valuable information about both total anticipated volume for a particular meal and the number of portion sales anticipated for each item on the menu. With this information in hand, a chef is better equipped to determine needs for perishable foods, for which orders will be placed, and for nonperishable foods, which would be requisitioned from the storeroom. Note that the form includes a column for adjusting the forecasted figure upward or downward on the basis of changes in the weather or other conditions likely to affect sales.

Ideally, changes in the forecast will be minor. In any case, adjustments can be made immediately before the forecasted date—the night before or even the morning of the date in question. The final figures in the "Adjusted Forecast" column are the final production goals for the kitchen for the date. With those goals in mind, the chef will proceed to produce the required quantities, ensuring that enough food preparation is ready for service, and seeing to it that leftover ingredients are used in meeting those goals whenever possible, provided that their use does not violate the establishment's quality standards.

In some operations, this very simple version of the production sheet would be considered inadequate. If additional control over production is necessary or desirable, a more elaborate form can be used. Such a form is illustrated in Figure 7.6.

• **FIGURE 7.6** •

A More Elaborate Production Sheet

Day _Thursday_   Date _February 11, 20XX_

Menu Item	Forecast	Adjusted Forecast	Portion Size	Production Method	Portions on Hand	Needed Production	Total Available	Left Over
Strip Steak	13	12	340 g	Broil	4	8	12	
Tournedos Bistro	11	10	170 g	Pan Sear		10	10	
Duck Breast	4	4	1 ea.	Roast		4	4	
Leg of Lamb	9	8	2 ea.	Roast	3	5	8	
Baby Back Ribs	4	3	113 g	BBQ		3	3	
Tamarind and Ginger Shrimp	11	10	6 ea.	Sauté		10	10	
Gnocchi	6	5	142 g	Sauté		5	5	
Darjeeling-Smoked Salmon	10	9	198 g	Broil		9	9	
Paella	7	6	1 breast	Sauté		6	6	
Big Eye Tuna	6	5	276 g	Broil	1	4	5	
Miso Glazed Black Cod	7	7	340 g	Sauté	3	4	7	
Chicken Breast	11	10	1 ea.	Sauté		10	10	
Tagliatelle	8	8	1 ea.	Sauté		8	8	
Scallops	6	5	6 ea.	Sauté		5	5	
Capellini	9	8	Recipe #1	Sauté		8	8	
Catch of the Day	12	10	276 g	TBA		10	10	
Total	134	120						

This form establishes greater control in several ways. It restates the portion size for each item, thus continually re-emphasizing management's concern that the size of each portion served be carefully controlled. This may be particularly important in establishments that offer portions of different sizes for luncheon, for dinner, and for banquets. It also directs the kitchen staff in the production method to be employed, which can be important when there are several recipes for the same item and management chooses to specify one particular recipe.

The purpose of the "Portions on Hand" column is to induce the chef to take an inventory of leftovers from the previous day or meal before starting production. Although this practice is inappropriate in some establishments because of their quality standards, it is permissible in others.

The figure in the "Total Available" column (the sum of leftover portions and additional portions produced) should equal the figure in the "Adjusted Forecast" column. As an additional control, there is a column for portions left over. Whenever possible, this figure should be carried over to the production sheet for the next day or meal, to ensure that these leftovers will be sold. If portions of uncooked meats have been left over and the number recorded cannot be located the following day or for the next meal, one can begin to suspect pilferage. If so, immediate steps can be taken to eliminate future problems.

Regardless of the degree of complexity of production sheets, their basic purpose is to establish control by setting goals for production. Controlling production is necessary to eliminate a major cause of excessive cost. Under ideal conditions, no unsold portions would ever be left over after a meal. Everyone recognizes that this is impossible, but it is a desirable goal nevertheless. If the number of unsold portions can be reduced or eliminated, food cost can be better controlled and excessive costs eliminated. It is with this goal in mind that management uses production sheets.

In most operations, the cost of main course items represents the major share of total food cost. Meats, fish, and other proteins usually account for the largest portion of food cost per customer served and require additional control procedures to reduce waste and inefficiency. Some of these additional procedures are covered later in this chapter.

To make judgements about the accuracy of a forecast, one must have detailed information about the forecast and about sales on the day for which the forecast was prepared. For the former, a copy of the forecast is necessary; for the latter, full details would be available in the sales history. Information from both sources can be recorded on a form such as that illustrated in Figure 7.7.

Examination of the specific information provided in Figure 7.7 indicates that the sales forecast differed from actual sales by only two portions. The total of actual portion sales was 98.3 percent of the total forecasted, a degree of accuracy that most foodservice operators would likely find acceptable. Examination of the figures for individual menu items suggests the following:

• FIGURE 7.7 •							
Comparison: Sales Forecast and Actual Sales							
Day *Thursday*			*Date* *February 11, 20XX*				
Volume Forecast							
Menu Item		*Sales Forecast*		*Actual Sales*		*Difference*	
Strip Steak		12		13		1	
Tournedos Bistro		10		8		−2	
Duck Breast		4		3		−1	
Leg of Lamb		8		10		2	
Baby Back Ribs		3		2		−1	
Tamarind and Ginger Shrimp		10		11		1	
Gnocchi		5		4		−1	
Darjeeling-Smoked Salmon		9		9			
Paella		6		6			
Big Eye Tuna		5		6		1	
Miso Glazed Black Cod		7		7			
Chicken Breast		10		10			
Tagliatelle		8		7		−1	
Scallops		5		6		1	
Capellini		8		7		−1	
Catch of the Day		10		9		−1	
Total		120		118		−2	

1. Strip Steak, Leg of Lamb, Tamarind and Ginger Shrimp, Big Eye Tuna, and Scallops were underforecasted. Total portion sales were six over the number forecasted, and one would question where these portions came from. It is possible that they were produced by reducing the size of other portions, so a number of customers received less than the standard portion size. Alternatively, these six additional portions may have been produced from inventory.

2. Darjeeling-Smoked Salmon, Paella, Miso Glazed Black Cod, and Chicken Breast appear to have been perfectly forecasted. However, it is possible that the kitchen ran out of these items before the end of the meal period, and late customers who had wanted to order one of these items were forced to make alternative selections. If this was the case, then actual sales of other items may be higher than they would have been otherwise. It is important, therefore, that someone make an appropriate notation in the sales history about the time any item runs out so that this information may be taken into account when other forecasts are made in the future. In many restaurants, the host or hostess notes this kind of information in a logbook that is kept in the dining room.

3. Items that sold fewer portions than were forecasted indicate a need to improve the accuracy of forecasts. In addition, these figures suggest the possibility of excessive costs if these items cannot be reused.

It is important to keep in mind that the data recorded in Figure 7.7 are not related to actual kitchen production in any useful way. Figure 7.7 merely compares numbers forecasted with numbers sold. The next logical step is to monitor the performance of the kitchen staff to judge how closely the chef has followed the production quantity standards provided on the production sheet for the day. To do this, it is necessary to establish a procedure for keeping records of portions rejected by customers and returned from the dining room. Such records may be kept on a form known as a void sheet, illustrated in Figure 7.8.

• FIGURE 7.8 •

Void Sheet

Day   <u>Saturday</u>   Date   <u>6-Feb</u>

Cheque	Server	Item	Reason for Return	Authorization		Sales Value
11031	6	Strip Steak	Too well done	PRD		$23.65
11034	6	Strip Steak	Dropped on floor	PRD		$23.65
11226	8	Gnocchi	Incorrectly ordered	PRD		$16.50

The Void Sheet

LEARNING OBJECTIVE 7.7
Describe a void sheet and explain its use.

Every restaurant offering steaks, chops, and similar à la carte main courses has had some experience with portions being rejected by customers and returned from the dining room for one reason or another. Sometimes portions are returned by customers who are difficult or impossible to please. However, there are many occasions when portions are returned because some staff member was not listening carefully. Sometimes it is a careless server, sometimes an indifferent or overworked cook. In any case, regardless of who failed to listen or why the item presented to the customer was returned. These returned portions are excellent examples of excessive cost and should not be ignored. Many restaurants record customer returns on a void sheet.

Whenever a portion is returned, an authorized individual, such as a manager, chef, or kitchen supervisor, records it on the **void sheet**, indicating the name of the item, the number of the cheque on which it appeared, and the reason for its return. These entries can be most revealing to an alert manager, chef, or food controller. For example, if one particular server appears on the list with greater than usual regularity, it is possible that he or she is not paying careful attention to customer orders. This can quickly lead to unwarranted and excessive costs for the restaurant and should be attended to quickly. By contrast, it may be noted that the number of grilled items returned is far greater when one particular employee is working. This may suggest the need for the chef to observe this employee's performance and, if warranted, take corrective action to improve it. If the number of returns is consistently high and evenly distributed among job classifications, investigation may indicate general understaffing. This finding may suggest a need for additional personnel to improve customer service.

There are other important uses of the void sheet, particularly when efforts are being made to control portions of preportioned mains (described in the following section). If all portions are not accounted for, kitchen personnel can easily claim that some were discarded after being returned by difficult customers. If all returned portions must be recorded on the void sheet and attested to by a member of the management team, it is more difficult for kitchen personnel to be careless with food. In addition, the recording of returned portions, along with other techniques previously described, makes possible the reconciliation of kitchen records of portions produced and records of portions sold.

Portion Inventory and Reconciliation

A useful means of determining how closely the chef has followed quantity production standards established for the day requires the use of the **portion inventory and reconciliation** sheet illustrated in Figure 7.9. The procedure follows logically from the production sheet illustrated in Figure 7.6. In fact, Figure 7.9 may best be viewed as an elaboration on Figure 7.6, although the production sheet is prepared before the meal period and the portion inventory and reconciliation sheet is prepared after the meal.

LEARNING OBJECTIVE 7.8
Complete a portion inventory and reconciliation.

Using this approach effectively requires that one follow a series of logical steps. First, each menu item should be listed on the form before kitchen production begins. Next, an inventory is taken of any portions left over from previous meals that may be used again. Reusing leftovers in this way is common in some establishments, but unacceptable in others.

If leftovers are to be used, the number of portions on hand is deducted from the quantity scheduled for production, and only the difference is prepared. That number is written in the "Portions Prepared" column. Additional quantities

• FIGURE 7.9 •

Portion Inventory and Reconciliation

Day Thursday   Date February 11, 20XX

Menu Item	Portion Production						Sales Reconciliation					
	Opening Inventory	Portions Prepared	Additional Preparation	Total Available	Closing Inventory	Portions Consumed	Portions Sold	Portions Voided	Total	Portions Consumed	Difference	Comment
Strip Steak	4	8	3	15		15	13	2	15	15		
Tournedos Bistro		10		10	2	8	8		8	8		
Duck Breast		4		4	1	3	3		3	3		
Leg of Lamb	3	5	2	10		10	10		10	10		
Baby Back Ribs		3		3	1	2	2		2	2		
Tamarind and Ginger Shrimp		10	1	11		11	11		11	11		
Gnocchi		5		5		5	4	1	5	5		
Darjeeling-Smoked Salmon		9	1	10		10	9		9	10	1	Given to Chef's Brother
Paella		6		6		6	6		6	6		
Big Eye Tuna	1	4	1	6		6	6		6	6		
Miso Glazed Black Cod	3	4	1	8		8	7		7	8	1	Comp. to Customer
Chicken Breast		10		10		10	10		10	10		
Tagliatelle		8		8	1	7	7		7	7		
Scallops		5	1	6		6	6		6	6		
Capellini		8		8	1	7	7		7	7		
Catch of the Day		10		10	1	9	9		9	9		
Total	11	109	10	130	7	123	118	3	121	123		

prepared, if any, are recorded in the next column. At the conclusion of the meal period, an inventory is taken of the portions on hand, and the information is recorded in the column headed "Closing Inventory." When these columns are completed, the form is given to a manager.

For each menu item, the manager adds opening inventory, portions prepared, and additional preparation to determine total available. Closing inventory is subtracted from the total available to obtain the number of portions consumed. Having determined the number of portions consumed according to kitchen records, the manager obtains from the cashier (or from the sales recorded in the computer) the record of portions sold from the sales history. These are recorded in the "Portions Sold" column. The number of portions voided or returned to the kitchen is recorded in the "Portions Voided" column and then added to "Portions Sold." The result is entered in the "Total" column.

The next step is to determine the difference, if any, between the kitchen records and the portion sales records. That difference is written in the appropriate column. In the example given, kitchen records show the production of 123 cooked portions, and sales records indicate only 121 portions sold. The difference (two portions) should be investigated immediately while events are still fresh in the minds of the personnel involved. Once the causes of the discrepancy have been identified, steps can be taken to eliminate them in the future. In this example, the discrepancy is explained in the comment column.

Although this technique is most useful to restaurants serving foods cooked to order, it can be helpful in other establishments as well. Its use requires that someone be able to estimate with some degree of accuracy the number of portions contained in, say, a steam table pan of beef goulash. The resulting information will not be precise, but it can be useful for identifying problems.

If portion sizes are carefully controlled and standard portion costs are known, the number of portions unaccounted for can be translated into dollars quite simply. In the previous example, if the missing portion of salmon has a standard cost of $5.75 and the portion of Black Cod has a standard cost of $7.75, then simple arithmetic determines that the loss of these portions has increased costs by $13.50 on that particular day. If there were no explanation for the missing two portions, an unacceptable loss would have occurred. While $13.50 is not a large amount, if equal losses occur seven days a week throughout the year, this would amount to a weekly cost of $94.50 and an annual cost of $4,914, a substantial amount. If this cost is considered excessive, management should find ways of eliminating it. If the cost can be eliminated without increasing other costs, profits will be increased by the amount saved.

As mentioned, two portions missing without explanation may seem to be too small a number to be concerned about, but these two portions represent 11.11 percent of the two items produced. The production of these portions has increased food cost figures. They have not been sold, so food sales figures have not increased by an appropriate amount. The net effect is an unwarranted increase in the food cost percent. Taking preventive steps would be advisable.

This procedure for reconciling portion production and sales is useful, but it is usually applicable only to main course items. In most instances, extending its use to cover other items on the menu would be unwieldy. Although it is true that main dish items usually represent the greatest proportion of cost, this does not mean that the cost of other items can be ignored. Overproducing appetizers, salads, and desserts can also lead to excessive costs if appropriate numbers for preparation and production are not established and followed.

The portion reconciliation also does not take into account any waste that may have occurred in the preparation of the number of portions that were finally listed on the form. It is possible, for example, that several steaks were improperly cut and so discarded, never having been listed on the reconciliation form.

Another problem is excessive **mise en place**, or preparation, of the ingredients that are served with the main. Often, restaurants serve costly garnishes and sauces with main course items. Production quantities for these preparations should, of course, mirror the numbers of corresponding mains that are to be produced, but this does not always happen. If a grilled steak comes with a red wine and shallot jus, roasted garlic and buttermilk mashed potatoes, and fresh steamed asparagus, and 10 portions of steaks are forecasted, then the appropriate amounts of sauce, potato, and asparagus should be made. If 5 millilitres of shallots in 55 millilitres of sauce is served with each steak along with 227 grams of mashed potatoes and 170 grams of fresh asparagus, then 10 times those amounts should be prepped. Most restaurants will not produce exactly 50 millilitres of shallots, 2,270 grams of mashed potatoes, or 1,700 grams of asparagus. More often than not they will use these items for other purposes as well and more production would be required. Preparing an amount appropriate for a day's sales is the preferred method and this amount is usually determined by observation rather than by using information from sales history. A daily production sheet of mise en place is often used as a control. Excessive cost can easily develop if these items are overproduced. They are not as valuable as steak or shrimp, but costs add up quickly when these items do not produce appropriate sales. These items also require extensive labour, perhaps even more than the main item they accompany. Excessive labour due to overproduction can be more onerous than excessive food cost. As always, establishing and monitoring proper forecasts and production quantity standards for these accompaniments is essential to profitability and should not be overlooked.

For these and other reasons, some large establishments, with the personnel and time necessary to complete the work, prepare various daily reports in addition to portion inventory and reconciliation, to determine the dollar difference between standard costs and actual costs. These topics are discussed in Chapter 10.

CONTROL OF PREPORTIONED MAINS

LEARNING OBJECTIVE 7.9
Describe a procedure used for controlling high-cost, preportioned main course items.

Another useful technique for controlling the preparation of quantities of specialized items is illustrated in Figure 7.10. Steaks, chops, and similar expensive main dish items are either purchased already portioned or portioned in the restaurant before cooking. These items are usually cooked to order and are typically held in a refrigerator close to the broiler or range. In such circumstances, the cook is usually responsible for putting the items on the fire when they are ordered.

Therefore, many managers and food controllers find it useful to make the cook fully responsible for these expensive items by requiring him or her to sign a form such as that illustrated in Figure 7.10. By signing, the cook acknowledges receiving the number of portions of each item indicated. If Bistro Quatre used this form, Figure 7.10 illustrates how it would apply to its menu.

The number of portions that the steward issues should be equal to the number of sales forecasted for each item. In case the forecasted number is incorrect, provision is made for additional issues, for which the cook will also sign. At the conclusion of serving hours, the number issued can be totalled in the next column. The number of portions returned, if any, will be entered in the "Returned to Steward" column, and the steward will sign for the returns. Total issues minus returns equals the number of portions consumed, and the steward fills in this figure before giving the completed form to the manager.

An advantage of this procedure is that it makes the cook accountable for a particular number of portions. Knowing the certainty of being questioned about missing portions, a cook is less likely to give any away to staff members.

• FIGURE 7.10 •

Control Sheet for Preportioned Mains

Day _Thursday_   Date _February 11, 20XX_

Menu Item		Portions Issued	Additional Issues	Total Issues	Returned to Steward	Portions Consumed
Strip Steak		12	3	15		15
Tournedos Bistro		10		10	2	8
Duck Breast		4		4	1	3
Leg of Lamb		8	2	10		10
Baby Back Ribs		3		3	1	2
Tamarind and Ginger Shrimp		10	1	11		11

(*continued*)

• **FIGURE 7.10** • (continued)						
Menu Item		Portions Issued	Additional Issues	Total Issues	Returned to Steward	Portions Consumed
Gnocchi		5		5		5
Darjeeling-Smoked Salmon		9	1	10		10
Paella		6		6		6
Big Eye Tuna		5	1	6		6
Miso Glazed Black Cod		7	1	8		8
Chicken Breast		10		10		10
Tagliatelle		8		8	1	7
Scallops		5	1	6		6
Capellini		8		8	1	7
Catch of the Day		10		10	1	9
Total		120	10	130	7	123
Issues Received		*Jack*				
Additional Issues		*Jack*				
Returned Portions Received *Paul Smith*, Steward						

A WORD OF CAUTION

In this chapter, we have illustrated many forms that are applicable to controlling the number of portions prepared and served. One should keep in mind that no establishment uses all of these forms. They should be used selectively to meet the needs of the particular foodservice operation. Bistro Quatre, for example, uses the forms illustrated in figures 7.3, 7.5, and 7.9. Management has determined that these three forms are all that is necessary to maintain control over portions produced. Other establishments will use other forms. For example, a steakhouse that prepares its mains over an open-hearth grill in the dining room might use the form shown in Figure 7.10. Most restaurants would choose only one of the forms shown in figures 7.2, 7.3, and 7.4.

THINGS TO CONSIDER

Operations that purchase portion-controlled main courses like steak or salmon realize that these items are expensive. But what they may not realize is that the true cost includes the cost of the food and the labour expense to clean and portion it, and all of the other associated costs of overhead, packaging, and distribution. There are some obvious control benefits to using these portion-controlled items, but there are also potential problems.

Restaurants that need to serve large numbers of covers in short periods of time, such as those located near a theatre, will often partially pre-cook these items. Most of the guests will order at the same time and need to leave at the same time, just before the show starts. Because of this, steaks may be marked on the grill, just before service, cooking them only to blue/rare, and salmon might be pan seared, also cooked only to rare. When a large number of guests order almost simultaneously, the steaks and salmon can be merely reheated and plated with the appropriate garnishes. This is an excellent way to facilitate service and meet the demands of the guests.

Pre-cooking does, however, require a high level of accuracy in forecasting portion sales. The cost of these items is higher now than it was as purchased, because it includes not only the significant cost of the portion control item but the additional labour costs to prepare it for expedited service as well. If the sales expectation is too low, guests will be unhappy if their chosen dish is unavailable, or conversely, costs will increase if portions go unsold. If these items go to waste, costs will suffer badly. Selling leftovers is another problem associated with over-production. Perhaps yesterday's steak and salmon portions, still in acceptable condition, can be reused today, but what about tomorrow or the next day? If guests notice diminished quality it could be more costly to the business in the long run than throwing out the portion and accepting the loss. These are difficult problems to deal with operationally. The best way to minimize and prevent them is to do your legwork and forecast well.

CHAPTER ESSENTIALS

In this chapter, we explained the application of the control process to the quantity production phase of foodservice operations. We described the standard for controlling production volume as determining and producing, for any menu item, the number of portions that is likely to be sold on any given day, and discussed techniques for establishing that standard. We defined sales history and described the means of collecting the data included in a sales history. We illustrated several possible patterns for maintaining sales histories. We defined the *popularity index* and illustrated its calculation. We explained how the sales history and popularity index are used to prepare a forecast of portion sales. We identified the production sheet and explained its use. We described several techniques for monitoring performance: comparing the sales forecast with actual sales in order to make judgements about the accuracy of the forecast, and comparing production records with sales records to determine the extent to which kitchen production has matched the production sheet and been converted into sales dollars. We illustrated a technique for controlling and accounting for such preportioned items as steaks and chops.

KEY TERMS IN THIS CHAPTER

Mise en place, p. 210
Popularity index (PI), p. 196
Portion inventory and reconciliation, p. 207
Production sheet, p. 202

Sales forecasting, p. 198
Sales history, p. 191
Void sheet, p. 207

QUESTIONS AND PROBLEMS

1. Calculate the popularity index for the following sales. Round each result to the nearest 1 percent.

   a. | Item | Portions sold |
      |------|---------------|
      | A | 60 |
      | B | 20 |
      | C | 80 |
      | D | 40 |

   b. | Item | Portions sold |
      |------|---------------|
      | A | 30 |
      | B | 42 |
      | C | 73 |
      | D | 115 |

   c. | Item | Portions sold |
      |------|---------------|
      | A | 86 |
      | B | 113 |
      | C | 55 |
      | D | 44 |
      | E | 25 |

2. Using the popularity indexes calculated in Question 1a, predict the sales for each item if total sales for all items are expected to be 300.

3. Using the popularity indexes calculated in Question 1b, predict the sales for each item if total sales for all items are expected to be 150.

4. Using the popularity indexes calculated in Question 1c, predict the sales for each item if total sales for all items are expected to be 450.

5. Using the forecast developed in Question 2, assume that this forecast must be adjusted to indicate 20 percent fewer sales than had been forecasted originally. Using Figure 7.5 as a guide, prepare a production sheet showing both the original forecast and the adjusted forecast.

6. Using the forecast developed in Question 3, assume that this forecast must be adjusted to indicate 10 percent more sales than had been forecasted originally. Using Figure 7.5 as a guide, prepare a production sheet showing both the original forecast and the adjusted forecast.

7. List and discuss four possible causes of discrepancies between figures listed in the "Portions Consumed" and "Portions Sold" columns on the form illustrated in Figure 7.9.

8. Explain the value of having a sales history available when attempting to create a restaurant sales forecast.

9. What advantages and disadvantages do you see in using each of the two methods described in this chapter for gathering information for a sales history?

10. Describe the procedure identified in this chapter that is used for controlling high-cost preportioned mains.

11. If a manager were looking for ways to reduce excessive food costs, would void sheets be of any use? Why?

12. What role can an electronic sales terminal play in developing a sales history?

13. Define each of the key terms in this chapter.

EXCEL EXERCISES

Exercise 7.1
Complete the sales history for Barnaby's Hideaway, as shown in Exercise 7.1 on the companion website for this text, and calculate the popularity index for each main during the entire 10-day period.

Exercise 7.2
Follow the instructions on the companion website for this exercise.

Exercise 7.3
Follow the instructions on the companion website for this exercise.

CHAPTER 8

Monitoring Foodservice Operations I: Monthly Inventory and Monthly Food Cost

• LEARNING OBJECTIVES •

After reading this chapter, you should be able to:

8.1 Explain the importance of monitoring a foodservice operation to assess monthly performance.

8.2 Describe the procedure for taking physical inventory at the end of the month.

8.3 Distinguish between opening (beginning) inventory and closing (ending) inventory.

8.4 List and describe five ways to assign unit costs to a food inventory and explain the effect on cost of each method.

8.5 Calculate cost of food consumed.

8.6 Calculate cost of food sold.

8.7 Prepare a simple monthly food cost report and calculate monthly food cost percent.

8.8 Explain the possible shortcomings of a system in which judgements about operations are made exclusively based on monthly food cost and food cost percent.

8.9 Define *inventory turnover* and explain how it is determined.

INTRODUCTION

LEARNING OBJECTIVE 8.1
Explain the importance of monitoring a foodservice operation to assess monthly performance.

In the preceding chapters, we examined the methods used to establish the control process through several phases of foodservice operations, including purchasing, receiving, storing, issuing, and production. It is useful to engage in a close examination of the individual phases of an operation. Foodservice managers must be able to do that, and be able to look at the whole operation and monitor its overall performance.

In Chapter 2, it was explained that the control process encompasses four critical steps:

1. Establish standards and standard procedures for operations.
2. Train all individuals to follow established standards and standard procedures.
3. Monitor performance and compare actual performance with established standards.
4. Take appropriate action to correct deviations from standards.

Thus, having addressed the establishment of standards and standard procedures over some of the more critical phases of foodservice operations, we now examine the techniques and procedures used by managers to monitor an entire operation. The most common approach to monitoring is one requiring that various procedures and calculations be completed at the end of each month. Some operators use 13 four-week units rather than 12 calendar months for a year's statement. The calendar month is the basic unit of time in the accounting process, and most of the procedures described in this chapter are actually accounting procedures designed to provide chefs and managers with monthly reports that measure the results of business operations. Although they might not be sufficiently detailed to pinpoint specific problems in an enterprise, they can provide some reasonable estimate of overall financial health through the end of the most recent month. For example, a restaurant with food and beverage costs of 30 percent, labour costs of 35 percent, and overhead of 20 percent is clearly in better financial health than an establishment with food and beverage costs of 40 percent, labour costs of 40 percent, and other costs of 20 percent. The latter has difficulty, obviously, but one cannot tell from this limited information which phases of operation are causing the difficulty. Imprecise as these figures are, without them management would have no idea of the existence or the extent of difficulty until it is too late to undertake some form of corrective action. Some operators think even a month is too long a wait to uncover problems and so they may do inventory weekly or bi-weekly.

In addition to providing management with information indicating the financial results of business operations, these monthly accounting procedures provide information that can be useful for assessing the various control procedures established for the operation.

This chapter describes the procedures for determining monthly food cost and food cost percent, and explains how these figures can be useful in assessing whether the operation is meeting its goals. To make these determinations, it is necessary to take several steps aimed at measuring performance. The first of these steps is taking physical inventory.

MONTHLY INVENTORY

Taking Physical Inventory

In most business establishments, including food and beverage operations, taking physical inventory is a universally accepted practice. Physical inventory is taken at the close of an accounting period, typically after the close of business on the last day of a calendar month. The purpose of doing this is to determine the actual cost of the foods and beverages used during the month, so that it can be determined that standards are being met and that cost-control measures are effective—in other words, the aim is to monitor how well the operation is performing.

Taking **physical inventory** requires counting the actual number of units on hand of each item in stock and recording that number in an appropriate place. The purpose of this process is to provide a list of goods on hand so that the value of the goods may be determined and recorded. Physical inventory may be recorded in an inventory book, as illustrated in Figure 8.1, or in some other type of permanent business record. It is normally considered good practice to list the items in stock in a book set up for that specific purpose and to list them in the same order in which they are maintained in stock. Arranging the list in this way facilitates the inventory-taking procedure that can be long and tedious, if there are numerous products on inventory.

LEARNING OBJECTIVE 8.2
Describe the procedure for taking physical inventory at the end of the month.

• FIGURE 8.1 •

Storeroom Inventory

Month	January			February		
Articles	Quantity	Price	Amount	Quantity	Price	Amount
Brought forward			$ 5,250.00			
Tomato paste #10	5	$ 14.72	$ 73.60			
Tomato paste #10	6	$ 11.20	$ 67.20			
Tomato puree #10	8	$ 10.50	$ 84.00			
Tomatoes crushed #10	16	$ 9.45	$ 151.20			
Tomato sauce #10	20	$ 9.75	$ 195.00			
Tomatoes, whole, peeled #10	15	$ 9.00	$ 135.00			

LEARNING OBJECTIVE 8.3
Distinguish between opening
(beginning) inventory and
closing (ending) inventory.

Taking a physical inventory in a storeroom, for example, commonly requires two people: one to count the units on the shelves and the other to record the numbers in the inventory book. If the storeroom is arranged as suggested in Chapter 5, it is possible for the two people to begin in one logical spot and work their way through the entire inventory in order, finding items on shelves in the same order as listed in the inventory book.

Once the units in inventory have been counted and the count has been recorded, total values can be determined for the items listed. To determine these totals, one records the unit cost of each product and multiplies it by the number of units of that product in the physical inventory. When the total value of each product has been determined this way, the totals are added to find the total dollar value of all items in the inventory. This figure, known as **closing inventory** for the period, automatically becomes the **opening inventory** for the next period.

Valuing the Physical Inventory

LEARNING OBJECTIVE 8.4
List and describe five ways to
assign unit costs to a food
inventory and explain the effect
on cost of each method.

One of the principal difficulties in valuing an inventory is assigning the unit value for each item, because all purchases may not have been made at the same price. It is not uncommon for prices to change several times during the course of a month. Determining the proper value to assign to units remaining in inventory at the end of the month raises a question as to which, if any, of the various purchase prices should be assigned to the unit remaining in the inventory. There are at least five possible ways of assigning values to units of product in a physical inventory:

1. Actual purchase price method
2. First-in, first-out method
3. Weighted-average purchase price method
4. Latest purchase price method
5. Last-in, first-out method

Because each provides a value to the units remaining in inventory at the end of any given month, anyone planning a career in foodservice management is well advised to become familiar with all five methods, any one of which may be selected as appropriate for use in a particular establishment, given a particular set of circumstances.

To simplify examples of each of the five methods, we will use only one item in the stores inventory: No. 10 cans of crushed tomatoes.

Inventory records for the month of May reveal the following:

Opening inventory on the 1st of the month: 10 cans @ $9.98 =	$99.80
Purchased on the 7th of the month: 24 cans @ $9.70 =	$232.80
Purchased on the 15th of the month: 24 cans @ $9.60 =	$230.40
Purchased on the 26th of the month: 12 cans @ $9.45 =	$113.40
Total value of purchases	$576.60
Value of opening inventory	+ $ 99.80
Value of total number of units available	$676.40

A physical inventory on the 31st of the month showed that 20 cans remain in stock. From this information, one can deduce that 50 cans were consumed during the month, as follows:

Opening inventory	10 cans	
+ Purchases during the month	60 cans	
= Total available	70 cans	
− Closing inventory	20 cans	(number of units still available)
= Units consumed	50 cans	(number of units no longer available)

Because both the value of the opening inventory ($99.80) and the value of the purchases ($576.60) are known, one can add the two values to determine the value of the total number of units available: $676.40. It should be obvious that one can determine the value of the units consumed only by determining the value of the units in the closing inventory and then subtracting it from the value of the total available. The following are five accepted methods for assigning values to units of the products in inventory.

Actual Purchase Price Method

Perhaps the most reasonable unit value to assign to the items in the closing inventory is their actual purchase price (**actual purchase price method**). This can be done only if those prices are marked on the units. If the cans of crushed tomatoes are marked with actual purchase prices, totalling their value is obviously a simple clerical job, requiring nothing more complex than addition. Assuming the cans are marked with the purchase prices indicated in the following list, the value of the 20 cans is determined as follows:

4 @ $9.98	=	$ 39.92
4 @ 9.60	=	38.40
12 @ 9.45	=	113.40
20		= $191.72

Note that the first four cans were part of the opening inventory. Thus, the stock of crushed tomatoes was not rotated during the month, as suggested in Chapter 5. If the actual purchase prices were not marked on the cans, an alternative procedure would be required.

First-In, First-Out Method (FIFO) (Latest Prices)

One alternative procedure is to assume that stock has been rotated properly during the period, so that the units consumed were the first to be placed on the shelf. In that case, those remaining on the shelf are those most recently purchased (**first-in, first-out method**).

To establish the value for the units in closing inventory using this method, it is necessary to know that the latest purchase on the 26th of the month was for 12 cans and that the previous purchase on the 15th was for 24 cans. With that information available, it is possible to determine the value of the 20 cans:

$$\begin{array}{ll}
12 @ \$9.45 = \$113.40 \\
\underline{8 @ \$9.60 = \$76.80} \\
20 = \$190.20
\end{array}$$

However, without some assurance that the stock on shelves had been properly rotated during the month, this procedure may lead to inaccurate valuation. After all, it is based on an assumption about rotation that might not be valid.

Weighted-Average Purchase Price Method

If there is no assurance that stock has been properly rotated and if large quantities of goods are involved, the **weighted-average purchase price method** offers a reasonable alternative. One can determine a weighted-average purchase price by multiplying the number of units in the opening inventory and in each subsequent purchase by their specific purchase prices, adding these values to determine a grand total for all units together, and then dividing this grand total by the total number of units.

By following this procedure, the weighted-average value of one unit can be determined by dividing 70 units into the $676.40 total value. The result is a weighted-average value of $9.66. Using that figure, the value of the closing inventory is

$$20 @ \$9.66 = \$193.20$$

It should be apparent that although this procedure makes logical sense, its use requires access to detailed records of purchases. Except in those operations that maintain computerized accounting records, the weighted-average purchase price method is seldom used in food and beverage operations. Attempting the necessary arithmetic manually may be too time-consuming.

Latest Purchase Price Method (Most Recent Price)

A simpler, faster, and more widely accepted approach is to use the **latest purchase price method** for valuing the closing inventory. A justification for this approach is that if it were necessary to replace the remaining cans, the cost of replacement at the present moment would likely be the latest price at which the items were purchased.

If this method is followed, as it frequently is in the food and beverage business, the value of the closing inventory of this item will be

$$20 @ \$9.45 = \$189.00$$

Last-In, First-Out Method (LIFO) (Earliest Prices)[1]

The last-in, first-out method is used only in certain special circumstances, such as when tax rates or inflation rates are particularly high. Management might choose to minimize profits on financial statements in order to decrease income taxes. To minimize profits, one might seek to maximize cost by minimizing the value of closing inventory. One merely values the units in the closing inventory by using the earliest and most costly purchase prices (**last-in, first-out method**).

If this method is used, the value of the 20 cans will be

10 @ $9.98 = $ 99.80
10 @ 9.70 = 97.00
————————————————
20 = $196.80

One should keep in mind that chefs and food controllers do not normally determine the method to be used in valuing inventories. Although they may be asked to contribute to the discussion of which method to use, the decision will probably be made by an owner or accountant. In addition, once the decision is made, it is usually not changed; various accounting conventions and Canada Revenue Agency regulations preclude frequent change.

Comparison of Methods

If the prices of goods purchased were fixed, selecting the method for valuing a closing inventory would be of no importance: All methods would yield the same figure. However, in times of fluctuating prices, which is the norm in the food and beverage business, selecting one method over another may be of considerable significance. Let's compare the values of the 20 cans in closing inventory described earlier to illustrate the point:

1. Value based on actual purchase price method: $191.72
2. Value based on first-in, first-out method: $190.20
3. Value based on weighted-average method: $193.20
4. Value based on latest purchase price method: $189.00
5. Value based on last-in, first-out method: $196.80

Using the lowest value, $189.00, as a base, there is a difference of 4.13 percent between the highest value and the lowest value established for these 20 cans of crushed tomatoes. Although the dollar differences for this single inventory item do not appear significant, the difference can be quite large if one is dealing with an entire inventory. For example, for an inventory that is valued at $10,000, a 4.13 percent differential amounts to $413.

---

[1] Canadian generally accepted accounting principles (GAAP), a standard framework of guidelines for financial accounting in Canada, allows the use of LIFO for reporting purposes, but Canada Revenue Agency (CRA) does not allow it to be used for tax filing. Since some Canadian companies file taxes in the United States as subsidiaries, a description of LIFO is included here.

Those establishments using one of the many restaurant computer programs will find that they almost always use the first-in, first-out method for evaluating inventory. These programs keep all purchases and issues in memory and assume that stock has been rotated properly during the period. Thus, it is very easy to get a "book" value for inventory at almost any time. Of course, it is also necessary to take an actual physical inventory in order to determine that all purchases and issues were recorded in the computer memory and that no spoilage, theft, or other shortage took place (a detailed discussion on this point is found at the end of this chapter). When this occurs, the "book" figure must be adjusted. One very good example of a computer program that provides inventory valuation is MenuLink Back Office, from Radiant Systems, which is included in the web links on this textbook's website.

Monthly Food Cost Determination

Drawing on previous discussions in this and earlier chapters, it is possible to turn our attention to the **monthly food cost** and food cost percent. The procedures discussed here are applicable to any foodservice enterprise, regardless of its size or the nature and complexity of control procedures in effect.

The **cost of food issued** for any month is determined by means of the following formula:

$$
\begin{array}{ll}
 & \text{Opening inventory} \\
+ & \text{Purchase} \\
\hline
= & \text{Total available} \\
- & \text{Closing inventory} \\
\hline
= & \text{Cost of food issued}
\end{array}
$$

The explanation is rather simple: Opening inventory for any accounting period is, by definition, the same as the closing inventory for the previous period. The figure is available from accounting records. To that, one adds the value of all purchases, directs and stores, during the period. The source documents for this information are the invoices for the period, which are summarized on the receiving clerk's daily reports. *Total available* thus indicates the total value of all foods available during the period for the production and sale of menu items. From this figure, one subtracts closing inventory, a valuation that is established by the means described earlier in this chapter. The result is a raw figure that indicates cost of food issued for the period. It includes the cost of all food, whether used productively or not.

It should be noted that the closing inventory figure often does not include the value of any directs that have been purchased but not consumed. Thus, the food cost figure is somewhat higher than it should be. In practice, this is routinely ignored, based on the theory that any error in this procedure in one month will be offset the following month. In other words, some directs that will be used at the beginning of each month will have been included in cost for the previous month. However, because directs are purchased in small quantities for immediate use, their value should be fairly constant from month to month. In some large organizations, these directs are in a category termed *foods in process,*

• **FIGURE 8.2** •

Comparison of Food Costs Using Five Different Methods

	Actual Purchase Price Method		First-In, First-Out Method		Weighted Average Method		Latest Purchase Price Method		Last-In, First-Out Method
Opening inventory	$ 99.80		$ 99.80		$ 99.80		$ 99.80		$ 99.80
Purchases	$ 576.60		$576.60		$576.60		$576.60		$576.60
Total available	$ 676.40		$676.40		$676.40		$676.40		$676.40
Closing inventory	$ 191.72		$190.20		$193.20		$189.00		$196.80
Cost of food issued	$ 484.68		$486.20		$483.20		$487.40		$479.60

mise en place, or *prepared foods in process,* which is subtracted from total available along with the closing inventory.

At this point it is useful to consider the effects of the various methods of establishing the value of closing inventory on the cost of food for a period, using the values established earlier in this chapter for the No. 10 cans of crushed tomatoes. These are summarized in Figure 8.2.

The illustration shows only one item in an inventory, but it should be apparent that these effects would be cumulative over an entire inventory. Although the selection of the method to use for valuing the inventory in a specific operation will be made by an owner and an accountant, a knowledgeable chef, manager, or food controller should be aware of the effects of the various inventory valuation methods on food cost.

Once food cost for a given period has been determined, food cost percent may be calculated. For purposes of illustration, we use Bistro Quatre. Financial records of the business reveal the following figures for the month of February:

Opening inventory	$ 9,010
Food purchases	$23,570
Closing inventory	$9,356
Food sales	$65,420

Given these figures, we may now begin to determine the cost of food for February by using the formula stated earlier.

	Opening inventory	$ 9,010
+	Food purchases	23,570
	Total available	$32,580
−	Closing inventory	9,356
=	Cost of food issued	$23,224

Once the cost of food issued is known, food cost percent can be determined by using the formula identified in Chapter 1:

$$\frac{\text{Cost}}{\text{Sales}} \times 100 = \text{Cost \%}$$

$$\frac{\$23,224}{\$65,420} = .355 \times 100 = 35.5\%$$

Saying that food cost percent is 35.5 percent is the same as saying that the cost of food has been $0.355 per dollar sold. As discussed in Chapter 1, these are merely two different ways of saying the same thing, and the two are used commonly and interchangeably in the industry.

At this point, it is important to recognize that, although the $23,224 figure is the cost of food issued, this is not necessarily the same as the **cost of food consumed**. Determining the cost of food consumed may require that the cost of food issued be adjusted to account for possible alternative uses of the food issued that do not represent the cost-to-sales ratio established as the standard for the operation. Some of the more common adjustments are identified and discussed in the following section.

Adjustments to Cost of Food Issued

Transfers

Transfers occur when goods are purchased by one unit or department and given to another. The goods represent value that must be credited to the unit or department that purchased them, and debited to the unit or department that was the recipient and end user. For example, if there have been any transfers between the kitchen and the bar, adjustments must be made to take the value of the transfers into account. Similarly, if there have been transfers from units in a chain to other units in the same chain, these must be totalled and used to adjust the cost figures of all units concerned. In some large hotels, where separate cost records are kept for the several food outlets in the property, similar adjustments must be made for food items transferred from one outlet to another. There are various kinds of transfers.

Intraunit transfers (those occurring within a given property) include:

1. Transfers of alcoholic beverages from bar to kitchen, such as wine used in food preparation. The term *cooking liquor* is commonly used to refer to these items. The cost of the cooking liquor is subtracted from the beverage department and added to the cost of food issued.
2. Transfers of directs from kitchen to bar, like lemons or limes, where they will be used for drink preparations or garnishes. The term *food to bar* (directs) is often used for these items. Food to bar transfers (directs) are

subtracted from the cost of food issued and added to the beverage department's cost.

Interunit transfers (those between properties in a chain) may involve any foods or beverages. For obvious reasons, interunit transfers seldom involve properties that are distant from one another. They are more common among urban units in a chain that may be only a few blocks from each other. The cost of food transferred from one unit to another in a chain is subtracted from the cost of food issued at the property where the food was transferred from and added to the cost of food issued at the property that received the food.

Transfers are not the only possible adjustments to food cost figures. To achieve more accurate food costs, many operations make one or more of the adjustments discussed in the following paragraphs.

Steward Sales

In some establishments—primarily large hotels and motels and a very few restaurants—employees may be permitted to purchase food at cost and take it from the premises for their own personal use (**steward sales**). Employees may take advantage of this opportunity for special occasions when, for example, they want a specific cut or grade of meat that is not normally available in their local markets. In those properties that permit steward sales, the amounts paid by employees are customarily treated as credits to cost rather than as revenue. In other words, steward sales are similar to reimbursements; they are considered cost reductions rather than revenue increases. If these sales are not treated as such, the cost of any foods sold to employees is included erroneously in food cost figures for the period. Many operations that allow staff purchases ask purveyors to directly invoice the staff, avoiding any transfers.

Gratis to Bars

In many establishments, the kitchen staff is expected to produce various hot and cold hors d'oeuvre that are given free to customers at the bar (**gratis to bar**). Because the purpose of this practice is to promote beverage sales, it seems logical to include the cost of the hors d'oeuvre in the cost of operating the beverage department. Alternatively, the cost could be made a cost to a promotion account if desired. Transferring this cost requires adjusting the cost of food issued by subtracting the value of the hors d'oeuvre from food cost, usually an estimated value, and adding that value to beverage or promotion costs.

Promotion Expense

In many properties, owners or managers entertain potential customers of banquet and convention sales. In large hotels and other properties that depend on group and party bookings for a major part of their revenue, sales managers, marketing directors, catering managers, banquet managers, and other sales personnel routinely entertain potential clients. They may invite people to the property for luncheon or dinner and discuss hospitality products and prices during the course of a meal. Food is provided from the menu for sampling. A server records it on a guest cheque, but sales revenue is not increased, because no one pays the cheque. Because the purpose of this practice is to promote sales (food, beverages, rooms, or all of these), it seems logical to include the cost of the food consumed during these meals in the cost of operating a sales, banquet, or marketing department. To do this, one must first adjust food cost by subtracting the value of the food. Thus, management may credit food cost for the value of foods consumed for these purposes and charge the cost to another account, such as promotion or sales expense.

Determining Cost of Food Consumed

LEARNING OBJECTIVE 8.5
Calculate cost of food consumed.

If some or all of the adjustments described in the preceding section are to be taken into account, the monthly determination of cost of food consumed is now determined as follows:

	Opening inventory
+	Purchases
=	Total available for sale
−	Closing inventory
=	Cost of food issued
+	Cooking liquor
+	Transfers in from other units
−	Food to bar (directs)
−	Transfers out to other units
−	Steward sales
−	Gratis to bar
−	Promotion expense
=	Cost of food consumed

However, although this procedure does enable management to determine a food cost figure that is more accurate than one that ignores the possible need for adjustments of various kinds, it is still not sufficiently accurate for some establishments. After all, some other foods consumed in many establishments also do not produce sales revenue. In many operations, meals are provided on the premises for employees as a matter of course. In most establishments, employees are either not charged for the food they consume while working or meals are sold to staff heavily discounted. Therefore, to determine a more accurate figure for food cost (cost of food sold), one must also subtract the **cost of employee meals** from the cost of food consumed.

Determining Cost of Employee Meals

There are numerous techniques for determining the cost of employees' meals. Some are in relatively common use in the industry, and others are comparatively uncommon. The four described here are among those in general use:

1. *Cost of separate issues.* This technique requires that employees be given food other than that which is prepared for customers. All food used in the preparation of employee meals must be issued separately and listed on requisitions, which are kept separately from all other food requisitions used in the establishment. If the food issued is listed on separate requisitions, one can readily determine its cost: a particular individual is assigned the task of pricing the requisitions, a procedure previously described in Chapter 5. For any given period, the total value of the foods listed on these special requisitions is equal to the cost of food for employee meals for the period. This technique is best suited to those operations large enough to maintain separate preparation and dining areas for their employees. Thus, it is used in a number of larger hotels but in comparatively few restaurants.

2. *Prescribed amount per meal per employee.* A somewhat more common approach is to direct the chef to give employees meals that will cost no more than a specific fixed amount per meal. For example, the fixed amounts established for meals may be $1.50 for breakfast, $2.50 for luncheon, and $3.50 for dinner. A procedure is established to keep daily records of the number of employees consuming each of these meals. These totals are added to cumulative figures for the period. The total cost of employees' meals for the period is determined by multiplying the fixed amount per meal by the number of employees who consume that meal during the period, and then adding together the totals for the meals. If employees have no choice of meals (if, for example, luncheon is the only meal they are permitted), or if the costs of the two or three choices offered are nearly identical, this technique for determining the cost of employees' meals is comparatively easy to use.

3. *Prescribed amount per period.* Because some establishments find it difficult to keep records of the numbers of employees consuming meals each day, they use another technique that requires no such records. Management simply informs the chef of a fixed amount that will be credited to food cost for employee meals for each period, regardless of the number of employees who actually have meals on the premises. It is up to the chef to estimate the number who will eat and then either prepare food that will not exceed the cost guideline or offer employees food prepared from the menu that does not exceed this permissible cost. Typically, the employees would be informed of which items they would be allowed to choose (if there is a lunch menu, this is often used as the employee meal menu as well).

4. *Sales value multiplied by cost percent.* Another technique requires that each employee who eats record the selections on a cheque. This may or may not be the same as the guest cheque used in the dining room. The menu price is recorded next to each selection. The cheque is totalled, but the employee is not asked to pay it. The cheques are totalled at the end of the period. This grand total is then multiplied by the average food cost

percent in recent periods to arrive at a reasonable cost figure for employee meals for that period.

By means of these or other alternative techniques, it is possible to arrive at a reasonable figure for the cost of employee meals. In operations that do not provide meals free of charge, it is common practice to require the employee to pay the dollar amount associated with the food cost for the meal. It is relatively easy, as well, to value the cost of staff meals in restaurants that charge a discounted price to employees ordering their meals from the menu. The cost for the portion of the employee meal to be credited is the restaurant's food cost percent multiplied by the amount the sale price is discounted.

Determining Cost of Food Sold

LEARNING OBJECTIVE 8.6
Calculate cost of food sold.

Once the total cost of employees' meals for a period has been established, the figure should be subtracted from the cost of food consumed to determine the **cost of food sold**. The amount subtracted is charged as a fringe benefit to labour cost by the accounting department. This procedure provides a final figure that should be used for calculating food cost percent (the cost-to-sales ratio) and for evaluating performance. Those who calculate cost of food sold and food cost percent without taking employee meals into account are likely to have overstated food cost and distorted food cost percent. This may even affect a chef's standing in the operation. If credits to food cost are not made, food cost percents will be inflated and the chef may be unfairly reprimanded or even dismissed. The same fate might befall a bartender who fails to record transfers for wine sent to the kitchen.

Using all of the preceding adjustments, the calculation of cost of food sold in the month of February for Bistro Quatre is as follows:

	Opening inventory	$ 9,010
+	Food purchases	23,570
=	Total available	$32,580
−	Closing inventory	9,356
=	Cost of food issued	$23,224
+	Cooking liquor	200
=	Subtotal	$23,424
−	Food to bar (directs)	170
−	Steward sales	80
−	Gratis to bar(s)	290
−	Promotion expense	250
	Total subtractions	790
=	Cost of food consumed	$22,634
−	Cost of employees' meals	1,050
=	Cost of food sold	$21,584

Using the sales figure of $65,420 identified earlier in this chapter, it is now possible to use this new and more accurate figure for cost of food sold to determine food cost percent for the period:

$$\frac{\text{Cost of food sold}}{\text{Food sales}} \times 100 = \text{Food cost \%}$$

$$\frac{\$21,584}{\$65,420} = .3299 \times 100 = 32.99\%$$

This is the same as stating that food cost in the period was $0.3299 per dollar sold, as discussed earlier. Food cost percent calculated with this more accurate figure, 32.99 percent, is actually 2.51 percentage points lower than that calculated before the adjustments were made. Similarly, cost per dollar sold was $0.0251 lower.

Although figures for food cost percent and food cost per dollar sale may be interesting, they become more useful when compared with figures for similar periods in the past. For example, if we know that food cost percent for January was 35 percent, we can compare the two and determine that the figure for February is lower than the figure for January by 2.01 percentage points. Comparisons of this nature are easier to make when the figures for current and past figures are recorded side by side on reports to management.

Food cost percent figures can also be compared with the industry averages for similar businesses, but care must be taken when comparing any business with another. Often seemingly comparable businesses have distinct differences in expenses, especially labour. It may be more beneficial to compare prime costs percentages when using industry averages as benchmarks.

REPORTS TO MANAGEMENT

Once cost of food sold and food cost percent have been calculated, they are normally reported to management. The nature of the report must be determined individually for each establishment or unit in a chain. That will be based on management's need for information, as well as the availability of the information. If the food control system is extensive and complex, more detailed information is likely to be available. When it is, management is more likely to be better informed and thus better equipped to make decisions and improve profitability.

Although the specifics of reports to management differ from one foodservice operation to another, they tend to have some similarities. The following illustrations are for two common types of reports used in foodservice establishments.

LEARNING OBJECTIVE 8.7
Prepare a simple monthly food cost report and calculate monthly food cost percent.

LEARNING OBJECTIVE 8.8
Explain the possible shortcomings of a system in which judgements about operations are made exclusively based on monthly food cost and food cost percent.

In some small establishments, where there are few formal control procedures and no specific control personnel, it may be impossible for anyone to prepare even the simplest reports without outside assistance. This assistance may be provided by a bookkeeper or professional accountant who comes in once a month, between the first and the tenth of the month, to make the necessary entries in the financial records of the business—the books of account. When the accountant has completed this work, the information required for preparing a basic report is available. After all, one only needs to know food sales and cost of food sold to determine food cost percent and food cost per dollar sale, as indicated earlier. A simple report can be prepared from that basic information. Report forms for foodservice operations are available from stationers catering to the industry. However, reports to management should always be based on management's need for specific information, rather than on the availability of a particular form. If no appropriate form can be obtained from a stationer, it is very easy to design one that will meet the need for specific information in a particular establishment.

The form illustrated in Figure 8.3 is one of the simplest that can be devised for a report to management. Figures for the current period are in the first column, and those for the same period in the previous year are in the second. When both can be seen on one form, side by side, it is possible to compare them and to make a judgement about the relative effectiveness of current operations. Thus, if the 34 percent cost-to-sales ratio for the same period last year was within the range of acceptability, it is likely that the 32.99 percent figure this year will also be acceptable, provided that there have been no significant changes in menu or operating procedure and no significant drop or change in sales.

• FIGURE 8.3 •				
Food Cost Report Comparing the Same Month in Two Different Years				
		February This Year		*February Last Year*
Food Sales		$65,420.00		$63,870.00
Net Cost of Food Sold		$21,584.00		$21,715.80
Food Cost %		32.99%		34%

In some instances, particularly when figures for previous periods have been unacceptable and corrective action has been taken to improve performance, it is desirable to have reports that make it easier to evaluate the effects of the corrective action. If the report is in a format that makes it easy to compare the figures for two consecutive months (e.g., January and February, as in Figure 8.4), one can readily make some judgement about whether the changes had produced the desired effect the following month.

Food Cost Report Comparing Two Consecutive Months

		January *This Year*		February *This Year*
Food Sales		$63,425.00		$65,420.00
Net Cost of Food Sold		$22,833.00		$21,584.00
Food Cost %		36.00%		32.99%

If the manager of Bistro Quatre had judged the January cost-to-sales ratio of 36 percent unacceptable and had taken corrective actions aimed at bringing the cost-to-sales ratio down in February, this format will make it easy to compare the two months and to make a judgement about the effectiveness of the changes. In the current instance, it is likely that the reduction in the cost percent from 36 percent to 32.99 percent will be considered acceptable. If so, the corrective actions taken to bring about the improvement will probably become the established standard procedures for the future.

In food service, cost percent is often used as a means for monitoring operations and judging the effectiveness of control procedures. Managers routinely compare cost percent for one period with cost percent for another. If the cost percent for a current month is approximately the same as it has been in other recent months, and that level of cost is acceptable, then no action needs to be taken. If there are no changes to sales or purchase costs, but food cost percent for the current month is considerably higher or lower than in the recent past, management will normally want to identify the reasons for the change. As we now know, there are many reasons for unacceptable food costs, which can be determined through diagnosis and analysis. Once the reasons are identified, action can be taken to prevent the recurrence of unacceptable costs.

Cost-to-sales analysis and comparisons should be done frequently to monitor progress. Judgements are made and, when necessary, corrective action is taken.

INVENTORY TURNOVER

It should be obvious that chefs and foodservice managers are responsible for ensuring that sufficient supplies of appropriate foods are available for use when needed. At the same time, they are expected to prevent the accumulation of excessive quantities of foods. The stockpiling of quantities greater than needed can lead to significant problems:

- Excessive food costs due to the spoilage of food stored too long
- Excessive amounts of cash tied up in inventory

LEARNING OBJECTIVE 8.9
Define *inventory turnover* and explain how it is determined.

- Excessive labour costs to receive and store foods
- Excessive space required for storage
- Unwarranted opportunities for misuse or theft

It is impossible to establish any valid industrywide standards for the foods, the number of units of those foods, or the valuation of food that should be on hand in a foodservice enterprise. The particulars vary from one operation to another and are likely to be related to such considerations as menus, size of operations, sales volume, distance from suppliers, and financial health, among others. Clearly, larger establishments tend to need more storage space and greater quantities of food in storage than do smaller establishments. And many foodservice establishments have slow periods during the year when smaller-than-usual quantities of food are needed. Nevertheless, managers are expected to make judgements to ensure that appropriate, not excessive, quantities of food are available for food preparation.

A technique commonly used to evaluate the adequacy of a food inventory is to calculate how often that inventory has been used and replenished during an accounting period. This frequency varies from one establishment to another and is influenced by many factors, including the amount of cash available for such purposes, the space available for storage, and the time necessary to receive foods ordered from purveyors. On one hand, if an operation were to purchase sufficient food to last one full year, most reasonable people would argue that the quantity was excessive and would lead to waste, inefficiency, and higher costs than were warranted. On the other hand, if just enough food was purchased to last only one day, some would argue that savings could result by purchasing larger quantities. Somewhere between these two extremes is an ideal amount of food to have on hand for a specific period. There is no standard of how many days of food supplies should be purchased at one time as the industry is too diverse, but for many foodservice operations, an amount sufficient to last more than one day and less than two weeks is normal, and we will use that range as our guide.

To measure how often a food inventory has been consumed and replenished during an accounting period, foodservice managers calculate a figure known as **inventory turnover**, or the *rate of inventory turnover*. The terms are used interchangeably. For example, if Bistro Quatre purchases, consumes, and replenishes its food inventory twice each month, its rate of inventory turnover would be 24 times each year. This is very close to the guideline cited earlier.

It is important to realize that not every item in the inventory turns over exactly twice during the period. Some items in the inventory are likely to turn over more frequently than twice a month, whereas others may turn over much less frequently. As discussed later, inventory turnover calculations are based on the dollar valuation of an inventory, not on the use of specific items in that inventory. Inventory turnover rates are calculated at the end of a month, soon after a value has been established for the closing inventory in the manner described earlier in this chapter.

Inventory turnover rate is calculated by means of the following formulas:

$$\text{Average inventory} = \frac{\text{Opening inventory} + \text{Closing inventory}}{2}$$

$$\text{Inventory turnover} = \frac{\text{Cost of food sold}}{\text{Average inventory}}$$

Using three figures taken from a previous discussion in this chapter, one can now proceed to determine inventory turnover for Bistro Quatre:

Opening inventory $9,010
Closing inventory $9,356
Cost of Food Sold $21,584

Next, one substitutes these figures in the formulas provided, as follows:

$$\text{Average inventory} = \frac{\$9,010 + 9,356}{2}$$
$$= \frac{\$18,366}{2}$$
$$= \$9,183$$
$$\text{Inventory turnover} = \frac{\$21,584}{\$9,183}$$
$$= 2.35$$

If the rate is the same each month, the inventory turnover rate for the year will be 28.2 times, or once every 1.844 weeks, slightly less than the guide indicated earlier.

Some will question the accuracy of the **average inventory** figure calculated here, which is based on an assumption that the opening and closing inventory figures are truly representative of the levels of inventory on hand during the month. That assumption is not always valid. Sometimes, when inventory value has been deemed too high early in the month, most purchasing may be stopped in order to bring overall inventory value down to an acceptable level before the end of the month. Although this practice, which is not uncommon, does tend to distort the average inventory figure, the alternative would be to determine the value of physical inventory more frequently. Most would find this too time-consuming and too costly to be considered a viable practice. If inventory software is used and records of all foods received and issued are entered in the computer terminal, it is easy to obtain a printout indicating the quantity of each item in inventory at any given time.

The most appropriate time to obtain this report is at the end of a month, when physical inventory is taken. This does not eliminate the need for physical inventory, because the inventory software does not report actual quantities in inventory. Instead, the printout indicates quantities that should be found in inventory, based on the data as input. This is an important distinction. If, for example, food has been taken from inventory without being recorded, then the number of units in the physical inventory will differ from the number on the computer printout. Therefore, if physical inventory is taken and compared item by item with computer records, management can determine the extent of unauthorized or nonstandard issues of food. This would be considered some measure of the extent to which employees were following the standard procedures established for operation.

A physical inventory provides information that can be used to update computer records of the inventory. With inventory records updated and current at the end of the accounting period, the software can perform all calculations necessary for determining the value of closing inventory, regardless of which of the methods previously discussed has been selected. Once the calculations are complete, one can obtain a printout that provides all necessary information. It should be obvious that the mathematical calculation of a closing inventory value can be completed much faster by computer than by manual means.

Given the aforementioned information, software currently available will calculate cost of food issued, cost of food consumed, and cost of food sold. It will also produce reports comparing figures for the current period with those for similar recent periods. The nature of these reports can range from the relatively simple variety illustrated in this chapter to any of a number of more extensive and detailed reports, similar to those illustrated in the following chapter.

THINGS TO CONSIDER

Food cost calculations are extremely important in assessing whether or not an operation is performing to standards. There are myriad things that affect this relationship of cost to sales, and we have covered many of them already. If costs are excessive it could be due to problems with standard recipes, purchasing, receiving, storing, issuing, production, or sales. As we have seen, establishing good standards and standard procedures for all phases of operations leads to profitability. If problems do develop, following a trail of all of these processes will lead to identifying and correcting them. This does require time and effort. Every aspect is important, including the proper use of transfers to adjust costs when the amounts involved are not insignificant. Occasionally, when procedures for recording transferred costs are not followed, time and money are wasted trying to find explanations for disproportionately high or low costs—problems that may not exist.

Perhaps when demand is unusually high during a dinner service and the saucier needs a bottle of red wine immediately to make a sauce, having unexpectedly run out, a transfer will not be made from the bar for the cooking liquor. Or maybe a transfer is just forgotten or filled out incorrectly. Perhaps the bookkeeper missed some transfers when calculating food costs. No matter the reason, transfers not accounted for will affect costs. As we mentioned, sometimes staff are reprimanded or even let go for missing cost targets, although if costs had been properly adjusted, it might have proven them to be good employees.

Food costs can be affected by small amounts of product and value, as those few dollars of cost add up quickly on a monthly report. When sales dollar amounts are small, cost tolerances are small as well. All of the things that contribute to costs must be controlled. Applying transfers properly can be just as important to food costs as using all of an ingredient as purchased without waste.

CHAPTER ESSENTIALS

In this chapter, we examined the simplest means of monitoring overall performance in food service. We described a series of monthly procedures used for this purpose in a large number of operations. We described the procedure for taking monthly physical inventory of food and identified five methods used to assign values to units of the products in an inventory. Having illustrated each of these methods, we showed the calculations necessary to determine food costs. We defined and differentiated among the terms *cost of food issued, cost of food consumed,* and *cost of food sold*. We described the procedure for calculating each of these and described various possible adjustments used in the calculations, including transfers, steward sales, promotion expense, and employees' meals. We illustrated the monthly determination of food cost percent and food cost per dollar sale and showed how these figures are commonly reported to management and used for making comparisons with similar figures for other operating periods and for judging operational performance. We described and illustrated the calculation of inventory turnover and discussed its significance to foodservice managers. Finally, we indicated that software can help assess employee adherence to standard procedures for issuing food, calculate the value of closing inventory and the cost of food for the current period, and prepare comparative reports for managers.

KEY TERMS IN THIS CHAPTER

Actual purchase price method, p. 221

Average inventory, p. 235

Closing inventory, p. 220

Cost of employee meals, p. 228

Cost of food consumed, p. 226

Cost of food issued, p. 224

Cost of food sold, p. 230

First-in, first-out method, p. 221

Gratis to bar, p. 227

Interunit transfer, p. 227

Intraunit transfer, p. 226

Inventory turnover, p. 234

Last-in, first-out method, p. 223

Latest purchase price method, p. 222

Monthly food cost, p. 224

Opening inventory, p. 220

Physical inventory, p. 219

Steward sales, p. 227

Weighted-average purchase price method, p. 222

QUESTIONS AND PROBLEMS

1. The following figures for November have been taken from the financial records of three units in the Pasta Pit. Determine total food issues for each:

   a. Opening inventory $ 1,500.00

      Purchases   4,600.00

      Closing inventory   1,722.00

   b. Closing inventory $12,083.00

      Opening inventory   10,371.00

      Purchases   28,468.00

   c. Purchases $65,851.08

      Closing inventory   18,335.10

      Opening inventory   19,874.77

2. Given the following figures for three units in a chain of restaurants operated under the name Grandma's Kitchen, calculate cost of food issued and cost of food consumed for each:

   a. Purchases $8,300.00

      Opening inventory   2,688.00

      Closing inventory   2,540.00

      Cooking liquor   94.00

      Gratis to bar   119.00

   b. Food to bar (directs) $ 189.00

      Closing inventory   6,647.00

      Transfers to other units   339.00

      Purchases   19,472.00

      Steward sales   53.00

      Transfers from other units   223.00

      Opening inventory   6,531.00

   c. Opening inventory $6,622.40

      Transfers from other units   47.35

      Cooking liquor   253.65

      Purchases   24,182.55

      Closing inventory   6,719.30

      Transfers to other units   347.60

      Food to bar (directs)   337.40

      Gratis to bar   177.35

3. For each of the following, determine cost of employees' meals:

   a. In the Meal Mall, employees were served 337 lunches and 381 dinners in March. Food cost is credited $0.70 per meal for lunch and $1.10 per meal for dinner.

   b. In Monty's Restaurant, employees are required to record their food selections on cheques and to enter the menu price next to each selection.

The total sales value of employees' meals in September was $7,826.95. In recent months, food cost percent has averaged 35 percent.

c. In Bartholomew's Pub, the chef was directed to prepare food for the employees at a cost not to exceed $25.00 per day, regardless of the number of employees fed. In February, the restaurant was open six days per week, but closed on Mondays.

4. Given the following figures from the financial records of three units in a small restaurant chain in Centreville, determine the cost of food sold for each:

a. Cooking liquor $210.50
   Steward sales   27.58
   Purchases   12,339.42
   Food to bar (directs)   201.38
   Gratis to bar   267.50
   Closing inventory   4,278.37
   Opening inventory   4,031.19
   Employees' meals: 328 lunches @ $0.65 each; 449 dinners @ $0.95 each

b. Closing inventory $3,427.30
   Purchases   11,230.45
   Opening inventory   3,012.80
   Transfers from other units   128.65
   Cooking liquor   298.40
   Gratis to bar   427.80
   Food to bar (directs)   312.45
   Transfers to other units   155.75
   Employees' meals: $2,576.45 sales value; recent average food cost percent: 34.0

c. Purchases $68,543.36
   Promotion expense   81.17
   Closing inventory   20,963.71
   Gratis to bar   58.73
   Transfers from other units   637.38
   Food to bar (directs)   296.35
   Opening inventory   22,687.40
   Transfers to other units   784.29
   Cooking liquor   543.18
   Employees' meals:
   Executives: $1,833.75 sales value; recent average food cost percent: 31.0 percent

   Other staff: 1,422 breakfasts @ $0.55
                1,208 lunches @ $0.80
                1,012 dinners @ $1.05

5. Using the figures for cost of food sold determined in Question 4, calculate food cost percent and food cost per dollar sale for each of the three restaurants, given the following sales figures:
   a. $ 26,173.55
   b. $ 25,819.45
   c. $191,405.95

6. The following information about one of the items carried in the food inventory of the Yellow Dog Restaurant is taken from inventory records for the month of January:

   1/1 Opening inventory 12 units @ $1.05 each
   1/5 Purchased 18 units @ $1.15
   1/12 Purchased 18 units @ $1.20
   1/19 Purchased 12 units @ $1.30
   1/26 Purchased 6 units @ $1.40

   On January 31, the physical inventory indicated nine units remaining on the shelf. Determine the value of both the closing inventory and the cost of units issued, using each of the five methods identified in this chapter.

7. The following information was taken from the May financial records of three restaurants in the same neighbourhood. Calculate inventory turnover for each:
   a. Opening inventory $3,287.40
      Closing inventory   3,322.60
      Cost of food sold   13,220.00
   b. Cost of food sold $18,448.30
      Opening inventory   6,327.65
      Closing inventory   6,581.75
   c. Closing inventory $21,971.38
      Cost of food sold   67,346.93
      Opening inventory   23,168.49

8. Determine inventory turnover for each of the three units in the Centreville chain identified in Question 4, using the information provided and the cost of food sold figures you calculated.

9. List as many possible causes as you can for each of the following changes from one month to the next:
   a. Increase in the food cost percent
   b. Decrease in the food cost percent
   c. Increase in the inventory turnover rate
   d. Decrease in the inventory turnover rate

10. Define each of the key terms in this chapter.

EXCEL EXERCISES

Exercise 8.1

Complete the storeroom inventory valuations for Barnaby's Hideaway and obtain a total inventory figure, using the form shown on the companion website for this text.

Exercise 8.2

Using the inventory value you calculated in Exercise 8.1 as a closing inventory, obtain a cost of food sold using the following information:

Opening inventory, $5,320.00
Purchases, $24,560.00
Cooking liquor, $183.00
Food to bar, $75.60
Steward sales, $365.50
Promotion expense, $87.30
Cost of employees' meals, $1,365.00

Exercise 8.3

Given the cost of food sold calculated in Exercise 8.2, calculate the food cost percent for Barnaby's Hideaway, assuming food sales are $66,419.15.

Exercise 8.4

Calculate inventory turnover for Barnaby's Hideaway using figures you calculated in Exercise 8.2.

CHAPTER 9

Monitoring Foodservice Operations II: Daily Food Cost

• LEARNING OBJECTIVES •

After reading this chapter, you should be able to:

9.1 Calculate food cost for a single day and for all the days to date in a period.

9.2 Calculate food cost percent for any single day and for all the days to date in a period.

9.3 Prepare a daily report of food sales, food cost, and food cost percent.

9.4 Differentiate between book inventory and actual physical inventory and identify various causes for differences between the two.

9.5 Determine book inventory value.

INTRODUCTION

Two effective and simple ways to control food costs are monitoring the garbage and watching the "back door." That means making certain that usable products are not wasted or stolen. If this was happening, it could be stopped immediately with good supervision. If foodservice operations were monitored from monthly cost figures alone, the length of time between monthly reports would present an obstacle. Many operators do not want to wait a month to find out that control problems have affected costs, as it is too late to resolve problems for that month. Those that wait for the month's cost report and find that the figures for the previous month reveal that problems have developed may take corrective actions to eliminate the problems, but must wait one more month to see the next report and determine whether the corrective actions have been effective. If by chance, management has made erroneous judgements about the causes of excessive costs, and the corrective actions taken have been based on those erroneous judgements, it will be another full month before the next report reveals that these corrective actions have not had the desired effect.

This delay can be very costly. To avoid the delay, and to make figures on which to base day-to-day operating decisions more timely, larger and better-organized foodservice operations calculate food cost daily.

DETERMINING DAILY FOOD COST

LEARNING OBJECTIVE 9.1
Calculate food cost for a single day and for all the days to date in a period.

It is possible to determine the daily food cost for any operation if certain procedures previously discussed are used. Because all foods can be categorized as either directs or stores in food control, the total costs for these two are the two basic components of the daily food cost.

As discussed in Chapter 5, directs are charged to food cost as received. Therefore, to determine food cost for any given day, one must know the total of directs received on that day. This figure is readily available if the Receiving Clerk's Daily Report or a similar form is completed each day. The sum of the entries in the "Food Direct" column on the report for any given day is the cost of directs for that day. Figure 9.1 shows the Receiving Clerk's Daily Report for February 5 at Bistro Quatre.

In contrast, stores are added to inventory and charged to the food cost when issued. Therefore, one must determine the value of stores issued on a given day, each day, to obtain the second principal component of food cost for that day. If all foods issued from inventory are listed on requisitions, the determination is not difficult. One merely prices and extends each requisition for foods issued on that day and then adds the totals for all requisitions to obtain the total cost of stores issued. If all foods are not listed on requisitions, it is important to distinguish directs from stores.

• FIGURE 9.1 •

Receiving Clerk's Daily Report

No. 1035   Date   5-Feb

Quantity	Unit	Description	Unit Price	Amount	Total Amount	Purchase Food Direct	Journal Food Stores	Distribution Sundries
		Market Price Meats						
9.99	kg	Duck	$ 8.38	$ 83.72				
6.64	kg	Strip loin	22.99	152.65				
20.01	kg	Chicken breast	7.15	143.07				
4.98	kg	Veal loin	27.17	135.31	$514.75		$ 514.75	
		Ottman Meats						
7	kg	Pork Ribs	$ 13.97	$ 97.79	$ 97.79		$ 97.79	
		Pier 1 Seafood						
1	bushel	Cherrystone clams	$ 11.75	$ 11.75				
1	bushel	Mussels	15.26	15.26				
4	kg	Lobsters	50.00	200.00				
5	kg	Shrimp	21.00	105.00	$332.01		$ 332.01	
		Contented Cows Inc.						
30	litre	Milk	$ 1.00	$ 30.00				
10	litre	Heavy cream	3.00	30.00	$ 60.00	$ 60.00		
		Daily Bread Bakery						
35	ea.	French bread	$ 0.82	$ 28.70	$ 28.70	$ 28.70		
		Jones Produce & Fruit						
4	kg	Shiitake mushrooms	$ 16.65	$ 66.60				
1	box	Lettuce	16.50	16.50				
1	bag	Onions	12.75	12.75				
1	box	Grapefruit	18.30	18.30				
1	box	Peaches	22.60	15.90				
					$130.05	$130.05		
Totals				$1,163.30	$1,163.30	$218.75	$944.55	

In smaller operations where there is no daily receiving clerk's report and no distinction made between directs and stores, invoices may be used to determine costs. The total of all purchases for the day is used for the daily food cost figure. This figure, however, may be inaccurate. Problems may result if a restaurant buys most of the week's goods on a Monday: daily food cost will be artificially high that day, and artificially low the rest of the week. Even when supplies are purchased daily, not all of the items will be consumed on the day they are invoiced, and those left over for tomorrow's use will somewhat invalidate cost figures for the day. To compensate for these problems, some operations will amortize the cost of these items over the week. For example, knowing that generally, a single two- kilogram box of frozen shrimp is used daily, the invoiced amount for the cost of one case of shrimp, containing six boxes, will be divided so that each day one-sixth of the price of the case is added to daily food cost. This type of adjustment will add accuracy to the daily food cost determination, but many small operators will not go to this much trouble. They will wait until a week's cost figures are accumulated, so that comparisons are averaged out and become more legitimate (we will discuss using cumulative to-date costs in the next section). Although this system is less timely and accurate than separating directs and stores, it may be effective if sales patterns are fairly consistent. If they are, cost patterns should also be consistent. When no unusual or uncommon spikes in the daily cost of purchases are noted, food cost should remain steady. If an unusual increase is noted, an investigation and corrective action should take place.

In operations where transfers are made between the food and beverage departments, or between units in a chain organization, or where any of the various other adjustments discussed in Chapter 8 are used (e.g., promotion expense, employees' meals, and steward sales), values for these should be determined daily and should be taken into account as well. For example, the values for any items that are received as directs, charged to food cost, but subsequently transferred to the bar for use in drink production are credited to daily food cost, just as they are credited to monthly food cost. These items—oranges, lemons, limes, and cream are common ones—should be listed on transfer memos or similar forms. One would determine their value and then credit the daily food cost for that amount. Similarly, the value of any alcoholic beverages transferred from the bar to the kitchen for use in food preparation should be charged to food cost. These, too, should be listed on transfer forms. In addition, many establishments credit daily food cost for the value of employee meals.

Thus, the **daily cost of food** can be determined in the following way:

Cost of directs (from the Receiving Clerk's Daily Report)
+ Cost of stores issued
+ Adjustments that increase daily cost (transfers from bar to kitchen; transfers from other units)
− Adjustments that decrease daily cost (transfers from the kitchen to the bar: food to bar (directs), gratis to bar, steward sales, promotion expense)
───────────────
= Cost of food consumed
− Cost of employee meals
───────────────
= Daily cost of food sold

The daily food cost for February 5 at Bistro Quatre is calculated as shown:

	Cost of directs	$ 218.75
+	Cost of stores issued	944.55
+	Adjustments that increase daily cost	90.00
−	Adjustments that decrease daily cost	70.35
=	Cost of food consumed	1,182.95
−	Cost of employee meals	99.65
=	Daily cost of food sold	$ 1,083.30

After determining daily food cost, the next step is to obtain a daily sales figure, usually from accounting records. When both food cost and food sales figures are known, a daily food cost percent can be determined. The food cost percent for February 5 at Bistro Quatre was calculated as follows:

$$\frac{\text{Food cost}}{\text{Food sales}} \times 100 = \text{Food cost \%}$$

$$\frac{\$1,083.30}{\$3,427.35} = .31608 \times 100 = 31.608\%$$

Calculating Food Cost Percent Today and to Date

By itself, the daily food cost percent for any one day may not be a very accurate figure. For example, many restaurants purchase directs every other day, and this will affect daily food cost, making it artificially higher on the days when directs are received and charged to food cost and correspondingly lower on the other days. In addition, some foods may be issued from stores one or more days before they will be used. Salt, flour, and various cooking oils, for example, may be issued to the kitchen once a week to avoid the need for daily requisitioning. In other instances, wholesale cuts of meat may be issued one full day in advance because of the time required for in-house butchering. These and any similar variances will raise food cost and food cost percent on the day of issue, because the food is not reflected in sales until one or more days later.

To help overcome the problem of artificially high food cost percent one day and low food cost percent the next, most operations also calculate **food cost percent to date**, which is defined as the cumulative food cost percent for a period. It takes into account all food costs and all food sales for all days so far in the period. Thus, the food cost percent to date on the fourth day of a period is based on the total food costs for the four days and the total food sales for the same four days. To determine this cumulative food cost percent (food cost percent to date), divide cost to date by sales to date:

$$\frac{\text{Food cost to date}}{\text{Food sales to date}} \times 100 = \text{Food cost \% to date}$$

LEARNING OBJECTIVE 9.2
Calculate food cost percent for any single day and for all the days to date in a period.

• FIGURE 9.2 •

Simple Daily Cumulative Cost Report

| Date | Directs | Stores | Adjustments | | Total Cost | | Total Sales | | Food Cost % | |
			Added to Cost	Subtracted from Cost	Today	To Date	Today	To Date	Today	To Date
1-Feb	$254.20	$ 977.30	$ 57.20	$255.30	$1,033.40	$1,033.40	$2,778.00	$ 2,778.00	37.199%	37.199%
2-Feb	$326.70	$ 944.10	$ 86.20	$253.40	$1,103.60	$2,137.00	$2,919.20	$ 5,697.20	37.805%	37.510%
3-Feb	$262.50	$1,040.40	$ 88.60	$177.80	$1,213.70	$3,350.70	$3,056.95	$ 8,754.15	39.703%	38.276%
4-Feb	$256.35	$ 965.30	$120.00	$220.00	$1,121.65	$4,472.35	$3,094.20	$11,848.35	36.250%	37.747%
5-Feb	$218.75	$ 944.55	$ 90.00	$170.00	$1,083.30	$5,555.65	$3,427.35	$15,275.70	31.608%	36.369%

Figure 9.2 is taken from the records of Bistro Quatre and is an example of the type of simple form that can be designed and inexpensively reproduced to give continuity to the procedure for determining daily food cost. To maintain simplicity for purposes of discussion, we have limited the number of adjustment columns to two: one for additions to cost and the other for subtractions. However, in practice there is no barrier to increasing the number of columns to whatever would be necessary for achieving the desired degree of accuracy in any particular operation. For example, the form does not show a separate figure for the cost of employee meals. Figure 9.2 combines that figure with other subtractions to food cost.

The procedure may be followed on a daily and cumulative basis for any number of days, depending on the needs of management. In many cases, these cumulative figures are maintained on a weekly or monthly basis as the figures become more accurate over time.

Comparing Similar Periods

Daily reports allow management to accurately assess daily costs and sales, but management often wishes to compare these costs and sales with similar periods. Doing this allows management to better assess operations and cost-control measures.

LEARNING OBJECTIVE 9.3
Prepare a daily report of food sales, food cost, and food cost percent.

Using the basic approach to monthly reports discussed in the preceding chapter, it is possible to design a report that does two important things:

1. It shows food cost, food sales, and food cost percent for any one specific day and for all the days to date in the period.
2. It compares these figures with those for a similar period.

Figure 9.3 is an example of a simple report from Bistro Quatre that accomplishes these objectives. This basic report includes daily figures for food cost, food sales, and food cost percent. In addition, the report includes cumulative figures for the period for food cost, food sales, and food cost percent. These are aligned with figures providing the same information about one or more recent periods. When the information is presented in this way, it is easier to monitor operations—to compare operating results for similar periods and to make judgements about the effectiveness of current operations. If results are judged undesirable or unsatisfactory, causes can be investigated while the events are relatively fresh in the minds of those concerned. In effect, by using readings or sightings taken daily, operational decisions can be made and corrective actions taken to get the operation back on course quickly.

If, for example, investigation in previous days had revealed that an undesirably high food cost percent is the result of overpurchasing directs, a decision can be made to use up those quantities on hand before additional purchases are made. This corrective action will have an immediate impact on the daily cost of directs, which should be lower than normal for a few days or so.

• FIGURE 9.3 •						
Simple Daily Food Cost Report						
Date 5-Feb						
		Today	Same Day Last Week		To Date This Week	To Date Last Week
Food sales		$ 3,427.35	$ 2,876.50		$ 15,275.70	$ 13,467.50
Food cost		$ 1,083.30	$ 1,050.40		$ 5,555.65	$ 5,010.30
Cost %		31.608%	36.517%		36.369%	37.203%

This, in turn, will tend to depress daily food cost percent and food cost percent to date for the balance of the period, and the ending to-date figures will be averaged out and more accurate.

In another instance, investigation may reveal that the undesirably high food cost percent is the result of excessive issuing of foods from stores. If this is the case, a decision may be made that quantities previously issued are to be used up before any additional quantities are requisitioned. Corrective action of this nature can have an immediate impact by keeping down the cost of issues for several days. Thus, subsequent daily and cumulative food costs and food cost percents will tend to be lower.

If there is a need for an even greater degree of detail than one can obtain from the forms in figures 9.2 and 9.3, it is possible to establish additional subdivisions for the categories. Figure 9.4 illustrates such a form. In order for the form shown in Figure 9.4 to be completed, detailed knowledge of directs and stores must be available. This thorough knowledge requires considerable effort to accumulate, so the benefit received from having it will not be worth the time and cost in most operations. Therefore one is unlikely to see this much detail in any but the larger establishments. If Bistro Quatre prepared such a report, it would look like Figure 9.4.

The cost of directs, for example, has been subdivided into four categories to provide detailed information about the daily cost of vegetables, fruits, dairy products, and baked goods. Similarly, the cost of stores has been subdivided into six categories to provide additional detail about the daily cost of beef, poultry, seafood, pork, lamb, and provisions. Given an accountant's analysis pad with an appropriate number of columns or a computer and a spreadsheet program, an establishment should be able to develop a reasonably detailed cumulative record of daily food costs, daily food sales, and daily food cost percents for a given operation. The specific subdivisions of the various categories will depend on specific needs identified in the particular operation. For example, the categories of stores shown in Figure 9.4 are consistent with the menu of Bistro Quatre.

• FIGURE 9.4 •

Daily Cumulative Cost Record Showing Costs Subdivided into Categories of Food

Date	Vegetables	Fruits	Dairy	Bakery	Total Directs	Beef and Veal	Poultry	Seafood	Pork	Duck
1-Feb	$118.30	$51.40	$49.75	$34.75	$254.20	$455.30	$65.30	$358.45	$22.30	$20.75
2-Feb	$178.15	$67.80	$65.15	$15.60	$326.70	$494.30	$77.20	$234.60	$32.00	$21.00
3-Feb	$176.30	$23.20	$34.30	$28.70	$262.50	$474.10	$75.20	$329.70	$40.30	$30.45
4-Feb	$166.35	$46.80	$33.20	$10.00	$256.35	$419.75	$65.30	$320.60	$43.20	$23.65
5-Feb	$95.85	$34.20	$60.00	$28.70	$218.75	$287.96	$143.07	$332.01	$97.79	$83.72
			Adjustments		**Total Cost**		**Total Sales**		**Food Cost %**	
Date	Provisions	Total Stores	Added to Cost	Subtracted from Cost	Today	To Date	Today	To Date	Today	To Date
1-Feb	$55.20	$ 977.30	$ 57.20	$255.30	$1,033.40	$1,033.40	$2,778.00	$ 2,778.00	37.199%	37.199%
2-Feb	$85.00	$ 944.10	$ 86.20	$253.40	$1,103.60	$2,137.00	$2,919.20	$ 5,697.20	37.805%	37.510%
3-Feb	$90.65	$1,040.40	$ 88.60	$177.80	$1,213.70	$3,350.70	$3,056.95	$ 8,754.15	39.703%	38.276%
4-Feb	$92.80	$ 965.30	$120.00	$220.00	$1,121.65	$4,472.35	$3,094.20	$11,848.35	36.250%	37.747%
5-Feb	$0	$ 944.55	$ 90.00	$170.00	$1,083.30	$5,555.65	$3,427.35	$15,275.70	31.608%	36.369%

When food costs and food cost percents are determined daily and to date and used as monitoring devices, the effects of these measures can be assessed daily, with the expected effect that by the end of the operating period, costs will be in line with management's goals. This is not always the case, but because this type of detail makes it easier to locate and diagnose problems and then correct them, excessive costs are unlikely to remain a problem for long.

Taking intelligent corrective action to eliminate undesirable effects is not possible until causes have been identified accurately. Occasionally, determining causes is a simple matter, but it is much more common to find that more than one cause exists and that the causes are not readily determined from the information on the report illustrated in figures 9.2 or 9.3. In many smaller operations, it may be possible to see first-hand any problems developing, or to go into the kitchen and make a complete first-hand investigation of all possible causes. In major hotels and other large operations, this is not usually the case. To reduce the amount of time and effort required for identifying the causes of unacceptably high food costs, some foodservice managers in large establish- ments rely on more complex reports. If Bistro Quatre wanted a more detailed report, it would resemble Figure 9.5.

A variation on this technique involves using the same form of report, but also showing the cost breakdown in terms of ratios. Ratios are established between direct costs and sales, both for today and to date, and the same is done for other costs as well. This can be a particularly useful approach in operations offering menus that seldom change.

In the example given in Figure 9.6, although sales figures to date are higher this week than last week, the ratio of cost components to sales has not changed dramatically. The food cost percent today is slightly lower and probably quite acceptable, but the food cost percent for the week to date is higher and might be a cause for concern. Further examination shows that the cost of directs expressed as a percentage of food cost is down both today and for the week, while sales for today and this week are higher. This might suggest overpurchasing of directs in the previous week and, consequently, some food spoilage or food waste. Stores, as a percentage of food cost, are about the same as the previous week. Subtractions from food cost were slightly higher last week, suggesting either employee food cost was higher than normal last week, or there was a higher figure for gratis to bar.

When a certain cost varies considerably from its level in the recent past, causes can be investigated and corrective actions taken if warranted. For example, if an increase in the overall cost-to-sales ratio were noted, along with a dramatic increase in the ratio of cost of seafood to total sales, while other ratios remain approximately the same as in recent weeks, the cause of the increase in the overall cost-to-sales ratio will be effectively localized. When seeking to identify a cause for the increase, one can disregard the total costs of directs and stores and concentrate on possible problems in the seafood

● FIGURE 9.5 ●

A More Detailed Daily Food Cost Report to Management

Date   5-Feb

	Today		Same Day Last Week		To Date This Week		To Date Last Week
Food sales	$3,427.35		$2,876.50		$15,275.70		$13,467.50
Food cost	$1,083.30		$1,050.40		$ 5,555.65		$ 5,010.30
Cost %	31.608%		36.517%		36.369%		37.203%
Cost Breakdown							
Directs	$ 218.75		$ 214.70		$ 1,318.50		$ 1,297.80
Stores	$ 944.55		$ 934.60		$ 4,871.65		$ 4,449.65
Additions	$ 90.00		$ 76.50		$ 442.00		$ 364.35
Subtractions	$ 170.00		$ 175.40		$ 1,076.50		$ 1,101.50
Stores Breakdown							
Beef and veal	$ 287.96		$ 406.50		$ 2,131.41		$ 2,162.30
Poultry	$ 143.07		$ 103.00		$ 426.07		$ 336.55
Seafood	$ 332.01		$ 286.40		$ 1,575.36		$ 1,261.80
Pork	$ 97.79		$ 28.60		$ 235.59		$ 170.00
Duck	$ 83.72		$ 22.30		$ 179.57		$ 120.00
Provisions	$ 0.00		$ 87.80		$ 323.65		$ 399.00
Totals	$ 944.55		$ 934.60		$ 4,871.65		$ 4,449.65

category. Note that the percentages shown in this figure are carried out to three decimal places, making it a more accurate report.

This approach is even useful for localizing problems and for facilitating more focused investigations. In some instances, changes in these ratios may be traced to changes in the sales mix caused by changes in customers' behaviour patterns for ordering. In cases in which customer demand has remained constant, however, and market prices have been relatively stable, increases in these ratios are likely to be traceable to production problems with kitchen operations. If, for example, directs or stores vary from week to week as a percentage of food cost, this indicates that a problem exists, as long as purchase prices and the menu has not changed, and the sales mix is relatively constant. Undoubtedly, when problems are localized and detailed, they may be more easily identified and assessed so that appropriate corrective actions can be taken.

• FIGURE 9.6 •

A More Detailed Daily Food Cost Report to Management, Including Percentages

Date ___5-Feb___

	Today		Same Day Last Week		To Date This Week		To Date Last Week	
Food sales	$ 3,427.35		$ 2,876.50		$ 15,275.70		$ 13,467.50	
Food cost	$ 1,083.30		$ 1,050.40		$ 5,555.65		$ 5,010.30	
Cost %	31.608%		36.517%		36.369%		37.203%	

Cost Breakdown as Percentage of Food Cost

	Today		Same Day Last Week		To Date This Week		To Date Last Week	
Directs	$ 218.75	20.193%	$ 214.70	20.440%	$ 1,318.50	23.733%	$ 1,297.80	25.903%
Stores	$ 944.55	87.192%	$ 934.60	88.976%	$ 4,871.65	87.688%	$ 4,449.65	88.810%
Additions	$ 90.00	8.308%	$ 76.50	7.283%	$ 442.00	7.956%	$ 364.35	7.272%
Subtractions	$ 170.00	15.693%	$ 175.40	16.698%	$ 1,076.50	19.377%	$ 1,101.50	21.985%

Stores Breakdown as a Percentage of Stores

	Today		Same Day Last Week		To Date This Week		To Date Last Week	
Beef and veal	$ 287.96	30.486%	$ 406.50	43.495%	$ 2,131.41	43.751%	$ 2,162.30	48.595%
Poultry	$ 143.07	15.147%	$ 103.00	11.021%	$ 426.07	8.746%	$ 336.55	7.564%
Seafood	$ 332.01	35.150%	$ 286.40	30.644%	$ 1,575.36	32.337%	$ 1,261.80	28.357%
Pork	$ 97.79	10.353%	$ 28.60	3.060%	$ 235.59	4.836%	$ 170.00	3.821%
Duck	$ 83.72	8.863%	$ 22.30	2.386%	$ 179.57	3.686%	$ 120.00	2.697%
Provisions	$ 0.00	0.000%	$ 87.80	9.394%	$ 323.65	6.644%	$ 399.00	8.967%
Totals	$ 944.55		$ 934.60		$ 4,871.65		$ 4,449.65	

BOOK VERSUS ACTUAL INVENTORY COMPARISON

In Chapter 8, we identified and explained procedures for determining the value of closing inventory at the end of each monthly period and discussed the reasons for doing so. The closing inventory value determined in that way is the value recorded in the financial records and statements. The value is real, or actual. It includes the value of all items counted in the inventory—those that were physically present and thus could be found, identified, counted, and valued.

Some foodservice operators also determine what the value of the closing inventory should be, based on records indicating purchases and issues. This is defined as **book inventory**. Those who determine a book inventory value normally do so to compare it with the actual inventory value.

A method of establishing the value of the book inventory is readily available to those who maintain daily food cost figures in the manner illustrated in figures 9.1 and 9.2. This form provides a means for maintaining cumulative book inventory figures for the period, as shown in Figure 9.7. This form is simply an extension of Figure 9.2. Additional columns are at the end of the form.

The closing inventory for any month becomes the opening inventory for the following month. This closing inventory should be the actual inventory as determined by a physical count of stores taken at the close of business the last day of the month. If the book inventory figure from the previous month is used instead, the opening inventory will not reflect true value. Thus, in Figure 9.7, the closing inventory for January ($9,010) has become the opening inventory for February 1. To find a closing balance for February 1, one must add to the opening balance any stores purchases received on February 1, and then subtract any stores issued on that day. As discussed in previous chapters, the value of stores purchases for any given day comes from the Receiving Clerk's Daily Report for that day. The value of stores issues comes from the day's requisitions. If the costs of issues from stores have already been recorded in the appropriate columns shown in Figure 9.6, one need only transfer the stores figure to the "Issues" column. Thus, to find the closing book inventory figure for any day, one merely starts from the closing inventory figure for the preceding day, adds any stores purchases, and subtracts any stores issues. This simple procedure can be followed daily through a period. If this is done daily for a calendar month, the final figure is the closing book value of the stores inventory for the month.

It is possible to determine the closing book value of the stores inventory in establishments that do not determine daily food cost figures, but only if some form of receiving report and daily issue requisitions are used. If so, book inventory value is determined as follows:

   Opening inventory (closing inventory for the preceding month)
+ Purchases (total stores purchases for the period, as listed on receiving reports)
= Total available (total value of the stores available for use during the period)
− Issues (total stores issues for the period, as listed on requisitions)
= Closing book value of the stores inventory

▪ **FIGURE 9.7** ▪

Simple Daily Cumulative Cost Record

| Date | Directs | Stores | Adjustments | | Total Cost | | Total Sales | | Food Cost % | | Inventory Balance | | |
			Added to Cost	Subtracted from Cost	Today	To Date	Today	To Date	Today	To Date	Purchases	Issues	Balance
													$9,010.00
1-Feb	$254.20	$977.30	$57.20	$255.30	$1,033.40	$1,033.40	$2,778.00	$2,778.00	37.199%	37.199%	$845.20	$977.30	$8,877.90
2-Feb	$326.70	$944.10	$86.20	$253.40	$1,103.60	$2,137.00	$2,919.20	$5,697.20	37.805%	37.510%	$756.35	$944.10	$8,690.15
3-Feb	$262.50	$1,040.40	$88.60	$177.80	$1,213.70	$3,350.70	$3,056.95	$8,754.15	39.703%	38.276%	$1,177.20	$1,040.40	$8,826.95
4-Feb	$256.35	$965.30	$120.00	$220.00	$1,121.65	$4,472.35	$3,094.20	$11,848.35	36.250%	37.747%	$1,055.40	$965.30	$8,917.05
5-Feb	$218.75	$944.55	$90.00	$170.00	$1,083.30	$5,555.65	$3,427.35	$15,275.70	31.608%	36.369%	$955.75	$944.55	$8,928.25

Theoretically, the value of the book inventory should be identical to the value established for the physical inventory taken at the end of the month. This is never true, however. There are many reasons for discrepancy, some normally acceptable but others never acceptable. Among the acceptable reasons are an occasional human error in costing out requisitions, the use of the most recent purchase price rather than actual purchase price in valuing the physical inventory, and the mismarking of actual purchase prices on items when that method is used. Reasons that are never acceptable include issuing stores without requisitions, allowing stores to age to the extent that they become unusable and must be discarded, and the theft of food.

Depending on the size of an operation and the volume involved, discrepancies of some small percentage between book inventory and physical inventory can often be attributed to acceptable causes and are of no further concern, except that the discrepancies should be pointed out, if possible, to the employees whose errors have caused them. When discrepancies reach an unacceptable level, however, management has a responsibility to investigate, identify causes, and take corrective action aimed at ensuring that the variance will be significantly reduced in future periods. This may involve reviewing control procedures for purchasing, receiving, storing, and issuing food and revising those procedures where necessary. It also may involve reviewing the work habits of employees responsible for carrying out control procedures and taking appropriate steps to ensure that established procedures will be followed more closely in the future. In extreme cases, management may find it necessary to review all procedures and all employee work habits in order to find causes. Once identified, the causes will be the basis of appropriate corrective action by management.

Comparing book and actual inventory values at the end of an accounting period can be an important element in the control process. The actual inventory, although necessary for accurately determining cost of food sold at the end of each month so that proper financial statements can be prepared, provides a value that can be compared with the value of the book inventory, enabling management to assess the effectiveness of receiving, storing, and issuing procedures. Significant differences between actual and book inventory figures signal that operations are not completely efficient and effective, and control procedures need investigation.

Using the following example, the actual physical closing inventory at the end of February is $9,120, and the book inventory as calculated on a form similar to Figure 9.7 is $9,620. The difference ($500) is a very significant amount and should be investigated immediately.

Opening Inventory	$9,010
+ Purchases	8,240
− Issues	7,630
= Book Value	9,620
− Actual Value	9,120
= Difference	500

One can analyze this discrepancy further by expressing it as a percentage of issues. This is done by using the following formula:

$$\frac{\text{Dollar difference between book value and actual value}}{\text{Total issues}} \times 100 = \%$$

Thus:

$$\frac{500}{2,600} = .192 \times 100 = 19.2\%$$

The dollar amount of $500.00 and the percentage 19.2% are significant and should be investigated by management to determine possible causes. One possibility is an incorrect actual closing inventory. Perhaps some of the calculations were incorrectly made or some food in storage was not counted when the inventory was made. Other possibilities include theft, food spoilage that had to be discarded, or food issued without a requisition.

THINGS TO CONSIDER

Time frame and scale of operations are two things to consider when determining food costs.

As we discussed, monitoring food costs on a shorter time frame than one month means that problems, if they develop, can be diagnosed sooner. Daily food cost calculations, even though somewhat inaccurate, can still be used as a tool to assess performance. When daily reports are combined and averaged into to-date reports, quality and accuracy improves and they become more helpful in diagnosing problems. The information obtained from daily and to-date cost-to-sales reports must be analyzed and acted on, if necessary, to correct any problems that arise. Working in these shorter time frames may have considerable implications over longer spans. When a physical inventory is done at the end of the month and acceptable cost figures are produced, it is possible the percentages ended the month satisfactorily because of the use of daily and to-date cost analysis. Monitoring shorter time frames can produce good long-term results.

Scale is another factor we discussed. Large operations have the time and resources to properly calculate daily and to-date food costs. Smaller operations can do this with somewhat diminished accuracy by totalling invoices daily, which takes very little time to do. They can even improve results by amortizing some of the purchases they know will not be sold immediately. When they operate on a smaller scale, chefs or kitchen managers can often do this quite easily because they know almost everything that comes into and goes out of the kitchen. The small scale of their operation also works to their benefit as they are able to monitor and correct any deviations quickly. Whatever the scale, it is wise and profitable to determine and analyze daily and to-date food costs.

CHAPTER ESSENTIALS

In this chapter, we described procedures used in some operations to determine food cost and food cost percent, both daily and cumulatively. This can be viewed as a basic management information system designed to provide data more frequently and in a more timely manner than that available from the monthly calculations described in the previous chapter. We illustrated and discussed various types of reports that provide basic information about the results of operations and that compare information about the current operating period with that of previous periods. We demonstrated how book inventory is calculated and explained how comparing book and actual inventory figures can be useful for evaluating the effectiveness of various control and reporting procedures.

KEY TERMS IN THIS CHAPTER

Book inventory, p. 255
Daily cost of food, p. 246
Food cost percent to date, p. 247

QUESTIONS AND PROBLEMS

1. Following the format illustrated in Figure 9.2, use the following information to determine food cost, food sales, and food cost percent today and to date for the Circle Diner for the first four days of May.

| | | | ADJUSTMENTS | | |
| | | | Added to | Subtracted | |
Date	Directs	Stores	Cost	from Cost	Sales
5/1	$350	$350	-0-	-0-	$1,400
5/2	$250	$175	$25	-0-	$1,000
5/3	$135	$125	-0-	$10	$1,000
5/4	$ 75	$135	$10	$20	$ 500

2. Following the format illustrated in Figure 9.2, use the following information to determine food cost, food sales, and food cost percent today and to date for the Magic Inn for the period September 4–9.

ADJUSTMENTS

Date	Directs	Stores	Added to Cost	Subtracted from Cost	Sales
9/4	$400	$500	-0-	$50	$2,550
9/5	$150	$325	-0-	-0-	$1,500
9/6	$350	$550	$60	-0-	$2,850
9/7	$200	$400	-0-	-0-	$2,850
9/8	$450	$450	-0-	$40	$3,325
9/9	$ 50	$290	-0-	$10	$1,300

3. Following the format illustrated in Figure 9.7, use the following information to determine food cost, food sales, and food cost percent today and to date, as well as book inventory balances for Ravel's Restaurant for the period November 1–5. The opening inventory balance for November 1 is $9,330.

11/1: Purchases: directs, $403; stores, $736
Issues: $591
Sales: $2,241

11/2: Purchases: directs, $261; stores, $108
Issues: $465
Sales: $2,121

11/3: Purchases: directs, $273; stores, $1,463
Issues: $821
Adjustments: cooking liquor from the bar, $33; food to bar (from the kitchen), $24
Sales: $2,740

11/4: Purchases: directs, $521; stores, $281
Issues: $944
Sales: $4,063

11/5: Purchases: directs, $334; stores, $372
Issues: $1,221
Adjustments: cooking liquor, $19; food to bar (from stores), $29
Sales: $4,682

4. Use the following information to determine the book value of the stores inventory on the morning of May 6.

Closing inventory for April: $11,353.40

DateStores	Purchases	Stores Issues
5/1	$742.38	$621.80
5/2	$397.49	$516.76
5/3	$619.66	$472.51
5/4	$273.16	$845.26
5/5	$824.93	$725.77

5. In each of the following cases, determine the book value of the closing inventory for the month of October.

a. Opening inventory:	$ 3,748.00
Purchases:	22,162.00
Issues:	21,477.00
b. Issues	$44,227.60
Purchases:	42,191.40
Opening inventory:	15,308.70
c. Purchases:	$10,601.58
Opening inventory:	4,219.66
Issues:	9,862.43

6. For each of the following examples, use the information given to find the book value of the closing inventory and the dollar difference between book and actual inventory for the month.

a. Opening inventory:	$ 400.00
Purchases:	1,200.00
Issues:	900.00
Actual value of closing inventory:	600.00
b. Purchases	$ 6,327.00
Issues	6,498.00
Opening inventory:	2,184.00
Actual value of closing inventory:	1,912.00
c. Issues:	$12,395.62
Opening inventory:	4,129.88
Purchases:	11,623.71
Actual value of closing inventory:	2,673.47

7. Using information from each of the examples in Question 6, determine the difference between book and actual closing inventory figures as a percentage of issues.

8. Given the dollar differences determined in Question 6 and the percentages determined in Question 7, which of the three examples in Question 6, if any, bear closer examination by a manager? Justify your answer.

9. Assuming that one or more of the examples in Question 6 needs closer examination, explain in detail how that examination should proceed. If you were manager, what steps would you take?

10. What are some of the potential advantages of using daily and cumulative figures for food costs and food cost percents, rather than relying exclusively on end-of-month calculations?

11. Discuss the possible advantages and disadvantages of the kinds of complex computer-generated reports described in the chapter.

12. Analyze the report shown in Figure 9.8 and provide a detailed report of unfavourable trends.

13. Define each of the key terms in this chapter.

● **FIGURE 9.8** ●

A More Detailed Daily Food Cost Report to Management, Including Percentages

Date ___6-Jun___

	Today		Same Day Last Week		To Date This Week		To Date Last Week	
Food sales	$2,986.95		$2,678.50		$13,179.25		$14,376.50	
Food cost	$1,337.75		$ 950.40		$ 5,455.50		$ 4,901.35	
Cost %	44.786%		35.488%		41.395%		34.093%	

Cost Breakdown as Percentage of Food Cost

	Today		Same Day Last Week		To Date This Week		To Date Last Week	
Directs	$ 209.50	15.661%	$ 204.70	21.535%	$ 1,438.50	26.368%	$ 1,229.30	25.081%
Stores	$ 985.65	73.680%	$ 922.50	97.049%	$ 5,081.65	93.147%	$ 4,336.65	88.479%
Additions	$ 190.00	14.203%	$ 89.50	9.416%	$ 722.00	13.234%	$ 346.25	7.064%
Subtractions	$ 340.00	25.416%	$ 166.40	17.506%	$ 1,760.50	32.270%	$ 1,011.60	20.639%

Stores Breakdown as a Percentage of Stores

	Today		Same Day Last Week		To Date This Week		To Date Last Week	
Beef and veal	$ 398.50	40.430%	$ 406.50	44.065%	$ 2,241.95	44.119%	$ 2,162.30	49.861%
Poultry	$ 77.65	7.878%	$ 103.00	11.165%	$ 360.65	7.097%	$ 336.55	7.761%
Seafood	$ 333.85	33.871%	$ 286.40	31.046%	$ 1,577.20	31.037%	$ 1,261.80	29.096%
Pork	$ 35.90	3.642%	$ 28.60	3.100%	$ 173.70	3.418%	$ 170.00	3.920%
Duck	$ 22.65	2.298%	$ 22.30	2.417%	$ 118.50	2.332%	$ 120.00	2.767%
Provisions	$ 117.10	11.880%	$ 75.70	8.206%	$ 609.65	11.997%	$ 286.00	6.595%
Totals	$ 985.65		$ 922.50		$ 5,081.65		$4,336.65	

EXCEL EXERCISES

Exercise 9.1

Complete the Daily Cumulative Record of Food Cost and Cost Percent for Barnaby's Hideaway, as shown on the companion website for this text as Exercise 9.1.

Exercise 9.2

Using the information calculated in Exercise 9.1, complete the report to management for October 3, as shown on the companion website as Exercise 9.2.

CHAPTER 10

Monitoring Foodservice Operations III: Actual versus Standard Food Costs

• **LEARNING OBJECTIVES** •

After reading this chapter, you should be able to:

10.1 Define *standard cost* and explain how it is calculated.

10.2 Calculate and compare actual and standard costs using the daily method.

10.3 Describe how to use a Menu Pre-Cost and Abstract form.

10.4 Define *potential savings* and list several conditions that affect it.

10.5 Calculate and compare actual and standard costs using the periodic method.

INTRODUCTION

Previous chapters were devoted to methods for establishing control over the purchasing, receiving, storing, issuing, and production phases of foodservice operations. Discussions focused on the establishment of various standards and standard procedures for operations, including standard purchase specifications, standard receiving and issuing procedures, standard portion sizes, and standard production methods, among many others. Establishing these standards makes it possible to establish one additional and very important standard: standard cost.

Standards can be set very tight, allowing almost no tolerance for waste or error, or management may adopt a more realistic set of standards that are within reach. After all, standards are somewhat like goals. In setting standards within a foodservice environment, management needs to consciously consider the proper level to adopt.

- Achievable standards are those that are realistically within reach. Such standards take into account normal variances and inefficiency.
- Ideal standards may never be reached. They represent what would result in a perfect situation (no spoiled goods, no worker errors, etc.). Many foodservice operations avoid ideal standards because they fear that employees will see ideal standards as meaningless since they cannot hope to achieve them.

Standard costs are compared with actual costs, and mathematical deviations between the two are termed **variances**. Favourable variances result when actual costs are less than standard costs, and vice versa.

Figure 10.1 demonstrates the relationship between actual cost and standard cost.

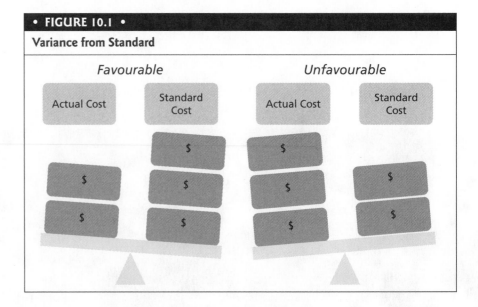

• FIGURE 10.1 •

Variance from Standard

Favourable   *Unfavourable*

Actual Cost   Standard Cost   Actual Cost   Standard Cost

If actual costs are equal to or less than standard costs, it is favourable, and conversely, if actual costs are greater than standard costs, it is unfavourable.

DETERMINING STANDARD COST

LEARNING OBJECTIVE 10.1
Define *standard cost* and explain how it is calculated.

Standard cost was defined in Chapter 2 as the agreed-upon cost of goods or services against which to compare costs. In Chapter 6, *standard portion cost* was defined as the amount that a standard portion should cost, given the standards and standard procedures for its production. For example, one portion of Strip Steak should cost $7.50 in Bistro Quatre, provided that the staff has followed all standards and standard procedures established for purchasing, receiving, storing, issuing, and producing the item. If these standards are not followed precisely, the actual cost of the portion may be different than standard.

By using standard portion costs in ways that will be illustrated in this chapter, management can measure operating efficiency with a greater degree of accuracy. Actual costs can be compared with standard costs, and any difference between them will be a useful measure of the extent to which the standards and standard procedures are being followed. This difference indicates both the degree of inefficiency in day-to-day operations and the extent to which costs can be reduced without compromising or reducing standards.

COMPARING ACTUAL AND STANDARD COSTS

In general, there are two methods for comparing actual and standard costs. The first requires calculations of standard costs and actual costs for the day and for all the days thus far in the operating period—the week or the month. Daily reports are prepared to compare actual and standard costs to date, and the last of these in a given period is a final summary report for the period. The second method does not require daily calculation, relying instead on periodic determination of standard costs from records of actual portion sales in the period. Choosing one method over the other is a matter for the management of any given operation to decide, and should be based on the type of menu in effect, management's need for information, and the availability of personnel to prepare the information.

The first method offers the advantage of immediacy and all its attendant benefits, but it does require considerable staff time daily. The second method, although saving many hours of staff time, lacks immediacy. Because of the considerable differences in the procedures required, both methods are discussed here.

DAILY COMPARISON

LEARNING OBJECTIVE 10.2
Calculate and compare
actual and standard costs
using the daily method.

If standard costs and selling prices for standard portions are established and forecasts have been made, it is possible to determine in advance what food cost percent should be. Of course, this forecasted cost percent will not be completely accurate and reliable unless the forecast is entirely accurate and all personnel follow all established standards and standard procedures precisely. This is seldom the case.

At the end of the day or after a service, when actual portion sales have been tallied to add to the sales history, this information can be used to determine what standard cost and cost percent those actual sales produce. In other words, management can use actual sales records to determine what the standard food cost percent should have been. Figure 10.2 is the sales forecast and actual sales for Bistro Quatre for March 5.

LEARNING OBJECTIVE 10.3
Describe how to use a Menu
Pre-Cost and Abstract form.

Figure 10.3 is the form where these daily procedures are accomplished, known as the **Menu Pre-Cost and Abstract**, which is divided into two parts. The section on the left—the forecast section—is based on a sales forecast prepared sometime before a day or a meal. The section on the right—the abstract section—is completed later, after the day or service for which the forecast was prepared. All menu items including appetizers and desserts are included on the form.

The Forecast

After sales have been forecasted, as described in Chapter 7, the food controller records in the first two columns on the form the names of the menu items and the number of portion sales forecasted for each. The entries in the third column, headed "Cost," are the standard portion costs for the items, as determined by means of the methods identified and discussed in Chapter 6: formula, recipe detail and cost card, butcher test, cooking loss test, and factors derived from the tests. In the next column, the figures entered are menu sales prices. Each of these, obviously, is the amount to be collected from each customer ordering the item named on that line. In the next column, headed "Food Cost Percent," the entry on each line is the ratio of cost to sales, given the standard portion cost and menu sales price identified for the item named on that line.

After all of these entries have been recorded, entries are calculated in the next column, "Total Cost," by multiplying the number of portion sales forecasted for any given item by the standard portion cost of that item. Thus, referring to the line for Strip Steak in Figure 10.3, one can see that the 15 portion sales forecasted have been multiplied by the $7.50 standard portion cost to determine total cost of $112.50.

$$15 \times \$7.50 = \$112.50$$

• FIGURE 10.2 •

Comparison: Sales Forecast and Actual Sales

BQ

Day ___Friday___   Date ___5-Mar___

Volume Forecast

Menu Item		Sales Forecast		Actual Sales		Difference
Bean Soup		12		12		
Fish Chowder		19		23		4
Duck Empanadas		13		11		−2
Vegetarian Tartlets		11		9		−2
Salmon Croustade		6		6		
Oysters Rockefeller		16		15		−1
Eggplant Roulade		6		6		
Shiitake Mushrooms		9		10		1
Strip Steak		15		13		−2
Tournedos Bistro		10		10		
Duck Breast		5		5		
Leg of Lamb		7		8		1
Baby Back Ribs		6		6		
Tamarind and Ginger Shrimp		7		8		1
Gnocchi		5		4		−1
Darjeeling-Smoked Salmon		12		13		1
Paella		8		7		−1
Big Eye Tuna		5		5		
Miso Glazed Black Cod		9		9		
Chicken Breast		9		11		2
Tagliatelle		7		7		
Scallops		6		6		
Capellini		13		9		−4
Catch of the Day		11		11		
Cheese Tartlettes		4		3		−1
Chocolate Torte		6		5		−1
Fresh Fruit Tart		5		5		
Total Covers		135		132		

• FIGURE 10.3 •

Menu Pre-Cost and Abstract

Day Friday Date March 5, 20XX

| | FORECAST | | | | | | ABSTRACT | | | | | |
| | FORECAST SALES AND FORECAST COST PERCENT | | | | | | ACTUAL SALES AND STANDARD COST PERCENT | | | | | |
Menu Item	Number Forecast	Cost	Sales Price	Food Cost Percent	Total Cost	Total Sales	Number Sold	Cost	Sales Price	Food Cost Percentage	Total Cost	Total Sales
Bean Soup	12	$1.55	$4.95	31.313%	$18.60	$59.40	12	$1.55	$4.95	31.313%	$18.60	$59.40
Fish Chowder	19	$2.60	$8.25	31.515%	$49.40	$156.75	23	$2.60	$8.25	31.515%	$59.80	$189.75
Duck Empanades	13	$2.40	$7.65	31.373%	$31.20	$99.45	11	$2.40	$7.65	31.373%	$26.40	$84.15
Vegetarian Tartlets	11	$2.00	$6.50	30.769%	$22.00	$71.50	9	$2.00	$6.50	30.769%	$18.00	$58.50
Salmon Croustade	6	$2.60	$8.20	31.707%	$15.60	$49.20	6	$2.60	$8.20	31.707%	$15.60	$49.20
Oysters Rockefeller	16	$3.00	$9.35	32.086%	$48.00	$149.60	15	$3.00	$9.35	32.086%	$45.00	$140.25
Eggplant Roulade	6	$1.75	$5.50	31.818%	$10.50	$33.00	6	$1.75	$5.50	31.818%	$10.50	$33.00
Shitake Mushrooms	9	$1.75	$5.50	31.818%	$15.75	$49.50	10	$1.75	$5.50	31.818%	$17.50	$55.00
Strip Steak	15	$7.50	$23.65	31.712%	$112.50	$354.75	13	$7.50	$23.65	31.712%	$97.50	$307.45
Tournedos Bistro	10	$8.70	$24.75	35.152%	$87.00	$247.50	10	$8.70	$24.75	35.152%	$87.00	$247.50
Duck Breast	5	$7.30	$21.40	34.112%	$36.50	$107.00	5	$7.30	$21.40	34.112%	$36.50	$107.00
Leg of Lamb	7	$6.90	$21.50	32.093%	$48.30	$150.50	8	$6.90	$21.50	32.093%	$55.20	$172.00
Baby Back Ribs	6	$6.30	$20.50	30.732%	$37.80	$123.00	6	$6.30	$20.50	30.732%	$37.80	$123.00
Tamarind and Ginger Shrimp	7	$5.20	$18.00	28.889%	$36.40	$126.00	8	$5.20	$18.00	28.889%	$41.60	$144.00

(continued)

• FIGURE 10.3 • (continued)

| Menu Item | FORECAST | | | | | | ABSTRACT | | | | | |
| | FORECAST SALES AND FORECAST COST PERCENT | | | | | | ACTUAL SALES AND STANDARD COST PERCENT | | | | | |
	Number Forecast	Cost	Sales Price	Food Cost Percent	Total Cost	Total Sales	Number Sold	Cost	Sales Price	Food Cost Percent	Total Cost	Total Sales
Gnocchi	5	$3.80	$16.50	23.030%	$ 19.00	$ 82.50	4	$3.80	$16.50	23.030%	$ 15.20	$ 66.00
Darjeeling-Smoked Salmon	12	$5.75	$19.20	29.948%	$ 69.00	$ 230.40	13	$5.75	$19.20	29.948%	$ 74.75	$ 249.60
Paella	8	$4.65	$16.50	28.182%	$ 37.20	$ 132.00	7	$4.65	$16.50	28.182%	$ 32.55	$ 115.50
Big Eye Tuna	5	$6.35	$20.85	30.456%	$ 31.75	$ 104.25	5	$6.35	$20.85	30.456%	$ 31.75	$ 104.25
Miso Glazed Black Cod	9	$7.75	$24.75	31.313%	$ 69.75	$ 222.75	9	$7.75	$24.75	31.313%	$ 69.75	$ 222.75
Chicken Breast	9	$5.20	$16.45	31.611%	$ 46.80	$ 148.05	11	$5.20	$16.45	31.611%	$ 57.20	$ 180.95
Tagliatelle	7	$5.90	$19.00	31.053%	$ 41.30	$ 133.00	7	$5.90	$19.00	31.053%	$ 41.30	$ 133.00
Scallops	6	$7.20	$19.95	36.090%	$ 43.20	$ 119.70	6	$7.20	$19.95	36.090%	$ 43.20	$ 119.70
Capellini	13	$7.90	$21.40	36.916%	$ 102.70	$ 278.20	9	$7.90	$21.40	36.916%	$ 71.10	$ 192.60
Catch of the Day	11	$5.30	$16.50	32.121%	$ 58.30	$ 181.50	11	$5.30	$16.50	32.121%	$ 58.30	$ 181.50
Cheese Tartlettes	4	$1.20	$ 3.85	31.169%	$ 4.80	$ 15.40	3	$1.20	$ 3.85	31.169%	$ 3.60	$ 11.55
Chocolate Torte	6	$1.40	$ 4.40	31.818%	$ 8.40	$ 26.40	5	$1.40	$ 4.40	31.818%	$ 7.00	$ 22.00
Fresh Fruit Tart	5	$0.90	$ 2.75	32.727%	$ 4.50	$ 13.75	5	$0.90	$ 2.75	32.727%	$ 4.50	$ 13.75
Total Covers	135			31.926%	$1,106.25	$ 3,465.05	132			31.838%	$1,077.20	$ 3,383.35

Because $7.50 is a standard portion cost, $112.50 is really a total standard cost for the required quantity of Strip Steak and the accompanying garnishes. It is the total that 15 portions of this item should cost. It presupposes that each of the 15 portions will be exactly as specified in terms of cost of ingredients, proportions, production method, and portion size.

The same procedure is followed for each item listed, and the standard cost of producing the forecasted number of portions of each item is determined. All entries in the "Total Cost" column are then added to determine the total standard cost for producing all items on the menu.

Completing the "Total Sales" column requires the same general approach. One multiplies the number of portion sales forecasted for each item by the sales price of that item. Thus, referring again to the line for Strip Steak in Figure 10.3, one sees that the 15 portion sales forecasted have been multiplied by the $23.65 sales price to determine total sales of $354.75. This is the total income that should result from selling 15 portions of this item after incurring costs projected at $112.50. Once total sales figures for all items have been determined in this way, the "Total Sales" column is added to determine total income that should be generated by the sales recorded in the forecast. In this manner, one can arrive at anticipated totals for forecasted standard costs and sales.

Once total costs and total sales have been forecasted, a forecasted cost percent can be predicted by simply dividing forecasted costs by forecasted sales and multiplying the result by 100. In the example cited, the total forecasted costs of $1,106.25 has been divided by the total forecasted sales of $3,465.05, and the resulting decimal answer, .31926, has been multiplied by 100 to determine cost percent of 31.926 percent.

$$\frac{\$1,106.25}{\$3,465.05} = .31926$$

$$.31926 \times 100 = 31.926\%$$

The foregoing discussion has presupposed the existence of a menu scheduled for production for a particular day in the near future, as well as a need or desire to predict the forecasted standard costs and sales associated with that menu. However, the forecast section of the Menu Pre-Cost and Abstract has another important application for the foodservice operator. Total forecasts for the individual menu items are added to project total standard costs and total sales for the proposed menu as a whole, based on a weighted average of the menu items sold. In fact, by using a popularity index in this way, and applying it to all menu items to extend costs and sales, food cost percent and gross profit can be anticipated. This is an excellent way to determine if a menu is suitable for the business. If the projections are judged satisfactory, the manager can send the menu to a printer. If they are not considered satisfactory, various changes can be made, because production has not yet started. Essentially, a new forecast can be developed. Standard cost and sales figures may be raised or lowered, depending on which is desirable, by the following means:

1. Sales prices may be changed.
2. Standard portion costs may be changed by altering portion standards—sizes, ingredients, recipes, or some combination of these.
3. Menu items may be added or eliminated.
4. The popularity index can otherwise be manipulated.

Conceivably, all of these means may be employed, and the final version of the new menu may bear little or no resemblance to that originally proposed. If the menu originally proposed may produce results that would be undesirable or unacceptable, the new menu should be successful, provided that good judgement and careful calculations have gone into its preparation. Further discussion of each of these means will be discussed in Chapter 11, "Menu Engineering and Analysis."

The Abstract

The **abstract**, or right-hand portion, of the form is prepared after the fact—after sales have taken place. The person preparing the abstract (a food controller or a manager) refers to the portion sales figures developed for inclusion in the sales history. These are recorded in the first column, "Number Sold." The next three columns, "Cost" (for portion cost), "Sales Price," and "Food Cost Percent," are merely copied from the forecast section of the form. To complete the "Total Cost" column, multiply the number of portions sold for each item by the standard portion cost for that item. Next, add the column to determine total standard cost of the portions sold. The "Total Sales" column is completed in similar fashion, by multiplying the number of portions sold for each item by the sales price for that item and then adding the column to determine a total for all portions sold. To determine a standard cost percent based on actual portions sold, divide total standard costs by total sales.

The next step is to compare the cost percent determined on the forecast (left) side of the form with that determined on the abstract (right) side. There invariably will be differences. The number of portions sold for each menu item will not be exactly the same as forecasted. And because each menu item has a different cost percent, the combined cost percents for the abstract side will not be the same as the forecasted side.

If a menu item has sold in greater quantities than forecasted, this may raise questions about the extent to which the kitchen staff is following production standards. Sales in excess of the number forecasted should always be investigated. Even though the sale of greater numbers of portions may have produced additional income, failure to follow production goals set by management indicates that at least one of the established control procedures is not working. It is quite possible that the kitchen staff produced the quantity called for on the production sheet and that the extra portions were made by reducing portion size. This is clearly undesirable and may lead to loss of business, because it really means that customers have been cheated.

Another important reason for comparing the forecasted cost percent with the percentage developed from the abstract is that any difference between the two indicates the extent to which the forecast was wrong, in terms of incorrect total volume, incorrect forecasted sales of particular items, or both. In addition, this difference will be an excellent indication of the extent to which one's forecasting techniques can be improved. The comparison is likely to suggest possibilities for improving forecasting performance, which may help bring future cost percents on abstracts more nearly in line with those of forecasts. After all, forecasted cost percents have received some measure of approval as acceptable goals, and therefore should not be ignored.

A forecasted cost percent indicates the level of food cost that management will approve to achieve a given level of dollar sales. In addition, a forecasted cost percent reflects plans for achieving those sales—plans that can be seen in the standards and standard procedures established for all phases of operation. So, to the extent that forecasted cost percents are not in line with those calculated after sales, overall performance, including forecasting, can be improved.

In an ideal situation, the cost percent calculated on the abstract side of the form should agree with the cost percent calculated on the forecasted side of the form, indicating that everything has gone according to plan. If the exact number of portions needed had been prepared in exact conformity to the standards and standard procedures established by management, and the sales of each item had been as forecasted, each side would be the same. However, this seldom, if ever, happens.

Computer users with application programs can easily calculate standard portion costs and prepare Menu Pre-Cost and Abstract forms. Even the most basic spreadsheet program makes it reasonably simple to prepare a Menu Pre-Cost and Abstract—a form that is always time-consuming to complete manually. Because computers are now universally common in foodservice operations, the Menu Pre-Cost and Abstract is becoming much more widely used than it was in the past. It is a comparatively simple worksheet to develop, provided that one has access to sales prices, standard portion costs, forecasts, and the sales history. The left, or pre-cost, section can be displayed on a monitor or printed before the forecasted date and then circulated to appropriate members of the management team for adjustment before the fact. The right, or abstract, section can be completed after the fact. The sales data can either be keyed in manually or through the use of an integrated software system, automatically input from the sales history. Formulas in the worksheet will quickly calculate any number of figures, including total standard cost, total sales, and standard cost percent, among others.

If the kinds of figures identified in this discussion are developed one meal at a time, or even one day at a time, and then put aside, they are not being used as effectively as they might be. For example, it is possible and desirable to develop abstracts of standard costs and sales over a period of some days or weeks and then summarize the results. Taken together, the days or weeks can be considered a test period, with the results offering a good indication of a realistic and acceptable level for food cost percent over time. Figure 10.4 illustrates a method for summarizing figures developed over a five-day test period.

• FIGURE 10.4 •

Summary of Daily Abstracts

Date		Standard Cost		Sales		Standard Cost Percent
1-Mar		$ 955.20		$ 2,715.70		35.178%
2-Mar		$1,060.60		$ 3,010.40		35.231%
3-Mar		$1,255.30		$ 3,588.90		34.977%
4-Mar		$1,050.75		$ 2,960.30		34.495%
5-Mar		$1,077.20		$ 3,383.35		31.838%
		$5,399.05		$ 15,658.25		
Total Standard Cost				$ 5,399.05		
Total Sales				$ 15,658.25		
Standard Cost Percent				34.481%		

In this case, Bistro Quatre should generally operate with a food cost-to-sales ratio of 34.481 percent for all items, assuming that the sales mix does not change dramatically. Such figures can be useful in judging effectiveness of operations from week to week or month to month.

If standards are in effect for every item served, if the standard portion cost for every item is known, and if a Menu Pre-Cost and Abstract prepared daily reflects the total menu, it is possible to regularly compare standard and actual food costs daily and to date during an operating period of any given length. Actual food costs are determined from direct purchases and storeroom issues including various adjustments, as discussed in Chapter 9. The standard cost of all the portions sold is taken from the Menu Pre-Cost and Abstract. Food sales figures come from register readings or accounting department records. All figures are recorded on a form such as that shown in Figure 10.5.

Actual cost percent for any given day equals actual cost for that day divided by sales for that day. Actual cost percent to date on any day equals actual cost to date for all the days thus far in the period, divided by sales to date for all the days thus far in the period. Similarly, **standard cost percent** for any given day equals standard cost for that day divided by sales for that day. Standard cost percent to date on any day equals standard cost to date for all the days thus far in the period, divided by sales to date for all the days thus far in the period.

• FIGURE 10.5 •

Summary of Actual and Standard Food Costs, Food Sales, and Potential Savings

Date	Actual Cost Today	Actual Cost To date	Standard Cost Today	Standard Cost To date	Sales Today	Sales To date	Actual Cost Percent Today	Actual Cost Percent To date	Standard Cost Percent Today	Standard Cost Percent To date	Potential Savings Today Dollars	Potential Savings To date Dollars	Percent Savings Today Percentage	Percent Savings To date Percentage
1-Mar	$1,033.40	$1,033.40	$ 955.20	$ 955.20	$ 2,715.30	$ 2,715.30	38.058%	38.058%	35.178%	35.178%	$ 78.20	$ 78.20	2.880%	2.880%
2-Mar	$1,103.60	$2,137.00	$1,060.60	$ 2,015.80	$ 3,010.40	$ 5,725.70	36.660%	37.323%	35.231%	35.206%	$ 43.00	$121.20	1.428%	2.117%
3-Mar	$1,277.80	$3,414.80	$1,255.30	$ 3,271.10	$ 3,588.90	$ 9,314.60	35.604%	36.661%	34.977%	35.118%	$ 22.50	$143.70	0.627%	1.543%
4-Mar	$1,100.60	$4,515.40	$1,050.75	$ 4,321.85	$ 2,960.30	$12,274.90	37.179%	36.786%	35.495%	35.209%	$ 49.85	$193.55	1.684%	1.577%
5-Mar	$1,186.50	$5,701.90	$1,077.20	$ 5,399.05	$ 3,383.35	$15,658.25	31.838%	36.415%	31.838%	34.481%	$109.30	$302.85	3.321%	1.934%

Typically, actual cost today and to date are greater than standard cost today and to date. The difference should be regarded either as waste or as its equivalent—excessive cost that can be reduced or eliminated if staff performance is improved. The raw dollar figures indicating that excessive costs have developed are not particularly useful for identifying specific causes of inefficiency or other operating difficulties. To determine specific causes, one must monitor and analyze data and operations to detect the areas in which waste and excessive costs have developed.

Potential Savings

Potential savings may be defined as the difference, or variance, between actual costs and standard costs. Potential savings may be recorded as dollars, as percentages of sales, or as both. Regardless of which one is used, potential savings must be regarded as reflecting the differences between existing conditions and those that would exist if all standards and standard procedures were followed to perfection. No foodservice operation will ever achieve that perfection, but it is usually possible to find ways to improve performance.

LEARNING OBJECTIVE 10.4
Define *potential savings* and list several conditions that affect it.

Figure 10.5 shows potential savings of $302.85 for the first five days in March. This amount may not appear to be significant, taking into consideration total costs of $5,701.90. The average is only $60.57 per day, but if this continued for one year, it would add up to $22,108.05—a significant amount.

Any number of problems can develop in day-to-day operations that will lead to differences between standard and actual costs. These include overpurchasing, overproduction, pilferage, spoilage, improper portioning, and failure to follow standard recipes, among many others. As we have seen before, each phase of operations must be controlled or excessive costs will result. When improvements are made and problems are reduced or eliminated, actual costs will be more closely comparable with standard costs, thus reducing any variance or potential savings. Ironically, potential savings and waste are synonymous. Reducing potential savings means reducing waste and excessive cost.

When potential savings figures are available daily and to date during an operating period, it is possible to make daily investigations of any variances. Understanding that the differences can be traced to instances in which actual performance is producing results other than those anticipated by established standards and standard procedures, a manager should be able to make hundreds of comparisons and judgements daily. Many believe that good managers can profitably spend many of their working hours comparing what they see with what they should be seeing and making judgements about any differences. Other managers avoid spending time in their offices, preferring to be out in those areas where employees are working. This, they believe, gives them opportunities to see where and how actual performance differs from the standards established so they can take corrective actions.

It will never be possible to completely eliminate discrepancies between actual and standard costs. Instead, management must make intelligent judgements about the extent to which reductions are possible and must be ready to accept some small discrepancy between the actual and standard costs. There are no industrywide figures to use as guides. However, once management has established a reasonable figure for acceptable variance, exceptions can be noted quickly, and investigations can begin at once. After all, an immediate investigation is more likely to uncover causes than one undertaken days or weeks later. As soon as causes are identified, one can take remedial action in the hope of correcting problems before their effects become pronounced. Immediate discussions with the chef, steward, and key personnel will often reveal causes and suggest simple corrective measures.

PERIODIC COMPARISON

LEARNING OBJECTIVE 10.5
Calculate and compare actual and standard costs using the periodic method.

In establishments where daily calculations of standard costs and potential savings are impractical, it is often possible to adopt an alternative method that relies on periodic calculations for determining potential savings. Like the daily method described in the preceding section, the periodic method presupposes that standards and standard procedures have been established for all phases of operations, that sales histories are maintained, and that standard portion costs are known. Under these circumstances, one can calculate standard cost for a test period (e.g., one week) and compare that figure to actual cost for the same period to determine the extent of potential savings. This can be done for a period of any length, long or short, depending on the need for information and the time available to accomplish the task.

Using a form such as that illustrated in Figure 10.6, one records menu items and portion sales for the test period. This information can be found in sales history. Standard portion costs are entered as well, derived from records of calculations based on formulas, recipe detail and cost cards, butcher tests, cooking loss tests, and cost factors. The total standard cost of the number of portions sold of a given item is found by multiplying the number of portions by the portion cost. Thus, for Strip Steak, one multiplies 55 portions by the $7.50 standard portion cost to determine the total standard cost of $412.50.

$$55 \times \$7.50 = \$412.50$$

The total of standard costs for all items sold in the period is determined by adding the entries in the "Total Standard Cost" column. Actual costs for the period are determined from records of direct purchases, storeroom issues, and any adjustments obtained from the accounting office. If the foodservice operation is already following the daily costing procedures described in Chapter 9, actual cost figures for the period will be readily available.

• FIGURE 10.6 •

Periodic Potential Savings Worksheet for Test Period March 11–16

Menu Item	# Sold	Portion Cost	Sales Price	Total Standard Cost	Total Sales
Bean Soup	60	$1.55	$ 4.95	$ 93.00	$ 297.00
Fish Chowder	115	$2.60	$ 8.25	$ 299.00	$ 948.75
Duck Empanadas	55	$2.40	$ 7.65	$ 132.00	$ 420.75
Vegetable Tartlets	45	$2.00	$ 6.50	$ 90.00	$ 292.50
Salmon Croustade	58	$2.60	$ 8.20	$ 150.80	$ 475.60
Oysters Rockefeller	75	$3.00	$ 9.35	$ 225.00	$ 701.25
Egplant Roulade	33	$1.75	$ 5.50	$ 57.75	$ 181.50
Shitake Mushrooms	52	$1.75	$ 5.50	$ 91.00	$ 286.00
Strip Steak	55	$7.50	$23.65	$ 412.50	$ 1,300.75
Tournedos Bistro	52	$8.70	$24.75	$ 452.40	$ 1,287.00
Duck Breast	23	$7.30	$21.40	$ 167.90	$ 492.20
Leg of Lamb	41	$6.90	$21.50	$ 282.90	$ 881.50
Baby Back Ribs	29	$6.30	$20.50	$ 182.70	$ 594.50
Tamarind and Ginger Shrimp	42	$5.20	$18.00	$ 218.40	$ 756.00
Gnocchi	22	$3.80	$16.50	$ 83.60	$ 363.00
Darjeeling-Smoked Salmon	59	$5.75	$19.20	$ 339.25	$ 1,132.80
Paella	46	$4.65	$16.50	$ 213.90	$ 759.00
Big Eye Tuna	27	$6.35	$20.85	$ 171.45	$ 562.95
Miso Glazed Black Cod	41	$7.75	$24.75	$ 317.75	$ 1,014.75
Chicken Breast	48	$5.20	$16.45	$ 249.60	$ 789.60
Taglliatelle	36	$5.90	$19.00	$ 212.40	$ 684.00
Scallops	29	$7.20	$19.95	$ 208.80	$ 578.55
Capellini	39	$7.90	$21.40	$ 308.10	$ 834.60
Catch of the Day	48	$5.30	$16.50	$ 254.40	$ 792.00
Cheese Tartlettes	14	$1.20	$ 3.85	$ 16.80	$ 53.90
Chocolate Torte	28	$1.40	$ 4.40	$ 39.20	$ 123.20
Fresh Fruit Tart	25	$0.90	$ 2.75	$ 22.50	$ 68.75
Total Covers	637			$5,293.10	$16,672.40

Sales For Test Period	$16,672.40
Actual Cost	$ 5,566.85
Standard Cost	$ 5,293.10
Potential Savings	$ 273.75

Actual Cost Percent	33.390%
Standard Cost %	31.748%
Potential Savings as a % of Sales	1.642%

With the necessary total figures for actual and standard costs for the test period recorded on the form, the difference between the two can be determined by subtracting. This difference can be stated in dollar terms and as a percentage of total sales for the test period. If the test period is truly representative of day-to-day operations, one can take the difference between actual and standard costs to indicate the extent of inefficiency or improper performance in the enterprise. When necessary, one can also institute appropriate corrective actions intended to improve actual performance before the end of the next test period.

It is usually advisable to select test periods (where sales patterns are typical) at random, after the fact. The figures developed also tend to be more truly representative if employees did not know in advance that a certain week was being used as a test period. If they knew, they might pay more careful attention to both the standards set by management and their own performance with respect to those standards. Although the results of their efforts might be entirely desirable, the comparison of actual versus standard costs for the period would clearly present distorted pictures of operations and of potential savings.

Once a valid standard cost percent for an operation has been determined, it may be compared with actual cost percents and used to evaluate day-to-day operations in the intervals between test periods. Thus, one has a reasonable means for making judgements about the efficiency of operations on a regular basis. For example, if actual cost percents are developed on a weekly basis, it may be much more useful to make comparisons with a recently calculated standard cost percent than with an actual cost percent from the previous week. This assumes that no significant changes have been made to menu contents, sales prices, or portion costs since the test period. Any significant changes in these factors will result in comparisons that will be less useful. The important point to remember is that a comparison of actual cost percent for any given period with actual cost percent for an earlier period may not provide useful information about whether there are excessive costs in an operation. That determination can be made only by comparing actual cost with standard cost or actual cost percent with standard cost percent.

To the extent that savings can be achieved without incurring other costs, profits will be increased. If, for example, some portion of the potential savings figure can be traced to overproduction, then by eliminating the overproduction while keeping other costs in line, one should see a reduction in excessive costs and an increase in profit. Furthermore, the increase in profit should be equal to the reduction in excessive costs. This is illustrated by the following:

	Actual	Standard
Sales	$10,000	$10,000
Food cost	3,800	3,400
Gross profit	$ 6,200	$ 6,600

It should be immediately apparent that a $400 reduction in actual food costs, bringing actual food cost in line with standard food cost, will bring an identical increase in gross profit. If this reduction can be achieved without increasing any other costs (e.g., the cost of labour), then literally every dollar saved will be an additional dollar in profit. This fact, perhaps more than any other, should point out the importance of regularly comparing actual cost with standard cost, determining the causes of any excess of actual cost over standard cost, and taking appropriate corrective actions. These actions, obviously, should be aimed at bringing actual performance in line with that anticipated by established standards and standard procedures and, by this means, reducing or eliminating excessive costs.

THINGS TO CONSIDER

In a restaurant where items are produced from raw ingredients, there is often a discrepancy between the ratio of food and labour costs for the various menu selections. Many operators are happy and successful if prime costs come in at approximately 60 percent of sales, regardless of the split between food and labour costs. When looking into the way prime costs break down, there may be food costs of 30 percent and labour costs of 30 percent. When further comparing individual main dish ratios, there could be substantial variations in these relationships. The food costs for some items may be 40 percent and the labour to produce them 20 percent, while others may be the other way around. There are infinite combinations of food and labour ratios that would yield 60 percent of sales. After seeing a financial statement for a fixed period, managers will be happy if menu mix yields prime costs of 60 percent knowing that the 40 percent margin is sufficient to pay all other costs and provide profit.

It may not be that simple when using the Menu Pre-Cost and Abstract to make decisions. It is important that the other prime cost, labour, maintains a similar ratio to sales for all of the items being considered. Special attention must be given if the deviation of labour cost from one menu item to another is too wide. Food and labour costs may have to be taken separately to ensure that decisions are based on an analysis of appropriate data.

When reconciling forecasted to actual numbers, if you uncover excess preparation, it would be wise to remember that not only should you reduce the production of expensive and perishable items to protect food costs, but you should also reduce the production of items that require extensive preparation to protect labour costs even when the food costs associated with them are minimal.

There are many other areas, like menu engineering and maximizing profit, where knowing both the food and labour cost components of menu items may be critical to proper analysis.

CHAPTER ESSENTIALS

In this chapter, we presented two methods for determining total standard cost for a given operating period. We explained the Menu Pre-Cost and Abstract, providing a step-by-step method for completing the form, and discussed the important information that can be obtained from it. We described how the Menu Pre-Cost and Abstract can be used to project and evaluate the consequences of offering a new or revised menu and identified four means that can be used to change projected costs or sales. We identified computers and spreadsheets as useful tools for preparing the Menu Pre-Cost and Abstract and for comparing actual and standard costs for an operating period. We defined *potential savings*, equated potential savings with waste and excessive costs, and explained how reductions in excessive costs result in increased profits. Finally, we explained how comparing actual and standard costs for a period can reveal inefficiencies in day-to-day operations, including poor forecasting, overproduction, failure to follow standard recipes, and overpurchasing, to name just a few. Students of this text should be able to add to this list of inefficiencies, knowing all of the areas where controls are necessary.

KEY TERMS IN THIS CHAPTER

Abstract, p. 273

Actual cost percent, p. 275

Menu Pre-Cost and Abstract, p. 268

Potential savings, p. 277

Standard cost, p. 267

Standard cost percent, p. 275

Variance, p. 266

QUESTIONS AND PROBLEMS

1. List and discuss five problems that can lead to differences between actual cost and standard cost for an operating period, pointing out how each increases potential savings.
2. It has been said that potential savings, taken as a percentage of sales, can be used as one possible measure of operating efficiency. Do you agree or disagree? Why?
3. Discuss the advantages and disadvantages of calculating and comparing standard and actual costs by the daily method rather than by the periodic method.
4. Using the figures that follow, determine actual cost percent, standard cost percent, and potential savings as a dollar figure and as a percentage of sales.

	Sales	Actual Cost	Standard Cost
a.	$ 400.00	$ 120.00	$ 100.00
b.	$ 860.00	$ 318.20	$ 301.00
c.	$ 3,486.00	$1,394.40	$1,324.68
d.	$11,198.00	$3,919.30	$3,695.34

5. Using the form illustrated in Figure 10.5, prepare a summary of actual and standard food costs, food sales, and potential savings for a four-day period, given the following figures:

	Actual Cost Today	Standard Cost	Total Sales Today
Monday	$110	$100	$300
Tuesday	$160	$145	$450
Wednesday	$175	$160	$505
Thursday	$185	$175	$520

6. Using the form illustrated in Figure 10.3 for a guide, prepare a Menu Pre-Cost and Abstract, given the following information:

Item	Portions Forecasted	Portion Cost	Sales Price	Number Sold
A	60	$2.50	$6.00	55
B	20	$3.25	$8.50	18
C	80	$2.25	$5.00	80
D	40	$2.70	$6.50	30

7. Use the following information to prepare a Menu Pre-Cost and Abstract:

Item	Portions Forecasted	Portion Cost	Sales Price	Number Sold
A	30	$3.70	$8.50	28
B	42	$3.00	$6.80	42
C	73	$2.75	$6.00	70
D	115	$2.50	$5.50	106

8. In an essay of approximately 300 words, compare and contrast the Menu Pre-Cost and Abstract to the Portion Inventory and Reconciliation (Chapter 7) as a method for controlling costs.

9. The owner of the Red Fox Inn has developed a new menu for use in her establishment. Each menu item represents a complete meal. She has determined standard cost for each item and has kept careful records of sales for the month of March. The data are as follows:

Menu Item	Number Sold	Standard Portion Cost
A	310	$5.50
B	270	7.80
C	540	3.80
D	425	5.25
E	175	8.70
F	340	6.50
G	510	5.70
H	480	4.20

Food sales for March totalled $50,028.50.

Using the information provided, calculate total standard cost for the period.

10. The following figures are from the accounting records of the Red Fox Inn, the restaurant identified in Question 9:

Opening inventory	$ 7,414.80
Closing inventory	6,327.35
Food purchases	17,642.80
Transfers: beverage to food	443.00
Transfers: food to beverage	226.00
Employees' meals	837.00

a. Calculate cost of food sold for the month of March.
b. Using information provided in Question 9, calculate each of the following:
   1. Actual cost percent
   2. Standard cost percent
   3. Potential savings in dollars
   4. Potential savings as a percentage of sales

11. Why might the increased use of computers in foodservice make the Menu Pre-Cost and Abstract more commonly used than has been the case?
12. Define each of the key terms in this chapter.

EXCEL EXERCISES

Exercise 10.1

Complete the comparison of sales forecast and actual sales for Barnaby's Hideaway for Friday, October 6. Calculate the difference between sales forecast and actual sales. Also, calculate total covers for both forecasted and actual sales, remembering that one main dish constitutes one cover.

Exercise 10.2

Complete the Menu Pre-Cost and Abstract using the information from Exercise 10.1.

Exercise 10.3

Complete the Periodic Savings Worksheet for Barnaby's Hideaway for the period October 10–15.

CHAPTER 11

Menu Engineering and Analysis

• **LEARNING OBJECTIVES** •

After reading this chapter, you should be able to:

11.1 Complete a menu engineering worksheet and analyze the resulting information.

11.2 Define the terms *star, dog, plowhorse,* and *puzzle* as they relate to menu analysis.

11.3 Prepare a chart showing stars, dogs, plowhorses, and puzzles.

11.4 Describe appropriate action to take for stars, dogs, plowhorses, and puzzles when changes are made to the menu.

INTRODUCTION

Cost-control procedures discussed in previous chapters were established to keep excess cost from developing and to help keep cost and cost percents within predetermined bounds. However, keeping food cost percents to a given figure (e.g., 35 percent), while critically important, does not mean that the most profit is obtained. In the final analysis, we take dollars, not percentages, to the bank. Many factors, including the contribution margin of menu items and number of covers served, determine how much profit there will be. As an example, two items found on the menu at Bistro Quatre are Strip Steak and Grilled Breast of Chicken. Strip Steak has a standard cost of $7.50 and a selling price of $23.65. Grilled Breast of Chicken has a standard cost of $5.20 and a selling price of $16.45. It is apparent that the contribution margin of the Strip Steak is considerably higher. At this point, it will help to reflect on the definition of *contribution margin* from Chapter 3, given as money available to cover fixed costs and provide profit.

Item	Selling Price	Cost	Contribution margin
Strip steak	$23.65	$7.50	$16.15
Grilled chicken breast.	$16.45	$5.20	$11.25
Difference in Contribution Margin			$ 4.90

If Bistro Quatre were to sell 100 orders of each of these two menu items over a period of two weeks, the restaurant would obtain $490 more in contribution margin from the steak. Further, it is very likely the labour cost in preparing the chicken might be greater than that of the steak. Generally, managers would rather sell items that provide the greatest contribution margin, because more profit can be obtained.

A very useful technique for analyzing menu sales and providing helpful information for evaluating every item on the menu relative to its popularity and contribution to bottom-line dollars is *menu engineering*. It provides a means for monitoring the effectiveness of efforts to maximize gross revenue from a menu. It follows naturally from our discussion of the Menu Pre-Cost and Abstract form in the previous chapter.

MENU ENGINEERING

LEARNING OBJECTIVE 11.1
Complete a menu engineering worksheet and analyze the resulting information.

The menu analysis technique described in the following pages was developed by Michael L. Kasavana and Donald I. Smith and was described in a book published in 1982. Known as **menu engineering**, the technique is now widely known and respected and has been the subject of numerous papers and articles. Although some do not agree entirely with the conclusions drawn by Kasavana and Smith, these authors' approach to menu analysis is still timely and is both interesting and revealing.

Menu engineering can best be explained by example. A Menu Engineering Worksheet showing sales of main dish items of Bistro Quatre for the month of February is illustrated in Figure 11.1. Initially, one notes many similarities to the Menu Pre-Cost and Abstract form illustrated and discussed in Chapter 10. Column headings on the worksheet such as "Menu Item," "Number Sold," "Food Cost," "Sales Price," "Menu Cost," and "Total Sales" are familiar. Although the terms differ slightly, these are much the same as those used on the Menu Pre-Cost and Abstract form. Specifically, the Menu Engineering Worksheet closely corresponds to the right, or abstract, side of the form in Chapter 10. The sources of the data and the required calculations are exactly the same.

There are several additional columns that distinguish the Menu Engineering Worksheet: (C) "Menu Mix %"; (F) "Item CM"; (L) "Menu CM"; (P) "CM Category"; (R) "MM Category"; and (S) "Menu Item Classification." At the bottom of the worksheet, there are several additional calculations. Both the additional columns and the calculations require some explanation.

Column C: Menu Mix Percent

The **menu mix percent** is the same as the popularity index, which was calculated in Chapter 7. The percentage for each item is calculated by dividing the number of units sold by the total number of units sold for all items. For example, 252 portions of Strip Steak were sold, and total portion sales for all items was 2,635. The menu mix percent for this item is calculated as 9.564 percent. In addition, 207 portions of Grilled Breast of Chicken were sold, and the menu mix percentage was calculated at 7.856 percent. The menu mix percent for each of the other items is calculated the same way.

Column F: Item CM

The student will recall from discussions in previous chapters that contribution margin (CM) is defined as sales price minus variable cost per unit. It is another term for gross profit (sales minus cost of sales), previously calculated for Strip Steak and Grilled Breast of Chicken. Thus, the CM for Strip Steak and all other menu items is determined by subtracting the portion cost for the item from its sales price, as previously illustrated.

For Strip Steak:

Sales price	$23.65
−Food cost	$ 7.50
CM	$16.15

The CM is the amount available from each sale to contribute toward meeting all other costs of operation, and, when those costs have been met, to provide profit.

• FIGURE 11.1 •

Bistro Quatre Menu Engineering Worksheet Month of February

A	B	C	D	E	F	G	H	L	P	R	S
Menu Item	Number Sold	Menu Mix %	Food Cost	Sales Price	Item CM (E-D)	Menu Cost (D*B)	Total Sales (E*B)	Menu CM (F*B)	CM Category	MM Category	Menu Item Classification
Strip Steak	252	9.564%	$7.50	$23.65	$16.15	$ 1,890.00	$ 5,959.80	$ 4,069.80	H	H	STAR
Tournedos Bistro	230	8.729%	$8.70	$24.75	$16.05	$ 2,001.00	$ 5,692.50	$ 3,691.50	H	H	STAR
Duck Breast	81	3.074%	$7.30	$21.40	$14.10	$ 591.30	$ 1,733.40	$ 1,142.10	H	L	PUZZLE
Leg of Lamb	102	3.871%	$6.90	$21.50	$14.60	$ 703.80	$ 2,193.00	$ 1,489.20	H	L	PUZZLE
Baby Back Ribs	98	3.719%	$6.30	$20.50	$14.20	$ 617.40	$ 2,009.00	$ 1,391.60	H	L	PUZZLE
Tamarind and Ginger Shrimp	204	7.742%	$5.20	$18.00	$12.80	$ 1,060.80	$ 3,672.00	$ 2,611.20	L	H	PLOWHORSE
Gnocchi	99	3.757%	$3.80	$16.50	$12.70	$ 376.20	$ 1,633.50	$ 1,257.30	L	L	DOG
Darjeeling-Smoked Salmon	238	9.032%	$5.75	$19.20	$13.45	$ 1,368.50	$ 4,569.60	$ 3,201.10	L	H	PLOWHORSE
Paella	195	7.400%	$4.65	$16.50	$11.85	$ 906.75	$ 3,217.50	$ 2,310.75	L	H	PLOWHORSE
Big Eye Tuna	98	3.719%	$6.35	$20.85	$14.50	$ 622.30	$ 2,043.30	$ 1,421.00	H	L	PUZZLE
Miso-Glazed Black Cod	164	6.224%	$7.75	$24.75	$17.00	$ 1,271.00	$ 4,059.00	$ 2,788.00	H	H	STAR
Chicken Breast	207	7.856%	$5.20	$16.45	$11.25	$ 1,076.40	$ 3,405.15	$ 2,328.75	L	H	PLOWHORSE
Tagliatelle	161	6.110%	$5.90	$19.00	$13.10	$ 949.90	$ 3,059.00	$ 2,109.10	L	H	PLOWHORSE
Fresh Scallops		143	5.427%	$7.20	$19.95	$12.75	$ 1,029.60	$ 2,852.85	$ 1,823.25	L	HPLOWHORSE
Capellini	155	5.882%	$7.90	$21.40	$13.50	$ 1,224.50	$ 3,317.00	$ 2,092.50	L	H	PLOWHORSE
Catch of the Day	208	7.894%	$5.30	$16.50	$11.20	$ 1,102.40	$ 3,432.00	$ 2,329.60	L	H	PLOWHORSE
Column	N					I	J	M	Q		
Total Covers	2,635	100.00%				$16,791.85	$52,848.60	$36,056.75			
						O		O			
					$ 13.68				0.04375	or 4.375%	

Column G: Menu Cost

The menu cost for the item is simply the number sold, as shown in column B, times the individual cost, as shown in Column D. It is the same as the "Total Cost" column in the Menu Pre-Cost and Abstract form.

> 252 portions of strip steak sold × $7.50 = $1,890 menu cost

Column H: Menu Revenues

Similarly, menu revenue (or total sales) for an item is the number sold, as shown in column B, times the sales price of the item, as shown in Column E.

> 252 units sold × $23.65 = $5,959.80 menu revenue

Column L: Menu CM

The **menu contribution margin** is found by multiplying the number of units sold for each menu item by its contribution margin. Thus, for Strip Steak,

> 252 units sold × $16.15 CM = $4,069.80 menu CM

This calculation shows the total contribution margin provided by the particular menu item. The sum of all the individual totals is found in Box M. For Bistro Quatre, the total contribution margins for all items for the month of February is shown as $36,056.75. This amount of money is available to be applied to all other costs in the restaurant and will hopefully provide a profit.

It is important to note that the amount shown in Box M represents the contribution margins for main course items only and does not include other sales such as appetizers, desserts, and beverages. There would be a larger total menu contribution if one were to include sales of other items. The Menu Engineering Worksheet shown in Figure 11.1 includes only main dishes, because the analysis would be skewed and invalid if sales of all menu items were included in one worksheet. This will be explained later in this chapter.

Box O: Average Contribution Margin

The figure in Box O is the **average contribution margin**, determined by dividing the total in Box M by the total number of units sold, found in Box N. For the illustrated worksheet, the calculation is as follows:

$$\text{Average contribution margin} = \frac{\text{Total CM}}{\text{Total number sold}}$$

$$= \frac{\$36,057}{2,635}$$

$$= \$13.68$$

Box Q: Item Percentages

The figure in Box Q requires careful consideration. This is the percentage of an entire menu represented by each item on that menu, multiplied by 70 percent.

There are 16 items on the menu used for Figure 11.1, so each is one-sixteenth, or 6.25 percent, of the menu. Similarly, if there were 10 items on the menu, each would be one-tenth, or 10 percent, of the total. The figure in Box Q is calculated by dividing one menu item by the total number of items on the menu and then multiplying the result by .7 (70 percent). Thus,

$$1/16 \times .7 = .04375 \text{ or } 4.375\%$$

This figure will be used when making entries in column R, as discussed in regard to that column.

The alert student will note that this percentage represents 70 percent of the average number of menu items. It will be used later in our discussion to determine if an item sold more or less than the average. Some will question why 70 percent is used. The authors of *Menu Engineering* simply stated that using 70 percent of the average makes the results more realistic. We will discuss this point further toward the end of this chapter. For the moment, we will accept the formula.

Column P: CM Category

The entries in this column, L for *low* and H for *high*, are made after comparing the contribution margin for each menu item (Column F) with the average contribution margin for the menu (Box O). If the contribution margin for a given menu item is lower than the average contribution margin, the entry for that item in Column P is L for low. If the contribution margin is higher than average, the entry is H for *high*. For example, the contribution margin for Strip Steak is $16.15, which is higher than the average contribution margin for the menu, $13.68. Thus, the entry for that item in Column P is an H for high. Grilled Breast of Chicken has a CM of $11.25, which is lower than the average contribution margin of $13.68, and the entry in Column P for that item is L for *low*.

Column R: MM Category

The entries in Column R (L and H for *low* and *high*) are determined by comparing the menu mix percentage for each item in Column C with the figure in Box Q. For example, the menu mix percentage for Strip Steak is 9.564 percent. Compared with the 4.375 percent figure in Box Q, this is high, so the entry for Strip Steak is the letter H. The menu mix percentage for Grilled Breast of Chicken is 7.856 percent, also higher than the 4.375 percent in Box Q. However, Roasted Muscovy Duck Breast represents only 3.871 percent and is lower than the 4.375 percent in Box Q, so it receives an L.

Because all entries in Column P and Column R must be one of two letters (either H or L), there are four possible combinations of letters: H/H, L/L, H/L, and L/H. These four possible combinations are used to categorize menu items. In the special language of menu engineering, each has been given a name:

- H/H is a **star**. A star is a menu item that produces both high contribution margin and high volume. These are the items that foodservice operators prefer to sell and maintain as menu items.
- L/L is a **dog**. A dog is a menu item that produces a comparatively low contribution margin and accounts for relatively low volume. These are probably the least desirable items to have on a menu and should be considered for removal.
- L/H is a **plowhorse**. A plowhorse is a menu item that produces a low contribution margin, but accounts for relatively high volume. These are items that have broad appeal to customers, but contribute comparatively little profit per unit sold.
- H/L is a **puzzle**. A puzzle is a menu item that produces a high contribution margin but accounts for comparatively low sales volume.

Because it provides a demonstration of the extent to which each menu item contributes to profitability, the Menu Engineering Worksheet can be of great use to restaurateurs who are interested in maximizing profit.

The illustrated worksheet contains main course items only. The thoughtful student will recognize that one cannot place appetizers and desserts on the same worksheet and obtain results that are meaningful. The costs, prices, and contribution margins for other menu items cannot be compared with main dish items. If, for example, appetizers were included, the results would be skewed, because the highest-priced appetizer would have a lower contribution margin than the lowest-priced main. All appetizers would be considered either dogs or plowhorses, and it would be difficult or impossible to use the Menu Engineering Worksheet, because average contribution margin and menu mix percentages would not be meaningful.

The Menu Engineering Worksheet can be much more useful when developed on a computerized spreadsheet. After the appropriate formulas are entered in the spreadsheet, the computer will do all of the calculations. Numbers, such as menu prices, can be changed, and the computer will automatically recalculate all financial results. This provides management with an opportunity to do what-if calculations to help determine the best course of action when changes to menu items or prices are made.

Several restaurant management programs incorporate menu engineering. These programs, such as Silverware POS Inc. and Compeat, make it easy to carry out what-if scenarios. Managers can substitute new prices, menu items, or quantities sold to determine the effects on food cost percents, average contribution margins, and sales.

██████████

MENU ANALYSIS

Description of Stars, Plowhorses, Puzzles, and Dogs

LEARNING OBJECTIVE 11.2
Define the terms *star, dog, plowhorse,* and *puzzle* as they relate to menu analysis.

Having completed the worksheet, a restaurateur can use the general guidelines offered in the following paragraphs to analyze the list of menu offerings and then determine the changes, if any, that would improve the menu and profitability.

Stars

Stars are both profitable and popular and should normally be left alone, unless there is a valid reason for change. Because of the popularity of stars, it is sometimes possible to increase their menu prices without affecting volume, thus increasing their profitability.

Plowhorses

Menu items classified as "plowhorses" are popular, but relatively unprofitable. They should be kept on the menu, but attempts should be made to increase their contribution margins without decreasing volume. One possibility is to decrease standard portion size slightly while improving the appearance of the product. Another is to raise prices on such items, assuming that the volume will not be adversely affected to any great extent.

Puzzles

Puzzles are comparatively profitable, but relatively unpopular. They should be kept on the menu, but attempts should be made to increase their popularity without decreasing their profitability substantially. There are any number of ways to do this, including repositioning the items to more favourable locations on the menu, substituting or adding a popular ingredient into the dish, featuring the items as specials suggested by servers, and changing the appearances or menu descriptions of these items to increase their appeal.

Dogs

Because menu items classified as "dogs" are both unprofitable and unpopular, they should be removed from the menu and replaced with more profitable items unless (1) there is a valid reason for continuing to sell a dog (as with an item that promotes other sales) or (2) its profitability can somehow be increased to an acceptable level. This will require that the item be changed in some way. One way of changing an item from a dog to a puzzle is to increase contribution margin per unit, which may be done by increasing sales price.

The Menu Engineering Worksheet in Figure 11.1 shows the following:

Stars: Strip Steak, Tournedos Bistro, and Miso Glazed Black Cod
Plowhorses: Tamarind and Ginger Shrimp, Darjeeling-Smoked Salmon, Paella, Grilled Breast of Chicken, Tagliatelle, Scallops, Capellini, and the Catch of the Day

Puzzles: Roasted Leg of Lamb, Barbequed Baby Back Ribs, Roasted Muscovy Duck Breast, and Big Eye Tuna
Dogs: Gnocchi

However, all stars, plowhorses, puzzles, and dogs are not the same. Some stars are truly outstanding, with very high volume and very high contribution margins. Examples of this are Strip Steak and the Tournedos Bistro. Darjeeling-Smoked Salmon, on the other hand, has very high volume, but its contribution margin is $13.45, very close to the average of $13.68. If its price were raised $0.25, it would be in the star category. Roasted Muscovy Duck Breast, by contrast, is classified as a puzzle, yet its contribution margin is $14.10. If its price were just $0.42 lower, it would be in the dog category.

Graphic Representation of Stars, Plowhorses, Puzzles, and Dogs

It is possible to better visualize the differences in the items by plotting them on a chart, as we have done in Figure 11.2. The numbers sold are shown on the vertical line at the left of the chart, and the contribution margins are shown on the horizontal line at the bottom of the chart. The horizontal line going across the chart at the 115 number, which is 70 percent of the average MM, represents 4.375 percent, the cut-off point that determines whether an item is classified as high or low for volume. All items shown above the 4.375 percent line are classified as high, and all items shown below the 4.375 percent line are classified as low. The vertical line in

LEARNING OBJECTIVE 11.3
Prepare a chart showing stars, dogs, plowhorses, and puzzles.

• **FIGURE 11.2** •

Graphic Representation of Stars, Plowhorses, Puzzles, and Dogs

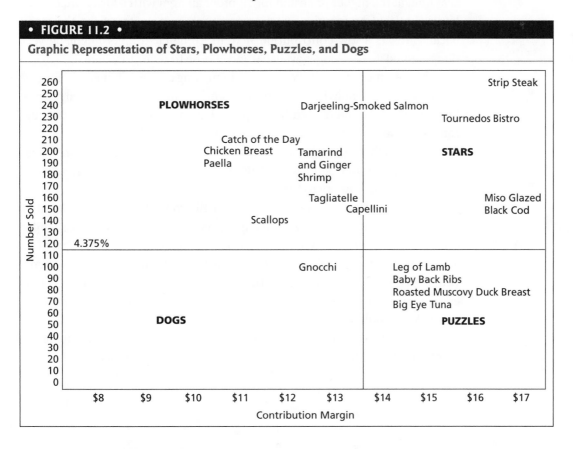

the centre of the chart represents the cut-off point that determines whether an item is classified as high or low for contribution margin. All items shown to the left of the line are classified as low, and all items to the right of the line are classified as high. We have placed each item in its approximate position on the chart so that a visual picture of all items can be shown.

Thus one can see that some items—Barbequed Baby Back Ribs, Gnocchi, Black Cod, Leg of Lamb, Roasted Muscovy Duck Breast, Scallops, Cappelini, Tamarind and Ginger Shrimp, and Darjeeling-Smoked Salmon—are very close to becoming classified in another category.

Using the Categories to Alter Menus

LEARNING OBJECTIVE 11.4
Describe appropriate action to take for stars, dogs, plowhorses, and puzzles when changes are made to the menu.

Having completed the Menu Engineering Worksheet and the Graphic Representation of Stars, Puzzles, Plowhorses, and Dogs, it is now possible to analyze the menu and make changes that will improve contribution margins. However, before doing that, the student should recognize that changes aimed at improving contribution margins might have effects on customer selection of menu items as well as the number of customers attracted to the establishment. The discussion of break-even analysis in Chapter 3 is very valid at this point. If prices are raised, it is possible that customers will view the menu as expensive, and the result could mean fewer customers. Further, customers who normally order a particular item with a low contribution margin might be unwilling to purchase that item at the higher price and might order an item with a lower price and a lower contribution margin. If management removes an item from the menu because it has a low contribution margin, some customers might be very disappointed it is no longer available and choose to dine elsewhere.

Management must be very careful in making changes in menu items and menu prices. Generally, it is wise to make small changes rather than large ones. Small changes are more readily accepted than large ones by restaurant customers. However, sometimes changes in menu items result in positive reactions by regular customers, as they frequently get tired of looking at the same menu selections. This is one of the reasons why many restaurants have daily specials. They want to add variety to the menu.

The average contribution margin for Bistro Quatre was calculated at $13.68. Because it is an average, one must recognize that it is impossible for every item on the menu to have a contribution margin that is above that average. No matter how much the average is increased, there will always be items with contribution margins below the average. It would also be unlikely that every menu item would have the same level of popularity. Invariably, some items will be less popular than others.

Figures 11.3 and 11.4 show the results of changes made in the menu for the month of March after the restaurant followed the guidelines discussed.

• **FIGURE 11.3** •

Bistro Quatre Menu Engineering Worksheet, Month of March

A	B	C	D	E	F	G	H	L	P	R	S
Menu Item	Number Sold	Menu Mix %	Food Cost	Sales Price	Item CM (E-D)	Menu Cost (D*B)	Total Sales (E*B)	Menu CM (F*B)	CM Category	MM Category	Menu Item Classification
Strip Steak	250	9.346%	$7.50	$23.65	$16.15	$1,875.00	$5,912.50	$4,037.50	H	H	STAR
Tournedos Bistro	225	8.411%	$8.70	$24.75	$16.05	$1,957.50	$5,568.75	$3,611.25	H	H	STAR
Duck à l'Orange	122	4.561%	$7.30	$21.40	$14.10	$890.60	$2,610.80	$1,720.20	H	H	STAR
Leg of Lamb	100	3.738%	$6.90	$21.50	$14.60	$690.00	$2,150.00	$1,460.00	H	L	PUZZLE
Baby Back Ribs	101	3.776%	$6.30	$20.50	$14.20	$636.30	$2,070.50	$1,434.20	H	L	PUZZLE
Tamarind and Ginger Shrimp	195	7.290%	$5.20	$18.00	$12.80	$1,014.00	$3,510.00	$2,496.00	L	H	PLOWHORSE
Gnocchi in Geai Bleu Cheese	125	4.673%	$3.80	$16.95	$13.15	$475.00	$2,118.75	$1,643.75	L	H	STAR
Darjeeling-Smoked Salmon	225	8.411%	$5.75	$19.20	$13.45	$1,293.75	$4,320.00	$3,026.25	L	H	PLOWHORSE
Paella	180	6.729%	$4.65	$17.00	$12.35	$837.00	$3,060.00	$2,223.00	L	H	PLOWHORSE
Veal Piccata	167	6.243%	$6.35	$20.85	$14.50	$1,060.45	$3,481.95	$2,421.50	H	H	STAR
Miso Glazed Black Cod	160	5.981%	$7.75	$24.75	$17.00	$1,240.00	$3,960.00	$2,720.00	H	H	STAR
Chicken Breast	195	7.290%	$5.20	$16.95	$11.75	$1,014.00	$3,305.75	$2,291.25	L	H	PLOWHORSE
Tagliatelle	140	5.234%	$5.90	$19.50	$13.60	$826.00	$2,730.00	$1,904.00	L	H	PLOWHORSE
Scallops	140	5.234%	$7.20	$20.45	$13.25	$1,008.00	$2,863.00	$1,855.00	L	H	PLOWHORSE
Capellini	155	5.882%	$7.90	$21.40	$13.50	$1,224.50	$3,317.00	$2,092.50	L	H	PLOWHORSE
Catch of the Day	160	5.981%	$7.90	$21.40	$13.50	$1,264.00	$3,424.00	$2,160.00	L	H	PLOWHORSE
Column	N					I	J	M			
Total Covers	2,675	100.000%				$17,088.60	$54,315.50	$37,226.90	O		
								O	Q		
								$ 13.92	0.04375	or 4.375%	

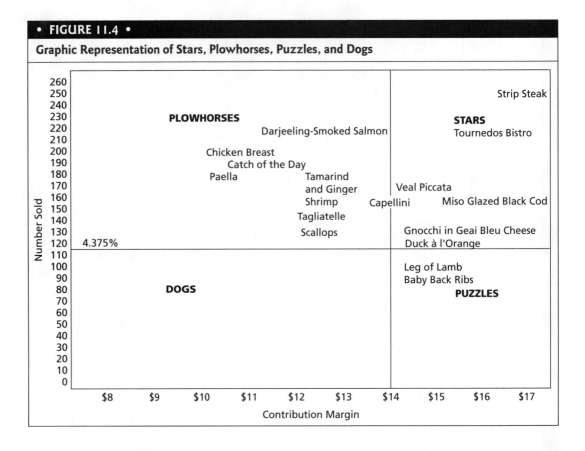

• **FIGURE 11.4** •

Graphic Representation of Stars, Plowhorses, Puzzles, and Dogs

1. *Dogs.* Gnocchi in Tomato Sauce was replaced with Gnocchi and Mushrooms in a Geai Bleu Cheese Fondue at a higher price and larger contribution margin. This action resulted in the vegetable dish becoming a star, as it was more attractive to customers.

2. *Plowhorses.* Menu prices for Paella, Prilled Breast of Chicken, Scallops, Tagliatelle, and daily special were increased $0.50. This resulted in somewhat fewer sales of these items, but raised contribution margins.

3. *Puzzles.* Big Eye Tuna was replaced with Veal Piccata and was more prominently displayed on the menu. It became a star. Roasted Muscovy Duck Breast was altered to Duck Magret à l'Orange to make it more attractive. This resulted in the duck also becoming a star. Lamb was left alone. Certain regular customers would be disappointed if it was replaced.

4. *Stars.* These items were left alone. Some of them had slightly lower sales as customers opted to order the new menu items with above-average contribution margins.

The overall result was an increase in the average contribution margin from $13.68 to $13.92, with a substantial increase in total contribution margins. Customers welcomed the changes, and there was a small gain in the number of customers. All of the dogs were eliminated. Further, the food cost percent was reduced from 35.7 percent to 34.89 percent, a positive improvement.

The effects illustrated here show clearly the value of menu engineering as an analytical tool that can be used for many purposes. It is possible to make menu changes that will increase menu contributions as well as customer satisfaction.

USING 100 PERCENT OF THE AVERAGE FOR NUMBER SOLD

It is possible that many foodservice operators might want to use 100 percent of the average number sold instead of 70 percent for Box Q. This would raise the horizontal cutoff line in Figures 11.2 and 11.4 from 115 to 165 and change the classification of some items. As shown in Figure 11.5, the classification for Tagliatelle and Scallops would be changed from plowhorse to dog, and the classification of Capellini would be changed from star to puzzle. Other items, such as Gnocchi and the Barbequed Baby Back Ribs, would appear even more unfavourable, as their relative sales would seem to be even lower than the average. The use of the 70 percent figure (as the original authors of *Menu Engineering* used) or the 100 percent figure (as many have suggested) is a matter of personal preference. Using either figure does not change the financial picture. As long as one understands that menu engineering is an analytical tool, the figure used—70 percent or 100 percent of the average sales—is not critical.

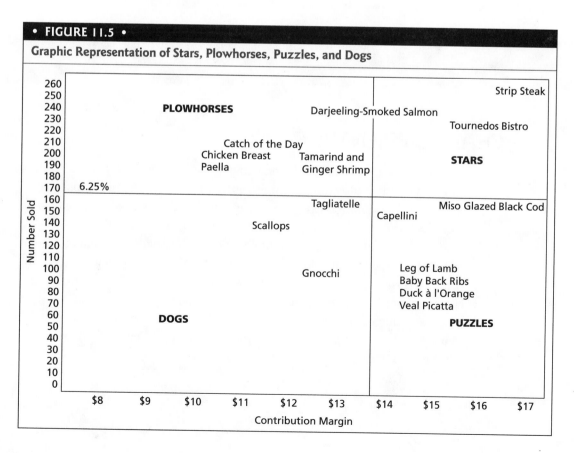

• FIGURE 11.5 •

Graphic Representation of Stars, Plowhorses, Puzzles, and Dogs

THINGS TO CONSIDER

The benefits of menu engineering are impressive. Used properly, it can lead to improved customer and staff satisfaction as well as to increased gross profits. It should not be used exclusively, though, despite its effectiveness.

There are many instances when other factors should be considered. Staff and guest feedback are important to pay attention to. Occasionally, this input conflicts with menu engineering analysis. A decision on menu item status should incorporate all available feedback, which could lead to a compromise solution. Perhaps something is currently so popular it must be included on the menu despite competitive pricing pressures and the consequent low contribution margin of a homogenous item, that is, an item that is undifferentiated, and that everyone sells. Other issues may also affect menu decisions. It may be difficult to remove an unpopular item, even if only a few regular customers would be upset by it. There is also something to be said for a good chef's or manager's intuition. Sometimes an item that starts out unpopular becomes extremely popular over time.

The point is that in addition to menu engineering, many other sources of feedback should be considered. Creating popular and profitable menus requires skill, knowledge, experience, hard work, creativity, and good analysis of all available data. Having all of these at your disposal usually results in success.

CHAPTER ESSENTIALS

In this chapter, we illustrated menu engineering as a technique for analyzing menu sales and providing helpful information for increasing gross profit. We defined *stars, puzzles, plowhorses,* and *dogs,* and suggested ways to change the classification of menu items to improve the profitability of the menu. We showed how plotting the menu items on a graph provides a visual picture of menu items and their relationship to each other. We explained that using a computerized spreadsheet can make the task of constructing and maintaining a Menu Engineering Worksheet much easier than a manual method. Finally, we discussed the use of the 70 percent and the 100 percent figure in Box Q on the worksheet to determine whether an item is to be classified as high or low for the number of an item sold.

KEY TERMS IN THIS CHAPTER

Average contribution margin, p. 289   Menu mix percent, p. 287
Dog, p. 291   Plowhorse, p. 291
Menu contribution margin, p. 289   Puzzle, p. 291
Menu engineering, p. 286   Star, p. 291

QUESTIONS AND PROBLEMS

1. George's Restaurant had the following menu sales during a period of one week:

Menu Item	Sales	Food Cost	Menu Price
Strip Steak	73	$6.50	$18.90
Fried Chicken	90	$3.90	$12.75
Lamb Chops	55	$7.00	$20.35
Fried Scallops	92	$5.90	$18.50
Broiled Haddock	85	$4.50	$15.65
Roast Turkey	92	$3.00	$12.00
Baked Stuffed Shrimp	77	$6.70	$18.50
Veal Marsala	65	$6.50	$18.75

   a. Calculate the menu mix percentage for each menu item.
   b. Calculate the menu contribution margin for the week.
   c. Calculate the menu food cost percent for the week.

2. Is the contribution margin for menu items more significant than the food cost percent when determining restaurant profit? Explain your answer. Does a large contribution margin for each menu item necessarily mean that the restaurant is profitable? Explain.

3. Would a Menu Engineering Worksheet that lists appetizers, main dishes, and desserts be useful to management in determining which menu items to delete, raise or lower in price, or otherwise change? Explain why or why not.

4. Under what circumstances might dogs be kept on the menu rather than eliminated?

5. What can be done to puzzles to increase menu profitability? Explain your answer.

6. Why are all stars not the same? Explain why one would be better than another.

7. Under what circumstances might you eliminate a plowhorse from the menu?

● FIGURE 11.6 ●

Menu Engineering Worksheet

Restaurant	Smuggler's Inn		Period	6/7–6/14							
A	B	C	D	E	F	G	H	L	P	R	S
Menu Item	Number Sold	Menu Mix %	Food Cost	Sales Price	Item CM (E–D)	Menu Cost (D*B)	Total Sales (E*B)	Menu CM (F*B)	CM Category	MM Category	Menu Item Classification
Grilled Chicken Breast	175		$3.00	$ 7.00							
Hanger Steak	190		$5.50	$13.00							
Pork Tenderloin with Black Bean Sauce	40		$4.00	$ 8.00							
Roasted Halibut	45		$7.00	$13.00							
Grilled Wild Salmon	80		$8.00	$15.00							
Lobster	60		$7.50	$16.00							
Braised Veal Brisket	90		$5.50	$14.00							
Roasted Venison	145		$6.00	$13.00							
Grilled Lamb Chops	125		$6.00	$ 9.00							
Beef Tataki	50		$3.50	$ 7.00							
Column	N					I	J	M			
Totals						$ —	$ —	$ —			
						K = I/J		O = M/N	Q = (1/no. of items × 70%)		

8. What are the possible positive and negative consequences of substituting different menu items for those with low contribution margins?

9. In what ways is the graphic representation of dogs, plowhorses, puzzles, and stars helpful in determining what to do about altering menu items?

10. a. Complete the Menu Engineering Worksheet reproduced in Figure 11.6, filling in the missing information.

    b. Prepare a graph similar to Figure 11.2 showing stars, plowhorses, puzzles, and dogs.

    c. Which items, if any, should be removed from the menu? Remain unchanged? Be increased in price? Be featured or repositioned on the menu? Why?

EXCEL EXERCISES

Exercise 11.1

Complete Barnaby's Hideaway Menu Engineering Worksheet for the period October 10 to October 15 as shown on the companion website for this text.

Exercise 11.2

Prepare a graph similar to Figure 11.2 showing stars, plowhorses, puzzles, and dogs.

Exercise 11.3

The following changes were made to Barnaby's Hideaway menu for the period October 16 to October 21:

Manicotti was replaced with veal piccata.
Prices for several items were adjusted.

Complete Barnaby's Hideaway's new Menu Engineering Worksheet showing the results of the changes. What has happened to gross profit and food cost percent?

CHAPTER 12

Controlling Food Sales

INTRODUCTION

Previous chapters have discussed in great detail the procedures for establishing control over costs. Chapter 11 discussed menu engineering as it relates to improving contribution margins. However, we must also discuss control with respect to the other side of the financial coin: sales.

For some, the term **sales control** is merely a synonym for **revenue control**, a collection of activities designed to ensure that each order placed by a customer results in appropriate revenue for the enterprise. Revenue control is critically important to the financial health of any enterprise; unless all of the revenue resulting from sales is realized, successful cost-control measures are less than effective. The financial health of a foodservice operation is not helped if cost-control measures result in savings of, say, $10,000, but lack of revenue control results in lost dollars that offset those savings. Revenue control is actually only one part of sales control.

One important maxim for any business is that "without sales it is impossible to control costs." Foodservice requires an interpretation of sales control that is somewhat broader than mere revenue control.

THE GOALS OF SALES CONTROL

LEARNING OBJECTIVE 12.1
List and explain the three goals of sales control.

There are at least two additional goals of sales control beyond revenue control. Because sales are necessary if management is to control costs, costs will benefit most when sales are at their best. That's why a second goal is to optimize the number of sales—maximize the number of customers—and attract a sufficient number of customers so that the enterprise can operate profitably. Remember, as sales rise, fixed costs are more easily met. Conversely, if an operation is losing money from variable costs that exceed sales, increasing sales will increase losses.

Success comes in part from a business knowing its clientele. Market surveys and feasibility studies are part of the planning process. Knowing what the customer wants and needs and meeting or exceeding their expectations is vital, along with many other factors, such as location, financing, expertise, timing, and differentiation. A target market must be chosen that is large enough to provide sufficient numbers of customers to achieve profitability. There are different ways to approach this. For example, fine-dining establishments typically succeed only in locations that have populations with relatively high income levels. Some ethnic restaurants are very popular in one community but not in another. Some multi-unit restaurants serving the same menu thrive in one location and not in another. Some concepts work well for two or three years and then their popularity fades. The right menu, pricing, and sales techniques are critical. Actually, everything is critical—from the concept to service quality and every other detail—but we will confine ourselves here to aspects of sales control.

The third goal of sales control is to maximize profit; that is, obtain the maximum gross profit from customers who patronize the facility. Profit maximization requires two essential activities: (1) pricing products properly and (2) selling those products effectively. Pricing products properly means that menu items should be priced so that the number of sales will result in the most profit for the foodservice operation. Selling products effectively has two essential requirements: a carefully crafted and well-designed menu and productive sales techniques employed by the staff.

In this broad sense, then, there are three principal goals of sales control:

1. Optimizing the number of customers
2. Maximizing profit
3. Controlling revenue

We will start this discussion with optimizing the number of customers.

OPTIMIZING THE NUMBER OF CUSTOMERS

Assuming that a good business plan was developed and that the marketplace is of sufficient size and opportunity, certain steps can be taken to maximize clientele. Many restaurateurs advertise and provide incentives to customers in the hopes of expanding their client base. These incentives may include discounts for meals during nonpeak hours, discounts to seniors, discounts on specific menu items, and free main dishes. Restaurants also improve and maximize sales volume by offering other products and services. For instance, a supper club may be a dining room until 10:00 p.m., when it becomes a night club with a DJ and dancing until close. Other restaurants expand sales by catering both to offices during the day and private clientele at night. These efforts are not necessarily fundamental or adequate to maximize the number of customers. The most productive efforts are established by the business plan, executed on start up, and improved on as the business matures. Those who understand why customers choose certain restaurants typically cite these eight factors as the most important to achieving the largest possible customer base:

LEARNING OBJECTIVE 12.2
List and describe eight determinants of customer restaurant selection.

1. Location
2. Menu item differentiation
3. Price acceptability and value
4. Decor and lighting
5. Portion sizes
6. Product quality
7. Service standards
8. Menu diversity

All customers have their own important reasons for patronizing restaurants, and these change under varying circumstances. For some, food quality is the single most important reason for patronizing a particular restaurant; for others, it is low prices or the variety offered on the menu. However, when time is short, the determining factor for these same individuals may be a convenient location. To be successful, a restaurant must meet enough of these needs to attract the number of customers necessary to cover costs and provide profit.

Location

If you were to take a given population centre and draw concentric circles around it, then place a restaurant on each of these concentric circles, as shown in Figure 12.1, you could judge the effect of location in relation to the population centre. Customers will normally choose the most convenient restaurant if there are no differences between them. In addition, there is a maximum time and distance that most customers will travel to reach any particular restaurant.

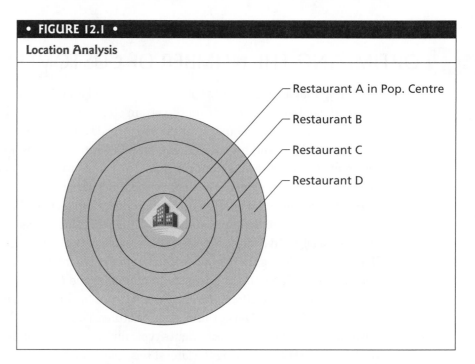

• FIGURE 12.1 •

Location Analysis

Restaurant A in Pop. Centre

Restaurant B

Restaurant C

Restaurant D

One would expect Restaurant A to have more customers than Restaurant B at any given time. Similarly, one would also expect Restaurant C to have fewer customers than Restaurant B and more than Restaurant D. Generally, the greater the distance from the population centre, the fewer the customers a restaurant owner can reasonably expect to attract from that population centre. Many people would be unwilling to travel extremely far distances to reach a restaurant, but there are always exceptions. Some well-known destination restaurants attract customers from far away. There are other factors to consider as well. As an example, restaurants located in Toronto's financial district do excellent luncheon business on weekdays, but, for lack of business, some are not open for dinner or on weekends. In contrast, large numbers of restaurants in good outlying neighbourhoods do little lunch business, but excellent dinner and weekend business. This is because many customers work downtown but live in the suburbs. Yet another factor is meeting a demand that others are not; the only Italian restaurant in a city with a population of 100,000 can expect to do quite well, even if its product quality or its prices are less than completely attractive to potential customers.

Having a good location is usually necessary for lower-priced businesses that depend on volume. The operators of fast-food restaurants have always recognized the importance of location. The managers of national fast-food chains know precisely the traffic patterns, number of potential customers, and the number of customers that can be expected to patronize one of their units located in a given population centre. That helps explain why one seldom hears of the failure of any of the units in these major national chains. Essentially then, all restaurants are local. Some are more local than others. Generally, fast-food restaurants are very local; that is, most people will not drive any appreciable distance to patronize one. Fine-dining restaurants are also local, but some customers will drive greater distances to dine at these establishments. Often, the closer a restaurant is to its target market, the more business it will do.

Menu Item Differentiation

Economists characterize goods and services as homogeneous or differentiated. This distinction is based on how similar or different goods or services are in relation to others or to competitors. A **homogeneous product** or service is one that is so similar to another that customers do not develop a preference and will purchase whichever costs less. Therefore, there is a general "market price" for homogeneous goods and services, and no individual operator can raise prices without substantial risk. Gasoline is a relatively homogeneous product. Many customers recognize that gasoline from all service stations will perform adequately; therefore, prices at most gasoline stations are about the same. Occasionally, customers find a service station that sells its gasoline at a discounted price. Such stations typically find that they sell much more gasoline than their competitors.

Differentiated products are sufficiently different from others in their class, so that customers may develop preferences for them. Customers may actually consider differentiated products unique. The perceived uniqueness can be real or imagined. As long as customers prefer one product or service over another, whatever their reasons for preference, that product or service is differentiated. Clothing is a good example of a product that can be frequently labelled as differentiated. The quality of clothing varies considerably from one manufacturer to another, and prices for particular items vary accordingly. However, many customers pay more for designer clothing, even though the quality may be no better than lesser known brands. To them there is a perceived difference, possibly a prestige factor, in clothing from a well-known designer and they are willing to pay more for it.

At the time of this writing, one of the most common homogenous restaurant menu items is the Grilled Chicken Caesar Salad; the quality may vary from one location to the next, but, when two or more establishments of similar quality standards offer this item on their menu, they will invariably have similar prices in order to remain competitive. But if an operator wanted to gain an advantage in the market, this same menu item could be differentiated by simply changing the grilled chicken to grilled tuna or by using local organic greens or adding grilled portobello mushrooms.

Comparatively few products and services can truly be labelled homogeneous. Most are differentiated, some more so than others. Differentiation is a matter of degree for most products and services, and the greater the degree of differentiation, the greater the degree of customer loyalty that may be generated. Differentiated menu items also allow owners more leeway in setting prices as this strategy prevents comparisons with competitor's prices.

The terms *homogeneous* and *differentiated* are useful for classifying menu items. To the extent that the foodservice operator can develop and include differentiated products in the menu, potential customers seeking those products are likely to be willing to travel greater distances and pay higher prices to obtain them. If Restaurant D in Figure 12.1 offers menu items that customers in the population centre consider both desirable and unique, the restaurant operator will have little difficulty increasing sales volume.

Unique menu items created for this purpose are called **signature items**. Signature items are often specially named for a restaurant, a chef, or a locality. Waldorf salad, for example, was originally a signature item created and served in one of New York City's most famous hotels, The Waldorf. Many restaurant operators create signature items in order to attract greater numbers of customers.

Price Acceptability and Value

One of the most important factors in customer selection of one restaurant over another is price and value. Given three foodservice establishments exactly alike in every respect except for menu prices, the one with the lowest prices might have the greatest sales volume. Of the restaurants shown in Figure 12.1, Restaurant A can be expected to have the highest sales volume, unless one of the others (e.g., Restaurant C) has lowered menu prices significantly. With lower prices, one would expect Restaurant C to increase volume by drawing some customers from Restaurants A, B, and D. If, however, Restaurant C has lowered quality to justify lowering prices, then perhaps it will lose the perception of value with the clientele and do even less business than before.

Restaurant menu items tend to be **price sensitive**; they have a high price elasticity. That means that there is a relationship between sales price and sales volume, such that demand drops as price rises. As the price of a menu item is increased, it can be expected that fewer customers will order that item. In the food and beverage business, the more homogeneous a menu item, the more price sensitive it is. By the same token, the more differentiated the item is, the less price sensitive it is. This helps explain why so many of the well-known national chains charge approximately the same prices for inherently similar or homogeneous menu items. For example, the prices of hamburgers at the national fast-food chains are similar, but the prices of hamburgers at established table service restaurants are typically higher. This is because customers may feel that the quality of the food is better, or they are willing to pay extra for table service or the enhanced environment or ambience in the table service restaurant. However, among similar table service restaurants in a given area, prices for hamburgers may be quite similar.

The customer must judge that the value received, including the food and all of the other items that make up the restaurant product, is sufficient to justify the menu price. Although some uniformity exists, every individual has a different perception of price acceptability. The challenge to foodservice operators is to establish menu prices that will be acceptable to those who make up their targeted market segments.

Decor and Lighting

Decor and design, including lighting, help differentiate one restaurant from another. Each establishment attracts customers who prefer—or at least accept—its ambience and decor. "Beauty is in the eye of the beholder," and although there are universally acceptable styles of decor, you cannot suit everyone's taste. Family groups, for example, tend to prefer informal, light, bright, and cheerful interiors; those patronizing restaurants offering gourmet cuisine are likely to expect a more formal setting. Some fine restaurants have very low lighting in order to create the proper ambience. Others are very bright. A restaurant's decor and lighting help determine not just the type of customer, but the number of customers as well. One key to restaurant success, then, is to select decor and lighting that will appeal to a sufficiently large segment of the targeted market, and thus will help maximize the number of customers. There are exceptions; some restaurants that spend a fortune on decor will fail and some do well with lacklustre designs. It's a good idea, nevertheless, to get help from a professional who specializes in designing restaurants, particularly someone with insight into what might work for a particular concept or market.

Portion Sizes

The quantity of the product given a customer must be appropriate to the clientele that a food and beverage operator wishes to attract. On one hand, young, active people are more likely to prefer larger portions, and some may select those restaurants that are the most generous with servings. Some more mature adults, on the other hand, may prefer smaller portions. It is clearly false to say that large portions always attract the greatest numbers of customers. Customers want value for their money, and portion size is only one of the factors they consider when determining whether any given establishment offers value. Portion sizes must satisfy the clientele a foodservice operator seeks to attract. If portions are too small, business will be lost. If they are larger than necessary, food may be wasted, food costs may be higher than necessary, and profits may be lower than they might have been. Again, there are always exceptions; some restaurants have made their reputation and success on oversized portions, maintaining enough margin and volume to achieve profitability.

Product Quality

Quality is a term that conveys different meanings to different people. Those with particularly refined tastes are more likely to seek perfection in food and may be inclined to accept only the best available. For them, this may mean that the quality of restaurant food must meet a long list of criteria: All ingredients must be of the highest quality, prepared by the most skilled and creative chefs using the best and latest techniques. Unless the food products offered in a particular restaurant meet their exacting quality standards, they will not patronize it. Many foodservice customers do not have these rigid standards. They are willing to consume and enjoy food products of lesser quality. Now more than ever, customers are able to find the information they desire about a restaurant's quality through guidebooks, newspaper reviews, and the Internet. The rating systems created by Zagat, Frommers, and the Mobil Travel Guide are some of the most common resources used by prospective customers. Mobil Travel Guide uses a star rating system and Zagat ratings use a 30-point scale based on surveys completed by customers. Figure 12.2 shows the criteria for the Mobil Travel Guide assessments, which are conducted by professional food critics and are regularly updated to ensure that quality is being maintained at each operation. Based on food and service quality and decor, restaurants are awarded from 1 to 5 stars. The Zagat Survey, another popular system, does not use professional food critics; instead the ratings are based on consumer comments, which are then rated on a 30-point scale.

At the same time, some patrons appear to be completely indifferent to all the quality standards for foodservice products that the majority seem to insist on. For them, food is food—a necessity similar to fuel for an engine. Their reasons for patronizing restaurants do not appear to be related to product quality as defined in terms that the majority would accept.

In any given population, various segments demand food products of various levels of quality. It is the management's responsibility to assess the market and then offer products of an appropriate level of quality that will appeal to and

---

• FIGURE 12.2 •

Mobil Travel Guide's Star Ratings

- *One Star* - Culinary specialty, local flair, or unique atmosphere. Value is considered in this category.

- *Two Star* - Freshly prepared food, cordial, efficient, and clean, often showcase a distinct cuisine.

- *Three Star* - Skillfully prepared food, specific style, professional service, décor of excellent quality.

- *Four Star* - Exceptional, creative, complex, refined personal service.

- *Five Star* - Elite, flawless, exceptional food, superlative service, elegant décor, and exquisite presentations.

---

reach a large enough segment of their market to ensure the level of sales volume required for profitability.

Service Standards

Anyone who has patronized restaurants and other foodservice operations can recognize that many different types of service are available. Some service is of very high quality; some much less so. Fast-food restaurants and cafeterias tend to provide comparatively little service beyond the basic requirements, whereas some fine hotel dining rooms and restaurants offer extraordinary levels of service. In establishments offering extensive service, it should be of the very highest quality: swift, unobtrusive, knowledgeable, and competent. At some lower-quality establishments, the service is likely to be less than competent.

Service quality (and every other component of a diner's experience) must be appropriate to the standards promised by the restaurant. All of the impressions and perceptions created by a business must be consistent and satisfying and lead to the customer's entire experience being positive and predictably pleasurable.

Each individual diner has a personal view, consciously or unconsciously, of the standards of service that he or she considers appropriate for the level of quality and value of a restaurant. Whenever possible, the customer tends to select a restaurant offering a type and level of service that he or she finds appropriate to the occasion. If the individual's time is strictly limited, he or she is likely to select a restaurant with limited service—one that allows a customer to eat within the limited time available.

When customers celebrate a special occasion, time is of less concern. For them, the pleasure of the dining experience, including food and service of the very highest quality, is of paramount importance. They may be entirely willing to travel some distance to reach a well-known and widely respected restaurant renowned for offering the finest food and service in the area.

Managers who seek to optimize customer counts should be aware of the extent and quality of service that their customers want. With that in mind, they may find it comparatively easy to adjust some aspects of service to increase customer satisfaction. For example, a family restaurant may find it desirable to reduce the amount of service by creating a salad bar and training servers to direct customers to the salad bar between the appetizer and main courses. This may make it possible to reduce the size of the wait staff and, at the same time, satisfy the needs of customers wanting to consume their meals as quickly as possible. It may have the added benefit of increasing turnover rate during peak dining hours. Another example of an adjustment to service might be a high-end dining room hiring a sommelier to increase wine sales and customer satisfaction, perhaps even gaining an advantage over competitors.

Menu Diversity

There are many restaurants that do well serving a themed menu. There are also many successful steak and seafood restaurants or pizza and noodle restaurants that do well. These businesses concentrate on one type of product and try to do it differently or better than the competition. Some have very limited menus and still do great business. Most restaurants, however, find it necessary to have a broad range of items on the menu. A menu that includes only two or three main course choices may have less appeal than one offering 12 or 15. A given diner might be more likely to find an acceptable item on the longer menu. In restaurants that depend heavily on repeat business, a limited menu can have significant negative impact on the number of times any given customer will return within a specific period of time.

The number and range of items on any menu are governed by several important considerations: the equipment available in the kitchen, the culinary abilities of the kitchen staff, and the cost considerations that may arise if the large number of items offered results in considerable leftover food. As a general rule, the greater the scope of the menu consistent with these other considerations, the larger the segment of the market to which the menu will appeal.

Despite the fact that there are exceptions to all eight of these factors that help to maximize the number of customers for a business, it is important to take them into consideration. It is also impossible to achieve all of the benefits we described. No location is perfect, and it is unlikely one could plan a menu consisting only of differentiated products offered at prices acceptable to all customers, and to do so in a setting that everyone would find pleasing. For a restaurant to have the best chance of success, management must keep all of these precepts in mind, taking care to satisfy as many targeted potential customers as possible.

MAXIMIZING PROFIT

There are two principal means for maximizing profit: (1) pricing products properly and (2) selling products effectively.

LEARNING OBJECTIVE 12.3
Describe the two principal means of maximizing profits.

Pricing Products Properly

Restaurants normally have standard sales prices for the menu items they offer. The prices are usually established by owners or managers and are communicated to customers via printed menus or conspicuously posted signs. Aside from playing a major role in attracting and satisfying guests, prices are critically important in determining the degree of profitability for any restaurant because the sum of the prices paid by all customers for their menu selections is the total food revenue for a restaurant.

Cost is normally the most significant consideration in establishing the sales price for any menu item. In any given restaurant, higher-cost items typically have higher sales prices than lower-cost items. Steak, for example, usually commands a higher sales price than spaghetti because the portion cost is higher. However, cost is not the only determinant of price.

Another important consideration is the desire to maximize sales. Restaurants with highly differentiated products have more flexibility to raise or lower menu prices than those with homogeneous products. For example, an exclusive French restaurant that increases menu prices may have very little adverse reaction from customers if they perceive the restaurant's products as highly differentiated and desirable. The student will recall that in the previous chapter on menu engineering, Bistro Quatre replaced Gnocchi in Tomato Sauce with Gnocchi and Mushrooms in a Geai Bleu Cheese Fondue. This change increased the sale of the dish at a higher price, primarily because it was viewed as a more differentiated product. By contrast, if there were two similar hamburger restaurants offering relatively homogeneous products in one mall, and one raised its prices substantially while the other did not, the one raising prices would be likely to lose a substantial number of customers. In fact, the increase in prices would probably result in decreases to total revenue and subsequently to profit.

It is important for foodservice managers to have some understanding of the relationship between the sales price of a menu item and the number of portions sold. If changes in the sales price of a given menu item result in changes in the number of portions sold, then the item is said to be price sensitive. To identify an item as price sensitive is to say that the number of portions sold will be influenced by changes in sales price. In the previous chapter on menu engineering, a $0.50 increase in many of the items considered Plowhorses resulted in fewer sales of those items.

Some menu items are more price sensitive than others, and although homogeneous products are clearly more price sensitive than differentiated products, there are variations within each classification. In other words, among products characterized as homogeneous, some are more price sensitive than others, and the same is true of differentiated products. Finally, price sensitivity is a function of the customers' attitudes, perceptions, and ability to purchase a given product. Therefore, among certain market segments, price sensitivity may be of greater significance than for others. In neighbourhoods where many residents have low disposable income, price sensitivity tends to be a more important consideration than in those where disposable incomes are higher. In any given restaurant, the proper sales price for a menu item is that which will produce an acceptable number of sales and yield an acceptable level of profit.

Changing conditions sometimes force changes in pricing policies. For example, a large restaurant had an excellent location on a major highway and catered primarily to travellers. Menu prices were comparatively low, and the restaurant served more than 500 customers each day. A new highway was built a short distance from the restaurant, and fewer cars drove past the restaurant. The number of customers immediately decreased to about 300 per day, and the large facility could not operate profitably with low menu prices and low volume. The owner attempted to attract the local population by offering products of higher quality at higher menu prices. She reduced the size of the dining area, turning some of it into a gift shop, and redecorated the establishment. Her efforts were successful. Profit margins were considerably higher, and the restaurant again became a profitable operation, even though it had fewer customers than before. By changing the business model, she survived.

There are several methods for establishing menu prices. Many of these, however complex they may appear, are variations on three basic approaches:

LEARNING OBJECTIVE 12.4
Explain the three most common methods of establishing menu prices.

1. Matching competitors' prices
2. Calculating prices from costs and cost percents
3. Adding desired contribution margins to portion costs

Matching Competitors' Prices

Perhaps the most widely used approach to menu pricing is one that may best be described as *follow the leader:* establishing prices that meet those of competitors. This approach is commonly employed by those who have little or no idea of the costs of the items they sell. Many who adopt this approach believe that if a nearby competitor manages to stay in business by, say, selling hamburgers for $5.00, then they can do the same. Many restaurateurs believe that if their prices are higher than those of nearby competitors, they will lose business to the competition. Tacitly, they are defining their products as homogeneous rather than differentiated. In many cases, they are correct: They are offering price-sensitive, homogeneous products. Restaurants featuring such common items as pizza, chicken fingers, or hamburgers can be very much alike in products, services, and prices. Decor might be the only element that renders one different from another. In such cases, accessibility to the market—location—is likely to be the primary determinant of the number of customers and sales. If that is the case, any increase in price over that charged by the competition may effectively destroy the small advantage offered by location and lead to an unacceptable loss in sales.

Although a policy of pricing to meet the competition may be satisfactory for some operators in some markets, it can lead to disastrous consequences for others. If menu prices are low, so are contribution margins; therefore, greater numbers of customers are required to cover fixed costs and provide a given level of profit. Not every restaurant in a given area can maintain the necessary volume to survive when all are offering low menu prices. If that is the case, only the most able operators survive, and the failure rate for restaurants in the area might be abnormally high.

Perhaps the best practice for most operators would be a hybrid approach taking into consideration all three pricing styles. Most restaurants whose menus combine both homogenous and differentiated items should probably take competitors' prices into consideration as necessary: not copying the prices, but deliberating their importance, and if necessary, integrating them into a process that builds market share, covers costs, and provides profit.

Calculating Prices from Costs and Cost Percents

The second approach to menu pricing, calculating prices from costs and cost percents, has two variations. In both cases, portion costs must first be determined by means of the techniques discussed in Chapter 6. The first variation proceeds as follows: Take the portion cost of an item and use a fixed percentage to determine a selling price. If, for example, a restaurateur wanted the food cost-to-sales ratio to be 35 percent, he or she could set a menu price for each item merely by dividing 0.35 into the portion cost and adjusting the resulting answer to a suitable amount to print on a menu. If this approach were followed with literally every menu item, the cost percent for the operation for any period would be 35 percent, provided that the staff followed all established standards and standard procedures for purchasing, receiving, storing, issuing, and producing food. The proper food cost percent to use could be taken from an industry average of similar restaurants or perhaps more accurately determined by subtracting profit, labour and other variable costs, and fixed cost, as percentages of sales, from 100 percent.

A better method is to take portion costs, then set tentative menu prices using a desired food cost percent, and then forecast sales volume based on expected covers. Projected figures for total cost, total sales, and food cost percent may be determined by using the Menu Pre-Cost and Abstract illustrated and discussed in Chapter 10. This type of costing using a weighted average against expected sales by menu mix gives a more accurate projection of total food costs. If the anticipated cost percent is judged unsatisfactory, then portion costs, menu prices, and perhaps even the forecasted sales volume (if done judiciously) can be adjusted until a realistic and satisfactory potential result is achieved. If the forecast has been reasonably accurate, and if the staff has observed the standards and standard procedures established for all phases of operation, the resulting cost percent for operation should conform to management's plans.

Adding Contribution Margins to Portion Costs

The third approach, adding contribution margins to portion costs, is becoming more common in the industry. This approach requires that the foodservice operator determine the average contribution margin required to cover all costs other than food and to yield the desired level of profit from the expected level of sales volume.

This average contribution margin is then added to the portion costs of menu items to determine their menu prices. An example of this approach can be illustrated with figures abstracted from the statement of income for Julio's, a hypothetical restaurant adjacent to a large shopping mall. The statement of income indicates the following for a period during which 30,000 customers were served.

	Food sales	$500,000
−	Cost of sales	200,000
=	Gross profit	$300,000
−	All other costs	250,000
=	Profit	$ 50,000

If one divides the $500,000 food sales by the 30,000 customers, it is apparent that each customer in this example spent an average of $16.67. This figure is known as the average sale per customer, as described in Chapter 1. By dividing the $300,000 gross profit by the 30,000 customers, it is also apparent that each customer contributed an average of $10.00 to cover costs other than food and provide profit.

This method suggests that each menu item or a combination of items representing the average cheque should be priced at $10.00 above portion cost, regardless of the food cost. For example, a steak with a portion cost of $8.00 would be priced at $18.00, and a pasta item costing $2.50 would be priced at $12.50. If this approach were followed, and if sales volume matched or exceeded forecasts, the minimum acceptable dollar profit would be ensured, provided that costs were kept strictly under control in all areas.

In addition, many operators may consider this a more equitable pricing method. Assuming that there is no significant difference in the cost of producing menu items, each customer is bearing only his or her fair share of costs and profits.

Some operators will add labour costs to food costs before subtracting those combined costs from sales to determine contribution margin. This is a more complex calculation, but may be more accurate and equitable when menu items have a wide range of labour-to-food-cost ratios.

These calculations are also necessary when preparing a business plan for a new operation. Determining pricing by establishing costs and using one or all of the three methods we discuss will help to determine average cheque when menu mix is considered. Forecasting sales by gauging expected number of covers or market share multiplied by average cheque is a necessary function in providing pro forma financial statements, which project future data rather than track historical data.

Marketing and Selling Products Effectively

The menu may be a simple list of what the restaurant offers for sale, but it is a critical sales and marketing tool. It can bring in customers when it is appealing. It can be popular for different reasons, because its items are inexpensive, house-made, different, currently popular, ethnic, or cutting edge. It is a critical sales tool. Essentially, the two principal means a restaurant has available for selling products effectively are:

LEARNING OBJECTIVE 12.5
Describe the two principal means of selling products effectively in a restaurant.

1. The menu
2. The sales techniques used by the staff

The Menu

The menu is the way items for sale are presented to clientele. The menu is the primary marketing and sales tool in many restaurants. It is responsible for sales and for determining sales mix, especially in operations that do not have the time to employ sales techniques by skilled servers. On a menu, the items that are presented most favourably (e.g., featured prominently on the menu) typically outsell other items. Conversely, those that are least favourably presented tend not to sell as well as they might. Because menu items normally have differing costs, contribution margins, and cost percents, the foodservice operator has an opportunity to exercise some measure of control over cost percent and gross margin by preparing menus that achieve maximum sales volume and profitability. Good menu design will help attain these goals. Menu preparation is a complete and separate subject that deserves more attention than we can give it here. Because the menu is such a key ingredient in efforts to maximize profits, we do want to offer general knowledge of the most important elements in menu preparation. They are:

1. Layout and design
2. Variety
3. Item arrangement and location
4. Descriptive language
5. Kitchen personnel and equipment

LEARNING OBJECTIVE 12.6
List and explain the five most important elements of menu preparation.

Layout and Design. The layout of a menu is the way in which the menu items will be placed on the menu. It is important to note that the menu mix, also known as the menu item popularity index, as discussed in the previous chapter, will usually be very different for two identical menus in which the only modification was to rearrange the order of the items. This knowledge has been used to identify areas of the menu known as *prime space:* this is the area that the guest is likely to read first. Studies have shown that customers are most likely to order items located in the prime space areas of the menu. Figure 12.3 illustrates this principle for one-, two-, and three-page menus. Note that the prime space on the one-page menu is the top one-third of the page; on a two-page menu it is in the top centre of the right-hand page; and on a three-page menu it is in the centre of the middle page.

Some operations that have menus in effect for long periods of time can spend considerable amounts on multi-coloured printing, expensive paper stock, and lamination. They are so elaborately designed and produced that they act as entertainment and add considerably to the appeal of the entire restaurant experience. It is not unexpected that the menus of some of the most expensive restaurants may use lower-quality stock and a more subtle, though not inelegant, design, usually because printing new menus everyday precludes spending enormous amounts of money on their production.

It should be apparent that the entire physical menu (the paper, the colour, the printing, and so on) should suit the character and style of the restaurant. One would not, after all, expect an elaborate menu printed in raised type on parchment stock at the average roadside diner, nor would one expect to see the menu of a high-priced and exclusive restaurant printed poorly on the cheapest paper available. Appropriate menu layout and design for a restaurant is an essential factor in achieving maximum revenue.

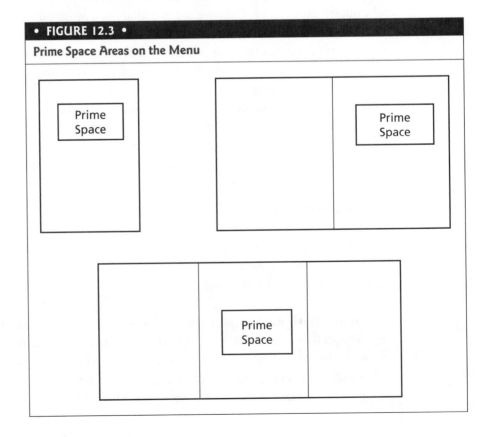

• FIGURE 12.3 •

Prime Space Areas on the Menu

Anyone unfamiliar with the principles of menu layout and design would be well advised to consult one or more of the several excellent books on the subject and to get an expert's opinion before printing a menu.

Variety. For a menu to have maximum public appeal, it should offer a suitable variety of foods, preparation methods, and prices. Variety will satisfy the needs of a broad market and will help the restaurant operator capture the largest possible number of customers. Even in specialty restaurants, fast-food restaurant chains, and those offering ethnic foods, variety is important.

Various restaurant specialists have suggested that a generally acceptable menu should include among the main courses several different types of meat, fish, poultry, and vegetarian dishes. In general, menus should also reflect various cooking methods. Some items should be sautéed, some roasted, some grilled, and so on. This not only ensures acceptance by customers with various preferences but also adds variety in the appearance of foods reaching the customers' tables. In addition, restaurant patrons are increasingly conscious of the nutritional value of their meals. More restaurants are including low-calorie and low-fat items on their menus, as well as providing nutritional information. Some municipalities require quick-service restaurants to provide nutritional information on their products in an effort to inform a more health-conscious public.

Appearance of foods is of great importance. The number of combinations of foods that may appear together on plates is vast, and some are more interesting and attractive than others. The possibilities for providing pleasant and appropriate contrasts in colour, contour, height, and texture are always in the mind of the experienced menu writer.

Item Arrangement and Location. One of the most significant menu-making principles involves the physical arrangement of items on the menu. Items on the menu seen first by customers tend to be ordered more frequently than those seen later. It is generally agreed that a person's eyes are first focused on the centre of a menu. And unless that person's attention is otherwise directed, items listed first and at the top of a list are seen first and make the greatest impression. It stands to reason that those items will probably sell in the greatest quantities, or at least will sell in greater quantities than if they were placed at the bottom of the list. That is why it is generally a good idea not to list the most expensive or least expensive dishes first: It is too methodical and it may lead to the quick conclusion that the restaurant is more or less expensive than it really is. It may even lead to decreased dollar sales. It is a good idea to mix up the prices within the list of menu items. Another way of bringing customers' attention to a particular menu item is to feature it in larger type than the items surrounding it. Sometimes a different typeface or colour can have the same effect. In some cases, not only is the type different, but the item is given its own featured spot on the menu. In addition, many restaurants use colour pictures, drawings, or photographs of some menu items to capture attention and to build sales volume for those items.

The significant point is that the items management wishes to sell in the greatest quantities should be the featured items. These may be those items in greatest supply in the kitchen during a particular season, those with the most favourable cost-to-sales ratios, or those that provide the greatest contribution margins. In some instances, the featured items are unique or are those whose sale would most greatly enhance the restaurant's reputation and thus help build sales volume. Many operators place items with the greatest contribution margins (such as steaks) in the most prominent places on the menu and relegate those with lesser contribution margins (such as pasta) to less conspicuous spots. On such menus, high-cost, high-price items will be more prominent, often appearing first. Other operators may feature signature items or items that require extensive preparation and cannot be used up as leftovers. On such menus, less perishable à la carte items, such as steaks cut and cooked to order, will be far less prominent. In the previous chapter on menu engineering, we indicated that one way to sell more puzzles—those items with high contribution margins but low sales volume—is to reposition them on the menu, giving them a more prominent location. We also noted that stars typically do not need changes in location, because they already sell well.

On a well-prepared menu, foods will appear in just those physical locations and with just those degrees of prominence that will induce customers to order what management wants to sell.

Descriptive Language. The dining experience begins well before customers taste the food they have ordered. It may begin with the first impression of the food operation, when the restaurant is first described by a friend, when potential customers read a review or an advertisement, or when they first enter the premises. The physical appearance of the establishment and its staff and the attitude of the staff toward customers will make or reinforce an initial impression, or change it.

The menu and the language used to describe menu items may make a good impression and induce customer orders. On one hand, the descriptions of foods may help make the customer hungry and may increase the number of sales to a level that might otherwise have been impossible. On the other hand, a menu that describes available items poorly may actually decrease sales. A food and beverage operator can exercise great influence over the amount of the average cheque by using written descriptions that make menu items sound interesting. Customers tend to react positively to foods that sound appealing .

Appropriate adjectives tend to increase customer satisfaction because they lead to higher levels of expectation. As long as the foods meet expectations, customers obtain greater satisfaction from foods that verbal description has suggested will be good. The successful operator knows that a menu item simply labelled "Broiled Steak" has considerably less appeal to the customer than one described as "Grilled Dry Aged Canadian Prime Sirloin Steak ," and that "Southern Style Fried Fenwood Farms Organic Chicken" does conjure up a different image for the diner than the simple "Fried Chicken." Descriptions shouldn't be overly elaborate or lengthy; customers aren't there to read. When writing is concise and descriptive without excess flourishes, menus are at their best. Correct grammar and spelling are also important.

In addition to appropriate descriptive adjectives, a good menu may include an indication of the portion size, method of cooking, major ingredients in the item, garnishes, and presentation. Descriptions that contain most or all of these factors provide the customer with a complete understanding of the item and will result in more satisfied clientele.

Ingredients that are known as common allergens, such as peanuts and seafood, and items with religious restrictions, such as pork, should be identified on menu items where they are not obvious or the primary ingredient.

To maintain the integrity of the foodservice industry, any claims must be substantiated. **Truth in advertising** is not only a legal requirement, it is also the proper ethical choice that will lead to good staff and customer relations.

Kitchen Personnel and Equipment. Over the years, there have been many examples of foodservice operators adding various items to their menus that were completely beyond the culinary skills of the kitchen staff. There have been instances of foodservice consultants creating menus with items requiring higher levels of culinary skill than were available in the local labour market. And everyone knows of at least one case in which a chef who was preparing fantastic and well-loved menu items quit suddenly, leaving behind a staff that was unable to prepare the items satisfactorily.

Anyone writing a menu should have a clear, unbiased view of the culinary abilities of current staff and should account for the possibility of having to replace any staff member with another of equal skill. At the same time, the menu writer should be aware not only of the equipment needed to prepare the foods on the menu, but also of the kinds of equipment available in the kitchen and its general condition. Before including a dish requiring precise oven temperatures to prepare, for example, one should be sure that oven thermostats are in proper working order, and before deciding to include french fries with every order, one should be sure of having adequate staff and equipment to prepare the needed quantity.

In many kitchens, particularly large hotel kitchens, employees are given workstation assignments and specific responsibilities. One individual may be assigned to the grill, one to sautéing, one to a garde-manger station, another to vegetable preparation, and so on. If this is the case, the menu writer must be sure that each station has a reasonable ratio of the total preparation and production work, so that none of the employees or workstations is either overloaded or underworked. If analysis of an existing menu suggests that the amount of work in the kitchen is not suitably balanced among employees or workstations, one should consider rewriting the menu, adjusting the number of employees at each workstation, providing additional equipment, or some combination of these suggestions. If situations of this nature are permitted to develop or continue, the turnover rate for kitchen personnel may increase significantly.

By taking these basic elements of menu preparation carefully into account, a menu writer can substantially increase the possibility of developing a menu that will produce an appropriate level of sales volume and a growing number of satisfied customers.

Sales Techniques

LEARNING OBJECTIVE 12.7
Explain management's attempts to maximize profits by establishing proper sales techniques.

The second means for selling products effectively is to develop appropriate sales techniques to be used by servers, who are a restaurant's sales force. In good table service restaurants, the sales staff may be more important in marketing and selling products effectively than the menu itself. The customer's decision to order an item (or not to order it) is influenced by the server. Because of this, restaurant managers are usually interested in developing appropriate sales techniques for their servers and in providing basic sales training.

In many restaurants, managers and chefs hold daily meetings with servers just before opening. They often use this time to go over the day's menu with servers to be sure they can describe each item to customers, naming the principal ingredients and identifying the preparation method. The time can also be used to go over new menu items, to enumerate the specials of the day, and to identify any dishes that servers are expected to make special efforts to sell.

Daily meetings normally have positive outcomes for management, for customers, and for servers. For management, these meetings help ensure that the sales force will have a thorough knowledge of the products they sell, a prime requirement for sales personnel in all businesses. For customers, these meetings increase the likelihood of being able to obtain immediate, accurate answers to questions about menu offerings. It is a distinct advantage to be able to learn from a knowledgeable server any information one needs or wants to know about a dish before it is ordered. This helps customers make realistic decisions about what to order or not to order, and it helps reduce the number of orders sent back to the kitchen by customers who made incorrect assumptions about food items. These things, in turn, benefit both the servers and the cooks.

For servers, daily meetings increase the likelihood of their being able to provide correct answers to questions arising from the menu. Most servers quickly comprehend that these meetings improve their ability to provide each customer with a satisfactory dining experience, and this leads to increased income from tips. It is clear that a server who can describe and explain the menu items as well as the daily specials is more convincing and appreciated than one who can only read a sheet of notes to the guest and is unable to answer basic questions.

The adoption of standard sales techniques can play an important role in increasing and maximizing sales. If properly used by the servers, standard sales techniques not only help build sales volume, but also help establish a relationship with the guest and provide customers with more personal attention than they might otherwise receive.

A useful sales technique that many successful restaurateurs train their personnel to use is to suggest menu items or courses to customers that they might not otherwise consider ordering. Suggestive selling can improve all aspects of sales and guest satisfaction when done properly. Common examples include drinks before dinner; soups; wine suited to a particular main dish; and liqueurs, cognac, or port after the meal. If the server takes orders for drinks before dinner, he or she is not just increasing sales revenue for the restaurant, but is also providing customers with some means of occupying their time while their orders are being prepared. Servers are often trained to suggest appetizers, salads, desserts, and cheese—courses that customers might not order otherwise.

A slight variation on this technique is to train servers to suggest specific menu items. In some restaurants, servers make suggestions for every course; in others, suggestions are made for the main course alone. For example, if the chef has prepared a limited quantity of a particularly desirable fresh fish item that is not normally on the menu, servers may be asked to suggest that item to customers to help ensure the sale of every portion. These suggestions, if made appropriately, can add a pleasant, personal touch to customer service while increasing sales.

Empowering employees to be able to directly interact with guests and solve problems can also be very beneficial to guest satisfaction. Long a part of **Total Quality Management** (TQM), it is a philosophy of leadership and responsibility. A server with enough authority to ensure a guest has a great experience can be invaluable to everyone concerned. Even in the best-run operation, problems arise that servers can help solve. For example, a server who can "comp" an item (make it complimentary by taking it off a customer's bill) or give a free drink without first having to get management permission may completely resolve a bad situation. Certain employees with enough experience or expertise may be able to do even more. In some cases the highest level management might be requested by a guest to solve a problem, but an immediate and effective solution by a front-line worker is often preferable. Management must also monitor this function sufficiently so that empowerment is not abused.

It is normally not difficult to secure employee cooperation in making suggestions to customers, particularly if the personnel are aware that customer tips are typically a percentage of the total cheque and that higher dollar sales tend to increase tips. In restaurants that hold daily meetings with servers and train personnel to use standard sales techniques, management normally engages in some sort of periodic review and evaluation of staff performance. Performance can be assessed in several ways. A common method is to determine gross sales per employee or average sales per employee for a given period (e.g., a week). Servers with performance levels significantly lower than those of their colleagues may need some coaching or additional training.

If management takes the steps described here to price products properly and sell those products effectively, there is a greater likelihood that sales revenue and numbers of sales in a restaurant will be maximized and that sales records will indicate increases in the number of sales of those items that produce the highest contribution margins and greatest profits. The benefits of satisfying guests and staff cannot be overstated.

LEARNING OBJECTIVE 12.8
Describe how technology has
affected sales techniques.

Technology and Sales. Restaurants that use a website for advertising have found it to be economical and useful in marketing. In some instances it is almost mandatory. It is an effective way to advertise and, if it is creative and interesting, will help to disseminate an image and a brand, and may directly bring in sales. Take out orders placed over the Internet are increasing every year as consumers become more comfortable buying on-line. Many large urban centres have companies that act as intermediaries for local restaurants, taking and delivering orders through their website.

Technology also helps boost sales for the many fast-food operators who take orders over the phone or the Internet. Some with multiple units use a central order number that then enters the order into a computer to distribute it to the nearest unit for filling and delivering. Pizza shops have used these systems for many years.

Self-service is a relatively new feature in the foodservice industry. Some businesses are using POS units that are customer operated. They are usually attractively integrated into a free-standing kiosk. A guest can punch in and pay for an order at the POS terminal. When it is easy to use, it is both a marketing tool and a way to reduce labour costs and improve service speed. Although not yet widely used in Canada, we may see them put into use in the near future.

Sales Information. One technique that is becoming more popular in the industry is **data mining**. It is a process of sorting and choosing relevant information from a base of historical data. Foodservice operators have used data mining for accounting and financial purposes for some time, but now they are beginning to use the software to uncover potentially useful information on customer preferences. Both in-house and external databases can be used, and with this information, operators can provide improved and more appropriate goods and services faster.

CONTROLLING REVENUE
The Goal of Revenue Control

LEARNING OBJECTIVE 12.9
Explain the importance of
revenue control.

Throughout the discussion of food control in previous chapters, there have been numerous references to food sales. With all of these references, there has been an unstated assumption that all food sales have been accurately recorded and that all have resulted in appropriate revenue to the establishment. Accurate recording of sales and inflows of appropriate revenue are both desirable and necessary to the successful operation of a restaurant, but neither can be assumed.

There are many possibilities for errors to occur in the recording of sales. Some are accidental; others are not. Sales may be incorrectly recorded; incorrect prices may be programmed into a computerized POS system or manually charged; cheques may be lost, stolen, or simply not used at all; and sales that have been correctly recorded may not always bring revenue to an establishment because of errors or the actions of dishonest employees or customers. Although these are but a few of the many possibilities, they suggest the need for establishing some control over revenue.

After reading the previous chapters on food control, one should be keenly aware of the proper method for establishing control over any phase of operations: instituting the four-step control process first discussed in Chapter 2. To control sales or revenues, then, one must institute the process, beginning by establishing standards and standard procedures. Standards and standard procedures for *revenue control* are aimed at one clear and simple goal: *to ensure that all food served produces the appropriate revenue for the enterprise.* For any menu item served to a customer, appropriate revenue is the price stipulated by the menu. When food is served in a different way, to an employee for instance, at the discretion of management, appropriate revenue may be a menu price, a discounted price, or no price at all, depending on management's policies. In any case, all food served must be accounted for appropriately even if served as a staff meal or a complimentary meal to a prospective banquet client. If one fails to account for all food served to customers and employees, the result will be a distortion of the cost-to-sales ratio. This may lead management to believe erroneously that cost-control procedures are not working as planned, and consequently waste time and resources trying to find the cause of the problem. Without proper revenue control, an establishment may be a financial failure even with excellent cost controls.

This point is best illustrated by example. Imagine that the cost controls in the Fidelity Restaurant are so successful that actual food cost for one week, $3,500, is nearly identical to standard cost for that period. Given a planned food cost-to-sales ratio of 35.0 percent, this food should produce sales of approximately $10,000. Without appropriate sales control procedures, it is quite possible that sales for the week may be $9,000, rather than $10,000, resulting in a food cost-to-sales ratio of 38.9 percent. If so, gross profit on sales is reduced by $1,000, and food cost percent is 3.9 percent higher than it would have been if all sales had been correctly recorded and collected.

If this is the case, additional cost controls and additional efforts aimed at improving employee performance to reduce costs will not be effective. The proper resolution would be to institute standard revenue control procedures. It is important for anyone planning a career in foodservice management to understand the nature of these procedures and to be prepared to establish them in any foodservice enterprise.

Theft can be a major issue also. An important aspect of revenue control is having trustworthy personnel in charge, especially for cash handling. Proper recruitment, screening, and background checks are necessary, even though background checks are difficult because many previous employers won't provide complete information. Hiring an outside company to do proper checks or conduct validated screening tests may be preferable. Many owners require control personnel be bonded, providing insurance from losses caused by abuse. Limiting the number of staff who handle money is a good way to prevent theft. As we will discuss later in this section, servers who also act as cashiers are responsible for and keep their sales until they cash out, limiting the amount of time the restaurant has a lot of cash on hand. Accepting credit cards is an excellent way to remove cash from an operation. Assuming merchant fees are not too onerous, credit cards are a great way to ensure that sales go straight to the business' bank account. Some credit card companies even provide promotions and marketing efforts to help businesses that use their products.

Security must be provided to prevent guests from stealing as well. "Dine and dash" guests who leave without paying are hard to completely eliminate, but if bills are given quickly when diners are finished and followed up by server visits to receive payment, problems will be prevented. Putting a greeter or cashier near the exit will also help to prevent walkouts. In addition, staff should be trained to spot the behavioural characteristics of this type of guest. We will discuss further what signs to look for when monitoring for fraud and theft in the section on beverage controls.

Establishing Standards for Revenue Control

LEARNING OBJECTIVE 12.10
List and explain the three standards established to achieve the goals of revenue control.

There are three standards for achieving the goal of revenue control—ensuring that all food served results in appropriate revenue to the establishment:

1. Documenting all sales
2. Pricing all sales correctly
3. Verifying that all sales are recorded and deposited

For establishments with computer systems similar to those described in Chapter 2, all orders for food prepared in the kitchen and bar are inputted into the computer terminal, and sales prices are automatically recorded, making revenue control easier. For establishments without computer equipment, the process is somewhat more complicated. Regardless of whether an establishment uses computer or manual means, management must establish standard procedures intended to ensure that food sales are documented, priced correctly, recorded, and deposited. Our discussion of revenue control will start with standard procedures needed in establishments using manual means of recording sales: documenting, pricing, and recording sales by hand, or using a mechanical or electronic register to record sales.

REVENUE CONTROL USING MANUAL MEANS

The specifics required to achieve the necessary level of control in those establishments using manual means require that guest cheques be used to record sales. A great many systems and procedures for manually controlling food sales using guest cheques are currently in use in the industry. The larger the organization, the more complex these systems are likely to be. Sometimes the standard procedures to manually control revenue using guest cheques in one restaurant appear to differ markedly from those used by another. On closer inspection, however, one is likely to find that they are merely variations. In the following pages, we describe the basics that one is likely to see used in foodservice operations that use guest cheques.

LEARNING OBJECTIVE 12.11
List and describe the standard procedures for controlling revenue.

Documenting All Sales

One of the most basic steps in manual food sales control is to require that each menu item ordered be recorded in some way. The traditional method for attending to this has been to require that servers record guests' menu selections and the menu prices of those selections on paper forms called **guest cheques** or sales cheques. Guest cheques are used almost universally to handle seven functions:

1. Help servers remember the specifics of guests' orders
2. Provide a written food order to kitchen personnel
3. Give itemized bills to guests
4. Maintain written records of portion sales to add to a sales history
5. Prove the accuracy of cashiers' work
6. Verify the accuracy of prices charged
7. Provide the records required for sales and deposit reconciliation and for tax purposes

Using Numbered Cheques

Most establishments that use guest cheques order sequentially numbered cheques. These are purchased from printers or stationers. When placing orders for new guest cheques, managers are careful to specify their serial numbers. This normally starts with the next number in a sequence of cheques previously ordered—not unlike the numbering system used on cheques from a chequing account with a bank.

A procedure often used in restaurants serving haute cuisine from à la carte menus is to require that personnel sign for individual cheques as needed. Figure 12.4 shows a sample sheet from one type of server's **signature book** used in this kind of operation.

Although some establishments fail to take full advantage of them, there are several benefits to using sequentially numbered cheques. For example, with the use of numbered cheques, it is possible at the end of any meal period to

• FIGURE 12.4 •				
Cashier's Record of Cheques Distributed to Servers				
Cashier H. Martin				Date 3-Sep
Cheque No	*Server No.*	*No. Served*	*Table No.*	*Server's Signature*
500	1	4	2	J. Jones
501	1	2	3	J. Jones
502	1			
503	1			
504	1			
505	2	3	5	Peter Smith
506	2	6	6	Peter Smith
507	2			
508	2			
509				
510				

reassemble the cheques in numerical order to see whether any are missing. If a cheque is missing, it is easy to look at the signature book to determine which server signed for it and then to question the server.

There are any number of explanations for missing cheques, none of which are acceptable. Missing cheques can be indications that a server or a cashier is dishonest, destroying cheques and pocketing the money. A missing cheque can also be a sign that a customer has taken the cheque from the restaurant and failed to pay for the food. In most establishments using numbered cheques, an immediate investigation is made whenever any cheque is missing, and someone is held accountable. In some restaurants, the server to whom the cheque was assigned is required to pay a flat amount in cash for a missing cheque or the amount determined from using the copies given to the bar and the kitchen to obtain orders if duplicates are used.

Assigning responsibility for specific individual cheques makes it possible to monitor other elements of servers' work as well. One of these is the legibility of the writing. If guest cheques provide the raw data that must be summarized before being added to a sales history, then it is obviously important that management be able to read the guest cheques. For this purpose, illegibility is likely to mean inaccuracy.

Although legibility is important for sales history purposes, it is equally important for purposes of determining whether employees are accurately recording the menu items ordered by customers. For example, when management insists on legibility, it is much more difficult for a server to get away with giving friends expensive main courses while charging them only for dessert and coffee.

It is normally advisable to monitor employee performance by conducting routine reviews of handwritten guest cheques on a regular basis, checking the legibility of handwriting, and verifying the accuracy of menu prices charged and arithmetic calculations. Some managers take the additional step of analyzing cheques periodically. This involves examining all guest cheques for one day, noting the nature and extent of each error, as well as the name or number of the server responsible. Errors in pricing, addition, and in calculation of taxes can be called to the attention of the individual servers. Sometimes the list of errors is posted on an employee bulletin board. Few people like seeing their errors posted for all to see, and this is often an inducement to improve.

Years ago, in order to eliminate some of the many possibilities for problems to develop in manual ordering, many restaurants (especially hotel restaurants) employed personnel who were known as food checkers. Food checkers were assigned to work at stations in the kitchen, near doors leading to dining rooms. The food checker's job was to verify that each food item leaving the kitchen was recorded on a guest cheque. In these establishments, menu prices were frequently recorded on guest cheques by food checkers, not by servers, and the entries on the guest cheques were made mechanically with a register similar to a cashier's register. This approach provided an extra measure of control, because at the end of any serving period, the total of the readings in the checker's register would equal the total of cash and charge sales recorded by the cashier, with allowance made for taxes and tips. When the total recorded in the food checker's register exceeded that in the cashier's register, management would investigate the cause of the discrepancy. An advantage of this system was that the independent recording of menu prices by the food checker provided some measure of protection against servers giving away food or undercharging for menu items purposely in a misguided effort to obtain larger tips.

Although some managers found some benefits in using food checkers, there were so many disadvantages that this approach to sales control has disappeared. A serious disadvantage was that lines tended to form at the food checker's station during busy periods. Consequently, service to customers slowed, turnover decreased, and some customers were served cold food and were dissatisfied. In addition, labour costs were obviously higher with food checkers than without them, and this has normally been a powerful inducement to reconsider the practice in foodservice. In some cases, attempts were made to combine the jobs of food checker and cashier, but with little success. Today, all control measures provided by food checkers in the past are available to those who have selected appropriate control-oriented computer systems from the growing numbers on display at hotel and restaurant trade shows and in the pages of the many foodservice periodicals.

To retain the desirable qualities of the food checker system while eliminating the problems, some restaurants follow a standard procedure that is usually referred to as the **dupe system**. *Dupe* is an abbreviation of the word duplicate. A standard requirement of this system is that a duplicate copy be made of each order. There are several means of doing this. One is to provide servers with pads of guest cheques, each of which produces a second and perhaps third copy, usually on a paper of a different colour and texture. Whenever a server records an order on a guest cheque, a duplicate copy of the order is made on the second copy or third copy. This is not the only way of producing a duplicate; there are several others. The important point is that the duplicate copy, the dupe, must be given to personnel in the kitchen before any food will be prepared or issued. Management usually instructs kitchen personnel to give servers only the food items recorded on the dupes in the quantities indicated. When food has been picked up by servers, the dupes are left behind in the kitchen. In some restaurants, these are then deposited in locked boxes to prevent their reuse. At the end of a serving period, dupes bearing the same numbers as the original cheques may be matched against the cheques to locate any discrepancies.

Although it is conceivable that dupes could be used for all food orders in some kitchens, it is not usually the case. In most instances, dupes are used only for main course items and certain other high-cost items (e.g., shrimp cocktails) over which management wants to exercise control. When dupes are used, many establishments match the duplicate to the original cheque to verify that nothing was given out from the kitchen without an original and that the cashier received all original cheques.

Pricing All Sales Correctly

Busy servers can make errors. Incorrect prices may be charged for menu selections, and incorrect selections can be written on cheques. Errors of this nature are normally accidental; sometimes they are purposeful. For example, a price of $19.95 may be written for a sirloin steak that is listed at $29.95 on the menu. Some establishments that use the dupe system require that servers write food orders, but no prices, on cheques as the orders are taken. Then, on the way to the kitchen to place the orders, each server records prices on the cheques and dupes with a machine similar to a cash register. The register dispenses a printed receipt, which is attached to the dupe before kitchen personnel will issue any food. When this procedure is followed, it is possible at the end of a meal period to compare the readings from the kitchen register with the cashier's register and to locate missing amounts.

For establishments that do not use the dupe system, it is necessary to audit guest cheques to verify that correct prices have been charged. In addition to verifying the accuracy of menu prices listed on guest cheques, managers are usually interested in the accuracy of the arithmetic on them: the accuracy of the subtotal determined by adding individual menu prices, the tax calculated as a percentage of that subtotal, and the grand total for the cheque. Some establishments require the cashier to verify that all guest cheques are priced and added correctly. Typically, the price of each item on the guest cheque is entered into the cash register, and the total of the guest cheque is then verified with the machine total. As the cashier is entering the price of each item into the register, he or she notes that all items are priced correctly.

Recording Revenue

Many restaurants employ cashiers who are assigned responsibility for taking payments from customers and recording sales as the customers leave the restaurants. They are usually stationed near restaurant exits, although some work in other locations. Some establishments have upgraded the equipment that cashiers use to record sales (cash sales, charge sales, and portion sales for a sales history), but continue to place cashiers at the familiar workstations adjacent to the front door. Although today's equipment is different, the basic requirements of the job are not. Restaurant cashiers today are following the same general principles established by restaurant managers in years past.

For proper revenue control, sales are always recorded in a register, and guest cheques may be endorsed in the register as the sale is recorded. If the guest cheque is endorsed, each cheque has to be inserted in the register as the sale is being recorded so that the amount recorded is printed on the cheque. Thus, all guest cheques are endorsed, regardless of how they were settled. The printed endorsement helps differentiate between guest cheques that had been settled and those that had not.

It is still common practice to require cashiers to record the breakdown of cheques into appropriate categories (food sales, taxes, and tips, for example, in one category, and cash sales and charge sales in another). Although this is no longer done on paper—mechanical cash registers, electronic cash registers, and now computers are used to do the breakdown—the results are perhaps best illustrated by the traditional **control sheet** shown in Figure 12.5.

In this illustration, it should be noted that the total of food sales, beverage sales, taxes, and tips is equal to the total of cash sales and charge sales. Thus, $301.75 + $113.10 + $24.90 + $52.00 = $491.75; also, $95.08 + $396.67 = $491.75. Traditionally, in restaurants using forms of this nature, cashiers were required to list the guest cheques in numerical order so that missing numbers would be readily apparent. If any were missing, the servers to whom the cheques had been assigned were questioned immediately.

Regardless of whether the breakdown is done using the traditional control sheet or by mechanical means, the resulting report provides management with

● **FIGURE 12.5** ●
Restaurant Sales Control Sheet

Cheque #	Server #	# Covers	Food Sales	Beverage Sales	Tax	Tip	Total	Cash	Charge	Detail
600	2	3	$ 35.75	$ 20.50	$ 3.38	$ 9.00	$ 68.63		$ 68.63	M/C
601	1	4	$ 56.80	$ 25.00	$ 4.91	$12.00	$ 98.71		$ 98.71	Visa
602	2	2	$ 42.80	$ 10.00	$ 3.17		$ 55.97	$55.97		
603	2	2	$ 36.90		$ 2.21		$ 39.11	$39.11		
604	1	4	$ 72.80	$ 22.00	$ 5.69	$18.00	$118.49		$118.49	Amex
605	1	4	$ 56.70	$ 35.60	$ 5.54	$13.00	$110.84		$110.84	M/C
Totals			$301.75	$113.10	$24.90	$52.00	$491.75	$95.08	$396.67	

the necessary sales information for accounting purposes as well as management analysis. Sales for the day can be recorded and analyzed. Management can determine the popularity of menu items, food cost percent, individual server sales, and other desired information.

REVENUE CONTROL USING COMPUTERS

Today, because of technological advances, many foodservice operators have been able to end their dependence on the traditional guest cheque. Fast-food operations with limited menus, for example, record guests' selections at computer terminals by depressing keys marked with the names of menu items. Even in restaurants dedicated to fine dining, servers can be observed recording guests' selections in small terminals located at sidestands, using three-digit or four-digit codes assigned to the menu items, or using touch-screen monitors that transfer orders to the kitchen or bar. Some innovative restaurants have incorporated the use of personal digital assistant (PDA) type devices with their computer systems. These wireless handheld devices allow servers to take orders tableside and send them to the computer system, then on to the kitchen and bar. These systems eliminate the need to wait at a busy terminal. In both fast-food and fine-dining establishments, additional features automatically look up correct menu prices for the items selected and then calculate both tax and total, printing itemized cheques, or bills, for guests.

Increasingly, restaurants with computer capabilities are using touch-screen programs similar to that illustrated in Chapter 2. With these systems, no guest cheque is used. Orders are taken on a plain piece of paper and inputted into the terminal located in the dining room. Liquor orders go directly to a printer at the bar, and food orders go directly to a printer in the kitchen. This saves considerable time and effort because the server does not need to go to the bar or kitchen to place an order. For example, a server places drink orders for guests at his terminal. He picks the drinks up without the usual delay of having to wait for the bartender to make these drinks. This is because the server has performed other duties while the drinks were being prepared and has timed his arrival at the bar when drinks are ready to be picked up. The same is true of food. After orders for food have been placed, the server is notified by various means that food is ready. He goes immediately to the kitchen, where he picks up his order. At the conclusion of the meal, the server obtains the guest bill from the printer at his terminal.

Assuming the programming of menu item prices into the database is accurate, all charges on the guest bill should be accurate, because the computer has kept in memory all inputted information, and has priced the guest bill according to information programmed into the computer. The only possibility that an item would not be posted to a guest bill would be those foods or drinks that would not normally be required to be inputted in order to be received by a server, such as coffee, or perhaps dessert. The guest bill is given to the guest, and the guest either gives cash or a credit card to the server, or the guest goes to the cashier to settle the bill. If cash or a credit card is given to the server, the server acts as a cashier or goes to the cashier, and returns to the guest with change or a charge voucher for the guest to sign.

There are many advantages in using computers to control revenue. All sales must be recorded because it is necessary for a server to record a sale in the computer in order to receive the food or drink. The computer is programmed to price each sale properly, as inputted, and the revenue is automatically recorded. The only possibility that a sale would be unrecorded is in those items—coffee or dessert—that can be obtained personally by the server without being inputted into computer memory. Using computers in a manner similar to the one illustrated in Chapter 2 also allows servers to provide better service to dining room patrons. Servers spend more time in the dining room looking after the needs of guests and less time in the kitchen or at the bar waiting for their orders to come up. No system is perfect. It is still possible for collusion between server and bartender or server and cook to occur, so that food or drinks are served without first being entered into the computer. However, when that occurs, it is usually noticed, and the offenders are caught.

Today, the number of restaurants requiring that servers also act as cashiers has increased. The individual servers, at the end of a day's work, determine their net receipts for the day from a computer printout. These printouts provide information similar to that provided in Figure 12.5. In many instances, the printouts resemble that form. When servers act as cashier, they settle with the manager or other designated person at the end of their shifts.

Another of the features of restaurant computer programs is that at any time during the meal, managers can monitor operations. They can find out which menu items are selling well and which are not. They can input a specific number of specials that are available for a service, monitor sales, and make the items unavailable when they are sold out. They can access sales figures, sales for each server, average cheque, and other desired information. At the conclusion of the meal period, the manager can obtain final daily information discussed in Chapter 1: sales mix, sales by category, sales per server, average sale, total covers, and standard cost percent.

Although electronic advances have made it easy to eliminate the use of many paper forms in the industry, some operators continue to prefer the traditional guest cheque to its alternatives. They find a measure of continuing security in familiar ways. They prefer systems that use paper forms, including guest cheques, which are less costly than computer systems. Most establishments, however, find computers appealing, as well as efficient and cost-effective for many of the control-related tasks that in years past required many hours and hundreds of repetitive calculations. In fact, the control possibilities previously discussed are all far easier to accomplish in the "chequeless" restaurant—the establishment that uses a computer system, not paper guest cheques, for control.

These are but a few of the methods and procedures that knowledgeable managers employ in their efforts to establish effective revenue control. The net effect of these efforts should be an accurate accounting of all sales.

THINGS TO CONSIDER

There are many factors that lead to success for retailers, and *restaurants are retailers*. We discuss many of these factors in Chapter 12. Menus are an important factor. They represent what you have to offer. Menu item prices are also important as they represent value and help to define your market. Prices can be critical to success. We discussed the three methods of pricing products properly, but it is such an important issue that we want to take it a bit further.

It is probably easiest to calculate costs from cost percents, but it is fairer and in many ways more accurate to price items by adding contribution margin to portion cost. If you start by using prices based on cost and cost percent and calculate expected covers by market research and experiential data, the product derived will be a fair estimation of total revenue. When you examine these figures using the contribution margin for the items that make up the average cheque, it will offer further insight as gross profit must now cover all additional costs, which can be calculated, and profit.

As we have indicated, some high food cost percent items offer excellent contribution margin and may be preferable under certain conditions to items that have low food cost percent. It depends on the market, sales mix, fixed costs, and other factors. Generally if the market will not accept high-price items it is better to offer pricing based on good food cost percents and try for more volume. If you sell a hot dog for $2.00 and your food cost is $0.50, you may be very successful in the right business environment with a 25 percent food cost. You might also do well if you sell lobster for $40.00 with a 50 percent food cost because your margin of $20.00 on each sale will pay your overhead quickly. Both strategies can work well under the right circumstances. In many cases, because of the market, using a hybrid approach to pricing that combines food cost percent and adding contribution margin to portion costs may produce better results.

There is one more thing to consider: as many operators realize, there is a certain amount of homogeneity in menu items and prices regardless of item differentiation. That means that competitors' prices should be considered. Operators should not match prices, but they should know the competition and carefully measure how they relate to or threaten them, especially regarding menu item prices. There should be a reconciliation of value between themselves and their competitors. In many cases, this competitive positioning should be incorporated into establishing menu prices after cost, cost percent, and contribution margins are considered. It may affect the menu items chosen or prices, increasing or decreasing them slightly, or it may be determined that altering items or prices is unnecessary. This decision can be made only after a proper analysis of the market and the competition.

Judiciously incorporating all three methods of pricing products should help operators arrive at popular and profitably priced menus.

CHAPTER ESSENTIALS

In this chapter, we explained the scope of sales control and listed its three goals: optimizing the number of sales, maximizing profit, and controlling revenue. We listed eight determinants of customer restaurant selection and explained how an understanding of these can help optimize the number of sales. We discussed two primary means for maximizing profits: pricing products properly and selling products effectively. We described the three most common approaches to menu pricing and identified the two principal means for selling products in a restaurant: the menu and sales techniques used by the staff. We listed the goals of revenue control and explained the most common standard procedures used to achieve these goals using manual means and computer systems.

KEY TERMS IN THIS CHAPTER

Control sheet, p. 331
Data mining, p. 324
Differentiated product, p. 307
Dupe system, p. 330
Guest cheque, p. 327
Homogeneous product, p. 307
Price sensitive, p. 308

Revenue control, p. 304
Sales control, p. 304
Signature book, p. 327
Signature item, p. 308
Total Quality Management, p. 323
Truth in advertising, p. 321

QUESTIONS AND PROBLEMS

1. Distinguish between sales control and revenue control.
2. List and explain the three goals of sales control.
3. Given two restaurants offering similar products at similar prices, one of which is located in a city centre, whereas the other is in a rural setting, which would you expect to achieve greater dollar sales volume? Why?
4. How can the portion sizes offered by a restaurant affect both the number and type of customers it attracts?
5. Distinguish between homogeneous and differentiated products.
6. List and explain the determinants of customer restaurant selection.
7. Describe the two principal means used by foodservice operators to achieve profit maximization.

8. List and explain the five most important elements of menu preparation.

9. Describe the three most common methods for establishing menu prices.

10. What sales techniques might management suggest that sales personnel can use to:

    a. Improve gross revenue and average cheque?

    b. Increase tips?

    c. Sell a menu item prepared in excess quantity that must be thrown away if not sold?

11. For each of the following number of covers, calculate the average sale:

Number of Covers	Total Sales
20	$ 70.00
87	$ 372.40
142	$ 863.45
463	$2,309.00

12. Why would each of the following adversely affect the average sale in a restaurant?

    a. Deterioration in service standards

    b. Customer dissatisfaction with food quality

    c. Inadequate sales promotion

    d. Changes in portion sizes

13. Show by example how improper recording of sales affects food cost percent.

14. a. The owner of Nagano Restaurant projects labour costs of 36 percent and fixed costs of 28 percent, and wants to plan for profit of 12 percent. What food cost percent should be projected? (Assume no alcoholic beverages are served.)

    b. Using the food cost percent from Question 14a, what menu sales prices would be suitable for each of the following?

Portion	Costs
Item A	$1.94
Item B	$2.26
Item C	$4.40
Item D	$2.88
Item E	$2.42

15. The owner of Gideon's Restaurant realizes that her establishment is offering homogeneous products that are extremely price sensitive. At current costs and sales, the business is unprofitable. She wants to take steps to turn the business around. What suggestions can you offer to help this owner make the business profitable?

16. The new manager of Frisbee's Restaurant has learned that there is always a waiting line of customers on Friday and Saturday nights. Because of the apparent need to serve customers as quickly as possible so that seating

can be made available to those waiting in line, to what extent should this new manager suggest the use of selling techniques that tend to prolong service and result in customers spending additional time at tables?

17. Define each of the key terms in this chapter.

EXCEL EXERCISE

Exercise 12.1

Follow the instructions on the companion website for this exercise.

PART III

BEVERAGE CONTROL

In previous chapters, the need for food, beverage, and labour control procedures was discussed, and specific control principles and procedures for food were described. In the following five chapters, specific control principles and procedures for beverages are described.

Beverage control is similar to food control in many ways. It requires that standards and standard procedures be developed for purchasing, receiving, storage, issuing, production, and sales. The standards and standard procedures of beverage control are akin to those used for food control. The principal differences between food controls and beverage controls can be traced to differences in the nature of the products: in general terms, foods tend to be more perishable than beverages, which can often be kept indefinitely.

Beverage control is as important as food control because of the nature of the product. The possibilities for excessive costs because of some forms of theft are probably greater with beverages than with food. Interestingly enough, although everyone recognizes the need for beverage control, it is an area in which, until recently, only limited controls had been successfully instituted by most establishments. The time and effort required and the vast amount of paperwork and calculations necessary for effective control meant that few establishments instituted meaningful control measures. However, the introduction of computer hardware and software specifically designed for the beverage industry has made it possible for all establishments to introduce effective control measures at reasonable costs and without management spending long periods of time taking inventory and performing myriad calculations.

Beverage Purchasing Control

• LEARNING OBJECTIVES •

After reading this chapter, you should be able to:

13.1 Identify and describe the three principal classifications of beverages.

13.2 Outline the process for brewing beer.

13.3 Identify the classifications of beers and distinguish between them.

13.4 Outline the process for making wine.

13.5 Identify and describe the colour classifications of wine.

13.6 Explain the purpose of the distillation process.

13.7 List the primary purposes for establishing beverage purchasing controls.

13.8 Identify the principal factors one must consider before establishing quality standards for beverages.

13.9 Identify seven principal factors used to establish quantity standards for beverages.

13.10 Explain the provincial and territorial regulations and practices for the sale of alcoholic beverages.

13.11 Identify the two principal methods for determining order quantities and calculate order quantities using both methods.

13.12 Describe several ways computer programs assist in calculating inventory balances and inventory usage.

13.13 Describe one standard procedure for processing beverage orders in large hotels and restaurants.

INTRODUCTION

The processes associated with beverage operations are the same as previously discussed in relation to food control; that is, like food, beverages must be purchased, received, stored, issued, produced, and sold. As with food, it is possible for excessive costs to develop in each area of operation. Sufficient beverages must be purchased so that a suitable supply of each beverage is on hand when needed. The beverages must be properly received and stored so that the quality is retained and all beverages are secure. The beverages must be issued, and drinks prepared, in a way that will control costs and quality. Finally, all sales must be recorded so that the establishment is ensured of receiving the appropriate revenue from drinks produced at the bar.

The term **beverage** requires some definition. Technically, any liquid intended for drinking is a beverage, so named by a word derived from French and Latin verbs meaning "to drink." In one sense, all beverages can be divided into two groups: those that contain some measure of alcohol and those that contain no alcohol at all.

This chapter discusses the various types of beverages, outlines the procedures for purchasing beverages, and discusses those control procedures that will ensure appropriate amounts of beverages are purchased at optimum prices. Succeeding chapters discuss receiving, storing, issuing, production, and selling of beverages. We begin with the first step in beverage operations—purchasing.

CONTROL PROCESS AND PURCHASING

In Chapter 2, *control* was defined as a process used by managers to direct, regulate, and restrain people's actions so that an enterprise's established goals may be achieved. The control process was described as having four steps:

1. Establish standards and standard procedures for operation.
2. Train all individuals to follow established standards and standard procedures.
3. Monitor performance and compare actual performances with established standards.
4. Take appropriate action to correct deviations from standards.

Previous chapters illustrated the application of this process to the significant phases of foodservice operations: purchasing, receiving, storing, issuing, producing, and sales. In this part of the text, the process is applied to these phases of beverage operations. As with the chapters on food control, the beverage chapters will not discuss training. This topic is left to the section on labour control. This chapter focuses on the application of the control process to beverage purchasing.

ALCOHOLIC BEVERAGES

Alcoholic beverages, obviously, are those that contain alcohol. They contain one particular type of alcohol, ethyl alcohol, which is produced naturally in the process of making alcoholic beverages. Other types of alcohol are unsuitable for human consumption. The amount of alcohol contained in alcoholic beverages varies considerably from one to another. Some have a very small percentage, as little as 0.5 percent. Most have substantially more.

There are three classifications of alcoholic beverages: beers, wines, and spirits. These are substantially different from one another, and anyone planning a career in food and beverage management should be able to both describe them and identify their differences. A full account of the history, production techniques, and various types of beers, wines, and spirits is not possible in this text. Students are advised to consult any one of a large number of books, other publications, and material on the Internet on these subjects for further information. The following description of each is intended to point out the differences among them, to motivate students to investigate further, and to explain why control procedures for each may vary.

LEARNING OBJECTIVE 13.1
Identify and describe the three principal classifications of beverages.

Beers

Beers are beverages produced by the fermentation of malted grain, flavoured with hops. The grain used in Canada is usually barley, predominately from Western Canada, but it can also be rice, wheat, or corn. Malted grain is grain that has been mashed and then steeped in water. Hops are the dried blossoms of the hop vine and are used to impart the typical bitter flavour to beer and contribute natural substances that help prevent bacteria from spoiling beer. Hops may be either domestic or imported from countries such as Germany, China, the Czech Republic, Poland, the United Kingdom, and France. Imported hops are commonly considered superior to domestic.

The Process of Brewing Beer

Although there are slight variations from one brewer to another, the following is the general process of brewing beer:

LEARNING OBJECTIVE 13.2
Outline the process for brewing beer.

1. Malting—the grain is mashed and steeped in water for several days until it begins to germinate. During this process, the grain is converted into a type of sugar called maltose. The resulting substance is called malt.
2. The malt is heated and dried (called kilning). The malt may be further roasted to produce a darker beer with different taste.
3. The dried malt is processed and transferred to a container called a mash turn, where hot water is added. The malt steeps in the liquid for about two hours, and this results in a liquid called wort.
4. The wort is transferred to a brewing kettle where it is boiled. Hops are added.

5. The wort is cooled and strained to make a liquid free of hop leaves and residue. The liquid is transferred to a fermenting tank.

6. Yeast is added, and the liquid ferments for up to two weeks. **Fermentation** is a natural process resulting from the addition of brewer's yeast to the wort. During fermentation, the starches in the liquid are converted to sugars. These sugars, in turn, are converted to carbon dioxide and alcohol. The carbon dioxide is dispersed and the alcohol remains. When the yeast is consumed, the liquid becomes beer.

7. The beer is transferred to an airtight container, called a conditioning tank, where a second fermentation occurs and the beer matures and develops. This aging process can last up to two months. During this process, it becomes naturally carbonated. Some brewers add carbon dioxide gas into the beer to give it more of a bubbly quality.

8. After aging, the beer will be filtered to remove any cloudiness. The beer is then bottled, canned, or put into kegs. If the beer is bottled or canned, it is then pasteurized to kill any bacteria that might be remaining. This process extends shelf life. If it is to be put into kegs for draught beer, it may or may not be pasteurized, but is cooled to prevent bacteria from multiplying and injuring the beer. Draught beer has a shorter shelf life than beer in bottles or cans, so it must be kept cool during the transfer of the kegs to retailers and during storage at the retailer. Draught beer is less carbonated than bottles or cans to prevent excessive foaming while pouring.

Types of Beers

LEARNING OBJECTIVE 13.3
Identify the classifications of beers and distinguish between them.

Although one might think that all products called beer are much the same, this is not the case. Beers are normally divided into two broad classifications: lager beers and ales. The yeast used in processing and the processing method determine whether the beer is to be a lager beer or an ale. There are two types of yeast used in making beer: lager yeast (bottom-fermenting yeast) and ale yeast (top-fermenting yeast).

Lager Beer. Lager beer, the type most commonly consumed in Canada, is a category that includes the popular brands of regular and light beer—Molson, Labatt, Kokanee, Moosehead, and many others. Light beer has become increasingly more popular in Canada as it has less alcohol content than regular beer, usually 4 percent instead of 5 percent. The major producers of lager make beer that is generally lighter, drier, crisper, and less bitter than ale, although this does not hold true for all lagers. Other names applied to lager beer are Pilsner, a golden lager; bock beer, a full-bodied darker beer with an alcoholic content by volume of up to 8 percent; ice beer, made by lowering the temperature of the beer below freezing and then filtering out the ice crystals that form; Japanese beers such as Asahi, Kirin, and Sapporo, which are made from rice and corn; and malt liquors, which are also classified as lager beers. Dry beers are made with less residual sugar. Nonalcoholic beers, nicknamed "near beer" (with an alcohol content of less than 0.5 percent), are produced in much the same way as regular beer, but most of the alcohol is removed.

In recent years regional microbreweries, or craft breweries—making their own lager and ale—have grown in popularity. With the increasing number of microbreweries, the variety of beers has increased dramatically. They frequently make beers for different seasons: lighter ones for the summer and more full-bodied ones for the winter.

Ale. Ales are becoming more popular in Canada, with familiar brands such as Rickard's and Alexander Keith's. Names associated with ales include porter (which is named after the train porters who drank this style) and stout, which are more popular in the United Kingdom. These are dark, dense ales, close to black in colour. Other ales found primarily in England, Ireland, and Scotland include mild ale, bitter ale, pale ale, and brown ale. The names of these ales describe their characteristics.

Wines

Wines are beverages normally produced by the fermentation of grapes, although various other fruits (such as apples, pears, and berries) and one grain (rice) are also fermented to produce comparatively small quantities of wine.

Wine Making

The fermentation process for wine differs considerably from beers.

LEARNING OBJECTIVE 13.4
Outline the process for making wine.

1. In the traditional method of wine making, grapes are crushed and then placed in tanks, where the yeasts occurring naturally on the grapes begin the fermentation process.
2. If the wine is to be white, the skins of the grapes are removed. If it is to be a red wine, the skins are left during fermentation.
3. The sugars in the crushed grape mixture are converted to carbon dioxide and alcohol. Left unchecked, this conversion will continue until all of the sugar is converted or the level of alcohol reaches 14 percent, at which point the yeast is killed by the alcohol and the process ceases. Grapes contain varying amounts of natural sugar, depending on the type of grape and the degree of ripeness when picked. Grapes with less natural sugar produce wines that are not as sweet as those with more natural sugar. The difference has to do with the amount of sugar, if any, that remains in the mixture when the yeasts are killed. If sugar remains unprocessed in the resulting wine, the flavour will have a certain sweetness to it. If no sugar remains, the wine will be designated as dry, a term used to describe wines that lack sweetness.
4. When fermentation ends, the resulting liquid is drawn off and stored in fresh wood casks. During the time it is stored, any residue will settle in the cask, so the new wine will be clear.

5. When the wines have "cleared" sufficiently, they are removed from the wood casks and placed in other containers to mature. The nature of these containers and the length of time required to reach maturity vary from one wine to another.

6. When the new wine is mature, it is filtered and then bottled. Once bottled, the wine is either shipped for immediate consumption or stored under carefully controlled conditions (or aged) for a period of time. The type of wine produced will determine whether it is shipped or aged and, if aged, the length of time appropriate for aging.

Sake Wine. Sake is a rice wine that has a higher alcohol content than traditional wines. This is because sake brewing combines the two chemical steps of converting the rice to sugar and the sugar to alcohol simultaneously. The process of brewing sake is much more precise than other wines, and the brewing temperature must be exact in order to achieve the desired result. Some brewers will fortify their sake to make the alcoholic content higher.

The preceding is an oversimplified description of the methods of making wine, used today primarily by those wineries producing high-quality, expensive wines. It should be noted that some makers, typically those producing large quantities of inexpensive wines for mass markets, use modern adaptations of traditional methods, such as producing wines in vast steel tanks rather than individual wood casks. Some pasteurize their wines, a process the traditional winemaker would never consider.

Classification of Wine

LEARNING OBJECTIVE 13.5
Identify and describe the
colour classifications of wine.

Wines are normally classified as red, white, or rosé. The colour of a wine is determined by the variety of grape used and the manner in which it is processed. Red wines tend to be drier than white wines and range from hearty and full-bodied to light and fruity. In contrast, white wines tend to be lighter-bodied than reds and range from very dry to very sweet. Red wines, normally served at room temperature, are often considered better accompaniments to red meat, whereas white wines, typically served chilled, more commonly accompany fish, poultry, and veal. Rosé wines, usually served chilled, may be used to accompany any main dish. These are general rules, commonly quoted in texts and practised by a number of wine connoisseurs. Today, however, most agree that individuals should follow their own tastes, and it is not uncommon to see restaurant customers ordering white wines to accompany beef.

The colour classifications discussed here are not the only means for identifying wines. The four terms in the following list are commonly used as well:

1. Varietal. A **varietal wine** is one named for the variety of grape that predominates the wine. Chardonnay, Zinfandel, Cabernet Sauvignon, and Pinot Noir, for example, are varieties of grapes that lend their names to wines—varietal wines.

2. Brand name. A **brand-name wine** is one known primarily by the name of the producer. Many winemakers produce wines under their own names.

Some are superior, whereas others are less so. These are normally blended wines, carefully produced so that their characteristics are the same from bottle to bottle, year after year. Lancers Vin Rosé is an excellent example.

3. Geographic. A **geographic wine** is one named for its place of origin. Many wines are named for the specific locations where they are produced. The location may be as large as a region or a district, or it may be as small as a particular vineyard, known in France as a château. Producers are normally required to follow standards and regulations established by some authority, usually a governmental agency, to ensure that the wine named for the area has identifiable and presumably desirable characteristics, given the climate and soil in the region. Examples of geographic wines are Château Margaux from the vineyard of the same name and Chianti, which is from the Chianti region of Tuscany, Italy.

4. Generic. A **generic wine** is named for a well-known wine-producing region, but is not produced in that region. Generic wines take their names from geographic areas, most commonly in France or Italy. Generic wines attempt to replicate the characteristics of the better-known geographic wines after which they are named. For example, some wines produced in California are known as burgundy, a name borrowed from the Burgundy region of France. A generic wine may be excellent, very poor, or anything in between. One must taste the wine to determine its quality.

There are several types of wines and wine-based beverages with characteristics that are sufficiently different to warrant separate discussion:

- **Sparkling wines** are carbonated. The carbonation may be natural or artificial, and the wines may be red, white, or rosé. Champagne, spumante, and cava are well-known examples of sparkling wines.

- **Fortified wines** are wines to which small quantities of brandy or spirits have been added to increase the alcoholic content. Port and sherry are the two best-known examples.

- **Wine coolers** are blends of wine and fruit juice. Consequently, wine coolers have comparatively low alcoholic content—commonly about 5 percent. With the growing trend to lighter drinks, wine coolers have become increasingly popular.

- **Blush wines** are characterized by their slightly pinkish colour. They are comparatively new to the market. One way to make blush wines is to ferment red and white grapes together to produce a wine similar in appearance to a rosé. Blush wines tend to be light-bodied and sweet.

Spirits

Spirits are alcoholic beverages produced by the distillation of a fermented liquid. The fermented liquid may be made from grain, fruit, or several other food products, including sugar cane and potatoes. A complete list of possible ingredients would be almost endless. Most spirits, however, are produced from the

• FIGURE 13.1 •	
Primary Ingredients in Distilled Beverages	
Distilled Beverages	*Primary Ingredients*
Bourbon	Corn
Brandy	Grapes
Gin	Any grain
Rum, dark	Molasses
Rum, light	Sugar cane
Whisky	Corn, rye
Scotch	Barley
Vodka	Potatoes; any grain

LEARNING OBJECTIVE 13.6
Explain the purpose of the distillation process.

aforementioned food products. Figure 13.1 lists some of the major alcoholic beverages produced by distillation and the primary food ingredients used to produce them.

Distillation is the process by which alcohol is removed from a fermented liquid. The process takes place in a device known as a still. In the still, the fermented liquid is heated to change the liquid alcohol to a gas. Alcohol vaporizes at a lower temperature than other liquids. Thus, as the liquid is heated, the alcohol in the liquid vaporizes first. The gas is then cooled, and the result is a condensed distillate that is principally alcohol, but with various impurities that are important in giving spirits their essential character. The nature of the final product is determined primarily by the basic food ingredient from which the fermented liquid was prepared and the alcoholic content of the distillate.

The alcoholic content of a distillate is stated in terms of proof. **Proof** is the term used to describe the strength of an alcoholic beverage or spirit. It is the relationship of pure alcohol (100 percent by volume) to water (0 percent alcohol by volume). In essence a spirit that contains 57.1 percent alcohol of volume at a temperature of 15.5°C is considered a proof spirit. Canada measures the alcohol in a spirit by the Gay-Lusac method, which expresses the alcohol as a percentage by volume of the liquid.

A distiller can control the proof of a distillate by regulating the temperature, duration, and other elements of the distillation process. In general, the lighter and clearer the final product, the higher the proof of the distillate. To produce vodka, for example, the process must be regulated so that the proof of the distillate is 85 or higher; in contrast, the proof of the distillate for bourbon is normally between 55 and 65.

With the exception of vodkas and some gins, spirits are stored in wooden barrels for some period of time before being bottled. This aging mellows and brings out the flavour and colour of the final product. The longer the aging, the better and more costly the final product. Thus, 12-year-old Scotch is considered better than 6-year-old Scotch and is more expensive. Just before bottling, all spirits are diluted, or cut, with distilled water to lower the proof and thus reduce the potency of the bottled product. When bottled, most spirits are between 40 and 50 proof. Once spirits are bottled, they can be stored at normal temperatures indefinitely.

A particularly interesting group of spirits is that known as liqueurs, or cordials. **Liqueurs** are spirits, typically brandies or neutral spirits that have been sweetened and combined with flavouring agents. Some, such as Drambuie, come from carefully guarded recipes; others, such as crème de menthe, are produced from well-known recipes by numerous distillers. Because liqueurs are sweet, they are commonly consumed as after-dinner drinks or combined with other ingredients in cocktails. Grasshoppers and Brandy Alexanders are examples of cocktails in which liqueurs are vital ingredients. The proof range of liqueurs is wider than that of spirits.

NONALCOHOLIC BEVERAGES

Nonalcoholic beverages include those normally found listed in restaurant menus under the "beverage" category: coffee, tea, and milk, as well as a host of others, some carbonated and some not. Carbonated nonalcoholic beverages include seltzer, club soda, tonic, ginger ale, and a wide range of other flavoured beverages known as pop or soda in various places. Nonalcoholic beverages that are not carbonated include fruit and vegetable juices, such as orange juice, clamato juice, and tomato juice.

Many of the nonalcoholic beverages are used to dilute alcoholic beverages and to produce a vast number of drinks with a wide variety of flavours. When used this way, nonalcoholic beverages are called **mixers**. A list of the most common mixers would include club soda, ginger ale, lemon-lime soda, cola, tonic, orange juice, tomato juice, clamato juice, and grapefruit juice.

For the purposes of these chapters, we use the term *beverage* alone to refer to alcoholic beverages and the term *mixers* to refer to nonalcoholic beverages that are typically used with alcoholic beverages to produce mixed drinks. Some mixed drinks, usually produced from recipes, require additional items, which will be referred to simply as other ingredients. These typically include olives, celery, pearl onions, sugar, cream, and two juices that are a bit too strong to be used as mixers: lime juice and lemon juice.

BEVERAGE PURCHASING

As with food purchasing, it is important to implement beverage purchasing controls. There are three primary purposes of beverage purchasing controls:

1. To maintain an appropriate supply of ingredients for producing beverage products

LEARNING OBJECTIVE 13.7
List the primary purposes for establishing beverage purchasing controls.

2. To ensure that the quality of ingredients purchased is appropriate for their intended use

3. To ensure that ingredients are purchased at optimum prices

As always, the key to successful control is to establish suitable standards and standard procedures. The starting point is to determine who is responsible for beverage purchasing.

Responsibility for Beverage Purchasing

The nature and size of an operation often dictate who is responsible for purchasing beverages. In small, owner-operated establishments, the responsibility is normally that of the owner. In others, it may be that of the manager. In some large operations, purchasing responsibility may be delegated to a purchasing manager or a beverage manager. The job title of the individual responsible for beverage purchasing is of little consequence. The important point is that one individual should be given responsibility and be held accountable for all beverage purchasing. For control purposes, it is desirable to assign the responsibility to someone who is not directly engaged in either the preparation or the sale of drinks. It is not common practice for a bartender to fulfill these duties.

Establishing Standards for Beverage Purchasing

For beverage purchasing, standards must be developed for the following:

1. Quality

2. Quantity

3. Price

Quality Standards

LEARNING OBJECTIVE 13.8
Identify the principal factors one must consider before establishing quality standards for beverages.

Alcoholic beverages purchased for bars may be divided into two classes according to use: call brands and pouring brands, also called a well brand. A **call brand** is one used only if the specific brand is requested by a customer; a **pouring brand** is one used whenever a customer does not specify a call brand. If a customer simply orders a "Scotch and soda" he or she would be given the pouring brand. In contrast, if a specific brand of Scotch is ordered (e.g., Dewar's White Label), the customer is given the call brand specifically requested, assuming it is available. The usual practice is for management to designate one low- to medium-priced brand in each category of spirits as the pouring brand. The specific brands selected as the pouring brands will vary with the clientele and the price structure. Once pouring brands have been identified, all other brands become call brands. The selection of pouring brands is an important first step in establishing both quality and cost standards.

Before establishing quality standards for alcoholic beverages, one must first weigh several considerations, including product cost, customer preferences, and product popularity, among others. Most people will agree on the extremes—that certain 25-year-old single-malt Scotch are of high quality and that particularly inexpensive gins are of very low quality—but between these extremes there is a vast area for legitimate differences of opinion.

The extent of the need for each of the three different types of alcoholic beverages must be determined before any purchase decisions can be made. After all, the possibilities for purchasing various beers, wines, and spirits are vast, and no establishment has the space or the need to purchase a massive variety of these products. Needs differ from place to place, depending on clientele and the inherent differences in the nature of operations. Some neighbourhood bars cater to customers whose tastes run primarily to domestic beer, inexpensive wines, and comparatively few whiskies. In contrast, cocktail lounges serving an upper-middle-income clientele commonly offer imported beers, a large assortment of spirits, and a few fine wines, whereas some expensive restaurants are widely regarded for their specialized wine lists that include the finest of imported wines. These are but a few of the many possibilities. Because all alcoholic beverages are comparatively expensive, defining customer taste carefully is particularly important. By doing so, management attempts to eliminate the purchase of beverages that will not sell.

Purchasing beverages requires the expenditure of cash for merchandise that must be carried as inventory until sold. It is usually undesirable to maintain an inventory of items that move very slowly. Once an operation is open and control procedures are in place, a manager can identify slow-moving items and restrict or eliminate their purchase. However, this is a partial solution at best. It is of great importance to restrict initial purchases to items that are likely to meet customer tastes. Thus, deciding on the specific alcoholic beverages and brands that are of suitable quality for the expected clientele is the responsibility of management in each operation.

Quantity Standards

Because beverage products are not highly perishable if stored properly, beverages can be purchased far less frequently than perishable foods. This is not to say that beverages are nonperishable, however. Canned and bottled beers should be used within approximately three months of packaging. Draught beers should be consumed within one month. Some wines have comparatively limited lives, whereas others, those that improve with age, can and should be stored for some period before use. Most spirits can be stored almost indefinitely. Thus, perishability is not a critical factor in establishing quantity standards for beverages. Other factors are far more significant.

LEARNING OBJECTIVE 13.9
Identify seven principal factors used to establish quantity standards for beverages.

There are seven principal factors used to establish quantity standards for beverage purchasing:

1. Frequency with which management chooses to place orders
2. Storage space available
3. Funds available for inventory purchases

4. Delivery schedules set by suppliers
5. Minimum order requirements set by suppliers
6. Price specials available
7. Limited availability of some items

Some of these considerations are more important than others. Most establishments, for example, have limited storage space, and this is clearly a factor in establishing quantity standards. So is the number of times that management will permit orders to be placed. It would be foolish to place orders for any item too frequently, so quantity standards must be such that the number of orders placed over time is kept to a minimum. Availability of funds can be another severely limiting factor. Beverage purchases require relatively large cash outlays, either at the time of delivery or very soon thereafter, depending on local regulations. Thus, if the necessary cash is not normally available for purchasing large quantities, it may be necessary to purchase smaller amounts and place orders more frequently. And although management may choose to order a given item frequently, the supplier may not be willing to deliver more often than once every other week. In addition, suppliers such as Brewers Retail in Ontario, more commonly known as The Beer Store, or Brewers Distribution Limited in western Canada may establish minimum order quantities for some items. In addition, wines must often be purchased by the case from suppliers.

From time to time, some beverage products, usually beer, are available at discounted prices for limited periods, and it is sometimes desirable to increase a current order beyond the normal order quantity to take advantage of the discount. Sometimes, some beverage products, especially wines, may not be readily available in the market, and it may be necessary to purchase a very large quantity when the item is available if one is to ensure an adequate supply for continuing needs.

To establish quantity standards for beverages, management must take several factors into account. This is best done by those who have considerable experience with beverage management and are fully informed about all aspects of the beverage operation, including its financial status.

Price Standards

LEARNING OBJECTIVE 13.10
Explain the provincial and territorial regulations and practices for the sale of alcoholic beverages.

Assuming that quality standards have been established and appropriate purchase quantities are known, the next step is to ensure that all beverage purchases are made at the optimum price. Any discussion of price standards is complicated somewhat by laws that vary across the country.

A government liquor authority controls the sale of alcoholic beverages in each province and territory. Most authorities own and manage retail stores and license private agency stores, which usually provide services to small and remote communities. Alberta is the only jurisdiction that has privatized all liquor retailing, although it continues to regulate the sale of alcoholic beverages as the importer and wholesaler of such products.

The process for selling domestic beer varies across jurisdictions. Most domestic beer in Ontario, for example, is sold through The Beer Store (legally known as Brewers Retail Inc.), a private company owned by the major breweries, and only a fraction of domestic beer is sold in government-run liquor stores. In Quebec, however, no domestic beer is sold in government stores; the breweries sell to consumers through grocery and convenience stores, and directly to hotels, restaurants, and other licensed establishments. Domestic beer is sold in convenience stores in Newfoundland and Labrador, but also in liquor stores. In the other provinces as well as the Yukon and Northwest Territories, domestic beer is sold in government-run stores and licensed agencies. Some jurisdictions (Alberta, British Columbia, Manitoba, Saskatchewan, and the Yukon and Northwest Territories) also allow appropriately licensed hotels to sell cases of beer to be consumed off their premises.

Currently, Nunavut does not have liquor stores. There are three types of alcohol policies in Nunavut. A few communities (such as Iqaluit) have no alcohol restrictions, which means that you can purchase alcohol and drink it at licensed establishments. The second type of community is one with no local purchasing of alcohol but it can be brought in with a permit endorsed by the local Alcohol Education Committee. The third type of community is one with a complete prohibition on alcohol.[1]

In general, anyone responsible for purchasing alcoholic beverages must be familiar with the laws, restrictions, and industry practices in effect in the area. If competitive pricing is the rule, the buyer should clearly take full advantage of it. If competition is minimal or nonexistent, the buyer must simply accept the fact and watch for special offers, if any, on appropriate beverages.

Establishing Standard Procedures for Beverage Purchasing

Having established standards for purchasing beverages, the next step is to establish standard procedures. In beverage purchasing, standard procedures are needed to do two things:

LEARNING OBJECTIVE 13.11
Identify the two principal methods for determining order quantities and calculate order quantities using both methods.

1. To determine order quantities
2. To process orders

Determining Order Quantities: Basic Methods

There are two basic methods for determining order quantities. The first, known as the periodic order method, is based on fixed order dates and variable order quantities; the second, the perpetual order method, uses variable order dates and fixed reorder quantities.

---

[1] Statistics Canada, *The Control and Sale of Alcoholic Beverages in Canada.* Catalogue no. 63-202-X , June 2008.

Periodic Order Method. The **periodic order method** requires that order dates be fixed so that there are equal operating periods between order dates. Ordering may be done weekly, biweekly, or on any other regular schedule, depending on the decisions of management with respect to such considerations as frequency of ordering, storage space to be devoted to beverages, and funds available for inventory purchases, as well as on suppliers' delivery schedules and the anticipated consumption of beverages.

Determining anticipated consumption is a key element: the person who sets order quantities must have some reasonable knowledge of the quantity of each beverage that is likely to be consumed in the interval between fixed order dates. There are two ways to determine this. The first, and by far the best, is to have records of the quantity of each beverage consumed during one such period. If bar requisitions of the type discussed in the following chapter are used, it is comparatively easy to determine quantities consumed. The second method is simply to estimate consumption, based on one's experience in the particular operation, experience in other similar operations, or both of these.

Having established for each beverage the anticipated consumption for a particular period, one increases that number by an amount that will allow for such unanticipated occurrences as increases in business volume, time required to receive delivery, and possible delay in receiving delivery. Some multiply the usage figure by 150 percent; others use some other percentage. Many round the results to whole case lots for pouring brands and any other beverages accounting for high volume. In the periodic system, the number so determined for each beverage item is defined as the **par stock** for that item—the maximum quantity of the item that should be on hand at any given time. Thus, at Bistro Quatre, the manager anticipates that the restaurant will use two bottles of Smirnoff vodka (its pouring vodka) each night, and that it should order liquor every two weeks. The restaurant will use 28 bottles in that period. Increasing that number to the next higher case lot, par stock is set at 36, or three cases of 12 bottles each.

There are thus two figures established for each beverage: anticipated usage and par stock. For each item in the inventory, both of these figures should be recorded on a label affixed to the shelf where the item is kept in the beverage storeroom. An example of such a shelf label is illustrated in Figure 13.2. On the established date for placing orders, the individual responsible for determining purchase quantities reviews the entire beverage inventory in an orderly manner to determine the correct purchase quantity for each item in the inventory. This is done by means of the following standard procedure:

1. Count the inventory (the number of units on the shelf).
2. Subtract the inventory from the par stock figure on the shelf label.
3. Obtain the purchase quantity, which is the result of the previous subtraction.

Referring to the information provided on the shelf label in Figure 13.2, if there were 8 bottles of Smirnoff vodka on the shelf, that number would be subtracted from the par stock figure, 36, to determine the proper order quantity: 28 units, or two cases plus four bottles.

> • FIGURE 13.2 •
>
> **Shelf Label**
>
> | ITEM | Smirnoff Vodka |
> | --- | --- |
> | Size | 750 ml |
> | Par Stock | 36 (3 cases) |
> | Anticipated Usage | 24 (2 cases) |

```
   Par stock            36
-  Current inventory     8
=  Purchase quantity    28
```

An order would be placed for the next full case lot, which is 3 cases, or 36 bottles.

If the actual usage is the same as the usage figure on the label, the purchase quantity determined in this manner will be the same as the usage figure. If the subtraction results in a purchase quantity that is substantially different from the usage figure on the label, that is a signal that actual usage is not as anticipated and that the figures on the shelf label must be reviewed. For example, if one finds 22 units of vodka on the shelf, the order quantity would appear to be 14. However, the fact that there are 22 units on the shelf means that usage has been considerably less than anticipated; thus, one should assess the need for a par stock of 36. Unless the decrease in the number of units consumed is a temporary phenomenon, par stock and usage figures on the label should be changed for future periods. In general, if the number of units in inventory on a given order date differs markedly from the difference between par stock and usage, the adequacy of these two figures for purchasing purposes must be reviewed.

Perpetual Order Method. The **perpetual order method** requires fixed purchase quantities and variable order dates. Its use depends on the establishment of a perpetual inventory system for beverages, with paper perpetual inventory cards on which all purchases and issues are recorded carefully and in a timely manner. Today, perpetual inventory records are more likely to be created in a computer database. The perpetual inventory is normally maintained in a location other than the beverage storeroom. However, as an alternative, some managers attach perpetual inventory cards to the shelves on which the beverages are stored.

To use the perpetual order method, several key figures must be established and recorded on the cards: par stock, reorder point, and reorder quantity. As previously indicated, par stock is the maximum quantity that may be on hand at any given time. It takes into account the storage space to be allocated to the item, the desired frequency of ordering, anticipated usage, and a safety factor to cover such considerations as unanticipated increases in quantities consumed. **Reorder point** is the number of units to which inventory should decrease before an order is placed. It must take into account the time required to obtain delivery of the order. **Reorder quantity** is the amount that should be ordered each time an order is placed. It is calculated by subtracting the reorder point from par stock and adding the number of units consumed between order date and delivery date.

Figure 13.3 illustrates a perpetual inventory card for a pouring gin in a restaurant open seven days a week. The card indicates that this gin is consumed at the rate of approximately three bottles per day. Management has determined that orders are to be placed at approximately one-week intervals, and experience has shown that it takes three days to obtain delivery. Therefore, par stock is calculated as follows:

> 3 bottles per day × 7 days × 150% (to include a safety factor) = 31.5 bottles

• FIGURE 13.3 •

Perpetual Inventory Card

Item	Gordon's Gin			Par Stock		32
Size	750 ml			Reorder Point		14
				Reoder Quantity		24

Date	Order #	Quantity	In	Out	Balance
31-Aug					32
1-Sep				2	30
2-Sep				3	27
3-Sep				3	24
4-Sep				3	21
5-Sep				3	18
6-Sep				4	14
7-Sep	#8	24		2	12
8-Sep				4	8
9-Sep				2	6
10-Sep			24	3	27
11-Sep				2	25
12-Sep				3	22

This is rounded to 32 bottles. Reorder point is determined by multiplying the number of units used in the three days required for delivery (9) by 150 percent to include a safety factor—9 × 1.5 = 13.5, rounded to 14 bottles. Reorder quantity is determined by subtracting the reorder point from par stock and then adding the number of units used in the three-day period before receiving delivery.

Thus, the reorder quantity is calculated as follows:

	Par stock	32	bottles
—	Reorder point	14	
	Total	18	
+	Units used in 3-day period	9	
	Reorder quantity	27	rounded to 24, or 2 cases

This number leaves a six-bottle safety factor.

The standard procedures suggested here for determining order quantities assume that supplies of the needed items are readily available. Although this is normally true for all mixers, most spirits and beers, and many wines, it is not universally true for all beverages. There are several complicating factors. For example, some wines (especially vintage wines, both imported and domestic) may be unavailable at any given time, and this unavailability may be either temporary or permanent. In some cases, supplies of various items may not always be adequate to fill an order completely, making adjustments necessary. The beverage buyer must be prepared to meet contingencies as they arise and must be able to deviate from established purchasing procedures when required. Sometimes one can anticipate problems, as with particular wines that one knows will be available at an appropriate price for only a short time. This is sometimes the case with fine wines. In such instances, one must be prepared to place one order for the total amount required over a very long period, possibly several years.

Determining Order Quantities: Using a Computer Program

Computer users sometimes use generic spreadsheet or database programs to record inventory values and to determine order quantities. However, many managers interested in using computers today are inclined to adopt one of the growing number of programs specifically written for beverage purchasing and inventory control. These software and hardware systems are of great benefit to management by providing critical information and by assisting the control of beverage operations so that planned costs can be more readily achieved. These systems:

LEARNING OBJECTIVE 13.12
Describe several ways computer programs assist in calculating inventory balances and inventory usage,

1. Allow easy input of purchases and issues so that accurate records can be kept without the need to hand write the information on receiving sheets and issue requisitions.
2. More easily provide an accurate inventory of liquor by keeping cumulative totals of liquor inventory in memory. Handwritten inventory cards are no longer needed.
3. Provide for easy inventory taking. Some programs allow full and partially empty bottles to be scanned, and then they automatically calculate inventory levels. Others keep inventory current by adjusting inventory as liquor is poured at the bar.

4. Provide management with daily reports showing purchase, usage, and cost information. Manual calculation for liquor cost and cost percentage is not necessary.

5. Allow management to more easily determine where liquor shortage is occurring. Some programs keep track of the usage of each brand of liquor as drinks are prepared. This allows management to compare the amount of liquor that should be used in drink preparation with actual usage of each brand.

One such system is the AZ 200 Controller, by Liquor Control Solutions. The controller measures and automatically deducts from inventory the exact amount of liquor poured each time a drink is prepared. Each day, management can get a report from the system showing usage and inventory balance (as well as other reports) for all beverages, effectively instituting a perpetual inventory system. This and similar programs will be discussed in further detail in Chapter 15, Beverage Production Control.

Other systems allow management to take inventory by estimating, weighing, or scanning bottles. Bar codes on each bottle are scanned to identify the brand. Full bottles are counted. Partial bottles are inventoried by scanning, weighing, or estimating.

One such program is provided by LiquidGuardian. Its software is downloaded to the computer at the establishment and provides forms for entering inventory of each product. Full bottles are counted, and partial bottles are inventoried by estimating amounts in each bottle. Each time an inventory is taken, the information is sent to LiquidGuardian. Various reports are produced for the establishment, including inventory usage and inventory balance.

Scannabar, another program, allows the establishment to scan bar codes on both full and empty bottles to determine the brand of liquor. Partial bottles are inventoried using a measuring ribbon attached to the bottle. The software at the establishment automatically calculates usage and inventory balances.

Still another program, AccuBar, also scans bar codes with a scanning device. Partial bottles are scanned by the operator tapping the scanner at the level of liquid in a bottle displayed on the scanner. The number of full bottles is entered into the scanner (see Figure 13.4). The information is downloaded and sent to AccuBar. Reports are sent to the establishment via e-mail.

Accardis Systems has a program named Cyclops. A scanner identifies bottles by scanning bar codes. Partially full bottles are weighed. All information is automatically sent to Cyclops. The counted inventory is uploaded to the Accardis software program, and various reports are quickly generated.

If an establishment does not want to take the time to do the inventory itself, it can hire a service firm. One such firm is Draught Prophets. They will send a representative to the establishment regularly to take the inventory, weighing open bottles and counting full ones. They provide necessary reports to management, including inventory usage, inventory balance, and suggested amounts to order. Further explanation of these systems as well as others is given in Chapter 15.

• **FIGURE 13.4** •

AccuBar's Inventory Report for Bistro Quatre

Brand	StockRm	Totals	Unit Cost	Ext Value
Alexander Keith's	168	168	$ 1.11	$
Amstel Light	48	48	$	
Blue Light	72	72	$ 1.00	$ 72.00
Bud Light	48	48	$ 0.70	$ 35.04
Coors Light	120	120	$ 0.73	$ 87.60
Corona Extra	168	168	$ 1.02	$ 171.36
Creemore Lager	48	48	$ 0.73	$ 35.04
Heineken	192	192	$ 1.09	$ 209.28
Kokanee	96	96	$ 0.72	$ 69.12
Moosehead	72	72	$ 1.02	$ 73.44
Rickard's Red	120	120	$ 0.99	$ 118.00
Sleeman Honey Brown	216	216	$ 1.00	$ 216.00
Beer Totals	**1368**	**1368**		**$ 1,324.32**
Jack Daniel's	37	37	$ 20.12	$ 744.44
Maker's Mark Bourbon	2	2	$ 21.53	$ 43.06
Wild Turkey	1	1	$ 17.70	$ 17.70
Bourbon Totals	**40**	**40**		**$ 805.20**
St. Remy	1	1	$ 10.22	$ 10.22
Brandy Totals	**1**	**1**		**$ 10.22**
Beefeater Gin	2	2	$ 20.87	$ 41.74
Bombay Gin	1	1	$ 19.63	$ 19.63
Bombay Sapphire Gin	3	3	$ 21.63	$ 64.89
Tanqueray Gin	3	3	$ 20.87	$ 62.61
Gin Totals	**9**	**9**		**$ 188.87**
Bacardi Light Rum	2	2	$ 11.80	$ 23.60
Lamb's White Rum	1	1	$ 17.53	$ 17.53
Rum Totals	**3**	**3**		**$ 41.13**
Baileys Irish Cream	1	1	$ 21.94	$ 21.94
Campari Liqueur	1	1	$ 20.03	$ 20.03
Cointreau Liqueur	1	1	$ 29.85	$ 29.85
Grand Marnier	3	3	$ 36.03	$ 108.09
Kahlua Liqueur	4	4	$ 22.62	$ 90.48
Martini & Rossi Sweet Vermouth	2	2	$ 6.08	$ 12.16
Martini & Rossi Very Dry Vermouth	2	2	$ 6.08	$ 12.16
Liqueur Totals	**14**	**14**		**$ 294.71**
Château des Charmes Cabernet	48	48	$ 23.46	$ 1,126.08
Gray Monk Pinot Noir	72	72	$ 22.13	$ 1,593.36
Jackson Triggs Cabernet Sauvignon	2	2	$ 20.13	$ 40.26
Kendall-Jackson Vintner's Reserve Cabernet	48	48	$ 10.63	$ 510.24
Ridge Lytton Springs Zinfandel	24	24	$ 20.13	$ 483.12
Jackson Triggs Pinot Noir	18	18	$ 5.96	$ 107.28
Wolf Blass Merlot	24	24	$ 10.96	$ 263.04
Wine Totals	**236**	**236**		**$ 4,123.38**
Grand Totals	**1671**	**1671**		**$ 6,787.83**

This report shows what you *actually* received from your supplier. The report can be made to show one delivery or everything delivered over a period of your choosing.

AccuBar allows you to update details of each item, such as their cost, on the handheld as you receive them, so it is simple to keep your unit costs updated in the system.

Taking inventory of draught beer using one of the aforementioned computer programs is similar to that of spirits. The Draught Prophets representative weighs partially used beer kegs, and thus determines the amount in inventory. Draught Prophets has a keg check, which is a measuring stick that hooks onto the edge of the keg. The stick has a scale, which shows the amount of beer in the keg when the keg is tilted. Draught Prophets sells a keg scale that allows management to weigh beer kegs to determine usage and amount in inventory. They also sell a draught beer measuring system that tracks the uantity of ounces poured from the tap. Other systems use similar means of determining beer inventory balances.

Determining which software program or computer system to purchase can be difficult. Some of the systems cost many thousands of dollars, whereas some software is relatively inexpensive. Thus, cost is a major factor in the purchase decision. The other major factor is the specific need of the establishment to control liquor purchasing and production. Smaller bars with owner supervision do not need complicated computer systems, but larger establishments where management is not present at the bar may benefit from them. Thus, a program like AccuBar or Scannabar is suitable for the typical restaurant or cocktail lounge of medium size. A small owner-operated establishment may not need a computer system at all, because the owner is present during working hours and can closely supervise the bar. For a large bar or one where there is little supervision over bar operations, a computer program similar to that described by Liquor Control Solutions might be appropriate. Bill Kowalchuk at Bistro Quatre looked at various computer programs for beverage control and chose AccuBar. See the sample inventory report shown in Figure 13.4.

Processing Orders

LEARNING OBJECTIVE 13.13
Describe one standard procedure for processing beverage orders in large hotels and restaurants.

Whenever practical, it is advisable to establish a purchasing routine that requires formal written purchase orders. In most large hotels and many large restaurants, formal purchase requests serve as the basis for ordering. In a large hotel, the purchasing routine may be the following: a wine steward, as the person in charge of maintaining the beverage inventory and stockroom, prepares a purchase request, similar to that illustrated in Figure 13.5, just after the first of the month.

• FIGURE 13.5 •

Purchase Request Form

Quantity	Item	Bottle Size	Purchase Unit	Supplier
3	Jim Beam Bourbon	1.75 L	case	LCBO
2	Beefeater Gin	750 ml	case	LCBO

Requested BY *J Sneed*   Approved By *H. Morgan*
Date *1-Oct*   Date *1-Oct*

The purchase request is prepared in duplicate, with the original forwarded to the purchasing agent in the accounting department. In some establishments, the purchasing agent is required to secure the manager's written approval on the purchase request before placing any order. The order placed is recorded on a form known as a purchase order, illustrated in Figure 13.6.

• FIGURE 13.6 •						
Purchase Order						
The Spanish Moon Bistro Lakefield, ON					Date Order Number	1-Oct C 267
To: LCBO						
Please Ship the Supplies Listed Below Via:					Your Truck	
Quantity	Purchase Unit	Bottle Size	Item		Unit Price	Amount Total
3	case	1.75 L	Jim Beam Bourbon		$155.40	$466.20
2	case	750 ml	Beefeater Gin		$128.40	$256.80
					Total	$723.00
Ordered By		H. Morgan				

The purchase order is made up in quadruplicate. The four copies are distributed as follows: (1) the original is sent to the agency from which the beverages had been ordered; (2) one copy is sent to the wine steward to confirm that the order has been placed; (3) another copy is sent to the receiving clerk so that he or she knows what deliveries to expect and will be able to verify that the quantities and brands delivered are correct; and (4) the final copy is kept by the purchasing agent.

Obviously, not all establishments follow such detailed purchasing routines for beverages. However, because written records reduce misunderstandings and disputes, it is advisable in all instances to maintain a written record of purchases, preferably on a purchase order, to verify the accuracy of deliveries received. Written purchase orders eliminate disputes over brands and quantities ordered, prices quoted, and delivery dates. Because the purchase of alcoholic beverages involves the outlay of considerable amounts of cash, it is wise to establish a system (the purchase order method or some other) to reduce or eliminate the possibilities for error.

In establishments located in provinces where the practice is permitted, salespersons may make site visits to meet with those who place the orders for beverages. It is not uncommon for purchase requests to be made on the basis of these meetings.

THINGS TO CONSIDER

Draught beer has become a very popular drink in bars and restaurants over the past two decades. Many operators do not use a qualified draught maintenance program, which is performed by many draught service companies. To optimize the sales potential of draught beer, you should regularly maintain your draught lines through cleaning, temperature checks, and general maintenance of your equipment. This can prevent unnecessary waste, foaming, overpouring, and spoilage.

CHAPTER ESSENTIALS

In this chapter, we defined beverages, distinguished between alcoholic and non-alcoholic beverages, and classified beverages into four categories: beers, wines, spirits, and mixers. We described basic methods for producing each of the three classes of alcoholic beverages and described the differences between them. We discussed the quality, quantity, and price standards required to establish control over beverage purchasing and identified the principal factors governing the establishment of these standards. We described two common standard procedures for determining purchase quantities and identified the most common standard procedure for processing purchase requests. We discussed several computer programs that provided means of determining inventory usage and inventory balances. Finally, we described the need for preparing purchase requests and purchase orders for some establishments.

KEY TERMS IN THIS CHAPTER

Beers, p. 343

Beverages, p. 342

Blush wines, p. 347

Brand-name wines, p. 346

Call brand, p. 350

Distillation, p. 348

Fermentation, p. 344

Fortified wines, p. 347

QUESTIONS AND PROBLEMS

1. What are the three classifications of alcoholic beverages?
2. What are the two broad classifications of beers, and how do they differ from one another?
3. What are the three colour classifications of wines?
4. Of what significance is the fermentation process in the making of alcoholic beverages?
5. What is the distillation process?
6. In Ontario, what agency sells the majority of beer to licencees?
7. How do liqueurs differ from other spirits?
8. Explain the importance of assigning responsibility for beverage purchasing.
9. Distinguish between call brands and pouring brands.
10. What are the primary purposes of establishing beverage purchasing controls?
11. What considerations should be taken into account by those responsible for establishing the quality standards that will be used when beverages are purchased for a particular hotel, restaurant, or bar?
12. List and explain the principal factors used to establish quantity standards for beverage purchases.
13. What province has privatized the sale of alcoholic beverages?
14. Name the two principal methods used in beverage purchasing to determine order quantities and identify the primary differences between them.
15. a. Given the following information, determine the proper order quantity for each item if the periodic order method is used:

Item	Par Stock	Usage	Quantity on Hand
Smirnoff Vodka	72	48	24
Gordon's Gin	36	24	3
Jack Daniel's	5	3	4
Canadian Club	9	6	4
Crown Royal	36	24	10

b. Should any adjustments to par stock or usage figures be considered for any of the beverages listed in Question 15a? Which? Why?

16. The new manager of the Philby Hotel plans to do the beverage purchasing for the property using the perpetual inventory method. She wants to reorder the items in the following list approximately every two weeks and plans to use a safety factor of 50 percent for calculating par stock and reorder point. Delivery requires six days. Storage space is ample. Given the daily usage figures listed here, determine par stock, reorder point, and reorder quantity for each item.

Item	Daily Usage
Gordon's Gin	4
Smirnoff Vodka	8
Captain Morgan Dark Rum	2
Cutty Sark Scotch	3
Bushmills Irish Whiskey	1

17. Identify four firms that provide computer hardware or software for bars, and explain how each is used to calculate liquor inventory usage and balances. How do they differ?
18. Define each of the key terms in this chapter.

EXCEL EXERCISES

Exercise 13.1
Barnaby's Hideaway uses the periodic method for ordering its beverages. Given the following information, use the form as shown on the companion website for this text to compute order quantities for each item:

Item	Par Stock	Usage	Quantity on Hand
Smirnoff Vodka	60	48	12
Gordon's Gin	54	36	36
Jack Daniel's Tennessee Whiskey	36	24	6
Canadian Club Whisky	12	6	6
Glenfiddich Single-Malt Scotch	18	12	3

Exercise 13.2
In light of the order quantities computed in Exercise 13.1, which of the par stock amounts should be changed?

Exercise 13.3
Follow the instructions on the companion website for this exercise.

CHAPTER 14

Beverage Receiving, Storing, and Issuing Control

INTRODUCTION

The previous chapter presented some of the common standards and standard procedures for beverage purchasing. The use of these standards helps ensure that adequate quantities of beverages of the proper quality are purchased at optimum prices. Management in a beverage operation identifies quality standards by selecting particular brands, determines needed quantities of those brands, and places orders at optimum prices. By doing so, one is, in effect, identifying the cost of the beverages that will be served in the establishment. By placing orders, one is tacitly accepting those costs, which may then be viewed as planned or budgeted costs. It is therefore clearly in the interest of any enterprise to take appropriate steps to ensure that no unwarranted, unbudgeted costs develop before the beverages are sold to customers.

This chapter focuses on the application of the control process to three critical areas of beverage operations in which excessive costs can develop: receiving, storing, and issuing. Standards and standard procedures for each of these areas are identified in the following text.

RECEIVING

Establishing Standards

LEARNING OBJECTIVE 14.1
Identify the objective of receiving control and explain the standards established for achieving receiving control.

The primary goal of receiving control is to ensure that deliveries received conform exactly to orders placed. In practice, this means that beverage deliveries must be compared with beverage orders in regard to quantity, quality, and price. The following standards and standard procedures for receiving apply to operations that receive orders from vendors.

1. The quantity of an item delivered must equal the quantity ordered. Verifying this normally requires examining bottles to be sure they have been filled and sealed, and then simply counting bottles or cases. It can also involve weighing kegs of beer to confirm the standard of fill or examining containers to confirm that those received conform to the order.
2. The quality of an item delivered must be the same as the quality ordered. For all spirits, wines, and beers, one would check to be certain that the brand delivered was the same as the brand ordered. For wines, verification may also require checking vintages or the bottling dates of wines that are best when young. For beers, it may require checking bottling or canning dates to ascertain freshness.
3. The price on the invoice for each item delivered should be the same as the price quoted or listed when the order was placed.

Because the basic standards for the job are rather clear and simple, any honest individual of suitable intelligence and ability can be trained to receive beverages correctly.

In many provinces, operators may also go directly to liquor outlets such as the Liquor Control Board of Ontario (LCBO) and purchase liquor from the store in the same way a consumer would go to a retail outlet to buy liquor, provided they use their licensee number. In most provinces and territories, each establishment is assigned a liquor licensee number when granted a licence to sell alcoholic beverages. Establishments must use this number when ordering products. Thus, the preceding standards for receiving may not strictly apply to those who purchase directly from provincial- or territorial-controlled liquor outlets. The manager must make sure the quantity, quality, and price of the liquor received conforms to the restaurant's requirements.

Establishing Standard Procedures

Standard procedures must always be established to ensure that standards will be met. The steps identified in the following list are generally considered those that make up a basic standard procedure for receiving beverages:

LEARNING OBJECTIVE 14.2
Describe the standard procedures for achieving receiving control over beverages.

1. *Maintain an up-to-date file of all beverage orders placed;* you may need these records for government liquor inspectors or tax auditors. Depending on the operation, these orders may be formal, informal, or a combination of the two. Major hotels, for example, commonly use formal purchase order systems. In contrast, the only record of an order placed by a small neighbourhood restaurant may be some notes taken during a telephone conversation between the owner and a salesperson. Regardless of the size of the establishment, there can be no effective receiving procedure without written records of the orders placed, and the individual responsible for receiving must have these records available.

2. *Verify that quantities, qualities, and prices on the invoice conform to the order.* Remove the record of the order from the file when a delivery arrives and compare it with the invoice presented by the delivery driver for verification. Figure 14.1 illustrates a typical beverage invoice.

3. *Complete the following before the delivery driver leaves the premises:* Check brands, dates, or both, as appropriate, to verify that the quality of beverages delivered conforms to the invoice. Count or weigh goods delivered to verify that the quantity received also conforms to the invoice.

4. *Compare the invoice with the order to verify that goods received conform to the order placed.*

5. *Call to the attention of both management and the delivery driver any broken or leaking containers and any bottles with broken seals or missing labels.*

6. *Note all discrepancies between delivered goods and the invoice on the invoice itself.* Call any discrepancy between an order and the delivery to management's attention immediately. Any such discrepancy may require a decision from management as to whether to accept delivery of the questionable items.

• FIGURE 14.1 •

Beverage Invoice

To:	The Spanish Moon Bistro Lakefield, ON					Invoice # 639-A142 Terms C.O.D.		

Date __3-Oct__   Order # __C267__   Account # __H108__   Ship __Truck__

Item No	Quantity Ordered	Quantity Shipped	Purchase Unit	Bottle Size	Description		Unit Price	Total Price
151	6	6	case	750 ml	Crown Royal		$155.40	$ 932.40
336	2	2	case	750 ml	Beefeater Gin		$179.40	$ 358.80
							Total	$1,291.20

7. *Sign the original invoice to acknowledge receipt of the goods, and return the signed copy to the driver.* Retain the duplicate copy for internal record keeping and government regulations.

8. *Record the invoice on the beverage receiving report.* Most smaller operations do not fill out beverage receiving reports, because they do not use purchase journals. They determine the cost of beverages received and issued weekly or monthly when a physical inventory is taken. Even if that is the case, establishments that use one of the many computer programs designed for beverage operation must input the quantities received and costs into their computer software at this point. If the program includes the use of a scanner, the bar code on each case or bottle is scanned to include it in inventory. If a bottle does not already contain a bar code, they are supplied by the firm that sold the program and are affixed to each bottle.

9. *Notify the person responsible for storing beverages that a delivery has been received.*

LEARNING OBJECTIVE 14.3
List the types of information contained in a beverage receiving report, and explain the report's use.

In many establishments, a form known as a **beverage receiving report** is filled out daily by the individual responsible for receiving beverages. A basic beverage receiving report is illustrated in Figure 14.2.

Many variations are possible, because forms of this nature are developed to the specifications of management in a given operation. As a rule, beverage receiving reports summarize the invoices for all beverages received on a given day. They include columns for listing quantities received and their values and for dividing purchases into essential categories (i.e., wines, beers, spirits, and mixers) for appropriate distribution in purchase journals. The need for separating purchases into these categories will be evident in Chapter 16 in the discussions on costs and management reports. In provinces or territories requiring deposits on bottles, kegs, and cans of beers, spirits, or wine, beverage receiving reports are likely to include columns for recording the charges and credits attributable to the deposits.

• FIGURE 14.2 •

Beverage Receiving Report

THE SPANISH MOON BISTRO
BEVERAGE RECEIVING REPORT

Date   3-Oct

Distributor	Item	Quantity Received	Purchase Unit	Size	Unit Cost	Total Cost	Purchase Journal Distribution			
							Wines	Beers	Spirits	Mixers
LCBO	Crown Royal	6	case	750 ml	$155.40	$932.40			$ 932.40	
LCBO	Beefeater Gin	2	case	750 ml	$179.40	$358.80			$ 358.80	
Brewer's Retail Inc.	Labatt Blue	12	case	375 ml	$ 11.95	$143.40		$143.40		
Canada Dry	Tonic	7	case	250 ml	$ 9.00	$ 63.00				$63.00
LCBO	Moselle	4	case	750 ml	$ 60.00	$240.00	$240.00			
LCBO	Château Rue	2	case	750 ml	$105.00	$210.00	$210.00			
Total							$450.00	$143.40	$1,291.20	$63.00

Filling out a beverage receiving report is a rather simple matter, merely requiring that essential data be transferred from an invoice to the report. The process for doing this can readily be inferred from a careful comparison of Figures 14.1 and 14.2. Because the beverage receiving report is an accounting document, its specific makeup will vary considerably from one beverage operation to another, depending on the nature and degree of complexity of the accounting practices in effect. It is generally advisable to require a receiving report for beverages that is separate and distinct from that for food and to design a form tailored to the individual establishment's needs.

It is generally considered good practice to require not only the individual receiving the beverages but also the individual responsible for storing the beverages (e.g., the food and beverage manager) to sign the beverage receiving report each day. By doing so, this individual acknowledges receiving the beverages listed on the report for addition to the beverage inventory.

STORING

Establishing Standards

LEARNING OBJECTIVE 14.4
Identify the objectives of storing control and explain the standards established for achieving storing control.

Storing control is established in beverage operations to achieve three important objectives:

1. To prevent pilferage
2. To ensure accessibility when needed
3. To preserve quality

To accomplish these objectives, standards must be established. The following standards are critical to effective storing control.

Preventing Pilferage

To prevent pilferage, it is clearly necessary to make all beverage storage areas secure. To establish the proper degree of security, access to storage areas must be restricted to authorized individuals, and steps must be taken to guard against unauthorized use of beverages by those who are permitted access to the storage areas.

Alcoholic beverages are among the items in hotels and restaurants that are most prone to theft by those who are inclined to steal. Unless appropriate steps are taken, beverage products will disappear. There are many reasons for this, including the dollar value of the products, addiction to alcohol, and irresponsible, impulsive behaviour, among others.

Ensuring Accessibility

To ensure accessibility of products when needed, the storage facility must be organized so that each individual brand and product can be found quickly. In practice, this means assigning a specific storage location (shelf or bin number) to each item in the beverage inventory.

Maintaining Product Quality

To maintain product quality, each item in the beverage inventory must be stored appropriately, under conditions that will maximize its shelf life. This requires taking into account such important elements as temperature, humidity, and the manner in which items are stored.

Although the quality of spirits will not be adversely affected in storage under most conditions, wines and beers are subject to rapid deterioration if improperly stored.

Establishing Standard Procedures

Standard procedures must always be established to ensure that standards will be met. The standard procedures required to achieve control over the storing of beverages normally include those discussed in the following paragraphs.

LEARNING OBJECTIVE 14.5
Describe the standard procedures for achieving storing control over beverages.

Procedures to Make Beverage Areas Secure

Because beverage products are prone to theft, keeping them in a secure facility is an urgent requirement. There are two ways to maintain the necessary degree of security. The first is to assign responsibility for the security of the stored items to one person alone. This responsibility can mean literally keeping watch over these items. In many hotels and some large restaurants, an employee may be assigned to work in the storage facility, maintaining the stock and issuing beverages as needed. Typically, this employee is the only person permitted in the facility, except for authorized managers. In operations that are open for long hours, responsibility may be shared by two or more employees working different shifts. Alternatively, the hours for storing and issuing beverages may be restricted so that one person can be held accountable for the beverage inventory.

The second way to maintain security is to keep the beverage storage facility locked, and to issue a single key to one person, who will be held accountable for all beverages in the inventory. The person with the key is required to open the lock and issue the needed beverages. An alternative provision can be made for issuing the needed beverages in the absence of this one individual. For example, a procedure can be established by which a manager can gain access to the beverage storage facility.

The difficulty with both of these procedures is that the individual assigned responsibility for the beverage inventory is not likely to be available 24 hours a day. At some point, the storage facility will be inaccessible, and no one will be able to obtain items that may be urgently needed. One way to prepare for this eventuality is to place a second key in a safe or a similar secure location and require that anyone using it sign for it and write a short explanation of why it is needed. Some managers may require both an explanation and a list of the items removed from the facility. However, making a second key available reduces both the degree of security and the possibility of holding one individual accountable for all beverages in the inventory. In general, the common standard procedure is to keep the number of keys to the minimum that management deems appropriate for efficient operation and maximum security. If there is more than one key or if more than one person has access to the single key, it is normally advisable to change locks regularly to minimize the possibility that some persons may obtain and use duplicate keys. It is also advisable to change locks whenever a worker with access to the beverage storage facility leaves the employ of the establishment.

Some hotels and large restaurants take the additional precaution of installing closed-circuit television cameras to observe various facilities and their entrances, such as the doors to beverage storage areas. A security guard in a remote area is responsible for monitoring traffic into and out of the area on a television screen. As an alternative, activity in the area may be monitored by means of a video recording that can be viewed by the security staff at a later time. One company sells a device that looks like a surveillance camera, but does not record anything. In theory, the mere presence of this device will deter theft.

Another means of monitoring is to install special locks that print on paper tape the times at which the doors are unlocked and relocked. The times printed on the tape inform management exactly when the door to a facility was unlocked and how long it remained so. This is a less costly alternative to a closed-circuit television system, but it provides less information. Maintaining the security of the beverage inventory is a clear imperative for any hotel or restaurant, requiring constant vigilance and careful monitoring.

Procedures to Organize the Beverage Storage Facility

Ensuring accessibility means storing beverage products in an organized manner, so that each stored item is always kept in the same place, and thus can be found quickly when needed. The physical arrangement of a storage area is important. Similar items should be kept close to one another. All gins, for example, should be kept in one area, rye whiskies in another, and Scotch whiskies in a third. This kind of arrangement simplifies finding an item when needed. It is helpful, too, for a floor plan of the storage area to be affixed to the door of the facility so that authorized personnel can easily locate items. One way of ensuring that items will always be found in the same locations is to institute the use of bin cards of the type illustrated in Figure 14.3.

Bin cards can be affixed to shelves and serve as shelf labels. When properly used, bin cards include essential information (e.g., type of beverage, brand name, and bottle size). They may also include an identification number for beverages. Some establishments assign a code number from a master list to each item in the beverage inventory and record that code number on the bin card. A newer trend in the industry is to use electronic systems such as magnetic strips for tracking purposes. Figure 14.4 provides an example of the kind of numbering code often used for wines, spirits, and beers in a beverage

• FIGURE 14.3 •

Bin Card

ITEM	Grey Goose Vodka			STOCK NUMBER			354
Date	In	Out	Balance	Date	In	Out	Balance
1-Oct			4				
3-Oct		1	3				
7-Oct		1	2				
11-Oct		1	1				
12-Oct	4		5				

• FIGURE 14.4 •

Beverage Code Numbers: Quatre Bistro

Canadian Whisky:	100 series
Rye whisky	100–139
Imported Whiskies:	200 series
Scotch	200–239
Bourbon	240–249
Irish	250–259
Other	260–269
Gins and Vodkas:	300 series
Gins, domestic	300–329
Gins, imported	330–349
Vodka, domestic	350–379
Vodka, imported	380–399
Rums and Brandies:	400 series
Rum	400–419
Brandy, domestic	420–429
Brandy, imported	430–439
Cognac	440–449
Cordials and Liqueurs:	500 series
Red Wines:	600 series
White Wines (still):	700 series
Other Wines:	800 series
Sparkling, Rosé, Dessert, Aperitif	
Beers and Ales:	900 series

inventory. Figure 14.5 is an example of how a beverage storeroom is organized using that numbering code.

In many establishments, indelible ink is used to stamp this code number on each bottle received. The stamped number on a bottle identifies that bottle as the property of the hotel or restaurant. This makes it impossible for an

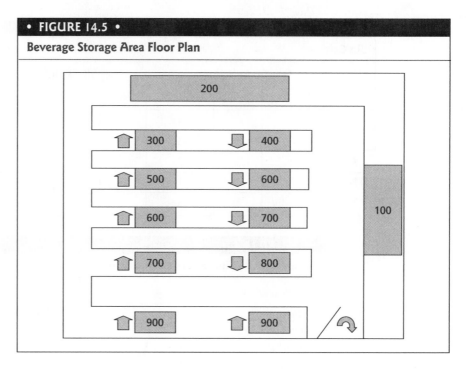

• FIGURE 14.5 •

Beverage Storage Area Floor Plan

employee to claim that such a bottle is personal property if one is found in his or her possession. In addition, empty bottles can be checked for numbers before they are replaced by full bottles, thus ensuring that no one is bringing empty bottles into the establishment and using them to obtain full bottles from the establishment's inventory.

The use of bin cards also enables a wine steward to maintain a perpetual inventory record of quantities on hand. By using this card to carefully record the number of units received as they are placed on the shelves, as well as the number of units issued as they are given out, the wine steward has a way of determining the balance on hand without counting bottles. In addition, the wine steward who carefully maintains such records has a way of determining that bottles are missing, so that this situation can be brought to management's attention immediately.

Internally, the storage area should be kept free of the debris that can pile up as the result of emptying cases and stocking shelves. Once opened, cases should be completely emptied. All units in a case should be stored on the appropriate shelf and the empty carton removed at once. In addition, care must be taken to ensure that some individuals do not purposely remove cartons that are not completely empty.

Procedures to Maximize Shelf Life of Stored Beverages

Procedures for maximizing the shelf life of stored beverages may be divided into two categories:

1. Those dealing with temperature, humidity, and light in the storage facilities
2. Those dealing with the manner in which bottles and other containers are handled and shelved

Temperature, Humidity, and Light in Storage Facilities. For every beverage product, there is a temperature range appropriate for storage that will tend to preserve quality and shelf life. For some, the range is extremely broad; for others, it is very limited. Spirits, for example, can be stored indefinitely at normal room temperatures without harming product quality. If necessary, they can be stored well above or well below room temperatures for considerable periods. As long as the storage temperature does not become extreme, they will not suffer loss of quality. In contrast, carefully controlled storage temperatures are critical for maintaining the quality of beers and wines. The problem of maintaining product quality for these items is complicated by the fact that various wines and beers require different treatments, depending on how they were made and the containers in which they are purchased.

It is normally advisable to learn from the maker, brewer, or distributor of each specific brand the temperature range recommended for the proper storage of the product. As a general rule, red wines should be stored at about 13°C. White wines and sparkling wines should be kept at slightly lower temperatures. Pasteurized beers can be stored for limited periods at normal room temperature without great harm, but they are normally kept under refrigeration, closer to the temperature at which they will be served. However, beer that has once been chilled should be kept chilled thereafter to maintain quality. Unpasteurized beers, including all draught and some bottled and canned beers, should be stored at about 4°C to reduce the risk of deterioration.

The degree of moisture in the air is of significance only for those beverages purchased in corked bottles. In general, wines are typically purchased in bottles with corks or screw tops, neither of which affect (or indicate) the quality of the wine. Low humidity will cause corks to dry out, thus permitting air to reach the product. Air is likely to harm product quality. Therefore, wines should be stored either in rooms that are naturally cool and damp or in special facilities, such as refrigerated rooms where both temperature and humidity can be controlled.

Bottled wines and beers should be kept away from light, which adversely affects product quality. Natural light is more harmful than artificial light, but any light will affect these products.

Vintners and brewers package their products in coloured glass bottles, commonly dark green or dark brown, to minimize the negative effects of light. However, although the dark glass reduces the impact, it merely slows the inevitable deterioration that light will cause if these products are not properly stored.

Shelving and Handling Bottles and Other Containers. Spirits can be stored upright on horizontal shelves for unlimited periods. In contrast, wines and other corked beverages cannot safely be stored in an upright position. If they are to be kept for any length of time, they must be stored on their sides, parallel to the floor. There are special racks designed to store wines in the proper position. In this horizontal position, the beverage in the bottle is kept in constant contact with the cork, helping to keep the end or "mirror" of the cork moist and thus keeping the bottle tightly sealed. Canned and bottled beers are usually not shelved at all. They are delivered in cases and are stored in those cases. The cases are typically stacked in the storage facility to save space.

Handling is an important factor in maintaining the quality of wines. They should be handled with great care as they are being positioned in wine racks and as they are being removed to fill customers' orders. Many wines, especially finer reds, develop a natural sediment that settles in the bottle. If the bottle is improperly handled, this sediment will be dispersed through the wine, destroying its clarity and making it unpalatable to those who appreciate and order fine wines. For all practical purposes, the wine becomes unusable until the sediment has resettled. Sparkling wines—those containing natural or artificial carbonation—must also be handled carefully for obvious reasons. Beers require careful handling as well. They are carbonated beverages, and shaking will cause them to foam excessively.

ISSUING

Establishing Standards

LEARNING OBJECTIVE 14.6
Identify the objectives of issuing control and explain the standards established for achieving issuing control.

Issuing control is established in hotel and restaurant beverage operations to achieve two important objectives:

1. To ensure the timely release of beverages from inventory in the needed quantities
2. To prevent the misuse of alcoholic beverages between release from inventory and delivery to the bar

It is important for managers to control the quantities of alcoholic beverages issued and to take all necessary steps to ensure that quantities issued reach their intended destinations.

To achieve these objectives, managers must establish two essential standards for issuing beverages:

1. Issue quantities must be carefully set.
2. Beverages must be issued only to authorized persons.

Authorized persons means those who have been assigned responsibility for the security of the issued beverages and will be held accountable for their disposition.

Establishing Standard Procedures

LEARNING OBJECTIVE 14.7
Describe the standard procedures for achieving issuing control over beverages.

To ensure that the essential issuing standards identified previously will be met, it is necessary to establish appropriate standard procedures for issuing beverages:

1. Establishing par stocks for bars
2. Setting up a requisition system

Establishing Par Stocks for Bars

As used in bar operations, the meaning of the term *par stock* is somewhat different from the definition used in wine cellar or liquor storeroom operations. In storeroom operations, par stock means the maximum quantity that may be on hand at any one time; it is a limit that the quantity on hand should never exceed. In bar operations, par stock is the precise quantity, stated in numbers of bottles or other containers, that must be on hand at all times for each beverage at the bar. For example, the stock of gin at a bar should be listed by brand name with bottle size and an exact number of bottles that should be at the bar at all times. One particular brand of gin, stocked in 750 ml bottles, may have a par stock of five bottles at a certain bar. This implies that someone can check the stock at any time and expect to find five bottles of that particular brand on hand. Not all would necessarily be full, but at least the number of bottles would be under control. An example of par stock at the Bistro Quatre is illustrated in Figure 14.6. This form can also be used as a requisition to replenish the stock at the bar to bring it back up to par.

• FIGURE 14.6 •

Par Sheet for Bar Operations: Bistro Quatre

Par	Item	Size	Price	On Hand	Needed		
	WHISKIES						
3*	Wiser's Deluxe	750 ml	$14.90				
1	Jim Beam Bourbon	1.75 L	$25.90				
1	Wild Turkey Bourbon	750 ml	$18.10				
2	Canadian Club	750 ml	$12.00				
1*	Seagram's V.O.	750 ml	$12.50				
1*	Jim Beam Rye	750 ml	$12.70				
1	Jack Daniel's Black Label	750 ml	$17.10				
1	Chivas Regal Scotch	750 ml	$25.80				
1	Cutty Sark Scotch	1.75 L	$36.50				
3*	Dewar's White Label Scotch	750 ml	$17.10				
1	J & B Scotch	1.75 L	$40.90				
1	Johnnie Walker Red Scotch	1.75 L	$40.90				
1	Jameson's Irish Whiskey	1.75 L	$39.90				
1	Glenfiddich Scotch	1.75 L	$18.90				

(*continued*)

● **FIGURE 14.6** ● *(continued)*							
Par	*Item*	*Size*	*Price*	*On Hand*	*Needed*		
	GINS						
2	Beefeater	1.75 L	$34.80				
2	Tanqueray	1.75 L	$39.40				
3*	Gilbey's London Dry	750 ml	$10.70				
1	Bombay Dry English	1.75 L	$34.50				
	VODKAS						
2	Absolut	1.75 L	$36.90				
2	Grey Goose	1.75 L	$32.90				
2	Smirnoff	1.75 L	$23.90				
3*	Polar Ice	750 ml	$ 8.90				
1	Skyy	1.75 L	$29.80				
	RUMS						
1	Bacardi Gold	1.75 L	$22.50				
2*	Captain Morgan	750 ml	$ 8.90				
	TEQUILA						
1	Cuervo Especial Gold	1.75 L	$34.90				
	BRANDIES						
2*	Courvoisier V.S. Cognac	1.75 L	$23.10				
1	Remy Martin VSOP	750 ml	$43.60				
	VERMOUTHS						
1	Martini & Rossi Ex. Dry	750 ml	$ 7.00				
1	Martini & Rossi Sweet	750 ml	$ 7.00				
	CORDIALS						
1	Amaretto di Saronno	750 ml	$19.00				
1	Bailey's Irish Cream	750 ml	$19.10				
1	Kahlua Coffee Liquor	750 ml	$17.80				
1	B & B	750 ml	$27.90				
1	Grand Marnier	750 ml	$15.50				
1	Drambuie	750 ml	$31.10				
1	Irish Mist	750 ml	$24.80				
1	Amarula Cream	750 ml	$ 7.70				
1	Antica Sambuca	750 ml	$ 8.90				
1	McGuinness Crème de Menthe	750 ml	$ 8.90				
1	Bols Blue Curacao	750 ml	$ 8.90				
1	Frangelico	750 ml	$ 9.50				
1	Bols White Crème de Cacao	750 ml	$ 9.50				
1	Meaghers Triple Sec	750 ml	$ 6.00				
1	Southern Comfort	750 ml	$12.10				

* Pouring brand

Essentially, there are three kinds of bars:

1. **Front bars**, where bartenders serve the public face-to-face
2. **Service bars**, where customers' orders are given to the bartender by the servers, who serve the drinks to the customers
3. **Special-purpose bars**, usually set up for particular events, such as a banquet

Par stocks vary greatly from one establishment to another. In every case, however, the par stock for any particular beverage should be related to quantities used and should be changed from time to time as customer demand changes. Drinks may go in and out of fashion for seasonal and other reasons, and par stocks at the bar should be adjusted to meet customer demand without being overstocked. In addition, because storage space at a bar is limited, the quantity of any item should be limited to the amount necessary to meet no more than two to three days' demand.

For front bars and service bars, specific par stocks should be established for each bar. However, this is not possible in the case of special-purpose bars, which present unique problems. When these bars are set up, sufficient stocks must be issued to meet anticipated demand for the length of time the bar is to be open. Typically, the quantities established are greater than needed, and the remainder is returned to the beverage storeroom at the conclusion of the event or merged with supplies at the front bar. In effect, a new par stock is established for a special-purpose bar each time one is needed for an event.

Setting Up a Requisition System

A **requisition system** is a highly structured method for controlling issues. In beverage control, a key element in the system is the **bar requisition form**, on which both the names of beverages and the quantities of each issued are recorded. No bottles should ever be issued without a written requisition signed by an authorized person, often the head bartender. A simple requisition form is illustrated in Figure 14.7. In most beverage operations, one type of requisition form is normally sufficient for maintaining the desired degree of control over issues. In more complex beverage operations, such as those found in many hotels, several kinds of requisitions may be required for specialized bars.

• **FIGURE 14.7** •				
Bar Requisition				
				Date _5-Oct_
Quantity	Description		Unit Cost	Total Cost
1	Smirnoff Vodka			
1	Dewar's White Label Scotch			
1	Gordon's Gin			
	Requisitioned by		_John_	
	Issued by			
	Received by			

The requisition form is filled out by either a head bartender or another authorized person who determines the quantities needed at the bar to replenish the par stock. For a special-purpose bar, the quantities are those established as the par stock for the specific occasion. The signed and dated requisition is given to a wine steward or beverage storeroom clerk—jobs and titles vary from one operation to another. This individual is responsible for obtaining the listed items and quantities from inventory shelves and issuing them to the person authorized to receive them—normally the person who has signed the requisition. In some establishments, the worker who receives the beverages is required to sign the requisition to acknowledge receipt of all listed items.

Later, after the beverages have been issued, the unit value of each beverage is entered on the requisition, and these individual values are extended. This means that each unit value is multiplied by the number of units issued to determine the total value of the quantity issued. A total value is obtained for all of the beverages listed on the requisition by adding the total values of the individual items.

Most establishments take the further precaution of requiring that each requisition from a front bar or a service bar be accompanied by empty bottles from that bar, to ensure that the units issued are actually replacing quantities the bartender has used. When this system is used, a par stock can be maintained at the bar. For example, suppose that the par stock of a particular brand of Scotch is five bottles. When one bottle is emptied, the bartender puts it aside. At the end of the night, the bartender lists it on a requisition form, along with all other bottles emptied in the course of the evening. This form is left for the morning bartender, who takes all empty bottles and the requisition on which they are listed to the wine steward. The wine steward checks each bottle against the requisition and then sends full bottles of those items—including that particular Scotch—to the bar before the beginning of business. This brings the stock of the bar—including the Scotch—back up to par. Such a system ensures a constant supply of beverages at the bar. Occasional comparisons of numbers of bottles at the bar with the par stock list can ensure that items are not missing from the bar. This affords an additional measure of control.

Establishments that operate more than one bar must prepare separate requisitions for each, so the various bars may be controlled separately. For example, special banquet requisitions are often used that make provision for all bottles issued, whether consumed or returned. An example is illustrated in Figure 14.8.

In hotels and catering establishments, requisitions of this type are often made by a banquet manager. They are given to a wine steward, who issues the items listed in time for the bar to be set up for an event. Provision is made for recording additional issues that may be required. At the end of the event, another individual (e.g., a beverage controller) checks that all full, empty, and partially used bottles are accounted for. Thus, the correct dollar amount can be recorded for the quantities actually consumed, and unused quantities can be returned to stock. Perpetual inventory and bin card entries can be made from the "Consumed" column on the banquet requisition.

• FIGURE 14.8 •

Banquet Bar Requisition

| FUNCTION | Lions Club | | BARTENDER | | Joe | | | |
| LOCATION | Green Room | | DATE | | 15-Oct | | | |

Item	Quantity	Original Issue	Additional Issue	Returns	Consumed	Unit Cost	Total Cost
J & B Scotch	2	2					
Beefeater Gin	2	2					
Smirnoff Vodka	2	2					
Crown Royal	1	1					
Canadian Club	1	1					
Sweet Vermouth	1	1					
Dry Vermouth	1	1					

Requisitioned By   Paul

Issued By   _____

Received By   _____

Returns Checked By   _____

Many of the beverage computer systems simplify control of special-purpose bars. For example, the AccuBar system allows for a separate inventory of special-purpose bars. At the conclusion of the event, usage from the special-purpose bar is calculated, and bar cost and sales are compared. The remaining inventory is calculated, and is either transferred to the inventory at the front bar or kept separate in the storeroom for use at a later date. All of this is done easily and automatically once the items are scanned before and after the event.

Automated Requisitions. Some beverage computer systems provide automated requisitions for bars in place of the manual requisition illustrated in Figure 14.7. For example, in the AccuBar system, bar inventory is taken daily using the hand scanner. Par stock for the bar inventory has already been established, and is programmed into the software. A report is automatically generated, showing the amount of each type of liquor used, the cost of liquor sold, the expected sales, and the amount of each liquor required to bring the bar back up to par. All of this is calculated by the software on the establishment's computer system. Some companies, such as Draught Prophets and Liquor Control Solutions, provide hardware and software that enable establishments to generate requisitions easily. These systems are described in the following chapter. Other systems, such as the one by Liquid Guardian described in Chapter 13, require the inventory amounts to be sent via the Internet to the restaurant's head office, which in turn supplies information.

In summary, liquor inventory management software can be purchased with a variety of features and purposes. In general, the goal of any program is to make the job easier for the manager; therefore, having a simple way to take a physical inventory is tantamount. Scales, Palm Pilots, and worksheets have all been used by various programs, but it is really about the level of comfort management has with a particular method that will determine which one is selected.

Other goals of using automated requisitions are tracking vendors, pricing inventory, product management, purchasing, and generating reports. Dealing with the large number of suppliers that is required to purchase intelligently and effectively has many challenges. A good inventory management program will alleviate that burden by tracking contact information, items purchased with the prices paid, and billing information. If that data is then coordinated with par stocks and desired frequency of ordering, the program can actually make recommendations for the amounts to purchase as well. Not only can these programs generate requisitions for restocking inventory, but they can also help with reports such as actual usage, cost of goods sold, and value of inventory on hand.

Additional Control Procedures

Many hotels and restaurants in which most wines are sold by the bottle, rather than by the glass, establish additional control procedures. In some, small supplies of the most popular wines are maintained at a front bar or service bar to eliminate the need for a trip to the wine cellar each time a bottle is ordered. Once the bottle of wine is taken from the bar and served to a customer in the dining room, it is effectively removed from the bartender's control. The bartender may not have an empty bottle to turn in with the requisition on the following day to bring the stock of the wine back to the par level. Therefore, many establishments maintain additional control over full-bottle sales by requiring that a **full-bottle sales slip** be filled out each time a bottle of wine is removed from the bar for service at a table. An example is illustrated in Figure 14.9.

Such a form is also useful in hotels that serve full bottles of wines and spirits to guests in their rooms, as well as in situations where par stocks of wines are not maintained at the bar, and each bottle must come directly from the wine cellar. The full-bottle sales slip serves as a requisition in such instances. When such a form is used, it is important to require that the server fill it out completely before

• **FIGURE 14.9** •				
Full-Bottle Sales Slip				
Date 5-Oct Table # 8		Cheque # 1230		
Code #	Description	Quantity	Size	Cost
602	Château LaGrim	1	Full	$95.00
Served by *Manny* Issued by *Joe*				

the bottle is issued, to guard against potential problems. When used correctly, the form provides an excellent means for verifying each sale of a full bottle. It is possible to compare full-bottle sales slips with the guest cheque numbers indicated and to hold the servers accountable for errors.

THINGS TO CONSIDER

Operators tend to forget the importance of maintaining proper beverage records. Government beverage inspectors may ask an establishment to produce various beverage invoices, so it is good practice to have secure, organized, and well-kept records. You may also be asked to produce these records in case you are audited by a government agency. In some provinces and territories, you may be required to keep records for six or seven years. Good records are also essential for management to control beverages, track costs, and change drink menu items—all ultimately to maximize profit. Your establishment's accountant will also need accurate beverage records for inventory valuation, bookkeeping, income tax, and financial statement purposes.

CHAPTER ESSENTIALS

In this chapter, we examined the application of the control process to the receiving, storing, and issuing phases of beverage operations. We identified management's objectives in establishing control over these three phases, and described the standards and standard procedures commonly employed to achieve the stated objectives. For receiving, deliveries received must conform to orders placed in three critical areas: quality, quantity, and price. Standard receiving procedures include maintaining records of orders placed, verifying that beverages received conform to those ordered, and making necessary entries on a beverage receiving report. For storing, the objectives are to prevent pilferage, to ensure product accessibility when needed, and to maintain product quality. Standard storing procedures include assigning responsibility to one person, keeping the storage facility locked when unattended, organizing the storage facility, and maintaining appropriate conditions for temperature, humidity, and light in the facility. For issuing, the objectives are to ensure the timely release of needed quantities and to prevent their misuse in the interval between their issue from inventory and their delivery to a bar. Standard issuing procedures include establishing par stocks for bars and setting up requisition systems to replenish the par stock.

KEY TERMS IN THIS CHAPTER

Bar requisition form, p. 379
Beverage receiving report, p. 368
Bin card, p. 372
Front bar, p. 379

Full-bottle sales slip, p. 382
Requisition system, p. 379
Service bar, p. 379
Special-purpose bar, p. 379

QUESTIONS AND PROBLEMS

1. What is the primary goal of receiving control in beverage operations?
2. List and explain the three standards for beverage receiving.
3. Identify the steps in the standard procedure for receiving beverages and explain the importance of each in achieving the primary goal of beverage receiving control.
4. List and explain the three objectives of storing control in beverage operations.
5. Discuss the importance of storeroom security, storeroom organization, and appropriate storage conditions in achieving the objectives of beverage storing control.
6. Describe two methods for maintaining security in the beverage storeroom.
7. Describe the procedures used to organize beverage storage facilities.
8. Describe the effects of temperature, humidity, light, handling techniques, and storing methods on the shelf life of beverages.
9. What are the purposes of bin cards in beverage storerooms?
10. Explain the reasons for using beverage code numbers.
11. Of what importance is each of the following in a beverage storage facility?
    a. Temperature
    b. Humidity
    c. Light
12. Why should corked wine bottles normally be stored on their sides?
13. What are the immediate effects of shaking a bottle of fine red wine? A container of beer? A bottle of spirits?
14. Identify the two objectives of issuing control in beverage operations.
15. What standards must be established for achieving the objectives of issuing control?

16. List and describe the three types of bars.
17. Define the term *par stock* as it is used in bar operations. How does this differ from the definition of par stock used in a beverage storeroom?
18. What is a requisition system?
19. Why are written requisitions considered necessary in beverage control?
20. How do computer programs make special-purpose bar control easier?
21. What is a full-bottle sales slip? Why are such forms used?
22. Define each of the key terms in this chapter.

EXCEL EXERCISES

Exercise 14.1

Complete the Beverage Receiving Report as shown on the companion website for this text. Show the amounts distributed to the purchase journal.

Exercise 14.2

Follow the instructions on the companion website for this exercise.

CHAPTER 15

Beverage Production Control

• **LEARNING OBJECTIVES** •

After reading this chapter, you should be able to:

15.1 Identify the two primary objectives of beverage production control.

15.2 Describe the standards and standard procedures necessary for establishing control over beverage production.

15.3 List four devices and means used to standardize quantities of alcoholic beverages used in beverage production.

15.4 Describe the use of standardized glassware in beverage control and the importance of stipulating specific glassware for each drink.

15.5 Explain the significance of standard drink recipes in beverage control.

15.6 Calculate the standard cost of any drink, given a standard recipe and the current market prices of ingredients.

15.7 Calculate the standard cost-to-sales ratio for any drink, given its standard cost and sales price.

15.8 Explain why bar operations should be monitored frequently and list four techniques for monitoring the performance of bartenders.

INTRODUCTION

Having established standards and standard procedures for purchasing, receiving, storing, and issuing beverages, the next logical step is to establish appropriate standards and standard procedures to control beverage production—the making of drinks. It should be apparent that failure to establish control in this area can lessen the overall impact of the standards and standard procedures carefully designed to establish control in other areas. Neglecting to establish control over drink production can lead to customer dissatisfaction resulting from improperly prepared drinks. It can also result in any number of unwarranted costs. Sales, profits, and the number of customers may all decrease if management fails to establish control over production. Additionally, beverage profit margin is extremely important to most restaurants and critical to establishments that serve primarily liquor. National averages for restaurants that serve liquor show that beverage sales amount to about 20 to 40 percent of their sales. The profit margin for liquor may be much higher than that for food, and in some establishments, liquor profit is the primary reason for making a satisfactory overall profit. After all, when one considers the relatively low cost percentage for liquor compared with food and the relatively minimal labour costs in preparing drinks compared with food, maintaining the profit margin for liquor may be critical to success. One must also take note of additional costs that may occur with the sale of liquor, such as entertainment, insurance, and increased security.

Since drinks are recognized in Canada as being prepared and sold in imperial units, the authors have used this system throughout the beverage chapters. Depending on the standards of the establishment where you work, you may use metric or imperial calculations. This means you may have to convert from one measurement system to another.

OBJECTIVES OF BEVERAGE PRODUCTION CONTROL

LEARNING OBJECTIVE 15.1
Identify the two primary objectives of beverage production control.

Control over beverage production is established to achieve two primary objectives:

1. To ensure that all drinks are prepared according to management's specifications
2. To guard against excessive costs that can develop in the production process

Specifications for drink production must take into account both the tastes of expected customers and management's desire to prepare drinks of appropriate quality and size. After all, customers who order drinks commonly have preconceived ideas of how the drinks will taste. A customer ordering a daiquiri, for example, may remember the enjoyable taste sensations provided in the past by the subtle blending of lime juice, sugar, and rum by skilful bartenders. A customer who is served a cocktail that does not meet expectations may be dissatisfied and complain, or simply not return. Therefore, any establishment selling drinks to the public must recognize and accept certain standards of customer expectation and drink preparation, and should establish procedures to ensure that these standards will be met. To achieve the two primary objectives, managers must establish appropriate standards.

ESTABLISHING STANDARDS AND STANDARD PROCEDURES FOR PRODUCTION

Standards must be established for the quantity and quality of ingredients used in drink preparation, as well as for the proportions of ingredients in a drink. In addition, drink sizes must be standardized. When standards are set for ingredients, proportions, and drink sizes, customers can have some reasonable assurance that a drink will meet expectations each time it is ordered. Once these standards have been established and procedures have been developed for training employees to follow them, they can be adhered to even during a high rate of employee turnover.

LEARNING OBJECTIVE 15.2
Describe the standards and standard procedures necessary for establishing control over beverage production.

By establishing and maintaining these standards, managers also establish a means for controlling costs. When drinks are prepared by formula and served in standard portion sizes, one portion of any drink prepared (e.g., a Caesar) should cost the same as every other portion of that same drink. In addition, because the sales prices for drinks are fixed, the cost-to-sales ratio for one portion of any drink should be the same as the cost-to-sales ratio for every other portion of that drink. If this is true, the cost-to-sales ratio for the overall operation should be reasonably stable, provided that sales remain relatively constant.

Simply stated, once standards and standard procedures for beverage production have been established, it becomes possible to develop a standard cost percent for operation with which the actual cost percent can be compared. This subject is discussed in greater detail in the next chapter.

Establishing Quantity Standards and Standard Procedures

As suggested earlier, one of the first steps in establishing control over beverage production is to standardize the quantities of the most costly ingredients used: the alcoholic beverages. The quantities used by the bartender must be controlled. To do so, one must determine in advance the specific quantities to be used for the production of drinks and then provide the bartender with a means of measuring those quantities.

Most drinks prepared with spirits are a combination of one kind of liquor and a mixer. Scotch and soda, gin and tonic, rye and ginger ale, and rum and cola are all examples of this type of drink. A manager must determine in advance the specific quantity of the expensive ingredient—the liquor—that a bartender should use to prepare any drink. The amount varies from bar to bar, but most have identified quantities that fall between two extremes—as little as ¾ of an ounce in some bars to as much as 2 ½ ounces in others, although the authors' experiences suggest that most bars serve 1 ¼ to 1 ½ ounces in their drinks. This quantity standard is established in advance by the manager and is the fixed quantity that will be given to a customer in return for the fixed sales price of a drink.

This is not to say that each type of drink should contain the same amount of liquor as every other drink. Clearly, this should not be the case. For example, management may specify that 1 ½ ounces is the standard measurement for mixed drinks, but cocktails such as martinis follow a recipe that calls for 2 ounces of gin or vodka. Once the quantity standard is established, managers must provide bartenders with a means for measuring this quantity each time a drink is prepared. One must keep in mind that wines, spirits, and some mixers are purchased in metric units, but bartenders preparing drinks measure the ingredients in ounces.

Devices for Measuring Standard Quantities

LEARNING OBJECTIVE 15.3
List four devices and means used to standardize quantities of alcoholic beverages used in beverage production.

There are four measuring devices commonly used by bartenders: shot glasses, jiggers, pourers, and automated dispensers.

The Shot Glass. In some establishments, bartenders are provided with small glasses, called **shot glasses**, that are used for measuring. There are two kinds of shot glasses: plain and lined.

A **plain shot glass** holds a predetermined quantity when filled to the rim. Plain shot glasses are available in a number of sizes, from fractions of an ounce to several ounces. In any given bar, all such glasses should be the same size. In many of the establishments that use shot glasses, bartenders are told to fill the shot glass and pour the exact measure into the drink. In others, bartenders are provided with shot glasses that hold slightly less than management is willing to give (3/4 ounce, for example, if 1 ounce is the standard measure). Bartenders are instructed to fill the shot glass, pour it into the drink, and then, in full view of the customer, pour an additional small amount directly from the bottle into the glass. Some believe there is positive psychological impact to this practice: customers think they are getting more than they are entitled to.

A **lined shot glass** is similar to a plain one, but a line is etched around the glass below and parallel to the rim. In some bars, the standard of fill is to the line, which is in full view of both the customer and the bartender. Some bars use shot glasses with deceptive lines, so that when the bartender fills to the line on the inside of the glass, it appears to the customer to go above the line on the outside. This is an optical illusion, but it can give the customer a sense of getting something for nothing. Another variation on the lined-glass approach is to use glasses that hold the standard measure when filled to the rim, but have lines etched in the glass at some level below the rim. These are used for the same psychological reasons.

The Jigger. A **jigger** is a double-ended stainless steel measuring device, each end of which resembles a shot glass. The two measuring devices that make up the jigger are of different sizes—one may hold 1 ounce and the other 1 ½ ounces. Many believe the jigger is necessary for the accurate measuring that ensures perfect cocktails. It can be used for measuring straight shots as well, but is more useful for preparing cocktails that call for varying quantities of ingredients. For measuring the ingredients required for these complex drinks, shot glasses are inappropriate. Some cocktails call for such varied measures as 1 ounce of one ingredient and 1 ½ ounces of a second. To measure exact quantities of each ingredient, it is necessary to use the jigger. Bistro Quatre uses a jigger for preparing all cocktails. It has 1 ½ ounces on one side and 1 ounce on the other.

The Pourer. A **pourer** is a device, fitted on top of a bottle, that measures the quantity poured from the bottle, limiting that quantity to a predetermined amount. This is another way to control the quantity of liquor used in preparing drinks. Several different types of pourers are available, but all operate on the principle of controlling the quantity poured each time a bottle is used. In an establishment where 1 ounce is the standard measure, all bottles can be fitted with devices that dispense just 1 ounce. Each time the bartender tips the bottle to pour, exactly 1 ounce is dispensed. The psychological effect, if any, of these pouring devices is widely disputed. Some think that the customer is given the illusion of the bartender pouring freely; others argue that customers may feel a certain resentment toward an establishment that neither trusts the bartender nor permits an extra drop to be dispensed to a customer. Still others believe that pourers are useful at service bars, which customers never see, but should not be used at front bars, where customers watch bartenders mixing drinks. Most bartenders do not like these devices, because it takes slightly more time to pour a shot than other means. There are many pourers and other devices associated with computer software, some of which are attached to liquor bottles. The following section discusses several of them.

Automatic Pouring Systems. All automatic pouring systems are designed to regulate the amount of liquor transferred from the bottle to the glassware. How that is achieved is probably the biggest difference between each system. The most common method has a special pourer that fits on each bottle; this is then used in conjunction with a ring or collar that slides over the pourer and activates it. Most of these rings or collars are attached to the cash register or to a piece of hardware that is designed to take the place of the cash register.

The wireless free pour is another system that is commonly in use in food-service operations dispensing liquor. This system has a radio transmitter, which transfers the data from the bottle to the software program and stores the information there in order to generate reports when the manager dictates. The benefit of this type of program is that there are no wires to interfere with the bartender's activities, and the data is stored and available to the manager to assist in important decisions. The downside to this system is that it does not control the portions; therefore, this system is intended for use in an operation that is confident that the bartenders are following standard recipes and are skilled enough to do so without the use of measuring devices.

Alcohol Controls sells a product called the Liquor Clicker. It is a liquor pour spout that fits on each bottle at the bar. It portions every shot to the amount determined by management and tracks the number of shots dispensed on an odometer-style counter. The software used with these pourers allows management to print a report that shows the number of shots poured from each bottle, the potential revenue, and the actual revenue.

Alcohol Controls also has a liquor control system called the Spirit. Bottles are capped with a brand ID control pour that will portion every shot of liquor or glass of wine dispensed. Liquor cannot be poured until the bartender inserts the control spout into the dispensing station's activator ring where the bartender mixes drinks. It is tied into a point-of-sale (POS) system that records the sale. Three different sales price levels can be programmed into the system, one for regular prices, one for happy hour, and another for special prices.

Liquor Control Solutions uses its AZ 200 controller with preprogrammed spouted bottles. The bottle needed for a particular drink is secured to an activator ring when a drink is prepared. The system identifies the brand, pours the exact quantity specified, and rings up the sale. If a wrong bottle is selected for a preprogrammed drink, the spout will not operate.

For draught beer, Liquor Control Solutions sells its Electronic Beer Head. It features both an automatic mode and a manual mode. A flow meter keeps track of the amount of beer poured. The automatic mode pours the exact quantity from one of four preprogrammed portion sizes. This feature works in conjunction with its AZ 200 controller.

The Automated Dispenser. Many companies have developed and successfully marketed various automated devices for dispensing predetermined measures of liquor. These range from comparatively simple systems for controlling only the pouring brands to elaborate electronic control systems that not only control ounces but also mix drinks at the push of a button. These systems, costing many thousands of dollars, are usually linked to cash registers in such a way that each sale is recorded on a guest cheque as the drink is prepared. In addition, meters record the quantities used, and this makes accurate inventory control possible. Many believe that these systems are best used in settings where bartenders have little or no direct supervision. Others think that such systems should be used in service bars but never at front bars, except in cases where repeat customers are rare, as in an airport bar.

Liquor Control Solutions has a system it calls the Cocktail Tower. It uses the AZ 200 controller, which is programmed with recipes of various drinks. Bartenders simply place a glass under the tower and press a labelled key for the desired drink. The system automatically makes and pours the drink into the glass. It is combined with a POS terminal that keeps track of all drink sales. At the end of the day, the system provides various reports, including inventory balances, sales, and cost of sales.

Free Pour. Another means of measuring quantity is to allow bartenders to **free pour**. This is a method by which bartenders pour without using any device to measure quantity other than their own judgement or eyesight. In some cases, bartenders are taught to count silently to measure the duration of the act of pouring, which is clearly related to the quantity dispensed. More often than not, however, managers are relying on the experienced bartender to use that expertise to gauge the quantities poured.

Although many experienced bartenders can free pour with considerable accuracy, the procedure clearly reduces a manager's control over bar operations. In the authors' view, free pouring negates any semblance of control in bar operations except where all bartenders are skilled at this method of pouring and are completely honest and dedicated. In addition, in bars that suffer from high rates of employee turnover, managers may find that they have no control at all over bar operations. Free pouring enables dishonest bartenders to operate more for their own advantage than for the general good of the business. However, many owners who permit free pouring seek to offset its costs by raising sales prices to ensure the desired level of profit. Free pouring is commonly used when bartenders are showing off their "flair." (Flair bartending includes flipping bottles, lighting drinks, and cascading drinks.)

Glassware

In addition to controlling the quantity of liquor used in preparing each drink, it is desirable to control the overall size of the drinks. Standardizing the glassware used for service makes this comparatively simple. It is the manager's responsibility to establish the standard portion size for each type of drink and to provide bartenders with appropriate glassware.

Beverage glassware is available in a wide variety of shapes and sizes. Therefore, it is very easy to furnish the bar with specified glassware for particular drinks. In The Spanish Moon Bistro, for example, stemmed cocktail glasses holding 4 ounces have been identified as the standard glassware for all cocktails. Because bartenders cannot fill glasses above the rim, it is impossible for them to serve a portion size greater than 4 ounces unless they use the wrong glassware or pour an extra measure, known as a dividend. By furnishing the bar with 4-ounce cocktail glassware, directing that all cocktails be served in these glasses, and declaring that no dividends may be given to customers, managers can effectively control portion sizes.

LEARNING OBJECTIVE 15.4
Describe the use of standardized glassware in beverage control and the importance of stipulating specific glassware for each drink.

Many fine hotels and restaurants, including Bistro Quatre, consider the 4-ounce cocktail glass too small. In these establishments, management is willing to give more generous portions in return for the higher sales prices charged. Thus, bartenders are instructed to use lined cocktail glasses holding 5 ounces, with lines etched around the glass, indicating a 4 ½ ounce measure.

To establish effective portion control, then, it is important to purchase glassware in appropriate sizes. Managers must determine the kinds of glassware that will be needed, based on present or anticipated customers and their preferences, and then determine portion sizes. The glassware purchased should be matched to the portion sizes established by the manager, and bartenders must be instructed on which glasses to use for serving specific drinks.

Although neighbourhood bars may be able to get by with just four or five types and a few sizes of glasses, fine restaurants and hotels cannot do so. Beverage service in these establishments may require as many as 10 to 15 different types and sizes of glassware. Fine hotels and restaurants often require an array of glassware similar to that listed in Figure 15.1. Samples of common glasses are pictured in Figure 15.2.

Thus, managers standardize portion sizes by purchasing specific glassware to be used for the service of specific types of drinks and then training bar personnel to serve drinks in the proper glasses. Although standardization of

• FIGURE 15.1 •		
Examples of Standard Glassware in a Fine Hotel		
Item	*Size*	*Par Stock at Bar*
Shot glass	1¼ oz.	72
Cordial	1¼ oz.	36
Cocktail	4½ oz.	72
Cocktail	6 oz.	72
Champagne	9 oz.	72
Sour	4½ oz.	72
Rocks	8¼ oz.	144
Brandy	8 oz.	36
Wine	7¾ oz.	72
Wine	9 oz.	72
Highball	8 oz.	48
Highball	10 oz.	144
Pilsner	8 oz.	72

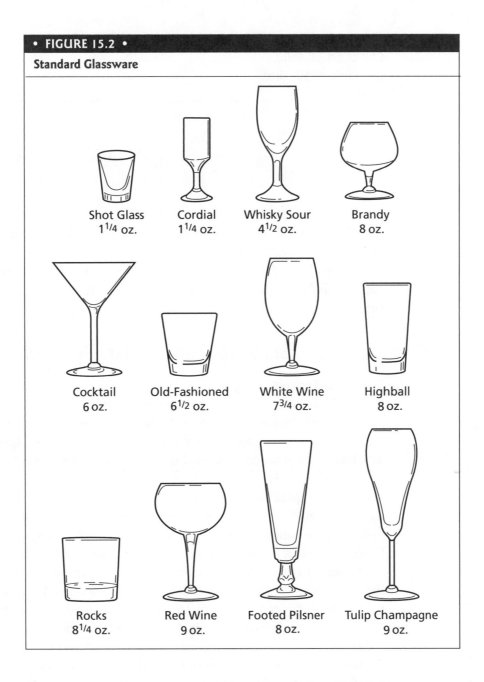

• FIGURE 15.2 •

Standard Glassware

Shot Glass
1¹/₄ oz.

Cordial
1¹/₄ oz.

Whisky Sour
4¹/₂ oz.

Brandy
8 oz.

Cocktail
6 oz.

Old-Fashioned
6¹/₂ oz.

White Wine
7³/₄ oz.

Highball
8 oz.

Rocks
8¹/₄ oz.

Red Wine
9 oz.

Footed Pilsner
8 oz.

Tulip Champagne
9 oz.

portion sizes helps control beverage costs, that alone is insufficient. It is useful to stipulate that gin and tonic be served over ice in an 8-ounce glass, yet this alone does not tell bar personnel what part of the standard portion should be gin and what part mixer. This consideration is particularly important in cost control because, after all, the cost of gin is greater per ounce than the cost of tonic water, and the relative amount of each used in making the drink will affect the cost and the taste. The following two examples clearly show the difference in the cost of ingredients affected by changing proportions:

Gin and Tonic

Cost of gin: $0.45/oz.

Cost of mixer: $0.04/oz.

Gin and Tonic A		Gin and Tonic B	
Gin—2 oz.	= $0.90	Gin—1 oz.	= $0.45
Mixer—6 oz.	= 0.24	Mixer—7 oz.	= 0.28
Total	$1.14	Total	$0.73

In both cases, the result is 8 ounces of gin and tonic. However, because the proportion has been changed, the cost of Gin and Tonic B is far less than that of Gin and Tonic A. If this particular drink were to be offered at a standard sales price of $4.00, there would be a considerable difference between the cost-to-sales ratios as well: 28.5 percent for Drink A versus 18.25 percent for Drink B.

Establishing Quality Standards and Standard Procedures

Standard Recipes

LEARNING OBJECTIVE 15.5
Explain the significance of standard drink recipes in beverage control.

It should be clear that to control costs, one must establish control over the ingredients that go into each drink, as well as over the proportions of the ingredients to one another. In other words, **standard drink recipes** must be established so that bar personnel will know the exact quantity of each ingredient to use in order to produce any given drink.

Generally speaking, bartenders prepare and serve two kinds of drinks that require liquor: straight shots with mixers, such as the gin and tonic identified earlier, and **mixed drinks** and **cocktails**, many of which involve several ingredients that must be combined in a specific way for the drink to be right.

For straight shots with mixers, the standard drink is controlled by providing the bartender with appropriate glassware of predetermined size, as well as a jigger or other device for measuring the liquor. The standard quantity of liquor for the drink is measured and poured over ice in the proper glass, and the glass is then filled with the mixer. In effect, this constitutes the standard recipe. Each time a customer orders a Scotch and soda, the bartender places a certain number of ice cubes in a glass of the proper size, adds one standard measure of the pouring brand of Scotch, and fills the glass nearly to the rim with soda. Every Scotch and soda prepared this way will be the same as every other. The customer's second drink will be the same as the first, and, if he or she returns to the bar in two weeks and orders a Scotch and soda, that customer will be served the same drink for the same price, barring changes in management policy. Preparing drinks that are consistently the same is a major factor in establishing customer satisfaction and developing repeat business.

With mixed drinks and cocktails, establishing control over ingredients, proportions, and cost while providing drinks that are consistently the same is somewhat more complex. There are normally two or more recipes for making any given cocktail, and the resulting cocktails are often quite different from one another. For example, the two recipes that follow for a cocktail known as a Manhattan have been taken from two different drink mixing guides.

Manhattan 1

2 ½ oz. blended rye whisky
¾ oz. sweet vermouth
Dash of bitters

Manhattan 2

1 ½ oz. blended rye whisky
¾ oz. sweet vermouth
Dash of bitters

Although mixing the listed ingredients in the prescribed manner will produce a Manhattan cocktail in either case, there are substantial differences between the two. In cocktail 1, the ratio of whisky to vermouth is more than 3 to 1; in cocktail 2, it is 2 to 1. In addition, recipe 1 produces a drink that is 1 ounce larger than that produced by recipe 2. Finally, recipe 1 costs more to make because it contains 1 additional ounce of blended rye whisky.

It is apparent that management must identify which of several recipes will be the standard recipe used to prepare the Manhattan. Similar decisions must be made for all cocktails. Although the most common solution is to adopt one of the standard bartender's recipe guides for use at the bar, it is by no means uncommon, particularly in chain operations, to find a book of standard recipes specifically prepared for companywide use. In every case, the standard recipe includes not only the measures of alcoholic beverages to be used in preparation, but also the quantities of all other ingredients, including garnishes, as well as mixing and serving instructions. In some cases, pictures of the drinks are provided to ensure uniformity, particularly in the face of high rates of employee turnover. Figure 15.3 gives examples of typical standard recipes for two common cocktails: the Manhattan and the Brandy Alexander.

Adopting a book of standard recipes also makes it possible for a bartender to prepare various unusual cocktails that are requested only on rare occasions. Although professional bartenders are able to mix virtually any drink requested, many have few occasions to mix cocktails as unusual as a Taco Fizz, an Opal, or an Earthquake. Thus, a standard recipe guide can help ensure the satisfaction of the customer requesting the unusual drink. Although standard bar recipes are a necessity for control purposes, many bartenders and some managers dislike them. In some establishments, therefore, any discussion of standard recipes is likely to result in heated debate.

It is theoretically possible to establish a standard recipe for every drink served by any bar, indicating the size of the drink and the specific quantity of each ingredient the drink should contain. As a practical matter, it is not possible to enforce the use of standard recipes in all instances at all bars. One illustration of the problem should suffice.

> **• FIGURE 15.3 •**
> **Standard Drink Recipes**
>
> **MANHATTAN**   S.P. _____
> 2½ ounces blended rye whisky
> ¾ ounce sweet vermouth
> dash of bitters
> 4 ice cubes
> stem cherry
>
> Combine the whisky, vermouth, and ice in a mixing glass and stir well. Strain into a 4-ounce stem glass. Garnish with a cherry.
>
> **BRANDY ALEXANDER**   S.P. _____
> ¾ ounce brandy
> ¾ ounce Crème de Cacao
> ¾ ounce heavy cream
> 3 ice cubes
>
> Combine all ingredients in a cocktail shaker and shake vigorously. Strain into a 4-ounce cocktail glass.

Most people are familiar with the martini, a cocktail made with gin and dry vermouth, stirred with ice, strained into a cocktail glass, and served garnished with an olive. For some, the best mixture for a 3-ounce martini is 2 ounces of gin to 1 ounce of vermouth; for others, it is 3 ounces of gin to one drop of vermouth. And there are an infinite number of variations. Because much of a bar's success depends on satisfying customer tastes, it is very difficult—many would say impossible—for a bar manager to establish an inflexible standard recipe for a martini. A single standard recipe may satisfy some customers but displease others. Many bar managers think that bartenders must be permitted a certain amount of freedom to alter standard recipes to suit the tastes and requests of customers. Some believe that the standard recipe should be a kind of average of all the martinis mixed in a particular bar over a period of time.

With standards and standard procedures established in the form of standard recipes and standard portion sizes, it is possible to calculate the standard cost of any drink.

LEARNING OBJECTIVE 15.6
Calculate the standard cost of any drink, given a standard recipe and the current market prices of ingredients.

LEARNING OBJECTIVE 15.7
Calculate the standard cost-to-sales ratio for any drink, given its standard cost and sales price.

Establishing Standard Portion Costs

Straight Drinks

Calculating the standard cost of a drink is generally much easier than calculating the standard cost for a portion of food. In determining the standard cost for food, sometimes a butcher's test or cooking loss test must first be performed for the main dish. Then the cost of all items that accompany the main dish must be determined and added to the cost of the dish. Calculating the cost of a straight drink simply entails calculating the cost of one ingredient—the liquor used—and then adding the cost of the mixer or other ingredient when necessary.

The cost of straight drinks, served with or without mixers, can be calculated by first dividing the standard portion size in ounces into the number of ounces in the bottle to find the number of standard drinks contained in each bottle. This number is then divided into the cost of the bottle to find the standard cost of the drink. Since we use the metric system in Canada it may be necessary to convert the metric contents of bottles into their ounce equivalents, as most all establishments use the imperial ounce method when preparing drinks.

Please note that although Canada uses the metric system, we commonly cost, prepare, and list drinks by the ounce. We will use the following conversion factor in this textbook (28.41 ml = 1 fluid ounce) and for bottle size we can translate 750 ml to 26.3[1] ounces (rounded to one decimal; amounts in the following calculations are expressed as decimals for ease of calculation). Therefore, it can be assumed that in a 750 ml bottle there would be 26.3 ounces or 26 1-ounce drinks. This is where the term a "twenty sixer" comes from.

For example, the standard portion size for the pouring brand of Scotch in the Bistro Quatre is 1.5 ounces. The bar uses 750 ml bottles of Scotch. A 750 ml bottle contains 26.3 ounces. Dividing the 1.5-ounce standard drink into the 26.3 ounces in the 750 ml bottle, one determines that each bottle contains 17.5 drinks, rounded to the nearest tenth.

$$\frac{26.3 \text{ oz.}}{1.5 \text{ oz.}} = 17.5 \text{ drinks}$$

Because there is a small amount of spillage and evaporation in all bar operations, this can be safely adjusted to an average of 17.2 drinks per bottle. If the purchase price of the bottle is $17.10, then the standard cost of each of the 17.2 drinks it contains can be determined by dividing the bottle cost, $17.10, by the number of drinks it contains, 17.2.

$$\frac{\$17.10}{17.2 \text{ drinks}} = \$0.994 \text{ or } \$.99, \text{ rounded to the nearest cent}$$

Bistro Quatre offers several call brands of Scotch as well, and the same technique is used to determine the standard cost of one standard drink of each call brand. For a premium Scotch costing $25.80 per 750 ml bottle, the standard cost of each drink is somewhat higher:

$$\frac{\$25.80}{17.2 \text{ drinks}} = \$1.50$$

---

[1]The exact amount should be 26.4 ounces, but we have allowed for 0.1 oz being lost/unsalvageable, which is usually the case when pouring from a bottle.

An alternative procedure for finding the standard cost per drink requires that one divide the cost of the bottle by the number of ounces it contains to find the cost per ounce, and then multiply the ounce cost by the standard drink size. For example, if the pouring brand of gin costs $10.70 per 750 ml bottle, the equivalent of 26.3 ounces, each ounce would cost $0.41, not taking into consideration any loss because of spillage or evaporation.

$$\frac{\$10.70}{26.3 \text{ oz.}} = \$0.41$$

This ounce cost, multiplied by the standard 1.5-ounce drink size for gin in Bistro Quatre (see Figure 15.4), yields a standard cost for the standard measure of $0.62, as indicated in the following equation:

1.5-ounce standard size × $0.41 per ounce = $0.62 per drink

• FIGURE 15.4 •

Example of Standard Costs for Straight Drinks

Bottle Code	Item	Bottle Size		Bottle Cost	Ounce Cost	Drink Size (oz.)	Drink Cost
		Metric	Imperial				
206	Dewar's White Label	750 ml	26.3 oz.	$17.10	$0.65	1.5	$0.98
332	Beefeater Gin	1.75 L	61.6 oz.	$34.80	$0.56	1.5	$0.84
354	Smirnoff Vodka	750 ml	26.3 oz.	$8.90	$0.34	1.5	$0.51
302	Gordon's Gin	750 ml	26.3 oz.	$10.70	$0.41	1.5	$0.62

Some who use this method prefer to subtract 1 ounce from the true number of ounces contained in a bottle to allow for evaporation and spillage, also referred to as the angel's share. Using this approach, one would treat a 750 ml bottle as 25.3 ounces, and a 1-litre bottle as 34.1 ounces.

The selection of one method over another depends on the preferences of those performing the calculations. Once these calculations have been completed, a common practice is to record the results on a form similar to that illustrated in Figure 15.4. These are updated regularly, whenever dealer prices change. In this way, up-to-date cost figures are readily available for managers to use in several ways. One use is to calculate the cost of mixed drinks and cocktails.

Mixed Drinks and Cocktails

It is particularly important to determine the standard costs of cocktails and other mixed drinks. These drinks, typically prepared from standard recipes, normally have several ingredients and may require two or more alcoholic beverages. Consequently, mixed drinks are usually more expensive to make than straight drinks. Knowledge of the cost per drink is important for making intelligent pricing decisions.

To simplify the task of determining standard costs of cocktails and other mixed drinks and maintaining records of the calculations, many bar managers obtain supplies of recipe details and cost forms similar to those illustrated in Figure 15.5 and Figure 15.6. Both forms are in common use, and both can be made up by a printer or by staff with access to computers and photocopiers.

• FIGURE 15.5 •

One Type of Standard Recipe Detail and Cost Card

Item	Gin Martini				Bar Recipe #		53
Drink sales price	$4.50						
Drink cost	$1.00						
Cost percent	22.22%						

Ingredients			Quantity		Cost	
Gordon's Gin			2 oz.		$0.82	
Martini & Rossi Dry Vermouth			½ oz.		$0.14	
Cocktail olive			1 ea.		$0.04	
Totals			2½ oz.		$1.00	
Glassware		4 oz. cocktail				
Procedure		Pour gin and vermouth into glass shaker. Add cracked ice.				
		Stir gently. Strain into cocktail glass. Add olive and serve.				

• FIGURE 15.6 •

Another Type of Recipe Detail and Cost Card

Item	Maurice Cocktail			Bar Recipe #		77
Date	11-Sep					

Drink sales price		$ 4.50		Drink Data			Cost
Drink cost		$ 0.81		¼ orange			$0.08
Cost percent		18%		½ oz. sweet vermouth			$0.14
				½ oz. dry vermouth			$0.14
Bottle Data				1 oz. gin			$0.41
Ingredient		Gordon's Gin		Dash of bitters			$0.04
Bottle size		750 ml					
Bottle cost		$10.70		Total Cost			$0.81
Glassware		4 oz. cocktail					
Procedure		Combine all ingredients in glass shaker. Add cracked ice.					
		Stir. Strain into cocktail glass.					

The first step in determining the standard cost of a drink is to record on the form all of the information from the standard recipe for the drink. It is essential to take into account all ingredients used by the bartender in preparing the drink. The cost of a drink should include the cost of any nonalcoholic ingredients used in its preparation—fruit juices, eggs, and heavy cream are but a few of the possibilities. In addition, any garnish for a drink must be included. Garnishes can include olives, stem cherries, cocktail onions, and slices of various fruits. To arrive at the true cost of a drink, the cost of all other ingredients must be added to the cost of the basic alcoholic ingredients.

Both of the forms illustrated include the standard preparation procedure and the standard glassware. With this information recorded, management has a complete set of standard bar recipes for ready reference. Depending on the type and size of paper used, these can either be kept in a loose-leaf notebook or in a card file. For ease of use, one may be better advised to rely on a computer.

After the standard recipe has been recorded on the recipe detail and cost card, the next step is to determine the cost of each ingredient, whether alcoholic or nonalcoholic. Determining the cost of alcoholic ingredients is easier if someone has previously completed a form such as that illustrated in Figure 15.7, which indicates the standard costs of straight drinks. If this information is not available, additional calculations are required. To do these calculations, one must have access to bottle costs and bottle sizes. In many hotels and large restaurants, someone in an accounting office may have perpetual inventory records that include bottle sizes and costs. Alternatively, the individual responsible for beverage purchasing may keep the information in an up-to-date price book.

In smaller bars and restaurants, managers may find it necessary to obtain the information from invoices, receiving sheets, or inventory books. For nonalcoholic ingredients, such as the food items transferred from the kitchen, it may be necessary to refer to transfer memos. Alternatively, one may ask the steward

• FIGURE 15.7 •

List of Standard Costs and Sales Prices for Straight Drinks

Straight Drinks: Scotch

Bottle Code	Item	Bottle Size Metric	Imperial	Bottle Cost	Ounce Cost	Drink Size (oz.)	Drink Cost	Drink S.P.
200	Glenfiddich	750 ml	26.3 oz.	$17.10	$0.65	1.5	$0.98	$4.50
201	Chivas Regal	750 ml	26.3 oz.	$25.80	$0.98	1.5	$1.47	$5.50
203	Cutty Sark	1.75 L	61.6 oz.	$36.50	$0.59	1.5	$0.89	$4.50
206	Dewar's	750 ml	26.3 oz.	$17.10	$0.65	1.5	$0.98	$4.50
207	J&B	1.75 L	61.6 oz.	$40.90	$0.66	1.5	$1.00	$4.50
210	Johnnie Walker	1.75 L	61.6 oz.	$40.90	$0.66	1.5	$1.00	$4.50

for the most recent purchase prices. Exact procedures vary considerably from one place to another. In general, the exact procedure followed is of no particular significance, as long as it results in the correct cost figures for each item in the recipe.

For each of the two forms illustrated, the techniques for recording the data differ slightly. For the form shown in Figure 15.5, one must determine the cost of the specific quantity used before making any entry on the form. In the example given, the cost of the 2 ounces of gin is recorded as $0.84. This is determined by referring to the chart in Figure 15.4, which shows that 1 ounce of the pouring brand costs $0.41 (the figure shown is rounded; the actual cost to four decimal places is $0..4068). This, multiplied by the 2 ounces in the recipe, gives the cost of the gin in the drink.

If a form similar to that shown in Figure 15.6 is used, the first step is to record the size and cost of a bottle of the pouring brand. In the example shown, the 750 ml bottle of gin is recorded as costing $10.70. The next step is to divide the number of ounces into the cost of the bottle and to multiply the result by the number of ounces of gin in the recipe. This is essentially the calculation required for developing the data included in Figure 15.7.

Once the costs of all ingredients in a drink have been determined, the figures are totalled. The result is the standard cost for a drink prepared according to the standard recipe. This cost is recorded on the line provided and divided by the sales price to determine the cost-to-sales ratio for the drink. This is recorded as the cost percent for the drink. If sales prices have not yet been determined, the cost per drink should certainly be one of the chief considerations used to set reasonable sales prices. Even if sales prices have been set before costs are calculated, all of these prices should be reviewed in light of the newly developed costs.

Computers can be used in beverage production control to maintain standard drink recipe files and to determine standard costs for drinks. If maintaining standard recipe files were the only objective, one could do so with any simple word-processing program. One approach would be to treat each standard drink as a document, give it a file name, and save it in a specified location. The individual files could be loaded, edited if necessary, and then filed or printed, depending on need. Alternatively, all standard recipes could be filed as one document, which would make it easier to print them for use in training.

A more practical approach is to maintain the standard recipes with one of the two more flexible programs: spreadsheet or database. Both permit the user to print the recipes for training and offer such other useful possibilities as determining standard costs of drinks and updating standard costs when ingredient costs change. With both the spreadsheet and database programs, information can be filed and printed selectively. For example, managers would certainly want bartenders to have the recipes, but would probably not want to give them cost data. Using the "report" function common to spreadsheet programs, the computer can be directed to print that section of the spreadsheet containing the recipe, but not the section containing the cost information. Using a database program can permit an even greater degree of flexibility.

Today, with the substantial number of software programs specifically written for beverage control, few managers are willing to devote the time and energy required to institute control with generic spreadsheet and database programs. Growing numbers of managers are simply adopting one or another of the beverage control programs similar to those illustrated at the beginning of this chapter. Software tailored to the hospitality industry is designed to accomplish far more than one could expect from any generic spreadsheet or database package.

Beverage control programs come in several forms and address different issues based on the type of operation. In an operation that has significant draught beer sales, one would be wise to adopt a draught beer control system, which can accurately meter or control portions for beer or wine. It should also have the ability to support multiple taps per control unit. Each tap should have the ability to pour a variety of sizes and support a variety of price levels as well. Many draught beer control systems have a flow meter system, which is designed to compensate for fluctuations in line pressure and flow rates, thus the portion size remains constant. This feature allows for maximum yield from each keg. Finally, and perhaps most importantly, the automatic portion control means that a bartender can place the glass or pitcher under the tap, press a button, and help another customer while the container is being filled, increasing customer service and reducing the time spent on each guest.

In an operation where the sales volume is primarily mixed drinks, a manager should consider a bottled liquor control system. This type of system was covered in detail earlier in the chapter in the discussion on automatic pouring systems. Both of these systems have similar goals: maintain control over the amount of liquor dispensed, give consistent portions to all guests, and track the sale of every beverage poured.

Establishing and Monitoring Standard Sales Prices

LEARNING OBJECTIVE 15.8
Explain why bar operations should be monitored frequently and list four techniques for monitoring the performance of bartenders.

When standard costs for standard drinks are known and recorded, a list of standard sales prices should be established. An obvious reason for this is to allow sales prices to be posted at the bar or listed in a menu, depending on the type of establishment. It is generally considered good practice to maintain a complete list of current standard sales prices in the manager's office. Success with some of the techniques to be discussed in Chapter 16 requires that one have access to an accurate list of sales prices.

Selling prices for similar alcoholic drinks obviously vary considerably among establishments. Reasons for the differences include the cost and quantity of the ingredients, the ambience of the establishment, the expectations of the clientele, and the desired cost-to-sales ratio. In most establishments, the cost-to-sales ratio for cocktails and mixed drinks will run between 15 to 25 percent, for beer 25 to 35 percent, and for wine 40 to 50 percent.

The techniques for maintaining up-to-date lists of standard sales prices are many and varied. As in so many other cases, the simplest is often the best. Many recommend that current sales prices for cocktails and mixed drinks be maintained on the recipe detail and cost cards, and that those for straight drinks be kept on an expanded version of the list first shown in Figure 15.4. This expanded version is illustrated in Figure 15.7.

It is absolutely essential in any bar operation that the sales price be standardized for each drink sold, for straight drinks as well as for cocktails and other mixed drinks. When sales prices are standardized, customers can be properly charged for the drinks they order, and the prices will not vary from day to day. The possibilities for customer satisfaction are increased: the customer who has been charged $4.50 for a particular drink on Tuesday has reasonable assurance that an identical charge will be made for the same drink on Wednesday. In some places, a list of standardized drink prices can be found posted on a sign over the bar. In others, they may be printed in the menu. These signs and menus eliminate any possible arguments over drink prices. Refer to the government agency policy in your province or territory regarding pricing regulations.

Establishing the standard price of wine is relatively easy. After all, wine is generally served only four ways: by the bottle, glass, half litre, or full litre. Each bottle has a known cost to the establishment. Thus the price charged to a customer is a function of that cost. In most establishments, the bottle price typically represents a 100 to 120 percent markup over cost, so the price is easily determined. For wines served by the glass, establishments typically establish the price per bottle and divide it by the number of glasses in that bottle. For example, if a bottle of Merlot is priced at $20 and there are four glasses poured from that bottle, each glass would be priced at $5.

Pricing of premium wines can be more complicated, because these wines are typically purchased when young and increase in value as they age. In those instances, management must continually reassess their value and make selling price adjustments.

Perhaps the most important purpose behind the standardization of sales prices is to maintain a planned cost-to-sales ratio for each drink. The drink costing $0.90 when prepared from a standard recipe and selling for $4.50 has a cost-to-sales ratio of $0.90 to $4.50—20 percent. The sale of one of these drinks results in the addition of $4.50 to daily sales and $0.90 to daily cost, the net effect being a gross profit on the sale of $3.60. For the drink in question, this is the desired, planned effect of each sale. It is not a matter of chance or a bartender's whim; it has been planned by the manager. Ingredients (and, consequently, costs) are planned. With costs established, sales prices are set that yield acceptable cost-to-sales ratios. Product cost has a known relationship to product sales price. In addition, each sale has a known impact on gross profit. In effect, the increase in gross profit attributable to each sale is planned when management establishes the cost and sales price of a drink. Thus, it becomes possible to plan for and maintain acceptable levels of profit.

It should be noted that unless management employs one of the computer programs or devices as previously illustrated, bar operations present unique opportunities for employees to deviate from established standards and standard procedures without management's becoming aware until well after the fact. For example, a bartender instructed to pour 1 ¼ ounces for a straight shot may instead pour 1 ½ ounces for customers for as long as a month (one full accounting period) before management obtains data revealing that excessive beverage costs have developed. The bartender may have simply misunderstood instructions or may have been pouring the larger shots purposely to increase tips. In either case, beverage costs would be higher than warranted, but this would not be known until beverage costs for the month had been determined and an investigation had uncovered the cause. One might think that the cost of an extra ¼ ounce is only a small amount of money, but assume that the additional ¼ ounce of gin costs $0.10 on average. If we multiply that additional cost by the number of drinks served in one day, say 200 drinks, we get $20 in additional costs per day. If we then multiply that by 31 days in a month, the potential savings figure is $620. Further, if management does not monitor bartenders' work or does not bother to verify beverage costs for the month, the yearly potential overrun would be $7,300.

For operators who do not use one of the many computer-based systems, one common approach to monitoring beverage production is to observe bartenders as they proceed with their daily work. The frequency of the observations may range from continual to occasional, depending on a given manager's perception of need. Some employees—those whose honesty, ability, or receptivity to training is questionable—should probably be observed rather frequently. In making these observations, a manager attempts to determine the type of corrective action, if any, that may lead to improved performance. Other employees, whose loyalty, interest, honesty, and willingness to follow standards and standard procedures have been demonstrated amply in their daily work, need not be observed so frequently. At most, the manager would probably spot-check their work to confirm previous evaluations. If, from time to time, a spot check suggests that a certain individual's performance has fallen below its previous acceptable level, the manager would be wise to focus attention more closely on the particular employee and increase the frequency of observation.

A basic prerequisite to monitoring beverage production is selecting the means to be used for observing employee performance. Essentially, there are four possibilities:

1. A manager can personally observe bar operations on a regular basis.
2. A designated employee, such as a head bartender, can observe others working at the bar and report unacceptable performance and problems to management.
3. Individuals unknown to the bartenders can be hired to patronize the bar, observe the employees, note problems, and report to management.
4. Closed-circuit television systems can be installed to permit observation of bartenders and bar operations from a remote location.

Managers who use one of the computer-based programs have a distinct advantage. Several of these programs provide nightly information comparing costs with sales, and others do not allow bartenders to pour greater amounts of liquor than those established by management. Even if an operation employs a computer program or device, observation of bartenders is desirable.

By using one or more of these approaches, managers have some reasonable means for assessing employee performance and uncovering operating problems. However, this is not to suggest that the manager of any bar operation can maintain perfect control merely by adopting these approaches. As will be shown in chapters 16 and 17, the opportunities for employees to purposely deviate from established standards are too many and too varied to be discovered by mere observation.

THINGS TO CONSIDER

Operators tend to forget that large amounts of cash change hands during the sale of alcoholic beverages. Therefore, as a security precaution, it is essential to monitor the activities of those employees who are handling the cash.

CHAPTER ESSENTIALS

In this chapter, we identified the two primary objectives for establishing beverage production control: to ensure that all drinks are prepared according to managers' specifications, and to guard against the development of excessive beverage costs in the production phase of operation. We described the standards and standard procedures commonly established to achieve these objectives, including the use of measuring devices, pourers, and other dispensing devices, and standard recipes. We discussed several computer programs and devices that allow managers to achieve the two objectives. We identified methods for determining standard costs for straight drinks and for mixed drinks, including cocktails, and explained the importance of determining standard costs as one basis for establishing sales prices. We explained the importance of monitoring employee performance. Finally, we identified four methods for monitoring employee performance at bars and discussed the problems inherent in relying on these methods as the sole means for controlling production.

KEY TERMS IN THIS CHAPTER

QUESTIONS AND PROBLEMS

1. Identify the two primary objectives of beverage production control.
2. List four noncomputer devices used to standardize quantities of alcoholic beverages used in beverage production.
3. Identify and explain three computer devices that prevent bartenders from pouring more than a standard shot per drink.
4. Identify the primary purposes for establishing standard drink recipes.
5. Why are standard sales prices necessary?
6. The cost of the pouring brand of Scotch is $0.58 per ounce, and the cost of club soda is $0.04 per ounce. Determine the cost of a Scotch and soda from each of the following standard recipes:

   a. 1 ounce of Scotch and 6 ounces of club soda
   b. 1 ½ ounces of Scotch and 7 ounces of club soda
   c. 2 ounces of Scotch and 6 ounces of club soda

7. In each of the examples in Question 6, determine sales price if the desired liquor cost percent is:

   a. 20 percent
   b. 25 percent
   c. 18 percent

8. In Fleezee's Bar, the standard measure for a straight shot is 1 ounce. How much does a straight shot of blended rye cost if the price of a 1-litre bottle is $13.50?
9. In the cocktail lounge at Fribble's Hotel, a straight shot of Irish whisky is 1 ½ ounces. The purchase price for a 1-litre bottle of the pouring brand is $16.95. If the desired cost-to-sales ratio is 20 percent, what should be the sales price for the drink?
10. In the Midway Bar, a straight shot of Canadian whisky is 1 ¼ ounces. The purchase price for a 1-litre bottle of the pouring brand is $14.95. If the desired cost-to-sales ratio is 20 percent, what should be the sales price for the drink?

11. In the Airport Lounge, a straight shot of Scotch whisky is 1 ounce. The purchase price for a 1-litre bottle of the pouring brand is $15.95. If the desired cost-to-sales ratio is 20 percent, what should be the sales price for the drink?

12. What steps can a manager take to institute portion control in a bar operation?

13. Why is production control necessary in bar operations? What measures can be taken to institute control?

14. Select recipes for any four common drinks from a book of drink recipes, obtain current market prices for the ingredients, and then determine the standard cost of one portion of each drink.

15. Why is frequent monitoring of bar operations essential?

16. List four techniques for observing the performance of bartenders.

17. Assume that you are the manager of a cocktail lounge. The bar register is an electronic sales terminal with automatic pricing. There is no other register in the establishment. It is 5:00 p.m. on a busy Friday afternoon, and the terminal has just become inoperable. What procedures would you direct the bartender to use to record sales until the terminal can be repaired?

18. Define each of the key terms in this chapter.

EXCEL EXERCISES

Exercise 15.1
Barnaby's Hideaway uses Jim Beam Bourbon to prepare its Manhattans. A 1-litre bottle of Jim Beam costs $12.50. It also uses Martini and Rossi sweet vermouth at $6.60 per litre in the drink. Compute the cost per ounce for the liquor and the vermouth.

Exercise 15.2
Complete the Standard Recipe Detail and Cost card for a Manhattan using the information calculated in Exercise 15.1. The sales price of the drink is $4.50.

Exercise 15.3
Barnaby's Hideaway uses Smirnoff Vodka to prepare its vodka martinis. A 1-litre bottle of Smirnoff Vodka costs $15.00. The recipe calls for dry vermouth, which costs $8.00 per litre. Compute the cost per ounce for the liquor and vermouth.

Exercise 15.4
Complete the Standard Recipe Detail and Cost card for a vodka martini using the information calculated in Exercise 15.3. The sales price of the drink is $4.50.

CHAPTER 16

Monitoring Beverage Operations

• LEARNING OBJECTIVES •

After reading this chapter, you should be able to:

16.1 Identify the three general approaches to monitoring beverage operations.

16.2 Calculate monthly amounts for the cost of beverages sold, cost percentages, and beverage cost percentages for wines, spirits, and beers separately.

16.3 Calculate the value of liquor issued to a bar, bar inventory differential, and cost of liquor consumed, and beverage cost percent.

16.4 List possible reasons for differences between actual and standard beverage costs.

16.5 Calculate daily amounts for the cost of beverages sold, beverage cost percentages, and cost percentages for wines, spirits, and beers separately.

16.6 Determine standard beverage cost for a given period.

16.7 Calculate potential sales value per bottle for beverages sold by the straight drink.

16.8 Determine a mixed drink differential and use it to adjust potential sales values.

16.9 Calculate potential sales values using the average sales value method.

16.10 Identify the formulas used to calculate beverage inventory turnover and explain how the results of this calculation can be interpreted for maintaining appropriate inventory levels of spirits and beers.

INTRODUCTION

LEARNING OBJECTIVE 16.1
Identify the three general
approaches to monitoring
beverage operations.

An important aspect of the control process is regularly monitoring operations to determine whether results conform to the manager's plans. One must assess the overall effectiveness of control procedures that, taken together, constitute the control system. In other words, one must evaluate the entire control process—the standards and standard procedures established, and the monitoring techniques used by the manager—to determine whether the controls instituted are producing the desired results.

Virtually any of the methods for monitoring beverage operations illustrated and discussed in this chapter may be integrated into a computer-based control system. This may be done by means of a generic database program, or the function may be incorporated into a beverage control package. A large chain may hire a programming firm to develop a database for its specific needs; an individually owned hotel or restaurant may purchase one of the beverage inventory programs that can be seen at hotel and restaurant trade shows. Assuming timely and accurate data entry for purchases and issues during a period, a printout of the inventory can be obtained to compare with the monthly physical inventory. Differences will show the extent of deviations from standard control procedures.

There are three general approaches to monitoring beverage operations. The first is based on *cost:* determining the cost of beverages sold, and comparing that figure with either actual cost or standard cost. The second is based on *liquid measure:* comparing the number of ounces of beverages sold with the number of ounces consumed. The third is based on *sales values:* comparing the potential sales value of beverages consumed with the actual sales revenue recorded. Each of the three approaches is incorporated into one of the computer programs available today. The decision as to which method to use depends on the size and scope of operations. Many operators use just one method; some use more than one. All three methods are discussed in detail in the following sections.

THE COST APPROACH

Cost Percent Methods

Monthly Calculations

LEARNING OBJECTIVE 16.2
Calculate monthly amounts for
the cost of beverages sold,
cost percentages, and beverage cost percentages for
wines, spirits, and beers
separately.

As illustrated in Chapter 1, raw dollar figures for directly variable and semivariable costs are seldom, if ever, of any particular significance for control purposes. Because these costs vary to some extent with business volume, they become significant only when expressed in relation to that volume with which they vary. Beverage managers calculate costs in dollars and compare those costs with sales in dollars. This enables them to discuss the relationship between costs and sales, sometimes described as the **cost per dollar of sale**, the ratio of costs to sales, or simply as the cost-to-sales ratio. The industry uses the following basic formula for calculating the cost-to-sales ratio.

$$\frac{\text{Cost}}{\text{Sales}} = \text{Cost per dollar of sale}$$

Students will recall from studying the food control section of this text that this same formula is used to calculate the cost per dollar of sale for food. In fact, this formula is used for cost per dollar of sale of all three elements that make up prime cost: food, beverage, and labour.

The formula normally results in a decimal answer, and any decimal can be converted to a percentage if one multiplies it by 100 and adds a percent sign (%). This is the same as simply moving the decimal point two places to the right and adding a percent sign. This is the formula used to calculate **cost percents**; it is commonly written as:

$$\frac{\text{Cost}}{\text{Sales}} = \text{Cost \%}$$

This formula can then be extended to show the following relationships:

$$\frac{\text{Beverage cost}}{\text{Beverage sales}} = \text{Beverage cost \%}$$

All beverage operations should compare cost and sales figures regularly to see whether the planned cost-to-sales ratio is being maintained. Methods for doing this vary considerably from one operation to another, so it will be useful to look at several that may be used in operations of different sizes.

Small operations, often owner-managed and with few employees, do not have beverage controllers. The task of determining the cost-to-sales ratio normally falls to the owner. In many establishments, the owner attends to this task daily, weekly, or monthly, with or without the help of an accountant. Beverage cost is determined from inventory and purchase figures in the following manner.

A physical inventory of the storage area is taken after the close of business on the last day of the month. Most operators do inventory on Sunday night or Monday morning. The number of bottles of each item in stock is counted, and the value of each item is determined by means of one of five methods for inventory valuation: (1) actual purchase price method; (2) first-in, first-out method; (3) weighted-average purchase price method; (4) latest purchase price method; or (5) last-in, first-out method (for internal inventory purposes only). The specifics of these five methods are described in detail in Chapter 8.

When the value of each item in stock is known, these values are added, and the result is the total dollar value of the closing inventory for the period.

Because the closing inventory figure for any period is, by definition, the opening inventory for the following period, it is necessary to look back at the records to determine the closing inventory for the preceding period. To this opening inventory valuation, one adds the cost of all purchases for the month, obtained from financial records. Opening inventory plus purchases equal the value of beverages available for sale during the period. To illustrate, the following are figures taken from the financial records of Bistro Quatre for the month of February:

LEARNING OBJECTIVE 16.3
Calculate the value of liquor issued to a bar, bar inventory differential, and cost of liquor consumed, and beverage cost percent.

Opening beverage inventory	$3,201.80
+ Beverage purchases this month	$3,666.80
= Total available for sale this month	$6,868.60

Of the total available for sale, some has been issued to the bar, but some has not. To find the value of the beverages issued to the bar, the closing inventory figure for the current month is subtracted from the total available:

Total available for sale this month	$6,868.60
− Closing inventory this month	$3,875.40
= Value of beverages issued to the bar	$2,993.20

Although this $2,993.20 figure is the value of liquor issued to the bar, it is not necessarily the cost of beverages sold at the bar, because that figure does not take into account the change in inventory at the bar when determining the cost of beverages sold. If the value of the inventory at the bar did not change, the issues figure would accurately reflect the cost of beverages sold. However, if, for example, the value of the inventory at the beginning of a period was $1,000 and it was $700 at the end of the period, there would be an additional cost of $300 in liquor sold that would not be accounted for in determining the cost of liquor sold. To determine the cost of beverages sold, the $2,993.20 must be adjusted by the change in the value of inventory at the bar from the beginning to the end of the month. This is called the **inventory differential**. To illustrate:

Bar inventory value at the beginning of the month	$1,041.50
− Bar inventory value at the end of the month	$ 876.20
= Bar inventory differential	$ 165.30

To determine the cost of beverages consumed in the month, one must take this bar inventory differential into account. In this case, $165.30 must be added to the $2,993.20 figure for issues. Thus,

Value of beverages issued to the bar	$2,993.20
+ Inventory differential	165.30
= Cost of beverages consumed	$ 3,158.50

If the bar inventory differential is positive, as in this case, it is added to the value of beverages issued to the bar. If it is negative, it is subtracted.

It should be noted that in operations using one of the beverage inventory programs, this last step, determining inventory differential, is incorporated into the normal inventory process. Thus, the cost of beverages consumed would be automatically calculated. For example, in the AccuBar system, the scanner used to take inventory allows management to also input inventory at the bar. The report received after completing the inventory shows the quantity of each drink of liquor, beer, or wine consumed during the period and compares it with the sales of each category of alcoholic beverage.

After the cost of beverages consumed at the bar has been determined, it is possible to calculate the **beverage cost percent**, or cost-to-sales ratio. The financial records of Bistro Quatre indicate beverage sales for the month to be $11,945.60. The calculation of beverage cost percent is as follows:

$$\text{Beverage cost percentage} = \frac{\text{Beverage cost}}{\text{Beverage sales}}$$

$$= \frac{\$3,158.50}{\$11,945.60}$$

$$= 26.44\%$$

This procedure can be used by the owners and managers of even the smallest bars because it entails a minimum of paperwork and calculation. The basic requirements are simple records of beverage purchases and a par stock at the bar. This par stock can be maintained rather easily by issuing full bottles in exchange for empties. From the point of view of a beverage controller, it is not the ideal approach, but it does enable the owner or manager of an establishment to determine beverage cost percent for a period even if no staff member is available to keep extensive daily records of issues.

Many managers find that these simple procedures result in beverage costs and beverage cost percents that are not sufficiently accurate for their particular operations. They feel a need to take into account some or all of the adjustments described in the following paragraphs. By doing so, they derive beverage cost figures to the degree of accuracy they require.

Adjustments to Beverage Cost

There are various possible adjustments to beverage cost that may be required.

Food and Beverage Transfers. One reason that some managers do not consider the preceding beverage cost figures sufficiently accurate is that they do not include the cost of all ingredients used in drink production, and they do include beverages issued from the bar and used in food production (**food and**

LEARNING OBJECTIVE 16.4
List possible reasons for differences between actual and standard beverage costs.

beverage transfers). First, accurate beverage costs should include the cost of such food items as oranges, lemons, eggs, and heavy cream, which are commonly used to make drinks but are typically purchased by the food department and transferred to the bar. The cost of these items can be significant and should be included in beverage cost, not food cost. You may also wish to set up a bar condiment account in your general ledger and charge these items directly to the account to eliminate the transfer of these goods. To ensure their inclusion, one keeps records of the transfer of these food items from the kitchen to the bar.

At the end of the accounting period, the total value of these items is added to beverage cost and subtracted from food cost. For those food items issued directly from food stores to the bar, such as olives, cocktail cherries, and pearl onions, separate bar requisitions are prepared, typically on paper of a different colour from that used for food requisitions. When these additional records are maintained, provision must be made for adding the cost of these items to the beverage cost as well. The effect of their use is reflected in beverage sales, so their cost should properly be reflected in beverage cost.

Second, in many hotels and restaurants, alcoholic beverages are used as ingredients in food production. It is rare to find supplies of these beverages kept in a kitchen. Instead, appropriate quantities of these ingredients are simply obtained from the bar when needed. If the value of the quantities used is deemed significant, separate records of these transfers are maintained as well. In a restaurant featuring a different parfait each day and using some quantity of a liqueur from the bar to prepare it, records of the liqueurs used and their values can be kept on transfer memos. These values are subtracted from beverage cost figures and added to food cost.

Other Adjustments. Other possibilities for additions to cost include:

- Cost of any foods used in beverage preparation, but not included in a transfer memo
- Cost of mixers, if not included as transfers (depending on your accounting system)

Possibilities for subtractions from cost include:

- Cost of any drinks consumed by managers that should more properly be charged to entertainment or to business promotion. In the event that sales revenue has been recorded for such drinks, this revenue should be subtracted from beverage sales and written off.
- Cost of the beverages used in other promotional activities, such as free drinks to couples celebrating 50th wedding anniversaries, complimentary drinks offered to diners ordering before 5:30 p.m., and so on. These costs should be charged to business promotion or another account. (You must check with the provincial or territorial government liquor control agency regarding the policy for complimentary drinks. Policies vary across provinces and territories.)

Costs subtracted from sales:

1. Officers' beverages, if their costs have also been subtracted
2. Special promotions, if their costs have been charged to another account

Taking into account a variety of the adjustments described here, the cost of beverages sold is determined as illustrated in Figure 16.1.

• **FIGURE 16.1** •

Calculations of Beverage Costs and Sales with Adjustments, Bistro Quatre

Period Covered   Feb 1–28

Cost Calculations			*Sales Calculations*		
Cost of Liquor Consumed		$ 3,158.50	Beverage Sales		$ 11,945.60
Add			Less adjustments		
Food to bar (directs)	$ 44.50		Officers' beverages	$ 33.35	
Storeroom issues	$ 15.20		Special promotions	$ 450.35	
Mixers	$ 115.60		Total	$	483.70
Subtotal		$ 3,333.80	Net Sales		$ 11,461.90
Subtract					
Cooking liquor	$ 144.90				
Officers' drinks	$ 10.00				
Special promotions	$ 119.35				
Subtotal		$ 274.25			
Cost of Beverages Consumed		$ 3,3059.55			

For Bistro Quatre, beverage cost percent equals adjusted beverage cost of $3,059.55 divided by beverage sales of $11,461.90, or 26.69 percent.

Once the beverage cost percent for a period has been calculated, it may be compared with the beverage cost percent for similar periods to evaluate the extent to which current results measure up to past results. If, for example, the beverage cost percent for the current period is 26.69 percent and records indicate that the beverage cost percent for each of the last six months has been between 25.0 and 27.0 percent, a manager is likely to conclude that the results for the current period are satisfactory, provided that the past results have been considered satisfactory. However, if the beverage cost percent changes dramatically (e.g., an increase of 5 percentage points), and the change is both unexpected and undesirable, the manager will try to find the reasons for the change. If causes can be identified, appropriate corrective actions can be taken to bring beverage costs back into line by the end of the next accounting period and to keep them in line in the future.

Cost Calculations by Category

Some managers believe that a single figure for beverage cost is too general to be of maximum value for their operations. They prefer to separate the beverage cost figure into its three components: spirits, wines, and beers. You may also separate these components into draught beer, domestic beer, and imported beer to further analyze costs. By doing so and by similarly separating beverage sales figures, one can calculate individual cost-to-sales ratios for these three categories. These cost-to-sales ratios are significantly different from one another, and changes from one period to another may not be apparent in a single cost percent figure that includes all three. Given appropriate data, a form such as that illustrated in Figure 16.2 may be used both to distribute cost and sales figures for these three major categories and to facilitate adjusting costs in the manner previously discussed.

In Chapter 15, in the discussion of standard drink recipes and standard costs for drinks, the point was made that standard costs are useful for determining sales prices for drinks. If, for example, prices for drinks made with spirits had been determined with a target cost percent of 18.5 percent, the single 26.44 percent cost-to-sales ratio identified earlier in this chapter would not be useful for evaluating whether that cost percent was being achieved. However, if the costs, sales, and adjustments for all wines and beers can be factored out, as in Figure 16.2, one can determine the cost percent for spirits alone for a period—in this case, 18.63 percent. A comparison of this figure with an 18.5 percent target suggests that the actual cost of drinks made with spirits is about the same as the planned cost. One should note that the additions to spirits costs include the cost of mixers and garnishes, such as olives, lemons, cherries, limes, cola, soda, and so on, on the assumption that all of these items are used in making drinks using spirits as the primary ingredient. The detail as shown in Figure 16.2 gives a better picture of the true costs of bar operations.

• FIGURE 16.2 •

Calculations by Category for Bistro Quatre

Period Covered   Feb 1–28

Beverage Sales

		Sales	Adjustments		Net Sales
Spirits		$ 6,950.70	$ 177.80		$ 6,772.90
Wine		$ 4,038.60	$ 189.25		$ 3,849.35
Beer		$ 956.30	$ 116.65		$ 839.65
Total Sales		$ 11,945.60	$ 483.70		$ 11,461.90
		Spirits	Wines	Beer	Total
Cost of Issues		$ 1,146.85	$ 1,615.20	$ 396.45	$ 3,158.50
Adjustments					
Additions					
Food to bar directs		$ 44.50			$ 44.50
Storeroom issues		$ 15.20			$ 15.20
Mixers		$ 115.60			$ 115.60
Subtotal		$ 175.30			$ 175.30
Total		$ 1,322.15			$ 3,333.80
Subtractions					
Bar to kitchen		$ 32.70	$ 42.20	$ 70.00	$ 144.90
Officers' drinks		$ 2.00	$ 8.00		$ 10.00
Special promotions		$ 25.35	$ 58.20	$ 35.80	$ 119.35
Subtotal		$ 60.05	$ 108.40	$ 105.80	$ 274.25
Net Adjustments		$ 115.25	$ (108.40)	$ (105.80)	$ (98.95)
Net Cost of Sales		$ 1,262.10	$ 1,506.80	$ 290.65	$ 3,059.55
Cost Percent		18.63%	39.14%	34.62%	26.69%
Cost per Dollar Sale		0.186	0.391	0.346	0.267

Daily Calculations

Analyzing the beverage cost-to-sales ratio just once each month presents some problems. The normal month is an accumulation of 30 or 31 days, and by the time the results of all those days are summarized into monthly cost and cost percent figures, it is too late to do anything about them. By the time monthly figures reveal that operating results for a previous month were disastrous, nothing can be done to change those results. It is now common to do daily or weekly beverage inventories. If, for example, the results for October have been terrible, the best a manager can hope to do is to show improvement in November and December, and thus offset the poor results for October. It may be possible to offset the effects to some extent over the course of a year by

LEARNING OBJECTIVE 16.5
Calculate daily amounts for the cost of beverages sold, beverage cost percentages, and cost percentages for wines, spirits, and beers separately.

striving for improved results in upcoming months, but nothing can be done to change the past.

It would clearly be preferable to have some indication of the probable beverage cost-to-sales ratio before the end of a period so that efforts can be made to improve operations while there is still time for the improvements to affect the figures for the current period. This is the aim of procedures for the daily calculation of beverage cost and cost percent.

If a manager obtains cost and cost percent figures for the first 10 days of a month and these figures indicate unsatisfactory operating results, corrective actions can conceivably be taken in time to have a positive impact on the final figures for the period. In some large operations with staff to maintain the necessary records, beverage cost and cost percent are calculated daily. It is not difficult to do. If beverages are issued to the bar daily on the basis of requisitions that accompany the empty bottles, it is rather easy to determine beverage costs daily. After beverages have been issued, unit costs are recorded on the requisitions, which are then extended and totalled to determine the cost of the issues for one day. This figure is recorded as the cost of beverages sold on the preceding day. After a beverage sales figure for the day is obtained, beverage cost and sales figures are used to determine a beverage cost percent for the day.

It is obvious that the figures obtained in this way are less than completely accurate. After all, an assumption has been made that every ounce in every empty bottle was sold on the preceding day; this does not account for the possibility that the contents of a bottle were probably sold over a period of several days. The daily cost percentage is, therefore, unreliable. However, if figures for the cost of daily issues are accumulated daily for all of the days thus far in a period, and if the same procedure is followed with daily sales, it becomes possible to determine beverage cost percent for all of the days thus far in the period. This new cost percent, beverage cost percent *to date*, is a more accurate and reliable figure. Cumulative cost and sales figures developed in this way tend to reduce the degree of inaccuracy inherent in figures for one single day. This approach, illustrated in Figure 16.3 for Bistro Quatre, provides a reasonably reliable picture of overall operations.

BQ

• FIGURE 16.3 •

Daily Beverage Cost Calculations, Bistro Quatre

Date	Cost		Sales		Cost %	
	Today	To Date	Today	To Date	Today	To Date
1-Feb	$ 130.85		$ 409.50		32.0%	
2-Feb	$ 125.60	$ 256.45	$ 420.70	$ 830.20	29.9%	30.9%
3-Feb	$ 90.40	$ 346.85	$ 390.65	$ 1,220.85	23.1%	28.4%
4-Feb	$ 88.90	$435.75	$ 370.60	$ 1,591.45	24.0%	27.4%
5-Feb	$ 90.30	$ 526.05	$ 432.85	$ 2,024.30	20.9%	26.0%
6-Feb	$ 110.60	$ 636.65	$ 422.70	$ 2,447.00	26.2%	26.0%

A more accurate picture of daily operations can be obtained if management can take daily inventory of the stock at the bar and determine a daily bar inventory differential analogous to the monthly differential discussed earlier in this chapter. If one can subtract a closing bar inventory for a given day from an opening bar inventory for that day, the daily bar inventory differential obtained can be added (or subtracted, in the case of a negative figure) to the daily issue figure to determine daily cost with greater accuracy. The beverage operations that do take a daily bar inventory typically record the amount remaining in each bottle in tenths. For example, a bottle of Scotch that is half full at the end of the day would be considered to be 0.5 full. This procedure makes it easier to calculate the value of each bottle at the bar.

If daily bar inventory differentials are used, it will be necessary to add two more columns to the form illustrated in Figure 16.3. These are inserted between the two columns headed "Date" and "Cost Today" and are headed "Beverage Issues" and "Bar Inventory Differential." With the addition of these columns, "Cost Today" becomes a net figure, incorporating daily issues and bar differential. This will yield a greater degree of accuracy in the figures for beverage cost percent for the day and for the period to date. This is illustrated in Figure 16.4. Note that the negative figures are subtracted and the positive figures are added to issues to arrive at a daily cost figure. For example, there is a –$22.35 figure entered as the bar differential figure for February 1. This means that the bar inventory was $22.35 greater than the previous day, so the differential figure would be subtracted from cost that day, as shown:

Bar inventory, March 31	$1,019.15
Bar inventory, February 1	$1,041.50
Bar inventory differential	–$ 22.35

For users of various computerized systems, it is possible to easily take a daily inventory without spending a great deal of time doing it, although most

• FIGURE 16.4 •

Daily Beverage Cost Calculations with Adjustments for Differentials, Bistro Quatre

Date	Beverage Issues	Bar Inventory Differential	Cost Today	Cost To Date	Sales Today	Sales To Date	Cost% Today	Cost% To Date
1-Feb	$130.85	($22.35)	$108.50		$409.50		26.5%	
2-Feb	$125.60	($19.10)	$106.50	$215.00	$420.70	$ 830.20	25.3%	25.9%
3-Feb	$ 90.40	$ 4.80	$ 95.20	$310.20	$390.65	$1,220.85	24.4%	25.4%
4-Feb	$ 88.90	$11.70	$100.60	$410.80	$370.60	$1,591.45	27.1%	25.8%
5-Feb	$ 90.30	$20.50	$110.80	$521.60	$432.85	$2,024.30	25.6%	25.8%
6-Feb	$110.60	($10.30)	$100.30	$621.90	$422.70	$2,447.00	23.7%	25.4%

operators would not take inventory more than once a week. For example, the AccuBar system employs a scanner that can easily be used to take a daily inventory.

Some programs keep track of liquor consumed each time a drink is prepared. One system from Bar Vision uses free-pour spouts that contain tiny radio transmitters. A receiver is placed in the bar. Each time a drink is poured, the system keeps track of the amount dispensed. At the end of a shift or a day, a report is issued showing the number of pours and the amount of liquor used from each bottle at the bar. This is compared with sales for the period to arrive at a beverage cost percent.

Cost percent to date reflects the net effect of all costs and all sales for the number of days thus far in the period. It is reasonable to compare this figure with cost percents to date for equivalent periods in the recent past. If this comparison reveals unsatisfactory performance in the current period, corrective action can be initiated to improve performance in the days remaining in the period. If this is done, it is possible that the final figures at the end of the period will be more acceptable than they may have been otherwise.

Adjustments to Cost. Just as several adjustments can be made to monthly figures, so too can daily figures be adjusted by those who prefer more precise numbers. If the records required as the basis for adjustments are available (e.g., transfer memos, sales cheques, and the like), the form illustrated in Figure 16.4 can be expanded to that illustrated in Figure 16.5.

Figure 16.5 makes provision for adjusting the daily cost of beverage issues, and as a result will differ from the data in Figure 16.4. It can be increased by recording such items as transfers of direct purchases (directs) from the kitchen to the bar, mixers purchased directly for the bar, and food storeroom issues to the bar in the "Additions" column. If bar inventory is taken daily, positive bar inventory differentials are to be included in this column. In the "Subtractions" column, one would include transfers of beverages to the kitchen (cooking liquor), the cost of drinks attributable to entertainment or promotion, and the cost of complimentary drinks used for special promotions. Negative bar inventory differentials can be included in this column. If desired, individual columns for all of these adjustments can be inserted in place of the two columns illustrated.

Using one or another of these forms, a manager can monitor bar operations, note significant deviations from acceptable norms, and then take corrective action while events are still fresh in the minds of participants and investigations are feasible.

To determine monthly cost, it is necessary to value the monthly physical inventory—a time-consuming task if done manually. However, any standard spreadsheet program can be used to maintain perpetual inventory and to value the physical inventory. So, too, can several of the beverage control packages available today from various software developers be used for this task.

• FIGURE 16.5 •

Daily Beverage Cost Calculations with Adjustments for Differentials, Bistro Quatre

Date	Beverages Issued	Additions	Subtractions	Total Cost Today	Total Cost To Date	Sales Today	Sales To Date	Cost% Today	Cost% To Date
1-Feb	$130.85	$ 9.65	$22.35	$118.15		$409.50		28.9%	
2-Feb	$125.60	$20.00	$30.15	$115.45	$233.60	$420.70	$ 830.20	27.4%	28.1%
3-Feb	$ 90.40	$14.80	$20.00	$ 85.20	$318.80	$390.65	$1,220.85	21.8%	26.1%
4-Feb	$ 88.90	$22.75	$32.70	$ 78.95	$397.75	$370.60	$1,591.45	21.3%	25.0%
5-Feb	$ 90.30	$44.60	$16.30	$118.60	$516.35	$432.85	$2,024.30	27.4%	25.5%
6-Feb	$110.60	$ 5.50	$33.40	$ 82.70	$599.05	$422.70	$2,447.00	19.6%	24.5%

Spreadsheets can also be used for calculating daily cost percents in the manner illustrated in figures 16.3, 16.4, and 16.5. Once the spreadsheet is set up, one merely records figures daily for issues, adjustments, and sales. The next logical step, printing a daily report for management, is easy.

Standard Cost Method

LEARNING OBJECTIVE 16.6
Determine standard beverage
cost for a given period.

In all of the methods discussed so far, the objective has been to obtain current cost figures to compare with historical figures (e.g., the cost percent for the current period with that for a previous period). Actual costs are determined in any of several possible ways, and actual sales figures are used to determine actual cost percents. Judgements are based on the acceptability of figures for the previous period and on the degree to which current figures match past figures. This is certainly the most common approach to monitoring and controlling beverage costs, but it is not necessarily the most desirable. After all, although current figures may compare favourably with figures for several previous periods, there is no adequate way to evaluate the figures for previous periods. Figures for previous periods may reflect unknown problems, and the comparison of current with past figures may merely confirm that past problems continue in the present. There is a clear need for a method that can be used to determine the extent to which problems exist. In short, a more reliable means for evaluating current costs is needed.

The **standard cost method** is a better means for evaluating beverage costs and judging the effectiveness of control procedures. By using this method, managers can compare actual cost for a period with standard cost for that period. It can be used only by those who have established standard recipes and have calculated standard costs for all drinks. The standard cost method requires very detailed records of drink sales and considerable calculation.

To calculate standard cost for a given operating period, one would need records of the number of sales of each specific drink sold during the period, as well as the standard cost of each drink. For example, the records of spirit sales would have to show the type of drink and brand of liquor. Types of drinks would include cocktails, mixed drinks, and straight shots. Records of beer sales would have to show both bottle sales and draught sales by brand. Equivalent detailed records of wine sales would also be needed. One would also have to know the standard cost of each.

With the necessary sales records and standard cost figures available, one can proceed to determine standard cost of beverages sold for the operating period. The first step is to multiply the number of sales of each type of drink by the standard cost of that drink to find total standard cost for each type of drink. This is done for each specific type of drink sold during the period. Next, the total standard cost for all drinks is added to determine total standard cost for the period. In Figure 16.6, the standard cost for one category of drinks, beer, is calculated this way. The same procedure is used to calculate standard cost for each of the other categories of drinks.

Once total standard cost for a period has been determined, it can be compared with actual cost for the same period. For example, assume that the actual cost of beer sold in March at The Spanish Moon Bistro was $4,098.90, and standard cost for beer for the period was $3,947.85, as calculated in Figure 16.6. Comparison of the two indicates a difference between actual and standard cost. The amount of the difference can readily be determined by subtraction:

• **FIGURE 16.6** •					
Determination of Standard Beverage Cost: Beer, The Spanish Moon Bistro					
Period Covered	March 1–31				
Item		Number Sold	Standard Cost	Total Standard Cost	
Bottled					
Canadian		1,178	$0.65	$ 765.70	
Blue		1,483	$0.65	$ 963.95	
Kokanee		674	$0.70	$ 471.80	
Draught					
Rickard's Red		2,005	$0.40	$ 802.00	
Sleeman		2,361	$0.40	$ 944.40	
Total				$3,947.85	

	Actual cost	$4,098.90
−	Standard cost	3,947.85
=	Difference	$ 151.05

Actual cost figures assume that an estimate of draught beer remaining in kegs has been determined and taken into account.

It is clear that actual cost is greater than it should be by $151.05. This difference is excessive cost—cost that is greater than warranted, given the standards, standard procedures, and standard costs established. Knowing that the cost of beer sold was excessive, a manager can immediately begin to investigate in order to determine the cause. Possible causes include breakage, pilferage, improper storage and handling of draught beers, and failure to record revenue from sales, among others. It is important to identify the causes so that corrective actions can be taken. Corrective actions would obviously be expected to result in improved performance in future periods.

Excessive cost is readily translated to everyday language as wasted money. After all, the excess cost determined in the preceding calculation ($151.05) should not have been required to produce these beer sales. This amount could have been used for some other purpose and would have been available for that purpose if employee performance had more nearly matched that anticipated by the standards and standard procedures established by management.

The standard cost methods for monitoring beverage operations are particularly difficult to use if one does not have a computer-based file of standard drink recipes and their costs, along with detailed records of sales showing the number of drinks of each type sold daily and for the period. The latter is best obtained from a computerized sales terminal.

THE LIQUID MEASURE APPROACH

Another technique for beverage control is the quantity or **ounce-control method**. As practised some years ago, it required taking daily physical inventory of bar stock, determining the number of ounces consumed each day, and calculating the number of ounces sold each day from detailed sales records. Ideally, the number of ounces consumed should equal the number of ounces sold; in practice, these amounts were never equal, because of spillage, evaporation, breakage, or other reasons. However, when bar operations were strictly controlled and bar personnel closely followed the standards and standard procedures established by management, the difference was kept to a minimum.

In this form, the ounce-control method has completely disappeared. An obvious reason is that the labour costs associated with it far outweigh the benefits that can be derived. However, modern technology has made possible the reappearance of ounce-control procedures in a variety of forms. Some use meters attached to bottles to measure the quantities used daily. Others require the use of complex and expensive computerized devices that dispense ingredients, mix drinks, record sales, and maintain bar inventory records automatically. Because complex equipment of this nature generally becomes comparatively less expensive with growing acceptance and use, it is not surprising that greater numbers of hotels and restaurants are taking advantage of it, particularly for use at service bars.

One computerized variation of the ounce-control method is found in Alcohol Control's Liquor Clicker. Each bottle at the bar has a pour sprout that is set to measure a predetermined-size shot. The system keeps track of the number of shots poured from each bottle and calculates the potential revenue from each bottle based on a price established by management. This is compared with actual revenue, and a variance is determined.

THE SALES VALUE APPROACH

LEARNING OBJECTIVE 16.7
Calculate potential sales value per bottle for beverages sold by the straight drink.

Another approach to controlling beverage operations is to determine the **potential sales value** of each full bottle of the various liquors issued from the storeroom. For example, if the standard drink of gin is 1 ¼ ounces and the pouring brand of gin is issued in 1-litre bottles, then each bottle potentially contains 28 drinks (35.1 ÷ 1.25). If the sales price for the standard 1 ¼-ounce drink is $4.00, then the potential sales value of each bottle of the pouring brand issued is equal to 28 drinks times $4.00 per drink, or $112.00. Hypothetically, then, each bottle of this gin issued should produce $112.00 in sales. Given standard drink sizes and standard sales prices, it is possible to determine the total revenue that should be generated by the issue of one bottle of any item kept at the bar. Therefore, when an empty bottle of any item is turned in with a requisition for replacement, it should be possible to find the potential sales value for that empty bottle reflected in actual sales. In a simple, hypothetical bar, for example, using only litre bottles and serving only straight drinks in 1 ¼-ounce shots for $4.00 per drink, the consumption of one bottle each of gin and rye should produce $224.00 in sales, calculated as follows:

$$\frac{35.1}{1.25} = 28 \text{ drinks per bottle}$$

$$2 \text{ bottles} \times 28 \text{ drinks} \times \$4.00 = \$224.00$$

Theoretically, one should find $224.00 in sales recorded in the register for the day.

As illustrated in Figure 16.7, it is possible to develop a chart of the standard sales values of bottles sold only by the straight drink.

• FIGURE 16.7 •

Calculation of Bottle Sales Value

Bottle Code	Item	Bottle Size	Drink Size	Drinks per Bottle	Sales Price	Value per Bottle
301	Dover Gin	1 L	1 ¼ oz.	28	$4.00	$112.00
107	Old Alberta Rye	1 L	1 ¼ oz.	28	$4.00	$112.00
217	Loch Ness Scotch	750 ml	1 ¼ oz.	21	$4.00	$ 84.00
352	Lenin Vodka	1 L	1 ¼ oz.	28	$3.75	$105.00
456	Burbles Brandy	750 ml	1 ¼ oz.	21	$4.50	$ 94.50

In practice, such a chart would necessarily include all brands sold at the bar and would obviously be considerably longer than the chart illustrated. However, most bars do not sell spirits only in straight shots. Beverage operations are seldom this simple. In most bars, cocktails and other mixed drinks account for some portion of sales, and such drinks require varying quantities of spirits and other ingredients. Therefore, if a control process is to be devised that uses the potential sales values of bottles, some way must be found to account for the complications that result from the production of mixed drinks. The potential sales values of bottles must be adjusted by means of a formula that takes into consideration variations in quantities of spirits used and in sales prices.

In fact, control procedures involving potential sales values are generally quite complex and require considerable time and calculation. For these and other related reasons, such procedures are not commonly used, except in some very large operations. However, some basic understanding of these procedures is necessary for anyone seeking to acquire a complete overview of beverage control. The major problem is to establish the sales values. Three different methods for doing so are discussed here. The first requires that potential sales values be established on the basis of sales of straight shots only and then adjusted daily or periodically by the means of a so-called mixed drink differential. These adjustments to the values of bottles issued and consumed are made after sales have taken place. The second method requires analyzing sales for a test period and determining weighted-average values for bottles in advance, based on historical sales records. The third method is really a modification of the second and is generally easier and more practical to use. However, it is sufficiently different from the second to warrant separate discussion.

Actual Sales Record Method

LEARNING OBJECTIVE 16.8
Determine a mixed drink differential and use it to adjust potential sales values.

If standard recipes are used to prepare drinks and detailed sales records are available, one can calculate the sales value of the ingredients in each type of drink sold (**actual sales record method**). For example, the preparation of a screwdriver may require 1 ¼ ounces of vodka. Assume that vodka as a straight drink is sold in 1 ¼-ounce measures for $3.75 (see Figure 16.7), and the screwdriver sells for $4.50. The sales value of the vodka is $3.75. The difference, $0.75, is known as a mixed drink differential. Each time a screwdriver is sold, sales revenue will be $0.75 greater than it would have been if the 1 ¼ ounces of vodka had been sold as a straight shot. **Mixed drink differential** is defined as the difference between the sales price of a given drink and the sales value of its primary ingredient if sold as a straight shot.

Once the sales value of the primary ingredient in a drink has been determined, it is possible to determine the mixed drink differential for that drink by subtracting the sales value of the primary ingredient from the sales price of the drink. Assume that gin is the primary ingredient in a martini and that the sales value for 2 ounces of gin in the martini is $6.38 as a straight drink of gin, calculated as follows:

$$\text{Sales value of 1 litre of gin} = \$112.00 \text{ (from Figure 16.7)}$$
$$\text{Number of ounces in 1 litre} = 35.1$$
$$\text{Sales value per ounce} = \frac{\$112.00}{35.1} = \$3.19$$
$$\text{Sales value of 2 ounces of gin} = 2 \times \$3.19 = \$6.38$$

The sales price of the martini is $4.50. Therefore, the mixed drink differential for a gin martini is a negative $1.88. Each sale of that particular drink decreases potential revenue by $1.88. That is, each time a martini is sold, the sales revenue is $1.88 less than it would have been if the gin in the martini had been sold as a straight drink.

Thus, to determine potential sales value of the quantity of gin sold, one must subtract $1.88 for each martini sold. The differential for each type of drink must be calculated and recorded for frequent reference.

Each day, after sales have been analyzed—either from guest cheques or from the register—the number of drinks of each type sold is multiplied by the differential for that drink, and the total bottle sales value for spirits consumed is increased by the total of all positive differentials and decreased by the total of all negative differentials.

Figure 16.8 illustrates the use of the method for calculating potential sales values. Bottle code numbers, item names, and numbers of bottles consumed

• **FIGURE 16.8** •

Daily Analysis of Potential Sales Values

Bottle Code No.	Item	Bottles Consumed	Sales Value per Bottle	Total Sales Value
301	Dover Gin	3	$112.00	$336.00
107	Old Alberta Rye	2	$112.00	$224.00
352	Lenin Vodka	2	$105.00	$210.00
			Total	$770.00

Mixed Drink	Primary Ingredient	Ounces Primary Ingredient	Straight Drink Price	Mixed Drink Price	Mixed Drink Differential	Number Sold	Total Differential
Martini	gin	2	$ 6.38	$ 4.50	($1.88)	8	($15.04)
Screwdriver	vodka	1¼ oz.	$ 3.75	$ 4.50	$0.75	18	$13.50
Martini	vodka	2	$ 6.00	$ 4.50	($1.50)	12	($18.00)
						Total	($19.54)

Sales Values Adjusted by Differentials

Sales Values of Empty Bottles from the Bar	$770.00
Adjustments for Mixed Drink Differentials	($19.54)
	$750.46

are taken from the bar requisition. Sales values per bottle are taken from a chart similar to that shown in Figure 16.7. Total sales values for the bottles consumed are determined by multiplying the number of empty bottles of each primary ingredient by the potential sales value per bottle. These are totalled to find sales values of the empty bottles from the bar. Next, this total is adjusted for mixed drink sales, as shown in the lower half of the form. The mixed drink differential for each type of drink is multiplied by the number sold to determine total differential per item. These, in turn, are added. In some instances, the differential is negative and is subtracted. The net of these two figures is the differential for the day, which is combined with the sales values of empty bottles to obtain an adjusted potential sales value. This adjusted potential sales value should be very close to the actual sales figure recorded in the bar register.

Determining potential sales values by this method requires considerable work each day. Although it results in highly accurate figures to use in evaluating actual sales data, it is somewhat cumbersome for day-to-day use in most establishments. However, new computerized liquor control systems have allowed daily sales value calculations of liquor consumed to come back into use.

One very good example of a computer system that uses potential sales is Liquor Control Solution's AZ 200 controller. Up to 255 different drinks and up to 16 different brands of liquor per drink can be programmed into the controller. Each time a drink is prepared, the system subtracts the amount of liquor from inventory and rings up a sale. At the end of each day, it provides a report showing sales of each brand, cost of liquor used, and other information including liquor cost percentage. In effect, the system automatically takes into account the differences in quantities of liquor used in each drink.

Average Sales Value Method

LEARNING OBJECTIVE 16.9
Calculate potential sales values using the average sales value method.

Many who formerly used the previously discussed potential sales value technique and who have not yet purchased one of the computer systems such as the AZ 200 controller have concluded that some simplification of this complex method would make it more feasible to use. Therefore, a method was developed that uses average potential sales values instead of potential sales values adjusted for actual mixed drink sales.

The **average sales value method** eliminates the need for daily sales analysis and daily calculation of a net mixed drink differential. Instead, this method depends on results determined during a test period when careful records are kept of the number of drinks sold of each type. These records serve as the basis for determining the average potential sales value of each bottle. Figure 16.9 illustrates the method used to analyze drink sales for the test period.

Assuming that actual drink sales during the test period truly represent the sales mix, a determination of the average sales value for 1 ounce of gin can be made by dividing 367.5 ounces sold into $1,005.00 total sales. In this case, the average sales value for 1 ounce of gin is $2.73. Because this primary ingredient

• FIGURE 16.9 •

Average Sales Value of Gin per Ounce

Primary Ingredients: Gin

Drinks	No. Sold	Ounces Per Drink	Total Ounces	Drink Price	Total Sales
Martini	90	2 oz.	180.0	$4.50	$ 405.00
Straight shots	150	1 ¼ oz.	187.5	$4.00	$ 600.00
Totals			367.5		$1,005.00
Sales Value per Ounce	$2.73				

is purchased and used by the litre, the average sales value of each litre is 35.1 ounces multiplied by the average sales value of each ounce, or $95.82. In some operations, the individual doing these calculations uses a figure that is 1 ounce less than the actual number of ounces in the bottle (e.g., 34.1 for the 1-litre bottle) to account for unavoidable spillage and evaporation. Many believe that this approach results in average sales values that are more realistic.

Once these calculations have been completed for all primary ingredients consumed during the test period, a chart is prepared showing the average sales value of each bottle used in the bar. Figure 16.10 illustrates a chart of this type.

• FIGURE 16.10 •

Chart of Average Potential Sales Values of Bottles

Bottle Code	Item	Bottle Size	Average Potential Sales Value		
301	Dover Gin	1 L	$ 92.27		
107	Old Alberta Rye	1 L	$ 98.30		
217	Loch Ness Scotch	750 mL	$ 76.56		
352	Lenin Vodka	1 L	$ 88.95		
456	Burble's Brandy	750 mL	$ 90.60		

This chart can be used in place of the chart of standard sales values of bottles sold only by the straight drink, illustrated previously in Figure 16.7. Once these average potential sales values have been established, it is comparatively easy to determine the potential sales value of the bottles consumed at the bar each day. One simply multiplies the number of empty bottles of each brand by the potential sales value per bottle, as shown on the chart. Figure 16.11 illustrates a form that can be used to organize the work required to determine a daily total.

Once determined, this total potential sales figure for the day is compared with actual sales for the day, as previously discussed. The manager making the comparison will be watching for any significant difference between actual and potential sales that may suggest some deviation from the standards and standard procedures established for bar operation.

• FIGURE 16.11 •

Total Sales Value of Bottles Consumed

Bottle Code	Item	Bottle Consumed	Sales Value Per Bottle	Total Sales Value
301	Dover Gin	3	$92.27	$ 276.81
107	Old Alberta Rye	2	$98.30	$ 196.60
217	Loch Ness Scotch	3	$76.56	$ 229.68
352	Lenin Vodka	4	$88.95	$ 355.80
456	Burbles Brandy	1	$90.60	$ 90.60
Total				$1,149.49

Although the average potential sales value method is more common than the method requiring the calculation of mixed drink differential, its use is by no means universal. It is simpler to use, but the average potential sales value method still requires many calculations, and it is not practical unless the work involved can be assigned to one individual who has time to do it each day. Most establishments lack the staff to do it. In addition, the average potential sales value method is useful only if the sales mix at the bar remains relatively stable. Major changes in the sales mix because of changing times and changing customer preferences make the calculated averages inaccurate. When this is the case, new average potential sales values must be calculated from data collected during a new test period.

The ounce-control and sales value methods, which have seldom been used in recent years because of the considerable time and high labour costs they require, have made a return to favour with the increasing use of computers for beverage control. Manual calculations consumed far too many hours to justify the adoption of these methods, but growing acceptance of beverage control software substantially improves the outlook for their increased use.

A Simplified Method of Monitoring Bar Operations

In the interest of further simplifying and eliminating frequent and time-consuming sales analyses of the types discussed, some managers have adopted a simplified method. This method requires the establishment of a test period, during which the manager takes all appropriate steps to ensure strict employee adherence to all standards and standard procedures for bar operation. In addition, all phases of bar operation are kept under close observation during the period to ensure compliance. At the conclusion of the test period, the number of bottles consumed is determined from records of inventory, purchases, and issues. Next, a potential sales value is determined for each type and brand of beverage issued. This potential sales value is based on bottle contents sold as straight drinks. The procedure for determining potential sales value is the same as that explained earlier in the chapter: If drinks are sold in 1 ¼-ounce shots for $4.00 per shot, then the sales value of a 1-litre bottle containing 35.1 ounces is $112.00.

Next, the total number of bottles of each type and brand consumed during the test period is translated into total potential sales value by multiplying the number of bottles by the potential sales value of the bottle. After a total for each type and brand is determined, these totals are added to determine a total potential sales value for all bottles consumed during this test period. The next step is to compare this figure with the actual sales revenue for the test period. Typically, the potential sales figure is greater than actual sales, and the difference between the two is assumed to reflect the sale of cocktails and other mixed drinks as well as the normal spillage to be expected at the bar. Because the bar operation has been under careful observation throughout the test period, this difference is taken as a standard difference, which can be used in the future for comparison purposes.

The difference is divided by the potential sales figure to determine, as a percentage, the extent of the deviation from the potential. If, for example, potential sales values were $10,000 and actual sales were $9,500, the $500 difference would be divided by $10,000 to determine that the difference amounted to 5 percent. Expressed in another way, one could say that actual sales during the test period were 5 percent less than potential sales. By reducing the potential sales figure by 5 percent to account for normal spillage and the sale of cocktails and other mixed drinks, it is possible to develop an adjusted potential sales figure, which can be used to monitor bar operations in the future, as long as the sales mix remains fairly constant.

Using this approach, one can calculate potential sales values for bottles consumed, adjust for the standard difference determined during the test period, and use the resulting figures to determine the extent to which bar operations are measuring up to expectations. As long as the sales mix does not change significantly, this approach makes it possible to monitor operations without dealing with extensive and elaborate calculations of the sort described earlier in the chapter. However, if there are major discrepancies between actual sales revenue and adjusted potential sales values of bottles consumed, one of the more complex methods may be required to determine the causes.

An important advantage to this method is that, when necessary, the differential can be recalculated with relative ease. As customers' tastes change and the sales mix changes accordingly, it is comparatively simple to establish a new test period and calculate a new differential to use for monitoring operations. Moreover, as costs or sales prices change, this differential as a percentage of potential sales should remain relatively constant.

Regardless of the techniques involved in their calculation, potential sales figures can be useful for monitoring bar operations. When compared with actual sales figures, they provide a means for measuring the extent to which actual operations are meeting management's expectations. For example, if actual sales of $14,000 are compared with potential sales of $15,000, it is apparent that the actual falls short of the potential by $1,000, or 6.7 percent. It is the manager's responsibility in a particular beverage operation to determine how great a difference is to be tolerated. Assuming that a potential sales figure is reasonably reliable, a difference between that and the actual sales figures is likely to mean that employees are not using beverages—the raw materials of drink production—in the manner prescribed by the manager. It can also mean that sales are being recorded incorrectly or that sales are not being recorded at all.

The difference between actual and potential sales figures reflects operational problems of all sorts, including failure to mix according to standard recipes, excessive spillage, errors in filling orders, overpouring, general waste, and even outright theft. Every one of these problems should be of concern to a manager, who should be taking steps to eliminate them. In most operations, however, some difference between actual and potential sales figures is inevitable. The question becomes one of determining the extent of the difference that can be tolerated, which will vary considerably from one beverage operation to another. In some operations, a difference of 1 percent between actual and potential sales may cause extreme concern and lead to careful and detailed analysis of all phases of the operation. In others, a 3 percent difference may be considered to be within the limits of tolerance. In general, managers are less tolerant of differences arising from failure to record sales. Poor pouring and mixing techniques may be a result of the pressures of business at the bar. But failure to record sales commonly indicates an intention to steal. For this reason, bar managers do not normally see it as an acceptable reason for the difference between actual and potential sales.

INVENTORY TURNOVER

LEARNING OBJECTIVE 16.10
Identify the formulas used to calculate beverage inventory turnover and explain how the results of this calculation can be interpreted for maintaining appropriate inventory levels of spirits and beers.

Although it is obviously important to monitor bar operations by one or another of the means identified here, no manager can afford to focus on these methods alone. Most would agree that it is important to monitor, on a regular basis, the size, value, and use of the beverage inventory. After all, one would not want to maintain a beverage inventory that was too large for the sales volume generated. A beverage inventory can easily reach excessive size and excessive value if beverage purchases are not suitably matched to beverage issues.

On the one hand, if beverage purchases are greater than warranted by beverage issues and sales volume, the value of a beverage inventory can quickly become excessive. When too much money has been spent to purchase unwarranted quantities of beverages, it should be quite clear that money has been expended unproductively. The funds could have been used more productively for other purposes. On the other hand, if the beverage inventory is not large enough, more frequent ordering of comparatively small quantities may be necessary, and this often means paying higher unit prices. It can also result in higher labour costs and increased costs for processing orders. Moreover, if the stock of some beverages is allowed to run too low, it may result in lost sales.

Suppose, for example, that the manager of Grady's Bar has records indicating that consumption of Rouge Valley Lager, a popular local beer, amounts to approximately 60 cases per month. Because this brand is known to have a very limited shelf life, it is apparent that an inventory of 600 cases would be too large. However, an inventory of two cases would clearly be too small unless daily delivery is possible.

Beverage managers require some routine procedure for monitoring the adequacy of beverage inventories. The normal method for doing this is to determine a turnover rate for the beverage inventory each month and then watch for significant changes. The **turnover rate** for a beverage inventory is calculated by means of the same formulas used for calculating turnover rate for a food inventory. These were identified and discussed in detail in Chapter 8. The formulas for beverages are as follows:

$$\text{Turnover rate} = \frac{\text{Cost of beverages sold for a period}}{\text{Average inventory for the period}}$$

$$\text{Average inventory} = \frac{\text{Opening inventory} + \text{Closing inventory}}{2}$$

For accuracy, both opening and closing inventory figures should include the values of all beverages in the beverage storeroom and at the bar. For example, given an opening inventory of $4,800, a closing inventory of $5,600, and a cost of beverages sold of $5,720, the turnover rate is calculated as follows:

$$\text{Average inventory} = \frac{\$4,800 + \$5,600}{2}$$

$$= \frac{\$10,400}{2}$$

$$= \$5,200$$

$$\text{Turnover rate} = \frac{\$5,720}{\$5,200}$$

$$= 1.1$$

This calculation yields the turnover rate for one month. One can infer from this that the average inventory is being consumed at the approximate rate of 13.2 times per year—just over once a month. Some individual items are consumed at higher rates, whereas the rates for others are lower. However, on average, the overall inventory is being turned over 1.1 times per month.

Although many use this single turnover rate, calculated for the beverage inventory in its entirety, others find it useful to calculate separate turnover rates for the three principal components of the beverage inventory: spirits, beers, and wines. There are generally accepted monthly turnover rates for spirits and beers:

- Spirits: 1.5
- Beers: 2.0

For a spirits inventory, a monthly turnover rate of 1.0 or less normally indicates an inventory larger than necessary for the current volume of business. This suggests that too many dollars have been used to purchase unneeded quantities of spirits—dollars that might better have been used for some other purpose. Some will disagree, arguing that if it is possible to obtain a sufficiently large discount by increasing the size of purchases, it may be perfectly appropriate to increase purchase quantities and temporarily accept a lower-than-normal turnover rate. If the monthly turnover rate is 2.0 or higher, it is quite possible that the inventory is smaller than it should be, which might lead to frequent purchasing, possibly at higher prices than may be obtained by purchasing larger quantities.

Because beers are perishable products that lose quality with age, monthly turnover rates for beers should be higher. Many beverage managers prefer to purchase beers weekly, which results in higher turnover rates with fewer dollars committed to inventory at any one time. Most would find a monthly turnover rate of 2.0 to be acceptable.

There is no accepted monthly turnover rate for wines. Some hotels and restaurants maintain extensive inventories of vintage wines, purchased young and stored in wine cellars until they reach maturity. Others offer more common wines, purchased for immediate use and turned over frequently; many stock a great variety of wines—some very fine and others simple table wines. The range of possibilities is too great for any accepted turnover rate to be determined.

THINGS TO CONSIDER

Many foodservice operators have their bartenders perform inventory. This is not a good practice as they are the employees controlling the pouring of drinks; in essence, they may manipulate the inventory to hide pilferage. Inventory should be performed by two employees, preferably management. Well-organized establishments will perform inventory daily or weekly because it is more timely than performing monthly inventories. The information can then be acted on more frequently.

CHAPTER ESSENTIALS

In this chapter, we identified the three general approaches to measuring the effectiveness of beverage controls: cost, liquid measure, and sales values. We described and illustrated calculations for several cost-based methods, including monthly cost and cost percent, daily cost and cost percent, and standard cost. We illustrated the ounce-control method and discussed its limitations. We explained three methods for using potential sales values to monitor beverage operations: actual sales record method, average sales value method, and a simplified method of monitoring bar operations. We demonstrated the determination of the beverage inventory turnover rate and discussed its use as a monitoring device. We also discussed computer-based applications of the various methods illustrated in the chapter and pointed out the impracticality of attempting several of the methods without computers.

KEY TERMS IN THIS CHAPTER

Actual sales record method, p. 428
Average sales value method, p. 430
Beverage cost percent, p. 415
Cost percents, p. 413
Cost per dollar of sale, p. 412
Food and beverage transfers, p. 415

Inventory differential, p. 414
Mixed drink differential, p. 428
Ounce-control method, p. 426
Potential sales value, p. 426
Standard cost method, p. 424
Turnover rate, p. 435

QUESTIONS AND PROBLEMS

1. Given the following information, determine beverage cost in each of the three bars:

Storeroom Inventory Data

	Opening Inventory	Purchases	Closing Inventory
Art's	$5,000	$ 8,000	$7,000
Chez Pierre	8,325	10,666	9,327
Carol's	4,872	7,454	3,856

Bar Data

	Opening Inventory	Closing Inventory
Art's	$1,000	$1,000
Chez Pierre	2,325	2,050
Carol's	1,867	1,988

2. Using the costs determined in Question 1, calculate beverage cost percent if:

a. the sales figure in Art's is $20,000.
b. the sales figure in Chez Pierre is $41,412.50.
c. the sales figure in Carol's is $29,817.85.

3. Using the figures from questions 1 and 2, as well as the following adjustments, calculate adjusted cost of beverages sold, following the format provided in Figure 16.1, and then calculate beverage cost percent based on adjusted costs.

Art's

Food to bar (directs)	$200
Issues from food storeroom	150
Mixers	475
Cooking liquor	110
Managers' drinks	120
Special promotions	160

Chez Pierre

Mixers	$925
Food to bar (directs)	500
Cooking liquor	335
Special promotions	320

Carol's

Issues from food storeroom	$235
Special promotions	$285
Managers' drinks	165
Mixers	695
Cooking liquor	185

4. Use the following information to prepare a report showing costs, sales, and adjustments by category, using the form illustrated in Figure 16.2:

Total beverage sales: $42,320, of which 10 percent represents beer sales, 18 percent represents wine sales, and the balance to spirits sales.

Total adjustments to sales: $424, of which 8 percent is allocated to beer sales, 12 percent to wine sales, and the balance to spirits sales.

Total cost of issues: $10,500, of which 55 percent is allocated to spirits, 35 percent to wines, and the balance to beer sales.

Mixers	$865
Food to bar (directs)	305
Bar to kitchen	440
Special promotions	520

Mixers and food to bar (directs) are all adjustments to spirits alone, but figures for bar to kitchen and special promotions must be allocated as follows:

Bar to kitchen: 70 percent to wines, 10 percent to beer, and the balance to spirits.

Special promotions: 60 percent to wines and 40 percent to spirits.

5. Using Figure 16.3 as a guide, prepare a cumulative and daily cost-to-sales ratio chart given the following information:

Date	Cost	Sales
10/1	$250	$ 910
10/2	225	850
10/3	270	920
10/4	290	1,070
10/5	240	900

6. Using the figures in Question 5, prepare a chart in the form illustrated in Figure 16.5 to include the following additional information:

Date	Food Transferred to Bar	Liquor Transferred to Kitchen
10/1	$15	$25
10/2	10	30
10/3	12	45
10/4	20	10
10/5	8	18

7. Determine the potential sales values of the bottle issues in the following list, assuming that only 1-ounce shots were poured, 1-litre bottles were issued, and the sales price for all straight shots was $2.95.

Liquor	Number of Bottles Issued
Gin	5
Scotch	3
Canadian rye	4
Rum	3
Vodka	4
Bourbon	2

8. During the period covered by the issues identified in Question 7, the following mixed drinks were served:

Gin martinis	20
Vodka martinis	10
Manhattan cocktails (prepared with rye whisky)	25
Whisky sours	13
Rob Roys	16

The sales price for each of these mixed drinks was $3.00. However, all martinis and Manhattans contained 1 ½ ounces of liquor, and all whisky sours and Rob Roys contained 2 ounces of liquor. Use this information and any additional information from Question 7 required to prepare an analysis of potential sales values in the form illustrated in Figure 16.8.

9. a. Using the following sales data, prepare a chart in the form illustrated in Figure 16.10.

Drinks Prepared	Number Sold	Ounces per Drink	Drink Price
Martinis	20	2	$4.95
Straight shots	120	1.5	$3.00

   b. Using the average sales value method, determine the potential sales value of 12 1-litre bottles of gin.

10. a. Compute the deviation from potential sales, as described in the text, given the following information for a recent test period:

   Actual sales for period = $12,000

   Potential sales based on straight shots = $12,500

   b. What should actual sales be if the potential sales based on straight shots in Question 10 a. were $9,000?

11. Refer to the figures provided in Question 1. Using this information, calculate inventory turnover for each of the three bars. Be sure to take both bar and storeroom inventories into account when determining average inventory.

12. According to this chapter, three general approaches can be used in monitoring beverage operations. List the three and discuss each briefly.

13. Most bar managers are interested in their monthly cost percents. Why? For what purpose are the figures used?

14. Why is it necessary to take bar inventory differential into account when calculating the cost of beverages sold?

15. The beverage manager of the Smart Hotel uses a single beverage cost percent for the entire month to monitor beverage operations. What are the disadvantages of relying exclusively on this figure as a means of monitoring operations?

16. Would you advise a bar manager who relied wholly on the monthly cost percent as a monitoring device to consider adopting a daily method? Why? What would be the advantages and disadvantages of the daily method, as compared with the monthly method?

17. As compared with the cost percent methods, would you consider the standard cost method more useful or less useful for monitoring operations? Why?

18. Compare and contrast the advantages of the average sales value method with those of the simplified method described in the chapter for measuring the effectiveness of beverage controls.
19. Define each of the key terms in this chapter.

EXCEL EXERCISES

Exercise 16.1

Complete the cumulative and daily cost-to-sales ratio chart for Barnaby's Hideaway, given the following information:

Date	Issued	Sales	Additions	Subtractions
11/1	$275	$1,018	$15	$23
11/2	$280	$1,115	$22	$30
11/3	$310	$1,192	$12	$21
11/4	$325	$1,230	$25	$10
11/5	$260	$ 950	$15	$12
11/6	$270	$ 980	$18	$25
11/7	$280	$ 995	$17	$13

Exercise 16.2

The manager at Barnaby's Hideaway has calculated the average sales value for the liquors shown on the companion website for this text in Exercise 16.2. Determine the total sales value for liquor consumed on the form from the period 11/1 to 11/7.

CHAPTER 17

Beverage Sales Control

• LEARNING OBJECTIVES •

After reading this chapter, you should be able to:

17.1 List and explain the three goals of beverage sales control.

17.2 Identify five reasons given by customers for patronizing establishments that serve drinks.

17.3 Describe two methods that can be used to maximize profits in beverage operations.

17.4 Identify and describe two important factors normally taken into account when establishing beverage sales prices.

17.5 List and describe 10 work practices considered unacceptable at bars because they inhibit the ability of bar managers to institute effective revenue control.

17.6 Describe the essential features of a precheque system.

INTRODUCTION

In previous chapters, we pointed out that establishing control over any phase of food and beverage operations requires that one have some understanding of management's objectives. Any controls established must be carefully designed to ensure that they facilitate reaching these objectives. A good beginning point then is to identify the objectives of beverage sales control.

THE OBJECTIVES OF BEVERAGE SALES CONTROL

LEARNING OBJECTIVE 17.1
List and explain the three goals of beverage sales control.

In the discussion of food sales control in Chapter 11, it was pointed out that many consider food sales control to have a single objective—revenue control—ensuring that each individual sale to a customer results in appropriate revenue to the establishment. In the earlier discussion, our position was that sales control is much more than a mere synonym for revenue control. Revenue control is clearly a critical objective of sales control, but it is not the only one. Sales control is a broad concept and has at least two other objectives. In this chapter, the discussion focuses on three objectives of **beverage sales control**

1. Optimizing the number of sales
2. Maximizing profit
3. Controlling revenue

Although these objectives may appear to be identical to those of food sales control, there are special considerations in bar operation—some legal, some ethical, and some moral—that lead to significant differences. For example, in food sales control, one of the means of maximizing profit is to increase sales to individual customers, to use any of several possible approaches to induce the average customer to purchase greater numbers of products. Bar operators who attempt to optimize the number of sales in this way will find their efforts restricted by various local, provincial or territorial, and federal laws and regulations affecting such considerations as customer age, hours of operation, drinking during pregnancy, and, perhaps most important, society's growing concern about those who drive while under the influence of alcohol. Other special concerns also create differences in the meanings of sales optimization and profit maximization in beverage sales control.

In most provinces and territories, licensees (or owners), managers, and employees are required to participate in alcohol-serving training sessions, such as Smart Serve in Ontario. These sessions provide practical rules for responsible sale and service of beverage alcohol, according to the laws of the province or territory. The owners, managers, and employees who are permitted to serve alcohol must possess this certificate and have it readily available to show to a government inspector during routine inspections.

Optimizing the Number of Beverage Sales

In beverage operations, **optimizing the number of sales** means engaging in activities that will increase the number of customers to the desired level, as defined by the individual operator. However, anyone seeking to increase beverage sales volume in this way must first understand why people patronize establishments that serve alcoholic beverages, including both restaurants and bars. At first glance, it may appear that people patronizing these establishments are usually motivated by a desire to consume alcoholic beverages. Although this is true for some customers, it is probably not the principal reason that people buy drinks in establishments serving the public. After all, alcoholic beverages can be obtained for home consumption in most communities, and drinking at home is considerably cheaper than drinking in a bar. It is necessary, then, to understand some of the many other possible reasons for a customer to decide to patronize beverage operations and restaurants that serve alcoholic beverages. These can include

LEARNING OBJECTIVE 17.2
Identify five reasons given by customers for patronizing establishments that serve drinks.

1. Socializing
2. Conducting business
3. Eating
4. Seeking entertainment
5. Killing time

Socializing

Perhaps the most significant factors motivating those who patronize beverage operations are social: meeting other people and engaging in conversation. There are endless numbers of examples: seeing colleagues after work, meeting neighbours after dinner, watching sporting events on a big-screen TV, and making new friends. The alcoholic beverages consumed are almost incidental; they are simply an accepted and expected element in the social setting. The incidental nature of the drinking may help explain the trend toward drinks with lower alcohol content, including wines, spritzers, wine coolers, and light beers.

Conducting Business

Considerable business is conducted in bars, cocktail lounges, and similar settings. For some people, discussing business in this type of setting is easier than it would be in a formal business office around a conference table. Many find that even the formal cocktail lounge in an elegant city centre hotel is more informal than a conventional office. The use of bars and lounges for business discussion is probably most common with sales personnel, who normally depend on establishing personal relationships with their clients. The bar setting can be an excellent one for the sales representative and the client to get to know one another.

In addition, one should not overlook the many people who frequent beverage establishments to conduct personal business. This type of business ranges from discussion of family problems and situations to myriad other important personal discussions among people.

Eating

Many customers patronize food and beverage establishments primarily to eat. They order alcoholic beverages as desirable enhancements to their meals. Beverage orders with restaurant meals include cocktails, mixed drinks, and aperitifs before meals; beer or wine to accompany meals; and such after-dinner drinks as brandy, ports, liqueurs, and dessert wines. The primary motivation for patronizing the establishment comes from the desire for food, and the food purchased can range from the hearty fare of pubs to the elegant cuisine of the finest restaurants and hotel dining rooms. The beverage purchases may even be incidental. For some customers, however, the availability of beverages may be an important factor in selecting one restaurant over another, and most successful restaurants would probably lose considerable business volume if they did not serve alcoholic beverages as accompaniments to lunch and dinner.

Seeking Entertainment

Many people go to bars, clubs, and other establishments offering alcoholic beverages for sale because they seek various forms of entertainment. Many of these people consume alcoholic beverages while enjoying the entertainment offered. In general, there are two types of establishments that offer entertainment: those deriving their primary revenue from beverage sales and providing entertainment to attract customers to buy the beverages, and those deriving their primary revenue from the entertainment and providing beverages to satisfy the expectations of customers. The former include nightclubs, discos, and piano bars—establishments that offer entertainment to increase the number of customers and thus increase beverage sales volume. The latter include sports facilities, gaming casinos, some theatres, and some concert halls—establishments that offer alcoholic beverages as a convenience, albeit a profitable one, to patrons.

Killing Time

There are many occasions when people waste time, either because they choose to or because they have no other useful option. It is common to hear of people doing this described as "killing time." Many of them are waiting: for boarding time at airports, for train arrivals at rail stations, for the appearance of a friend or business associate for lunch, for curtain time at a theatre, and so on. Time must be passed—some number of hours or minutes must somehow be consumed. For many people, a bar is a suitable place to wait while time passes. So many bars are conveniently located, offering shelter, a place to sit, a television set to watch, and something to do: drink. Bars and cocktail lounges at airports are examples of establishments that cater almost exclusively to those who must pass time while they wait for flights to arrive or depart.

Clearly, anyone who operates an establishment that serves beverages should understand the beverage market and the various subgroups within that market. These subgroups should be taken into account by anyone attempting to make plans to maximize sales by increasing the number of customers to the necessary level. Any customer may be included in one subgroup of the beverage market one day and another subgroup the next. An individual's reasons for patronizing a beverage establishment may change from day to day. For example, the person who patronizes a neighbourhood bar for social reasons one evening may be killing time in an airport bar the following afternoon and then going out to dinner in the evening to celebrate a special occasion.

Each of these subgroups is called a **market segment**. The owner or manager of a beverage operation must determine which market segment or segments he or she intends to attract, or target. Once the target segments have been identified, numerous decisions must be made as to brands and types of drinks, portion sizes, selling prices, entertainment, lighting, decor, ambience, dress codes, giveaways, advertising, promotions, hours and days of operation, extent of service, classifications of employees, and suitable uniforms, among others. The decisions made will have significant impact on whether the target market will be attracted to the establishment in sufficient numbers to achieve the desired level of sales. For example, the owner of a bar attempting to attract a late-afternoon clientele of office workers may decide to offer moderately priced, large drinks made with high-quality liquor, to maintain an informal atmosphere, to provide free hot and cold hors d'oeuvres, to advertise by means of handbills distributed throughout neighbouring office buildings, and to make a conscious effort to learn and use customers' names. You must check with the provincial or territorial alcohol governing agencies to determine the criteria for advertising, drink specials, happy hours, and food giveaways. Many provinces and territories do not allow this practice as it may entice customers to consume more alcohol. In contrast, the management of a fine hotel, targeting a different market segment for the late-afternoon cocktail hour, may prefer to offer expensive, high-quality drinks in a more elegant atmosphere, with formal service, and to provide such amenities as soft piano music and elegant hors d'oeuvres, and to restrict advertising to small, tasteful signs in the elevators and guest rooms.

It should be apparent that optimizing the number of sales is a complex process, requiring not only substantial time and effort, but also considerable experience in the beverage business and some reasonable knowledge of both marketing and the techniques of market research.

Maximizing Profits

In the chapter dealing with food sales control, one element of profit maximization was identified as increasing customer purchases. This approach is of very limited use to those interested in maximizing profits from beverage sales. It is important to understand the reasons for this difference.

LEARNING OBJECTIVE 17.3
Describe two methods that can be used to maximize profits in beverage operations.

Today, most people appear to reject the notion that the amount of alcohol an individual consumes is wholly his or her own affair. They point out that those who have consumed excessive amounts of alcohol frequently behave in ways that have adverse, sometimes lethal, effects on others. Drunk drivers are the most common examples. As a consequence, there is a growing tendency to hold both the consumer of alcohol and those responsible for serving that consumer accountable for any harm the drinker may do as a result of excessive drinking. Many jurisdictions have passed relevant laws, known as **dram shop laws**, that hold the serving establishment and the server financially liable for damages if any employee in the establishment has served an alcoholic drink to an intoxicated person who, in turn, causes harm to a third party. In some countries without dram shop laws, third parties can still recover damages under common-law liability. Because of changes in society's outlook and the passage of various laws, it is both advisable and necessary for beverage operators and their employees to restrict customers' purchases of alcoholic beverages, rather than attempt to increase them in the manner common with food sales. As previously mentioned, there are many educational programs available to managers on serving alcoholic beverages safely, and it is critical and sometimes mandatory that employees receive instruction on this topic. Beverage operators can, however, adopt various merchandising techniques to influence the customer to select a drink with a greater contribution margin rather than another.

In beverage operations, profit maximization is accomplished in two ways:

1. Establishing drink prices that will maximize gross profit
2. Influencing customers' selections

Establishing Drink Prices

LEARNING OBJECTIVE 17.4
Identify and describe two important factors normally taken into account when establishing beverage sales prices.

Unlike food sales prices, drink prices are not primarily determined by the costs of ingredients and labour. Beverage ingredient costs and labour costs per dollar sale can both be significantly lower than those for food, so they are not as important in establishing sales prices. This is not to say that labour costs can or should be wholly ignored; in fact, many operators tend to charge more for drinks that require more labour to produce. However, the ingredient and labour costs associated with a particular drink tend to be similar from one operation to another. Other considerations are of greater importance in establishing drink prices. These include overhead costs (e.g., occupancy, insurance, licences, and entertainment, to name a few) and significant market considerations.

Overhead costs for a beverage operation typically account for a large percentage of total costs. This is true regardless of differences in location, sales volume, and specific dollar costs. For example, rents for airport locations tend to be very high, inducing beverage operators to set higher sales prices for drinks than would otherwise be necessary. In contrast, neighbourhood bars in low-rent areas can charge considerably lower prices and still be profitable. Insurance premiums vary dramatically from one area to another, depending in part on the legal climate in the region. The passage of dram shop laws, for example, normally increases the cost of liability insurance for a bar owner. The costs associated with purchasing and maintaining licences are considerably different from one place to another.

Establishments that offer live entertainment must either charge drink prices that are high enough to cover these costs or cover the cost of entertainment in some other way, such as charging an admission fee. Market considerations must also be taken into account before setting sales prices for drinks. Chief among these is the clientele targeted. Many operators rely heavily on regular customers, those who patronize an establishment frequently, often because they live or work close by. Such customers tend to be concerned with the prices charged, and operators serving this kind of clientele are usually careful to charge prices their customers consider reasonable and to avoid price increases unless absolutely necessary. By these means, they attempt to maintain as large a base of regular customers as possible, thus maximizing profits. In contrast, other beverage operations cater to transient, rather than regular, customers. The transient customer may have no practical choice of establishments (at an airport, for instance), and the choice may be limited to paying the high price charged by the only bar available or not drinking. Some transient customers are travelling on expense accounts and may be unconcerned about the prices charged for drinks. In general, bar operators serving transient customers can charge high prices for their drinks.

Other market considerations that a beverage operator must take into account in establishing drink prices include average income in the area served, prices charged by the competition, special advantages offered by a specific location (such as the top floor of the city's tallest building), and even a manager's desire to maintain exclusivity through pricing, among others. For these and many other reasons, sales prices for drinks must be established by the individual operator after carefully weighing both the cost structure and the relevant market considerations for that specific establishment.

For example, Bistro Quatre caters to the population in the immediate area and depends on repeat business. The average income in the area is relatively high, and most people are well educated. However, management recognizes that its customers are concerned with paying high prices for their food and beverages, so it has prices that are somewhat moderate, yet high enough to be profitable. Additionally, management recognizes that its customers appreciate and demand quality food and beverages. Thus, the pouring brands used at the bar are mid- to high-priced name brands. The bar does not stock any inexpensive liquor and carries a supply of excellent liquors. See Figure 14.6 for the list of liquors used at Bistro Quatre.

No discussion of drink prices can be concluded without a consideration of pricing differences between call brands and pouring brands (well brands). Call brands, selected by the customer, are normally considered to be of higher quality. They are typically of higher cost. It is therefore logical that they are given higher sales prices. Pouring brands, selected by the bar operator for the customer who expresses no preference, are commonly of somewhat lower quality, less costly, and are therefore given lower sales prices. In general, the contribution margins of drinks made with pouring brands are likely to be lower than those of drinks made with call brands. Although it is to the operator's advantage for customers to request specific call brands, most customers do not.

Influencing Customer Selections

As with food products, contribution margins for beverage products vary greatly from one drink to another. For the bar operator, it is obviously desirable to sell more drinks with high contribution margins and fewer drinks with low contribution margins. If a customer is having difficulty deciding which of two drinks to order, it is clearly to the bar operator's advantage for the customer to select the one with the higher contribution margin. In fact, under these circumstances, a bar operator may want employees to help the customer decide in favour of the drink with the higher contribution margin. This is done in several ways:

1. Training servers to up-sell (to use suggestive selling)
2. Featuring and promoting specialty drinks
3. Preparing carefully designed beverage menus

Training Servers to Up-sell (Suggestive Selling). Unfortunately, servers in the beverage industry are seldom properly trained to up-sell. **Up-selling** means suggesting drinks that will bring a higher contribution margin. Customers who intend to order a beer with a relatively low contribution margin can frequently be persuaded to order a beer with a higher contribution margin. Customers who order the least expensive wine sometimes can be persuaded to order the higher-priced one. Customers who order a whisky can frequently be persuaded to order one with a higher price. All of this is done by suggesting that the higher contribution beverage is being featured, or is becoming very popular, or has better quality. Many innovative operators have introduced in-house up-selling contests for their serving staff. Contests may resemble filling a "bingo card" wherein sellers must complete the card by up-selling targeted high-contribution margin items and thus become eligible for incentives. Those with high up-sells may be rewarded with better schedules or prizes such as cash, concert tickets, gift certificates, or even trips.

Featuring and Promoting Specialty Drinks. Some bar operators attempt to maximize profits by featuring and promoting selected drinks, often specially created for the purpose. These drinks may be given enticing names, be served in unusual ways (e.g., in hollowed fruits or with exotic garnishes), or be made from unusual combinations of ingredients. These special drinks are normally sold for higher-than-average prices, and they normally have higher-than-average contribution margins. A few of the many hundreds of specialty drinks offered include names such as:

Absolut Trouble
Almond Cocktail

Bahama Mama
Banana Sunrise
Bermuda Bouquet
Bill's Tropical Depression
Cosmopolitan
Dragon Slayer
Firewall

Preparing Carefully Designed Menus. Another technique for influencing customer selections is to produce a carefully designed beverage menu that includes pictures (colour photographs or artists' drawings) of the drinks that management would prefer to sell, along with appropriate descriptive language, to entice customers. Customers' orders would not necessarily be restricted to the listed drinks, but the drink menu would include only those drinks management prefers to sell.

Understanding and using the many creative possibilities for influencing customer selections is a key element in maximizing profits that is too often ignored by some bar operators, but is used wisely and to full advantage by others.

Controlling Revenue

Revenue control consists of those activities established to ensure that each sale to a customer results in appropriate revenue to the operation. In beverage operations, the opportunities for revenue control are often somewhat limited. In general, effective control procedures in business are likely to depend on division of work among several employees. For example, larger restaurants may facilitate revenue control by employing cashiers to collect sales revenue, servers to write sales tickets (guest cheques), and cooks to prepare meals. But the possibilities for dividing work in this way do not exist in most bars. In many bars, one employee—the bartender—is responsible for virtually all of the work: taking orders from customers, filling those orders, recording the sales, and collecting cash or obtaining signatures on charge vouchers. This dependence on one individual tends to minimize the possibilities for instituting and maintaining control. In addition, it often sets the stage for the development of several control problems.

A common means for determining whether control problems exist in a particular establishment is to assess the work practices of the bartender. Most of the problems in the following list are considered unacceptable in most well-managed bars, because the owners or managers are aware of the kinds of control problems that are likely to develop under these work practices.

1. *Working with the cash drawer open.* This practice makes it possible for dishonest employees to make sales transactions without recording the sales in the register. This is a serious problem if the bartender is held responsible at the end of the shift for only those sales recorded on the register tape.

LEARNING OBJECTIVE 17.5
List and describe 10 work practices considered unacceptable at bars because they inhibit the ability of bar managers to institute effective revenue control.

2. *Under-ringing sales, either as "No Sale" or as an amount less than the actual sale.* Doing so enables an employee to steal the difference between the cash in the register drawer and the sales recorded on the tape.

3. *Overcharging customers, but ringing correct amounts in the register.* This, too, provides a dishonest employee with a source of cash equal to the difference between the amounts collected and those recorded in the register.

4. *Undercharging customers.* This may be done to accommodate a bartender's personal friends or to increase tips. It may be done in various ways, such as by using call brands but charging for pouring brands, or by overpouring.

5. *Overpouring.* Giving customers more than they pay for, often through failure to measure, typically results in unfavourable cost-to-sales ratios and in reduced profits from operation.

6. *Underpouring.* This technique is sometimes adopted by bartenders who selectively overpour. If they overpour for some customers (e.g., those who tip well), they may be able to avoid being detected by underpouring for others. One may offset the other. Moreover, the bartender who keeps track of the extent of underpouring may later use the reserved amounts to prepare drinks. These drinks may then be given to friends or sold to customers, with the sales revenue going to the bartender rather than to the bar.

7. *Diluting bottle contents.* This practice involves pouring out some of a bottle's contents to reserve for later use and replacing it with an equal amount of water. The liquor poured out and reserved is typically used later to make drinks that are sold to customers. However, the revenue for those drinks goes directly into the bartender's pocket rather than to bar revenue.

8. *Bringing one's own bottle into the bar.* This practice enables a bartender to become a silent partner in the bar operation. The bartender can prepare drinks using his or her own liquor and take the sales revenue without his or her performance being detected through changes in the figures used to monitor bar operations.

9. *Charging for drinks not served.* By charging a customer or a group of customers for drinks that were never served, a bartender can then serve equivalent drinks to other customers and steal the sales revenue.

10. *Drinking on the job.* In addition to the unprofessional appearance and cost this practice is likely to cause, an employee who is drinking is more likely to make mistakes in pouring, mixing, and recording sales than one who does not drink on the job.

To reduce the number of control problems, management must establish standards and standard procedures for bar operation. Effective revenue control requires that employees adhere strictly to these standards and standard procedures and that the performance of bartenders be monitored by management.

GUEST CHEQUES AND CONTROL

Some bars use guest cheques; others do not. It is important to understand the fundamental differences between these two approaches because of the impact they have on management's ability to establish effective control over sales revenue.

Bars without Guest Cheques

Many bars, especially small, owner-operated neighbourhood bars, do not use guest cheques. Customers pay cash. The bartender is often the owner, who collects all cash personally. This owner-bartender does not perceive any revenue control problem and sees no need for guest cheques. Some owner-bartenders require each customer to pay for each drink as it is served; others serve customers more than one drink without requiring payment and somehow remember what each customer has consumed. Cash is collected after each customer has finished his or her last drink. This system offers the advantage of simplicity, saves time that would be required to prepare guest cheques, and is clearly less expensive than alternatives. It works well enough as long as the owner is also the bartender.

If the owner does not tend the bar and collect the cash personally, someone else must be hired to work behind the bar. This individual must do the work that the owner would otherwise do, including making the drinks and collecting the cash. But the hired bartender may be guilty of some or all of the unacceptable work practices identified earlier. If so, sales revenue will be recorded incorrectly or not at all. To reduce the number of errors, accidental or intentional, the owner will be likely to spend some amount of time at the bar observing the bartender. Someone other than the owner (sometimes referred to as a "mystery shopper") can also be stationed at the bar to monitor the bartender, with or without the bartender's knowledge. This approach, with some variations, works well in many establishments. However, if no one is available to monitor the bartender, another operating procedure must be found.

Bars Using Guest Cheques

When visual monitoring methods are impossible or impractical, some degree of control is made possible by the use of numbered guest cheques. A standard procedure is established that requires all drink orders to be recorded on numbered cheques. If all employees follow the procedure, records of all sales are available for daily audit. In its simplest form, such an audit consists of verifying that no numbered cheques are missing, that correct prices have been charged for all drinks, and that total sales recorded on the cheques equal the total of cash and charge revenues recorded in a register or a sales terminal. With sales records available, it becomes possible for an owner or manager to monitor revenue by conducting a simple audit of the type described earlier.

The system has essentially two disadvantages: (1) recording orders on guest cheques takes time and tends to make customer service slower than would otherwise be the case, and (2) the standard procedures must be followed if the revenue control system is to be effective. However, if no one is available to monitor bartenders, it is conceivable that they will purposely fail to follow those procedures, especially those who demonstrate some or all of the poor work practices described earlier. Guest cheques are used in a variety of ways. Three of the most common are

1. Precheque systems
2. Automated systems
3. Other types of computer systems

Precheque Systems

LEARNING OBJECTIVE 17.6
Describe the essential features of a precheque system.

A **precheque system** incorporates at least one register that enables bartenders to record sales as drinks are served and to accumulate the sales to any one customer on one cheque. The use of such registers makes it feasible to require that a guest cheque be placed in front of each customer at the bar. When the customer is ready to leave, the cheque is inserted into the register or terminal, and the total sales to the customer are recorded as cash or charge, depending on how the customer settles the cheque. At the end of the day's operation, the total drink sales recorded in the terminal, plus taxes, should equal the total of cash and charge sales. Readings taken from the terminal at the end of a day would be similar to those illustrated in Figure 17.1.

• FIGURE 17.1 •		
Cash Register/Point-of-Sale Reconciliation		
Register 1		*12-Jun*
Liquor	$456.50	
Beer	$235.60	
Wine	$335.00	
Tax	$ 82.17	
Tip	$ 65.00	
Total		$1,174.27
Cash	$578.50	
Charge	$575.02	
Void	$ 20.75	
Total		$1,174.27

A void key is used to record such instances as drinks that were rejected by customers, made with errors, or unprepared because customers walked out. The void key must be closely monitored by management to ensure bartenders are not voiding items and keeping the cash. Most point-of-sale systems generate a void report that can be reconciled by management. An accountant or bookkeeper reduces the beverage sales figures by the total of the voids before making entries in the accounting records for the day's sales.

Automated Systems

Another approach to controlling revenue, used particularly when close supervision by a manager is either impossible or impractical, is to install an automated bar. An **automated bar** is both an electronic sales terminal and a computerized dispensing device for beverages. The dispensing device is controlled by the sales terminal. In some systems, bottles are inverted, with flexible tubing connecting the bottles to the dispensing device. The automated bar apparatus may be in full view of the customers or in some nearby location, out of sight. In either case, the bartender cannot pour directly from the bottles; their contents may be dispensed only by depressing keys on a sales terminal.

As mentioned in Chapter 16, Liquor Control Solutions' Cocktail Tower is a good example of an automated dispenser. When a customer orders a drink, the bartender places the proper glassware under the dispensing device, inserts a guest cheque in the terminal or in a separate printer controlled by the terminal, and depresses the terminal key with the name of the drink on it. When the key is depressed, the name of the drink and its pre-assigned sales price are printed on the cheque. Simultaneously, the terminal signals the release of the proper quantities of the correct ingredients, which are automatically dispensed. Both the drink and the cheque are given to the customer or to a server who delivers them to the customer, depending on the type of bar.

At the end of each day, management obtains a report showing the number of each type of drink sold and the total dollar sales recorded in the terminal, as well as other information. A type of perpetual inventory is maintained for beverages connected to the system, and the number of ounces in the inventory is reduced appropriately with each drink order recorded.

In other automated systems, a control sprout is attached to each bottle. A drink cannot be prepared until the control sprout is attached to an activator ring, which is part of the sales terminal. The sales terminal records each sale as the drink is prepared. Automated systems are available in a variety of sizes and configurations. Some hold a comparatively small number of bottles and can prepare only a limited number of drinks. Others can accommodate many bottles and produce hundreds of different drinks.

There are some significant advantages to automated systems over traditional methods of preparing drinks: (1) the proportions of ingredients are exactly the same each time a given drink is prepared, and thus the drinks are of uniform quality, prepared according to the standard recipes programmed; and

(2) the quantity of each ingredient is measured exactly, and thus the sizes of all drinks of any given type are uniform. In general, automated systems help reduce the possibilities for the development of excessive costs through pilferage, spillage, charging incorrect prices, and various bartender errors.

However, there are also some important disadvantages to these systems. Some cannot accommodate customers' requests for drinks made according to recipes other than the standard recipes programmed. For this reason, they are more commonly used at service bars than at front bars. At front bars, many customers have negative reactions to automated dispensers. They are accustomed to watching the bartender go through the ritual of drink mixing—many bartenders are accomplished artists who enjoy displaying their skills. For these customers, having drinks prepared by a machine takes something away from the experience. In addition, traditional methods of drink preparation often give customers the impression that the bartender is giving them more than the standard measure—a dividend, so to speak. This may or may not be true, depending on the bar and the bartender, but the customer who believes that it is true may not react well to machine-prepared drinks. This customer is likely to think that the measure is miserly.

Although no system guarantees that all sales will result in appropriate revenue for the establishment, any sensible system designed to take into account the realities and needs of a particular operation will provide some desirable measure of control.

Other Types of Computer Systems

Many computer systems allow the bartender to pour drinks in the usual way—free pour, shot glass, or measuring device—but help maintain revenue control. One good example is the AccuBar system used at Bistro Quatre. Bartenders measure the amount of liquor going into a drink using a jigger. Drinks served by dining room servers are automatically recorded when servers input drink orders into their terminals in the dining room. Drink orders are printed at the bar using the remote printer located there. Sales at the bar to customers waiting to be seated are recorded in the register at the bar. At the end of the day's business or the following morning, management uses the hand scanner to take inventory at the bar. This information, along with a recorded inventory of the storeroom, is sent to AccuBar. A report showing sales and usage of liquor is returned. Sales can be compared with usage, and management can determine that appropriate revenue was recorded. The AccuBar system is one of many systems that are not fully automated, but enable revenue control to be established.

THINGS TO CONSIDER

It is essential that operators are aware of government regulations and liabilities associated with serving beverage alcohol. The untrained server, bartender, or manager may not recognize the symptoms of an intoxicated patron or for that matter may feel it is acceptable to serve an already intoxicated person. Through the legal concept of "vicarious liability," owners, servers, and managers have been held financially responsible to victims of drunk drivers and, in some cases, have lost their businesses as a result. Establishments can also lose their liquor licences. In one example in Ontario, a man was charged with impaired driving causing death after three teenagers were struck and killed while walking on a road outside a small community. The man allegedly had been drinking at a local bar. Soon after the tragedy, the Alcohol and Gaming Commission of Ontario issued an interim liquor licence suspension for the bar while it investigated the incident

The defence "but we only served them a few drinks" does not hold up in court. In today's society, it is no longer acceptable to allow "regulars" to over-consume and drive their vehicle, even if you think they are fine. You will be held accountable.

CHAPTER ESSENTIALS

In this chapter, we defined the scope of beverage sales control and explained essential differences between food sales control and beverage sales control. We identified the three goals of beverage sales control as optimizing the number of sales, maximizing profit, and controlling revenue. We pointed out various special considerations in beverage operations that lead to significant differences in the interpretation of these goals. We identified the principal reasons that customers patronize establishments that offer alcoholic beverages for sale. We discussed some of the market segments that beverage operators attempt to target, and suggested some specific steps that management can take to reach these target markets. We identified the two means considered appropriate to maximizing beverage profits: setting suitable drink prices and influencing customer selection of drinks. We listed several poor work practices that bartenders and other bar employees may exhibit and explained how these limit management's ability to institute revenue controls. We identified three basic operating patterns for beverage revenue control and described variations on them, including a common automated system for beverage operations.

KEY TERMS IN THIS CHAPTER

Automated bar, p. 455

Optimizing the number of sales, p. 445

Beverage sales control, p. 444

Precheque system, p. 454

Dram shop laws, p. 448

Revenue control, p. 451

Market segment, p. 447

Up-selling, p. 450

QUESTIONS AND PROBLEMS

1. What are the three goals of beverage sales control?
2. Why is selling the maximum number of drinks to each customer an inappropriate goal for a bar operator?
3. List and explain five possible reasons for a customer to patronize an establishment that offers alcoholic beverages for sale.
4. Identify two ways in which profit can be maximized in a beverage operation.
5. How do dram shop laws typically affect bar operation?
6. What are the principal factors considered by managers when establishing beverage sales prices?
7. Select a beverage operation in your area, list the primary target market it attempts to reach, and describe features of the operation that attract that market. If possible, identify specific steps that management has taken to increase the appeal of the operation for that market.
8. Select a beverage operation in your area and list the market considerations that have been taken into account by management in establishing sales prices for drinks.
9. Two months ago, Fred Sneed became the owner of a small bar in Centreville. When he assumed ownership, beverage cost percent was 24.5 percent. Since Fred assumed ownership, beverage cost percent has increased to 29.5 percent, although there have been no increases in purchase prices and the sales mix has not changed. The bartender has been employed in the establishment for the last eight years. Fred has concluded that the increase in beverage cost percent is somehow related to the bartender and has decided to observe his performance closely. Given the list of poor work practices identified in this chapter, rank in order of importance the five that he should watch for as he observes the bartender at work.

10. If the owner of a bar does not mandate the use of guest cheques, how can he or she establish some degree of control over revenue?

11. What are the essential features of a precheque system?

12. List the possible advantages and disadvantages of automated bars compared with traditional methods for pouring and mixing drinks.

13. What are the advantages of a computerized beverage sales control system compared with a manual system using guest cheques?

14. Define each of the key terms in this chapter.

EXCEL EXERCISE

Exercise 17.1

Follow the instructions on the companion website for this text to complete this exercise.

PART IV

LABOUR CONTROL

Most customers of restaurants and other foodservice operations have at one time or another witnessed situations that suggest a need for labour control. Sometimes it seems nearly impossible to get any service; the few servers in sight clearly have more customers to serve than they can possibly handle, and even when a customer has managed to place an order, it seems like an eternity before the food is served. At other times, there appear to be more servers on duty than there are customers in the dining room, and one wonders how the management can afford to have so much help around when there is no business to support it.

In the first example, one can readily imagine the number of customers who walk out in disgust without ordering at all, as well as those who silently resolve never to return after waiting 15 minutes or more to order and another 45 minutes to be served. Customers who are not satisfied with the service at an establishment will most likely comment to friends, family, and colleagues. This snowball effect will have a serious impact on the operation, as the bad news may continue to spread. An adage states that one disgruntled customer will inform 10 friends, who in turn will tell 10 other friends. When service is slow and otherwise lacking, the total sales for the day are undoubtedly less than they might have been if adequate service had been provided; total sales for future days may also be affected because of customers who have decided to take their business elsewhere.

In the restaurant where more staff members are on duty than are warranted by current business, the wages paid to unnecessary staff increase payroll costs. At the very least, this will lead to owner dissatisfaction, and probably to dissatisfaction among those employees whose incomes depend largely on the tips they receive from customers. Achieving proper ratios of employees to sales volume will be discussed at greater length in Chapter 19.

In either case, one certain effect will be the reduction of net profit from current operations, caused by lower sales in the first instance and by increased costs in the second. Clearly, there is a need to manage staffing levels and control payroll costs to maximize sales while minimizing costs.

Labour control is an attempt to obtain maximum efficiency from staff without compromising standards of operating performance. By that we mean labour control attempts to have the right number of staff with appropriate skills on duty for the number of customers in attendance at any given time. As discussed in the following chapters, labour control is most difficult to achieve because of the relative unpredictability of the number of customers in a restaurant at any given time, among other factors.

CHAPTER 18

Labour Cost Considerations

• **LEARNING OBJECTIVES** •

After reading this chapter, you should be able to:

18.1 Define *compensation* and list the principal types of compensation common in food and beverage operations.

18.2 Explain the difference between direct and indirect compensation.

18.3 Explain why each of the following is a determinant of labour cost or labour cost percentage: labour turnover rate, training, labour legislation, labour contracts, use of part-time staff, outsourcing, sales volume, location, equipment, layout, preparation, service, menu, hours of operation, weather, and competent management.

18.4 Explain why labour costs and labour cost percentages vary from one establishment to another.

18.5 Define *labour cost control* and explain its purpose.

INTRODUCTION

In hotels, restaurants, and all other related food and beverage establishments, the cost of labour accounts for considerable amounts of money, as labour is a major prime cost. Taken as a percentage of total sales, labour cost varies widely from one foodservice establishment to another. It generally ranges from 15 percent to 45 percent. At Bistro Quatre, labour cost is 25 percent of total sales when employee benefits are included in the total cost. This relatively low cost is one important reason why the restaurant is able to be profitable. In some isolated instances, labour cost percents are as high as 60 percent, although this tends to be true only in establishments operated on a not-for-profit basis. Because labour cost is such a major consideration in the typical food and beverage enterprise, an ability to deal with it effectively is an important requirement for food and beverage managers.

The objective of this and subsequent chapters is to provide an introduction to the elements of labour cost and some of the procedures and techniques for controlling labour cost in food and beverage establishments. However, any discussion of labour cost control must be preceded by a basic introduction to the following:

1. Employee compensation
2. The determinants of total labour costs and labour cost percents

EMPLOYEE COMPENSATION

LEARNING OBJECTIVE 18.1
Define *compensation* and list the principal types of compensation common in food and beverage operations.

Because labour cost, or employee compensation, consumes such a major share of sales dollars in food and beverage operations, it is important to understand the various components of labour cost before proceeding to the discussion of labour cost control.

The term **compensation** is used to refer to all forms of pay and other rewards going to employees as a result of their employment. In the hospitality industry, as in many industries, employees receive two forms of current compensation: direct and indirect. In addition, many receive deferred compensation.

Current Compensation

Direct Compensation

LEARNING OBJECTIVE 18.2
Explain the difference between direct and indirect compensation.

Direct compensation is directly related to that person's job. It is base pay plus overtime, if applicable, or incentive pay that an employee receives, and includes salaries, wages, tips, bonuses, and commissions. Traditionally, the term **salary** is used to refer to a fixed dollar amount of compensation paid on a weekly, monthly, or annual basis, regardless of the actual number of hours worked. **Wages**, in contrast, always take the actual number of hours worked into account. Wages for a given employee are calculated by multiplying the employee's hourly rate by the number of hours worked, up to the number of hours at which overtime rates apply. At that point, the hourly rate increases; however, the same procedure is followed to calculate overtime wages.

Tips, also known as **gratuities**, although not paid from an employer's revenues, are also compensation in the eyes of the Canada Revenue Agency. Tips must be claimed when employees file their annual government income tax returns. It is the employee's duty to accurately provide this information to the government. Many workers in the hospitality industry earn more from tips than from wages.

Bonus is a term that refers to a dollar amount exceeding an employee's regular wages or salary, given as a reward for some type of job performance, or to show appreciation for service to the business, such as at holiday time. **Commissions**, by contrast, are dollar amounts calculated as percentages of sales. Banquet managers commonly earn commissions on their sales. So do many convention and event planners and catering sales staff.

Indirect Compensation

Indirect compensation is a benefit to a current employee other than direct compensation. It is a contract between employee and employer, and is typically designed to attract and keep loyal employees. It includes everything from legally required programs to those that the employer decides to provide. It may include paid vacations, health benefits, life insurance, free meals, free living accommodations, use of recreational facilities operated by the employer, discounts on accommodations at other properties within a chain, and many other possibilities, including the use of a company vehicle, reimbursement for outside classes, child care while the employee is at work, counselling of various kinds, sick leave pay, and funeral leave. In some instances, such as health benefits, indirect compensation may be partially paid for by the employee. The part that the employer pays for is considered indirect compensation.

Paid vacation is among the most common forms of indirect compensation available to employees in the hospitality industry today. It should be noted that in Canada, paid vacations are required by law. Paid vacations are typically linked to length of service with the employer. In many instances, employees are awarded a basic vacation period with pay amounting to two weeks per year, or a period pro-rated based on time of service if less than a year. This would equate to roughly 4 percent of an employee's current annual earnings. Those whose length of service reaches some predetermined number of years (e.g., five in Alberta, British Columbia, and Ontario) are given an additional week with pay, so that they are able to take three weeks off with pay each year. This would be roughly 6 percent of annual earnings. Vacation pay may be paid in each pay period or accrued until the employee chooses to take a vacation, depending on the establishment's policies. You must check the employment standards for the rules that apply in your province or territory.

Health benefits, including extended medical, dental, and optical insurance, are among the most sought-after forms of indirect compensation. They are also among the most costly. Health benefits are commonly in the form of an insurance plan, some or all of the costs of which are paid by the employer, who also assumes the entire cost of administering the health insurance plan, hiring personnel in the human resources office to process forms, maintain records, and generally attend to the myriad details associated with any such plan. Payroll companies may administer this function for an operation at an added charge.

Life insurance coverage, another popular form of indirect compensation, provides protection for the families of covered employees, thus saving these employees the considerable costs that can be associated with life insurance coverage.

Many establishments provide meals to employees during their working hours. Thus, foodservice employees assigned to work from 7:00 a.m. to 3:00 p.m. may be permitted to have breakfast and lunch on premises. In hotels and other large properties where this is permitted, special facilities may be set up to be used by employees. In some cases, one or more members of the kitchen staff may be assigned exclusively to the preparation of employees' meals. Including meals or a reduction in the price of meals in a compensation package is generally very popular with employees, who gain substantially from this very tangible benefit.

Increasingly, employers are offering counselling of various forms, including alcohol and drug counselling or counselling for various family problems such as divorce, death in the family, and so on. The use of employee assistance programs (EAPs) is becoming common in large hotel and restaurant chains. In some regions, providing EAPs becomes an employer responsibility, particularly when alcohol is involved. Before an employer terminates employees with addictions, it has a certain obligation to offer to help employees with their issues.

In some lodging properties, part of the employees' compensation package may include living accommodations. This is particularly true in resort hotels, but not uncommon in some large transient hotels. In the former, living accommodations may be available to all employees; in the latter, accommodations are likely to be limited to some of the managerial staff who are expected to be on call 24 hours a day.

Many resort properties include in their employees' compensation packages the right to use various recreational facilities during the hours they are off duty. Thus, employees at ski resorts may have access to the slopes, those at beach resorts may be able to use special beaches and such equipment as water skis and sailboats during their off hours, employees at hotels with swimming pools and/or exercise facilities might be granted use of these facilities during off-peak hours, and workers at golf and tennis resorts may be able to use those facilities during certain times of the day.

Many hotel and motel chain organizations offer their employees special discounted rates on accommodations. Those who choose to travel during their vacation periods find this an extremely useful and valuable form of indirect compensation. Some forms of indirect compensation may be considered taxable benefits and will be taxed by the federal, provincial, or territorial governments. For instance, if a cook eats for free and the weekly value of the meals is $50.00, the employee would be taxed on that amount. It is important to research tax law through a reputable accountant to prevent any prosecution for the incorrect handling of taxes and payments.

Deferred Compensation

Deferred compensation is defined as compensation received by an employee after the conclusion of his or her period of employment, most commonly known as retirement. The most important form of deferred compensation is company pension plan benefits. More and more hospitality organizations are introducing company pension plans to entice potential employees during the recruitment process.

It is obviously important for the owners and managers of food and beverage operations to have broad and comprehensive knowledge of the various forms of compensation found in the industry, all of which have some impact, direct or indirect, on the overall cost of labour in an establishment.

DETERMINANTS OF TOTAL LABOUR COSTS AND LABOUR COST PERCENTS

The cost of labour is affected by several important considerations. Some of these are within the scope of a manager's control but others are not. Each plays a role in determining total cost of labour and labour cost percent in food or beverage operations. Each can therefore be described as a determinant of labour cost or labour cost percent. Direct employee costs, indirect costs, and deferred costs are considered part of the total labour costs.

The determinants discussed in the following sections all have a direct effect on the total cost of labour or on the cost of labour expressed as a percentage of total sales. Some affect both. The significance of each varies from one establishment to another. Although the following discussion treats each determinant briefly and individually, one must keep in mind that these determinants are so interdependent that managers do not normally have the luxury of dealing with them one at a time in this fashion.

LEARNING OBJECTIVE 18.3
Explain why each of the following is a determinant of labour cost or labour cost percentage: labour turnover rate, training, labour legislation, labour contracts, use of part-time staff, outsourcing, sales volume, location, equipment, layout, preparation, service, menu, hours of operation, weather, and competent management.

Labour Turnover Rate

The **labour turnover rate** is a ratio relating the number of departing employees to the total number of employees on the staff. It is usually expressed as a percentage in a given period of time, usually a year. The labour turnover rate has traditionally been very high in the foodservice industry. It has been commonly measured at 90 to 100 percent per year across the industry, with some establishments having rates as high as 300 percent, meaning essentially that the staff changed three times in one year! This does not compare favourably with turnover rates in Canadian industry in general, which tend to range between 10 and 30 percent.

When jobs become vacant and managers decide that those jobs must be filled, an individual manager must be assigned responsibility for recruiting, interviewing, selecting, and hiring replacement personnel. Large organizations often have dedicated human resource personnel to attend to much of this work, but small restaurants do not. Instead, the work must be done by restaurant managers, possibly with help from assistant managers, chefs, stewards, dining room managers, and others. It can be time-consuming and expensive work, depending, in part, on the level of skill and experience required of the new employee. If a manager is engaged in recruiting and hiring, he or she must defer some other tasks. If personnel work consumes a great portion of the manager's time, it may become necessary to hire an assistant for the manager. If turnover is so great that it becomes necessary to hire a human resource manager to fill vacancies, the additional cost is obvious.

High labour turnover rates generally result in higher labour costs, which of course will affect net income profits. It has been estimated by some authorities that the cost of replacing a hospitality employee may be as high as $2,500 to $10,000 (depending on level of experience), to pay for advertising, interviewing, checking backgrounds and references, training, and so on. Using this figure, it is easy to calculate that the potential expense to a restaurant with 50 employees and a turnover rate of 100 percent can be as high as $125,000 to $500,000 per year. This number seems very high; however, it is not uncommon in the hospitality industry.

Training

The need for some degree of training exists in all foodservice establishments. Training is one of the most integral components of running such a business. The amount of quality training that takes place in an establishment cannot be overemphasized. Managers, after all, are not typically able to find employees with complete and accurate knowledge of the jobs for which they are hired. All jobs require some level of training. At the most elementary level, training may entail merely showing a new dishwasher the location of the dish machine and explaining the operation of the controls. With an experienced cook, training may involve a meeting to familiarize the cook with the nature of the menu or the preferences of the restaurant's clientele. On another level, training may include pre-shift daily meetings and morning meetings or "huddles" with servers to make sure that each understands the menu fully and is aware of which items it is most beneficial to sell. Then again, training may mean taking completely inexperienced people and teaching them everything they need to know to perform particular jobs. This may be done on premises or in facilities provided by such outside agencies as unions, public schools, community colleges, or proprietary schools.

Training can be a key factor in reducing the labour turnover rate in a restaurant. Over the years, many studies have shown some relationship between the extent of training and the turnover rate. Generally, restaurants with training programs that are both extensive and effective tend to have employees who report greater job satisfaction than those in restaurants where training is ignored. In restaurants with good training programs, customers often report that they receive better service and that staff members appear to be friendlier and more attentive. Where this is the case, the working environment is more pleasant, and this makes for lower turnover rates.

Detailed discussion of training is found in Chapter 20. For purposes of this chapter, it is sufficient to state that the extent of training carried on in any particular establishment is an important determinant of the overall cost of labour.

Labour Legislation

Labour legislation differs considerably from province to province, and thus the net effect of legislation on labour cost for any particular food operation must be discussed in terms of the legislation in effect in the particular province or territory where the operation is located. However, it is possible to generalize a discussion of a significant area covered by legislation in all provinces and territories: minimum wages and provisions for overtime.

A **minimum wage** is the lowest dollar wage before deductions that an employer is permitted to pay each employee in a covered category. It is usually expressed as an amount per hour. Minimum wage legislation normally defines a maximum permissible number of hours per day for work at that hourly wage; beyond that number of hours, an overtime rate may be paid. In addition, a maximum number of consecutive working days per week is specified, and the overtime rate must be applied beyond that maximum. Legislation differs from province to province and contacting any designated provincial or territorial agency will provide regulations regarding wages and overtime for hospitality workers. Tips or gratuities are not considered wages and will not be considered in determining whether an employee is receiving at least minimum wage.

In Canada, minimum wages are established by the provinces and territories. Minimum wages for hospitality workers may be different than for someone who works in other industries, such as a factory. Again, checking with your provincial and territorial agencies will clearly define what the proper minimum wage will be for your operation. As an example, the minimum wages set by the Province of Ontario rose on March 31, 2009, to $9.50 per hour for general minimum wage (this rate applies to most employees) and $8.90 per hour for student minimum wage (this rate applies to students under the age of 18 who work 28 hours a week or less when school is in session or work during a school break or summer holidays). For those serving liquor, the Ontario minimum wage became $8.25 per hour. This hourly rate applies to employees who serve liquor directly to customers or guests in licensed premises as a regular part of their work. "Licensed premises" are businesses for which a licence or permit has been issued under the *Liquor Licence Act*. In essence, the hourly wage paid to back-of-the-house employees (those working in the kitchen and other places away from customers) is traditionally higher than front-of-the-house employees (those working with customers) as the latter usually receive tips.

Provincial legislation sets a maximum number of hours and times of the day that minors can be employed. These vary according to province as to whether work is done during a school day, weekend, or summertime. For example, in Alberta, an employer can hire an "adolescent" (defined as a person between 12 and 14 years old) to work two hours on a school day or eight hours on a non-school day, only between the hours of 6 a.m. and 9 p.m. A parent or guardian must provide written consent to the employer. A permit is required from the Director of Employment Standards. In Nunavut and Northwest Territories, those under 19 years old cannot work where liquor is sold or kept for sale. In Ontario, an 18-year-old may serve liquor; however, they may not consume it until they are 19. Normally the hospitality industry in Canada does not hire employees under the age of 14. Many restaurant companies use the age of 16 as an entry-level age. As noted earlier, checking the legislation in your province or territory is essential. Ages of employees will also be determined by the type of establishment. For example, quick-service restaurants tend to hire younger employees than fine dining establishments.

The industry employs large numbers of minors. Foodservice establishments must be very careful that they follow the laws with regard to hours and time of work for minors. Many restaurants have been fined large sums for allowing minors to work at illegal times and/or more hours than permitted by law.

As a labour-intensive industry, the foodservice industry has traditionally employed a large number of unskilled individuals, many of whom have been paid the prevailing minimum wage. Thus, as provincial legislatures have steadily increased minimum wages, labour cost in the restaurant industry has been significantly affected.

Federal and provincial legislation also mandates other costs that affect total labour cost. These include premiums for the Canada Pension Plan, workers' compensation, and Employment Insurance. Federal requirements are uniform, whereas provincial requirements vary. Review the employment standards acts that pertain to your particular region.

Labour Contracts

The presence or absence of labour contracts will always be an important factor affecting labour cost. Where employees are organized (i.e., members of unions) and labour contracts exist, wages for each category of employee are likely to be higher than they would be in the absence of a union. In addition, such fringe benefits as extra vacation pay, sick pay, employees' meals, and extended health insurance are more likely to be found where union organizations and contracts exist.

Although the effects of wages and fringe benefits on labour cost are apparent in situations where labour contracts exist, other factors also have a significant effect. Of primary concern are provisions in labour contracts that limit management's freedom to change work rules. Such contracts typically restrict management's ability to arbitrarily alter the duties of an employee in a particular job category. One effect of this may be to force the employer to hire someone for a job even when existing employees may have the time and ability to do the job. This would obviously increase total labour cost.

Use of Part-Time Staff

The use of part-time staff in place of full-time staff can have a significant impact on labour cost. The extent of the impact depends, obviously, on the difference between the full-time wage and the part-time wage for specific types of work and on the extent to which part-time help is used. One example will be sufficient to illustrate the point. Suppose the Circle Diner has seven full-time cooks, each of whom works 35 hours a week (five, seven-hour shifts each week). The prevailing wage in the area for full-time cooks is $15.00 per hour, plus the cost of a package of employee benefits amounting to an additional 20 percent. The labour cost for these seven full-time cooks is calculated as follows:

$$\text{Wages: 7 cooks} \times \text{35 hours} \times \text{\$15 per hour} = \$3{,}675$$
$$\text{Benefits: \$3,675 x 20\%} = \underline{\$\ \ 735}$$
$$\text{Total labour cost} = \$4{,}410$$

Now suppose the manager decides to cover some of the shifts by hiring part-time cooks with adequate skill at $10.00 per hour, plus the cost of a smaller package of employee benefits—an additional 10 percent. If it is possible to keep four full-time cooks, and to hire part-time cooks to cover the remaining 15 shifts, the new labour cost will be calculated as follows:

Full-time cooks
Wages: 4 cooks $\times$ 35 hours $\times$ $15 per hour = $2,100
Benefits: $2,100 $\times$ 20% =   420

Part-time cooks
Wages: 15 shifts $\times$ 7 hours $\times$ $10 per hour = $1,050
Benefits: $1,050 $\times$ 10% = $\underline{\$\ \ 105}$
New total labour cost = $\overline{\$3{,}675}$

Thus, it would be possible for the manager of the Circle Diner to reduce labour cost from $4,410 to $3,675 (16.7 percent) by reducing the number of full-time cooks from seven to four and hiring part-time cooks at lower hourly wages to cover the 105 hours previously covered by full-time cooks. If, in the manager's judgement, part-time cooks are able to produce work equal to that of full-time cooks, there are likely to be some staffing changes in the Circle Diner. In the foodservice industry today, many managers are hiring growing numbers of part-time employees to keep labour costs lower than they would be if all work were done by full-time personnel. Thus, the use of part-time staff is another determinant of labour cost.

Outsourcing

Outsourcing is arranging to have work done on a contract basis by outside organizations rather than by full-time employees. It can also affect labour cost. Some establishments, for example, no longer rely on full-time employees to clean the premises at night, after the close of business. Instead, the owners and managers have engaged firms that contract to perform night cleaning services for a fixed amount per month. Similarly, many foodservice organizations now use contract services to calculate payrolls and prepare paycheques, rather than have the work done by their own employees. Others no longer employ skilled kitchen personnel to prepare such items as baked goods, desserts, and ice carvings. Still others are purchasing frozen, portioned main dishes, rather than hiring high-cost chefs. Many are finding it less costly to rely on outside contractors for various goods and services that were commonly provided by in-house personnel in years past. Where this is the case, there is a significant effect on labour cost.

Sales Volume

For a restaurant of any given size, increases in sales volume will result in increased productivity per employee up to his or her maximum capacity to perform. For example, in a hypothetical restaurant selling only hamburgers and employing only one cook, 100 hamburgers are typically prepared and sold during one busy hour of the lunch period. During the slack period of the afternoon, the same cook prepares only 10 hamburgers during a one-hour period. If the cook is being paid $12.00 per hour, the labour cost per unit produced during the peak period is equal to the hourly wage of $12.00 divided by the 100 hamburgers produced during that period, or $0.12 per unit. The labour cost per unit for hamburgers prepared during the slow period is equal to the $12.00 wage divided by the 10 hamburgers sold, or $1.20.

It is clear from the example that the cook in question is working at less than his proven capacity during the slack hour, obviously because of the absence of customers. We can see that as the sales volume increases, the cook's labour is used more efficiently. At the same time, as his efficiency increases, the cost of labour per unit produced actually decreases. Therefore, it is apparent that an increase in sales volume results in greater employee efficiency at lower labour cost per unit.

In the previous example, one employee is the minimum number that can be hired for that particular job. However, in larger establishments that require greater numbers of employees as the minimum, it is possible to better schedule employees for greater efficiency, thus keeping each employee busy a greater amount of time. It is desirable to schedule fewer employees during slack periods and more during busy periods, thus increasing individual efficiency.

In addition, large restaurants are often able to take advantage of the economies of large-scale production. In simplest terms, this may also be described as the division of labour, assigning individuals to the tasks they are best qualified to complete and paying each a wage commensurate with level of ability and training. For example, the single cook cited earlier may be required to wash dishes, keep the counter clear, or act as cashier, all for the single wage of $12.00 per hour. In effect, the jobs of cook, dishwasher, counterperson, and cashier are all being paid $12.00 per hour. Furthermore, the particular individual in the job might not be very good at the side jobs assigned, and his performance at those tasks may be less efficient than that of someone hired at a lower hourly wage but specifically trained for the job. The small restaurant can usually do nothing about this, but the large restaurant frequently can hire dishwashers and counterpersons at considerably lower wages.

In large establishments where there is enough work to keep a specialist in any category busy most of the time, it is usually cheaper to hire the specialist at the prevailing wage for the job category, thus reducing the labour cost per unit produced. Consider an illustration: if the hamburger restaurant cited earlier were large enough, it could hire cooks at $12.00 per hour, dishwashers at $10.00 per hour, and a counterperson at $8.50 per hour, thus resulting in a reduction of the overall labour cost per unit produced. As an additional benefit, the specialists should be more efficient at their jobs and capable of performing higher-quality work. In the long run, this should reduce the labour cost per unit still further.

Location

It is well known that labour costs vary from one part of the country to another. In many rural areas, particularly where jobs are scarce and competition for those jobs is intense, employers can often pay comparatively lower hourly rates (while conforming to employment standards) and so keep labour costs down. The same condition can often be noted outside rural areas, particularly in depressed areas and in areas where living costs are low. However, although such conditions as these may result in lower labour costs in dollars, labour costs as percentages of sales may not be lower at all because of the lower menu prices in effect in such areas.

In contrast, the opposite effect can often be noted in metropolitan areas, where living costs are greater and wage scales are higher. Under such conditions, labour costs in dollars may be quite high by some standards, but, as percentages of sales, they may be identical to those found in rural and depressed areas. For example, consider a certain item produced in a kitchen in one area at a labour cost of $1.50 and sold at a menu price of $5.00, contrasted with that same item produced in another area at a labour cost of $3.00 and sold for $10.00. In the second instance, the labour cost in dollars is twice what it is in the first. In both cases, the relationship between labour cost and sales price is the same.

Equipment

Given such tasks as peeling potatoes, making pasta, chopping vegetables, and slicing meats, lower labour costs can often result from doing this work with modern equipment, rather than by traditional hand methods. For example, a machine can peel 50 kilograms of potatoes in less than 20 minutes, whereas the same job done by hand may require many hours. Pressing out 5 kilograms of fettuccini with modern slicing equipment may take less than 5 minutes, but doing the same job manually will take much longer. Chopping cabbage for coleslaw by hand may require four to six times the amount of time needed to do the job with up-to-date machinery. In addition, old equipment in poor condition often requires more time to accomplish a given job than equipment that is newer or in better condition. In general, from the point of view of one seeking to control labour cost, doing work by machine is cheaper than doing it by hand, and doing a job with good equipment is cheaper than doing it with poor equipment. The amount of equipment in use, as well as its variety and condition, has considerable effect on labour cost.

Layout

Labour cost is directly affected by the manner in which space is used. Within the work area, equipment must be arranged to facilitate, rather than impede, employees' ability to perform their tasks. In new establishments, equipment and facilities can be suitably arranged during construction; in converted properties, arrangement is often less than satisfactory because of walls that cannot be moved, plumbing that cannot be readily relocated, and room sizes that are less than ideal for a given purpose. If equipment is poorly arranged, employees may have to walk excessive distances. In extreme cases, it may even be necessary to hire employees who may not have been required if the equipment and facilities had been arranged better. For example, if the person working at the broiler does not have ready access to a reach-in refrigerator, he or she may have to walk a considerable distance each time a broiler order is placed. If the broiler is extremely busy, it may be necessary to assign one person to bring items from a refrigerator when they are required at the broiler station. In some older hotels, the kitchen is so far removed from the dining room that a larger-than-necessary staff of servers is required.

In all of these instances, equipment and facilities have been poorly or improperly arranged, with the effect of raising labour costs to higher levels than would otherwise be necessary. It is not a question of the workers being inefficient, but rather the poor layout of the restaurant virtually forces them to be so.

Preparation

Theoretically, one could rate all foodservice operations on a scale of 0 to 100 to reflect the amount of preparation required on the premises. At the 0 end of the scale would be any establishment that purchased all items precooked, fully prepared, and preportioned, thus requiring minimal preparation beyond reheating prior to sale. At the opposite end would appear those establishments that prepared everything on the premises, including such basic ingredients as mayonnaise and ketchup. In places falling near the 0 end of the scale, labour costs could clearly be kept minimal. Foods could be served in the disposable packages in which they were purchased, thus eliminating the need for dishwashing. Clearly, this type of establishment would require largely unskilled personnel in the kitchen. "Cooking" would merely be a matter of reheating, and the services of a traditional chef would not be required. Conversely, restaurants at the other end of the scale would require kitchen personnel with special talents for comparatively complex and conceivably elaborate preparations, probably under the expert guidance of a highly trained and highly paid executive chef. In addition, such an establishment would require additional personnel to take charge of the many responsibilities involved in the purchasing, receiving, storing, and issuing of the expensive and highly perishable basic ingredients required for many of the preparations.

Although few, if any, restaurants would appear at either absolute end of such a scale, a reasonable number would be near either end. Typical fast-food restaurants would appear at the lower end, and traditional restaurants offering haute cuisine would appear at the higher end. Clearly, fast-food restaurants have considerably lower labour costs than those offering dishes to customers with gourmet tastes.

Service

Foodservice establishments could also be charted on a scale of 0 to 100 based on the amount of service offered to the customer. At the lower end of the scale, one would find vending machine operations offering no service. At the other end would be establishments offering French-style service that includes some cooking as an element in the service. Typically, the finishing of main dishes and some other items is accomplished in the dining room by highly trained staff on specialized trolleys known as gueridons. In the middle range, one would find typical Canadian restaurants where food is plated in the kitchen and served by a server, whose station includes a number of tables.

For those establishments at the lower end of the scale, labour costs for service tend to be minimal. Establishments near the opposite end of the scale require not only considerable numbers of skilled servers, but also appropriate personnel to prepare and plate food properly. Labour costs would clearly be lower in restaurants in the former category and higher in those in the latter category.

Menu

From the point of view of a manager interested in controlling labour cost, it is less costly to prepare 300 portions of an item than it is to prepare 30 portions each of 10 different items. This is especially true if those 10 items require several types of preparation, such as braising, broiling, baking, roasting, and boiling. This is because one employee could conceivably prepare all 300 portions of the single item, but the preparation of 10 different items by several different methods would probably require employees in several job categories, particularly if all portions were needed at one time, as in the case of a banquet. This is one of the primary reasons that many establishments restrict their menus to only a few items. In the case of some fast-food operations, the menu may even be structured around one basic main dish: the hamburger. Clearly, limiting the numbers and varieties of menu items is a factor of considerable importance in the control of labour cost. During times of a severe labour shortage, which was experienced in Alberta and British Columbia, establishments have been known to remove labour-intense menu items or reduce the amount of items in response to a diminished number of staff.

Hours of Operation

Obviously, the number of hours that a restaurant operates will have a significant impact on labour cost. A restaurant open only for dinner will have lower labour costs than that same operation open for three meals each day. However, decisions concerning hours of operation involve more considerations than the mere cost of labour.

Every operation has overhead costs that exist regardless of whether the restaurant is open or closed. These typically include rent or mortgage payments, salaries not based on hours of work (managers' salaries as distinguished from those of service personnel paid hourly wages), insurance premiums, depreciation, property taxes, and so on. These fixed costs are independent of business volume. As a general rule, as long as additional revenue gained by staying open is greater than the additional cost incurred during that period of time, remaining open is desirable from a financial viewpoint.

For example, assume that a restaurateur is trying to determine whether to extend the dinner hours from 9:00 p.m. to 10:00 p.m. Additional wages for that hour will be $148; heat and light are estimated at $11. These additional costs can be considered fixed once the decision to remain open for the extra hour is made. Variable costs, including food, beverages, linen, and miscellaneous, are estimated at 38 percent of each dollar of sale. Thus, from the formulas in Chapter 3:

$$\text{Break-even point (BE) for the additional hour} = \frac{(FC)}{(CR) \text{ (equal to } 1 - (VR))}$$

$$BE = \frac{\$159.62}{.62}$$

$$= \$256.45$$

If management can project sales volume in excess of $256.45, it will be financially advantageous to remain open. Thus, assume sales volume of $350 for the additional hour. Costs for that period would include the $159 previously cited plus 38 percent of $350, or $133. Total costs for the additional hour at the projected sales level would be $292, leaving a net revenue of $58 ($350 − $292) that would be available to cover overhead costs and additional profit. Management must decide whether the additional $58 of net revenue is worth the time and effort required. Employee morale and long-term effects on overall sales volume must also be considered.

Weather

Of all the determinants of labour cost, weather is clearly one that is completely beyond any manager's control, but can have a significant impact on labour cost percentages. Weather often affects sales volume, which, in turn, affects staffing levels in our industry. Bad weather, such as heavy rain or snow, deters potential customers from venturing out to restaurants. Interestingly, identical weather conditions typically increase sales volume in hotel dining rooms for the very same reason: those who may have gone out to other restaurants remain in the hotel to avoid the weather.

To the extent that one can obtain accurate weather forecasts, one can plan staffing levels suitable for anticipated demand. The problem is that weather forecasts are not always accurate, and unforeseen weather changes may render planned staffing levels inappropriate. When this occurs, it is often too late to modify the employee schedule. Sometimes employees can be sent home early if the restaurant is overstaffed, although this may have negative consequences, particularly on employee morale, labour turnover, and performance. On the other hand, weather changes that render planned staffing levels inadequate may cause other types of problems, including poor service and even lost sales, as well as an overworked staff. These consequences can sometimes be avoided by scheduling a number of "on-call" employees. These employees would simply call into the establishment to see if they are needed for that day's shift. For example, during times of the year when patio season is about to begin, the changes of weather can be quick and dramatic. It may be anticipated that the patio will not be open due to inclement weather and suddenly the sun appears, requiring more staff to service the patio. Bear in mind that in some provinces a person filling a scheduled on-call shift must be paid a minimum of hours as it is a regular scheduled shift. Some managers use the on-call person to fill the position of last-minute absences (such as covering an employee who suddenly becomes ill; this can lead to low morale under certain circumstances). To the extent that a restaurant is unable to adjust staff schedules quickly to accommodate unforeseen changes in the weather, labour cost percents will be affected.

Competent Management

The cost of labour is always affected by management's ability to plan, organize, control, direct, and lead the organization in such a way that the desired level of employee performance is obtained at the appropriate level of cost. Competent management requires, among other things, that managers have clear conceptions of important elements of the work at hand, including the nature of the work to be done; the number and types of employees required to do it; the measurement of suitable performance; the scheduling of employees to optimize performance levels; the training, facilities, equipment, and other materials required; and how, when, and in what quantities these resources are to be used. The manager's ability to motivate, direct, and lead will determine the quality of work and level of performance.

This may be summed up by saying that good management will have positive effects on labour costs, whereas poor management will have negative effects. A good manager, merely by being a good manager, will create a work environment conducive to optimal performance at minimal cost.

Labour Costs across Establishments

In light of the previous discussion on the determinants of labour cost, it is apparent that each of these must be taken into account in analyzing labour costs. Moreover, because of the many differences that are readily apparent from one establishment to another within this vast industry (which includes operations ranging from hot dog stands to the finest hotels, and from fast-food chains to award-winning gourmet-style restaurants), it is impossible to arrive at industry-wide standards or averages for a particular manager to use as guides for his or her own establishment.

Each owner or manager must base the desired and optimal labour cost and labour cost percentage for an operation on an array of relevant factors and must recognize that labour cost in a particular operation will be affected to a greater or lesser extent by the various determinants discussed here: labour turnover rate, training, labour legislation, labour contracts, use of part-time staff, outsourcing, sales volume, location, equipment, layout, preparation, service, menu, hours of operation, weather, and competent management. Clearly, the impact of each of these varies considerably from one establishment to another.

Indeed, two identical restaurants located in different areas do not and probably should not have the same labour costs or the same labour cost percentages. In fact, two such restaurants will normally be found to have significantly different cost structures for food, beverages, and overhead, as well as for labour.

It is worthwhile, at this point, to recall an important point made in Part I of this text, namely, that the basic categories of cost (fixed, directly variable, and semivariable, also identified previously as overhead, food, beverages, and labour) must add up to a figure that is less than total sales if the operation is to show a profit: these costs must total less than 100 percent of sales. Therefore, the proportion of total sales that must be allocated to cover each of the three types of costs partly depends on the proportion required to cover the other two. Figure 18.1 illustrates this point.

• FIGURE 18.1 •					
Cost Comparison: Two Restaurants					
	Restaurant A			**Restaurant B**	
	Dollars	*Percentages*		*Dollars*	*Percentages*
Sales	$ 1,200,000	100%		$1,200,000	100%
Fixed costs	$ 360,000	30%		$ 360,000	30%
Semivariable costs	$ 240,000	20%		$ 420,000	35%
Directly variable costs	$ 480,000	40%		$ 300,000	25%
Profit	$ 120,000	10%		$ 120,000	10%
Total Costs + Profit	$ 1,200,000			$1,200,000	

In the illustration, fixed costs account for equal percentages of sales in both restaurants, as well as for equal numbers of dollars. Profits are equal as well. The differences between the two restaurants are seen in the dollars and percentages attributable to semivariable costs (labour) and to directly variable costs (food and beverages). In Restaurant A, food and beverage costs and cost percents are comparatively high, which means that labour costs must be kept comparatively low for the restaurant to earn the 10 percent profit. In contrast, food and beverage costs and cost percents are comparatively low in Restaurant B, meaning that labour costs can be comparatively higher than those in Restaurant A without causing profit to be lower than 10 percent. Whenever directly variable costs account for a high percentage of the income dollar, semivariable costs (primarily labour costs) must be kept down. By the same token, if fixed and directly variable costs are comparatively low, semivariable costs can be proportionally higher.

An increase in the percentage of sales attributable to any cost category will have an effect on the remaining cost categories, on profit, or on both. If the semivariable cost of labour increases from 20 to 25 percent, then a manager must somehow reduce the percentages for the remaining costs or be prepared to accept a decreased percentage of profit. Similarly, if the percentage of variable costs increases, then the manager must be prepared to exercise some restraining influence on fixed or semivariable cost percentages if the percentage of profit is to be held constant.

In the final analysis, all restaurant owners and managers must control combined food, beverage, and labour costs so that their operations will earn satisfactory levels of profit. The combined costs of these three typically should not exceed 60 to 70 percent of sales if establishments are to cover overhead and earn profits. Having addressed the elements of employee compensation and some major determinants of labour cost and labour cost percent, it is now appropriate to turn our attention to the primary subject of this part of the text: labour cost control.

LABOUR COST CONTROL

LEARNING OBJECTIVE 18.5
Define *labour cost control* and explain its purpose.

In the preface to this subject, we defined labour control as an attempt to obtain maximum efficiency from staff without compromising standards of operating performance. **Labour cost control** is a significant part of labour control. It is a process used by managers to direct, regulate, and restrain employees' actions in order to obtain desired levels of performance at appropriate levels of cost. To the inexperienced owner or manager, labour cost control is sometimes mistakenly taken to suggest the mere reduction of payroll costs to their irreducible minimum. This can be achieved by employing a bare minimum number of people paid the minimum legal wage. But there is much more to labour cost control than just minimizing dollar wages, a fact sometimes ignored by owners and managers who take the short-term view of operations, thinking only of immediate profits and not taking into account the long-term effects of their policies and actions.

Short-term policies geared strictly to minimize immediate costs may have undesirable long-term effects, including decreased dollar sales, increased operating costs, and even business failure. For example, hiring a full staff of employees at minimum wage may minimize immediate labour costs but lead to poor-quality products, high labour turnover, customer dissatisfaction, decreasing sales volume, and a host of other long-term problems. Obviously, management should pay the wage rates necessary to attract and retain qualified personnel, but not more. To overpay may make for an operation that cannot be profitable.

Appropriate performance levels differ from establishment to establishment. For some (fast-food restaurants serving frozen, portioned products that need only be heated and served by comparatively unskilled labour), desired levels of performance may be such that minimum-wage employees are appropriate; for others (fine restaurants attempting to offer the finest food, wines, and service in their areas), appropriate levels of performance may be such that wages considerably above those prevailing in the area may be required.

But level of performance is not simply a function of wage rates. Unskilled employees in fast-food establishments cannot perform at appropriate levels unless they are provided with appropriate equipment, given suitable training, placed in a working environment conducive to getting work done, and supervised in a manner that will inspire them to work and remain on the staff. This is also true for highly skilled employees in the finest restaurants. Suitable wage levels do not guarantee appropriate performance. Many other factors are involved in ensuring suitable levels of performance.

The Purpose of Labour Cost Control

The primary purpose of labour cost control is to maximize the efficiency of the labour force in a manner consistent with the established standards of quality and service. Ideally, each employee's services will be used as effectively as possible. There should be a sufficient number of dishwashers working to ensure that dishes are washed as efficiently as possible, but there should be no time when dishwashers stand around without any work to do. Similarly, a sufficient number of servers should ensure that all customers are served as quickly as possible while standards of service are maintained, but at no time should there be more than a sufficient number to serve the customers then in the restaurant.

Control Process

Before proceeding to the topics to be discussed in the remaining chapters on labour cost control, it will be useful to review the four-step control process identified and discussed at length in Chapter 2 and used as the focus for parts II and III of the text:

1. Establish standards and standard procedures for operation.
2. Train all individuals to follow established standards and standard procedures.
3. Monitor performance and compare actual performance with established standards.
4. Take appropriate action to correct deviations from standards.

These four steps are as important to labour cost control as they are to both food cost control and beverage cost control. They will provide the framework for the discussion of labour cost control that occupies the chapters that follow.

THINGS TO CONSIDER

Managing labour cost is definitely a major contributor to the success of an establishment. Many operators are under pressure to maintain a "lean" labour force, which often results in inadequate service to their guests. Managers who are overly concerned with labour dollars will sometimes send employees home early, not start them at all, or call and tell them not to come to work in order to save labour dollars. This practice can often backfire, leading to a lack of proper service and leaving a poor impression on the guest's mind. Well-trained staff and management can easily manage the challenge of handling workload. There is really no point in reducing labour by half an hour if it is going to result in lost revenue.

Minimum wages, staff ages, hours of work, overtime, and public holidays are all governed by the provinces and territories. It is essential that operators are aware of and understand the guidelines set out by these legislations (see the web links on the textbook's companion website).

CHAPTER ESSENTIALS

In this chapter, we discussed the elements of employee compensation, identifying direct, indirect, current, and deferred compensation and distinguishing between the terms *salary* and *wage*s. We listed and explained 16 major determinants of labour costs and labour cost percentages: labour turnover rate, training, labour legislation, labour contracts, use of part-time staff, outsourcing, sales volume, location, equipment, layout, preparation, service, menu, hours of operation, weather, and competent management. We explained why labour costs and labour cost percentages vary from one establishment to another by illustrating the comparative cost structures of two common types of restaurants. We defined *labour cost control* and explained that minimal labour costs are not necessarily optimal labour costs. Finally, we reviewed the four steps in the control process, which are the themes of the following chapters on labour cost control.

KEY TERMS IN THIS CHAPTER

Bonus, p. 465

Commission, p. 465

Compensation, p. 464

Deferred compensation, p. 467

Direct compensation, p. 464

Gratuities, p. 465

Indirect compensation, p. 465

Labour cost control, p. 480

Labour turnover rate, p. 467

Minimum wage, p. 469

Outsourcing, p. 472

Salary, p. 464

Tips, p. 465

Wages, p. 464

QUESTIONS AND PROBLEMS

1. Distinguish between direct compensation and indirect compensation.
2. Distinguish between current compensation and deferred compensation.
3. List five forms of indirect compensation.
4. Distinguish between salaries and wages.
5. List and discuss four hidden costs of labour turnover.
6. In a short paragraph, discuss the possible effects on labour cost of a newly negotiated labour contract.
7. Select and describe a reasonably well-known restaurant in your area and discuss the effect of each of a minimum of five of the determinants identified in this chapter on that specific establishment's labour cost.
8. Research the following types of dining-room service: Canadian, French, Russian, and cafeteria. Rank them according to the extent of labour cost normally associated with each, and justify the ranking of each.
9. Discuss considerations that a restaurant owner or manager should take into account before deciding between the following alternatives: purchasing an expensive piece of equipment to make hamburger portions of uniform size, or employing people on hourly wages to do the same work, along with buying inexpensive portion scales for them to work with.
10. Identify several laws affecting labour cost in your region. What is the specific effect of each?
11. The Alibi Restaurant is normally open for business until 8:00 p.m. Recently, business has been getting better during the period just before closing, and the manager is attempting to determine the viability of remaining open until 9:00 p.m. She estimates her additional costs for the extra hour as follows:

Labour	$75
Heat, light, and gas	$12
Variable cost of food, beverages, etc.	40% of sales

a. What additional sales are necessary for the manager to break even exactly on the extra hour of opening?

b. If the manager were able to obtain $280 in sales volume for the extra hour, what income could be applied to normal overhead expenses?

12. A restaurant's income statement shows the following cost and sales structure:

Sales	$450,000
Fixed costs	$135,000
Directly variable costs	$120,000

What must the semivariable cost figure be if the restaurant is to show a profit of $30,000?

13. In Erphalene's Restaurant, fixed costs are 30 percent of sales, and directly variable costs are 25 percent. What percentage of sales should semivariable costs be if the restaurant is to show a 10 percent profit?

14. Rank the foodservice operations listed here in order of probable labour cost percent, from low to high. Justify the rank you have assigned each establishment.

    a. An industrial cafeteria using only convenience foods
    b. A seafood restaurant using only fresh fish
    c. A restaurant specializing in tableside cookery

15. A restaurant selling hamburgers employs only one cook. During the peak lunch hour, the cook is able to produce 120 hamburgers per hour. During the slack afternoon period, he produces only 30 hamburgers per hour. If each hamburger sells for $0.60 and the cook is paid $8.00 per hour, calculate the labour cost per hamburger for one hour during each of the two periods described.

16. Define each of the key terms in this chapter.

EXCEL EXERCISES

Exercise 18.1

Calculate gross wages, total deductions, and net pay for each of the following employees of Barnaby's Hideaway. Assume a 40-hour work week, with hours worked over 40 hours (overtime wage) calculated at 1.5 times regular wages. Deductions from wages are as follows:

CPP @ 7.30% of gross wages
Federal tax @ 8.8% of gross wages
Provincial tax withholding @ 5% of gross wages

Name	Total Hours Worked	Hourly Rate	Gross Wages	Total Deductions	Net Pay
Caroline Adolpho	46	$ 7.75			
Anita Corliss	55	$ 8.25			
Adam Lockheart	42.5	$ 9.55			
Charles Osprey	48.5	$11.70			
Claudia Shrenk	57	$12.25			

Exercise 18.2

Barnaby's Hideaway currently accepts dinner reservations up to 8:00 p.m. each night. Recently, there have been requests for dinner reservations as late as 9:00 p.m. Given the following information, calculate the needed revenue for the restaurant to break even if it should stay open the additional hour.

Additional fixed costs to remain open one extra hour (includes heat, light, and power as well as additional wages for the hour) = $160
Variable cost percentage = 44%

CHAPTER 19

Establishing Performance Standards

• LEARNING OBJECTIVES •

After reading this chapter, you should be able to:

19.1 Explain the meaning and significance of quality and quantity standards in labour control.

19.2 Identify the three steps used to establish standards and standard procedures for employees.

19.3 Explain the need for an organizational plan.

19.4 Describe an organization chart and explain its purpose.

19.5 Describe *job analysis*, and explain its importance in developing job descriptions and making employment decisions.

19.6 Identify the three parts of a job description and use these to prepare a job description.

19.7 Differentiate between variable-cost personnel and fixed-cost personnel.

19.8 Explain how records of business volume are used in scheduling.

19.9 Differentiate between the scheduling of variable-cost personnel and the scheduling of fixed-cost personnel and prepare a schedule for each.

19.10 Describe how to develop performance standards based on a test period.

19.11 Explain how to determine appropriate staffing levels for an establishment given a table of standard staffing requirements and a sales forecast.

INTRODUCTION

In the previous chapter, discussion of the considerations affecting labour cost suggested that job categories and numbers of personnel involved vary greatly from one foodservice establishment to another. That is true: as the extent of preparation increases, the number of job categories and the degree of specialization increase as well. In addition, as the nature and extent of service increase, on a continuum from self-service to elaborate service, the number of personnel and the degree of expertise required also increase. Regardless of the extent of preparation and the type and extent of service, managers should work to ensure that every employee is performing as effectively as possible. This is best accomplished by establishing standards and standard procedures.

ESTABLISHING PERFORMANCE STANDARDS AND STANDARD PROCEDURES

LEARNING OBJECTIVE 19.1
Explain the meaning and significance of quality and quantity standards in labour control.

In Chapter 2, *standards* were defined as rules or measures established for making comparisons or judgements. Management establishes standards for many reasons, including to determine the extent to which the results of organizational activities match those anticipated by plans. Other chapters illustrated the importance of standards for judging the effectiveness of food and beverage cost controls. Now it is appropriate to discuss using standards for evaluating employee performance and controlling labour costs.

Earlier chapters explained that there are three kinds of standards used in cost control: quality, quantity, and cost. These three are also used in labour cost control. Quality standards and quantity standards are discussed in the following sections. The discussion of cost standards is deferred to the end of the chapter.

Quality Standards

Before developing quality standards for employee performance, a manager must first have a clear and detailed understanding of the establishment, including the quality standards for food and beverage products. Obviously, the food and beverage standards differ in restaurants. Some restaurants serve food that comes prepackaged or in cans, and preparation involves only heating, broiling, sautéing, or frying. The standards for food quality in these restaurants are not as high as those in a restaurant that uses few convenience foods, uses fresh vegetables, prepares its own sauces, does its own butchering, and so on. With the standards for food preparation clearly in mind, a manager can then begin to establish quality standards for employee performance.

For example, the standards for employee performance in a diner are considerably different than in a fine-dining establishment. Diners typically serve a variety of wholesome food in an informal setting, catering to customers looking for a wide variety of relatively plain food ranging from breakfast items to sandwiches to dinner items. Employees must be able to follow standard recipes and provide fast service. A fine-dining establishment, by contrast, caters to guests looking for superior-quality food in an unobtrusive atmosphere. Employees must be highly trained, and their knowledge of food, food preparation, and service must be greater than that of diner employees. The quality standards for employee performance in a diner need not be as exacting as those in a fine-dining establishment. As an illustration, standards for serving sandwiches typically do not require the same polished service as that appropriate for serving Tournedos Rossini in a fine-dining establishment. Those serving sandwiches typically need only be cordial and put the food in front of the customers within a reasonable period of time. Those serving Tournedos Rossini require a greater degree of knowledge about the food itself and skill in service procedures.

Quantity Standards

Once appropriate quality standards have been established, corresponding quantity standards must be developed. The manager must determine the number of times a task can be performed within a certain time period at a given level of quality. The typical time period is the same as that used for payroll purposes—the hour. In effect, the manager must determine the quantity of performance to be expected per hour and, by extension, per meal and per day from employees in each job classification. In the diner just illustrated, a cook is expected to turn out foods rapidly, and servers will wait on a large number of customers per hour, because of the relatively fast customer turnover in the establishment. By contrast, in a fine-dining establishment, cooks will spend more time preparing each meal, and servers will wait on fewer customers per hour because of the relatively slow customer turnover.

In other industries, various sophisticated techniques have been developed for establishing quantity standards. These have been successfully used by those scheduling personnel for factory and office jobs that are essentially repetitive in nature. On an assembly line, for example, one person is typically responsible for one task and can reasonably be expected to perform that task a certain number of times per hour. Time and motion studies can be used to analyze each job. A time and motion study breaks a job down into component parts and specific body movements to find the most efficient way of doing the work. This must be clearly defined and taught to the workers. The key to such an approach lies in the repetitive nature of the tasks to be performed and in the fact that management has the ability to control the rate of production. Further, in a typical manufacturing business, production is normally linked to demand in the long run, but not on a day-to-day basis. A factory can turn out items that can be stored in inventory for appreciable periods. In the long run, management must schedule production in such a way that the supply of an item produced does not exceed demand, which can be done by increasing or decreasing (or even by ceasing) production for a period of time.

However, food and beverage managers do not have this luxury. In our business, production must be linked to immediate demand. If a restaurant has 120 customers in a given time period, food is produced for those 120 people. If during the next time period only 50 customers are in the restaurant, food is produced only for those 50 people. We do not normally prepare most food today for sale in the next day, week, or month, except to the extent it can be frozen or otherwise preserved for service at a later time. A time and motion study can be used to determine appropriate techniques that a cook may use to make, for example, omelettes of acceptable quality at peak efficiency for one hour. Such a study may result in a determination that the cook can produce 30 omelettes per hour by following certain carefully specified procedures. However, this would be of little use unless the cook actually had to produce 30 omelettes per hour for each hour of work. Generally, this is not the case. Thus, industrial approaches have not been widely applied in food and beverage operations.

One exception is found in the fast-food industry and in some food-processing firms. Some fast-food operators and food-processing firms that cater to fast-food restaurants have been able to take advantage of production techniques used in typical manufacturing enterprises and have used time and motion studies and other related techniques to establish quantity standards. Certain preportioned fast-food items can be produced, frozen, and stored by a food-processing firm or by a fast-food operator. In some instances, such items as hamburgers can be produced by employees doing repetitive assembly-line jobs. These cooked products can then be stored for limited periods. If not sold within a predetermined period, they are discarded. However, most foodservice operators are not able to use these assembly-line techniques. Even those that do use them to some limited extent find that they are applicable only to certain specialized products. Therefore, in our industry, other ways must be found to establish quantity standards.

Establishing standards and standard procedures for employees requires three steps:

LEARNING OBJECTIVE 19.2
Identify the three steps used to establish standards and standard procedures for employees.

1. Organizing the enterprise
2. Preparing job descriptions
3. Scheduling employees

In the next several sections, we will look at these steps in more detail.

ORGANIZING THE ENTERPRISE

Few activities designed ultimately to control labour cost can be undertaken sensibly until management has devoted appropriate time, thought, and energy to organizing the operation, establishing jobs, and identifying the relationships between them. Organizing an enterprise properly normally requires that one design a rational **organizational plan**.

Establishing an Organizational Plan

Establishing an organizational plan requires the owner or manager to first develop a clear picture of the nature of the operation. This includes the type of clientele, the nature of the products offered, and the extent and type of service rendered, as discussed earlier in this chapter. In addition, it should include some reasonable estimate of the number of meals to be prepared and served. Once the owner or manager has developed this basic idea of the nature and scope of the operation, he or she can begin to think in terms of specific jobs that must be performed.

LEARNING OBJECTIVE 19.3
Explain the need for an organizational plan.

As an illustration, consider a very small establishment serving fast food from a limited menu and offering counter service rather than table service. The manager can order a comparatively small selection of frozen, preportioned foods and oversee the simple preparation of these items by a small number of cooks of limited ability, who can also serve as counter help. If the serviceware—plates, cups, and so on—were all disposable paper and plastic, the services of a dishwasher might not be needed. And if the manager were able to work the cash register, no cashier would be needed. The restaurant could exist with only two categories of employees: manager and cook/counter worker. With that understanding clearly in mind, the manager can begin to think of hiring a staff.

In contrast, a large restaurant offering gourmet cuisine prepared from fresh ingredients by highly skilled kitchen personnel and served by a highly professional dining room staff would require a comparatively large staff consisting of several specialists. The kitchen staff would include several types of skilled professionals, carefully trained in the arts of butchering meats, preparing soups and sauces, decorating cold platters, and doing other jobs appropriate to such a restaurant. Typically, one individual could not attend to managing such an enterprise while covering one of the workstations (e.g., that of cashier). To operate this type of establishment successfully requires the services of specialists, including receiving clerks, stewards, storeroom clerks, hosts, cashiers, and many others.

In addition to establishing the general categories of employees needed to operate an establishment, a manager must think in terms of the relationships that should exist among employees in the various job classifications. In essence, the manager must decide which employees will be responsible for overseeing the work of other employees. The manager must decide, for example, that an executive chef will have complete responsibility for the production of food items and that, to carry out this responsibility, that chef will be placed in charge of specialists who will serve under his or her direction and guidance, including sous chef, saucier, legumier, and garde manger, among others. In turn, the executive chef must know and understand that he or she reports to the manager and works under the manager's direction. The chef and the steward must realize that there must be a special working relationship between them, that they are equals in the organizational structure, and that they must cooperate fully if the best interests of the restaurant and its customers are to be served.

Preparing an Organization Chart

LEARNING OBJECTIVE 19.4
Describe an organization chart and explain its purpose.

In order to see all of these distinctions and relationships in their proper perspective, the owner or manager of a restaurant is usually well advised to set them down on paper in the form of an **organization chart**, such as that illustrated in Figure 19.1. Such a chart shows the positions and describes reporting relationships within an organization.

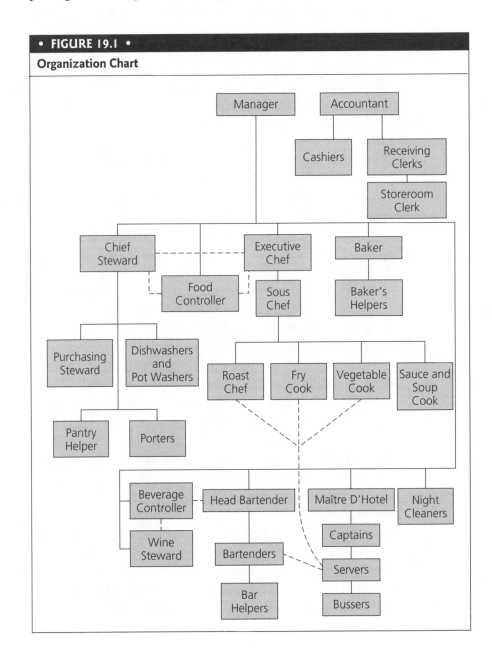

• FIGURE 19.1 •
Organization Chart

The lines drawn from one position to another signify the lines of authority. An unbroken line from one position to another indicates that the person below reports to and takes direction from the person immediately above on the chart. The dotted lines show communication and cooperation between the two positions, but one does not have authority over or responsibility for the actions of the other. The lateral dotted line between the executive chef and the chief steward shows that the two are expected to cooperate in every possible way in accomplishing their respective tasks, but that neither takes direction from the other. The student should note that the organization chart illustrated in Figure 19.1 is suitable for a large operation, perhaps the food and beverage operation in a 300-room luxury hotel. Bistro Quatre is a smaller restaurant with only 75 seats. The organization chart for it is shown as Figure 19.2.

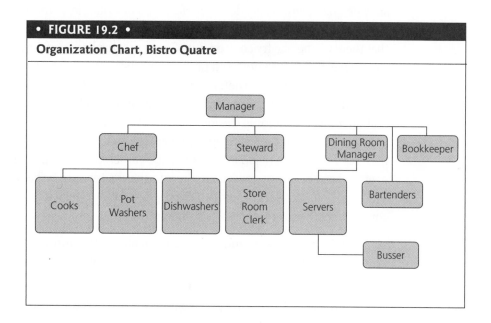

• **FIGURE 19.2** •

Organization Chart, Bistro Quatre

There are many fewer employees and fewer specialized positions. At Bistro Quatre, the manager is also the food controller and the beverage controller, and the chef is a working chef and not an executive chef as is shown in Figure 19.1. There is no sous chef, and the cooks do not specialize in any particular position. The steward does the ordering and receiving. The head of the dining room is called the dining room manager instead of a maître d'hotel. There are no captains in the dining room as all servers and bussers report directly to the dining room manager. The head bartender acts as wine steward in addition to mixing drinks. The position of bar helpers is eliminated. Finally, there is only one bookkeeper and no cashiers, as each server acts as his or her own cashier.

PREPARING JOB DESCRIPTIONS

Once the organization chart is completed and accurately reflects the organizational plan of the owner or manager, particularly with respect to the job titles needed for successful operation, it is necessary to gather the information required to prepare an appropriate job description for each job title on the chart. The term given to the process of gathering this information is **job analysis**.

Job Analysis

LEARNING OBJECTIVE 19.5
Describe *job analysis* and explain its importance in developing job descriptions and making employment decisions.

Organizing an enterprise is much more complex than simply listing the various job titles commonly used in food or beverage operations and determining the number of workers needed in each position. Instead, it requires that one identify the nature of each job as well as the skills, the level of education, and any other specific qualifications needed to perform it. For example, planning for personnel in the kitchen of a restaurant is more complicated than simply determining that there will be one fry cook on duty for every eight-hour shift, every day of the week. One must also know and understand the nature of the fry cook's job in the specific restaurant, the specific duties assigned to that job, the skills required to carry out those duties, and any other qualifications or attributes that an individual holding the job should possess or demonstrate.

Job analysis is the first step in preparing job descriptions. The information necessary to complete job analysis may be gathered in any of several ways. In new food and beverage operations, the information tends to be based on a manager's previous experience in the industry. In existing operations, the two most common methods are:

1. Interviewing workers and supervisors to obtain the information
2. Observing workers on-site as they perform the jobs

Complete analysis requires effective use of both methods. One approach is to conduct in-depth interviews with workers and supervisors during the course of a normal workday. These interviews are typically conducted on premises in a reasonably quiet area, somewhat removed from the actual worksite. In some instances they are videotaped to facilitate review. Each interview is carefully structured to elicit the specific information required for the job analysis. Later, interviewers will observe both workers and supervisors, taking extensive notes to supplement those taken during the interviews. The interviews and observations are designed to provide information about the following:

1. Job objectives
2. Specific tasks required to achieve objectives
3. Performance standards

4. Knowledge and skills necessary

5. Education and experience required

In addition to the information gathered through interviews and observations, the manager must have thorough knowledge of the standards and standard procedures established for the purchasing, receiving, storing, issuing, preparing, selling, and serving of all menu items—foods and beverages—as discussed in chapters 4 through 17. For example, in the chapters dealing with food production and beverage production, the concept of the standard recipe and its importance for cost control was stressed. Now, in analyzing jobs to determine the nature and extent of skills needed for such jobs as cook and bartender, it is important to take into account the need for individuals in those jobs to be able to read and follow the standard recipes developed.

Unless job analysis is thorough, any resulting job description or job specification will not accurately indicate the specific duties of a job and the qualifications required to perform it. If job analysis does not uncover a need for reading and following standard recipes, the job description and job specification resulting from the faulty analysis will not accurately reflect the real duties of the job and the qualifications needed by the job holder. The information gathered in job analysis is reported in the form of job descriptions, used for informing employees of their duties and for developing training plans, and job specifications, used for making employment decisions.

Writing Job Descriptions

Once job analysis is completed, job descriptions can be written. As the term implies, **job descriptions** are written statements that describe jobs. They can be quite detailed. In some instances, job descriptions list specific duties and directions for performing jobs. Job descriptions for particular jobs should answer three important questions:

LEARNING OBJECTIVE 19.6
Identify the three parts of a job description and use these to prepare a job description.

1. What is to be done?

2. When is it done?

3. Where is it done?

Today, growing numbers of experts in the field of human resources development advocate including performance criteria in job descriptions. **Performance criteria** are statements that describe an acceptable level of job performance. Included in performance criteria are standards of job performance that should be known and understood by each job holder, because each is likely to be evaluated on the basis of these standards. For example, if the job description for a server includes a statement such as "Customers are greeted and dealt with in a polite and helpful manner at all times," then there is a standard established that can be used as a basis for evaluating servers' behaviour toward customers. A job description typically has three parts:

1. *A heading that states the job title and the department in which the job is located.* In some organizations, the heading may include such information as the number of positions with that particular job title; the specific hours, days, or shifts worked by those with the job title; and the supervisor to whom those with that job title report.

2. *A summary of the duties of the job, typically written in paragraph form.* The summary enables the reader to quickly gain some basic understanding of the nature and purpose of the particular job. By reading the summaries of all the jobs in a particular department, one can obtain a great deal of information about the department in a very short time. This can be of great benefit to a new manager, for example.

3. *A list of the specific duties assigned to the job.* These will be as detailed as possible, to the point that well-written job descriptions can be used as step-by-step instructions for doing the specific work required of those holding these jobs. As shown later, having detailed job descriptions of this nature can be of great value to those charged with appraising employee performance.

A job description is particularly important for prospective employees. If they have access to detailed descriptions of the duties assigned to particular jobs, job applicants and newly hired workers have a means of knowing the work that is to be done by someone holding a particular job.

Job descriptions are also very important for employers. They enable employers to hold employees accountable for doing the specific work assigned to a particular job. Employees who have read job descriptions but fail to perform the assigned work cannot successfully use the age-old excuse, "Nobody ever told me I had to do this."

Job analysis and the resulting job descriptions have the added benefit of forcing managers to assign specific work to each job holder. If all the normal duties of a department are identified within specific job descriptions, the department will be better organized and will operate more smoothly.

Figure 19.3 is written for a server at Bistro Quatre and is an example of the kind of job description that one may find in a foodservice enterprise. Note the degree of specific detail provided. Job descriptions that include this level of detail can be of great assistance to those responsible for developing employee training programs.

Job Specifications

A **job specification** outlines the qualifications needed to perform a job. It is a second outcome of job analysis. A job specification describes the specific skills needed for a given job and the kinds and levels of education and experience required. The job specification is an important standard that can and should be used by anyone assigned to interviewing applicants for employment and

---

• FIGURE 19.3 •

Job Description—Server, Bistro Quatre

SUPERVISOR: Dining Room Manager

JOB TITLE: Server

WORKING HOURS: 4:00 p.m. to close

JOB SUMMARY: Servers greet guests, take food and beverage orders, serve food and drinks, present cheques with last service, collect cash or process credit for customers, and clear/reset tables.

DUTIES:

1. Report to dining room manager at 4:00 p.m. (one hour prior to opening) to assist in preparing dining room for opening and to discuss menu, special guests, and service techniques.
2. Pour water; take food and drink orders; plate orders; pick up and serve food and drink; present and process guest cheques; clear and reset tables.
3. Follow standard service procedures: serve food from left and beverages from right. Remove all china, glassware, and silver from the guest's right.
4. Pool all tips: 10 percent of tips go to bartenders; 20 percent to bussers; remainder divided equally among servers; tips distributed the following day.
5. Provide own uniform as follows: black pants and white long-sleeved shirt with buttoned cuffs; black bow tie; polished black shoes with flat heels. No high heels. Pants and shirt to be clean and ironed daily. Servers will be given an allowance of $20 weekly to care for their uniforms.
6. Standards for personal appearance: showered or bathed prior to work; underarm deodorant required; clean fingernails (no long nails); hair clean and neat; no excessive jewellery.

Males:

a. Clean shaven. Moustache permitted if neat and trimmed.
b. No facial or ear jewellery.
c. Hair cannot extend beyond shirt collar.

Females:

a. No excessive jewellery, makeup, or perfume.
b. Long hair must be in a hair net.
c. No long false nails.

---

judging their suitability for particular jobs. Job specifications typically include minimum qualifications that are used to determine which applicants are qualified to fill particular positions and which are not. Applicants who possess the qualifications indicated in the job specification are normally deemed suitable for further consideration; those who lack the listed qualifications are not.

With the foregoing discussion of job analysis, job descriptions, and job specifications as background, we turn our attention to another important element in developing standards and standard procedures for labour: scheduling.

SCHEDULING EMPLOYEES

One popular scheduling method is commonly used in operations where menus seldom vary and sales change little from week to week. Managers routinely review staffing levels in the most recent weeks. Purely on the basis of recollection, they decide whether the level of staffing was sufficient to meet customers' needs. Then, to the extent to which previous schedules were adequate, they are repeated, thus making these schedules standards of sorts. If recollection suggests that staffing was excessive or inadequate, changes are made and a new schedule is prepared. It should be noted that this entire scheduling process depends on remembering the details of past performance; intuitive judgement is the essential factor in determining increases or decreases in the number of scheduled work hours.

Because this approach fails to recognize essential differences between fixed-cost and variable-cost personnel and neglects to take sales records into account, it does not normally provide the most effective labour cost control. Improved labour cost control can be obtained by taking these factors into account.

Labour Classifications for Control Purposes

LEARNING OBJECTIVE 19.7
Differentiate between variable-cost personnel and fixed-cost personnel.

It is important for any manager attempting to develop schedules for employees and to control labour costs to recognize that there are two classifications of employees:

1. Variable-cost personnel
2. Fixed-cost personnel

Because there is a difference between scheduling variable-cost employees and fixed-cost employees, they are discussed separately.

Variable-Cost Personnel

Variable-cost personnel are those whose numbers are linked to business volume. As business volume increases, it becomes necessary to hire more personnel in this category. As a consequence, the total labour cost increases for this category of employees. The reverse should also be true: As business volume decreases, it is possible to decrease the number of employees in this category and thus to decrease the total labour cost for this category of employees. Typical examples of variable-cost employees are servers and bussers. When business volume reaches a peak, as it typically does during normal meal hours, more of these workers are needed. During nonpeak times (e.g., the middle of the afternoon), reduced levels of business volume can be handled with comparatively fewer servers, bussers, and other such variable-cost employees. For this category of employees, the total cost of labour is higher during peak hours than it is during nonpeak hours. Other examples of variable-cost employees are dishwashers and certain food preparation personnel. As business volume increases, so does the volume of work for these employees.

It is interesting to note that the hours of work for some variable-cost employees correspond to the hours of peak sales, whereas the work hours of others may not. For example, preparation personnel are needed in comparatively large numbers before the hours of anticipated peak sales so that food will be ready when needed. In contrast, there is usually a time lapse between the onset of peak sales in the dining room and the beginning of peak dishwashing needs in the kitchen. Moreover, the period of peak dishwashing usually continues for some time after peak food sales have ended. In general, an increase or decrease in business volume will dictate the need for an increase or decrease in the number of variable-cost personnel, but their hours of work will not necessarily coincide with the hours of peak business volume.

It is important to recognize that the points made in the foregoing discussion also apply in those establishments that experience periodic or seasonal changes in business volume. During slow periods, fewer variable-cost personnel are needed to handle reduced business volume; as volume increases during busier periods, more of these employees must be hired. A typical example is a restaurant at a popular east coast seashore resort, which does comparatively little business during the winter months, but operates at near capacity during the summer. The number of variable-cost personnel is kept to a minimum during the slow season and is greatly expanded during the busy summer season.

Fixed-Cost Personnel

Fixed-cost personnel are those whose numbers are unrelated to business volume. Although business volume in a given establishment may increase or decrease, the number of these employees remains relatively constant, as does the cost of their services. Typical examples of fixed-cost personnel include managers, bookkeepers, chefs, and stewards, as well as maintenance personnel and cashiers.

Regardless of the increases and decreases in business volume, there will be only one manager. The same is true of the chef. As business volume changes, it becomes necessary to vary the number of personnel working under the chef's jurisdiction, but the chef, whose job as a result will vary in difficulty, will be the single constant factor in the kitchen. The same is usually true of the bookkeeper. During a slow period, the sales figure recorded in the accounting records of the business may be only $1,000 for a given day, but it takes neither more nor less time to make that entry than it does to enter a sales figure of $10,000 for a single day during a busy period. Depending on the particular duties assigned to the bookkeeper, preparation for making the bookkeeping entry may take longer in the case of $10,000 in sales, but it is highly unlikely that any additional bookkeeping help will be hired during busy periods.

Keeping and Using Records of Business Volume

A very important step that managers should take before scheduling employees is to keep records of business volume. These are typically in the form of tallies

LEARNING OBJECTIVE 19.8
Explain how records of business volume are used in scheduling.

of numbers of covers served. For best results, these tallies should be made both daily and hourly.

Daily Tallies

Several techniques are commonly used for determining the number of covers served daily. Perhaps the simplest is to take the information from records being prepared for a sales history, as discussed in Part II of this text, which deals with food control. If a cashier, for example, is developing records of the number of portions of each main dish served in the dining room, one may determine the total number of covers served by totalling the number of portions served for all items on the menu. In small restaurants, where sales histories are not developed but where guest cheques are used, it is reasonably simple to determine the number of persons served from information on the cheques after the close of business. A third approach, which is the most common in the industry today, is to use electronic means to record sales. This may be done with either point-of-sale (POS) computers or their close relatives, electronic cash registers. Either of these provide up-to-the-minute data, indicating the number of persons or covers served. In the last analysis, each restaurant manager must find a technique appropriate to his or her operation to determine the number of covers served daily.

Any manager or owner is in a better business position if he or she can determine today what conditions and sales volume are likely to be encountered in a future period. Forecasting is an attempt to make these determinations. Because experience has shown that history tends to repeat itself in food and beverage operations, any owner or manager can use historical records to predict what is likely to occur in the near future. As discussed in previous sections of the text, such forecasts enable a manager to exercise some degree of control over food and beverage purchasing and production, for example, and thus to gain some control over food and beverage costs. Similarly, a manager can exercise greater control over labour costs if he or she is able to predict the establishment's labour requirements with some reasonable degree of accuracy. This can be accomplished if the manager can predict business volume and then schedule an appropriate number of variable-cost personnel for those days and times when they are needed.

With data collected over a suitable period, business volume can be forecasted with some reasonable degree of accuracy. Many restaurants have found, for example, that the number of customers served varies from day to day during the week. Many have found that Monday is normally slower than Friday. Knowing this in advance, a manager is able to schedule an appropriate number of employees for each of the days, with fewer on Mondays and more on Fridays.

In addition to helping forecast the appropriate numbers of employees needed to meet anticipated sales volume on various days of the week, such records also enable a careful manager to spot such things as seasonal variations in business volume, which should always be taken into account in scheduling staff. Obviously, nontypical days and weeks resulting from such unforeseen circumstances as bad

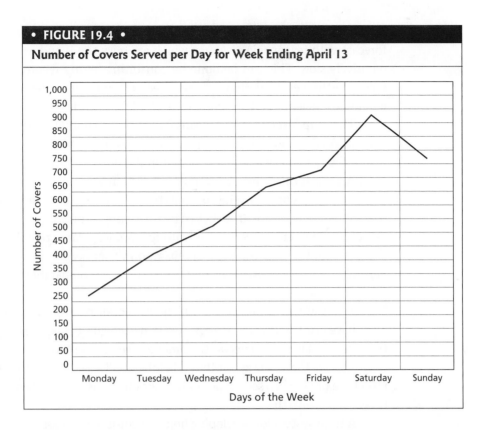

• FIGURE 19.4 •

Number of Covers Served per Day for Week Ending April 13

weather, strikes, and road construction must be dealt with as they occur. A graphic illustration of business volume by day of the week appears in Figure 19.4.

Collecting and analyzing sales volume for purposes of forecasting can be more easily done with the aid of one of the many computer programs available today. For example, Silverware POS is a computer program for the hospitality industry that provides technology capability in restaurant labour control and enables a restaurant to forecast sales revenue based on historical data maintained by the computer system. This in turn allows the restaurant to establish schedules for employees, as discussed later.

Hourly Tallies

The daily record of business volume described earlier helps in controlling labour cost by enabling the manager to schedule employees' workdays and days off in accordance with anticipated needs. However, it does not help with problems posed by hourly fluctuations in demand. Most establishments, for example, find that the middle of the afternoon is a very slack time between two periods of peak volume: the luncheon and dinner hours. In such cases, the maximum number of dining room personnel on duty are clearly necessary during the luncheon and dinner hours. However, from the standpoint of a manager attempting to keep labour cost at the optimum level, it is undesirable for the dining room personnel on duty during the busy lunch hour to be idle through the slack afternoon while waiting for the start of a busy dinner hour. This is the kind of problem that can sometimes be reduced or eliminated by more efficient scheduling. However, improved scheduling is possible only if the manager can forecast with reasonable accuracy which are busy times and which are comparatively slow. This can be done by consulting hourly records of business volume—the key to designing employee schedules intended to maximize employee efficiency and minimize excessive labour cost.

There are several manual means for developing hourly records of business volume. A common way is to require the dining room manager to count and record the number of customers seated in the dining room every hour on the hour. Although this is by far the simplest system, it is not the most accurate. Many customers order several cocktails before ordering food, and others linger over coffee after eating. In either case, the hourly count does not accurately reflect the number of covers served during any particular period. To the extent that this count is used to schedule preparation personnel as well as dining room personnel, it may be misleading and may result in the preparation of inefficient work schedules.

To offset the inadequacy of this hourly counting procedure, some managers have instituted a system requiring that each guest cheque or duplicate be time-stamped in the kitchen as the order is given to the cooks. The cheques or duplicates are then analyzed at the end of the day. These results more accurately reflect the times when service personnel take orders, as well as when preparation personnel receive them.

A third system for developing hourly records of business volume requires that the cashier in the dining room record the number of covers served as customers settle guest cheques. Each guest cheque reaches the cashier as the customer leaves the restaurant. Therefore, a simple system can be instituted to have the cashier record covers on a form such as that illustrated in Figure 19.5. This form is included to show the theory behind the principle; however, most point-of-sale systems can provide you with accurate hourly data.

When the guest cheque has been settled and the transaction is completed, the cashier determines how many covers are reflected on the cheque and records that number in the space on the form for the one-hour period then current. This system is not as accurate with respect to preparation and service as is the one involving time stamps in the kitchen, but it has the advantage of being relatively simple and inexpensive. It must be noted that manual means for developing hourly customer counts are rapidly being rendered obsolete by the growing use of sophisticated computer systems in foodservice, as mentioned above. Detailed discussion of a typical system is included in Chapter 2.

By one or another of these means, the owner or manager can quickly accumulate a useful set of figures reflecting the hourly volume of business in the establishment. By developing and maintaining this information regularly, he or she can better schedule variable-cost employees and thus control labour cost more effectively, as described in the following paragraphs.

• FIGURE 19.5 •

Tally of Covers Served

WEATHER Clear   DATE 1-Apr

EXTERNAL CONDITIONS AFFECTING SALES   Cool

Hourly Period					Number of Covers	
11:00 a.m. to Noon	𝍸	𝍸	𝍸	𝍸		
	𝍸	𝍸	111		33	
Noon to 1:00 p.m.	𝍸	𝍸	𝍸	𝍸		
	𝍸	𝍸	𝍸	𝍸		
	𝍸	𝍸	𝍸	𝍸		
	𝍸	𝍸	𝍸	𝍸		
	𝍸	𝍸			90	
1:00 to 2:00 p.m.	𝍸	𝍸	𝍸	𝍸		
	𝍸	𝍸	𝍸	𝍸		
	𝍸	𝍸	𝍸	𝍸		
	𝍸	𝍸	𝍸	𝍸		
	𝍸	1111			89	
2:00 to 3:00 p.m.	𝍸	𝍸	𝍸	𝍸		
	𝍸	𝍸	𝍸	𝍸		
	𝍸	𝍸	1		51	
3:00 to 4:00 p.m.	𝍸	1			6	
4:00 to 5:00 p.m.	𝍸	11			7	
5:00 to 6:00 p.m.	𝍸	𝍸	𝍸	𝍸		
	𝍸	𝍸	𝍸	𝍸		
	𝍸				45	
6:00 to 7:00 p.m.	𝍸	𝍸	𝍸	𝍸		
	𝍸	𝍸	𝍸	𝍸		
	𝍸	𝍸	𝍸	𝍸		
	𝍸	𝍸	𝍸	111	78	
7:00 to 8:00 p.m.	𝍸	𝍸	𝍸	𝍸		
	𝍸	𝍸	𝍸	𝍸		
	𝍸	𝍸	𝍸	𝍸		
	𝍸	𝍸	𝍸	𝍸		
	𝍸	𝍸	𝍸		95	

(continued)

• FIGURE 19.5 • *(continued)*						
Tally of Covers Served						
WEATHER <u>Clear</u>				DATE	<u>1-Apr</u>	
EXTERNAL CONDITIONS AFFECTING SALES					<u>Cool</u>	
Hourly Period					*Number of Covers*	
8:00 to 9:00 p.m.	TᕼᕮJ	TᕼᕮJ	TᕼᕮJ	TᕼᕮJ		
	TᕼᕮJ	TᕼᕮJ	TᕼᕮJ	TᕼᕮJ		
	TᕼᕮJ	TᕼᕮJ	TᕼᕮJ	TᕼᕮJ		
	TᕼᕮJ	TᕼᕮJ	TᕼᕮJ	TᕼᕮJ		
	TᕼᕮJ	TᕼᕮJ	TᕼᕮJ		95	
9:00 to 10:00 p.m.	TᕼᕮJ	TᕼᕮJ	TᕼᕮJ	TᕼᕮJ		
	TᕼᕮJ	TᕼᕮJ	TᕼᕮJ	TᕼᕮJ		
	TᕼᕮJ	TᕼᕮJ	TᕼᕮJ	TᕼᕮJ		
	TᕼᕮJ	TᕼᕮJ	111		73	
9:00 to 10:00 p.m.	TᕼᕮJ	TᕼᕮJ	TᕼᕮJ	TᕼᕮJ		
	TᕼᕮJ	TᕼᕮJ	TᕼᕮJ	TᕼᕮJ		
	TᕼᕮJ	111			48	
Total					710	

The first step in using this information is to tabulate the hourly volume of business for a given day, as has been done in Figure 19.5. These tabulated figures are shown on the graph in Figure 19.6.

In this graph, the degree of fluctuation in hourly volume of business for this particular restaurant is readily apparent. However, this graph represents only one day—a certain Friday in April—and no manager can safely assume that one specific day is typical. Clearly, it would be unwise to base general scheduling on such limited information. Therefore, it is necessary to accumulate similar data for other Fridays and for other days of the week as well. The broader picture of operations that will emerge can provide a better basis for making scheduling decisions. A second step in scheduling is to tabulate the hourly volume data for a series of days (e.g., Fridays) on a form similar to that shown in Figure 19.7.

Charts of this nature may be prepared for each day of the business week. Together, they present a history of the hourly volume of business that management can use to plan future schedules and thus improve control over the cost of labour. One of the keys to labour cost control is effective scheduling, and it is very important to schedule labour according to anticipated requirements, based on experience.

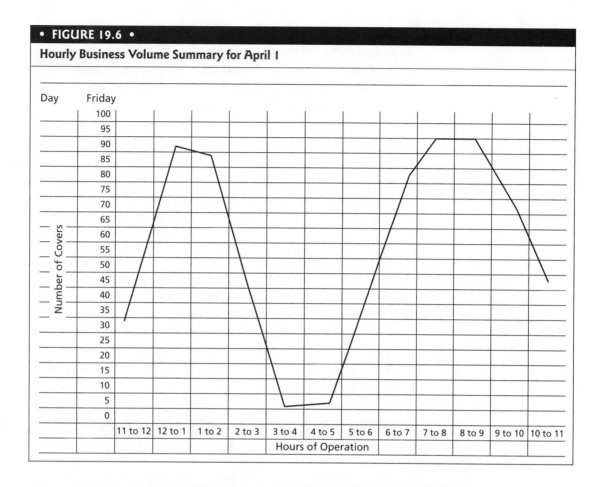

• FIGURE 19.6 •

Hourly Business Volume Summary for April 1

Day   Friday

Number of Covers (y-axis: 0 to 100)

Hours of Operation (x-axis: 11 to 12, 12 to 1, 1 to 2, 2 to 3, 3 to 4, 4 to 5, 5 to 6, 6 to 7, 7 to 8, 8 to 9, 9 to 10, 10 to 11)

• FIGURE 19.7 •

Tabulation of Hourly Data for Fridays during April

Hourly Time Periods	1-Apr	8-Apr	15-Apr	22-Apr	29-Apr
11 a.m. to Noon	33	30	50	40	60
Noon to 1:00 p.m.	90	85	105	100	107
1:00 to 2:00 p.m.	89	85	105	100	107
2:00 to 3:00 p.m.	51	50	63	60	65
3:00 to 4:00 p.m.	6	5	15	10	18
4:00 to 5:00 p.m.	7	5	12	10	18
5:00 to 6:00 p.m.	45	45	55	50	60
6:00 to 7:00 p.m.	78	75	96	90	100
7:00 to 8:00 p.m.	95	95	100	100	105
8:00 to 9:00 p.m.	95	85	95	95	100
9:00 to 10:00 p.m.	73	70	77	75	85
10:00 to 11:00 p.m.	48	45	55	50	60

An important third step in scheduling is to translate the raw numbers, such as those in Figure 19.7, into a graph that reflects the hourly volume experienced over a reasonable period. The graph shown in Figure 19.8 is a picture of the hourly volume of business for Fridays in the month of April.

The figures on the vertical axis show volume of business, and those on the horizontal axis show hourly periods of the operating day. Three lines are plotted on the graph to show various levels of volume for each hour. The upper dotted line shows the maximum volume experienced at each hour during the period covered by the graph. The lower dotted line shows the minimum. These are the extremes to which the hourly volume has gone during the period covered. The solid middle line shows the median.

The **median** is the value of the middle item in a group. It is not an arithmetic average, but a middle point. Figure 19.8 shows that business volume on the five successive Fridays between the hours of noon and 1:00 p.m. ranged from 85 to 107 covers. The numbers of covers during that hour for the five days, taken in ascending order, were 85, 90, 100, 105, and 107. From this list of five days, the two with the highest values were the days when volume reached 105 and 107 covers per hour. The two days with the lowest volume were those on which it was 85 and 90 covers per hour. By eliminating the two highest and two lowest values, one is left with the value in the middle—the median. If the list of values

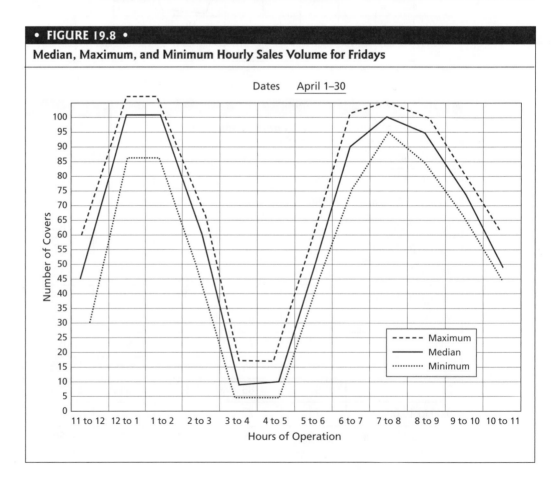

• FIGURE 19.8 •

Median, Maximum, and Minimum Hourly Sales Volume for Fridays

Dates   April 1–30

Number of Covers

Hours of Operation

---- Maximum
—— Median
·········· Minimum

had covered 15 days, one could identify the median by eliminating the seven highest and seven lowest values.

The advantage of determining the median number of covers served during an hour rather than the arithmetic mean, commonly known as the average, is that the median shows the central tendency, unaffected by either high or low extremes. For example, if the number of covers served between 1:00 and 2:00 p.m. on five successive Fridays were 65, 66, 68, 71, and 25, the arithmetic mean, or average, would be the total of 295 divided by the five periods represented, or 59 covers. The median, however, is 66, which is clearly more representative of the typical number of covers served. In this case, the average is weighted too heavily by the one extremely low number of covers served on one particular day. Because these figures are to be used for staff scheduling, it will be far safer to plan on the basis of the median rather than on the arithmetic mean. The presence on the graph of both the maximum and minimum numbers served, as discussed earlier, provides the manager with a complete picture of the hourly volume of sales: the typical number of covers served, as well as the maximum and minimum extremes.

Developing Schedules for Employees

With appropriate information obtained from records of daily and hourly business volume, a manager is prepared to develop schedules for employees, an important element in controlling labour costs. Because of marked differences in the scheduling of variable-cost employees and fixed-cost employees, the scheduling techniques and procedures for employees in these groups are discussed separately.

Variable-Cost Employees

Referring to the limited data in Figure 19.4, one notes a greater daily volume of business on Friday and Saturday than on Monday and Tuesday. If the graph represents the historical record of median volume over an appropriate period, it will be advisable to plan a schedule for variable-cost employees geared to the data in the graph, assuming that similar conditions are expected for the week to be scheduled. A manager should also use the records of hourly volume to plan schedules that have adequate numbers of variable-cost employees on duty at appropriate times through the workday. Their working hours should be staggered to meet anticipated hourly demand.

A preliminary step in the scheduling of variable-cost employees is determining the types and numbers of employees needed at given levels of business volume. These are used to develop staffing tables. Staffing tables for variable-cost employees are estimates of the numbers of these employees required at various levels of business volume, given the quality and quantity standards established for their work. Each manager must determine the number needed in each job classification affected by hourly volume. For servers, the manager must determine the number of covers that each can serve in a given hour while maintaining the established service standards. For dishwashers, the manager must determine the quantity of dishes that each can process in an hour. A similar decision must be made for each job category.

Determining the number of employees required at various levels of business volume is typically an intuitive process, based on a manager's experience. Figure 19.9 is a staffing table for servers in a given restaurant. To develop this table, the manager first had to use intuitive means to set the number of covers that each server could reasonably be expected to serve per hour. Having set that number at 20, she then referred to Figure 19.8, indicating the number of covers served per hour on Fridays. She assumed that the expected number of customers for the coming Friday would be approximately the median number served on previous Fridays. As the figure indicates, the median number of covers served between 12:00 and 1:00 p.m. was 100. If one server could serve 20 covers per hour, then five servers should be needed for any hour when 100 customers must be served. The rest of the staffing table is prepared from similar estimates for the other hours of the day.

With records of the daily and hourly volume of business available, and with staffing tables developed from those records, a manager is suitably equipped to schedule variable-cost employees for a specific Friday. The manager can then prepare a schedule showing the total number of servers needed for that day and the time periods they will work. Figure 19.10 is an hourly schedule for servers for a particular Friday.

• FIGURE 19.9 •

Staffing Table for Servers Based on Median Sales

Hours of Operation	Anticipated Sales Volume in Covers		Servers Required
10:00 to 11:00 a.m.	0		2
11:00 to noon	40		2
Noon to 1:00 p.m.	100		5
1:00 to 2:00 p.m.	100		5
2:00 to 3:00 p.m.	60		3
3:00 to 4:00 p.m.	10		1
4:00 to 5:00 p.m.	10		1
5:00 to 6:00 p.m.	50		3
6:00 to 7:00 p.m.	90		5
7:00 to 8:00 p.m.	100		5
8:00 to 9:00 p.m.	95		5
9:00 to 10:00 p.m.	75		4
10:00 to 11:00 p.m.	50		3
11:00 to 12:00 p.m.	0		2

• **FIGURE 19.10** •

Sample Schedule Worksheet: Hourly Schedule for Servers

Day __Friday__   Date __6-May__

	a.m.		p.m.										
Server	10 to 11	11 to 12	12 to 1	1 to 2	2 to 3	3 to 4	4 to 5	5 to 6	6 to 7	7 to 8	8 to 9	9 to 10	10 to 11	11 to 12
A														
B														
C														
D														
E														
F														
G														

In the exhibit, the manager has scheduled two servers to begin work one hour before opening and two to remain one hour after closing to clean up and prepare for the following day. To increase efficiency, she has also scheduled some part-time workers. It is apparent that seven servers are needed for the day, three of them part-time and four full-time, of whom three are working split shifts. Other possible schedules can also be devised. For example, employee B may become a full-time employee by working his normal shift and, in addition, taking on the shift of employee G. This would reduce the number of servers from seven to six.

By following this procedure for all days and hours of operation during the workweek being planned, while keeping in mind the number of days and hours that each employee can or will work, the manager can develop a work schedule based on both anticipated sales volume and judgements about servers' abilities to provide each customer with the established level of service quality. In addition, because the schedule is based on realistically anticipated needs, it can be set up to keep labour costs at a suitable level for the forecasted number of covers. Once complete, a schedule such as that illustrated in Figure 19.11 is prepared and posted for employees, so that each will know his or her scheduled work hours for the coming week.

• FIGURE 19.11 •

Sample Schedule for Servers

Week   May 2–May 8

Server	Mon.	Tues.	Wed.	Thurs.	Fri.	Sat.	Sun.
A	Off	Off	10–6	10–6	10–6	10–6	10–6
B	Off	10–6	10–2	10–2	10–2	10–2	10–2
C	Off	Off	12–3; 5–10	12–3; 5–10	12–3; 5–10	12–3; 5–10	12–3; 5–10
D	12–3; 6–11	Off	Off	12–3; 6–10	12–3; 6–11	12–3; 6–11	12–3; 6–11
E	10–2; 5–9	10–2; 5–9	Off	Off	12–2; 6–12	12–2; 6–12	12–2; 6–12
F	10–6	6–12	Off	Off	6–12	6–12	6–12
G	Off	5–9	5–12	5–9	5–9	5–10	Off
H						6–9	

Fixed-Cost Employees

Although the scheduling of variable-cost employees is linked directly to daily and hourly records of business volume, the scheduling of fixed-cost employees is not. Before fixed-cost personnel can be scheduled with any degree of certainty, the manager must determine the specific requirements of the job that should be taken into account in scheduling. For a storeroom clerk, such requirements may include a need to have the storeroom open during hours of preparation, so that food supplies can be issued to the production staff, or a need for the storeroom clerk to be available to accept food deliveries taken in

• **FIGURE 19.12** •							
Sample Schedule for Some Fixed-Cost Personnel							
Week May 2–May 8							
Employee	*Mon.*	*Tues.*	*Wed.*	*Thurs.*	*Fri.*	*Sat.*	*Sun.*
Purchasing steward	9–5	9–5	9–5	9–5	9–5	9–5	Off
Storeroom clerk	Off	8–4	8–4	8–4	8–4	8–4	8–4
Receiving clerk	7–3	7–3	7–3	7–3	7–3	7–3	Off
Porter 1	Off	7–3	7–3	3–11	3–11	7–3	Off
Porter 2	3–11	3–11	3–11	Off	Off	3–11	3–11
Vegetable preparer	Off	8–4	Off	8–4	8–4	8–4	8–4
Cashier 1	Off	5–12	10–5	10–5	10–5	10–5	10–5
Cashier 2	5–12	Off	5–12	5–12	5–12	5–12	5–12

by the receiving clerk. These details should be considered before establishing the work schedule for the job.

When all such requirements have been considered, a manager can establish and post a schedule for fixed-cost personnel resembling that illustrated in Figure 19.12.

Although schedules for fixed-cost employees tend not to change from one week to the next, major changes in business volume for protracted periods may cause management to reassess both schedules and costs for fixed-cost personnel. Substantial decreases in business volume, for example, may suggest the need for a substantial decrease in labour costs generally, including a reduction in the number of fixed-cost personnel. When such a step is necessary, it is important to ensure that any reduction in staff does not lead to a decrease in operating efficiency.

As with food control and beverage control, labour scheduling can be more easily accomplished using one of the many computer programs available today. One program from Silverware POS discussed earlier enables the establishment to create a schedule template specific to the restaurant's requirements and projected sales for any day. This allows management to easily prepare a schedule for employees. Actoris, another online firm, has a program called Xpress Schedule that allows the employer to "drag and drop" employee names by clicking on the employee and dragging her name to where he wants her to be scheduled.

This is a very basic approach to labour cost control commonly used by many food and beverage managers. It establishes performance standards for staff, but does so informally. Because the resulting performance standards are based on a manager's recollections about the adequacy of performance, they are not sufficiently accurate and reliable to meet the needs of managers in highly structured organizations. In these kinds of organizations, management has found that the intuitive approach to establishing performance standards is not sufficient. A better approach is to base one's standards on written evaluations of performance accumulated over a period of time. The results will be more objective and are likely to be better suited to monitoring performance.

Managers in large organizations are better equipped to establish performance standards for work in this way and to use the resulting standards for evaluating the degree of efficiency with which managers of individual units schedule employees. In such organizations, standards of employee performance have been established, and various means have been found to compare these performance standards with actual performance. Preliminary aspects of this approach to establishing standards are discussed in the following section.

PERFORMANCE STANDARDS BASED ON TEST PERIOD

LEARNING OBJECTIVE 19.10
Describe how to develop performance standards based on a test period.

Performance standards developed from records kept during a test period take both quantity and quality standards for work into account. A test period of a particular number of days or weeks is established for gathering data. During this period, detailed sales records are kept, indicating the number of covers served per day or per meal, depending on the type of establishment being analyzed. Managers also record the number of staff members on duty in each fixed- and variable-cost job and review each, judging sufficiency of staff and efficiency of employee performance. These judgements are key to establishing standards for use in future periods, as discussed later in "Standard Staffing Requirements."

Variable-Cost Personnel

Figure 19.13 relates numbers of variable-cost personnel to sales volume in covers for a particular test period and shows one manager's judgements about staffing during that period. As the chart shows, with sales of 275 covers and seven servers scheduled for lunch on May 1, the manager judged performance to be highly inefficient because of overstaffing and recorded his observations for future reference. As the one-week period progressed, he continued to note his estimates of labour efficiency, relating the number of servers working to the total number of covers served. Although Figure 19.13 has been set up to record estimates of labour efficiency for an entire meal period, it is also possible to do this on an hourly basis if a more detailed view is required.

Fixed-Cost Personnel

It also is feasible to prepare a similar chart that relates numbers of fixed-cost personnel to numbers of covers sold for a period , which allows the manager to estimate employee efficiency by the day or meal or even by the hour. However, as has been noted, the nature of the work of fixed-cost personnel is such that

• FIGURE 19.13 •

Evaluation of Employee Efficiency

Date	2-May	3-May	4-May	5-May	6-May	7-May	8-May
No. of Covers Served	275	450	400	350	400	425	500
Servers Scheduled	7	7	7	7	7	7	7
Efficiency of Performance	Poor; 5 servers needed	Excellent	Very good	Poor; 6 servers needed	Very good	Excellent	Poor; 8 servers needed
Dishwashers Scheduled	3	3	3	3	3	3	3
Efficiency of Performance	Poor; 2 needed	Excellent	Good	Poor; 2 needed	Good	Excellent	Poor; overtime required
Preparation Personnel Scheduled	4	4	4	4	4	4	4
Efficiency of Performance	Poor; 3 needed	Excellent	Good	Poor; 3 needed	Good	Excellent	Excellent

the numbers on duty in any category cannot be varied in normal circumstances. Under extraordinary conditions (e.g., when sales increase or decrease abnormally for protracted periods), such charts can reflect the need for increasing staff or for laying off staff and combining jobs. However, under normal circumstances, such volume/staffing review charts are prepared only for variable-cost personnel.

STANDARD STAFFING REQUIREMENTS

Once appropriate charts have been prepared for a test period and the manager has a record of sales volume, numbers of variable-cost employees working, and his or her own personal estimates of the employees' efficiency, it is time to take

LEARNING OBJECTIVE 19.11
Explain how to determine appropriate staffing levels for an establishment given a table of standard staffing requirements and a sales forecast.

the next logical step: to develop a table of **standard staffing requirements**, traditionally known as workforce requirements, for variable-cost personnel at several levels of business volume. Figure 19.14, a typical example, shows standard staffing requirements for variable-cost personnel in each category. It is apparent from a comparison of figures 19.13 and 19.14 that this manager judged seven servers excessive for serving 275 covers on May 2, and therefore set five as a more appropriate number. Similarly, he judged seven as insufficient for serving 500 covers on May 8, and determined that this number of covers could be satisfactorily served by eight servers. Thus, by judging performance carefully and recording these judgements over a period of time, a manager can set standards for staffing. Referring to these two tables of standard labour requirements and to forecasts of anticipated sales for a coming week, the manager can establish better control over labour cost by scheduling the number of personnel necessary to meet the establishment's preparation and service standards.

• FIGURE 19.14 •

Standard Staffing Requirements—Luncheon

Covers	200–299	300–399	400–499	500–599
Servers	5	6	7	8
Dishwashers	2	2	3	4
Preparation personnel	3	3	4	4

This technique can be further refined. Records may be analyzed to establish hourly standards for performance, and suitable tables may then be developed. When hourly tables are used, the manager can achieve an even greater degree of control over payroll. Clearly, hourly records of the sort discussed earlier in this chapter and tables of standard labour requirements developed from these hourly records can offer a more complete and detailed means for scheduling staff efficiently.

STANDARD WORK HOURS

Before attempting to describe an approach to improving labour efficiency, it is necessary to introduce another way of looking at standards for labour productivity. Here we consider **standard work hours**: the number of employee work hours required to perform a given volume of work. The term is normally related to the work of those in specific job categories, such as servers, dishwashers, or cooks. If, for example, eight servers are needed to serve 500 covers in a three-hour luncheon period, the standard work hours required for servers are calculated as follows:

> **8 servers × 3 hours = 24 work hours**

The 24 work hours would become the standard for serving 500 covers over a luncheon period. Given a forecast of 500 covers, the scheduling of any number of servers' work hours in excess of 24 would be an indication of poor scheduling. Fewer than 24 would also be an indication of poor scheduling and would further suggest that unsatisfactory levels of service quality will be provided to customers. Varying numbers of standard work hours should be established for varying levels of sales volume, and it is management's responsibility to establish these standards.

The number of standard work hours required do not necessarily vary directly with changes in the volume of business. In the previous example, 24 work hours for servers was the standard for 500 covers during the luncheon period. For the three-hour time period, this was 20.83 covers per standard work hour. At a lower level of sales volume (e.g., 300 covers), six servers equalling 18 standard work hours may be established as the standard. This is 16.7 covers per standard work hour, suggesting less efficiency than that at the higher volume level. High levels of efficiency are more difficult to achieve at lower volume levels.

By employing the techniques previously discussed, management can develop tables of standard work hours for all job categories at various levels of business activity. Figure 19.15 illustrates a table of standard work hours for variable-cost personnel for a particular restaurant. Used in conjunction with forecasts of sales volume, these figures are helpful both in forecasting work hours required and in scheduling employees as efficiently as possible. For example, assume that the manager of a given restaurant, after referring to the establishment's sales history, has forecasted 500 covers for a given luncheon period. Given that level of sales volume, one can determine from the chart illustrated in Figure 19.15 that the standard work hours required for that level of sales are as follows:

Service personnel: 24
Dishwashing personnel: 12
Preparation personnel: 12

• FIGURE 19.15 •

Standard Work-Hour Requirements for Variable-Cost Personnel

Number of Covers	Service Personnel	Dishwashing Personnel	Preparation Personnel
200–299	15	6	9
300–399	18	6	9
400–499	21	9	12
500–599	24	12	12

Forecasts would be made for each meal or day, depending on the nature of the operation. Then the number of standard work hours required at those levels of volume would be determined. The standard work hour requirements would form the basis for developing work schedules for employees, following the procedures discussed earlier in this chapter. Obviously, all of this would be done far enough in advance so that employees would have appropriate notice of their work schedules for the week.

STANDARD COST

The development of standard work hours makes possible the development of **standard labour costs**. This may be done by simply multiplying the number of standard work hours required to perform a given volume of work by the hourly wage paid those performing the work. For example, assume that servers are paid $8.50 per hour and that 24 standard work hours are required to serve 500 covers in a three-hour luncheon period, as indicated in Figure 19.15 and described earlier. Standard cost for this can be calculated by multiplying the number of standard work hours by hourly wage, as follows:

> 24 hours × $8.50 per hour = $204.00 standard cost

Note that standard cost calculated in this way takes only the hourly wage into account and not the additional cost of various payroll taxes, deductions, and fringe benefits.

Thus, the standard cost for servers serving 500 covers in a three-hour period is $204.00. Similar calculations are used to determine standard costs for other categories of employees (e.g., cooks, dishwashers, and others). Calculated standard costs are useful for evaluating the efficiency of scheduling.

As discussed previously in so many ways in this text, a principal requirement for gaining control over cost in food and beverage operations is the establishment of standards to be used for making comparisons and judgements. Quality and quantity standards have been cited as critical standards that must be established before management can begin to control costs. Quality and quantity standards for labour are established by the means described earlier: organizing an enterprise, preparing job descriptions, and scheduling employees. Having established these standards, one can turn to the second step in the control process: training all individuals to follow standards and standard procedures, which is the subject of the next chapter.

THINGS TO CONSIDER

Scheduling of employees can be a time-consuming task. Those with knowledge of the establishment are best suited to perform this task. In some operations, the server/busser/bartender schedule may be compiled by a senior server or junior manager. Back-of-the-house schedules may be assigned to a chef, sous chef, or senior cook with knowledge of business fluctuations and kitchen preparation requirements. Schedules can be used as a motivational tool for some departments; servers who establish the highest sales may be rewarded with preferred schedules and table sections to work in. All schedules must be approved by management before posting to employees. Schedules should be posted on a given day each week (or biweekly in some cases) to allow plenty of time for employees to plan their personal lives. Generally, the earlier in the week the schedule is posted, the more at ease employees will be. A good rule of thumb is to post the employee schedules on Thursday no later than 5 p.m. for the next week's business.

CHAPTER ESSENTIALS

In this chapter, we identified three steps used to establish standards and standard procedures for staff. The first of these is organizing an enterprise, which includes identifying the types of jobs needed and designing an organization chart that shows the relationships of jobs within the enterprise. The second step is preparing job descriptions based on job analysis, which makes possible the development of job specifications. The third step is scheduling employees, which requires developing hourly, daily, or weekly records of business volume. We distinguished between variable-cost and fixed-cost personnel and discussed basic approaches to preparing schedules for both. We discussed the importance of developing performance standards, both as guides to efficient scheduling and as means for judging performance. Finally, we described how computers can aid in keeping the records of business volume used to develop staffing tables.

KEY TERMS IN THIS CHAPTER

Fixed-cost personnel, p. 497
Job analysis, p. 492
Job description, p. 493
Job specification, p. 494
Median, p. 504
Organization chart, p. 490

Organizational plan, p. 489
Performance criteria, p. 493
Standard labour cost, p. 514
Standard staffing requirements, p. 512
Standard work hours, p. 512
Variable-cost personnel, p. 496

QUESTIONS AND PROBLEMS

1. List the three steps used to establish standards and standard procedures for personnel.
2. What does an organization plan include? Why is it necessary to develop one?
3. Describe an organization chart.
4. Distinguish between variable-cost personnel and fixed-cost personnel.
5. Define the term *job analysis* and explain the importance of job analysis in developing job descriptions.
6. Define the term *job description*. What are the three elements of a job description?
7. What are performance criteria? What purpose do they serve?
8. Using the appropriate chapters in the food control or beverage control section of this text as a reference, develop a job description for a receiving clerk.
9. What is a job specification? For what primary purpose are job specifications used?
10. The following chart is an hourly record of business volume for a typical day in a neighbourhood restaurant. Servers are expected to attend to 25 customers per hour, and each server is scheduled for an eight-hour workday whenever possible. Part-time help is often used, and split shifts are permitted. Two servers are always scheduled to come in one hour before the 11:00 a.m. opening to set up the dining room, and two remain from 10:00 p.m. to 11:00 p.m. for cleanup.

Time Period	Covers Served
11:00 a.m.–noon	50
Noon–1:00 p.m.	200
1:00 p.m.–2:00 p.m.	100
2:00 p.m.–3:00 p.m.	25
3:00 p.m.–4:00 p.m.	10
4:00 p.m.–5:00 p.m.	10
5:00 p.m.–6:00 p.m.	60
6:00 p.m.–7:00 p.m.	150
7:00 p.m.–8:00 p.m.	100
8:00 p.m.–9:00 p.m.	50
9:00 p.m.–10:00 p.m.	20

a. Prepare a chart similar to that in Figure 19.6, showing a record of the volume of business per hour on a typical day.

b. Prepare an hourly schedule for servers similar to that in Figure 19.10.

11. Refer to the record of the volume of business per hour in Question 10. Assume that the restaurant is open seven days per week and that the first five days follow the pattern of business indicated here, but the last two days of the week normally have business volume equal to 50 percent of that on other days. Full-time servers work a five-day week, part-time servers work four-hour days, and the manager prefers to use as few part-time servers as possible. Given this information, prepare a weekly schedule for servers similar to that found in Figure 19.11.

12. Developing work schedules for variable-cost personnel requires taking into account some considerations that are quite different from those used in developing work schedules for fixed-cost personnel. List and discuss two such considerations.

13. Of what value are performance standards in controlling labour costs?

14. List and describe the methods for establishing performance standards.

15. Which of the methods identified in Question 14 would be most practical for most foodservice establishments? Why? Which would be the least practical for small operations? Why?

16. Why might managers of small restaurants decide not to adopt the standard work hour approach to controlling labour cost?

17. Many object to the standard work hour approach to labour cost control on the grounds that it ignores the human relations element in the workplace. What do you think they mean by this? What possible drawbacks are inherent in the standard work hour approach?

18. Assume that the numbers in Figure 19.15 are applicable to a foodservice establishment that you are managing. Prepare a list of staffing requirements for the five days forecasted.

Monday, June 6	200 covers
Tuesday, June 7	350 covers
Wednesday, June 8	450 covers
Thursday, June 9	475 covers
Friday, June 10	575 covers

19. You are the manager of the Hearthside Restaurant, a 150-seat evening dining establishment. Recently, patronage at the restaurant has become unpredictable. An example of the number of covers served for the past three weeks is shown as follows:

Number of Covers Served

Week	Monday	Tuesday	Wednesday	Thursday	Friday	Saturday	Sunday
1	80	70	110	140	160	180	75
2	30	110	50	100	180	150	60
3	60	55	80	160	120	170	100

As a result of not being able to accurately predict the number of covers on any given night, labour scheduling has been almost impossible to do accurately, food has been wasted on those nights when fewer than expected covers were served, and the kitchen has run out of menu items on nights when more covers than expected were served.

a. As manager of the restaurant, how would you deal with this situation in order to keep your labour cost to a minimum and at the same time provide excellent service to your customers?

b. What action would you take to keep food waste to a minimum?

20. Define each of the key terms in this chapter.

EXCEL EXERCISES

Exercise 19.1

The manager of Barnaby's Hideaway is concerned that he is scheduling too many servers during some days and too few on other days. In order to get a clearer picture of business volume, he has asked you to prepare a graph similar to Figure 19.8 for Friday nights, showing the maximum, minimum, and median volume for those days. Below you have tabulated the following numbers of customers served for Fridays of the previous month. Enter the numbers in Excel and create a graph for the manager.

	Customers Served				
Time Period	**9/2**	**9/9**	**9/16**	**9/23**	**9/30**
4:00–5:00 p.m.	25	28	35	20	30
5:00–6:00 p.m.	75	80	90	60	84
6:00–7:00 p.m.	100	110	118	92	105
7:00–8:00 p.m.	114	122	130	95	125
8:00–9:00 p.m.	83	90	110	80	92
9:00–10:00 p.m.	27	35	44	20	29

CHAPTER 20

Training Staff

• **LEARNING OBJECTIVES** •

After reading this chapter, you should be able to:

20.1 Define *training*, and differentiate between training and education.

20.2 Identify the objectives of training.

20.3 Explain the relationship of training needs assessment to the development of a training plan.

20.4 List and explain the 10 elements commonly covered in a training plan.

20.5 Describe the advantages and disadvantages of centralized and local training for multiunit organizations.

20.6 Identify the four content areas normally included in training manuals.

INTRODUCTION

As previously discussed, the second step in the labour cost control process is training employees to follow the standards and standard procedures established. This is a critical step in the successful control of labour cost: employees who are properly trained will be more efficient, enabling management to keep labour costs to their practical minimum. This should result in better financial performance for the establishment. For example, a properly trained server will be better able to quickly take customer food orders, place them with the kitchen, and complete the service procedure. This allows for shorter service time and results in faster customer turnover, enabling the server to handle greater numbers of customers, and providing increased revenue to both the server and the establishment.

There are several other benefits to training. A key one is safety: properly trained employees have fewer accidents. A cook who is properly trained in the use of a knife or a server who is properly trained to stack dishes on a serving tray will be less likely to have an accident. Additionally, they will be able to do their jobs in the manner that presents the establishment in its most favourable light. For example, properly trained servers will make favourable impressions on guests both by their approach to guest relations and by their professional use of proper serving techniques. They will speak to guests in the manner intended by management, suggest appropriate items to guests, take orders efficiently, and serve food using proper techniques, thus providing an excellent dining experience for a guest. Finally, well-trained employees are more likely to continue working for the employers who have provided their training, thus keeping the labour turnover rate lower in establishments with effective training programs.

A DEFINITION OF TRAINING

LEARNING OBJECTIVE 20.1
Define *training*, and differentiate between training and education.

Training is a process by means of which individuals acquire the skills necessary to perform particular tasks. For this discussion, we will assume that these tasks are job related and that the individuals acquiring the skills do so for employment purposes. Many are given training by their employers; some seek training to become qualified for employment in a specific job.

Training is narrowly focused on particular skills and tasks. It normally includes some education, but it is not the same as education, which is a broader-based concept. The objectives of education include increasing one's knowledge of a given subject and developing the capacity of the mind to address complex topics and to analyze critically.

THE PURPOSE OF TRAINING

The primary purpose of training is to improve job performance. Many employers provide training for this specific purpose: to improve their employees' on-the-job performance. Some provide training only for new employees so that each newcomer will learn the specifics of the job he or she is expected to do, as well as learn the performance criteria associated with the job. Others also provide training for long-term employees so that each will have an opportunity to maintain or improve the skills required in a specific job. A particularly important step in training, most would agree, is to develop a healthy climate for training. In some organizations, management has devoted considerable time and attention to developing an organizational climate that treats training as a necessary and important element for its health and well-being. Training is considered a positive factor in achieving organizational and personal goals, and employees learn early in their careers to look forward to the training that will increase their skills inventories and enhance their ability to contribute to the organization.

Whether it is done properly or improperly, training does consume resources in any organization: it requires time and money. Because training is costly, one must take care to develop an approach and a program that will meet the organization's needs. The training program starts with a needs assessment.

LEARNING OBJECTIVE 20.2
Identify the objectives of training.

THE TRAINING PROGRAM

Assessing Training Needs

Training needs should be based on assessments of current and new staff. For current staff members, one should be concerned about their ability to carry out their tasks and to meet the standards and standard procedures established for their jobs. In addition, one must bear in mind that the purchase of new equipment, the development of new standards and standard procedures, or both of these, may lead to the need for additional training. Often, employers find that employees who have been at their jobs for some time require some training. Long-term employees may need training to work with new equipment that is purchased and new methods and procedures that are developed. For example, a foodservice operator who has purchased a complex computer system to be used for dining room and kitchen operation must spend considerable time training servers and others to use the system.

Another consideration for some employers is the extent of the need to institute cross-training. **Cross-training** is defined as teaching a worker

LEARNING OBJECTIVE 20.3
Explain the relationship of training needs assessment to the development of a training plan.

to perform the duties of a job or jobs other than his or her own. Some employers consider it important to provide cross-training so that employees are prepared to perform the duties of those who are absent or ill or so that jobs can be combined during slow periods. Sometimes employees are reassigned to jobs for which they have been cross-trained so that they will not lose their new skills. In some cases, employers have found it desirable to reassign employees in this way to prevent the feelings of boredom that can be experienced by those with routine jobs. Employees may be reassigned for several weeks and then either return to their regular jobs or be reassigned again. The process of periodically reassigning employees to other jobs is known as *job rotation*.

In well-managed organizations, training is generally required of all new employees, even those who come to an organization with considerable experience. Every foodservice operation has its own way of doing things—its own methods for performing tasks and accomplishing work. It is very important that people who already know how to perform a job be shown the specific methods and procedures used by the organization for which they have just started to work. Those who are inexperienced will likely require more formal training.

Every new employee needs some amount of training in the methods and procedures of the foodservice operation. This can range from a mere tour of the establishment for a highly skilled and experienced professional to urgently required basic-skills training for some newcomers to the industry. Once an assessment has been made of the nature and extent of the training that will be required, a plan for undertaking the training can be developed.

Developing Training Plans

LEARNING OBJECTIVE 20.4
List and explain the 10 elements commonly covered in a training plan.

A **training plan** is a series of elements that constitute a method for teaching a specific employee the skills required to perform a job correctly and in the manner anticipated by management when the standards and standard procedures for the job were developed.

Although the specifics of training plans vary from one organization to another, the following 10 elements are most commonly included:

1. Objectives
2. Approaches to training
3. Training methods
4. Instructional timetables
5. Location
6. Lesson plans
7. Trainer preparation
8. Trainee preparation
9. The training session(s)
10. Evaluation

Objectives

Training objectives identify the skills, tasks, and behaviours that a specific employee will have mastered by the time training is complete. These skills, tasks, and behaviours are the basis for developing lesson plans for training, as described later in this chapter.

Training objectives are developed from a job analysis and from a carefully developed job description that lists the duties of a job and the performance criteria for that job. Each job description should identify the specific duties and performance criteria associated with the particular job. Given the specific duties and performance criteria, one must determine the specific skills, manual and otherwise, that each job holder will require to carry out the duties of his or her job. Once these skills have been identified, training becomes possible.

In a food and beverage operation, there are many different kinds of jobs, and management must devise one set of training objectives for each job title for which training is to be done. For example, the most basic training objectives for a dishwasher would include the ability to handle five functions:

1. Start the equipment at the beginning of the day.
2. Load soiled china, glassware, and flatware properly to avoid breakage.
3. Operate the equipment properly, in accordance with manufacturer's directions.
4. Unload clean china, glassware, and flatware properly, stacking and storing in accordance with company rules.
5. Shut down the equipment at the end of the day, cleaning it in accordance with manufacturer's directions and local health codes.

Some managers are inclined to add many other training objectives to this short list. These may include objectives related to personal hygiene, foodservice sanitation, and other issues.

Approaches to Training

Several approaches to training must be considered before selecting one of the training methods available. These approaches are characterized and described as follows.

On-the-Job versus Off-the-Job. Training can be done on the job or off the job. **On-the-job training** means that the new employee is taught the techniques of doing a job while actually performing that job during business hours. It is more commonly used with experienced workers who need only to be shown the methods used by the hospitality operation. For example, a new cook may be put to work immediately under the guidance and instruction of an experienced cook, who will show the new cook how to fill out requisitions for supplies, how orders are placed for menu items, and how the establishment garnishes plates of food going into the dining room.

For inexperienced employees, on-the-job training can be used effectively in situations where the work they do can be easily monitored and corrected before it has a negative impact on guests or where a new employee can work side by side with an experienced worker. For example, a new dishwasher can be trained effectively if assisted by an experienced dishwasher. The experienced dishwasher can show the new dishwasher the normal routine for preparing the dishwashing machine for operation. He or she can show the new dishwasher the best way to place dishes, glassware, and other pottery and glass to be washed in the dish racks, as well as how to do all of the other tasks that go into washing dishes.

The experienced dishwasher can monitor the work performed by the new dishwasher, correct mistakes, and suggest improvements to ensure that the work is done in the most efficient manner possible without damage or breakage to the machine or dishes and glassware. Other related instances of on-the-job training include apprenticeships and internships.

Sometimes the type and level of job for which training is required is such that off-the-job training is more suitable. **Off-the-job training** means that the new employee is trained in a location away from the business or at the business while it is not in operation. Although this kind of training would not be provided for a dishwasher, it may be for a loyal kitchen worker whom management wanted to train to be a cook. Rather than attempt the training in-house, management might enroll the worker in one of the culinary programs offered by community colleges or proprietary schools or under the sponsorship of hotel and restaurant unions in some major cities.

Structured versus Unstructured. Training may be structured or unstructured. **Structured training** is characterized by a formal approach to instruction. The structured approach requires extensive planning, with considerable time and attention given to the nature of each formal step in the specific training plan being undertaken. It might include lesson plans, manuals, training films and DVDs, and webcasts developed specifically for use in the training program. In contrast, **unstructured training** is commonly undertaken with relatively little thought given to the specifics of the training. It is quite informal and often involves a trainee being directed to follow and carefully observe an experienced worker doing the job.

The unstructured approach tends to work well in situations where high levels of skills training are not required. For example, a garde manger who has been newly hired to replace a retiring employee and comes to the job with extensive skills, honed over a period of many years, may be able to gain all the training needed by working closely with the retiring garde manger for a period of several days. He or she would come to the job with all of the requisite skills and would have to learn only the standards and standard procedures established by the new employer. This approach would be unproductive if a trainee came to the job without garde manger skills.

Individual versus Group. Training can be done on an individual basis, as described earlier, or it may be done in groups. Individual training is undoubtedly more effective, but it is very expensive: The trainer must devote time to training only one person at a time. In contrast, some of the major foodservice organizations rely heavily on group training sessions because of the large number of employees requiring training.

There are many specific methods used for training employees. Some of those described in the following section are more commonly used to train groups. Others are best suited to the training of individuals. Some are equally effective in either setting, provided that suitable adjustments are made.

Decisions as to approaches and methods vary from one establishment to another and include such considerations as the type and level of the jobs for which training is to be done; the number of individuals to be trained; the number of trainers available; and time, space, and funds available for training purposes.

Training Methods

Many training methods are available to those desiring to institute employee training. Eight of these more common methods are identified and described in the following paragraphs:

1. Lecture/demonstration
2. Role playing
3. Seminars
4. Individual assignments
5. Field trips
6. Case studies
7. Panels
8. Programmed instruction

Lecture/Demonstration. The lecture/demonstration method requires that a trainer explain a subject or task to one trainee or to a group of trainees, demonstrate the skills involved, and respond to questions during or after the lecture/demonstration. For example, a trainer may explain to new servers the proper procedures for taking orders and serving food and then demonstrate those procedures to the trainees. The lecture/demonstration method typically has limited effectiveness unless combined with other training methods that provide trainees with immediate opportunities to practise the techniques and standard procedures explained and demonstrated.

Role Playing. Role playing can be a very effective method of training, particularly when coupled with the lecture/demonstration approach. Role playing enables each learner to play a part in a scene created by the trainer. For example, servers can be divided into small groups, with each member of the group taking a turn at practising the various serving techniques that a trainer has previously demonstrated.

Seminars. **Seminars** are group discussions of particular subjects led by trainers. They are most useful for management training, where the input of the trainees is an important part of the learning process. Significant questions are typically raised by the seminar leader, and each member of the group is asked for his or her opinions. For example, a foodservice chain may hold a seminar on guest relations for restaurant managers. Participants may be asked to discuss the best way to handle guest complaints about food quality or service in the dining room. Each manager is expected to participate actively in the seminar, and each individual's expressed point of view is discussed by the others, enabling all present to benefit from the thoughts of their colleagues. Training sessions of this type can be extremely valuable when conducted as part of an ongoing training program.

Individual Assignments. Individual assignments are very effective for undertaking the training of employees for particular types of jobs at or near the management level. This method is most effective for trainees who are comfortable with self-paced learning, a characteristic this method shares with programmed instruction.

The individual assignment method includes a broad array of techniques, including assigning specific readings, requiring research into a specific topic, having a trainee observe experienced personnel performing their tasks and duties in a specified setting, and requiring a trainee to practise the skills and techniques learned via one of the other methods. Many have found that this method works best when preceded by more formal training delivered via one of the other methods. It is frequently used with the seminar method and makes it possible, for example, for the seminar participants to gain first-hand experience and to verbally share their experiences with others attending the seminar.

Field Trips. Field trips offer an excellent means for individuals or groups to observe others at work and to study the standards and standard procedures they follow in carrying out their job assignments. Group field trips are preferred by many because of the opportunities they afford for a leader to call attention to key points and to ensure that all participants note the particular elements they are expected to observe. In addition, the leader can serve as a discussion leader, effectively linking the field trip method to the seminar method in a very useful way.

Field trips for single individuals, rather than groups, offer a valuable means for a learner to observe settings, standards, and processes as they normally occur. Group observation can sometimes disturb the normal work environment, in which case participants in a group field trip may get a somewhat distorted view of the work behaviour of those being observed.

Case Studies. The **case-study method** bears some similarity to the seminar method, except that the participants are asked to read a prepared case involving a real or hypothetical situation. The case should provide sufficient information so that the participants can discuss the particulars of the case, providing their personal views about the meaning, significance, or importance of all that has occurred. In addition, all participants are commonly expected to develop or to assist a group in developing solutions to the problems posed by the case.

The case-study method is best suited for use in management training and is often used to assist managers attempting to learn how to cope with such common problems as dealing with difficult guests and settling interpersonal disputes among employees.

Panels. **Panels** consist of groups of experts called in by trainers to express their opinions on specific questions for the benefit of an audience of trainees, usually management trainees. The panel members are typically asked to comment on timely subjects under discussion. They may agree with each other or provide differing and contrasting opinions, thus giving trainees the benefit of hearing several views.

Like the seminar method, the panel method offers an excellent means of eliciting the opinions of participants. However, the opinions are those of the panel members, not those of the trainees. In some instances, especially with management training groups, trainees are encouraged to question members of the panel and to challenge their views.

Programmed Instruction. The **programmed-instruction method** is considered by its supporters to be among the most effective means of providing individual training. Programmed instruction is individual instruction that can be accomplished via books or dedicated equipment. Study guides and work-books are good examples of the materials used. These are commonly designed to accompany texts and thus to help students acquire more knowledge and understanding than may otherwise be possible. Today, much programmed instruction is delivered by computer. The tutorials that normally accompany computer software are common examples of programmed instruction. The learner is presented with information, walked step by step through a process, and then asked to demonstrate that he or she has acquired the knowledge and skills that the programmed instruction was designed to teach. If the learner is unable to complete a necessary task satisfactorily, the program will indicate this and then conduct the learner through the instruction once again.

Given today's technology, programmed learning aids can be employed to provide employee training on premises. In an establishment with a major computer system, designated workstations can be used for regular and ongoing training. In smaller establishments without computer systems, management can take advantage of decreasing prices for increasingly complex technology to purchase and install computers and related devices for programmed learning. At the same time, growing numbers of interactive programs for training are coming into the market. Some of these use multimedia techniques, and a growing number simulate real conditions to add new dimensions to training. In addition, any organization choosing to do so today can develop and print training manuals and other learning aids using one of the many desktop publishing programs available. If such materials are published in-house, they can readily be revised and reprinted at far lower cost than without desktop publishing.

An obvious advantage of programmed instruction is that it provides immediate feedback to the learner. Another is that instruction is totally under the control of the programmer, effectively preventing the learner from straying beyond the bounds written into the program. In addition, the program can be repeated endlessly by the learner until he or she has acquired the knowledge or skills that the program was designed to teach.

Each of these training methods may be used for any of several different levels of training. However, their purposes vary slightly. Lecture/demonstration and role playing are excellent for teaching specific skills. Seminars, case studies, and panels are fine methods to use in programs designed for employee development, to improve levels of job performance, and to qualify participants for higher levels of responsibility within the hospitality organization. Depending on their particular uses in a given setting, individual assignments, field trips, and programmed instruction are also excellent methods for assisting individuals and groups to learn about and follow the standards and standard procedures established for successful hospitality operation.

From the several approaches to training and the array of training methods available, one must select those that can best be employed for achieving the training objectives established. For example, to teach a new employee how to perform the job of a dishwasher, one would probably use the individual rather than the group approach, as well as the lecture/demonstration method. One may combine this training with the role-playing method or with the individual assignment method, both of which can reinforce the valuable lessons imparted during the lecture/demonstration. If role playing or individual assignment were selected, one would supervise the trainee's activity so that incorrect behaviours would be subject to timely corrective action.

Instructional Timetables

Once a suitable training method has been selected, it is necessary to assess the amount of time training will take—the number of days, hours, or minutes that should be allotted to each phase of training, as well as the overall length of time required to complete the training.

The amount of new material that learners can absorb in a given training session is limited. Although the amount varies with the nature of the material to be presented, the capabilities of the trainer, and the degree of concentration required of the learners, any qualified trainer understands that this limit exists and takes great care not to go beyond it in any one session. This limit, known intuitively by experienced trainers, helps determine both the length of a given training session and the number of sessions required to achieve a specific training objective. Provision for the development of suitable instructional timetables is a major requirement in training plans.

Location

The nature of the training to be done is key to selecting a training method, which helps determine the type of location that will be most suitable for training.

On-the-job training typically requires that trainees be present at the job site during normal business hours. Off-the-job training carries no such requirement and enlarges the list of potential training locations. The structured approach to learning is more likely to require that specific locations be set aside for regular use as instructional sites. In contrast, the informality of the unstructured approach can make this unnecessary. Similarly, the individual approach is not as likely as the group approach to require the assignment of a classroom or similar specific site for training activities. For the individual approach, the job site is often the proper location for training.

Determining the proper location for training is often a very simple exercise. For example, if one intends to train servers, it would be sensible to undertake some of the training in a setting that resembles the area in which they will work: a dining room. Some of the training may take place in a classroom setting, but a great deal of it should be done in a dining room. Similarly, most—possibly all—of the training for a dishwasher should be done at the dish machine and should be specifically directed at learning to load, start, run, stop, unload, and clean the machine properly.

Finding suitable space for training can be a severe problem in some organizations and may play a role in determining the hours when training can take place. If servers should be trained in a dining room, then the specific times set aside for training must coincide with the hours when the room is closed to the public. If a dining room normally opens at 11:00 a.m., and the staff preparing the room for opening begin their work at 10:00 a.m., then training sessions for servers may be restricted to the hours between 7:00 a.m. and 10:00 a.m. If these hours are unsuitable for any reason, then some other location may have to be identified. This may be another part of the building that can be made to resemble a dining room, or it may be a suitable space located in another unit, in the case of a chain establishment. In fact, some chain organizations prefer to schedule training in centralized locations, as discussed later in this chapter.

Lesson Plans

With training objectives clearly established and appropriate decisions made as to approach, method, instructional timetable, and location, it becomes possible to devise a lesson plan that will ensure that the appropriate training takes place.

A **lesson plan** is a written, step-by-step description of the training required for a specific job, including an objective, detailed notes about content, the instructional timetable, and any items that may be required during instruction, such as specific pieces of equipment, materials, and other audiovisual aids. The objective of the lesson plan is to ensure that a trainee learns to accomplish the skills and tasks that make up the job. Ideally, the lesson plan will be so complete and detailed that any qualified trainer will be able to follow it and deliver the necessary instruction to an individual or group. Figure 20.1 is a lesson plan for training a server, based on the job description for a server illustrated in Chapter 19.

• FIGURE 20.1 •

Lesson Plan

OBJECTIVE: Train servers to perform all job duties, including use of computer terminal.

Location for Training: Dining room

Timetable: 8 hours of instruction, divided into 6 training sessions. Training to take place between 7:00 a.m. and 10:00 a.m., when dining room is not open to the public.

Training Methods: Lecture/demonstration and role playing

Material and Equipment: For each trainee—one complete place setting, service tray, tray stand, coffee carafe, and water pitcher. Use of computer terminal located in dining room.

Session 1: Introduction to Training and Introduction to the Establishment—2 Hours
  1. Introduction to supervisory management: dining room manager, chef, and restaurant manager
  2. A tour of the facility, including employee locker rooms and kitchen
  3. Discussion of payroll matters, handling of tips, employee parking, work schedules, station assignments, health benefits, employee meals, vacation, sick leave, and employee evaluation
  4. Uniforms and standards for personal hygiene and appearance
  5. Rules for behaviour while on the job
  6. Location of supplies and equipment needed by serving staff
  7. Off-limits areas for serving staff

Session II: Instruction in Use of Computer Terminal—1 Hour
  1. Signing in
  2. Placing orders
  3. Retrieving guest bill
  4. Payment of guest bill

Session III: Preopening Duties—1 Hour
  1. Preparation of dining room for opening
  2. Table setting and *mise en place*

(continued)

● **FIGURE 20.1** ● *(continued)*

Session IV: Taking Initial Order for Drinks and Food—1 Hour

1. Approaching the guest's table
2. Taking drink orders
3. Explaining menu and describing specials
4. Taking food orders
5. Role playing (Trainees will be divided into groups of three, taking turns as guests placing food and drink orders and server taking orders.)

Session V: Meal Service—2 Hours

1. Serving beverages
2. Serving food
3. Serving wine
4. Server conduct during meal
5. Removing plates, glassware, and flatware
6. Taking dessert orders
7. Serving dessert
8. Presenting cheque
9. Handling guest complaints

Session VI: Role Playing—1 Hour

The trainees will be divided into teams of three and will take turns being guest and server, going through the entire sequence. Role playing will continue until trainer is satisfied trainees are fully prepared to serve.

Without lesson plans, training sessions tend to be less effective than intended. Trainers working without lesson plans are more likely to lose sight of the particular objectives of training and to neglect specific points that ought to be covered in training a given individual to perform a specific task. In general, the absence of a lesson plan makes for highly informal and largely ineffectual presentations that are less likely to meet the carefully defined training objectives.

Trainer Preparation

With considerable effort having been devoted to establishing training objectives, creating job descriptions, writing job breakdowns, developing performance criteria, determining suitable approaches and methods, developing lesson plans, establishing timetables, and choosing locations, the essentials for training are in place.

At this point, it becomes the trainer's responsibility to make sure that all is ready for training to begin. Many components are likely to require attention. Lesson plans must be available to the trainer. Arrangements must be made for individual employees to be available for training at specific times. Transportation arrangements from job site to training site may sometimes be required. Some checking may be required to confirm that a given worker has been informed that he or she will be "shadowed" by a less experienced worker on Thursday mornings for the next two weeks. In some cases, it may mean that a particular room set aside for training must be made ready for a scheduled session—for example, materials must be taken to the room and placed on the chairs that trainees will occupy. In other cases, it may mean that specific pieces of equipment must be prepared for use during a training session or that particular supplies must be taken to a training site for the use of trainees. Sometimes it means that special workstations must be made ready for trainees to use during a training session. Sometimes it may be important to gather paper, pencils, chalk, felt-tip markers, or other materials required for a training session. It may even mean checking to see that lights are on and heating or air-conditioning equipment is working properly in the room being used as a training site. These are a few simple examples of the many details for which trainers are commonly responsible. Most are mere details, seemingly minor, but each can be a critical factor in determining whether a training session meets the objectives established for it.

Trainee Preparation

After particular employees have been selected and are at the point of beginning their training, it is important to take some preliminary steps before the training begins. Adults learn best when they understand the need for learning and both the personal and organizational benefits that will result from it. These needs and benefits can usually be communicated to learners in an introduction to training that explains the following:

- The objectives of the training
- The instructional method being used
- The skills they will learn

Most employees have some degree of apprehension when faced with any kind of change. This may show itself as reluctance or fear and can be an impediment to successful training. An introductory explanation by a skilled trainer can have several positive effects on learners' attitudes. For example, it can help change employees' negative feelings and reduce their fears of inability to complete the training or to learn new skills. Thus, trainee preparation plays an important role in improving the climate for learning and skills improvement.

The Training Session(s)

With objectives, approach, method, instructional timetable, location, and lesson plan all established, and with trainer and trainee prepared to begin, the actual training process can start. The trainer is expected to follow the lesson plan, proceeding at a reasonable pace. A good trainer will normally respond to any question raised by a trainee and will sense trainees' concerns, spoken or unspoken. In addition, good trainers help trainees to feel at ease during training sessions, speaking clearly and distinctly, using words and phrases appropriate to the language level of the trainees, correcting helpfully, and praising appropriately for good work. Under these conditions, the training is more likely to achieve its intended goals. Under less suitable conditions, this is less likely to be the case.

Evaluation

After training of any kind has taken place, it is important to evaluate the training to see whether established training objectives have been met and to learn whether those trained are able to meet the performance criteria for their positions. After all, men and women trained as servers should be able to work as servers in a dining room, meeting the performance criteria established by management for servers.

It is normally advisable to begin the testing of trainees during their training period to assess learning as it progresses. This can take place at various stages of training and may be accomplished by various means. In general, one seeks to determine the extent to which the trainee is making progress toward acquiring the skills required by a worker in the position for which he or she is being trained. The practical testing techniques used by trainers include oral questioning, written examinations, supervised practice of newly acquired skills, and required demonstration of those skills.

However, unless their training has taken place in an entirely realistic work environment, one cannot fully evaluate the future ability of trainees during training. The ability of individuals to meet established performance criteria cannot be fully tested until they take their places in the workforce, alongside others similarly trained and performing the same duties under the same pressures.

CENTRALIZED VERSUS LOCALIZED TRAINING

LEARNING OBJECTIVE 20.5
Describe the advantages and disadvantages of centralized and local training for multiunit organizations.

Many multiunit organizations, including chains of company-owned and franchised units, face very complex training problems. Some of these organizations have hundreds of units and must find some means of providing employees across the organization with the training they need. In addition, it is important that each individual in a given job title receive training that will enable him or her to meet the same performance criteria as others in very distant locations.

Many large organizations employ professional human resources personnel to develop training programs that can be implemented throughout the organization. Essentially, there are two alternatives available for any companywide program:

1. **Localized training** requires that trainers be sent to the individual units, either to train the staff at their normal worksite or at an appropriate site nearby.

2. **Centralized training** allows trainees to be sent to a central training facility, often located at the national or regional headquarters of the organization.

The first of these is more commonly used to train servers and others in similar capacities. The latter is more common for management personnel.

The first alternative is a good choice when many individuals in a single unit require the same training. It is clearly less costly to send one trainer to the unit than to send all employees to a distant training location. In contrast, the second alternative is a better choice when numerous individuals in various locations require the same training. Rather than send the trainer on a tour of the locations to provide costly one-on-one training to numerous individuals, it is quicker and probably less expensive to bring all those needing the training to a central location to receive their training together.

Although each of these alternatives offers excellent means to ensure that personnel with particular job descriptions receive appropriate training, each must be employed in those situations to which it is best suited.

TRAINING MANUALS

LEARNING OBJECTIVE 20.6
Identify the four content areas normally included in training manuals.

Many large organizations also employ human resources professionals to develop training manuals for use throughout the organization. These can be used any time training is required, regardless of whether the training is done centrally or locally. Under optimum conditions, an organization will develop a training manual for every job that is common to all units in the organization. Any time training is required, that training will be based on the information printed in the training manual. This approach provides for standard training and standard results in all units. In addition, the existence of a training manual makes it unnecessary to reinvent the wheel each time training is required.

Training manuals take different forms, depending on the intended audience. Some are written as guides for trainers and give the trainer specific information and tips that will help provide the best possible training sessions for staff. Others are aimed at trainees and are designed to give the trainee the information required even if no trainer is available to provide instruction. Some of these may better be termed *programmed-instruction aids* than training manuals.

Some training manuals are little more than collections of written paragraphs, photocopied and then stapled together. Others are more attractive booklets, produced with modern desktop publishing techniques and containing written materials and useful illustrations. Still others may best be described as books, printed at great expense by managers who believe that providing training to staff is one of management's most important functions.

Although the specific contents of training manuals vary, most attempt to include information that can be categorized in four areas:

1. *General background.* The manual should include an introduction to the organization, its principal goals and objectives, its philosophy, and its view of the role of the individual within the organization. In addition, it should provide an introduction to the specific jobs, indicating the specific role of each job in the organization and the position of the job within the unit structure. This is normally the first section in a training manual.

2. *Specific duties of a job.* The manual should include a detailed list of the duties of each job, taken from the job description, as well as the performance criteria established for each task. In order for a trainee to be able to understand the duties clearly, these should be described in great detail and in comprehensible language. Any terms that the trainee might not know should either be avoided or carefully and fully explained. Sometimes a manual includes questions designed for trainees to self-test as they use the manual. When such questions are included, answers are provided so that the trainee can have immediate feedback.

3. *Specific procedures for carrying out the duties.* The manual must list all standard procedures established for performing the duties and tasks assigned to each job. If possible, the standard procedures should be listed with the duties, tasks, and performance criteria associated with the job. It should be obvious that separating these components would make learning more difficult for the trainee. In some instances, complexity or limitations of space may make it impossible to list all of these together. If so, it is of great importance that the arrangement be such that it does not impede the trainee's learning. Whenever feasible, line drawings, diagrams, and even cartoons can be included to illustrate and thus clarify the standard procedures for the trainee. Here, too, questions and answers for self-tests can be an important learning aid for the trainee.

4. *Summary.* This section of the manual normally re-emphasizes the critical points made in the earlier sections, including the importance of the job, of the major duties associated with each job, and of those specific and distinctive standard procedures that render the proper performance of the job critical in the organization. In addition, the summary often restates—and thus reinforces for the trainee—the organization's commitment to him or her as a developing long-term member of a very important team.

PROFESSIONAL TRAINING ORGANIZATIONS

Many professional organizations will provide training assistance to foodservice organizations. They conduct training on or off premises, or provide training materials on-line. For example, one organization that provides on-line or on-site assistance in Canada is TrainCan Inc., whose programs conform to the Canadian *Food Retail and Food Services Code*. Owners can download training manuals for servers, hosts, dishwashers, line cooks, bussers, and bartenders from its website.

THINGS TO CONSIDER

An employee new to the foodservice industry might feel a bit intimidated and overwhelmed by the requirements of the job, their inexperience, or their introduction to the work environment. Good training helps ease this transition as the employee will feel more comfortable in their abilities, thus reducing the stress involved in their desire to do a good job and appear competent in the eyes of their peers. There have been many cases where new employees leave their job after a short period of time simply because they feel they don't fit in due to lack of confidence in their abilities. Proper training can rectify this situation, reduce costly employee turnover, and provide a positive working environment.

CHAPTER ESSENTIALS

In this chapter, we provided a definition of training, distinguished it from education, and identified its purpose. We discussed the assessment of training needs, the first step in training. We listed and discussed 10 elements commonly covered by training plans: objectives, approaches to training, training methods, lesson plans, instructional timetables, location, trainer preparation, trainee preparation, training sessions, and evaluation. We discussed the alternatives faced by organizations engaged in centralized and localized training, and we described the typical contents of training manuals.

KEY TERMS IN THIS CHAPTER

Case-study method, p. 527
Centralized training, p. 534
Cross-training, p. 521
Lesson plan, p. 529
Localized training, p. 533
Off-the-job training, p. 524
On-the-job training, p. 523
Panels, p. 527

Programmed-instruction method, p. 527
Seminars, p. 526
Structured training, p. 524
Training, p. 520
Training manual, p. 534
Training objectives, p. 523
Training plan, p. 522
Unstructured training, p. 524

QUESTIONS AND PROBLEMS

1. Define *training*.
2. Distinguish between training and education.
3. What is the primary purpose of training?
4. Why is it important to complete a training needs assessment before developing a training plan? What does a training needs assessment examine?
5. Define *cross-training*. Why might a manager want staff members cross-trained?
6. What is job rotation? Why might a manager institute job rotation?
7. What do training objectives identify?
8. Identify and distinguish between the following approaches to training:
   a. On-the-job versus off-the-job
   b. Structured versus unstructured
   c. Individual versus group

9. List and explain eight methods that can be employed in training. Which are best suited to use with groups? With individuals? For structured training? For unstructured training?
10. Given the following jobs, identify appropriate locations for training staff to accomplish each:
    a. Dishwasher
    b. Server
    c. Bartender
    d. Greeter
    e. Manager

11. What is a lesson plan? What should a lesson plan include?
12. What is the purpose of trainee preparation? What positive effects can an introductory explanation by a skilled trainer have on learners' attitudes toward training?
13. List five performance characteristics of a good trainer that help make employees feel at ease during a training session.
14. Why should training be evaluated? Against what two criteria should training be measured?
15. Identify four practical testing techniques that trainers can use to evaluate the progress being made by trainees.
16. Distinguish between centralized and localized training. Which approach would be more commonly used to train management personnel? Which for servers?
17. The information included in training manuals can be categorized into four areas. Identify these four areas, and describe the material typically covered in each.

18. Identify two computer applications that are of specific value for training.

19. You are the newly hired manager of the Westfield Fine Dining Restaurant. You note that the servers are not properly trained. They do not greet guests properly, their explanation of the evening main dishes is cursory, and their service techniques are fit only for a diner.

    a. What training method would you use to correct their service deficiencies?

    b. Write a one-page description of the proper guest greeting, explanation of the evening main dishes, and service techniques appropriate for a fine-dining facility employing Canadian table service.

20. As the newly hired manager of the Westfield Fine Dining Restaurant, you are concerned about the sanitary habits of the kitchen staff. They do not wear plastic gloves when handling food, they store much food in refrigerators in uncovered containers, and the kitchen floor is constantly littered with garbage and discarded food.

    a. What training method would you use to correct this situation before the health inspector arrives?

    b. Would you include all kitchen personnel in the initial training or just the chef? Justify your answer.

21. Define each of the key terms in this chapter.

EXCEL EXERCISES

Exercise 20.1

Develop a training lesson for a job of your choice (since time is a factor, a simple task such as setting a table or handling customer complaints is sufficient) using one or more of the eight training methods. Deliver the lesson to the class. Use the performance evaluation spreadsheet on the companion website for this text, and have the class evaluate the training lesson.

Exercise 20.2

Take the results of the evaluations and compile them onto the trainer evaluation spreadsheet on the companion website for this text. Discuss the results with the class.

CHAPTER 21

Monitoring Performance and Taking Corrective Action

• LEARNING OBJECTIVES •

After reading this chapter, you should be able to:

21.1 Define the term *monitoring* as it is used in labour cost control and differentiate between direct and indirect monitoring of employee performance.

21.2 Identify the two means of direct monitoring of employee performance and provide examples of each.

21.3 Describe four sources of information used for indirect monitoring and provide examples of each.

21.4 Outline the five-step approach used to identify the specific cause of some discrepancy between actual and standard performance.

21.5 List and describe the three general causes of discrepancies between actual performance and that anticipated by standards.

INTRODUCTION

In the preceding chapters, we discussed the application of the first two steps in the control process: establishing standards and standard procedures for operation, and training all individuals to follow these established standards and standard procedures. This chapter is devoted to the remaining steps: monitoring performance, comparing actual performance with established standards, and then taking appropriate action to correct deviations.

Training employees to follow established standards and standard procedures does not guarantee that they will always work as trained. Some trained employees will follow their training initially, but may begin to forget after some weeks or may begin to be influenced by poor work habits of long-term employees whose training dates from some time in the distant past. Some merely become indifferent to details after they have done one particular job too long. There are many other reasons. Because there is a strong possibility that employees' work will not always conform to the established standards, it must be monitored to assess whether it meets those standards.

MONITORING PERFORMANCE

LEARNING OBJECTIVE 21.1
Define the term *monitoring* as it is used in labour cost control and differentiate between direct and indirect monitoring of employee performance.

Monitoring the performance of employees is gathering information about their work and the results of that work. This is the necessary third step in the control process—the step that enables managers to make those judgements about performance that can suggest whether corrective action will be required. Employees' work may be monitored directly, indirectly, or by a combination of the two, as discussed in the following sections.

Direct Monitoring

LEARNING OBJECTIVE 21.2
Identify the two means of direct monitoring of employee performance and provide examples of each.

Direct monitoring of employee performance normally means direct observation by a manager or supervisor of an employee at work, or direct examination of the results of that employee's work by a supervisor or manager. For example, the host in a hotel dining room normally spends some time in direct observation of the servers assigned to work in the room to determine the extent to which each is conforming to the standards and standard procedures established for servers and covered during their training (e.g., serving plates of food from the left and removing soiled dishes from the right). Similarly, the steward in a foodservice operation will watch those whom he or she is responsible for supervising to be sure they are doing their assigned work correctly (e.g., putting away deliveries of frozen food as quickly as possible after they have been received).

Although direct observation often takes place in this manner—as an employee is actually attending to a task—this is not always the case. Another possibility is for the supervisor to examine the results of the work and make a judgement about it immediately after it has been done. This would be the approach adopted by a chef who waited until after a cook finished plating a main dish and handed it to a server to examine the appearance of the plate. Similarly, a steward would be unlikely to watch an employee storing cans of food on shelves in a storeroom. He or she would be more likely to monitor the employee's performance by examining the storeroom after the food had been put away.

There are many examples of direct monitoring of employees' performance seen every day in any food and beverage operation, such as any time there are supervisors on hand and time is available for direct monitoring. The extent to which direct monitoring can take place depends on the number of employees working under the jurisdiction of a supervisor and how closely the supervisor is able to monitor each employee. For example, supervisors in most dining rooms seldom have the ability to closely watch all the movements of servers under their jurisdiction. They typically cannot listen to the greetings given to customers by an individual server, nor can they hear explanations to customers of the methods used to prepare particular menu items. Dining room supervisors have limited ability to monitor employees directly. To a greater or lesser extent, they must rely on indirect monitoring.

At the same time, there are many examples of establishments with other kinds of supervisory problems (e.g., inadequate numbers of supervisors or supervisors with inadequate training). In such establishments, it may be difficult or impossible to monitor employees' performance adequately by direct means. Indirect monitoring becomes necessary.

Indirect Monitoring

Indirect monitoring is accomplished by developing a variety of means or methods for assessing work without directly observing it. This approach to monitoring is very common in food and beverage operations. Four sources provide the information needed for indirect monitoring:

LEARNING OBJECTIVE 21.3
Describe four sources of information used for indirect monitoring and provide examples of each.

1. Customers
2. Employees
3. External agencies, organizations, and groups
4. Managers

Customers

It is interesting to note that restaurant customers typically have little to say to dining room servers and dining room supervisors about the high or low quality of food or service. They have very little to say when food quality and service exceed their expectations, and they seldom complain to dining room servers or supervisors when they receive poor service or when food quality does not meet their expectations. Even when questioned by supervisors upon leaving restaurants, customers frequently do not admit that their dining experience was poor. They seldom take time to write positive or negative letters to management, although occasionally an individual writes a letter of complaint if an experience with restaurant food or service was extremely bad. Instead, customers typically accept the level of service or food quality, good or bad, and then pay their bills and leave. Privately, their innermost reactions are likely to determine whether they ever return.

In contrast, in conversations with co-workers, neighbours, and friends, people describe many of their dining experiences in great detail. They are particularly inclined to describe the good ones and the bad ones, not the indifferent, and they will dwell on those experiences that have been particularly bad. These experiences are described endlessly, and the impressions they create are carried verbally throughout the community. In fact, the overall reputation of a restaurant may actually be little more than the sum of statements and comments, positive and negative, made about that restaurant by its customers in conversations with their friends, relatives, neighbours, and co-workers.

When comments about service quality and food quality are made by customers, management must take them seriously. When the comments are complaints, they are frequently indications that other, more serious, problems exist. Complaints or compliments may result from questions customers are asked by employees or supervisors. These may be verbal or written. Most servers today are trained to ask customers a question such as, "Is everything all right?" at some time during a meal. Asking this question has several purposes, including showing interest in and concern for the customer's dining experience and determining whether the meal is progressing satisfactorily. Sometimes the answer to the question may be no.

A server asking the question may learn that the soup is not hot, that a desired condiment is missing from the table, or that the meat is too well done. A supervisor asking the question may be told that the service is too slow, the room too cold, or the server misinformed about the nature of a dish. However, negative responses to such questions are rare in most establishments, even if service quality or food quality is not up to customers' expectations. Customers typically say, "Everything is fine," even when it is not, because many are unwilling to express their real views openly. Some customers undoubtedly are self-conscious, perhaps embarrassed to complain; others do not want to be labelled complainers. Thus, the accuracy of these comments solicited from customers is questionable.

Because a relatively small percentage of customers state their true views to servers or dining room supervisors about the quality of food and service, many foodservice establishments ask their customers to formally evaluate the quality of their service and food. They ask customers to write answers to specific questions. Figure 21.1 is an example of the kind of survey form that customers are often asked to complete. Forms of this nature are available for customers to complete at the end of a meal. It is recommended that they be coded or marked in a way that will help identify particular servers and particular menu items. Customers frequently are more willing to answer questions honestly when presented with a form of this kind because their responses are anonymous and because they know that they will be gone by the time the form is read.

• **FIGURE 21.1** •

Customer Satisfaction Survey

We need your help. By responding to several questions below, you can help us maintain the levels of service and food quality you look forward to when you come to our restaurant. On the basis of the following scale:

5 = excellent
4 = very good
3 = average
2 = poor
1 = unacceptable

circle one of the numbers below to rate each of the following:

1. The host's greeting	5	4	3	2	1
2. The appearance of the table	5	4	3	2	1
3. The server's demeanour and friendliness	5	4	3	2	1
4. The server's professionalism	5	4	3	2	1
5. The quality of the drinks	5	4	3	2	1
6. The food:					
Appearance	5	4	3	2	1
Quantity	5	4	3	2	1
Quality	5	4	3	2	1
7. Your overall impression	5	4	3	2	1

Any comments you choose to write will be carefully considered and greatly appreciated.

_____

_____

_____

_____

Thanks for all your help,
The Management

Employees

Another means for indirect monitoring are reports about co-workers from their fellow employees. Good managers encourage all employees to care about the establishment and to want to maintain established standards and standard procedures. When loyal employees see that co-workers are not maintaining standards, some will suggest to their colleagues that they return to accepted methods for doing the work, as they were trained to do. Others may be more inclined to alert their supervisors.

When reports about co-workers come to supervisors, it is important that they be carefully considered. Supervisors must make judgements about the individuals providing the information and their reasons for doing so. Frequently, the report is based on a loyal employee's deep concern for the best interests of the establishment—a true concern that standards and standard procedures are not being met. Sometimes other motives prompt such a report. For example, it is not uncommon for an employee to exaggerate or to make a false report about a co-worker's behaviour because of a personal quarrel or a genuine dislike. In all instances, it is important that information be verified before corrective action is taken.

External Agencies, Organizations, and Groups

Across Canada, one finds an array of external agencies, organizations, and groups engaged in monitoring the performance of hospitality employees. The following are the most common.

Government Agencies. Various agencies inspect food and beverage operations to assess their adherence to the standards and standard procedures established by government for foodservice operation. In effect, they monitor performance with respect to government standards that should be incorporated into the establishment's own standards and standard procedures. Local fire departments, for example, routinely inspect restaurants, bars, and related operations to verify compliance with local laws designed to protect the lives of customers and employees. They commonly check to see that fire extinguishers are available and suitably charged, that grease filters over cooking equipment have been cleaned as required by law, and that fire exits are neither locked from the inside nor blocked by stored materials.

If job descriptions list the tasks and responsibilities related to fire safety and if training adequately prepares employees to carry out those tasks and responsibilities correctly, a fire inspection should not be a matter for great concern: monitoring in the form of a fire department inspection should merely confirm that standards and standard procedures are being followed. The same can be said of inspections carried out by representatives of any number of other agencies—local, regional, provincial, territorial, or federal. These may include health and safety inspectors from a health department. Usually in Canada, health inspections are performed by local municipalities or regions. Many of these inspections are unannounced and usually occur when the establishment is busy. Inspectors monitor adherence to various standards and standard procedures.

Chain Organizations. Many foodservice chains employ inspectors to perform a monitoring service by visiting and inspecting units in the chain. These units may be company owned, franchised, or both. The aim is to verify that every unit bearing the corporate name and logo is following the standards and standard procedures established by headquarters. The nature and extent of these inspections vary. They may be announced or unannounced. They may be brief, or they may take several days. They may be confined to tasting the food and beverage products prepared in the kitchen, or they may include observation of actual preparation.

Food Critics. Another kind of performance monitoring is carried out by food critics: those who patronize foodservice operations as customers and then inform the public at large about their professional views of these establishments. Some write for the daily press, some for magazines; some comment on radio; and others report on local television news, syndicated cable programs, or on the Internet. All are interested in the quality of food, beverages, and service, and many notice decor, cleanliness, and other conditions in an establishment. The results of their monitoring can have a substantial positive or negative impact on the success of a restaurant, so both owners and managers of the establishments that these powerful people are likely to visit are normally careful to be ready for such a visit at any time.

Rating Organizations. The better foodservice enterprises are likely to have annual visits from representatives of organizations that are in the business of rating restaurants and publishing their ratings. There are any number of these, ranging from local agencies serving major cities to national organizations covering North America and beyond. These, too, monitor and rate the performance of all employees in a given establishment and publish their views in an appropriate book or periodical.

All of these reviewers provide monitoring services that, although conducted by a variety of external entities, help provide management with a means of verifying that the established standards and standard procedures covered in employees' training are being carried out in day-to-day operations.

Managers

Managers at all levels may be the most important of those engaged in monitoring the performance levels of staff. There are any number of means by which this may be accomplished, the most significant of which is to require the preparation of records and reports that reflect employee performance. The basic daily reports discussed in the food and beverage sections of this text provide an indication of the performance of all employees working as a group. Suppose, for example, that a daily report is prepared that shows that food cost percent to date for the first four days of this week is 36.5 percent, as compared with 32.5 percent for the similar period last week. Assume that other data reveal approximately the same menu mix, number of covers, and dollar sales for the two weeks. If 32.5 percent is considered an acceptable level of cost under the circumstances, it is likely that the 36.5 percent level will not be considered acceptable.

The results of the two weeks are determined by a form of monitoring designed to keep management abreast of employee performance. When monitoring reveals unexpected and negative results, management normally begins to look for an explanation. Further investigation may lead to explanations rooted in inadequate employee performance: improper portioning of foods, excessive preparation of foods, or failure to follow standard recipes, to name but a few possibilities.

Monitoring Labour Costs

Another important consideration that requires regular monitoring is labour cost. In fact, many managers find today that labour cost requires more careful monitoring than food and beverage cost. As with all costs, the key to control lies in establishing standards.

Chapter 19 described several methods for establishing quality, quantity, and cost standards for labour. If a way can be found to compare actual performance with established standards for performance developed by management, differences can be noted, particularly those that reflect inefficiencies in labour productivity. Once these differences, or variances, are identified, it is possible for management to seek an explanation for each and to work toward eliminating them in the future, to bring labour productivity up to established standards.

Once standards for work hours have been established, it becomes possible to make judgements about the number of actual work hours used in an establishment, given an actual level of business volume for a period (e.g., hour, meal, day, or any other period). This may best be illustrated by an example. Figure 21.2, a duplicate of Figure 19.15, provides a list of standard work-hour requirements at various volume levels for three classifications of variable-cost personnel (in service, dishwashing, and preparation categories) in a particular restaurant.

• FIGURE 21.2 •

Standard Work-Hour Requirements for Variable-Cost Personnel

Number of Covers		Service Personnel	Dishwashing Personnel	Preparation Personnel
200–299		15	6	9
300–399		18	6	9
400–499		21	9	12
500–599		24	12	12

Assume that a sales forecast has been prepared for the coming week, which includes Tuesday, June 7. According to the forecast, 500 covers are expected to be served during the normal three-hour luncheon period on that date. Given that forecast, the manager has consulted the chart of standard work-hour requirements and prepared an appropriate schedule.

Sometime after the June 7 luncheon period, it becomes possible to compare the actual number of employee hours worked with the number that should have been worked, based on the number of covers actually served. For example, on

June 7, with a forecast of 500 covers, 24 work hours were scheduled. If 24 standard work hours were scheduled and 500 covers were actually served, then management's standards for service and cost would have been met. However, assume that the actual number of covers served was 400 instead. According to the chart, the number of standard work hours appropriate for serving 400 covers is 21. Because of faulty forecasting, a managerial responsibility, too many standard work hours were scheduled. In fact, if the manager had been able to prepare a more accurate forecast, only 21 standard work hours would need to have been scheduled, which would have resulted in labour cost savings. Given a wage rate of $8.50 per hour for servers, 24 work hours would cost $204.00 in wages, whereas 21 hours would cost $178.50. The three extra hours would amount to $25.50 in excessive labour cost for servers alone in this single three-hour luncheon period.

To some, this amount does not seem to be large enough to be concerned about. However, $25.50 is 14.3 percent of $178.50, indicating that this small segment of labour cost for the day was 14.3 percent higher than necessary to provide the standard of service established by management. In addition, this excessive cost of $25.50 per luncheon period multiplied by 365 days a year amounts to $9,307.50 in unnecessary costs for servers alone, without considering the amount of such other costs as benefits, Employment Insurance (EI), and Canada Pension Plan (CPP) deductions.

To the extent that more work hours than the standard have been used, it is apparent that greater efficiency is possible. It is also desirable: greater efficiency will translate to lower payroll cost. If fewer work hours than the standard have been used, it is likely that the quality of service was less than standard.

The next step is to prepare a report that assesses the efficiency of labour utilization by period—the same period used for forecasting volume and scheduling work hours. In some establishments, this will be by meal period; in others, it will be by the day. In the present instance, because forecasting and scheduling were by meal period (luncheon), the assessment report should also be by meal period. An appropriate report would be similar to that illustrated in Figure 21.3.

• **FIGURE 21.3** •

Reconciliation of Standard and Actual Work Hours, Based on Actual Covers Served

DAY: Tuesday   DATE: June 7   MEAL: Luncheon
                                            WEATHER: Fair

Number of covers:
    FORECAST: 500   SOLD: 400

Personnel		Actual Work Hours		Standard		Difference Work Hours		Explanation
Service		24		21		3		Covers fewer than forecasted.
Dishwashing		12		9		3		
Preparation		12		12		0		

Note that the report shows both the forecasted number of covers and the actual number of covers for the meal period, which facilitates judging the accuracy of the forecast. If the forecast was quite close to the actual number of covers, one could ignore any difference. However, if there is a considerable difference between forecast and actual covers, it will be desirable to make some attempt at explanation. If a satisfactory explanation can be found, it may be possible to develop more accurate forecasts in the future.

The number of hours in the "Standard Work Hours" column requires explanation. The number of standard work hours recorded for each job category are those required for the actual number of covers, not the forecasted number. If there is a significant difference between the forecasted number of covers and the actual number, then the standard work hours recorded in the "Standard Work Hours" column will be somewhat different from the actual number of hours worked by employees.

In this instance, it is quite apparent that although scheduling has been efficiently accomplished on the basis of the forecast, a degree of inefficiency has resulted from the overscheduling of personnel. If this result were repeated frequently, the owner or manager might have to find ways to improve the accuracy of the forecasts. Other possible reasons for differences between standard work hours and actual hours worked may be unforeseen variations in weather and in other conditions affecting sales, such as repairs to the street in front of the restaurant, improper attention to standard work hour charts (resulting in poor scheduling), and absenteeism. The important point is that management now has some means of monitoring labour efficiency.

Monitoring Labour Costs Using Cost Percentage

Many foodservice operations monitor labour costs by comparing forecasted and actual sales with forecasted payroll percentages and actual payroll costs in a similar fashion to the food Menu Pre-Cost and Abstract discussed in Chapter 10. This requires that previously discussed employee schedules be prepared for both fixed-cost and variable-cost employees. Every employee's wage or salary is calculated for the period based on the prepared employee schedule, and a total labour cost figure is calculated, including CPP, EI, health insurance costs, and employee benefits. Health insurance premiums are determined by each province or territory. The forecasted labour cost is compared with the forecasted sales for the period, and it becomes the payroll percentage goal for the establishment. Adding CPP, EI, health insurance, and employee benefits to wages and salaries allows the organization to come up with a labour cost percentage that is realistic and can be added to food and beverage cost percentages to arrive at a prime cost, as discussed in Chapter 1. At the conclusion of the period, the actual labour cost is compared with actual sales to arrive at an actual labour cost percentage. This is compared with the forecasted labour cost percentage to determine the accuracy of the forecast. Those operations that use computers can obtain scheduling software programs. These programs make it considerably easier and less time consuming to forecast and compute labour costs and cost percentages.

As a result of the various monitoring methods, techniques, and procedures described and discussed here, information is available that must be evaluated, normally by a capable, experienced manager. Increasingly, the person who does this evaluation has completed coursework in a post-secondary institution and has acquired the knowledge and skill to make the necessary judgements. *Judgement* is the key word here. Today, a foodservice manager must be able to read financial and statistical reports, evaluate related data, make judgements about the significance of the information, and determine which of various possible courses of corrective action to pursue in order to improve operational performance in the near term and over the long term.

TAKING CORRECTIVE ACTION TO ADDRESS DISCREPANCY BETWEEN STANDARDS AND PERFORMANCE

If actual performance brings results that deviate significantly from those anticipated by established standards and standard procedures, some corrective action must be taken to bring actual performance into line with the standards.

Once evaluation reveals a discrepancy between actual performance and that anticipated by standards and standard procedures, a generally accepted five-step approach can be used to identify the cause and find a suitable solution to the problem:

LEARNING OBJECTIVE 21.4
Outline the five-step approach used to identify the specific cause of some discrepancy between actual and standard performance.

1. Meet with appropriate staff to point out the problem and to determine its cause.
2. Identify all appropriate corrective measures that may be adopted.
3. Select the best corrective measure from among the alternatives.
4. Institute the selected measure.
5. Monitor performance to be sure that the corrective measure has the desired effect.

The initial difficulty lies in identifying the reasons for the discrepancy. Essentially, there are three possibilities:

LEARNING OBJECTIVE 21.5
List and describe the three general causes of discrepancies between actual performance and that anticipated by standards.

1. Inadequate performance
2. Unsuitable standards
3. Inappropriate organization

Inadequate Performance

If the reason for a discrepancy is identified as inadequate performance, one must seek the cause. There are any number of possibilities, some of which are attributable to employees and others that are not. In fact, some may even be traceable to poor management performance manifesting itself as poor employee performance.

A complete list of all the possibilities would be impossible to produce. It would be as long and as varied as the list of names of those working in food-service operations. Among the more common causes of poor employee performance are the following: improper materials provided to workers; lack of required equipment or tools; need for additional training; inadequate management or supervision; poor union–management relations; personal problems away from the job; difficulties with interpersonal relations on the job; inadequate compensation, as compared with that derived from other jobs or employers; illness, including due to substance abuse and addiction; poor working conditions, including improper heat, light, or ventilation; and improper work schedules. And this is just the beginning.

For those contemplating careers as foodservice managers, it is probably distressing to learn that the list of possibile causes of poor employee performance is so long. It will be equally distressing to learn that there is no single best approach to dealing with any one of the causes on the list. Treating any of these causes requires the attention of an experienced manager, who must take great care in determining the proper approach in a given instance. It will depend on the particular situation and the specific personalities involved.

Unsuitable Standards

If standards and standard procedures for staff have been established by knowledgeable and experienced managers, one would expect that these would be well suited to the operations in which they were designed to be used. However, this is not always the case. Sometimes conditions change and render standards and standard procedures inappropriate. This may be the case in an establishment adopting a new menu and new service techniques to accompany renovations to the physical plant. Sometimes the managers who develop standards for a given operation are not experienced at doing so, and their efforts result in standards that are not well suited to the operation for which they were developed. In other instances, consultants may develop standards and standard procedures that are wholly unrealistic for the staff members who will be expected to work with them.

When evaluation and analysis reveal that standards and standard procedures are unrealistic, it would make no sense to waste time and effort in attempting to bring employee performance up to the level anticipated by the standards. It would make obvious sense simply to change the standards so that they are better suited to an operation and its staff.

Inappropriate Organization

It would be impossible to compose a complete list of the conditions that have led restaurant owners and managers to conclude that their basic organization structures had been rendered inappropriate. Those with experience in food and beverage management are quick to agree that many have decided to reorganize their establishments. **Reorganization** is another word for *restructuring*. It means changing the organization structure so that titles and duties of the various jobs change. It may mean adding, subtracting, or combining jobs.

In most cases, the conditions that have led an operation to restructure its organization include increases in costs, decreases in sales, or both. We will address the need for reorganization and consequent restructuring of the labour force, on the assumption that all other possibilities have been ruled out. This will enable us to make certain points about reorganization in general, as well as to continue pertinent discussion of labour cost control.

Any manager planning reorganization must have some clear, basic objectives in mind. Without these, it is difficult to imagine how one could proceed in any logical, orderly fashion. Just as in every other area of human endeavour, basic objectives give direction to activity and provide benchmarks against which to measure and judge any plans for change. For purposes of the following discussion, we will assume that the primary objective of reorganization is a reduction in labour cost, and we will use this objective to judge the effectiveness of the reorganization that will be proposed.

The techniques for reducing labour costs as part of a reorganization program do not differ markedly from those employed by managers seeking to reduce costs temporarily. These include combining jobs, hiring part-time rather than full-time employees where possible, adding duties of variable-cost employees to the normal work of fixed-cost personnel, and appropriately using various pre-prepared food and beverage items to reduce the labour cost of preparation.

The chief differences between a temporary reduction of labour cost and a permanent reduction through reorganization typically involve the degree of change, as well as the degree of impact on the labour force as a whole and on particular jobs. Clearly, the manager who decides in favour of reorganization is reacting to a situation that has become untenable, one that dictates the need for a steady and reasoned reversal from unacceptable financial statements to an acceptable level of profit. The manager knows what must be done: reduce the cost of labour to the extent necessary to ensure profit, particularly if there can be no increase in revenue. To the extent to which the manager can do this, each dollar reduction in labour cost should be a dollar increase in profit, assuming no change in overall dollar sales.

As an example of what may be done, Figure 21.4 shows the effect of reorganization on the organization chart of the restaurant first described in Chapter 19 and pictured in Figure 19.1.

Note that reorganization has had a major impact on several positions in the kitchen. For example, the sous chef has been eliminated, and the executive chef is now a working chef. In addition, the work of the purchasing steward has been taken over by the chief steward. Both the fry cook and vegetable cook positions have been eliminated and replaced by a new worker whose duties include those of both the former job titles. The entire baking department has been eliminated, resulting from a decision to buy rather than make baked products.

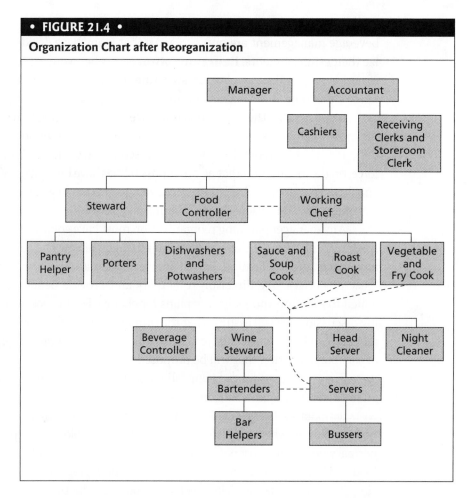

• FIGURE 21.4 •

Organization Chart after Reorganization

These and other changes have resulted in a net reduction of five fixed-cost employees, as well as an indeterminable number of variable-cost employees. This reorganization represents an annual payroll savings of thousands of dollars, by which amount net profits should be increased.

Note that, in this case, management decided to eliminate the jobs of both the fry cook and the vegetable cook in favour of creating a new position for a combination vegetable/fry cook. This new worker could probably not perform all the duties of the former employees, so management would need to undertake another important aspect of reorganizing: writing new job descriptions. As a result of the reorganization and the consequent elimination of some jobs and combining of others, new areas of responsibility have been created, and it is important that each be covered clearly and concisely by a job description.

THINGS TO CONSIDER

The manager who is visible on the "floor," constantly coaching, mentoring, assisting, and working with the team, will have greater results in monitoring employee performance. Being part of the team and not just a figurehead will instill a sense of competent leadership among employees, and the results will be noticeable. Regular performance reviews of employees will keep their performance in check as well as provide the feedback they require. It is always important to remember that managers are not just managing people, they are also managing personalities.

CHAPTER ESSENTIALS

In this chapter, we defined the term *monitoring* as it relates to labour control. We distinguished between direct and indirect monitoring and identified and discussed various sources of the information used for indirect monitoring. We identified a generally accepted five-step approach that can be used to determine the cause of a discrepancy between actual and standard performance and to find a suitable solution to the problem. Finally, we listed and discussed three possible reasons for these discrepancies, including inadequate performance, unsuitable standards, and inappropriate organization.

KEY TERMS IN THIS CHAPTER

Direct monitoring, p. 540   Monitoring, p. 540

Indirect monitoring, p. 541   Reorganization, p. 551

QUESTIONS AND PROBLEMS

1. Define the term *monitoring* as used in labour cost control.
2. Distinguish between the two types of direct monitoring identified in the chapter, and provide examples of each.
3. Distinguish between direct monitoring of employee performance and indirect monitoring.
4. List the four sources of information used in indirect monitoring of employee performance.
5. Do the majority of foodservice customers readily and voluntarily provide management with useful information about the quality of food or service? Why?
6. Suppose you are the manager of a foodservice operation. One of the employees reports to you that another employee does not do his work correctly except when you are watching. What should you say to the employee making the report? What should you do about it?
7. Identify three government agencies that inspect and report on foodservice operations. What kinds of information do they provide? How does this help managers monitor employee performance?

8. "Food critics are not valuable sources of information that management can use to monitor employee performance." Do you agree or disagree? Why?

9. Develop a customer questionnaire, along the lines suggested by Figure 21.1, for a college foodservice operation or for a specific foodservice operation of which you are an employee or a customer. How would the data developed from the use of this form help management monitor employee performance?

10. In a certain restaurant, the manager has determined that six servers are needed for between 320 and 380 covers over a three-hour luncheon period; seven servers are needed for between 381 and 440 covers; eight servers are needed for between 441 and 520 covers; and nine servers are needed for between 521 and 600 covers. Prepare a table of standard work hours along the lines suggested by Figure 21.2.

11. Using the data in Question 10, prepare a report, along the lines suggested by Figure 21.3, for servers only, assuming 520 covers forecasted and 420 covers actually served during the three-hour luncheon period on Tuesday, June 14.

12. Sashi Kavi is the manager of the Eastern Star Restaurant. He has been examining his labour cost and has compared it with the previous period. The following are the figures he has been looking at:

	Current Period	Previous Period
Sales	$185,650	$216,667
Overall Labour Cost as a % of Sales	41.3%	35.0%
Service staff salaries	$ 15,600	$ 15,300
Cooks' and prep personnel salaries	$ 21,750	$ 21,198
Dishwashers and other kitchen personnel wages	$ 6,650	$ 6,655
Receiving and storeroom clerk salary	$ 3,280	$ 3,280
Bartenders' salaries	$ 12,400	$ 12,400
Chef, Dining Room Manager, and Restaurant Manager salaries	$ 17,000	$ 17,000
Total Labour Cost	$ 76,680	$ 75,833

The standard labour cost for the restaurant established by Sashi Kavi is 36%.

a. Identify the excessive costs for the current period.

b. Suggest possible reasons for the excessive costs.

c. Suggest a method for correcting the excessive costs.

13. Define each of the key terms in this chapter.

EXCEL EXERCISE

Exercise 21.1

Follow the instructions on the textbook's companion website to complete this exercise.

GLOSSARY

The definitions included in the text and collected in the following glossary tend to be those common in food and beverage operations. Some people will point out that many of the terms have broader applications than suggested by these definitions. Although this is clearly true, we have chosen to restrict the definitions to those specific to food, beverage, and labour cost control and to this text. Thus, they are intentionally limited.

Abstract The right-hand portion of the Menu Pre-Cost and Abstract.

Actual beverage cost The cost of beverages sold as determined from inventory and purchase figures, with adjustments, if any, taken into account.

Actual cost percent The ratio of actual cost of sales to total sales for a given period.

Actual food cost The cost of food sold, as determined by adding the cost of direct purchases to the cost of issues from inventory, calculated either from requisitions or from valuation of inventory. At the discretion of management, actual food cost may also take various adjustments into account.

Actual inventory value The total value of the physical inventory, determined by pricing each item in that inventory.

Actual purchase price method A method used for determining the value of a physical inventory that requires each unit to be valued at the price at which that particular unit was purchased.

Actual sales record method A method for monitoring bar operations that translates quantities of alcoholic beverages consumed into potential sales values, taking into account actual numbers of various drinks sold.

Aging A process for improving the flavours of alcoholic beverages by storing the beverages under carefully controlled conditions for periods of time that vary from one beverage to another. Also, a process for improving the flavour and texture of meat, especially beef.

As purchased The amount or the price of a product as it is purchased from a supplier, before it is trimmed or processed.

Automated bar A computerized device for dispensing beverages and simultaneously registering sales.

Average cheque See *average sale*.

Average contribution margin The difference between average sale and average variable cost; the amount remaining after average variable cost is subtracted from average sale.

Average sale (cheque) Total dollar sales for a period divided by the number of sales. Also referred to as average cover, average sale per cover, and average sale per customer.

Average inventory The sum of opening and closing inventory for a period, divided by 2.

Average number of covers Total number of covers for a given time period, divided by some other number, such as number of hours in a meal period or the number of servers on duty during a time period.

Average potential sales value The calculated sales value of a bottle of liquor based on detailed records indicating actual sales in a test period.

Average sale per customer Total dollar sales for a period, divided by the number of customers served in that period; an average dollar figure representing the average amount spent by customers.

Average sale per server Total dollar sales attributable to a particular server in a given time period, divided by the number of customers served.

Average sales value method A method for monitoring bar operations that calculates the potential sales value of all bottles of liquor consumed, based on the number of empty bottles at the bar multiplied by the average potential sales value of each bottle.

Average variable cost Total variable cost for a period divided by the number of customers served in that period.

Average variable rate The ratio of average variable cost to average sale, normally expressed in decimal form.

Bar requisition form See *requisition*.

Beers Alcoholic beverages produced by the fermentation of a malted grain flavoured with hops.

Beverage Any liquid intended for drinking. There are two general classifications of beverages: alcoholic and nonalcoholic.

Beverage cost The expense to an establishment for beverages consumed, regardless of the reason. Beverage cost includes the cost of beverages sold, given away, stolen, and spilled.

Beverage cost percent The ratio of beverage cost to beverage sales, expressed as a percent.

Beverage profit maximization An approach to maximizing beverage profits by (1) establishing drink prices that will maximize gross profit and (2) influencing customers to purchase those drinks with the highest contribution margins, rather than attempting to sell greater numbers of drinks to customers.

Beverage receiving report A form used to summarize the invoices for all beverages received on a given day, indicating both quantities received and their values and providing columns for dividing purchases into essential categories (wines, spirits, beers, and mixers) for purchase journal distribution. See *Receiving Clerk's Daily Report*.

Beverage requisition A form used to record the names and quantities of beverages ordered and issued from inventory.

Beverage sales control The sum of various processes used by managers to optimize the number of sales, maximize profits on sales, and ensure that all sales result in appropriate revenue to the establishment.

Bin card A card, label, or other device affixed to a storage shelf, used for recording the number of units of a particular item added to and issued from inventory, and for determining the inventory balance that should be found on the shelf.

Blush wines Wines named for or described by their distinctive pale reddish colour.

Bonus Dollar amount exceeding an employee's regular wages or salary, normally given as a reward for some type of job performance.

Book inventory The stores inventory balance, determined from records of transactions affecting inventory (not from a physical count). Book inventory value is calculated as follows: opening inventory balance, plus purchases (from Receiving Clerk's Daily Report or from invoices), minus issues (from requisitions alone or from requisitions and meat tags).

Brand-name wines Those wines that are given identifying names (sometimes unusual names) by their producers, often to differentiate them. Blue Nun is an example.

Break-even point The point at which the sum of all costs is equal to sales, so that profit equals zero.

Budget A realistic statement of management's goals and objectives, expressed in financial terms.

Budgeted cost A planned cost included in the financial plan, or budget, of an enterprise.

Butcher test A procedure used to determine the standard cost of one standard portion of a product portioned before cooking. It is used for products that cannot be portioned as purchased, but that require some further processing before portions are produced. Butchering is an example of the kind of processing required. The butcher test is also used to determine yield factors and cost factors.

Call brand An alcoholic beverage that a customer must specifically request by brand name, for example, Canadian Club.

Case-study method A method of training that requires participants to read a prepared case involving a real or hypothetical situation.

Centralized purchasing A system used by chains, franchises, and groups of independent operators that results in purchases for all participating units being made by one central office.

Centralized training Training that takes place at a central training facility, rather than at a given trainee's job location. Central training facilities are often located at the national or regional headquarters of an organization.

Closing inventory The physical inventory at the end of a period, expressed in terms of units, value, or both.

Cocktail A drink consisting of the appropriate measures of two or more alcoholic beverages.

Commission Compensation calculated as a percentage of sales.

Compensation All forms of pay and other rewards going to employees as a result of their employment.

Contracts Documents used in a method of purchasing that guarantee a certain price for a product for a given term.

Contribution margin The amount resulting from the subtraction of variable cost from sales price.

Contribution rate The percentage (expressed as a decimal) of the sales dollar available to cover fixed costs and profit. It is calculated by subtracting the variable rate from 1 (1 − variable rate).

Control A process used by managers to direct, regulate, and restrain the actions of people so that the established goals of an enterprise may be achieved.

Controllable cost A cost that can be changed by management in the short term. Examples include food cost, beverage cost, and labour cost.

Control process The means employed by managers to institute control, consisting of four essential steps.

Control sheet A traditional method of controlling revenue. Cashiers list guest cheques by number on a cashier's sheet. Missing cheques are spotted and revenue is verified.

Control system The collection of interrelated and interdependent control techniques and procedures in use in a given food and beverage operation.

Cooking loss test A procedure used primarily to determine the standard cost of one standard portion of a product that is portioned after cooking. It is used for products that cannot be portioned uncooked. The cooking loss test is also used to determine yield factors and cost factors.

Cost The expense incurred for goods or services when the goods are consumed or the services rendered.

Cost–benefit ratio The relationship between costs incurred in instituting and maintaining a single control or control system and the benefits or savings derived from doing so.

Cost control The process used by managers to regulate costs and guard against excessive costs.

Cost factor per kilogram The ratio of the cost of a usable kilogram of edible product to the dealer price per kilogram for the product as purchased. Cost factor per kilogram is obtained from butcher test or cooking loss test calculations and is used to update standard costs when dealer prices change.

Cost factor per portion See *portion cost factor*.

Cost of employee meals The dollar value of foods used for employees' meals. This dollar amount is used as an adjustment when calculating cost of food sold.

Cost of food consumed The cost of food issued plus or minus all adjustments, except employees' meals.

Cost of food issued The sum of opening inventory and purchases, less the value of closing inventory.

Cost of food sold Cost of food consumed, less the cost of employees' meals.

Cost per dollar of sale The cost percent expressed as a dollar figure, or the ratio of cost to sales expressed as a dollar figure.

Cost percent The ratio of cost to sales, expressed as a percent.

Cost plus An agreement in which the buyer pays the supplier's cost for a product(s), plus an agreed upon percentage or dollar mark-up. This arrangement is usually negotiable only for large buyers (small operations may have to pay a higher mark-up).

Cost/volume/profit equation An equation stating that sales is equal to the sum of variable costs, fixed costs, and profit (or loss).

Cover A diner; one customer who has purchased food in a restaurant, regardless of the number of items purchased.

Covers per hour　The average number of diners per hour of operation; total covers, divided by the number of hours of operation; usually calculated for particular meal periods (i.e., breakfast, lunch, dinner).

Cross-training　Teaching a worker to perform the duties of a job or jobs other than his or her own.

Current compensation　Direct and indirect compensation received by an employee while he or she is employed.

Daily cost of food　See *food cost today/food cost to date.*

Daily food inventory balance　The inventory book value of food at the close of business on a given day.

Data mining　A process of extracting patterns from data and transforming them into information. In retail applications, it is commonly used in customer relationship management and marketing.

Deferred compensation　Compensation received by an employee after the conclusion of his or her period of employment.

Desired ending inventory　An established quantity of product, sufficient to last until the next delivery is received.

Differentiated product　A product that is sufficiently different from other similar products so that customers may consider it unique and develop a preference for it.

Direct compensation　Salaries, wages, tips, bonuses, and commissions.

Directly variable cost　A cost that varies directly with sales volume, such that every change in sales volume brings a corresponding change in that cost.

Direct monitoring　Direct observation of employee performance at work, or direct examination of the results of employee work.

Directs　Those foods (typically perishables) charged to cost on the day they are received.

Distillation　A process by which alcohol is evaporated from a fermented liquid and then condensed and collected as a liquid.

Dog　In menu engineering, a menu item for which both contribution margin and sales volume are judged to be low.

Dram shop laws　Statutes that hold the serving establishment and the server financially liable for damages to third parties resulting from the serving of alcoholic beverages to intoxicated customers.

Dupe system　A system for recording customers' orders that provides for two copies of each order, one on a guest cheque for the customer and the other on a dupe used by the server to place the order in the kitchen. Additional uses of the dupe are possible. (*Dupe* is an abbreviation of the term duplicate.

Edible portion The amount of usable product remaining after trimming or cleaning.

Extending the requisition A two-step process for determining the total value of all items listed on a given requisition. The first step is to multiply the quantity of each item listed by its unit price to determine a total value of the quantity issued. The second step is to add these individual totals to determine a grand total for the requisition.

Fermentation A natural chemical process by which sugars in a liquid are converted to ethyl alcohol and carbon dioxide.

First-in, first-out method of stock rotation A method for determining the value of a physical inventory, based on the assumption that units are used in the order of purchase, such that those remaining in the physical inventory are the units most recently purchased. The values of these units can then be determined from recent invoices or other records of recent purchases.

Fixed cost A cost that is normally unaffected by changes in sales volume; a fixed cost does not increase or decrease significantly as business volume changes and thus is said to have little direct relationship to the volume of business.

Fixed-cost personnel Those employees whose numbers do not normally change because of increases and decreases in the volume of business. Changes in their numbers are unlikely unless there are extraordinary changes in volume over an extended period. Chef or manager are examples.

Flexible budget A budget prepared for more than one level of business activity.

Food and beverage transfers Foods or beverages received by one cost centre from another. The values of the foods or beverages transferred are normally recorded, and these values are used later for end-of-period adjustments.

Food cost The expense to an establishment for food, incurred when food is consumed for any reason. Food cost includes the cost of food sold, given away, stolen, or wasted.

Food cost percent today/food cost percent to date The daily and cumulative ratio of food cost to food sales as shown on various reports to management.

Food cost today/food cost to date The daily and cumulative cost of food sold as shown on various reports to management.

Food sales today/food sales to date The daily and cumulative dollar sales of food as shown on various reports to management.

Forecasted sales Predictions of unit sales, dollar sales, or both, normally based on historical data.

Fortified wines Wines to which small quantities of brandy or other spirits have been added to increase alcoholic content. Sherry and port are examples of fortified wines.

Free pour A technique for pouring alcoholic beverages that permits a bartender to "measure" the quantity poured visually, without such physical devices as jiggers or shot glasses. Quantities poured thus depend on the judgement of the individual doing the pouring.

Front bar A fixed counter for beverage service, open for business on a regularly scheduled basis and directly accessible to customers. A front bar includes various facilities for beverage production and is staffed by a bartender to whom customers have direct access.

Full-bottle sales slip A special beverage requisition form used to record the issue and sale of full bottles of beverages.

Generic wine A wine that takes its name from a specific geographic area. California burgundy is an example.

Geographic wine A wine produced in a specific location and named for that location. Château Latour is an example.

Gratis to bar(s) The dollar value of foods given away without charge at the bar that has been previously added to food cost. This dollar amount is used as an adjustment when calculating cost of food consumed.

Gratuity Another term for tip. A gratuity is a form of direct compensation—an amount voluntarily given to employees by customers for services rendered.

Guest cheque A special type of invoice used in restaurants and similar food and beverage operations to provide customers with itemized bills for their menu selections and purchases. The guest cheque lists the specific items sold to the customer, identifying quantity and sales price for each, and indicates the total amount the customer is to pay. The total includes any applicable sales tax.

Historical cost A past cost that has been documented in business records.

Homogeneous product A product that is so much like other similar products that customers have no preference for any one over the others and will purchase the one with the lowest price.

Hourly analysis of business volume A record of the number of covers served each hour of one or more business days.

Indirect compensation All current compensation that is not direct compensation. Examples of indirect compensation include paid vacations, extended health benefits, life insurance, meals, accommodations, use of recreational facilities operated by the employer, and use of company automobiles.

Indirect monitoring Obtaining information about employees' performance or the results of their performance by some means other than directly observing the employees.

Interunit transfer A food or beverage transfer between units in a chain.

Intraunit transfer A food or beverage transfer between departments in a single hotel, restaurant, or similar enterprise.

Inventory differential The difference between start-of-month and end-of-month dollar values of the bar inventory, used as an adjustment in calculating cost of beverages consumed at the bar.

Inventory turnover The ratio of cost of food or beverages sold to average inventory of food or beverages for a period.

Invoice A bill from a vendor for goods or services, often presented as the goods are delivered or the services are performed.

Invoice stamp A rubber stamp used by a receiver to overprint a small form on an invoice to record the date on which goods were received, as well as the signatures of the several individuals verifying the accuracy of data on the invoice.

Jigger A double-ended, stainless steel measuring device used by bartenders to measure the alcoholic ingredients in drinks.

Job analysis The process of identifying the nature of a job, as well as the skills, level of education, and other specific qualifications needed to perform the job. It is the first step in preparing a job description.

Job description A formal definition of a job, which typically includes a summary of the work to be done and a list of specific tasks and duties.

Job rotation The process of periodically reassigning employees to other jobs.

Job specification A document that outlines the qualifications needed to perform a job. It is an outcome of job analysis and describes the specific skills, level of education, and experience required for the job.

Kilogram cost factor See *cost factor per kilogram.*

Labour cost Payroll cost, which includes salaries, wages, and employee benefits.

Labour cost control A process used by managers to direct, regulate, and restrain the actions of people in order to obtain a desired level of employee performance at an appropriate level of cost.

Labour turnover rate The ratio of the number of departing employees to the total number on the staff, expressed as a percentage.

Last-in, first-out method A method for determining the value of a physical inventory that assigns to remaining units the earliest prices paid for units in that category during the period. This method is currently used in Canada for reporting purposes only; it is not allowed for tax filing purposes. It is still used in the United States.

Latest purchase price method A method used for determining the value of a physical inventory that assigns the most recent price paid for units in a given category to all units counted in that category.

Lesson plan A written, step-by-step description of the training required for a specific job.

Lined shot glass A shot glass with a line etched below the rim at a point to which the glass must be filled to measure a given quantity.

Liqueur An alcoholic beverage consisting of spirits that have been sweetened and combined with one or more flavouring agents.

Localized training Training that takes place at the normal worksite or at an appropriate facility near the worksite.

Make versus outsource determination The decision whether to make a menu item on the premises from scratch or buy a prepared convenience product from a supplier.

Market quotation(s) Current prices obtained from suppliers for use in determining the best purchasing option.

Market Quotation List A form often used by food purchasers for taking daily inventory of perishable foods, determining suitable order quantities, recording market quotations, and selecting vendors.

Market segment A subgroup of potential patrons with similar characteristics. Market segments can be based on such characteristics as age, sex, income level, and occupation.

Median The value of the middle item in a group.

Menu contribution margin See *contribution margin*.

Menu engineering A technique used to evaluate a menu by assessing sales volume and contribution margin for each item on a given menu and thus to evaluate the individual menu items.

Menu mix percent As used in menu engineering, the ratio of the number of sales of one menu item to the total number of sales of all menu items, expressed as a percentage.

Menu Pre-Cost and Abstract A form used to calculate standard costs and standard cost percents for both forecasted and actual sales.

Minimum wage The least gross dollar amount that an hourly employee can legally be paid.

Mise en place All of the preparation needed in the kitchen before production can begin. In French, literally, it means "put in place."

Mixed drink A drink typically prepared before being poured into the glass or other container from which it is consumed. Mixed drinks are normally stirred, shaken, or blended before being poured for the customer.

Mixed drink differential An adjustment to the potential sales value of a bottle of liquor, calculated to take into account the varying quantities of liquor used in preparing mixed drinks.

Mixer A nonalcoholic beverage used both to dilute an alcoholic beverage and to produce a drink of distinctive flavour.

Monitoring A process used to gather information about employees' work and the results of their work.

Monthly food cost The cost of food sold for one month.

Noncontrollable cost A cost that management cannot change in the short term. Examples include rent, real estate taxes, and licence fees.

Nonperishable foods Foods that have a comparatively longer useful life than those known as perishables. Because of their longer useful life, nonperishable foods can be ordered less frequently than perishables and can be ordered in comparatively greater quantities.

Off-the-job training Training that takes place when an employee is not engaged in performing his or her normal job duties.

On-the-job training Training that takes place while the employee is engaged in performing his or her job.

One-purveyor (supplier) buying Also known as one-stop buying, defined as purchasing all necessary goods from one supplier to reduce the numbers of orders placed and received, as well as reduce bookkeeping costs. Its main disadvantage is the possibility of increased costs due to the reduction of competition between suppliers.

Open bid A request to suppliers to provide price quotations on specific products, with contracts generally awarded to the lowest price bidder.

Opening inventory The physical inventory at the beginning of a period. It is expressed in terms of units, value, or both.

Operating budget A forecast of sales activity and an estimate of costs that will be incurred in the process of generating those sales.

Optimizing the number of sales In beverage operations, increasing the number of customers to the desired level.

Organization chart A chart that shows positions and describes reporting relationships within an organization.

Organizational plan A plan prepared by management to organize an enterprise that identifies the jobs and job titles required for day-to-day operations.

Ounce-control method A method for monitoring bar operations that compares the number of ounces of alcoholic beverages consumed at the bar with the number of ounces sold, as recorded on sales records.

Outsourcing Arranging to have work done on a contract basis by outside organizations rather than by full-time employees.

Overhead All costs other than prime costs.

Panel A method of instruction whereby a group of experts provides their opinions on a given subject and answers questions from the trainees.

Par See *par stock*.

Par stock In this text, the maximum quantity of an item that should be on hand at any given time. Other definitions are possible.

Par stock control A control technique requiring cooks to sign for and thus accept responsibility for particular numbers of portions of high-cost menu items.

Par stock for bars The exact number of bottles or other containers that must be on hand at the bar at all times for each item.

Payroll costs See *labour cost*.

Performance criteria Written statements describing the minimum level of performance acceptable for a job.

Performance standards Measures established for judging the quality and quantity of employees' work.

Periodic order method A method for ordering food or beverages based on fixed order dates and variable order quantities.

Perishable foods Those foods, typically described as "fresh," that have a comparatively short useful life. Consequently, these must be ordered quite frequently and in relatively small quantities.

Perpetual inventory card   A card or other device used in the perpetual inventory method for recording additions to and issues from inventory, inventory balance, and such other pertinent information as supplier, size, par stock, reorder point, and reorder quantity.

Perpetual inventory method   A method for determining suitable order quantities for nonperishable foods that enables a purchaser to place orders for fixed reorder quantities on varying dates.

Perpetual order method   A method for ordering food or beverages based on variable order dates and fixed order quantities.

Physical inventory   The actual number of units of goods in storage. For food control purposes, there are two physical inventories: (1) directs, which are counted daily to determine order quantities, and (2) stores, which are counted monthly to determine values.

Plain shot glass   A shot glass without a line, which holds a predetermined quantity when filled. See also *lined shot glass*.

Planned cost   An anticipated cost, projected by management, that reflects business plans for the future.

Plowhorse   In menu engineering, a menu item for which contribution margin is judged to be low and sales volume is judged to be high.

Popularity index   The ratio of the number of portions sold of a given menu item to the total number of portions sold of all menu items.

Portion cost factor   The ratio of the standard cost of a standard portion of a menu item to the dealer price per kilogram for the item as purchased. Portion cost factors are derived from butcher tests or cooking loss tests. When dealers' prices change, one uses portion cost factors to recalculate and update the standard costs of standard portions of menu items.

Portion inventory and reconciliation   A comparison of portion sales records and production consumption records to ensure that management is able to account for all portions produced.

Potential sales value   The dollar sales value of a given quantity of alcoholic beverage. It is based on the sales value of the number of drinks in each bottle, assuming that each is sold as a straight drink.

Potential savings   The difference between actual and standard cost. The cost savings that could have been realized if all activities associated with food production and sales had been conducted in strict conformity to the standards and standard procedures established by management.

Pourer   A device that replaces an original bottle top and facilitates the pouring of predetermined quantities of the contents.

Pouring (well) brand An alcoholic beverage served to any customer who does not request a call brand.

Precheque system A method for controlling revenue that requires that sales be recorded on cheques as drinks are served, that revenues resulting from sales be recorded when customers settle their bills, and that sales records and recorded revenues be reconciled.

Price sensitive The relative effect of sales price on sales volume. The greater the effect of price on volume, the more price sensitive the product.

Primary ingredient The principal alcoholic beverage in a drink, the determination of which is necessary for the calculation of mixed drink differentials.

Prime cost The sum of food cost, beverage cost, and labour cost for a given operating period.

Procedures Methods used to prepare products or perform jobs.

Production sheet A form on which one lists the names and quantities of all menu items that are to be prepared for a given date.

Programmed instruction method Instruction using books, computers, or other means that allows a student to learn individually at his or her own pace.

Promotion expense The dollar value of goods and services given away to promote sales in an establishment.

Proof A measure of the percentage of alcohol in a beverage. Canada measures the alcohol in a spirit by the Gay-Lusac method, which expresses the alcohol as a percentage by volume of the liquid.

Purchase Journal Distribution That portion of the Receiving Clerk's Daily Report used to separate invoice amounts for delivered items into food direct, food stores, and sundries.

Purchase order A buyer can issue a purchase order document to a seller, indicating specifics of product quality, quantity, and agreed-to price that will constitute a legal offer to buy when accepted by the seller.

Puzzle In menu engineering, a menu item for which contribution margin is judged to be high and sales volume is judged to be low.

Quality standards Rules or measures established for making comparisons and judgements about the degree of excellence of raw materials, finished products, or work.

Quantity standards Measures of weight, count, or volume used to make comparisons or judgements.

Receiving Clerk's Daily Report Those forms used in food and beverage operations to record data from invoices for goods received on a given day and, for accounting purposes, to distribute purchases into appropriate categories. Sometimes referred to simply as a Receiving Report or Receiving Sheet. There are normally separate forms for foods and beverages, each of which may provide varying numbers of columns for separating purchases into categories. Specifics vary from one establishment to another.

Receiving Report (or Sheet) See *Receiving Clerk's Daily Report*.

Recipe detail and cost card A form used to record a standard recipe and to calculate the standard cost of producing the quantity stipulated in the recipe, as well as the standard cost and standard cost percent for one standard portion.

Reorder point The number of units to which an inventory should decrease before an order for additional units is placed.

Reorder quantity The amount of a particular item that will be ordered each time the quantity of that item diminishes to the reorder point.

Reorganization Restructuring the staff of an enterprise to create a different organizational structure.

Requisition A form prepared by a staff member that lists items and quantities the staff member needs in his or her work area.

Requisition system A formal system that makes provision for recording specific items and quantities needed and issued from inventory.

Revenue control The process used by managers to ensure that all sales result in appropriate dollar income to the enterprise.

Rotation of stock The storing of goods in such a manner that the units received most recently are placed behind those already in storage, resulting in the first units stored being the first units used. This is commonly known as the first-in, first-out (FIFO) method of stock rotation.

Salary A fixed dollar amount paid on a weekly, monthly, or annual basis, regardless of the actual number of hours worked.

Sales Revenue resulting from the exchange of products and services for value.

Sales control The several processes used by managers to optimize numbers of customers, to maximize profits, and to ensure that all sales result in appropriate revenue.

Sales control sheet A form used to record cash and credit sales after guest cheques have been settled by customers.

Sales forecasting The estimating of future sales, based on sales history and other information deemed relevant by management.

Sales history A record of the number of portions of each menu item sold each time that item has appeared on a menu.

Sales mix The ratio of the number of sales of one menu item to the total number of sales of all menu items. Usually calculated for particular segments of a menu (e.g., appetizers, main dishes, or desserts).

Sales per seat Total dollar sales for a given time period, divided by the number of seats in the restaurant.

Sales per serving person Total dollar sales attributable to a particular server in a given time period.

Sales price The dollar amount charged for each unit of any given product or service sold.

Seat turnover The number of seats occupied during a given period, divided by the number of dining seats in the restaurant; the number of customers (or covers) served in a given period, divided by the number of dining seats available.

Seminars Group discussion of particular subjects led by trainers.

Semivariable costs A cost that has both fixed and variable elements, such that one component would not change as sales volume changes, whereas the other component would change.

Service bar A permanent or temporary beverage production and sales facility accessible to servers alone, rather than directly to customers.

Shot glass A small glass used for measuring alcoholic beverages.

Signature book A procedure adopted by some haute cuisine restaurants that use sequentially numbered manual cheques, requiring a server to sign for individual guest cheques as needed.

Signature item A unique food product created for a restaurant to help increase sales volume. A signature item is a differentiated product.

Sparkling wines Those wines containing carbonation, natural or artificial. Asti Spumante and sparkling burgundy are examples of sparkling wines.

Special-purpose bar A beverage production and sales facility, established for customers attending a particular function and normally staffed by a bartender.

Spirits Alcoholic beverages produced by the distillation of a fermented liquid.

Standard cost The cost of goods or services identified, approved, and accepted by management.

Standard cost method   The method of monitoring operations that compares calculated standard product costs with actual product costs to determine whether actual costs should be judged excessive.

Standard cost percent   The ratio of standard cost to actual dollar sales for a given period.

Standard deviation method   A method for monitoring bar operations requiring a test period, careful monitoring of operations, and calculations of difference between actual dollar sales and potential sales value of bottles consumed in the period. This difference, assumed to be attributable to mixed drinks sales, is expressed as a percentage of potential sales for the period and used in succeeding periods to adjust potential sales.

Standard drink cost   The calculated cost of a drink prepared from a standard recipe.

Standard drink recipe   A set of instructions, including ingredients, proportions, and preparation method, intended to be followed each time a drink is prepared.

Standard labour cost   The dollar amount calculated by multiplying the number of standard work hours required to perform a given volume of work by the hourly rate paid to those performing the work.

Standard portion cost   The dollar amount that a standard portion should cost, given the standards and standard procedures for its production.

Standard portion size   The specific quantity of any given menu item that is to be served to every customer ordering that item.

Standard procedures   Those procedures that have been established as the correct methods, routines, and techniques for day-to-day operations.

Standard purchase specifications   Carefully written descriptions listing in appropriate detail the specific and distinctive characteristics that best describe an item to be purchased. Standard purchase specifications commonly identify grade, size, weight, degree of freshness, colour, and other similar characteristics.

Standard recipe   A recipe that has been designated the correct one to use in a given establishment for the production of a given food or beverage product.

Standards   Rules or measures established for making comparisons and judgements.

Standard sales price   The established sales price for a given food or beverage product, to be charged each time that product is sold.

Standard staffing requirements The established number of employee work hours required to perform a given volume of work.

Standard work hours The number of employee work hours required to perform a given volume of work.

Standing orders Arrangements made between purveyors and foodservice operators that result in regular delivery of goods without specific orders preceding each delivery.

Star In menu engineering, a menu item for which both contribution margin and sales volume are judged to be high.

Static budget A budget prepared for one level of business activity.

Steward sales The dollar value of foods from inventory sold at cost. These are typically sales to employees. Steward sales are cost recoveries and thus decrease food cost in the period during which they occur.

Stores Those foods added to inventory when received and charged to cost as issued.

Straight drink A drink consisting of the appropriate measure of one of the many types of spirits, prepared in the glass or other container from which it is consumed. It may or may not contain a mixer.

Structured training A formal approach to training involving a lesson plan and other means of structuring the training so that it proceeds from beginning to end.

Tip Another term for gratuity.

Total available The sum of opening inventory and purchases for a period. Total available may be expressed in terms of units, values, or both.

Total cost The sum of all unit costs for a given period of time.

Total covers The total number of all covers for a period, usually a meal or a day.

Total dollar sales by category The total volume of sales revenue for a given period of time for a particular category of food, such as main dishes, beverages, and so on.

Total number sold The total number of a menu item sold during a given period of time.

Total Quality Management A management process and set of disciplines that are coordinated and inclusive, to insure that customer demands and quality standards are consistently met and exceeded. They involve the participation of all levels of the organization, and the pursuit of continuous improvement.

Total sales Total volume of sales revenue for a given period of time, expressed in terms of dollars or units.

Total sales per seat Total dollar sales for a given time period, divided by the number of seats in the establishment.

Total sales per server Total dollar volume of sales for which a given server has been responsible in a given time period.

Training A program for teaching individuals the skills necessary to perform particular tasks.

Training manual A manual that provides for standardized training directed toward standardized results. Training manuals take different forms. Some are written guides for trainers; others are aimed at trainees and are designed to give trainees the information required, even if no trainer is available to provide instruction.

Training objectives Objectives that identify the skills, tasks, and behaviours that specific employees will have mastered by the time their training is complete.

Training plan A series of elements or steps that constitute a method for teaching a specific employee the skills required to perform a specific job correctly, in the manner anticipated by management when the standards and standard procedures for the job were developed.

Transfers from kitchen(s) to bar(s) Intraunit transfers of food previously charged to food cost. The values of such items are commonly determined, recorded, and used to adjust food and beverage costs, thus increasing their accuracy.

Truth in advertising The concept, and federal regulation, that customers have the right to know what they are buying, and that statements or product claims must be substantiated.

Turnover rate The number of times a food or beverage inventory is used and reordered in a given time period. It is calculated by dividing the cost of food or beverages for a period by the average inventory of food or beverage for the period.

Unacceptable costs The unplanned, unwarranted costs that normally develop from spoilage, waste, or pilferage.

Unit costs The cost of one or many like units, such as one portion of a particular menu item (e.g., one steak or one martini) or one hour of labour.

Unit sales required to break even The number of average sales required to reach the break-even point.

Unplanned costs Any unanticipated costs.

Unstructured training Informal training characterized by a trainee being directed to observe and follow the procedures and techniques of an experienced worker.

Up-selling (or suggestive selling) Management may instruct servers to concentrate on selling certain items that may increase profits, and/or cash flow.

Variable cost A total cost that changes when sales volume changes. Variable costs are linked to business volume, such that total variable cost increases and decreases as sales volume increases and decreases.

Variable-cost personnel Those employees whose numbers and total cost increase or decrease as business volume increases and decreases. An example would be a server.

Variable rate The ratio (expressed in decimal form) of variable cost to dollar sales.

Variance Standard costs are compared with actual costs, and mathematical deviations between the two are termed variances. Favourable variances result when actual costs are less than standard costs, and vice versa.

Varietal wines Those wines that are named for the varieties of grapes that predominate the wines. Chardonnay is an example.

Void sheet A form used to record information about portions rejected by diners, or mishandled during preparation.

Wages Compensation based on an hourly rate of pay. Calculated by multiplying the number of hours worked by the hourly rate.

Weighted-average purchase price method A method used for determining the value of a physical inventory that is based on calculating a weighted-average value for each unit purchased in a particular category and then applying this value to each of the remaining units in that particular category.

Wine Alcoholic beverage produced by the fermentation of grapes or various other fruits.

Wine cooler Blends of wine and fruit juice.

Work schedule A graphic presentation showing the names of workers and days/hours they are scheduled to work.

Yield The number of portions produced by a given standard recipe.

Yield factor The ratio of the weight of part of a product to the weight of that product as purchased. Yield factors are used to make judgements about the values of comparable products and to determine purchase quantities, among other purposes. The term tends to be used interchangeably with yield percentage.

Yield percentage The percentage of a whole purchase unit of meat, poultry, or fish available for portioning after any required in-house processing has been completed. The term tends to be used interchangeably with yield factor.

INDEX